Chaucer's World

CHAUCER'S WORLD

Compiled by Edith Rickert

Edited by Clair C. Olson

and Martin M. Crow

Illustrations selected by

Margaret Rickert

Published in New York by

Columbia University Press

1948

Foreword

THE ORIGINAL IDEA of editing and publishing the contents of the present book was to use this material for a memorial volume to Edith Rickert, whose major scholarship and interests centered in the work and world of Chaucer. The book was to include also a memoir and a bibliography of all her published writings. Subsequently, war conditions caused first a postponement of the publication altogether, and later, when the project was revived, a proposal to reduce its size so drastically, owing to shortages of materials, as to necessitate the elimination of the memorial features as well as much of the text. Now, at last, when publication of the textual material in its original complete form is again possible, so long a time has elapsed since Edith Rickert's death on May 23, 1938, that a volume intended primarily as a memorial to her seems to have lost some of its appropriateness.

Yet it will occur inevitably to many readers of this book that the material itself constitutes a peculiarly suitable memorial to Edith Rickert even though the more personal features have been omitted. Many of the items were hitherto unknown and were discovered by her and her assistants in their exhaustive search of the public records in London and elsewhere for new facts bearing on the life of Chaucer and on that of his friends and contemporaries. The appearance of Edith Rickert represented facing page vi was familiar to those who frequented the Public Record Office during the years following the initiation of the Chaucer studies in 1924. The tireless enthusiasm with which she herself worked day after day, often with hands numb from the chill of a room only partially heated by an open fire (a truly medieval experience from which, one must believe, she derived some delight, if little comfort) was the result of no mere scholarly thoroughness but of her passionate eagerness not to miss any single item which could contribute an additional detail to her knowledge of Chaucer's world. Those who were associated closely with her during these times well remember the vividness with which she often would sketch some vignette of medieval life, the result of a fresh discovery in a document or an illuminated manuscript. Housekeeping equipment and routine of the fourteenth century were of infinitely greater interest to her than conveniences in her own household. Medieval ladies' dress she always admired, contrasting it with the oddities of many modern fashions, but admitting reluctantly that it was unsuitable for modern women's lives. Many of the recipes recorded in medieval manuscripts tempted her to try her hand at cookery, and some of her friends and students will remember the joy and triumph with which she occasionally prepared a medieval repast and served it in the medieval manner, even though the process demanded more of her time than would have been required for an ordinary meal.

It was obvious that more than the bare facts entered into this re-creation of a past world, and it was in no small measure Edith Rickert's keen imagination which, playing over the scenes and interpreting their recorded details, brought everything to life, so that there evolved in her mind an ever-clearer impression of Chaucer's London—how it looked and smelled, what a din of sounds filled the narrow streets. She accompanied Chaucer in and out of his house in Aldgate, walked with him to and from the Custom House, rowed with him on the Thames to Westminster, saw what he saw and heard what he heard as he came and went on his daily rounds.

Many of the documents which helped to construct this living picture are contained in this volume, and some of the illustrations were taken from illuminated manuscripts of which slides and photographs had been collected by Edith Rickert for use in her own lectures and later had been given to the University of Chicago. The framework on which this material is arranged suggests the vividness of her participation in medieval life in the time of Chaucer, and the clarifying light with which her mind and heart flooded the meager details which make up the picture may be reflected still in the memories of those who knew her and perhaps vaguely sensed even by those who did not.

Yet fascinating as this phase of her research was to Edith Rickert, it held second place in relation to her two major labors. Foremost of these was the comparative study of all the known manuscripts of Chaucer's *Canterbury Tales* with the purpose of establishing a definitive critical text. Although the results were not published until nearly a year and a half after her death, this monumental work, in which she collaborated with John M. Manly, occupied practically all the time she could spare from her teaching during the last fourteen years of her life. During the early part of this time her tremendous enthusiasm for the proposed work, with its implications of new methods in textual criticism, carried her

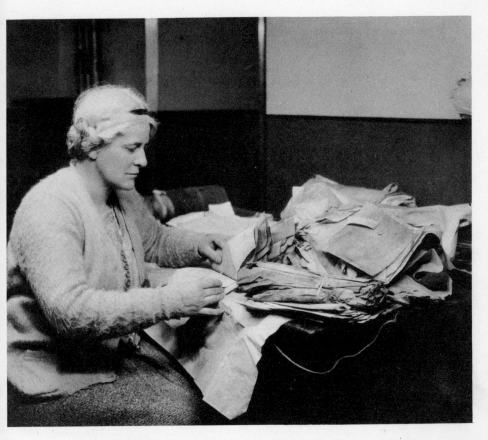

EDITH RICKERT, photographed at the Public Record Office, London, *ca.* 1928, when she was examining records such as Chaucer himself would have kept in connection with his work as Controller of the Customs and Clerk of the Works. In Miss Rickert's hands are some Exchequer "bille" —bits of parchment used for the current work of the office, as it were—and on the far side of the table, the large enrollments upon which the accounts would finally be entered. These records are the fourteenth-century version of the modern civil servant's files of typescript minutes and reports.

through many self-imposed work weeks of seven days, the day often fifteen hours long, almost her only relaxation being an occasional concert or theater. Six months of the year were spent in Chicago, teaching at the university and working in the Chaucer "laboratory" with a staff which at the height of the work numbered some fifteen persons, chiefly graduate students. The other six months were spent abroad, the first few weeks, perhaps, on a reluctant vacation in southern France or in Italy—at any rate somewhere within easy reach of London, where the major part of the research went on. Although the project was not completed within the lifetime of Edith Rickert, all the many parts of *The Text of the Canterbury Tales* as it finally appeared had been written and worked over by the editors together, and all the important theories and conclusions incorporated in it were the result of this complete collaboration. It was tragic that this enormous labor did not yield her the ultimate satisfaction of seeing it finished.

The second main purpose of the documentary search, which was instituted primarily for the study of the *Canterbury Tales* manuscripts, was a revision of the Chaucer *Life-Records*. For this work a staff of trained helpers in London, headed by Miss Lilian Redstone and supervised by Edith Rickert in her "spare moments," turned up much new material bearing on Chaucer's life, as well as many items of more general interest which are included in the volume. The *Life-Records* material still lies in the files of the University of Chicago library awaiting an editor and publication.

These two major projects carried on concurrently in addition to full-time teaching for half the year would seem to have been enough to absorb a normal person's energies, but there was still another side of Edith Rickert's creative nature, which demanded expression in the form of fiction. One novel was published during this time (1930), in England under the title *Olwen Growing* and in America as *Severn Woods;* it was written largely during one of those so-called "vacation" periods between the teaching term and the sojourn in London. Previously, five other novels had been published and a considerable number of short stories. Even during the later period of teaching and research one or two additional novels were written more or less completely, but not published, and a number of stories and sketches, most of the latter also unpublished. The published stories of this period might surprise anyone who did not know Edith Rickert well, for they are children's stories, told with the rare

simplicity and charm with which she used to tell them to the occasional
child who came to visit her. The most successful is still *The Bojabi Tree*,
the earliest of the group (1923).

A love for children and an understanding of their minds are evident also
in Edith Rickert's contributions to a series of readers, known as *Good
Reading* (1926–28). Many of the selections supplied by her were her own
translations or versions of old material, and she also found and adapted
and even herself wrote some entirely new selections. Other textbooks,
which she published in conjunction with Mr. Manly, were *The Writing
of English* (1919 and subsequent editions) and a volume each on English
and American contemporary literature, which went through several re-
visions and editions. Her most revolutionary ideas were contained in the
New Methods for the Study of Literature (1927), which grew out of
some novel and promising experiments in the analysis of literary forms
conducted through several successive university classes in modern literature.

And so, finally, to her teaching, which represents still another side of
Edith Rickert's interest, no less intense than that expressed in her research and in her literary and critical work and no less suitably com-
memorated in this volume, so carefully and excellently prepared by the
well-trained, scholarly minds of certain of her students. The twenty-odd
years of her university teaching were enriched by student friendships in-
creasing in number with each succeeding class and renewed from time to
time by letters and visits from returning students. To Edith Rickert her
students were more than members of successive classes. On them she
tried out her new theories, as in the studies of modern literature, hoping
to stimulate in them independent mental activity; into them she poured
her own joyous enthusiasm which lightened what must have seemed to
them at first the drudgery of research; with them she shared her own
exciting intellectual and personal experiences and discoveries; in each
new student she sought to find a new recruit for the ranks of distinguished
scholars and teachers. And running through all these stimulating mental
contacts was her deep and sympathetic interest, even in their personal
problems, and her genuine desire to help them in any way possible. Probably every one of her students cherishes the memory of some personal
kindness shown to himself, but no one person can ever know the many
thoughtful acts which endeared her to them all. As Edith Rickert's sister
I might have been jealous of her students, so much of her interest and
affection did they receive. But the source was boundless; there was always

plenty for us all. It is a satisfaction to remember, too, that our gratitude for what we received was more than equaled by her joy in the giving.

What more need be said? To have lived broadly and deeply and to have brought the beauty and grace and integrity of her personality into the lives of many; to have produced richly and in varied kinds; to have found at the end of her life the sheer force of will to dominate the crippling illness that drained her physical strength, but could not conquer her mind and spirit; and to have carried forward unremittingly even in the face of death the work to which long before she had dedicated herself—this is the measure of Edith Rickert's stature.

M.R.

Chicago, Ill.
October, 1947

Preface

THE COLLECTION of material for this book was one of several projects growing out of the research done by the late Professors John M. Manly and Edith Rickert which resulted in the publication of *The Text of the Canterbury Tales* in 1940. As early as 1925 or 1926 Miss Rickert had begun gathering source material, assisted by Miss Lilian J. Redstone and her staff in England, who were searching documents of many kinds for additions to the Chaucer *Life-Records*. Miss Rickert's original idea for organizing the material to illustrate phases of fourteenth-century life in general was finally crystallized by Miss Redstone's suggestion that the selections be grouped about the life of a typical fourteenth-century person. During Miss Rickert's last visit to England, in 1936, she and Miss Redstone agreed upon the final plan of the book. After Miss Rickert's death, in 1938, Professor Manly suggested that Clair C. Olson, who had done his doctoral research under Miss Rickert's supervision, should take charge of completing the editing of this material, with the idea that it be published as a memorial to her and with the understanding that he would ask as many of Miss Rickert's former students as seemed practicable to assist him. Mr. Olson therefore invited Martin M. Crow to become coeditor, and later they asked others to assist. The illustrations were selected by Miss Margaret Rickert, who, through long association with the project, was familiar with the body of material and with many of her sister's ideas for incorporating it into a book.

The distinctive features of *Chaucer's World* are the limitation of the material largely to Chaucer's period and its focus on aspects of life with which he was familiar. Many of the selections deal with people, places, or events that Chaucer himself knew or knew of. The items, from widely diverse sources, are fitted into a pattern which forms a mosaic of fourteenth-century life, picturing Chaucer's London and illustrating chronologically typical aspects of the life span of people from various social classes and occupations.

Although both editors have to some extent worked over the entire book, Mr. Crow was primarily responsible for Chapters I, VI, VIII, IX, and X, and Mr. Olson for Chapters II, III, IV, V, and VII.

Because the bulk of the material which came to the editors was so great, the problem of selection and organization according to the general plan laid out by Miss Rickert and Miss Redstone was difficult. The editors devised the chapter organization and headings to carry out Miss Rickert's conception of the book, made the final selection and grouping of the items, chose certain additional material, checked the transcriptions and translations of all previously published selections as well as the bibliographical information, translated certain items from Latin and Old French, where necessary, modernized Middle English passages, supplied footnotes, prepared a bibliography of the sources used, and obtained permission to reprint hitherto published material. A complete check of the manuscript material has not been possible, owing to war conditions; but since much of it had already been checked before it reached the editors and since it was felt that the unpublished material constitutes the most valuable contribution of the book to scholarship, it has all been included.

The exact amount of editing Miss Rickert had done on certain of the items it has been impossible to ascertain, although her handwriting on the manuscript shows that she had gone carefully over many of the selections, modernizing, annotating, and indicating material to be omitted. Even the parts apparently most nearly finished may not be just as Miss Rickert would have published them, but they have been left as they were unless further editing seemed absolutely necessary. The number and length of the explanatory comments introducing chapters and selections vary greatly, because Miss Rickert had prepared them only for certain parts. The editors have retained practically all of these introductions and have supplied certain others.

Introductory passages and notes written by Miss Rickert or constructed by the editors from material in her files are indicated by R. The authorship of footnotes based on the publications of other scholars has also been acknowledged. Footnotes which were added by the editors and those which were typed or written in unidentified hands in the original manuscript have no attribution. Glossarial notes have been made in accord with Miss Rickert's practice: that is, only for words not included in Webster's *New International Dictionary*, or not defined there in a sense appropriate to their use in the manuscript.

In accordance with Miss Rickert's editorial method, the original language has been translated, modernized, and in some cases summarized. In order to preserve the stylistic flavor of the medieval originals, the Middle English material has been modernized only enough to render

the selections intelligible to modern readers. The translations from
French and Latin are free renditions.

The editors have not tried, however, to attain absolute uniformity in
these or other matters. For example, only those geographical proper
names which have been identified and the names of all well-known
persons concerning whose identity there can be no doubt have been
modernized. Certain inconsistencies in spelling, resulting from hand-
written copies of the unchecked, unpublished material, have been queried.

For published material, the style of the entries in the bibliography is
based upon the form used by the Library of Congress. Entries for unpublished material agree with those used by Miss Rickert and Miss Redstone
in their work on the yet unpublished revision of the Chaucer *Life-Records*.

The editors wish to thank the many people and institutions that have
aided them in preparing this volume, primarily Miss Redstone, whose
interest and work represent the latest collaboration with Miss Rickert.
A number of Miss Rickert's graduate students helped in the early stages
of preparation; in the completion of the work, Mrs. Virginia Everett
Leland and Miss Mary Giffin rendered most valuable assistance. Of the
many members of library staffs who assisted, Miss Winifred Ver Nooy
should be especially mentioned. The resources of several libraries were
freely placed at the disposal of the editors. Various scholars have answered questions and checked translations. The University of Texas Research Institute made to Mr. Crow a grant of three hundred dollars to
help defray expenses. Finally, the editors wish to thank Mrs. Grace A.
Olson for preparing the manuscript for the press, compiling the bibliography of source materials, and assisting them in many ways.

So many people have co-operated in the preparation of *Chaucer's
World* and the work has been carried on over so long a period of time and
across such large distances that errors and inconsistencies can scarcely have
been avoided. The editors have done their best to reduce them to a
minimum; but if some have remained, neither Miss Rickert nor the
many friends who have aided in preparing the manuscript for publication
should be held responsible.

The editors wish to thank the following for their generous permission
to print material used in *Chaucer's World*: Rear Admiral H. T. Baillie-
Grohman; Bishop of London's Registry; Department of Manuscripts of
the British Museum; Cambridge (England) Antiquarian Society; Cambridge University Press; His Grace the Archbishop of Canterbury (per

Miss Irene J. Churchill, Assistant Lambeth Librarian); Chatto and Windus; University of Chicago Press; The Clarendon Press; "The Columbia Studies in History, Economics, and Public Law"; The Worshipful Company of Drapers; Early English Text Society; The Grolier Club; William Gronau, Verlagsbuchhandlung; Controller of His Britannic Majesty's Stationery Office; Henry Holt and Company; Treasurer of the Inner Temple; Messrs. Jackson, Son & Co.; Kegan Paul, Trench, Trubner & Co., Ltd.; Corporation of the City of London; Library Committee of the Corporation of the City of London; London and Middlesex Archaeological Society (per Major N. G. Brett-James, honorary editor); Longmans, Green & Co., Ltd.; Lutterworth Press; Manchester University Press; Dr. John M. Manly; Sir Herbert Maxwell's executors; Professor Ellis H. Minns; Oxford University Press; Principal Probate Registry; Public Record Office; Dr. Bertha H. Putnam; Mr. Vincent B. Redstone; Royal Historical Society; Royal Society of Literature; The Sheldon Press; Simpkin Marshall, Ltd.; The Society for Promoting Christian Knowledge; Society of Antiquaries of London; Elliot Stock; Suffolk Institute of Archaeology and Natural History; Surtees Society; The Times Publishing Co., Ltd.; United Society for Christian Literature; Dr. Andrew F. West; and the Right Honorable, the Earl of Westmorland.

The editors also wish to thank the following for their generous permission to reproduce the illustrative material used in *Chaucer's World:* the Bodleian Library, the British Museum, His Grace the Archbishop of Canterbury, the Huntington Library, the Pierpont Morgan Library, the Walters Gallery, the Public Record Office of London, the Bibliothèque Royale.

C. C. O.
M. M. C.

October, 1947

Contents

CONTENTS

9. RELIGION

10. DEATH AND BURIAL

Illustrations

Chaucer's World

1. London Life

THE CITY

To London [1]

Wright, ed., *Reliquiae antiquae*, I, 205–206.

London, thou art of towns A *per se*,[2]
Sovereign of cities, most seemliest by sight,
Of high renown, riches, and royalty,
Of lords, barons, and many [a] goodly knight,
Of most delectable lusty ladies bright,
Of famous prelates in habits clerical,
Of merchants of substance and might;
London, thou art the flower of cities all.

. . . .

Above all rivers thy river hath renown,
Whose boreal streams, pleasant and preclare,
Under thy lusty walls runneth adown,
Where many a swan swimmeth with wing [so] fair,
Where many a barge doth row and sail with air,
Where many a ship resteth with top royal.
O town of towns patron, and not compeer,
London, thou art the flower of cities all.

Upon thy lusty bridge with pillars white
Been merchants full royal to behold;
Upon thy streets goeth many a seemly knight,
In velvet gowns and chains of gold.
By Julius Caesar thy Tower founded of old
May be the house of Mars victorial,
Whose artillery may not with tongue be told.
London, thou art the flower of cities all.

Strong be the wall [that] about thee stands,
Wise be the people that within thee dwells,

[1] Usually attributed to the Scottish Chaucerian, William Dunbar (1460?–1520?).
[2] First by itself, without rival, as the letter A heads the alphabet.

Fresh be thy river with its lusty strands,
Blithe be thy churches, well sounding thy bells.
Rich be thy merchants in substance that excels,
Fair be thy wives, right lovesome, white, and small,
Clear be thy virgins, lusty under kells.
London, thou art the flower of cities all.

THE CITIZENS' HOMES

1. Houses in Bow-Lane Vintry, 1365

Chaucer's father was a vintner of Vintry Ward. In 1381 his house stood between the houses of William le Gauger and John le Mazelyner, in upper Thames Street. Probably his house was similar to theirs, and we know from two wills in the Gauger family (1324 and 1335) what the Gauger house was like. It contained two cellars, over one of which was built a hall, a "parlour," a bedchamber with a chimney and privy, a kitchen with a pantry, larder, and other offices. Probably there were also garret chambers (cf. Chaucer, Canterbury Tales, ed. by Manly, p. 61).

If Geoffrey Chaucer lived, as is supposed, in his father's house in upper Thames Street, the district known as the Vintry was the part of London with which he was most familiar in his early years.

The house probably faced on upper Thames Street and backed on the Walbrook, then a fair-sized stream of fresh water, not yet walled over as later became necessary because of its contamination. Almost next door was his parish church, St. Martin Vintry, where he would certainly have been baptized. There were three other churches within a stone's throw: St. Michael Paternoster Royal, St. James Garlick-hithe, and St. Thomas the Apostle. Little Geoffrey would certainly have played on (or in) the Walbrook and on the docks where the ships from France and Spain unloaded their cargoes of wine by means of cranes. Other wine merchants, friends of John Chaucer, had large houses and wharves on this part of the river, with cellars for stowage of wine. One large house directly opposite St. Martin's church was owned by Henry Picard, son-in-law of John de Gisors (see Stow, A Survey of London, I, 106), and in 1363 it was the scene of a sumptuous banquet at which four kings were entertained.

Three church schools were in this part of London: St. Mary-le-Bow was nearest, St. Paul's next, and beyond that St. Martin-le-Grand, whose bells rang the curfew (see London, Corporation, Calendar of Letter-Books, G, p. 3). Whichever one Geoffrey may have attended (see below, p. 121), his way there would have taken him through Cheapside, where he must often have loitered to watch a street brawl or a procession passing by, or a tournament, or to listen to the chatter that went on at the various market stations around the great Cross.

Newgate by St. Paul's was used as a prison; Ludgate, the old Roman west gate, was crowded with the continuous throng going to and from Westminster and the thickly populated suburbs lying along the Strand. Baynard's Castle and probably also Montfichet's Tower had been incorporated in the site of the Black Friars' monastery, although the name of the former still lingered in the nearby wharf.

In the district thus outlined, bounded by Gracechurch Street leading to London Bridge, Lombard Street, Cheapside and Newgate Street, the city wall on the west and the Thames on the south, there were no less than thirty-nine parish churches.

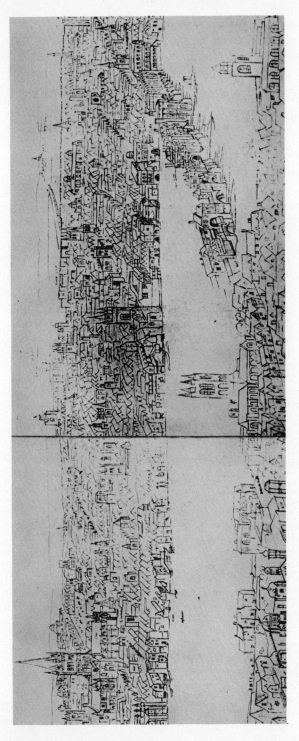

A PANORAMA OF LONDON as seen from the Southwark side of the
River Thames, showing London Bridge and St. Paul's Cathedral,
ca. 1550; drawings by Antonie van den Wyngaerde
London, Brit. Mus., Maps 63.e.8

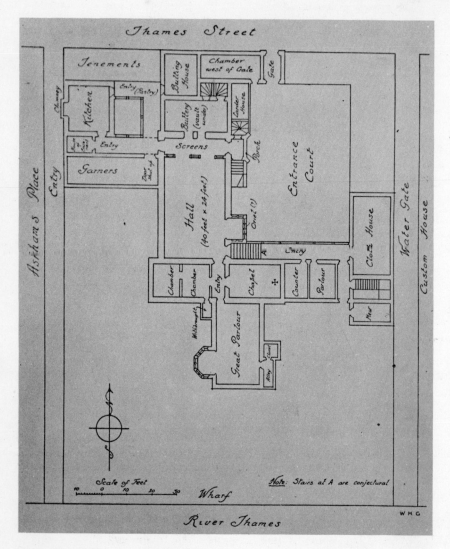

PLAN OF A MERCHANT'S HOUSE
Known as Browne's Place, in 1463
Kingsford, "A London Merchant's House and Its Owners,
1360-1614," *Archaeologia*, LXXIV (1923-1924), 155

The network of narrow streets about St. Paul's was densely populated and contained centers for many trades, some of which are suggested by the names of streets such as Bread Street, Milk Street, Ironmonger Row, Poultry, etc. Other important craft centers in this district were those of the skinners, the goldsmiths, the fullers and dyers; in the "flesh shambles" within Newgate were the butchers.

There is frequent mention in contemporary records of the various features of this district, as it was one of the liveliest parts of London. [R.]

Great Britain, Public Record Office, *Descriptive Catalogue of Ancient Deeds*, II, 72, No. A. 2387.

Indenture is hereby made between Robert de Marny, knight, and Alice his wife [et al.] . . . of the one part and Katherine, late wife of John atte Pole . . . of the other part concerning the partition of lands, etc. in London. . . . It is agreed at the husting before . . . the mayor that [the parties of the first part] shall have for their share of the tenements in St. Michael Paternoster Church parish those between the church and Bow-Lane on the south, tenements that Domengo de Espayne holds on the north, the highway called "la Reole" on the west, and Walbrook and a long stable on the east, with all stone walls, light for four windows towards the north, "les distillations" and other watercourses, etc. . . . and Katherine shall have the said tenements that Domengo holds and the said stable. . . .

Saturday the Feast of St. Luke the Evangelist [October 18] 39 Edward III.

2. *A Merchant's House Next the Customs Wharf (in Building While Chaucer Was Controller at the Wharf)*

MEMORANDUM (15TH CENTURY) OF A BUILDING LEASE OF PACKENHAM'S WHARF, 1384

Kingsford, "A London Merchant's House and Its Owners, 1360–1614," *Archaeologia*, LXXIV (1923–1924), 155 (Anct. Deed [P.R.O.] A 1779).

Memorandum of an indenture, executed 7 Richard II, whereby John Chirteseye of the shire of Hertford, gentleman, makes estate . . . unto Richard Willysdon and to Agnes his wife of all his wharf called "Pakkemannys Wharf" . . . in the parish of St. Dunstan's in the East . . . unto the end of one hundred years . . . paying John Chirteseye, his heirs, and his assigns £12 [a year]. . . . Richard Willysdon shall undertake . . . within ten years . . . to enlarge, in the direction of the Thames, the said wharf by eighty feet, the wall to be all of Maidstone stone . . . and he shall take down all manner of housing upon all the ground and build all the ground [up] only with new timber, putting in none of the old timber. . . . All the front of the said ground upon the high street [*i.e.*, Thames Street] and forty feet inward, is to be of stories of [good] height, the first story twelve feet, the second ten feet, the third seven feet, constructed of sufficient timber all only of heart of oak . . . with all manner of dividing, garnishing, and covering that should belong to said building. Also, the said Richard Willysdon shall . . . build upon the said ground inward a chief dwelling place above-stage, *viz.*, a hall forty feet in length and twenty-four feet in breadth, [and] a parlor, kitchen, and buttery, as to such a hall should belong. And the rest of the ground, except the cartway and the said wharf of eighty feet, shall be used for building chambers and houses sufficient for merchandise. It is provided that the said hall, parlor, kitchen, buttery, and all the said chambers shall be cellared underneath the ground seven feet in height and [that] all the said building to be done shall belong to John Chirteseye or his assigns.

THE SAME PROPERTY, STYLED "BROWNE'S PLACE," IN 1463

Kingsford, "A London Merchant's House and Its Owners, 1360–1614," *Archaeologia*, LXXIV (1923–24), 156–157 (P.C.C. 33 Wattys).

[The property is described as including] all such parcels as ensue: The garret, or coalhouse, set over the great gate towards Thames Street and over two tenantries by the street side set on the west side of the same great gate. Also, a chamber underneath the east part of the same garret, and a bolting house adjoining the same chamber. Also, an entry called a pastry house, leading eastwards from a kitchen of the said house to the same bolting house, and from the same bolting house—[*sic*] feet southwards toward the garners thereunto a door there now shut up. Also, the same kitchen with an entry leading from it to the hall of the said house, with a house of easement set in the west side of the entry. Also, a cellar vaulted at the north end of the hall, with a shed without the east door of the cellar called a larder house, adjoining the cellar and extending northwards to the door of the vault there next to the said gate. Also, the buttery over the said cellar, with the stair leading down to the cellar. Also, the hall with the porch at the east door and leads over the porch and a stair with nine steps leading to the porch. Also, a chamber at the north end of the hall over the buttery with a stair leading thereto. Also, an entry leading from the south end of the hall southwards unto a great parlor. Also, a closet with a little alley thereby to draw water in, set at the south end of the same great parlor. Also, two chambers and a privy on the west side of the entry leading to the said parlor, set betwixt the said hall and the same parlor, with three chambers, otherwise called garrets, set over the same two chambers, privy, and great parlor. Also, a chapel set on the east side of the same entry, with the leads over the same chapel. Also, another entry leading from the south end of the same hall eastwards unto a house called the cloth-house, with a closet called a counter set on the south side of the same entry, with the leads over the same closet. Also, a parlor set on the south side of the same entry. Also, the same cloth-house. Also, another entry leading from the door of the same cloth-house southwards unto a stair leading up unto three garrets over the same two entries and parlor, with the same stair and three garrets. And also, the leads over all the bay windows, with all other manner of leads above any of the said housing and garrets above assigned. Also, a little mew for poultry, set on the south side of the same stair, with the leads over the same mew. Also, a great cellar under the said hall, with a little house adjoining thereto on the east side of the same great cellar. Also, a little house under the stair whereby the going up is into the hall. Also, the third part of all the ground called the Wharf and Crane, and the third part of a latrine set upon the said wharf, and the third part of a house called a "water-house," set upon the same ground and wharf, with the third part of all manner of wharfage, cranage, and other profits which shall come, grow, or be taken of the same ground called the Wharf and Crane or by reason of them or any one of them.[3]

3. A Tavern in Paternoster Row, 1342

SPECIFICATION FOR A MASON TO MAKE THE VAULTED CELLARS

London Bridge Estate Deeds, G 16–17.

Indenture, being a covenant of Philip de Cherche, mason, with William le Marbrer, vintner, to dig beneath the place belonging to the said William in Paternoster Row in the parish of St. Michael at Corn, an excavation seventeen feet deep and to make at the end thereof, in the corner towards the northwest, beneath the floor, a vault with a garderobe, the

[3] From the Plea and Memoranda Roll A 33 m. 1 b we have the following details concerning the house of another London merchant, Richard Toky, grocer or pepperer, member of Parliament for the City in 1358. His house, which may be considered as typical of middle-class dwellings, consisted of a hall, or living room, a solar, or chamber, pantry and buttery, countinghouse, and storehouse (see London, Corporation, *Calendar of Select Pleas and Memoranda, A.D. 1381–1412*, pp. 209–213). Cf. below, pp. 62–65.

same to be built of chalk, and the pipe thereof of stone; the walls of the vault of the cell are to be of good ragstone as high as the first jetty towards the place and tenements of Thomas Leg, and the vault and the arches of freestone and the "parfurnir" of the vault of chalk and the wall thereof towards the street of ragstone to the height of two feet above the pavement, with few windows overlooking the street; and the steps of the stairs of the same cellar and the jambs of the door to be of ragstone; and another stair of chalk, with steps of rag, to be made between the first floor above the vault of the cellar and the floor of the same cellar; and the steps of the door of the room to be of rag; and two fireplaces (*chymenys*) to be built, one at either end of the said cellar, and carried up to the height of the jetty in stone; and beneath the aforesaid stairs a vaulted "cawet," with a doorway of stone; and the said Philip to find the materials—stone, chalk, lime, and sand—as well as the labor, and to receive therefor £26 and 13s. 4d. for a robe.

SPECIFICATION FOR A CARPENTER TO BUILD THE HOUSE AND PUT IN THE FIXTURES FOR THE TAVERN

London Bridge Estate Deeds, G 16–17.

Covenant of Richard de Felstede, carpenter, with William Marbrer, taverner, to build upon the land of the said William in Paternoster Row, between the room beneath the gate of the tavern of Thomas Legge which is held by John de Okebroke, chaplain, on the east and the tenement of the said Thomas on the west and south, a new house with two gabled roofs toward the street, each with two jetties; and above the two stories, beneath the one roof, a garret with puncheons six feet in height, and beneath the other roof, towards Paternoster Row, a room on the highest story, and at one end thereof, towards the north, a buttery and a kitchen; and all the partitions throughout the whole house; and upon the lowest floor above the vault a partitioned room, and on the rest of the same floor thirty seats for the tavern; and a partition extending along the whole length of the said lowest floor; and on the second floor above, thirty seats for the tavern; and in the room (*sale*) a bay window towards the street and on either side thereof a linteled window; and in the bedroom another bay window, with other such linteled windows on either side; and everywhere windows, doors, and steps as they are required; and in the bedroom the canopy over the bed; the said William supplying the timber and "le syer" of timber, and the said Richard receiving for his carpenter's work £24 and a gown worth 20s. or its value in money.

4. A Building Next the Grey Friars, 1391

Summarized from London Letter-Book H, fol. cclxvii b.

Building permit, granted by Robert Hyndon, warden of Friars Minor in London and convent of the same, to Adam Bamme, the mayor, the aldermen, and the commonalty, of a parcel of land on the west side of their church, extending toward the maintenance of London Bridge:— The land to be built upon was ninety-five feet and two inches long; at the east end seven feet and four inches wide; at the west end seven feet and nine inches wide. The ground wall, of stone, was to be eleven feet high. On this was to be erected a building of the height of three solars. The first floor was to have a "gette" [jetty] of two and one-half feet beyond the wall; the second floor the same; the third floor a "gette" of one and a half feet. These three stories were to be faced with Flemish tiles, as were those of the convent opposite them. [This specification applied only to the walls facing the convent.] The windows facing the convent were all to be not less than six feet from the floor and not more than seven inches wide; they were also to be suitably barred with iron and glazed.

LONDON'S STREETS AND STREAMS

1. The Thames as a Highway

Glimpses of daily occurrences on London streets are found in the fragmentary Coroners Rolls, of which the scanty remains have been published by R. R. Sharpe. They consist of the findings of the coroner's jury holding inquest on persons who died deaths "other than their own" (*i.e.*, unnatural deaths). The first entries which have survived are from 1301, and the latest from 1378; most of the material for the years between has been lost. What remains, however, is of great interest, not only for its allusions to medieval ways of living but also for its pathetic-humorous side-lights on human nature. Several entries concern Chaucers, some of them probably kinsmen of the poet. [R.]

WAITING FOR THE TIDE, 1367

London, Coroner, *Calendar of the Coroners Rolls*, pp. 272–273.

On Wednesday [September 15, 1367], at dusk, John Farnaham entered a boat belonging to John Sevar of Portsoken, which boat lay in the Thames near Botolph's Wharf, in the ward of Billingsgate, desiring to voyage in her to the village of North Wokyngdon. While he and his fellow travelers lay asleep waiting for the tide, a great storm of wind and rain arose and overturned the boat, so that John fell into the water and was drowned. His corpse was carried hither and thither until Wednesday after the Feast of St. Michael,[4] when it was found cast by the water in the Fleet,[5] at "le Lymhostes." [6] The vessel and its belongings were appraised by the jury at 20s. Having been asked what became of the boat, they said that John Sevar the same night took it and sailed away. Precept was sent to the sheriff to attach the boat, etc., when found in their bailiwick.

CITY, COURT, AND TEMPLARS DISPUTE THE USE OF THE RIVER, 1360

Riley, *Memorials of London*, I, 306 (from London Letter-Book G, fol. lxxxviii).

Time out of mind the commonalty of the city have been wont to have free ingress and egress with horses and carts from sunrise to sunset for carrying and carting all manner of victuals and wares therefrom to the water of Thames and from the said water of Thames to the city aforesaid, through the great gate of the Templars, situate within Temple Bar, in the ward [of Farringdon Without], in the suburb of London; and the possessors of the Temple were wont and by right ought to maintain a bridge [7] at the water aforesaid and a common latrine there, well covered and with four apertures therein over the same water. And the possessors of a certain structure in Fleet Street in the suburb of London ought to pave the road on either side of that structure. Also, the Prior of St. John of Jerusalem in England, who is the possessor of the Temple aforesaid, molests the citizens of the said city so that they cannot have their free ingress and egress through the gate aforesaid as of old . . . and . . . by default of the said Prior . . . the pavement . . . is worn out and broken and dangerous to all persons passing or riding thereby.

2. *Care of Streets and Quays*

The care which fourteenth-century London gave to street repair and to sanitation is attested by excerpts from the Letter-Books: On November 12, 1364, ordinance was made by the mayor that "scawageours" (superintendents of scavengers or "rakyers") should have full power to survey the pavements and see that they were kept in good repair, and also the streets and lanes that they be kept clean (London, Corporation, *Calendar of Letter-Books*, G, p. 198).—On July 28, 1366, the order was repeated, charging constables, "escawangers," and beadles to cause the streets to be paved and cleared of rubbish (*ibid.*, p. 208).—On November 1,

[4] The Feast of St. Michael is September 29.
[5] One of the "lost rivers" of medieval London. It entered the Thames west of St. Paul's.
[6] Lime Hurst, Lime Host, corruptly called Lime House (Stow, *Survey of London*, ed. by Kingsford, II, 71). Apparently there is some error here in nomenclature.
[7] A pier, or jetty, for landing, called Templebridge [Riley's note].

1372, proclamation was made that no one by night or day, secretly or openly, should place rubbish, dung, etc. in the water of the Thames or the City ditches; that each one keep his street clean according to the ordinance thereon made; that no one cast water or anything else out of the window, but bring it down and put it in the kennel, under penalty of paying 2s. for default (*ibid.*, p. 300).—On October 9, 1385, a similar proclamation was made, fining anyone found placing rubbish before his neighbor's door 4s. (*ibid.*, H, p. 275).—On September 16, 1390, the surveyor of streets and lanes was ordered to kill all pigs, geese, etc. he might find at large and sell them at the best price he could get, paying one half of the proceeds to the chamberlain and keeping the other half for his trouble (*ibid.*, p. 355). Cf. below, p. 421.

CLEANING THE CITY STREETS AND THE BANKS OF THE THAMES, 1357

Riley, *Memorials of London*, I, 295–296 (from London Letter-Book G, fol. lxiv).

The King to the mayor and sheriffs of our city of London, greeting: Considering that the streets and lanes and other places in the city and the suburbs thereof, in the times of our forefathers and our own, were wont to be cleaned from dung, laystalls, and other filth and were wont hereto-fore to be protected from the corruption arising therefrom, from which no little honor did accrue unto the said city and those dwelling therein, and whereas now, when passing along the water of Thames, we have be-held dung and laystalls and other filth accumulated in divers places and have also perceived the fumes and other abominable stenches aris-ing therefrom, from the corruption of which, if tolerated, great peril as well to the persons dwelling within the said city, as to the nobles and others passing along the said river, will, it is feared, ensue, unless, in-deed, some fitting remedy be speedily provided for the same; we, wish-ing to take due precaution against such perils and to preserve the honor and decency of the city . . . do command that you cause as well the banks of the said river as the streets and lanes of the city and the suburbs thereof to be cleaned of dung, laystalls, and other filth without delay, and the same when cleaned so to be kept; and in the city and the suburbs thereof public proclamation to be made, and it on our behalf strictly forbidden that any one shall, on pain of heavy forfeiture unto us, place or cause to be placed dung or other filth to be accumulated in the same. And if any persons, after proclamation and prohibition so made, you shall find doing to the contrary hereof, you are to cause them so to be chastised and pun-ished that such penalty and chastisement may cause fear and dread unto others perpetrating the like. And this, as you would preserve yourself safe and would avoid our heavy indignation, you are in no wise to omit.

A LEVY TO REPAIR THE ROAD OUTSIDE ALDGATE, 1376

For about twelve years beginning in May, 1374, Chaucer and his wife, Philippa, occupied an apartment over Aldgate, which he "obtained rent-free from the municipality, on condition that he keep it in repair and that the city retain right of entry for purposes of defense in time of war" (Chaucer, *Canterbury Tales*, ed. by Manly, p. 20).

London, Corporation, *Calendar of Letter-Books*, H, p. 54.

Commissioners were appointed under the seal of the mayoralty by Adam Stable, the mayor, and the aldermen to levy twopence a week on every iron-bound cart bringing victuals to the city by way of Aldgate and every cart and car bringing blood and entrails of slaughtered beasts entering the city or returning the same way, a penny a week on every cart or car not iron-bound bringing dung, etc., and a halfpenny a week on every horse laden with grain, etc., the money to be expended on the repair of the highway outside Aldgate.

Similar commissions for the highways outside Bishopsgate, Cripplegate, and Aldersgate.

KEEPING PAVEMENT CLEAN NEAR THE WOOL QUAY, 1377

On the Wool Quay, Chaucer, as "controller of the customs on wool, hides, and sheepskins in the port of London," kept "a counter-roll, or check-roll, of the customs accounts, to verify the roll of the two collectors" (Chaucer, *Canterbury Tales*, ed. by Manly, p. 17).

London, Corporation, *Calendar of Letter-Books*, H, p. 63.

Nicholas Brembre, the mayor, and the aldermen appointed John Stokyngbury, John Bamptone, water bailiff, Simon atte Bole, John Salpertone, and Ralph Evenynge to be collectors of certain prescribed tolls on merchandise entering any quay or port between London Bridge and the quay called "Wool Quay" and to render account of the same to the chamberlain, the said tolls to be applied to keeping clean the pavement, etc., within that district.[8]

[8] Compare with the following excerpt, dated 1379: "John Hadley, the mayor, and the aldermen, under the mayoralty seal, appointed John de Kenle, Nicholas Pays, and Thomas Fraunkeleyn, 'chandler,' to collect and levy on every boat coming to the City with rushes for sale the sum of twelve pence, and on every boat with straw or hay [to strew on floors; used instead of carpets], eight pence, the money to be devoted to cleaning and keeping clean the ports, quays, etc., where such boats discharge" (London, Corporation, *Calendar of Letter-Books*, H, p. 152).

SHORTENING THE ALESTAKES, 1375

Riley, *Memorials of London*, II, 386–387 (from London Letter-Book H, fol. xxii).

On Friday the Feast of St. Matthew the Apostle [September 21] at the prayer of the commonalty, making plaint that the alestakes projecting in front of the taverns in Cheap and elsewhere in the city extended too far over the king's highway, so as to impede those riding there and other persons, and by reason of their excessive weight did tend to the great deterioration of the houses in which they were placed, it was ordained and granted by the mayor and aldermen, as a befitting remedy for the same, and all taverners of the city being summoned, orders were given unto them, on pain of paying forty pence to the Chamber of the Guildhall every time the said ordinance should be contravened, that in future no one should have an alestake bearing his sign or leaves,[9] projecting or extending over the king's highway more than seven feet in length at the utmost—the said ordinance to begin to take effect at the Feast of St. Michael [September 29] then next ensuing, and always in future to be in force.

3. Traffic Problems

A HIT AND RUN DRIVER, 1337

London, Coroner, *Calendar of the Coroners Rolls*, pp. 181–182.

On Thursday [February 13], about the hour of vespers, two carters taking two empty carts out of the city were urging their horses apace, when the wheels of one of the carts collapsed opposite the rent of the hospital of St. Mary, Bishopsgate, so that the cart fell on Agnes de Cicestre, who immediately died. The carter thereupon left his cart and three horses and took flight in fear, although he was not suspected of malicious intent. The cart and its trappings were appraised by jurors of the ward of Bishopsgate at 6s. 8d.; the first horse, of a dun color, at 10s., the second, a gray, and blind of both eyes, at 4s., and the third, a black, at 6s.; also five old sacks and five pounds of candles of "coton" [10] which were in the cart at the time of the accident at 16½d. Total 28s. ½d., for which John de Northhalle, one of the sheriffs, will answer.[11]

[9] A bunch of leaves, or "bush," indicating that wine was sold within. Cf. the proverb "Good wine needs no bush."
[10] That is, with cotton wicks (*O.E.D.*). Cf. below, p. 79.
[11] Cf. the following Common Pleas case [1386], in which Margery atte Hill of London sued Richard Tulby, carter, for damages of £40 for injuries [breaking her right leg] in consequence of his negligent driving (Common Pleas, Plea Roll 502 m. 385 d).

SPEED LIMIT FOR EMPTY CARTS, 1419 [12]

The *Liber albus*, or *White Book*, was compiled in 1419 under the auspices of John Carpenter, who was common or town clerk of London. The purpose of the book, as he himself says in the preface, was "that there might be a trustworthy record of the customs and proceedings of the city." The value of such a book in his time is evident from this statement: "When, as not unfrequently happens, all the aged, most experienced and most discreet rulers of the royal city of London have been carried off at the same instant, as it were, by pestilence, younger persons who have succeeded them in the government of the city have been often at a loss from the very want of such written information," the result of which has repeatedly been disputes and perplexity among them as to the decisions which they should give. The book throws light upon social conditions of London in the thirteenth and fourteenth centuries. [R.]

London, Corporation, *Munimenta Gildhallae Londoniensis; Liber albus*, I, 453–454.

No carter within the liberties shall drive his cart more quickly when it is unloaded than when it is loaded, for the avoiding of divers perils and grievances, under pain of paying forty pence unto the Chamber and of having his body committed to prison at the will of the mayor.

CARELESS RIDING IN THAMES STREET, 1321

London, Coroner, *Calendar of the Coroners Rolls*, pp. 34–35.

On Monday, October 19, at vesper time, one Thomas atte Chirche, esquire to the Earl of Arundel, and an unknown man were riding together through Thames Street towards the Tower. As they were passing the house of Olive Sorweles, a widow, in the ward of Billingsgate, Thomas atte Chirche nearly threw to the ground with his horse an unknown woman carrying a child in her arms. Because John de Harwe, a porter, begged the two men to ride more carefully, Thomas angrily drew his sword and struck John in the right side, inflicting a mortal wound two inches long and five inches deep. Thus wounded, John walked as far as the solar which he rented in the parish of St. Martin, in the ward of Vintry, where he received his ecclesiastical rights and died of the wound on the next day.

Thomas atte Chirche and the unknown man immediately fled toward the Tower, but, although there were many passersby, no one knew what became of them. Thomas had no chattels except the horse on which he fled.[13]

[12] Date of compilation of *Liber albus*.
[13] Compare with the following case of damages for an accident caused by a runaway horse in 1398: John Wherewell of London, defendant, hired a horse from Alice Stok, "hakenay

4. Street Quarrels

A FIGHT ABOUT EELSKINS, 1326

London, Coroner, *Calendar of the Coroners Rolls*, pp. 169–170.

On Friday [August 15] at the hour of prime, Roger Styward was walking in Cordwainer Street carrying eels in a bucket for sale. He threw down on the street some skins of eels opposite the shops of Simon de Peckham [14] and John de Keslyngbury; whereupon Simon and Richard de Keslyngbury, apprentice of John, remonstrated with him. A quarrel arising, the apprentice left the shop and struck Roger with the palm of his hand under the left jaw and returned to the shop. Simon followed Roger as far as the churchyard of St. Mary-le-Bow and there struck him with his fist on the head under the left ear, so that he fell to the ground, and then kicked him as he lay. Roger rose with difficulty and went towards Cheapside, when he again fell and immediately died. Simon and Richard, on hearing of his death, took refuge in the church of St. Mary-le-Bow. Richard, after the inquest was held, surrendered and was taken to Newgate, but Simon refused to surrender.

A FATAL DISPUTE ABOUT APPLES, 1301

London, Coroner, *Calendar of the Coroners Rolls*, pp. 14–15.

On Thursday before the Feast of the Conversion of St. Paul,[15] after the hour of curfew, a certain costermonger came before the building of Master Gilbert the marshal, at the top of the street near Gracechurch, crying "Costard apples for sale." Copin le Kyng and a certain William Osbern bargained for some of the apples and wished to carry off five of them against the will of the bearer; thereupon he made a noise and clamor. There came a certain Thomas le Brewere, who reprimanded Copin and William for taking the apples against the wish of the vendor, so that

---

woman," to ride on business to Eltham. After he mounted the horse, it took the bit between its teeth and bolted along Woodstreet and Cheap to St. Martin-le-Grand, knocking down Nicholas Whitlock, plaintiff. Case tried in Court of Common Pleas; jury returned that the defendant had not been warned of the bad disposition (*de malis condicionibus*) of the horse before he had mounted it. Summarized from Common Pleas, Plea Roll 551 m. 119; cf. Common Pleas, Plea Roll 548 m. 221.

[14] There is strong reason to believe that Simon de Peckham was Simon Chaucer, brother of Richard, the poet's step-grandfather. Simon Chaucer's murder in 1336 was the subject of inquest in Coroners Roll F, No. 4 (cf. *Life-Records of Chaucer*, IV, 144–45). [R.]

[15] The Feast of the Conversion of St. Paul is January 25.

angry words arose between them, and Copin and William assaulted Thomas le Brewere, following him with abuse as far as Fenchurch, where, at the top of the street, Thomas turned and struck Copin on the left side of the head with a staff called "balstaff," [16] inflicting a wound an inch long and two inches deep, and another wound on the right side of the head of the same length and breadth. Copin lingered until Thursday before the Purification [17] and then died of his wounds at the hour of prime.

A SQUABBLE BETWEEN BEGGARS, 1399

Coram Rege Roll 553 m. 18 d.

John Dray, beggar, had been attached to answer Ralph Goodson in a plea of assault and battery [etc.]. Goodson by his attorney stated that on Thursday before the Feast of SS. Tiburtius and Valerian,[18] 22 Richard II [1399], in the parish of S. Faith, ward of Farringdon Within, Dray attacked him and caused him to suffer damage to the amount of £20.

John Dray in his own person denied the charge and said that on the day and in the place mentioned he and the said Ralph were sitting together and begging, when John Stowe, a monk of Westminster, came by and gave them a penny in common. Ralph received the penny, but would not give Dray his share. A quarrel arose and Ralph assaulted him with a stick. Any injury Ralph received was done in self-defense.

Ralph denied any grounds for John's assault; they put themselves on the country. Dray found mainpernors.

5. *Street Noises*

BLACKSMITHS, CA. 1350

Wright, *Reliquiae antiquae*, I, 240 (from Arundel MS [B.M.] 292, fol. 72 b).

Swart smoky smiths smutted with smoke
Drive me to death with the din of their dints;
Such noise at night heard no man ever,
Such crying of knaves and clattering of knocks;
The pug-nosed bumpkins cry for "Coal! coal!"
And blow with their bellows till their brains are all bursting.

[16] A balkstaff, or quarterstaff. See Thomas Wright, ed., *Dictionary of Obsolete and Provincial English.*
[17] The Feast of the Purification (of the Virgin Mary) is February 2.
[18] The Feast of SS. Tiburtius and Valerian is April 14.

"Huff! puff!" says the one; "Haff! paff!" the other.
They spit and they sprawl and they tell many stories;
They gnaw and they gnash, and they groan all together,
And hold them hot with their hard hammers.
Of a bull's hide are their big aprons;
Their shanks are sheathed against sparks of the fire.
Heavy hammers they have that are hard to handle;
Strong strokes they strike on a stock of steel:
"Lus! bus! las! das!" they roar in a row.
Like a dreadful dream—may it go to the devil!
The master stands apart; his stroke is the lighter;
Between the two of them he twines out a treble:
"Tick! tack! hic! hac! ticket! tacket! tick! tack!
Lus! bus! las! das!" such a life as they lead us!
All our clothes they smut—Christ give them sorrow!
No man for such water-burners can get a night's rest.

MINSTRELS, 1324

London, Coroner, *Calendar of the Coroners Rolls*, pp. 85–86.

On Wednesday after the Feast of Invention of Holy Cross,[19] it happened
that a certain Thomas de Lenne, "pelleter,"[20] lay dead in the house
held by Walter de Lenne, "pelleter," of Hugh de Waltham, in the
parish of St. Michael in the ward of Cornhill. On hearing this, the coroner
and sheriffs proceeded thither, and having summoned good men of that
ward and of the three nearest wards, *viz.* Broad Street, Langbourn, and
Walbrook, they diligently examined how it happened. The jurors said
that on the preceding Thursday, after the hour of vespers, a certain
Thomas Somer, a "menestral," came playing to the house, and Thomas
de Lenne, moved with anger, took a staff called "durbarre" [doorbar]
in his hand and pursued Thomas Somer to kill him as far as the Tun [21]
upon Cornhill, and therewith struck him on the head; that Thomas
Somer at last drew his knife and with it struck Thomas de Lenne on the
breast, inflicting a mortal wound an inch long and four inches deep; that
Thomas, so wounded, returned to the house and there had his ecclesiastical rights; that he lingered until midnight [and then died]. Thomas

[19] The Feast of the Invention of Holy Cross is May 3.
[20] Dealer in skins or hides of animals; fellmonger. (*O.E.D.*)
[21] A prison for vagrants, said to be so called from its being built "in fashion of a Tunne
standing on the one ende" (cf. Stow, *A Survey of London*, I, 188).

Somer was forthwith taken and committed to Newgate. Having been asked who were present when this happened, the jurors said no one except those two, so far as they could learn, nor did they suspect anyone of his death.

CURFEW BELLS, 1370

London, Corporation, *Calendar of Letter-Books*, G, pp. 270–271.

Proclamation was made December 4, 44 Edward III [1370] . . . that no one wander in the City after curfew sounded at the churches of St. Mary-le-Bow, Barking Church in Tower Ward, St. Bride, and St. Giles without Cripplegate, unless he be of good repute and carry a light, on pain of imprisonment.

That no taverner or brewer keep open house after curfew sounded at the above churches, and that curfew be not sounded at any other church later than at the above churches.[22]

MIDNIGHT ROISTERERS, 1321/22

London, Coroner, *Calendar of the Coroners Rolls*, pp. 46–47.

At midnight on a certain Tuesday in January [1321/22], Reginald de Freestone "settere," [23] John Bocche, Walter le Skynnere, and eleven others whose names were unknown were passing the shop of William de Grymesby in the ward of Broad Street. [They were] singing and shouting, as they often did at night, when William de Grymesby, who was in his shop, begged them to allow him and the neighbors to sleep and rest in peace.

Whereupon Reginald de Freestone, John Bocche, Walter le Skynnere,

---

[22] Another church where curfew was rung was St. Martin-le-Grand (*ibid.*, pp. 3, 150). An ordinance of 1282 required that at every parish church curfew be rung at the same hour as at St. Martin-le-Grand, so that they begin together and end together (Riley, *Memorials of London*, I, 21).

Bells other than curfew are mentioned by Stow: "[King Edward III] also builded to the use of this chapel [St. Stephen's at Westminster] . . . a strong clochard of stone and timber, covered with lead, and placed therein three great bells, since usually rung at coronations, triumphs, funerals of princes and their obits. Of those bells men fabled that their ringing soured all the drink in the town" (Stow, *A Survey of London*, II, 120; cf. Hunter, "Notices of the Old Clochard or Bell-Tower of the Palace at Westminster," *Archaeologia*, XXXVII [1857], 23–26).

The bell in the great steeple of St. Paul's was in the fourteenth century rung to call the inhabitants of the city together to the place of assembly of their folkmoots in the east part of the churchyard (Stow, *A Survey of London*, I, 325).

[23] Arrow-head maker. [Sharpe's note.]

and their companions invited William de Grymesby to come out of his shop if he dared.

At last he seized a staff called a "balstaf" [24] and did run after them. He struck Reginald with the staff on the left side of the head and smashed the whole of it. Reginald fell to the ground at the entrance of the tenement of Jordan de Langelegh and there lingered without speaking until break of day on Tuesday, when he died of the blow.

Alice de Breynford first discovered Reginald lying dead, and she raised the cry so that the country came.

The goods of William de Grymesby were appraised and found to be: two small pigs, at 3s.; one "shippingbord," at 3d.; one broken chest and a table, at 6d.; one pair of worn linen sheets, at 4d.; a blanket, a worn linen cloth, and other small things, at 2s. 9½d. Total, 6s. 11½d., for which Richard de Hakeneye, the sheriff, was to answer.

BUYING AND SELLING

The citizens of medieval London were of two very different types, "freemen" and "foreigners," to use the old terms; but as there were also some thousands of Italians, Flemings, and Frenchmen, to say nothing of Germans, Spaniards, and other non-English nationalities dwelling in this crowded town, it is better to make three groups: freemen, outsiders, and foreigners.

The freemen were the members of the twenty-four gilds, each duly admitted after serving his apprenticeship and proving his knowledge of his craft or trade, and upon payment of a fee. Each gild was under the supervision of two masters to see that the standard of work was kept up and that no frauds were perpetrated. When offenses against their regulations concerned the gild alone, it was a self-governing body; when they concerned outside citizens, the problem was transferred to the mayor's or municipal court.

The outsiders were the "nonunion" men of the city; that is, they included people from the country and people in the city who were not members of any gild. They were without, of course, the special privileges which the freemen arrogated to themselves, and they could not hold municipal offices.

The control of the city, indeed, was in the hands of a closed corporation: the members of the gilds, which were largely localized in the twenty-four wards, elected the twenty-four aldermen, and by annual election the two sheriffs and the mayor were chosen from the aldermen—as they are still.

The most interesting and perhaps surprising fact about this oligarchy was its benevolence. The high officials of medieval London showed continual concern that their city should be well managed. Their regulations and records of infringements of them are preserved in a series of municipal documents which is perhaps the most complete and certainly the most interesting in the world—and this, too, although they suffered the irreparable loss of the entire body of records of the mayor's court for the fourteenth century in the Great Fire of 1666. By a lucky chance, three dif-

[24] See above, p. 16n.

ferent types of documents have survived:[25] the original Letter-Books, or day books, of the municipality, in which the most varied matters of concern to the community were recorded from late thirteenth century to late fifteenth century; the Husting Rolls, each of many skins of parchment, on which were recorded the wills and deeds of London freemen; and the Plea and Memoranda Rolls, approximately one hundred in number, each commonly consisting of eight to twelve skins, which are believed to be informal records of cases in the mayor's court.

Of these records, a calendar, or digest, of the Husting wills has been edited by R. R. Sharpe (former clerk of the records at the London Guildhall); but the deeds are still unpublished; a Calendar of the Letter-Books, in nine volumes (A–L) has also been edited by Sharpe, and many of the more interesting documents have been published almost or quite in full in H. T. Riley's *Memorials of London*; a *Calendar of the Plea and Memoranda Rolls* has been made by the clerk of the records, A. H. Thomas. Besides these, there is a great store of documents at the Guildhall, unpublished, uncalendared, and still largely unexplored.

From records of these regulations, then, and their infringements has been taken most of the body of material which follows. As many of the records are in French or Latin, they are given in translation, with the continually recurrent formal elements cut. [R.]

1. Keeping up the Standards

WEIGHER OF THE GREAT BALANCE, 1375/76

London, Corporation, *Calendar of Letter-Books*, H, p. 22.

On February 18, 50 Edward III [1375/76], John Lokes was elected by the good men of the mystery of pepperers to be weigher of the Great Balance,[26] and sworn before John Warde, the mayor, to execute the office faithfully, he taking for the use of the sheriffs one penny for every thousand weighed and for his own trouble one farthing for every hundred weighed and more, and rendering an account of all profit weekly to the sheriffs.

SEA COAL METERS, 1369

Riley, *Memorials of London*, II, 338–339 (from London Letter-Book G, fol. ccxxx).

On the eleventh day of July [1369] John Wirhale, Roger Cooke, Henry Cornewaille, and Geoffrey Prudhomme were chosen to hold the office of meters of sea-coal coming into the city of London; and sworn that they would well and trustily make measure of coals so coming thither, taking for their trouble as from of old they were wont. And they gave sureties that they would well and trustily do all things which unto the said office pertain.

[25] These documents have survived the ravages of the second World War.
[26] The mercers elected the weigher of the Small Balance (see London, Corporation, *Calendar of Letter-Books*, G, p. 2).

CHARCOAL, 1368

Riley, *Memorials of London*, I, 335–336 (from London Letter-Book G, fol. cxcix).

Whereas the common people of the city of London have suffered great loss for a long time past for that foreign folks [*i.e.*, not freemen of the city] of divers counties have brought charcoal in carts and upon horses for sale in the said city and given the common people to understand that every sack into which such charcoal was put contained fully one quarter; therefore . . . the Mayor of the said city caused divers sacks brought as well by cart as by horse into which charcoal had been put for sale to be essayed by the standard of the city. Of these sacks one was found to be two bushels short and another sack was deficient by one bushel and a half; and in all the other sacks fully one bushel was wanting. For avoiding such damages and falsities committed against the common people, it is ordained by the assent of the mayor, aldermen, and good folks of the commonalty to the Guildhall summoned . . . that all those who shall be convicted of such deceit and falsity shall be put upon the pillory and the sacks burned beneath them.

FIREWOOD, 1379

Riley, *Memorials of London*, II, 437–438 (from London Letter-Book H, fol. cxvi).

Be it remembered that on the twentieth day of December [1379], it was published at Billingsgate on behalf of the mayor that all persons who had any wood called "bilet" (billet, or firewood) either stored in houses or laid up upon their wharves should sell the same before the Feast of Our Lord's Nativity [December 25] then next ensuing on pain of forfeiture of the same; and that no one in future should buy such wood coming by water for resale on pain of forfeiting the same, but that all such wood should be sold to the commonalty from the vessels without any of it being housed or laid up upon the wharves for resale upon the pain aforesaid, as from of old was wont to be done.

PURE FOOD REGULATIONS, 1379

Riley, *Memorials of London*, II, 438 (from London Letter-Book H, fol. cxvii).

Because the pastelers (pie bakers) of the city of London have heretofore baked in pasties rabbits, geese, and garbage (entrails),[27] not befitting and sometimes stinking, in deceit of the people, and have also baked beef

[27] Giblets were probably included under this uninviting term. [Riley's note.]

in pasties and sold the same for venison, in deceit of the people; therefore, by assent of the four master pastelers and at their prayer, it is ordered and assented to:

In the first place—that no one of the said trade shall bake rabbits in pasties for sale, on pain of paying, the first time, if found guilty thereof, 6s. 8d. to the use of the Chamber and of going bodily to prison, at the will of the mayor; the second time, 13s. 4d. to the use of the Chamber and of going, etc.; and the third time, 20s. to the use of the Chamber and of going, etc.

Also, that no one of the said trade shall buy of any cook of Bread Street or at the hostels of the great lords, of the cooks of such lords, any garbage from capons, hens, or geese to bake in a pasty and sell, under the same penalty.

Also, that no one shall bake beef in a pasty for sale and sell it as venison, under the same penalty.

Also, that no one of the said trade shall bake either whole geese in a pasty, halves of geese, or quarters of geese for sale, on the pain aforesaid.

BURNING A FALSELY MADE ARRAS, 1374

Riley, *Memorials of London*, II, 375–376 (from London Letter-Book G, fol. cccxv).

On Monday next after the Feast of St. Valentine [28] . . . [various] tapicers, masters of the trade of tapicers in London, caused to be brought here a coster (hanging) of tapestry, wrought upon the loom after the manner of work of Arras and made of false work, by Katherine Duchewoman in her house at Finch Lane, being 4 yards in length and 7 quarters in breadth. Seeing that she had made it of linen thread beneath but covered with wool above, in deceit of the people and against the ordinance of the trade aforesaid, they asked that the coster might be adjudged to be false and for that reason burned, according to the form of the articles of their trade.

[It was accordingly burned.]

THE PILLORY FOR SELLING BAD FISH, 1382

Riley, *Memorials of London*, II, 464 (from London Letter-Book H, fol. cxlv).

On the eighth day of May [1382], after dinner . . . [five citizens] of the county of Somerset came before the Mayor, sheriffs, and certain of the aldermen [of London] and showed to them two pieces of cooked

[28] The Feast of St. Valentine is February 14.

fish commonly called conger, rotten and stinking and unwholesome for man, which they had bought of John Welburgham, a cook in Bread Street, at noon on the same day, and which the said cook warranted to them to be good and wholesome for man, and not putrid.

And hereupon the said John Welburgham was immediately sent for, and, being questioned, he said that he did sell to the said complainants the said fish so cooked and that he warranted it to them as being good and wholesome and still did warrant it; and this he demanded to be proved in such manner as the court should think proper, etc. Whereupon, the said Mayor caused to be summoned [twelve] reputable men . . . neighbors of the said cook . . . who said upon their oath that the said pieces of fish were rotten, stinking, and unwholesome for man. Wherefore it was awarded that the said John Welburgham should repay to the said complainants six pence, which he acknowledged he had received for the fish aforesaid, that he should also have the punishment of the pillory for one hour of the day, and that the said fish should then be burned beneath him.[29]

2. *Grouping the Trades*

A PLACE FIXED FOR THE MARKET GARDENERS, 1345

Riley, *Memorials of London*, I, 228–229 (from London Letter-Book F, fol. cxi).

Be it remembered that on Wednesday next before the Feast of St. Bartholomew the Apostle [30] a certain petition was presented to John Hamond, mayor of the city of London, in these words:

"Unto the mayor of London show and pray the gardeners of the earls, barons, and bishops, and of the citizens of the same city.[31] May it please

---

[29] Equally appropriate was the punishment of John Penrose, who, having been convicted of selling wine "unsound and unwholesome for man," was forced to drink a draught of the same and have the remainder poured on his head (*ibid.*, I, 318–319 [from London Letter-Book G, fol. cxli, 1364]).—Robert Porter, convicted of inserting a piece of iron in a penny loaf of bread, with intent to make the bread weigh more, was put in the pillory for an hour of the day, the loaf and piece of iron being hung about his head and the reason for his punishment being publicly proclaimed (*ibid.*, II, 498 [from London Letter-Book H, fol. ccxxiv, 1387]).—Alice, wife of Robert de Caustone, convicted of selling ale in a quart measure in the bottom of which was put an inch and a half of pitch, so that six such quarts would not make one proper gallon of ale, was forced to undergo the punishment of the pillory, to which was tied in sight of the common people one half of the same false measure (*ibid.*, I, 319 [from London Letter-Book G, fol. cxxxvii, 1364]).

[30] The Feast of St. Bartholomew the Apostle is August 24.

[31] Cf. below, pp. 69–70.

you, sire, seeing that you are the chief guardian of the said city and of the ancient usages therein established, to suffer and to maintain that the said gardeners may stand in peace in the same place where they have been wont in times of old, in front of the church of St. Austin at the side of the gate of St. Paul's churchyard in London, there to sell the garden produce of their masters and make their profit as heretofore they have been wont to do; seeing that they have never heretofore been in their said place molested and that, as they assert, they cannot serve the commonalty nor yet their masters as they were wont to do, as to the which they pray for redress."

By reason of which petition on the Friday next after the Feast of St. Bartholomew there were assembled in the chamber of the Guildhall of London . . . the Mayor . . . and [certain aldermen] . . . [who], seeing that the place aforesaid opposite the said church of St. Austin near the gate of St. Paul's churchyard is such a nuisance to the priests who are singing matins and mass in the church of St. Austin, and to others, both clerks and laymen, in prayers and orisons there serving God, as also to other persons passing there both on foot and on horseback, as well as to the people dwelling in the houses of reputable persons there, who, by the scurrility, clamor, and nuisance of the gardeners and their servants there selling pulse, cherries, vegetables, and other wares to their trade pertaining, are daily disturbed—gave order to the said gardeners and their servants that they should no longer expose their wares aforesaid for sale in that place.

And after conference had been held between the mayor and the aldermen as to a place in which the gardeners might sell their wares, it was agreed that all gardeners of the City, as well aliens as freemen, who sell their pulse, cherries, vegetables, and other wares aforesaid in the City, should have as their place the space between the south gate of the churchyard of the said church [St. Paul's] and the garden wall of the Friars Preachers at Baynard's Castle, that so they should sell their wares in the place by the mayor and the aldermen thus appointed for them and nowhere else.

REGULATION OF THE POULTRY MARKET, 1357

Riley, *Memorials of London*, I, 299–300 (from London Letter-Book G, fol. lxxi).

No poulterer or other person, a freeman of the city, shall stand at the Carfax of the Leadenhall with rabbits, fowls, or other poultry on sale; but let such persons stay within their own houses with their poultry for sale; or otherwise let those who wish to carry out their poultry to sell stand and expose the same for sale along the wall towards the west of the church of St. Michael on Cornhill, and let them be found nowhere else, either going or standing with their poultry for sale, on pain of forfeiture of all such poultry. . . . And no person, of whatsoever condition he be, shall bring or expose any poultry for sale that is rotten or stinking or not proper for man's body, on pain of forfeiting the same poultry and of imprisonment of his body. . . . Also, that no poulterer or other person in his name shall go anywhere to meet any manner of poultry coming towards the said market, to make any bargain or purchase in forestallment of the same.

3. Markets

CLEANING SMITHFIELD CATTLE MARKET, 1372

Riley, *Memorials of London*, II, 366–367 (from London Letter-Book G, fol. ccxci).

On Wednesday next after the Feast of St. Margaret the Virgin [32] came reputable men, the horsedealers and drovers, and delivered unto the mayor and aldermen a certain petition in these words: "To the mayor, recorder, and aldermen show the dealers of Smithfield, that is to say, the coursers and drovers, that for the amendment of the said field they have granted and assented among them that for the term of three years next ensuing after the date of this petition for every horse sold in the said field there shall be paid one penny, for every ox and cow one halfpenny, for every eight sheep one penny, and for every four swine one penny by the seller and the same by the purchaser who buys the same for resale." . . . [This petition was enrolled and became an ordinance.]

Afterwards, on the eleventh day of August in the same year, Adam Fernham, keeper of the gaol at Newgate, Hugh Averelle, bailiff of Smithfield, and William Godhewe, weaver, were chosen and sworn faithfully to collect and receive the said pennies in form aforesaid and to clean the field of Smithfield from time to time during such term of three years when necessary.

EVENING MARKETS IN THE STREETS, 1393

Riley, *Memorials of London*, II, 532–533 (from London Letter-Book H, fol. cclxxviii).

From of old it has been the custom to hold in the city of London on

[32] The Feast of St. Margaret the Virgin is July 20.

every feast day two markets called eve-cheapings—one in Westcheap and the other on Cornhill—and that, too, by daylight only, between the first bell rung and the second for the said markets ordained.

And now on the tenth day of March in the sixteenth year [1393], etc., William Staundone, the mayor, and the aldermen of the said city have been given to understand that divers persons at night and by candle-light do sell in the common hostels there and in other places, in secret, divers wares that have been larcenously pilfered and some falsely wrought and some that are old as being new, and that other persons do there practice the sin of harlotry under color of the sale of their said wares, to the very great damage and scandal of good and honest folks of the said city.—Therefore, the said Mayor and aldermen, in order to put the said markets under good control and governance, have ordained that from henceforth on every such market night each of two bells shall be rung by the beadle of the ward where it is hung, one hour before sunset and then again half an hour after sunset. At which second ringing all the people shall depart from the market with their wares, on pain of for-feiture to the Chamber of all such wares as shall, after the said second bell rung, be found in the same. As to which the beadle, if he be acting, or other officer by the Chamber of the Guildhall thereunto assigned, shall have two pence in every shilling for his trouble in taking them.

4. Some London Shops

A SHOPPING TOUR, EARLY 15TH CENTURY

"London Lickpenny," attrib. to John Lydgate,[33] in Nicolas, ed., *A Chronicle of London*, pp. 266–267 (from Harl. MS 367, fol. 126, 127).

> Then unto London I did me hie;
>> Of all the land it beareth the prize.
> "Hot peascods," one began to cry;
>> "Strawberries ripe," others coaxingly advise.
>> One bade me come near and buy some spice;
> Pepper and saffron they gan me bid.
> But for lack of money I might not be sped.
>
> Then to Cheapside I went on,
>> Where much people I saw for to stand.
>> One offered me velvet, silk, and lawn;

[33] Lydgate's authorship of the poem is questioned by many present-day scholars.

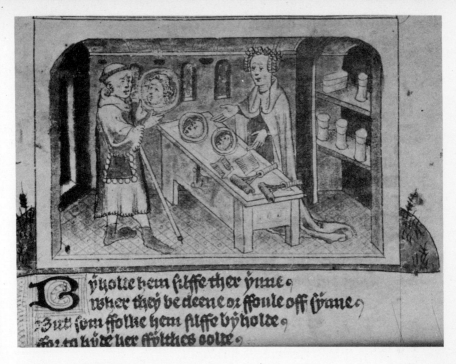

B y holte hem silffe ther ynne ·
wher they be cleene or ffoule off sname ·
But som ffolke hem silffe by holde ·
for to hyde her ffylthes colde ·

A SHOP; early fifteenth century
London, Brit. Mus., Cott. Tib. MS A.VII, fol. 90

O lui les · v · puceles / qui li font au gieron
T isu pozus lindois / qui or cuer de lyon

ARMORERS AT WORK; early fourteenth century
(Cf. "Blacksmiths," on page 16, *supra*)
Oxford, Bodl., MS 264, fol. 83

MIXING AND BAKING BREAD; early fourteenth century
Baltimore, Walters Gallery, MS W. 88, fols. 14v-15

COOKING; early fourteenth century
Oxford, Bodl., MS 264, fol. 84

Another he taketh me by the hand,
 "Here is Paris thread, the finest in the land."
I never was used to such things indeed,
And wanting money, I might not speed.

Then went I forth by London Stone,[34]
  Throughout all Canwick [35] Street;
Drapers much cloth me offered anon.
  Then met I one, cried, "Hot sheep's feet."
  One cried, "Mackerel"; "Rushes green," another gan greet.
One bade me buy a hood to cover my head;
But for want of money I might not be sped.

Then I hied me into Eastcheap;
  One cried, "Ribs of beef and many a pie";
Pewter pots they clattered on a heap;
  There was harp, pipe and minstrelsy.
  "Yea, by Cock!" "Nay, by Cock!" some began cry;
Some sang of Jenken and Julian for their meed,
But for lack of money I might not speed.

Then into Cornhill I took my road,
  Where was much stolen goods among;
I saw where hung my own hood,
  That I had lost among the throng; [36]
  To buy my own hood I thought it wrong,
I knew it well as I did my creed;
But for lack of money I could not speed.

A TRICKY MERCER, CA. 1376–1379

Gower, *Mirour de l'omme*, ll. 25, 273–25, 308.

Fraud also of its trickery
Oftentimes in mercery
Cheats people diversely,
Being full of artifice,

---

[34] London Stone, a fragment of which has been fixed in the exterior wall of St. Swithin's church, is deemed a *milliarium*, marking a starting point for the measurement of distances along the Roman roads; but there is no actual evidence of its purpose (*Encyclopaedia Britannica*, article "London").
[35] Candlewick Street.
[36] See below, p. 32.

Of joking and of nonsense,
To make fools of silly people
So as to get their money.
And smooth and soft he talks to them
And is the best of company
With his mouth, but in his thinking
He is slyly after his lucre
Under pretense of courtesy.
He who is born of such a nest
Is never dumb for lack of words,
But cries out like the sparrowhawk,
When he sees people he doesn't know,
Pulls them and drags them with hue and cry,
Saying: "Come on! Come in!
Beds and kerchiefs, ostrich feathers,
Silks and satins, and cloths imported—
Come, I will give you a look at them,
For if you are thinking of buying,
You have no need to go farther;
Here is the best in the street!"
But about one thing be careful
In entering his premises:
Have a mind to your buying;
For Fraud does not show his true colors,
But by subtle flattery
Chalk for cheese he can sell you.
You would think by his language
That the wild nettle he offers
Was a precious rose,
So much courtesy he will show you;
But if you wish to go uncheated,
Have no faith in his pretenses.

A HABERDASHER'S WARES, 1378

London Letter-Book H, fol. ccxii.

Articles that were in the shop of Thomas Trewe, haberdasher of London,
in the Parish of St. Ewen in Farringdon Ward Within . . .

1 doz. caps, half of them red, half green	2s.	8d.
5 blue caps, & 1 cap of russet	2s.	6d.

1 red cap . . . .   7*d*.
1 other cap of russet . . . .   7*d*.
2 doz. woolen caps, divers colors . . . .   16*s*.
6 caps of black wool . . . .   4*s*.
1 doz. white nightcaps . . . .   2*s*.   3*d*.
5 children's caps, red and blue . . . .   2*s*.   1*d*.
1 doz. black hoods . . . .   4*s*.
1 black hood . . . .   4*d*.
1 hat of russet . . . .   6*d*.
1 white hat . . . .   3*d*.
2 hair camises (loose shirts) . . . .   12*d*.
1 black girdle of woolen thread . . . .   2*d*.
1 pair children's boots of white woolen cloth . . . .   2*d*.
2 doz. laces of red leather . . . .   8*d*.
1 gross of tagged laces of red leather . . . . . .   18*d*.
2 pounds linen thread, green and blue . . . . .   2*s*.
3 pieces of whipcord . . . .   3*d*.
1 doz. cradlebows made of wool and flax . . . . .   18*d*.
3 cradlebows made of wool and flax . . . . . .   3*d*.
1 cloth painted with *Him Crucified* [37] and other figures . . 2*s*. 4*d*.
1 purse called "hamondeys" of sea-green color . . .   6*d*.
6 purses of red leather . . . .   4*d*.
1 set of beads of jet . . . .   6*d*.
1 set of beads of black alabaster . . . .   4*d*.
3 sets of beads of wood . . . .   3*d*.
2 sets wooden beads called "knottes" . . . . . .   4*d*.
1 double chain of iron . . . .   10*d*.
1 other iron chain . . . .   6*d*.
8 white chains of iron for ferrets . . . .   8*d*.
4 pairs of spurs . . . .   2*s*.
4 eyeglasses . . . .   2*d*.
2 permis (jewel cases?) . . . .   2*s*.
4 articles called "kombes" of boxwood . . . . .   4*d*.
1 wooden block for shaping caps . . . .   2*d*.
2 wooden cosynis (cushions with wooden frames?) . . .   2*d*.
2 wooden coffins (or coffers) . . . .   8*d*.
2 wooden boxes . . . .   3*d*.
1 fly-cage of wood . . . .   3*d*.

[37] Probably a mistake for *Ihm* (*Jhesum*) *Crucified*.

2 gaming-tables with the men	16*d.*
1 wooden gaming-table with set of men	6*d.*
1 osculatory called a paxbred [38]	3*d.*
2 wooden mills for grinding pepper	3*d.*
1 wooden whistle	2*d.*
2 papers covered with red leather	12*d.*
2 papers, one covered with black leather, the other red . .	8*d.*
13 quires of paper . . . . 6*s.*	8*d.*
other paper, damaged	6*d.*
7 leaves of paper	1*d.*
6 skins of parchment called "soylepeles"	6*d.*
2 pencases	6*d.*
2 pairs of pencases with inkhorns	8*d.*
18 horns called "inkehornes"	18*d.*

A WESTMINSTER COOK SHOP, EARLY 15TH CENTURY

"London Lickpenny," attributed to John Lydgate,[39] in Nicolas, ed., *A Chronicle of London*, pp. 262, 266 (from Harl. MS 542, f. 102 and Harl. MS 367, f. 126, 127).

> Then to Westminster gate I presently went,
>   When the sun was at high prime.
> Cooks on me they were all intent,
>   And proffered me bread, with ale and wine,
>   Ribs of beef, both fat and full fine;
> A fair cloth they began for to spread,
> But wanting money, I might not be sped.

PRICES IN COOK SHOPS, 1378

Riley, *Memorials of London*, II, 426 (from London Letter-Book H, fol. xcix).

Ordinance of the cooks, ordered by the mayor and aldermen, as to divers flesh-meat and poultry, as well roasted as baked in pasties:

The best roast pig	8	*d.*
The best roast lamb	7	*d.*
Best roast goose	7	*d.*
Best roast capon	6	*d.*
Best roast hen	4	*d.*

[38] A tablet to be kissed during Mass. It came into use during the thirteenth century as a symbolic substitute for the kiss of peace (*O.E.D.*).
[39] See above, p. 26*n.*

Best roast pullet	2½d.
Best roast rabbit	4 d.
Best roast river mallard	4½d.
Best roast dunghill mallard [40]	3½d.
Best roast teal	2½d.
Best roast snipe	1½d.
Five roast larks	1½d.
Best roast woodcock	2½d.
Best roast partridge	3½d.
Best roast plover	2½d.
Best roast pheasant	13 d.
Best roast curlew	6½d.
Three roast thrushes	2 d.
Ten roast finches	1 d.
Best roast heron	18 d.
Best roast bittern	20 d.
Three roast pigeons	2½d.
The best capon baked in a pasty	8 d.
The best hen baked in a pasty	5 d.
For the paste, fire, and trouble upon a capon [41]	1½d.
For the paste, fire, and trouble upon a goose	2 d.
Ten eggs	1 d.

LAW COURTS AND PRISONERS IN THE CITY

1. The Plight of a Poor Suitor, early 15th century

"London Lickpenny," attrib. to John Lydgate,[42] in Nicolas, ed., *A Chronicle of London*, pp. 260–262, 265–266 (from Harl. MS 367, fol. 126, 127).

> To London once my steps I bent,
>   Where truth in no wise should be faint;
> To Westminster-ward I forthwith went,
>   To a man of law to make complaint;
>   I said, "For Mary's love, that holy saint,
> Pity the poor that would proceed!"
> But for lack of money I could not speed.

[40] The river mallard was the wild duck; the dunghill mallard, the domesticated duck. [From Riley's note.]
[41] The customer finding the capon himself. [Riley's note.]
[42] See above, p. 26*n*.

And as I thrust the press among,
  By froward chance my hood was gone;
Yet for all that I stayed not long,
  Till to the King's Bench I was come.
  Before the judge I kneeled anon,
And prayed him for God's sake to take heed;
But for lack of money I might not speed.

Beneath him sat clerks a great crowd,
  Who fast did write by one assent,
There stood up one and cried aloud,
  "Richard, Robert, and John of Kent."
  I knew not well what this man meant,
He cried so rapidly there indeed.
But he that lacked money might not speed.

Unto the Common Pleas I did go,
  Where sat one with a silken hood;
I did him reverence, for I ought to do so,
  And told my case as well as I could,
  How my goods were defrauded me by falsehood.
I got not a mum of his mouth for my meed,
And for lack of money I might not speed.

       .   .   .

In Westminster Hall I found out one,
  Who went in a long striped gown of ray;
I crouched and kneeled before him anon,
  For Mary's love, of help I him pray.
  "I know not what thou meanest," he gan to say.
To get me thence he did me bid;
For lack of money I could not speed.

Within this hall neither rich nor yet poor
  Would do for me ought, although I should die.
Which seeing, I got me out of the door,
  Where Flemings began on me for to cry,
  "Master, what will you purchase or buy?
Fine felt hats, or spectacles to read?
Lay down your silver, and here you may speed."

2. *Starvation in a City Prison, 1322*

London, Coroner, *Calendar of the Coroners Rolls*, p. 53.

William, son of John de Brich', who had been attached for burglary of the house and carrying off the goods of Geoffrey le Rook of Little Burstead,[43] died of starvation [44] in the prison of Newgate on Thursday before the Feast of St. John "ante Portam Latinam" [45] and of no felony. The corpse was viewed, on which no hurt appeared.

3. *Prison Regulations, 1430/31*

ORDINANCES FOR NEWGATE AND THE PRISONERS THEREIN

London, Corporation, *Calendar of Letter-Books*, K, ed. by Sharpe, pp. 124–127.

On February 23, 9 Henry VI [1430/31], ordinances were made by the mayor, aldermen, sheriffs, and commonalty in common council assembled for guarding and governing the gate of Newgate . . . to the following effect:

First, that in order to diminish the number of officers in Ludgate and Newgate who waste the alms of the poor prisoners, and also to curtail the charges made by porters of the compters, it is decreed that henceforth all prisoners who wish and ought to live by the common alms of the people shall not remain in a compter for more than a day and a night, but shall be removed by the sheriffs and their clerks to the said gate,[46] there to remain as prisoners until lawfully delivered, *viz.*, freemen of the city and other honest persons in the chambers which have chimneys and privies near the hall and fountain on the north part of the prison, and the free and other honest women in the like chambers on the south; that strangers (*foreins*) and others of inferior condition shall occupy less convenient chambers, whilst felons and others suspected of great crimes be safeguarded in the basement cells and strongholds on the south part of the prison and not allowed any intercourse with other prisoners.

Also, whereas the common people suffer from the importunity of a

---

[43] In Essex County.
[44] Prisoners in Newgate and Ludgate (if without private means) were largely, if not wholly, dependent upon charity in those days (see the following excerpt from Letter-Book K).
[45] The Feast of St. John "ante Portam Latinam" is May 6.
[46] In or about 1393 it was ordained . . . that prisoners in certain cases might remain in the compters, on terms, instead of being removed to Newgate or Ludgate. See *Liber albus*, I, 523; cf. Letter-Book H, fol. cclxxxvi b. [Sharpe's note.]

number of persons daily soliciting alms for the prisoners, who profit little thereby owing to the large payment demanded by those so soliciting, it is decreed that in the future only two couples of prisoners shall solicit alms, one by the river side and the other on the land, each couple having a box and saucer so marked that they may be recognized as belonging to the prison.

Also, whereas the keepers of the prisoners and their servants often appropriate the alms given to the prisoners, it is ordained that the said boxes be sealed by one of the sheriffs or the chamberlain for the time being, and that their contents be used for paying the collectors and buying food and other necessaries for the prisoners. . . .

Also, it is forbidden that any officer or servant of the prison sell any manner of victual, charcoal, candles, etc. (except beer, in manner prescribed), but the prisoners may buy their victuals where they please.

Also, it is decreed that no keeper or servant of the prison shall prevent any freeman or woman from having and using their own bed, if they have one, without any charge, nor shall they take more than a penny a night for a bed with blankets and sheets, as is done at hostelries, or more than a penny a week for a couch, or more than fourpence toward the maintenance of the prison lamps for the whole time the prisoner may be there. . . .

Also, inasmuch as the said prison is sufficiently strong, it is ordered that the keeper . . . shall not put any freeman or woman in irons if imprisoned for a debt of less than a hundred shillings (100s.), on their finding surety for good behavior. . . .

Also, inasmuch as the basements and dark places often cause infection, it is ordained that the keeper shall allow all freemen of the city and other honest persons, on their finding sufficient surety for good behavior, to go every day at convenient times for devotion and recreation to the chapel and the two spacious and well-lighted chambers on each side of the chapel, and the women to the large chamber near the hall on the south side, without demanding any payment but desiring them to pray devoutly for the souls of Richard Whittyngtone [47] and Alice his wife.

[47] The famous Dick Whittington (d. 1423), wealthy London merchant, thrice mayor of the city and public benefactor, out of whose goods the prison had recently been rebuilt. Reference to Whittington appears earlier in the document, though omitted in the present transcript.

THE PAGEANTRY OF LONDON

1. A Royal Visit: Richard II's Reconciliation with the City, August 29, 1392

Richard de Maidstone, *De concordia inter Ricardum Secundum et civitatem London,* ed. by Wright, pp. 33-42.[48]

Here the city prepares to meet the King. The knight whom the King has appointed warden of the city speaks to the citizens thus on that glorious day: "Make ready to meet your King, and let him see publicly how welcome he now is. Let there be a procession of the clergy of the whole church, and let each Order carry before it its crosses. Let there be no craft of the city which does not in its own livery, more splendid than of wont, ride forth on horseback across the river. Whatever good there is in the City, let it be brought forth; for on that day, you shall rejoice that peace shall be given."

Stirred by these words, the whole body works together and prepares itself with splendid array. At the same time every street is decorated beautifully; with cloths of gold innumerable the city gleams. Every street is fragrant with varieties of sweet-smelling flowers, and there is no lack of purple hangings among the houses. Gold, scarlet, cotton, and colored garments paint here, with the aid of art, a new heaven. . . .

Lo, the day is at hand. They hasten out of the city to meet the King and his Consort. Who can count the number of the immense crowd which pours forth more thickly than the stars [are strewn] in heaven? Twenty thousand young men on horseback are counted; but of those who go forth on foot the number is countless.

The warden rides first and with him go the twenty-four aldermen whom the city has as its rulers. By senatorial right, as in Rome, the city is governed by them, and over them is the mayor, whom the people have chosen. Their livery of red and white, their parti-colored robes, distinguish them from the others.

With the keys and the sword of the city, the warden rides at the head of the aldermen, and they follow close behind. After them comes the gild of each craft, its livery showing its kind. Here is the goldsmith; here the fishmonger; following him the mercer and the vintner. Here is the apothecary, the baker, the painter, the mason; here the cutler, the bar-

[48] John Stow in *The Annales,* pp. 482-483, gives [an] account of the King's reception in the capital, which forms the subject of the poem of Richard de Maidstone. [Wright's note.]

ber, and the armorer. Here the carpenter, the tailor, and there the shoe-maker; here the skinner, the fuller, the monger, the smith. Here are craftsmen; there butchers, there a tiler; there a spurrier and a draper to-gether. There is a sheathmaker, there a girdler, there a weaver; here a tallow chandler and a wax chandler side by side. Here is the brewer; there the stirrup maker, there the joiner; there is the fruiterer and also the dealer in birds. A (*Anne*) over R (*Regina*) is everywhere in pleasing designs among these crafts. . . . Here is the glover, the pouchmaker, the hosteler, and the cook: the craft of each gild is seen by its livery. . . . Each is drawn up in its own bands; the whole roadway for four miles is filled.

Here the citizens meet the King. "Sing now, citizens, sing now to your King. Lo! your King draws near; sing that he may hear you." As the King approaches, the young lords of his household crowd round him. . . .

Where he sits on his white horse, they draw back so that the good King himself may be seen by his people. How fresh-colored his face crowned with yellow hair, his combed locks shining under the garland; gleaming with gold is the red robe that covers too much his fair body. . . . He is girt, as is fitting, by the nobles of the realm. Near at hand is the Queen Consort, with her maidens, Anna her name—may she be Anna (grace) indeed, I pray! Beautiful she stands among her beautiful maidens; under these Amazons, New Troy conquers. Her robe is be-sprinkled with shining gems; from head to foot nought but gems can be seen. With diamonds, carbuncles, beryls—all kinds of precious stones—her head is covered. They shine on her white forehead, sparkle in her ears; they dazzle the sight which could never have enough looking at them.

Here the city surrenders to the lord King. While the King pulls at his golden bridle and forces his charger to stand, the nobles and the people are silent. The warden approaches, and with him the aldermen. In his left hand he holds the keys, in his right the sword, with the point toward himself, as if he were an abject prisoner, and thus he speaks:

"Hail! King, whose power is no less to be loved and worshipped than it is to be feared. Hail! Your humble citizens, prostrated at your feet, sur-render to you at once themselves and all that they have. With these keys and this sword, the city freely now yields and comes ready to submit to your will. She earnestly begs, amid her tears, that the merciful King will deign to enter his chamber. Let not the most beautiful walls of the realm be torn down and destroyed; for they are his and everything in them. . . ."

At this the King takes the sword and also the keys of London and quickly gives both to his attendants. "We accept," he says, "both you and what is yours to give; and this splendid array pleases me now. But I shall go on to see what is being done in my city, whether my people have learned to recognize their King."

Here the citizens come to the Queen. Meanwhile the warden and his twenty-four companions cross over and are behind the King's back. They draw near to the Queen and with humble demeanor earnestly beseech her, and she promises her favor. She is gracious to them but grieves deeply because so illustrious a city has fallen under the wrath of the King. "Yet there is hope," she says.

Here the King with the whole company goes toward the city. After this, the progress to the city continues. Gild follows gild, but now the last is first. Each holds the place due to its rank, and each is proud of its honor and precedence. In mantles dyed in grain of black, purple, white, golden, green, red, and crimson and in gowns particolored as befit craftsmen are the different crafts of the procession. This craft in front, that one after, they move toward the city; the road is scarcely wide enough for the army. Crowd presses upon crowd; here one is thrown down; there another is falling. . . .

Nor is there lack of music, singing, shouting, and uproar; and the sweet song beats against high heaven. At the same time choruses of friars chant in greeting to the King, and he proceeds to honor with his worship the crosses. He kisses them, and his Consort does likewise; and each asks that God may preserve the kingdom.

Of the rain that then happened. Then a heavy wind blew up, before a storm; and it rained so hard that men and women were troubled, fearing that all would be spoiled by so heavy a storm. But as the south wind blew over and a gentle breeze from the west took its place, the clear air shone, and the city trembled no longer.

.   .   .

Here the King with the whole company proceeds toward Cheap. After [the presenting of gifts to the King and Queen, and her coronation], they move on joyously [from Southwark] into the city. Crowd presses against crowd, so does the street confine them. When the Queen comes to the gate of the bridge, good fortune plainly gives a new omen. For there follow her two chariots full of her ladies. Phaeton is driving them, for one falls. When a woman shows her woman's legs, the crowd can scarcely control its laughter. A good thing that this accident should happen, I ask, because to me it means that all unholy and evil love shall fall.

They arrive in the city; the streets are shining, gleaming, and full of array; in every lane there is applause and singing. Pretty girls are looked at while they are looking; there is no window but is full of them. He who would be looking for girls' faces in the heart of the city would think nothing of them, they were in such numbers.

At a slow pace the procession moves on in the city, for the concourse of people blocks the way. But when they have reached the midst of the city and the entrance of the street which is called Cheap, how it is adorned with figures woven and painted—who could write? Nothing can be seen from roof to road save wealth and angelic faces.

How the conduit gives wine. The Conduit brings forth Bacchus, and no Thetis is there; that liquor reddens the cups of a thousand men. On the roof stands a heavenly being, who with great skill sings heavenly songs. Gold in dense leaves or flowers flows about everywhere, scattered by a maiden hand.

Of the marvelous tower in the midst of Cheap. As the King, proceeding, comes to the midst of an open space, he sees there a castle, stands still, and wonders greatly at it. A whole tower by means of ropes hangs in mid-air. And on this tower stand a youth and a beautiful girl; he is dressed as an angel, and she wears a crown. Whoever looks upon their forms would not, I think, believe that anything under heaven could please him more.

The King and the Queen stand discussing what this high tower and these young people are there for. Then the youth and the girl together come down from the tower—no stairway and no steps are to be seen. They come surrounded by clouds and they hang in mid-air, by what device I do not know, believe me. He holds a beaker full of wine; she, twin crowns of glittering gems. These are newly made of shining gold, the rich material bears witness, and the work is superior to the material, as is seen in the new delicacy of art and artifice. Then the girl offers her crowns to the warden, who, holding one in each hand, speaks as follows:

Here the warden offers the crowns to the King and Queen. "Illustrious King," he says, "and noble Queen, may God always keep you both safe! May He who gives you diadems of earthly rule grant you also eternal rule in heaven. You see now your people who joyfully greet you and are proud to honor you as they can."

2. *The Mayor's Show, 1419* [49]

In 1389 the extravagance of municipal processions had been somewhat curtailed, as shown by the following enactment:

"Whereas the men of divers trades, at the presentation of the sheriffs on the morrow of St. Michael the Archangel [*i.e.*, on September 30] . . . had been wont to array themselves in a new suit and to hire horses for riding upon and to incur many other expenses; and then shortly afterwards, upon the mayor's riding to Westminster on the morrow of St. Simon and St. Jude [*i.e.*, on October 29] . . . they again incurred the like expenses . . . and forasmuch as it seemed . . . a matter of necessity to diminish such expenditure . . . it was agreed unanimously that no sheriff should in future, for the day of his presentation, give any vestments to any other persons than the servants of the city and his officers and sergeants; or should on that day, himself or by others, have any riding; but that the sheriffs . . . together with their servants and others . . . should go by water in barges and boats, or else proceed by land to Westminster and in like manner return to London, without there being any arraying of men of the trades in like suit for that purpose." (Riley, *Memorials of London*, II, 515–516 [from London Letter-Book H, fol. cccxlvi].) The following account, however, describes the Mayor's Show in all its splendor.

London, Corporation, *Munimenta Gildhallae Londoniensis; Liber albus*, I, 24–26.

On the morrow of the Feast of the Apostles Simon and Jude [50] it was the custom for both the new and the past mayor and the aldermen as well, in a like suit of robes, attended by the sheriffs and as many as were of the mayor's livery and of the several mysteries arrayed in their respective suits, to meet on horseback upon the place without the Guildhall about nine of the clock, the sword being borne upright before the person nominated as mayor. Departing thence, they rode together along Cheap through the gate of Newgate and then turning into Fleet Street passed on to Westminster. [The ceremony of oath-taking then took place.] Which done, they returned, the commons preceding on horseback in companies arrayed in the suits of their respective mysteries. Those, however, who were members of the mystery to which the mayor belonged, as also those who were of his livery, proceeded next before the mayor.

[49] Date of composition of *Liber albus*.
[50] The Feast of the Apostles Simon and Jude is October 28.

No person, however, moved so close to the mayor but that there was a marked space between; while the sergeants-at-arms, the mace-bearers, and his sword-bearer went before him, with one sheriff on his right hand and the other on his left, bearing white wands in their hands. The recorder and the other aldermen followed next in order and accompanied him through the middle of the market of Westcheap to his house; after which they returned home, as many, that is, as had not been invited to the feast.

3. *The Midsummer Watch, 1378*

Riley, *Memorials of London*, II, 419–420 (from London Letter-Book H, fol. lxxix).

On Wednesday next after the Feast of St. Barnabas the Apostle,[51] in the first year, etc., a letter was sent to every alderman, in form as follows:

"We do command you that, together with the good men of your ward, you be well and sufficiently armed, arrayed in red and white, parti-colored, over your armor, to keep the watch on the Eves of the Nativity of St. John,[52] and of St. Peter and St. Paul[53] next to come, in manner as done heretofore, for the honor of the city and for keeping the peace; and this you are not to omit, on the peril which attends the same, and as you would save the honor of the city."

And upon this, by advice of the mayor and aldermen, the said watch was made in manner as follows: that is to say—all the aldermen, with the good men of their wards, assembled in Smithfield on the Eve of St. John, arrayed as aforesaid, and from thence passed through the city, first the aldermen, and then the men of their wards, as follow.

First, the wards of Tower, Billingsgate, Aldgate, Lime Street, with cressets and white lances powdered with red stars.

Second, the wards of Bridge, Candlewick Street, Dowgate, Walbrook, with lances all red.

Third, Bishopsgate, Langbourn, Cornhill, Broad Street, with white lances environed, that is to say, wreathed, with red.

Fourth, Farringdon, Castle Baynard, Aldersgate, with black lances powdered with white stars.

Fifth, Cheapside, Cripplegate, Coleman Street, Bassishaw, with lances all white.

Sixth, Bread Street, Queenhithe, Vintry, and Cordwainer Street, with lances—[54]

[51] The Feast of St. Barnabas the Apostle is June 11.
[52] That is, on June 23.   [53] That is, on June 28.
[54] The description abruptly closes here. [Riley's note.]

KEEPING THE CITY

1. Hue and Cry by Horn and Voice, 1302

London, Lord Mayor's Court, *Calendar of Early Mayor's Court Rolls*, pp. 124–125 (from City of London, Mayor's Court R., E, m. 4).

Six men (servants and young men) were accused of attacking and assaulting the watch of Walbrook Ward, June 14, 1302.

Afterwards on Thursday a jury . . . found on oath that the defendants committed the assault when midnight was striking at St. Paul's, and were captured after the hue and cry had been raised by horn and voice and the neighboring wards had come to help . . . [The young men] had filled an empty cask with stones on Monday midnight and set it rolling through Gracechurch Street to London Bridge to the great terror of the neighbors.

The young men were arrested and put in the Tun.[55]

2. Fire Regulations and Others, 1376–1378

London, Corporation, *Calendar of Letter-Books*, H, pp. 28, 92.

Precept was sent, July 25 [1376], to each alderman to see that a large vessel of water be kept outside every house in case of fire, the season being very dry and hot, and further that ladders and hooks be provided and that thoroughfares be conveniently made [*i.e.*, kept open].

Proclamation was made in 1378 on the eve of Pentecost [56] to the effect that no one wander abroad after ten of the clock, unless he be of good character or on his master's service, and then only with a light; that no taverner or brewer keep open house after that hour; that every one of estate keep a barrel or "tyne" (hogshead) of water before his house by day and night on account of the dryness of the season in case of sudden fire; and that no one conspire by day or night to break the peace, under penalty of fine and imprisonment.

3. Smoke Nuisance, 1371

Riley, *Memorials of London*, II, 355–356 (from London Letter-Book G, fol. cclxxiii).

Petition to the mayor and aldermen of London: "Whereas certain plumbers, namely, Robert Belcampe [and] Richard Diche, do purpose to melt their solder in a vacant place called "Wodhawe" (or Wood-yard) in the Parish of St. Clement [London], . . . to the great damage

---

[55] See above, p. 17*n*.   [56] That is, on June 5.

and peril of death of all who shall smell the smoke from such melting
. . . may it please your honorable and rightful lordships, at the request of [John Walcot and others], for the saving of human life to ordain a befitting remedy as a work of charity, in such manner that such
perilous work may not be done within the city. . . ."

By reason of which petition, precept was given to John Chamberleyn,
sergeant, to summon here on the Thursday after the Feast of St. Dunstan [57] then next ensuing the aforesaid Robert Beauchampe [Belcampe]
and Richard atte Diche, to make answer as to the matters aforesaid. . . .
Upon which Thursday the parties appeared, and the said Robert and
Richard asked to hear the petition; which being read and heard, they
said that they had hired the said vacant place, which had a furnace therein,
for doing their melting and following their trade there, as had been accustomed for about the last forty years there to be done; and they said
that the vacant place was not so noxious as had been alleged, and this they
were ready to prove . . . and they asked that they might follow their
trade and do their melting in that place. . . . [The complainants] said
that the shaft of the furnace was too low and that the smell of the smoke
issuing therefrom at the time of melting their lead was rendered all the
more offensive thereby, to the nuisance, etc. And they asked that the
mayor and aldermen should find a remedy for the same.

And afterwards, conference being held by the mayor and aldermen
thereupon . . . it was agreed and granted by the mayor and aldermen
that the same Robert Beauchampe and Richard atte Dyche and others of
their trade might follow their trade at the place and furnace aforesaid
and do their melting in manner as theretofore they had been accustomed
to do—provided, however, that the shaft of the said furnace should be
heightened for the benefit of the neighbors there.

4. Shutting out the Lepers, 1375

Riley, *Memorials of London*, II, 384 (from London Letter-Book H, fol. xx).

William Duerhirst, barber, porter of Aldgate, and the several porters of
Bishopsgate, Cripplegate, Aldersgate, Newgate, Ludgate, Bridgegate,
and the Postern have sworn before the mayor and recorder . . . that
they will well and trustily keep the gates and postern aforesaid . . .
and will not allow lepers to enter the city or to stay in the same or in the
suburbs thereof, and if anyone shall bring any leprous person to any

[57] The Feast of St. Dunstan is September 7.

such gate or to the postern abovesaid, or if any leper or lepers shall come there and wish to enter, such persons shall be prohibited by the porter from entering. . . .

William Cook, foreman at Le Lock, and William Walssheman, foreman at Hackney,[58] were sworn that they will not bring lepers or know of their being brought into the city aforesaid, but that they will inform the said porters and prevent the said lepers from entering, so far as they may.

5. Watch and Ward within the City, 1311

Riley, Memorials of London, I, 92–93 (from London Letter-Book D, fol. cxlvii).

On [August 15, 1311,] it was ordered that the gates of the city should be watched day and night, in form as follows:[59] At Ludgate [two citizens] were sworn to keep the key of the said gate. Also for the safe-keeping of the said gate there were to be found each night from the ward of Cordwainer Street eight men well armed and strong. And from one half of the ward within of Nicholas de Farringdon, namely, that on the western side, eight men well armed.

At the gate of Newgate there were to be found at night eight men of the ward of Cheap well armed, of the ward of Walbrook eight men well armed, and of the half of the aforesaid ward of Farringdon Within on the north side of Cheap, eight men well armed. And [four citizens] were sworn to keep the keys thereof.

At the gate of Aldersgate there were to be found at night from the ward eight men well armed; and from the ward of Bread Street eight men well armed. And [two citizens] were sworn to keep the keys of the said gate.

At the gate of Cripplegate there were to be found at night, from the same ward within, eight men well armed; and from the ward of Bassishaw six men well armed; and from the ward of Coleman Street six men well armed. And [two citizens] were sworn [to keep the keys thereof].

At the gate of Bishopsgate there were to be found at night from the same ward six men well armed, and from the ward of Bread Street six men well armed, and from the ward of Cornhill six men well armed, and from the ward of Lime Street two men well armed. And . . . [two citizens] were chosen to keep the keys of the gate aforesaid.

At the gate of Aldgate there were to be found at night from the same

[58] Both lazar houses for lepers. [Riley's note.]
[59] These regulations were made in the King's behalf, who was then at variance with his nobles. [Riley's note.]

ward six men well armed, and from the ward of Langbourn eight men well armed, and from the ward of Candlewick Street six men well armed. And [two citizens] were sworn to keep the keys of the said gate.

At the Bridgegate there were to be found at night six men of the ward of Billingsgate and eight men of Bridge Ward. And . . . [two citizens] were sworn to keep the keys of the said gate.

And to guard the bankside of the River Thames there were to be found each night six men of the ward of Dowgate, twelve men of the ward of Vintry, twelve from Queenhithe, and eight from the ward of Castle Baynard.

The great gates of the city were to be closed each night at the beginning of curfew being rung at St. Martin-le-Grand, and the wickets were then to be opened; and at the last stroke of curfew rung the wickets were to be closed and were not to be opened afterwards that night unless by special precept of the mayor or aldermen.

A chain was to be drawn across at Castle Baynard each night and to be fastened at the hour aforesaid, and . . . [two citizens] were sworn before the mayor and the aldermen to keep the same.

To keep the postern near the Tower there were to be twelve of Tower Ward, well armed.

6. *The Citizens' Arms, 1380*

London, Corporation, *Calendar of Letter-Books*, H, p. 153.

Precept [was] sent to each alderman to see that the men of his ward [were] suitably armed with "basinet" (helmet), gauntlets of "plate," habergeon, sword, dagger, and hatchet, according to their estate, and inferior men arrayed with good bows, arrows, sword, and buckler, and to return their number before Monday next. Dated August 20, 4 Richard II [1380].

7. *A Guard against the French, 1377* [60]

London, Corporation, *Calendar of Letter-Books*, H, pp. 64–66.

[Immediately after the death of Edward III, June 21, 1377,] ordinances [were passed] for safeguarding the city, to the effect that the gates of the city be fortified with portcullises and chained and have barbicans in front; that breastworks be built along the quays between the

[60] Precautions taken on the decease of Edward III, when the French were threatening the south coast. [Sharpe's note.] Cf. below, p. 297.

Tower and London Bridge, and the keys of the city gates be kept by two persons of the neighborhood; that the aldermen keep the names of hostelers (innkeepers) in their wards and cause each inhabitant to swear that he will be ready with his harness (armor) to maintain the peace if affray arise; that all hostelers and those dwelling with them be taxed according to their estate, except servants and apprentices, at the discretion of the aldermen; that special guard be kept at the gates in view of the forthcoming expedition [of the French]; that no one carry any arms except a baselard by day, but a knight to have his sword borne after him, his page having a baselard, but not a dagger; that each alderman put his ward into array under his pennon, bearing his arms in relief, and lead his men whithersoever commanded for the defense of the city; that the alderman of Tower Ward take special precautions against an attack by way of the Thames; that the alderman of Candlewick Street guard the Wool Quay and all the wharves up to the wharf late belonging to Reynold Love; the alderman of Billingsgate guard the said wharf of Reynold Love up to Billingsgate; the alderman of Walbrook keep guard between Billingsgate and the Bridge; the alderman of Bridge keep guard of the Bridge and of the wharves as far as Ebbgate and have good ordnance on the Bridge with stone and shot; the alderman of Dowgate keep guard between Ebbgate and Dowgate; the alderman of Vintry between Dowgate and Queenhithe; the alderman of Queenhithe between Queenhithe and Paul's Wharf; the alderman of Baynard Castle guard Paul's Wharf up to the water of the Fleet and thence to Ludgate; the alderman of Farringdon keep the gates of Ludgate and Newgate; the alderman of Aldersgate the gate and ditches between Newgate and Aldersgate and thence to the house of the Lord Neville; the alderman of Cripplegate guard the house of the Lord Neville as far as Cripplegate; the alderman of Bassishaw and Coleman Street, the ditches between Cripplegate and Bishopsgate; the aldermen of Bishopsgate and Broad Street, the gate of Bishopsgate and the walls as far as Aldgate; the aldermen of Aldgate, Lime Street, and Langbourn, the gate of Aldgate and the walls up to the Postern; that the aldermen of Cheap, Cordwainer Street, Bread Street, and Cornhill, with their pennons and men in array, gather at the Standard in Cheap; and that the sheriffs have six sergeants, well mounted and armed, to report matters to the mayor.

Precept [was made] to the several aldermen that they make a return of all hostelers in their ward, the number of men fully armed or otherwise, the number of those who can provide themselves with arms by the

Feast of St. John Baptist [June 24]; also the number of those who can pay a certain sum a week for the city's protection and those who can give one day's labor in three weeks for the same purpose, etc.

Another precept [was made] for putting the wards in array and for providing a sufficient number of shields for those who act as shield-bearers, not being able to incur the charge of other arms. The names of those capable of bearing arms to be returned to the Guildhall by Monday after the Feast of St. James.[61]

THE SOUL OF THE CITY

1. St. Paul's Cathedral Towers above Ludgate Hill

REPAIRS TO ST. PAUL'S, 1314

Simpson, "St. Paul's Cathedral, London," *Transactions of the London and Middlesex Archaeological Society*, V (1881), 316–317 (from Lambeth Palace Library, MS 590, with additions from MS 1106, fol. 96b).

In this year were taken down the cross and the ball of the belfry of St. Paul's because they were weak and dangerous, and a new cross with a ball well gilded was set up, and many relics of saints for the protection of the belfry and of the whole edifice attached to it were with a great and solemn procession replaced in the cross by the bishop. May God the All Powerful, by the glorious merit of all his saints whose relics remain in that church, vouchsafe to preserve the steeple from all danger of storm! By the favor also of the bishop to all those who helped in the erection of the said edifice, one hundred and fifty days' indulgence are granted annually to endure for twenty-seven years.

In this same year was the said church measured; its length is 690 feet, its breadth 130, the height of the roof of the west part to the floor 102, the height of the vault of the new fabric [that is, east from the steeple] 88 feet; the body of the church is 150 feet in height. In all, the space of the ground on which it stands extends to 3½ acres, a rod and a half, and 6 perches (*virgas*). The height of the belfry tower from the ground up measures 260 feet; the height of the wooden spire, 274 feet. The height in all does not exceed 500 feet. The ball of the steeple could contain in its hollow 10 bushels of wheat. The length of the cross above the ball is 15 feet. The transverse of the cross is 6 feet in length.

[61] The Feast of St. James is July 25.

RELICS AT ST. PAUL'S, 1314

"French Chronicle of London," in Riley, ed., *Chronicles of the Mayors and Sheriffs of London*, p. 251.

In the old cross certain relics were found,[62] that is to say, a corporal with which they sing mass, white and entire, without any defect; and in this corporal was found a part of the wood of the cross of Our Lord Jesus Christ wrought in the form of a cross, a stone from the sepulcher of Our Lord, and another stone from the place where God stood when He ascended into Heaven, and another stone from Mount Calvary, where the cross of Our Lord was erected. There was also found a purse, and in this purse a piece of red sendal in which were wrapped some bones of the eleven thousand virgins [63] and other relics, the names of which were unknown. These relics Master Robert de Clothale [chancellor of the cathedral] showed to the people during his preaching on the Sunday before the Feast of St. Botolph,[64] and after the same the relics were replaced in the cross, and many other new ones as well, on the day of St. Francis [July 16].

2. *Preaching and Rioting in St. Paul's Churchyard, 1327, 1378*

St. Paul's Churchyard from earliest times was used for preaching, reading proclamations, statutes, etc., and for assemblies such as trade meetings and love days (times of reconciliation), as well as for sports such as wrestling, javelin hurling, and leapfrog.

Love days often ended far otherwise than intended, and trade feuds overflowed into the cathedral precincts, as the following incidents show.

Riley, *Memorials of London*, I, 158–159 (from London Letter-Book E, fol. clxxvi); *ibid.*, II, 415–416 (from London Letter-Book H, fol. xcii).

. . . Whereas contumelious words had arisen between William de Karletone, saddler, and William de Stokwelle, painter, and by reason of such words six good folks of the one trade and six of the other did interfere therein and appoint a day of love at St. Paul's Church as between the aforesaid William and William . . . the aforesaid William de Stokwelle, compassing mischief, did cause all the painters, joiners, lorimers (bit-makers), and gilders to be collected together with other workmen in order to act by force of arms and in affray of the said city; they took counsel to make the saddlers aforesaid concede by compulsion that if

---

[62] That is, when the cross and the ball were taken down in 1314.

[63] Who, with St. Ursula, according to legend, were martyred by the pagans at Cologne. [Riley's note.]

[64] The Feast of St. Botolph is June 17.

any man of the one trade should have cause of offense as against anyone of the other trade, then in such case all the painters together with all the [other] trades should no longer be bound to work, but should close their selds (shops).

.   .   .

On Sunday . . . before the hour of noon a conflict arose in Westcheap between certain persons of the trade of goldsmiths and others of the trade of pepperers, from a certain rancor that had existed between them; by reason of which conflict no small affray arose throughout the whole city, and that, too, while the bishop of Carlisle was preaching in St. Paul's churchyard. In which place, because of such conflict, and the wounded fleeing thither with great outcry, no little tumult and alarm ensued. Upon which Nicholas Brembre, the then mayor,[65] being informed thereof, together with other aldermen, immediately went to Westcheap to restore peace there and to maintain it.

3. *Excommunication for the Traders in the Cathedral and the Boys Who Play in and out of the Church, 1385*

Letter of Robert Braybroke [66] (printed in Wilkins' *Concilia*, III, 194).

Truly according to persistent reports of many trustworthy persons it has been brought to our notice that both men and women are frequenting our cathedral church for the purpose of selling their merchandise, articles, and goods almost every day, and especially on holy days and feast days, so that what was ordained to the honor of God, by the growing wickedness of the people has been changed into an abuse. There in their stations, as if they were in the public square or market place, they are so bold as to display and sell their wares and merchandise. . . .

Certain [boys], also, good for nothing in their insolence and idleness, instigated by evil minds and busying themselves rather in doing harm than good, throw and shoot stones, arrows, and different kinds of missiles at the rooks, pigeons, and other birds nesting in the walls and porches of the church and perching [there]. Also they play ball inside and outside the church and engage in other destructive games there, breaking and greatly damaging the glass windows and the stone images of the church, which, having been made with the greatest skill, are a

[65] See below, p. 158.
[66] Bishop of London from 1381 to 1404.

pleasure to the eyes of all beholders, adorning the fabric and adding to
its refinement. This they do not without great offense to God and our
church and to the prejudice and injury of us as well as to the grave peril
of their souls.

Wishing therefore to the utmost of our ability to put a stop to this kind
of injurious, malicious, and wicked deeds, . . . we ourselves enjoin
upon all persons that out of reverence for God and for His holy church
which He willed and ordered to be called His special charge upon earth,
they stop these nefarious acts and refrain and desist from them on pain
of sentence of major excommunication,[67] which by these writings we
bring against the persons of those thus delinquent and the perpetrators
themselves, on grounds of hindrance, deceit, blame, insolence, rebellion,
and offense, according to this our present warning herein before stated
to take effect from now henceforth. . . .

We command by virtue of sacred obedience all and sundry of the
rectors, vicars, presbyters, and curates ordained throughout our city of
London and enjoin upon them very strictly to proclaim solemnly that
any malefactors whatever of this kind whom it is possible to catch in
the aforesaid actions after this our warning have been and are excommunicated. . . .

And let this be announced on the days at the hours and in the places
where the greatest number of people convene. Given in our palace at
London, November 9 in the year of our Lord 1385.

[67] See pp. 393–394, below.

2. The Home

1. Marriage

A FOURTEENTH-CENTURY BEAU, 1371

La Tour-Landry, *The Book of the Knight of La Tour-Landry*, pp. 33–34.

Three ladies sat together in a private chamber and talked of their adventures, until one happened to say, "Very close-mouthed is anyone of us that will not tell, of good fellowship here among us three, that which she shall be asked, that is, if she has been this year made love to."

"Truly," said the first, "I've been made love to." The second and the third said the same.

"Now," said the boldest lady, "sorry love hath she that telleth not the name of him that last made love to her"; and they agreed to tell.

"Forsooth," said the first, "it was Boucicaut that made love to me."

"And in good sooth," said the second, "so did he to me."

"By my troth," quoth the third, "and to me also."

"In good faith," said the three ladies, "he is not so true a knight as we thought, for he is but a deceiver and a mocker; however, let us send for him."

And when he came he said, "My ladies, what would ye?" and they bade him sit down on the ground by them. And he said, "Since I am come and must sit, let me have some cushion or a stool, for I might, if I sat low, break some of my points." So they granted him a stool; and when he had sat down, they, full of ire and wrath, said, "Boucicaut, we are foul deceived in you the time past, for we thought that ye had been a true knight, and ye are but a mocker and a deceiver of ladies, and that is a foul blemish."

And he answered, "Ladies, how know ye that?"

"For, sir, ye have here made love to my cousin and also to me, and ye said ye loved us and that each of us had your heart, which was false lying. Ye might not love us all three best, for ye are not three persons, nor have ye three hearts, and therefore ye are false and deceitful, and ye ought not to be set in the number of true knights."

Then said he, "Ladies, ye are wrong, and that will I show you if ye will give me leave to speak, and I will tell you why. For at that time I spake with each of you, I loved her best that I spake with, and thought truly the same, and methinketh therefore ye be in the wrong to have such language on me; but I must suffer it."

And when they saw him no more abashed, they said they would draw cuts among them there, to know to whom he should abide.

"In good faith," said the first lady, "I will draw no cut for him, for I quit my part of him"; and the other two ladies said, "So do we our part, for we will not of him."

"Ah!" said the knight, "ye need not strive; for she is not here that shall have part of me." And with that he rose and rode on his way, and let the three ladies stay there all abashed and ashamed . . . for there is many a woman who beginneth language with a man and cannot end it well.

VANITY LOSES A GOOD HUSBAND; A TALE OF 1371 [1]

La Tour-Landry, *The Book of the Knight of La Tour-Landry*, pp. 165–167.

There was a knight that had three daughters, of which the eldest was wedded, and there was a knight that asked the second daughter both for land and marriage, insomuch that the knight came to see her that should be his wife, and to be assured and affianced together if they were pleased each with other, for neither of them had seen the other before that time.

And the damsel, that knew of the knight's coming, arrayed herself in the best guise that she could, to have a slender and a fair-shapen body, and she clothed her in a coat-hardy [2] unfurred and unlined, which sat right strait upon her, and there was great cold, great frost, and great wind; and because of the simple vesture that she had on, the color of the maid was defaced, and she waxed all pale and black with cold.

So this knight that was come to see her beheld the color of her, all dead and pale, and after that he looked upon that other sister that she had, and saw her color fresh and ruddy as a rose, for she was well clothed and warm against the cold, as she that thought not upon marriage at so short a time. The knight beheld first that one sister and after that other. And when he had dined, he called two of his friends and of his kin and said unto them, "Sirs! we be come hither to see the daughters of the lord of this place, and I know well that I should have the one I choose, wherefore I would have the third daughter." And his friends

---

[1] Slightly condensed.
[2] A close-fitting garment with sleeves, formerly worn by both sexes. (*O.E.D.*)

answered him that it was more honor unto him to have the elder. "Fair friends," said the knight, "ye see but little advantage therein, for ye know well that they have an elder sister, which is wedded; also, I see the youngest, the fairest and freshest of color, more pleasant than her second sister, for whom I was spoken unto to have in marriage; therefore it is my pleasure to have her."

And the knight asked for the third daughter, which was granted him; whereof folk marveled, especially the maid that thought to have been wedded to the same knight.

So it happened within a short time after they married that the young damsel which the knight refused, when she was well clothed and furred and the weather was changed to warmer, got back her color and fairness again, so that she was fresher and fairer an hundred part than was her sister, the knight's wife; and so the knight said unto her, "My fair sister, when I was to wed and I came to see you, ye were not so fair by the seventh part as ye be now, and now ye pass your sister, my wife, in fairness, whereof I marvel greatly."

And then the knight's wife answered and told him how it was and what her sister had done. "And I," said she, "that thought as much to have such wealth and worship as to have you unto my lord, without any vanity I clothed myself in warm furred gowns that kept my body warm, wherefore I had better color than she had, whereof I thank God, for therefore I got your love; and blessed be that hour that my sister clothed herself so light, for if it had not been so, ye had not taken me and left her."

A FORWARD LADY GETS HER JUST DESERTS, 1371

La Tour-Landry, *The Book of the Knight of La Tour-Landry*, p. 18.

It happened that my friends spake to me to be married into a noble place, and my father brought me to see her that I should have, and there we had great cheer, and my father set me in language with her, that I should have knowledge of her speech, and so we fell to talking of prisoners, and I said, "Damsel, it were better to fall to be your prisoner than to many another, for I trow your prison should not be so hard to me as it should be if I were taken by Englishmen."

And she answered, "I have seen some not long since that I would were my prisoner."

"Would you," I asked her, "put them in evil prison?"

"Nay," she said, "I would keep them as I would my own body."

I said, "Happy is he that might come into so noble a prison."

What shall I say? She loved me enough, and had a quick eye, and a light, and there were many words. And so at last she waxed right familiar with me, for she prayed me two or three times that I should not wait long before coming to see her again; at which I marveled, seeing that I was never acquainted with her, nor had spoken or seen her before that time; and she knew well that folk were about to marry us together. When we were parted, my father asked me, "How liketh you? Tell me your opinion." And I said she was both good and fair, but she should be to me no nearer than she was. And I told my father how it seemed to me, and of her estate and language; and so I said I would not of her, for she was so pert and so light of manners that she caused me to be displeased with her; for which I have thanked God divers times since.

CONTROL OF MARRIAGE THROUGH FEUDAL TENURE A FINANCIAL ASSET, 1312

Harleian Charters, 55 C 18. Ipswich, Saturday after St. Matthew [3] in September, 5 Edward II.

To all faithful who shall see or hear the presents, Robert de Reydon, knight, greeting in the Lord. Whereas the marriage of Robert, son and heir of Roger Maukel of Hintlesham, belongs to me by reason of certain lands and tenements which he holds of me by knight's service, and whereas the said Robert, without my license or will, hath married himself to Joan, daughter of Thomas Stace [4] of Ipswich; know that I have pardoned and altogether released to the said Thomas Stace and to Robert, son of the said Roger, for twenty marks silver which they have given me in hand, all actions, claims, and demands which I ought to have had against them or either of them, or may henceforward have, by reason of the said marriage or the custody of the said lands or tenements by reason of the minority of the said Robert belonging to me. . . .

Witnesses: Hugh Horaud, Walter de Westhale, Robert de Reymes . . . Ranulphus [5] le Taverner.

[3] The Feast of St. Matthew is September 21.
[4] The Staces and the de Westhales of Ipswich were relatives of Chaucer; Mary le Chaucer, his grandmother, was a de Westhale (Chaucer, *Canterbury Tales*, ed. by Manly, pp. 4–5); cf. below, pp. 54–55.
[5] Raño written over an erasure.

THE KING'S MINISTERS HASTEN TO SECURE THE MARRIAGE OF A
WEALTHY HEIRESS, CA. 1325

Chancery Warrants (Internal) 1767/31.

Greetings and affectionate regards. My lord, we have learned since our
departure from London that the Foliot marriage concerns a demoiselle,
wherefore we consider the thing more noble and rich than we had
thought. We therefore beg and counsel you, my lord, that for the profit
of our lord the King, as soon as you have seen these letters, you cause the
said demoiselle to be seized into the King's hand, and put in good ward,
so that the lord King may profit thereby; for you know that the wardship
of a woman is often perilous, and there is also danger that our lord the
King may not profit because she is not in his hand. So be pleased to hasten
the matter before others set hand to it, and so that our lord the King may
profit from it as is abovesaid. . . . Written at Isleworth, June 9.

The thing was even richer and more noble than the writer thought; for there were
two coheiresses, Margery and Margaret Foliot, for whose marriage the King had
£200 each. Margery was in the keeping of the Constable of the Tower of London
until she was handed over [for £200] to Isabel de Hastyng.[6] [R.]

In another case, about 1377, William de Brantingham considered the custody of an
heiress so valuable that he was charged with hiring an impostor to impersonate her,
in order to show that she had not died while on a trip to the Holy Land, as had been
asserted. William de Brantingham had purchased the custody of the lands and marriage of the heiress which had been originally made to John de Beverle, the King's
esquire, in 1370, just as the custody of the lands and marriage of the heirs of
Edmund de Staplegate and of John Solys was granted to Geoffrey Chaucer as the
King's esquire in 1375.[7]

As Edmund de Staplegate was the heir of a wealthy Canterbury merchant, this
wardship paid Chaucer £104, which was equivalent to about $15,000 today. In
1378 Chaucer and John de Beverle were mainpernors for Sir William de Beauchamp
in his guardianship of the lands of the Earl of Pembroke in Wales and elsewhere,
involving responsibility to the King for £400 a year, which would be about $60,000
today.[8]

Records of several cases in which people were kidnaped because of their value as
marriageable persons have survived. For example, John Basyng and wife Agnes and
John, brother of Agnes, were attached to answer John Wilcotes, William Makkeney,
and John Orwell, executors of the will of Richard de Adderbury, knight, in a plea
why they abducted (*rapuerunt et abduxerunt*) Philippa, daughter and heir of John
Hanwell, within age, whose marriage belonged to Richard in his lifetime at Glymp-

[6] Gt. Brit., P.R.O., *Calendar of the Fine Rolls*, 1319–1327, p. 357.
[7] Gt. Brit., P.R.O., *Calendar of the Patent Rolls*, 1367–1370, p. 416; *ibid.*, 1374–1377,
p. 178, and Ancient Petitions 5026 and 5110.
[8] Chaucer, *Canterbury Tales*, ed. by Manly, pp. 20–21.

ton, because John Hanwell, her father, held a messuage in Glympton of Richard.[9]

Two similar cases occurred in Chaucer's family, one involving his father, John Chaucer, who was kidnaped by two members of the related Stace family and by his own aunt, Agnes de Westhale, in order that he might be married to Joan, the daughter of Agnes, and thus consolidate their property. In 1380 Chaucer himself was accused of connection with the abduction of Cecilia Chaumpaigne, but was exonerated through the testimony of Cecilia and of several men, one of whom was Sir William Beauchamp, for whom he and John de Beverle had acted as mainpernors in 1378.[10]

A STUDENT'S MARRIAGE, 1380

Common Pleas, Plea Roll 487 m. 625.

John Melburne of Bernes [probably an attorney in the courts of the city of London, was] summoned to . . . pay John Chiterne . . . £200 . . . because he had not kept a covenant made . . . in the Feast of St. Lawrence [August 10], 4 Richard II [1380], [whereby] it was agreed that William, the son of Melburne, should marry Agnes, the sister of Chiterne, for which marriage Chiterne should give Melburne fifty marks, and . . . Melburne should enfeoff divers persons . . . of the manor of Wytecombe . . . and [make other settlements upon the issue of William and Agnes], should . . . sustain all the costs and charges of William and Agnes and of their children . . . should support William at the Schools of Oxford continually until he should be sufficiently learned in the art of grammar, and afterwards should enable him elsewhere to study the law of the land, where the King's Court should for the time be, and also should provide Agnes with reasonable food, sufficient clothing, and other necessaries.

> This case turns upon a quibble raised by Melburne, that Chiterne should not first have sued him in the Marshalsea court because neither party was of the King's household, although the agreement was made within the Verge. A record of the financial arrangements in connection with the marriage of a student who was a minor is found in the account, drawn up by auditors, for John Pothowe of Melton, defendant, for the time he was bailiff of tenements in York for ten years during the minority of Richard Lonud, plaintiff. The latter had married a ward of Pothowe, and both lived with him at Melton for one year. Pothowe claimed, among other items, £60 for food, clothing, and other necessaries for Lonud and his wife, and 60s. for Richard's expenses in attending grammar school a year. In addition, Pothowe claimed 40s. as the expenses of a nurse and one child of the Lonuds maintained at Pothowe's house at Melton for one year.[11] [R.]

[9] Common Pleas, Plea Roll 561 m. 204 [East. 2 Hen. IV].
[10] Chaucer, *Canterbury Tales*, ed. by Manly, pp. 5, 21. See above, p. 53.
[11] Common Pleas, Plea Roll 511 m. 202 [Mich. 12 Ric. II].

MARRIAGE CUSTOMS, 1317 AND 1321

Stapleton, "A Brief Summary of the Wardrobe Accounts of the Tenth, Eleventh, and Fourteenth Years of King Edward the Second," *Archaeologia*, XXVI (1836), 338–340.

The Wardrobe Accounts of King Edward II contain the following items:

In money thrown over the heads of Oliver de Bourdeaux and the Lady Maud Trussel [12] during the solemnization of their nuptials, at the door of the chapel within the park of Woodstock, on the twenty-sixth day of June, 10 Edward II, £2, 10s.

Ninth day of February [14 Edward II], in money thrown by the King's order at the door of the King's chapel, within the manor of Havering-atte-Boure, during the solemnization of the marriage between Richard, son of Edmund Earl of Arundell, and Isabella, daughter of Sir Hugh le Despenser,[13] junior, £2.

Delivered, for a veil to be spread over the heads of Richard de Arundell and Isabella, daughter of Sir Hugh le Despenser, junior, at their nuptial mass in the King's chapel, at Havering-atte-Boure, the ninth day of February, one piece of Lucca cloth.

2. *Choosing a House*

A BARON ARRANGES QUARTERS FOR HIS LADY AND HIMSELF IN HIS MOTHER'S COUNTRY HOUSE, 1383

"Early Deeds Relating to Shropshire," *Collectanea topographica et genealogica*, V (1838), 180–181 (from Ashridge Muniments).

This indenture, made between my very reverend Lady Alyne Lestrange, lady of Knokyn, of the one part, and the Lord Lestrange, Sir John, her son, of the other part, witnesses that the said Sir John shall have board and lodging in the household of my said very reverend lady—that is to say, he himself, the Lady Maude Lestraunge his spouse, one esquire, one lady (*damoisele*), two yeomen (*vadlets*), a nurse, and a page, from the date of the execution of this indenture until the completion of one full year following: rendering and paying to my said very reverend lady for their lodging during the time aforesaid £50 of good money in her manor of Mudle. . . . And if the aforesaid lord, Sir John, the Lady Maude his spouse, or any of their retainers be away from the said house,

[12] The marriage of Lady Maud Trussel came into the hands of the King because of the death of her previous husband.   [13] Isabella le Despenser was the King's niece.

during the time until their return there shall be abated of the said sum
—for himself 7*d.* a day, for the Lady Maude, his spouse, after the same
manner, for the esquire 4*d.* a day, and for the damoisele as much; for
a yeoman 3*d.* a day, the nurse likewise, and for the page 1*d.* a day.
And in case the household of my said very reverend Lady Lestraunge be
charged with the retainers of the said lord her son, the Lady Maude his
spouse, or any of their followers aforesaid other than is contained in
this indenture, that the said Sir John shall be obliged to pay for their
dwelling [there] at the end of each quarter . . . that is to say for a
knight (*bachiler*) 8*d.* a day, an esquire 6*d.*, a yeoman 3*d.*, and a page 2*d.*
a day. And these retainers shall be accounted for by the steward of the
household of my said very reverend lady for the time being and one
other [living] with the said lord whom it shall please him to appoint.
. . . [Provisions follow for collecting arrears of payment.] Written
at Mudle on the Feast of St. Katherine [November 25], 7 Richard II
[1383].

A MARRIAGE SETTLEMENT, INCLUDING PROVISION FOR QUARTERS WITH
THE BRIDE'S FATHER, 1379

Common Pleas, Plea Roll 476, Deeds Enr. m. 3 d.

These indentures, made between the most honorable lady the Countess
of Norfolk and Thomas de Mikelfeld of the one part and William Berard
of the other part, witness their agreements and covenants as follow, to
wit: that the said Thomas will marry Margaret, the daughter of the
said William; and that the said William will have charge of the said
Margaret, [his] daughter, and will bear the expenses of the said Margaret, his daughter, and of the issue begotten of the bodies of the said
Thomas and Margaret sufficiently and fitly, in food, clothing, and other
expenses and charges, at his own expense, for the term of the life of the
said William, for any time which it pleases or shall please the said Thomas
that Margaret his wife or their issue shall remain in company with
the said William, her father; also, as for the coming and staying of the
said Thomas, the said William grants that at whatever time it please the
said Thomas to come or stay in company with the said William, he shall
stay at the expense of the said William for himself, his servants and
horses, without anything being taken from the said Thomas for the
charges or expenses of the said Thomas.

Also, they are agreed that the said William will grant to the said

Thomas for the life of the said William ten marks rent to be taken from all the lands and tenements in Whatfeld and Neuton in the county of Suffolk. . . .

Also, they are agreed that the said William, Thomas Morieux, knight, Roger de Bergham, and the feoffees in Whatfeld shall demise to John de Mikelfeld, Robert Melton, William Vavasour, and others whom the said countess and Thomas will name all the lands and tenements with their appurtenances clear and discharged of all actions and charges as they were at the time of purchase of the said William . . . and that those feoffees shall reënfeoff of the manor of Whatfeld and the advowson . . . the said William for term of his life with remainder to the said Thomas and Margaret . . . and the heirs of their bodies, and in default of issue remainder to William Berard and his heirs forever. . . .

Also, that, as for the manor of Neuton called Netherhalle . . . the said William Berard and John Cakestrete and those who have estate in the same shall enfeoff the said persons of the said tenements . . . and that they shall reënfeoff the said William Berard and Isabel his wife and the heirs of their bodies with remainder to Thomas Mikelfeld and Margaret his wife and the heirs of their bodies, and in default remainder to the right heirs of William. . . .

And for the good and faithful performance of all these covenants, the said William binds himself to the said countess and Thomas in two hundred marks. Given at London, November 16, 3 Ric. II.

RENTING A HOUSE, CA. 1380

The Stonor Letters and Papers, 1290–1483, ed. by Kingsford, I, 23–24 (from *Anct. Correspondence* [P.R.O.], xlvi, 22).

Very dear and beloved, I should like you to know that my honorable cousin, Monsieur Henry le Scrope, has bought a house in London to live in there, but he cannot have possession of the said house at his convenience until a certain time. Therefore I ask you kindly that you would lease to my very honorable cousin your London house in which Sir William Mulso has been living recently, until he can take possession of his own house, it being understood certainly, Sir, that he will pay you for your said house, in the mean time, whatever is reasonable, so that you shall be well satisfied. And, dear Sir, I wish you would do this at my request and would ask one of your household to give up your said house to him.

And may the Almighty have you always in His keeping.
Written at London, the 14th day of January.

Richard Le Scrop [14]

To very dear and beloved Edmund de Stonor

DIFFICULTY OF GETTING A HOUSE BUILT TO TIME, 1390

Common Pleas, Plea Roll 516 m. 463 d.

John de Anne of Wyghtreshamme has been attached to answer for not building a new house at Wyghtreshamme in the time specified.[15]

3. *Furnishing a House*

AN ESQUIRE'S SUMMARY OF THE CONTENTS OF HIS HOUSE AT SALISBURY, 1410

Prerogative Court of Canterbury, 21 Marche.

George Meryet, Esquire, of St. Thomas's Parish, Salisbury, included in his will "all my goods and utensils in my inn (*hospicio' meo de George*)." [16] To wit, covers, blankets, linens, coverlets, mattresses, testers, painted cloths, rugs, napkins, towels, wash basins, candelabra of bronze, marble, and silver-gilt, bronze pots and pans, twelve silver spoons, spits, poles, iron pots, vessels of silver-gilt and lead for beer, silver-gilt salt cellars, three iron braziers, and boards for tables, with trestles.

INVENTORY OF THE GOODS IN A FISHMONGER'S CITY HOUSE, 1373

London, Corporation, *Calendar of Plea and Memoranda Rolls, A.D. 1364–1381,* ed. by Thomas, pp. 154–156 (from Plea and Mem. R. A 18. m. 6).

Thomas Mocking, "late citizen and fishmonger," had an eight-room house, furnished as follows:

In the chamber:	*Value*	
A new bed and a tapestry	42s.	
Another bed with a tapestry	6s.	8d.
3 quilts and 1 mattress	8s.	

[14] If, as C. L. Kingsford thinks, the author of this letter was the first Lord Scrope of Bolton, he was the man whose claim to the arms azure, a bend or, Chaucer supported with testimony at the Scrope-Grosvenor trial in 1386.

[15] That this was a fairly common difficulty is shown by the survival of several records of the same type. In one instance the man for whom the house was to have been built claimed £20 damages (Common Pleas, Plea Roll 519 m. 562).

[16] In the fourteenth and fifteenth centuries private dwelling houses were commonly referred to as "inns" (cf. Chaucer, *Canterbury Tales*, ed. by Manly, p. 624).

3 rugs (*chalones*) ⎫
1 framework (*supellex*) ⎪
1 tester   ⎬   18*s.*
1 blanket ⎪
2 pillows (*cervical*) ⎭
4 pairs of sheets   8*s.*
5 feather beds   17*s.*
5 pillows (*wongers*)   2*s.*
panels around the bed (*tabule circa lectum*)   3*s.*
2 curtains (*rydelli*)   3*s.*
2 chests and 2 counters (*computoria*)   10*s.*
1 silver girdle   20*s.*
2 pairs of amber paternosters   6*s.*

In the hall:

3 dorsers ⎫
3 bankers ⎬   £4 15*s* 8*d.*
6 cushions ⎭
3 old bankers and 5 cushions   3*s.* 4*d.*
1 board (*tabula*) ⎫
2 trestles   ⎬   8*s.*
5 stools ⎭
3 checker boards (*scacar'*)   2*s.*
1 fireplace of iron [17] and 1 pair of tongs   31*s.* 3*d.*
5 basins, whereof one is round
7 wash bowls (*lavatoria*), whereof one is a hanging bowl
4 candelabra weighing ½ cwt., 15 lb. at 2*d.* a pound 16*s.* 3*d.* [*sic*]

In the storehouse (dispensa):

7 cloths (*nappe*) ⎫
6 hand towels (*manutergia*) ⎬   24*s.*
4 napkins (*manapia*) ⎭
1 cupboard or locker (*aumbry*) ⎫
4 vats (*fates*)   ⎬   4*s.*
5 barrels   2*s.*

---

[17] "An inventory . . . of the goods of Sir Richard de Vernon at the Manor of Harlaston mentions iron furnaces in the hall for burning sea coal." Sir Richard de Vernon flourished *ca.* 1360. (Carrington, "Haddon: the Hall, the Manor, and Its Lords," *Journal of the Derbyshire Archaeological and Natural History Society*, XXII [1900], 10–11.)

1 gallon jug	all of pewter, weighing 35 lbs. at 2*d.* a lb.	7*s.* 3*d.* [*sic*]
5 pottle jugs		
2 quart jugs		
3 chargers	all of pewter weighing ½ cwt., 17 lbs., at 2½*d.* a pound	13*s.* 11*d.* [*sic*]
12 small platters (*platerell'*)		
12 plates		
12 salt cellars		
1 broken silver cup called a biker	weighing by goldsmith's weight £8 5*s.* at 25*s.* a goldsmith £, £10 6*s.* 3*d.*	
1 silver gilt cup with a silver foot		
4 silver cups without feet		
24 silver spoons		
3 nuts (*nuces*) [18] with silver feet		40*s.*
4 broken cups of mazer		
1 broken cup of warre (*werr'*) [19]		46*s.* 8*d.*

In the parlor (*interlocutorium*):
1 dorser and 1 banker .... 10*s.*
1 board (*tabula*) and 1 counter .... 5*s.*
1 board (*tabula*) for cups, called a cupboard ... 4*s.*

In the chamber next the parlor:

1 cupboard or locker (*aumbry*)	4*s.*
3 chairs	

In the workmen's room:

1 chest	2*s.*
1 board	

In the solar above the same, called the apprentices' chamber:
2 boards .... 12*d.*
4 forms .... 3*s.*

In the kitchen:
2 mortars .... 2*s.*
2 vats (*fates*) .... 7*s.*
1 water tankard .... 2*s.*
5 tubs .... 12*d.*

---

[18] Cf. p. 64*n.*, below.
[19] Warre or werre, a knotty excrescence of a tree, which gave bird's-eye grain when carved; possibly boxwood. [Thomas' note.]

1 sieve called a hairsieve (*hersive*)   4*d.*

1 board for a form   8*d.*

2 large spits

3 small spits

2 tripods

2 gridirons (*creticula*)   weighing in all

1 frying pan (*patella frixoria*)   220 lbs. at   27*s.*   6*d.*

1 hook (*grom*)   1½*d.* a lb.

1 firepan (*ferpanne*)

4 iron rods for curtains

5 pitchers (*urcieli*)

7 pots (*olle*)   weighing 2 cwt.,

7 pans   3 quarters, 10 lbs.,   47*s.*   6*d.* [*sic*] [20]

2 caldrons   at 2*d.* a lb.

Total value of furnishing: £238 16*s.* 3*d.*

INVENTORY OF SOME ARTICLES IN THE HOUSE OF RICHARD TOKY, A LONDON GROCER, 1393

Although the house of Richard Toky, which has been described on p. 7*n.*, was evidently somewhat smaller than that of Thomas Mocking, the inventory of Toky's goods and chattels is much more detailed than that for Mocking. For the most part only those articles in Toky's house are here listed which are not mentioned in the inventory of Thomas Mocking's possessions:

London, Corporation, *Calendar of Select Pleas and Memoranda, A.D. 1381–1412,* ed. by Thomas, pp. 209–213.

In the hall (weapons and armor):   *Value*

1 lance with a shield   2*s.*

poleaxes   3*s.*

1 arblast [cross-bow] with the tackle   2*s.*

In the chamber (mostly clothing):

1 small press for caps   4*d.*

5 ells of linen at 7*d.* the ell   35*d.*

3 ells of cloth of Cologne   20*d.*

---

[20] Four sums in this inventory have been marked *sic* because it is impossible to determine whether any of them are correct. Evaluating the hundredweight at 100 lbs., which, however, is its American value, the third and fourth sums so marked are correct; but evaluating the hundredweight at any of the values it has had in England, *i.e.*, 108, 110, 112, or 120 lbs., all the sums so marked are wrong.

1 long shirt (*camisia*)	
1 night gown (*flameolum*)	12*d*.
1 night cap	
1 vernicle	4*d*.
1 pair of gloves	8*d*.
3 handbags (*mantice*)	3*s*.
1 gown (*gonella*) slashed (*bipartita*) with russet and furred with lambswool	6*s*. 8*d*.
2 pairs of top-boots (*ocrearum*)	16*d*.
1 pair of spurs	4*d*.
2 lances	3*s*.
2 pieces of woolen cloth of shot colors (*stragulatus*)	6*s*. 8*d*.
1 slashed gown of the Grocers' livery	3*s*. 4*d*.
1 gown of russet with caps	2*s*. 6*d*.
1 gown of black fresed [21]	4*s*.
1 otter fur	5*s*.
1 white fur	2*s*.
1 pilche [22] of black	2*s*. 6*d*.
3 kirtelles	18*d*.
1 doublet	2*s*.
6 caps	3*s*.
5 pairs of hose (*caligarum*)	2*s*. 6*d*.
2 pairs of mittens	10*d*.
1 beaver hat	12*d*.
1 gown of blood-color (*sanguinei*) furred with crestigray [23]	33*s*. 4*d*.
1 gown of *blod* [24] color furred with crestigray	20*s*.
1 russet gown furred with *bys* [25]	8*s*.
1 gown of scarlet	4*s*.
1 gown of violet	2*s*.
1 tunic of scarlet	20*d*.
1 kirtle of violet	8*d*.
1 kirtle of russet	18*d*.
2 other old kirtles	16*d*.

[21] Friesed, *i.e.*, combed out into a woolley nap. (All glossarial notes for this inventory are Mr. Thomas'.)

[22] A fur coat.

[23] A variety of gray fur taken from the back of the squirrel in winter.

[24] Either blood color or blue.

[25] Dark gray.

1 kirtle of blanket		20d.
2 pieces of crestigray	4s.	
3 caps	2s.	4d.
1 cloak of *blod* lined with blanket	5s.	
1 other old cloak		16d.
1 worn-out cloak		8d.
1 cradle		12d.
2 paunchers [26]		6d.
1 pilche		8d.

Jewels in the chamber:

1 gold signet		9s.	
1 silver seal with a chain weighing 3½ oz. 4 dwt.		9s.	9d.
1 pair of tables of ivory			12d.
3 plain pieces of silver with a covercle, weighing 2½lbs., 1½oz., at 26s. the pound	£3	8s.	3d.
1 nut [27] with a covercle		20s.	
1 mazer bound with silver, with silver covercle and foot		13s.	4d.
1 cup bound with silver		10s.	
1 small cup bound with silver		6s.	8d.
2 cups of mazer		2s.	
13 silver spoons		19s.	10d.
1 baselard harnessed with silver		6s.	8d.
1 small baselard		3s.	
1 belt partly garnished with silver		3s.	4d.
1 horn with a braser [28] harnessed with silver		6s.	8d.
1 dagger harnessed		2s.	
1 buckle and 1 pendant of silver			26d.
broken silver		4s.	11d.
1 knoppe [29] of pearls			6d.
1 pair of coral beads with an *agnus dei*		23s.	4d.
1 pair of red coral beads		6s.	8d.
1 pair of amber beads		5s.	
1 pair of beads		2s.	
3 jet buttons and 3 silver conies (*coniculi*)			6d.[30]

[26] Either a piece of armor to cover the stomach, or else a belt or girdle.
[27] A cup made of a coconut.
[28] Probably a strap.
[29] A knob or ornamental boss.
[30] A list of the objects in the pantry, buttery, and kitchen is here omitted.

In the counting house:

1 large box bound with iron	12s.
1 small chest (*forcer*)	8d.
1 book of the statutes	3s. 4d.
1 quire of paper	8d.
3 hooks of latten	4d.
1 lock of latten and 1 balance of latten	12d.
3 pieces of *blod carde*	8d.
4 bows	2s. 6d.
18 arrows and 2 bolts	16d.
3 *stantifs* [31], 36 counters, and 1 pair of pincers	18d.
1 pair of balances	4d.
1 pencase (*pennar*) and 1 inkhorn (*hincornu*)	4d.
1 pair of tables of box	8d.
1 pyx, bound with iron, for silver	12d.
1 ell of old canvas	4d.
2 pieces of deer hide	14d.
1 basinet with aventail	13s. 4d.
1 breastplate	13s. 4d.
1 *polett* [32] with aventail	4s.
1 pauncher of mail	2s.
1 legharness	10s.
1 pair of vambrace and rerebrace	4s.
1 pair of gauntlets of plate	3s.
1 image of the Blessed Mary in alabaster	2s.
1 image of St. John the Baptist in alabaster	16d.
1 yard of *blod frised*	10d.
9 heads for arrows	4d.
bags for silver	4d.
1 breastplate	10s.

PURCHASING A CLOCK, 1394

Clocks were fairly common in Chaucer's day. In 1368 three clockmakers from
Delft were given permission to live in England and exercise their trade.[33] In 1397
the Duke of Orleans bought two clocks for 240 shields, and in 1407, 60 shields were
paid for a small clock to be placed in the chamber of the Duchess of Orleans.[34] There

[31] Probably pen trays.
[32] A headpiece with visor.
[33] Thomas Rymer, *Syllabus*, I, 447.
[34] La Borde, *Les Ducs de Bourgogne*, Pt. 2, III, 147, 228.

were clocks at Canterbury, Westminster, and St. Albans which showed the tides, as well as the time,[35] and the clock at St. Paul's, which was repaired in 1344, had a dial made with an angel pointing to the hours.[36] Dafydd ap Gwilym, a Welsh poet writing about 1340, compared the sound of a clock to that of a drunken cobbler, or the "ceaseless chatter of a cloister." In his imprecation he describes it: "May its head, its tongue, its pair of ropes, and its wheel moulder; likewise its weights of dullard balls, its orifices, its hammer, its ducks quacking as if anticipating day, and its ever-restless works." [37]

Common Pleas, Plea Roll 530 m. 479.

Robert Ragenhill, clerk, *vs.* Stephen atte Hegge, of London, brewer, and wife Joan, and Richard "that was Hans-servant Clokmaker"—whereas Robert bargained with Joan and Richard for a clock (*horologium*), they, knowing it was "poorly made and defective," warranted it as "well made and sufficient."

BEQUESTS OF HANGINGS, 1386–1428

Commissary of London. 149 Courtenay.

Laurence Gleseworth, citizen and vintner of London, 1386: Left to his daughter, among other things, one coverlet and one red tester covered (*operat'*) with unicorns, another coverlet and one tester colored green and gray, and three hangings (*tapit?*) of blood color covered (*operatis*) with gray trefoils.

Prerogative Court of Canterbury, 7 Luffenam.

Sir William Esturmy, 1426: Among the bequests of Sir William Esturmy are two costers portraying the deeds of Rowland and Fyrumbras.

Prerogative Court of Canterbury, 9 Luffenam.

Elizabeth, the widow of Richard Ruyhale, 1428: Left in her will one bed with all hangings embroidered with mermaidens.

THE ROYAL ARRAS, 1413

In the account of Thomas Carnica, Keeper of the Great Wardrobe, and of Thomas Dalton, clerk, deputy of the said keeper, appears the following list of pieces of arras, which reads like a catalogue of medieval romances.

Exchequer, King's Remembrancer, Accounts 406/15.

[35] Smyth, "Description of an Astrological Clock belonging to the Society of Antiquaries of London," *Archaeologia*, XXXIII (1849), 10–11.
[36] Madden, "Agreement between the Dean and Chapter of St. Paul's, London, and Walter the Orgoner, of Southwark, relating to a Clock in St. Paul's Church," *Archaeological Journal*, XII (1855), 173–174.
[37] Smyth, "Supplement to the Description of an Astrological Clock, belonging to the Society of Antiquaries," *Archaeologia*, XXXIV (1852), 5–6.

Arras:

5 pieces of the History of Troy.

1 piece de Castro Virtutat dict' de Amor'.[38]

2 pieces of the History of Beaufitz de Hampton.

2 pieces of the History of Kings.

1 piece of the History of Ootoman.

1 piece of the History of Furmentz.

1 piece of the History of the Seven Joys.

1 piece of the Twelve Peers.

1 piece of the History of the King of Love.

1 piece of the History of Percival.

1 piece of the History of Bayard.

1 piece of the History of the Siege of Jerusalem.

1 piece of the History of the King of Cyprus.

1 piece of the History of King Saul.

1 piece of the History of King Alexander.

1 piece of Amis and Amylon.

1 piece of the History of the Nine Conquestors.

1 piece of the Five Joys of the Blessed Mary.

1 piece of the History of Gingebras.

PRICES OF TAPESTRY, 1389–1399

Some idea of the cost of tapestry in Chaucer's time may be obtained from the following entries in the accounts of the Dukes of Burgundy.

LaBorde, *Les Ducs de Bourgogne*, Pt. 2, III, 117.

May 3, 1396. To Nicholas Bataille, 1700 francs for three tapestries, one of which, 15 ells long and 4¼ ells high, depicted the history of Penthesilia; another, 20 ells long and 3½ ells high, dealt with Beves of Hampton; and the third, 20 ells long and 3⅝ ells high, gave the history of the youthful exploits of Regnault de Montabau and of Riseus de Ripemort.

LaBorde, *Les Ducs de Bourgogne*, Pt. 2, III, 171–172.

February 8, 1398/99. To Nicholas Bataille, 200 crowns for a tapestry showing a tree of life on which there are a crucifix and several prophets among the branches of the tree, and beneath which are the earthly paradise, the Virgin Mary, St. John, and other saints, male and female.

[38] The romance here illustrated was, no doubt, "The Castle of the Virtues of Love."

LaBorde, *Les Ducs de Bourgogne*, Pt. 2, III, 63–64.

1391. To Colin Bataille, 1,200 francs paid by the Duke of Touraine for a tapestry showing the story of Theseus and the Golden Eagle.

LaBorde, *Les Ducs de Bourgogne*, Pt. 2, III, 42.

1389. Jehan de Croisetes, a Saracen tapestry-maker living at Arras, acknowledges that he has received from Jehan Poulain, treasurer of the Duke of Touraine, 800 gold francs which were owing to him for a golden Saracen tapestry giving the history of Charlemagne, which had been purchased from him at the inn of Beaute.

LaBorde, *Les Ducs de Bourgogne*, Pt. 2, III, 109.

November 24, 1395. To Jaquet Dordin, merchant and citizen of Paris, 1,800 francs for three tapestries,[39] of which two show the history of the Credo, with twelve prophets and twelve apostles, and the other shows the coronation of the Virgin Mary.

4. *Planting a Garden*

OF SOWING AND SETTING OF WORTS, 15TH CENTURY

Gardener, "A Fifteenth Century Treatise on Gardening," [40] *Archaeologia*, LIV (1894), 163–164.

> Worts we must have
> Both for master and for knave;
> Ye shall have mind here
> To have worts young all times of the year.
> Every month hath his name,
> To set and sow without any blame:
> May for summer is all the best,
> July for autumn is the next,
> November for winter might the third be,
> March for lent, so may I thrive.
> The land must well dunged be,
> Delved and stirred, sir, pardie!
> When thou hast sowed thy seed along,

[39] They are described as having a vertical warp and a woof of threads which formed a vertical design. They were made of fine Arras thread worked with gold.
[40] The poem from which the following excerpt is taken is entitled "The Feats of Gardeninge." It deals with the setting and grafting of trees, cutting and setting of vines, sowing and setting of seeds, sowing and setting of worts of the nature of parsley and of other kinds of herbs of the nature of saffron.

Four weeks thereafter thou let them stand;
When the four weeks be all over gone,
Take thy plants every one
And set them in good fat land,
And they will fair worts be and long.
Within two weeks that they be set
Thou may pull them for thy meat.
And so from month to month
Thou shalt bring thy worts forth.
They that shall bear seed less and more
Let them grow to make the store.
Of worts can I no more tell;
Of other herbs hereafter I shall.

TO MAKE CHERRIES GROW WITHOUT STONES, TIME OF EDWARD IV

Halliwell-Phillipps, ed., *Early English Miscellanies*, p. 71.

Cleave a young shoot of a young cherry tree that is a span long or two from the top even down to the root, but let it stand still on the stock. Then draw out the pith on every side with some manner of iron, join every part together, bind it well, and smear it well with clay on every side from the top to the root. When a year is past where its wound is, graft on the same stock a shoot that never bore fruit, and thereon shall grow cherries without any stones. Also grapes will grow without pips when the pith of the vine is taken out. The same is true of all other like [fruits].

JOHN OF GAUNT'S GARDENER AT THE SAVOY, 1372

John of Gaunt's Register, II, 61 (No. 999).

The Savoy, June 30, 1372. John [King of Castile, etc.] to . . . our receiver general. Whereas we have ordained our servant, Nicholas Gardiner, to be the gardener of our manor of the Savoy during our pleasure, receiving every day . . . two pence for his wages; and also we will that he have for his own use all manner of fruit and herbs growing therein to make his profit thereof,[41] saving to us what we shall expend for the expenses of our household at our comings; and the said Nicholas shall till and work the said gardens at his own charges and [shall provide] all things needful and necessary for the work of the said gardens, except that we shall find him rails and rods for the time of paling; we will that you . . . pay the said Nicholas the said two pence a day and also

[41] Cf. above, p. 23.

by controlment of our beloved clerk, Sir John de Yerdeburgh, clerk of our wardrobe, whom we have assigned to be his controller in this respect, you can know that the said Nicholas has paid or will pay for the same palings.

A GARDEN WALL

Great Britain, Public Record Office, *Descriptive Catalogue of Ancient Deeds*, V, 55, No. A. 10849.

Memorandum of an agreement between John de Laufar, clerk, and William de Auverne, citizen of London, that, whereas William had removed the earth in his garden next a stone wall in front of John's solar without John's assent, he shall construct three stone buttresses to support the said wall, and keep them in repair; the water running off the said solar he shall catch in his garden. John shall have two windows opening on the same garden, but so barred with iron that William may incur no loss thereby. William may not block the view of the said windows by buildings.

A GOLDSMITH'S CLOSE AT WESTMINSTER

Coram Rege Roll 538, m. 57 d.

John Henle[y], clerk, and another attached to answer Richard Noke, goldsmith, for breaking the close and houses of Richard at Charring in Westminster and felling pears, apples, figs (*vices*), poplars, oaks, beech trees, ash trees, willows, thorns, and other trees bearing walnuts, and carrying them off.

AFFODILLE, LATE 14TH CENTURY

Stephens, "Extracts in Prose and Verse from an Old English Medical Manuscript," *Archaeologia*, XXX (1844), 382–383.

> Affodille, a precious plant,
> Is not at all red [42] in English.
> Some say there are leeks five,
> But the best that is alive,
> Garlic the one, leek the other,
> Squirle is the great brother,

[42] *Red* may possibly be the participle of *read* and mean here "expressed." The poet may, perhaps, mean that the word *affodille* has no native form, but is a borrowed word. As there was some red in the continental flower, however, this statement may refer to an English variety.

Gracia Dei that groweth in mead;
Affodille, the fifth child,
In February he beginneth to spring;
In May he beginneth down to hang;
First in Piscibus [43] his springing is,
But soon in Cancer away, I wis;
In March and April will he flower,
None so fair herb to him is in color.
The flower is yellow, very little white,
I know no flower like to it.
The stalk is a foot and a quarter long;
The leaf is of the same length.
On the stalk are leaves none,
But stalk and leaves out of the ground go;
Stalk and leaves all of one height,
Nigh as it were of a white oat.[44]
The taste is somewhat also the same,
Though it little be, as of leek;
It beareth a top with many seeds
Black polished as jet is;
This herb in a clean cloth, and its root
Against the falling evil is medicine.
Affodille in clean cloth kept thus
Shall suffer no fiend in that house;
If ye bear it on you day and night,
The fiend of you shall have no might.

FAMILY LIFE

1. Husband and Wife

A PARISIAN'S IDEA OF THE MODEL WIFE, CA. 1393

Le Ménagier de Paris, ed. by Pichon, I, 168–169.

Take pains to cherish the person of your husband, and I beg of you to keep him in clean linen, for that is your business; and since men have the trouble and pains of outside matters, so must a husband take pains to go and come and to run from one place to another, through rain,

---

[43] The twelfth sign of the zodiac.
[44] Professor Hulbert has suggested this translation for the extremely difficult line, "Ny as it were of on heyte wheyte."

through winds, through snow and through hail, wet one day, dry the next, sweating one day, shivering the next, ill-fed, ill-lodged, ill-warmed, ill-bedded. Yet no real harm is done him, because he is consoled by his confidence in the care which his wife will take of him upon his return, and in the ease, the joys, and the pleasures which she will give him, or cause to be given him in her presence: to have his hose taken off before a good fire, to have his feet washed, and fresh hose and shoes, to be well fed and given good drink, to be well served and cared for, to be put to sleep in clean sheets and clean nightcaps, to be well covered with good furs and solaced with other joys and entertainment, privities, loves and secrets, about which I do not speak. And the next day, fresh underlinen and garments. . . . Therefore I advise you to prepare such comforts for your husband whenever he comes and stays, and to persevere therein; and also to keep peace with him and remember the country folk's proverb that three things drive a goodman out of his home: a leaky roof, a smoking chimney, and a scolding wife.[45]

A FOURTEENTH-CENTURY BUTTERFLY, 1371

La Tour-Landry, *The Book of the Knight of La Tour-Landry*, p. 35.

I will tell you of a lady that caught a great blame and slander at jousting without cause. She was a fair young lady and made there good cheer and danced and sang with knights and squires, and all her heart was set on the world's pleasure, notwithstanding her husband was not best pleased with her for her outgoing. But she was always glad when she was asked to go out, and she found means to her husband that she was always asked that she might go. Her husband refused her not, for fear lest those that prayed him would be wroth and lest men would think that he was jealous of his wife. He spent much money to make her fresh and gay at the said feasts, out of respect for her friends, but she might have perceived many times that it was against her husband's will that she went to such feasts. And so it happened once at a feast that she was at by night they quenched the torches suddenly and made great noise and cry, and when the light was lighted again, the lady's husband's brother was there and saw his sister-in-law a little aside with a knight in a corner. In truth, I am sure there was nothing done amiss, but nevertheless the brother told her husband, who all his life after mistrusted that his wife had done amiss and loved her never afterward so well as he did before. So there was never peace between them, but ever glooming, lowering, and chiding.

[45] Cf. Chaucer's use of this saying in the *Canterbury Tales*, D 278–280 and B² 1086.

La Tour-Landry, *The Book of the Knight of La Tour-Landry*, pp. 26–27.

It happened once there were three merchants that rode homeward from a fair, and as they fell to talking, riding on the way, one of them said, "It is a noble thing for a man to have a good wife that obeyeth and doth his bidding at all times."

"By my troth," said another, "my wife obeyeth me truly."

"By God," said the other, "I trow mine obeyeth best to her husband."

Then he that began first to speak said, "Let us lay a wager of a dinner, and whose wife obeyeth worst, let her husband pay for the dinner." And thus the wager was laid. And they agreed among themselves . . . that every man should bid his wife leap into a basin that they should set before her, and they were sworn that none should let his wife know about their wager, but all they should say was, "Look, wife, that which I command be done."

However it happened that after one of them bade his wife leap into the basin he had set before her on the ground, she answered and asked why, and he said, "For it is my wish, and I will that ye do it."

"By God," quoth she, "I will first know wherefore ye will have me leap into the basin." And for nothing her husband could do would she do it. So her husband up with his fist, and gave her two or three great strokes. Then they rode to the second merchant's house; and he commanded . . . his wife to leap into the basin . . . but she asked whereto, and said she would not for him. And then he took a staff, and beat her. Then they rode to the third merchant's house. There they found the meat on the board, so he whispered in the ear of one of his fellows, "After dinner I will try my wife, and bid her leap into the basin." And so they set them down to dinner.

And when they were set, the good man said to his wife, "Whatever I bid, look it be done, however it be." And she that loved him and feared him, heard what he said, and took heed to that word; but she knew not what he meant. It happened that they had for their dinner soft eggs, and there lacked salt on the table; so the goodman said, "Wife, sele sus table." The wife understood her husband had said, "Seyle sus table," which is in French, "Leap on the board." And she, that was afraid to disobey, leaped upon the board, threw down meat and drink, brake the glasses, and spilt all that there was on the board.

"What," said the good man, "then know ye no other sport, wife?"

"Though ye be angry, sir," she said, "I have done your bidding, as ye bade me to my power, notwithstanding it is your harm and mine; but I had rather both ye and I had harm than I disobeyed your bidding. For ye said, 'Seyle sus table.'"

"Nay," quoth he, "I said, 'Sele sus table,' that is to say, salt on the board."

"By my troth," she said, "I understood that ye bade me leap on the board," and there was much mirth and laughing.

And the other two merchants said there was no need to bid her leap into the basin, for she had obeyed enough; whereby they consented that her husband had won the wager, and they had both lost.

A FIGHT ABOUT A BADLY-COOKED HERRING, 1353

Chancery, Criminal Inquisition, 41/9.

[The jurors in a criminal inquisition say that]. On Thursday after the Feast of St. Bartholomew,[46] 27 Edw. III, when John de Lincoln, spicer, had sat down to supper in his own house in Lincoln with Margaret his wife and Thomas de Huddeswell, "harpoure," because the said Margaret had brought the said John a herring which was not well cooked, as it seemed to the said John, the said John being annoyed thereat struck Margaret with his hand below the cheek. This was told to Robert, son of John de Dunham of Lincoln, as he was going past the door of the house. Upon hearing it Robert entered the house and spoke fiercely to the said John, who was still sitting at supper, about what he had done, and dragged John's hood over his face and hit him again and again upon the head and below the cheeks with his fists and buffeted him. Whereupon John begged him humbly not to maltreat him, as he did many times. Thereupon Robert drew his long knife, called a baselard, and struck John on the head and wounded him and ran upon him, aiming the point of his knife at John's heart and swearing that he should not depart from that place alive. At which, John turned aside the point of the knife with his hand and . . . the blow somewhat. But yet John struck Robert on the left side and wounded him severely. And while Robert was following up the said blow fiercely and rashly, John struck him to the heart with the knife with which he had been cutting his supper, which was still in his hand; whereof Robert died that day, unconfessed and immediately.

[46] The Feast of St. Bartholomew is August 29.

A HUSBAND'S LAST LETTER TO HIS WIFE, 1419

Furnivall, ed., *The Fifty Earliest English Wills in the Court of Probate, London,* pp. 40–41 (P.C.C. 45 Marche).

Codicil to the Will of Stephen Thomas of Leigh in Essex: [47] And also I will that my will be fulfilled as I ordained when I went from home, and all that is contained in this codicil; that is to say, my will is to have a trental of masses if I have died before I come home. And also I pray you that you would brew ten bushels of malt to give poor men of my parish, and also that you would bake six bushels of wheat in small half-penny loaves and give every man and woman a loaf and a gallon of ale, as far as it will go. And also I pray you and charge you, in God's name, that you send a man to the Holy Prior of Bridlington to offer for me, and before anything, that this way [48] to Bridlington and the trental be both before Easter if I die ere I come home.

And I also wish you to know that it is my will that Thomas Chesse shall have me if I die in his boat with him and also that he shall have my best gown of the King's livery that is at home at my house, and my gold ring, and my whistle. And . . . it is my will that Thomas Albwe shall have the next best gown that is at home after that, and a hood. And that George Thomas, my cousin, shall have all the goods and the harness that I have at Hampton in the ship, and beside, and this that is on the sea with me at Rouen he shall have all together, save that Richard Smytheot shall have my russet gown that I wear and my black hood and an old basinet.

More write I not unto you, but the Holy Trinity keep you now, dear and trusty wife. Here I make an end, wherefore I pray you, as my trust is wholly in you over all other creatures, that this last will shall be fulfilled, and all other that I ordained at home, for all the love that ever was between man and woman.

Written at Rouen, the Sunday next before the Feast of the Purification of Our Lady.[49]

[47] The will and codicil were proved July 20, 1419.
[48] Journey. (*O.E.D.*)
[49] The Feast of the Purification (of the Virgin Mary) is February 2.

2. *The Servant Question*

CHOOSING SERVANTS IN FRANCE, CA. 1393

Le Ménagier de Paris, ed. by Pichon, II, 57–59.

Know that of those chambermaids out of a place, many offer themselves and clamor and are at great pains to seek out masters and mistresses; and of these take none until you know beforehand where they were last, and send some of your people to get their character; that is, whether they talked or drank too much, how long they stayed, what work they did and knew how to do; whether they have homes or acquaintances in the town; from what part of the country and what kind of home they come; how long they stayed there and why they left; for you shall find out by their past service what expectation or hope you may have of their service in time to come. And know that such women from distant parts of the country frequently have a reputation there for some vice, and this it is which brings them into service away from their own district. . . .

And if you find from the report of her master and mistress, neighbors, or others that she is likely to fill your requirement, find out from her, and cause the butler to enter into his account book in her presence, on the day when you engage her, her name and those of her father and mother, and some of her relatives; the place where they live, her birthplace, and her sureties. For servants will be the more afraid to do wrong if they think that you are registering these things and that if they run away from you without notice or commit any offense, you will complain of it in writing to the justice of their country or to their friends. And, nevertheless, remember the saying of the philosopher called Bertram the Old, who saith that if you engage a chambermaid or a man who answers back proudly, you will know that when she leaveth she will speak ill of you if she can; and if she is not of that kind, but soft-spoken and accustomed to flatter, you shall not trust her, for she is trying to trick you in some way; but if she blushes and is silent and modest when you correct her, love her as your daughter.

WRITING TO LONDON FOR A BUTLER, 1402

Rickert, "Some English Personal Letters of 1402," *Review of English Studies*, VIII (1932), 260 (Excheq. K.R. Accts. 512/10 m. 1).

[Elizabeth Lady Zouche from Eaton Bray in Bedfordshire to Her Friend, John Bore, in London]:

Right well beloved friend, I greet you well and desire to hear of your welfare. And I pray you for my love that you will think about my butler as you promised me, for you know well yourself that it is difficult for me to be so long without [one], and unless you can get me another and that he be humble, in any way, I pray you, and I trust that you will not fail me. I can say no more, but I commend you to God. Written at Eaton the twenty-ninth day of May.

HIRING HOUSEHOLD SERVANTS AT A HIGHER-THAN-LEGAL WAGE, 1357

Latin original printed in Putnam, *The Enforcement of the Statutes of Laborers, 1349–1359*, p. 227* (Assize R. 971 [Warwick], m. 3 d.).

The jurors of the hundred of Barlichway present that Alice Portreve, wife of William Portreve of Henley, gives excessive salaries to spinning women.

Item, they present that Geoffrey de Welneford, rector of the church of Kynenarton, gave to his two household servants for the winter term eight shillings with their liveries, and with their daily food to be taken in his hall.

A CASE OF SERVANT GRABBING AT WOOLWICH, 1382

Common Pleas, Plea Roll 486 m. 349 d.

Kent. Goscelin Osbarn, who sues as well for the Lord King as for himself, offers himself the fourth day against Richard Oxford of London and Richard Hare in a plea why, whereas it was ordained by the lord Edward, late King of England, grandfather of the present King, for the common utility of the same Kingdom, that if anyone withdrew a servant retained in the service of anyone else before the end of the agreed term from the said service without reasonable cause or leave, he should undergo the penalty of imprisonment, and no one should presume to receive or retain such an one in his service, the said Richard Oxford withdrew the said Richard Hare, late servant of the said Goscelin, lately retained in his service at Woolwich, before the end of the term agreed between them and without reasonable cause or license, and although he was often requested to restore the said Richard Hare to the same Goscelin, he retained him in contempt of the King and to the great damage of the said Goscelin. [Adjourned until Michaelmas.]

THE SERVANTS' TABLE, CA. 1393

Le Ménagier de Paris, ed. by Pichon, II, 69–70.

[Set your people to their work, wherever it may be], for laziness and idleness bring about all manner of ills. Nevertheless, at the proper times, cause them to sit down to table and have them fed generously upon meat of one kind only, and not upon more or on dainties or delicacies; and order for them drink of only one variety, nourishing but not heady, whether it be wine or not, and not several; and tell them to eat well and to drink plenty, for it is right that they should eat straight-off, without sitting too long over meals, and all at once, without resting at meat or lingering or putting their elbows on the table.

And as soon as they begin to tell tales or to argue, or to lean upon their elbows, tell the [housekeeper] to make them get up and clear away; for it is commonly said, "When the servant holds forth at table and the horse grazes in the ditch, it is time to take them away, for they have had their fill." . . .

And after they have done their next work, and upon feast days, let them have another meal, and after that, to wit in the evening, let them be fed well and generously, as before, and if the weather demands it, let them warm themselves and take their ease.

3. *Life by Candlelight*

A YEAR'S SUPPLY OF TORCHES AND CANDLES, 1418–1419

Large houses were lighted with torches, candles, and tapers of varying size, as is shown by the following stock-account of the steward of Dame Alice de Bryene,[50] at Acton in Suffolk, for the year from Michaelmas, 1418, to Michaelmas, 1419.

Bryene, *Household Book of Dame Alice de Bryene*, pp. 120–121, 137–138.

Wax. [The steward accounts] for 112 lbs. remaining, and for 40 lbs. purchased of the lady's providing. Sum, a hundred and 40 lbs., which make 152 lbs., *viz.*, 112 lbs. to the hundred. Of which in making one torch as below, 24 lbs. Item, in making 2 "tortys," as below, 28 lbs. Item, in making 20 "prykettes," as below, 10 lbs. Item, in making tapers and candles, as below, 50 lbs. Sum, a hundred, which makes 112 lb. And there remain 40 lbs. of wax.

Torches, tortys, prykettes, and candles. [And] for 1 torch and ⅔ of a torch, 10 prykettes, 1 tortys and ¼ of a tortys remaining. And for one torch containing 24 lbs., 2 tortys containing 28 lbs., 20 prykettes con-

taining 10 lbs., 50 tapers and 30 candles called "percheres" containing 50
lbs., made this year. . . . Of which, expended in the said household,
¼ and the third part of a torch . . . 1 tortys and ½ a quarter of a tortys.
Item, expended in the same household, 20 prykettes. Item, expended
in the chapel and in the household of the lady, 50 tapers and 30
candles. . . .

Paris candles.[51] And for 80 lbs. of Paris candles remaining. And for
525 lbs. of Paris candles made of tallow from stock. And for 52 lbs. of
candles purchased by the said steward. Sum, 657 lbs. Of which expended
in the said household, 506 lbs.

Purchase of wax. For 40 lbs. of wax bought by the lady, 15s., price
4½ the lb. For 13 lbs. of wick, 2s. 2d. In stipend of John Blast for making
the said wax into torches, tortys, prykettes, and candles, 2s. Sum, 19s. 2d.

Purchase of Paris candles and clarified tallow. For 52 lbs. of candles,
5s. 10d. . . . For 180 lbs. of clarified tallow, 14s. 3d. . . . For 4 lbs.
of cotton, 2s. 5½d. . . . Item, for 8 lbs. of cotton bought by the lady,
4s. 4d. . . . For wages of John Bocher with his servant for 5 days, for
making 525 lbs. of Paris candles this year by agreement in the gross,
3s. 8d., besides [their] board in the household. Sum, 30s. 6½d.

WOMEN SHOULD BE MORE CAREFUL WITH CANDLES, 1326

London, Coroner, *Calendar of the Coroners Rolls*, p. 171.

On Monday, the Feast of the Nativity [December 25], John Rynet and
Alice his wife were alarmed at midnight by a fire which had been caused
by the fall of a lighted candle, as they were going to sleep, and hurriedly
left the burning shop. Immediately afterward John, blaming Alice for
causing the disaster, violently pushed her back into the shop and fled, but
whither the jurors knew not. Alice was thus injured by the fire and again
leaving the shop lingered until the following Tuesday, when she had
her ecclesiastical rights and died of her burns.

CARRYING FIRE ABOUT THE HOUSE, 1321

London, Coroner, *Calendar of the Coroners Rolls*, p. 41.

When on Sunday [December 29] at dusk, Elena Scot, a servant, left
the solar of the house to get some fire, she slipped from the top step

---

[51] The torches, tortys, prykettes, and candles were of wax. Paris candles were of tallow. All
were homemade. A tortys was a kind of very large wax candle and was usually distinguished from a torch. A prykette was a candle or taper made to be used on a pricket
candlestick. (*O.E.D.*)

of the entrance of the solar and fell backwards down the steps upon a stone at the bottom and broke her neck and forthwith died in consequence of that and from no other felony. Being asked who were present when this happened, the jurors say Margaret de Sandwich, her mistress, and one Cristina Lovel, and Margaret first discovered the corpse and raised the cry, so that the country came; nor do they suspect any man or woman of the death, but only mischance. The corpse was viewed, on which the broken neck appeared and no other hurt.

4. The Toilet and Home Remedies

A RICH MAN'S TOILET AND BATH, CA. 1447

Russell, "Book of Nurture," *The Babees Book*, ed. by Furnivall, pp. 175–183.

The duty of a chamberlain is to be diligent in office, neatly clad, his clothes not torn, hands and face well-washed, and head well-kempt.

He must be ever careful of fire and candle. And look you give diligent attendance to your master. . . .

See that your lord has a clean shirt and hose, a tunic, a doublet, and a long coat, if he wear such, his hose well-brushed, his socks at hand, his shoes or slippers as brown as a water-leech.

In the morning, against your lord shall rise, take care that his linen be clean, and warm it at a clear fire, not smoky, if [the weather] be cold or freezing.

When he rises make ready the foot-sheet, and forget not to place a chair or some other good seat with a cushion on it before the fire, with another cushion for his feet. Over the cushion and chair spread this sheet so as to cover them; and see that you have a kerchief and a comb to comb your lord's head before he is fully dressed.

Then pray your lord in humble words to come to a good fire and array him thereby, and there to sit or stand pleasantly; and wait with due manners to assist him. First hold out to him his tunic, then his doublet while he puts in his arms, and have his stomacher well-aired to keep off harm, as also his stockings and socks, and so shall he go warm all day.

Then draw on his socks and his hose by the fire, and lace or buckle his shoes, draw his hose on well and truss them up to the height that suits him, lace his doublet in every hole, and put around his neck and on his shoulders a kerchief; and then gently comb his head with an ivory comb, and give him water wherewith to wash his hands and face.

Then kneel down on your knee and say thus: "Sir, what robe or gown doth it please you to wear today?" Then get him such as he asks for, and hold it out for him to put on, and put on his girdle, if he wear one, tight or loose, arrange his robe in the proper fashion, give him a hood or hat for his head, a cloak or cape for the house, according as it be fair or foul, or all misty with rain. . . . Prepare his pew before he goes to church; then return in haste to your lord's chamber, strip the clothes off the bed and cast them aside, and beat the feather-bed, but not so as to waste any feathers, and see that the blankets and sheets be clean. When you have made the bed properly, cover it with a coverlet, spread out the bench-covers and cushions in the chamber, set up the head-sheet and pillow, and remove the basin. See that carpets be laid round the bed and dress the windows and the cupboard with tapestries and cushions. See there be a good fire brought into the chamber, with plenty of wood and fuel to make it up. . . .

You must attend busily to your lord's wardrobe, to keep clothes well, and to brush them cleanly. Use a soft brush, and remember that over-much brushing easily wears out cloth.

Never let woolen clothes or furs go a sevennight without being brushed or shaken, for moths are always ready to alight in them and engender; so always keep an eye on drapery and skinnery.

If your lord take a nap after his meal to digest his stomach, have ready kerchief and comb, pillow and headsheet; yet be not far from him —take heed what I say—for much sleep is not good in the middle of the day, and have ready water and towel so that he may wash after his sleep.

When he has supped and goes to his chamber, spread forth your foot-sheet, take off his gown or whatever garment he wears, and lay it up in such place as ye best know. Put a mantle on his back to keep his body from cold, set him on the foot-sheet, and pull off his shoes, socks, and hose, and throw these last over your shoulder, or hold them on your arm. Comb his hair, but first kneel down and put on his kerchief and nightcap. Have the bed ready; and when he is in bed, there to sleep safe and sound, draw the curtains round about the bed, set there his night-light with wax or Paris-candle, and see that there is enough to last the night; drive out the dog and the cat, giving them a clout, take no leave of your lord, but bow low to him and retire.

If your lord wishes to bathe and wash his body clean, hang sheets round the roof, every one full of flowers and sweet green herbs, and have five or six sponges to sit or lean upon, and see that you have one big sponge to sit upon, and a sheet over so that he may bathe there for a while, and have a sponge also for under his feet, if there be any to spare, and always be careful that the door is shut. Have a basin full of hot fresh herbs and wash his body with a soft sponge, rinse him with fair warm rose-water, and throw it over him; then let him go to bed; but see that the bed be sweet and nice; and first put on his socks and slippers that he may go near the fire and stand on his foot-sheet, wipe him dry with a clean cloth, and take him to bed to cure his troubles.

A NORTH COUNTRY CHARM FOR THE TOOTHACHE, CA. 1430

Wright, *Reliquiae antiquae*, I, 126.[52]

Say the charm thrice until it be said nine times, and always thrice at a charming:

> I conjure thee, Loathly Beast, with that same spear
> That Longinus in his hand did bear,
> And also with a hat of thorn
> That on my Lord's head was borne,
> With all the words more and less,
> With the office of the Mass,
> With my Lord and his twelve apostles,
> With our Lady and her ten maidens,
> Saint Margaret, the holy queen,
> Saint Katherine, the holy Virgin,
> Nine times God has forbidden, thou wicked worm,
> That ever thou make any resting,
> But away must thou wend,
> To the earth and the stone!

HOW TO RELIEVE HEADACHES, LATE 14TH CENTURY

Stephens, "Extracts in Prose and Verse from an Old English Medical Manuscript," *Archaeologia*, XXX (1844), 350.

> Now at the head I will begin,
> For often sickness falleth therein.
> If a man or woman, more or less,
> In his head hath great sickness,

[52] Taken from a MS. written on paper, in the library of Lincoln Cathedral, marked A.1,17, and compiled by one Robert Thornton of the North Riding of Yorkshire, probably between the years 1430–1440. (Wright's note.)

Or any grievance or any working,
Averoyne he take without letting,
Which is called southernwood also,
And honey and vinegar stamp thereto,
And this drink fasting let him drink,
And all his headwork away shall sink.

A medicine I have in mind
For headwork to tell as I find,
To take vinegar, wild thyme, royal,
And camomile and seethe withal;
And with the juice anoint the nostrils well
And make a plaster of the other part
And put it in a good great clout
And wind your head therewith about.
As soon as it be laid thereon
All the headwork shall away go.

Also it is good for the headache
Ten kernels of pepper to take
And grind them well with vinegar,
And drink or bind upon thy cheek.

5. Household Hints, 15th century

TO MAKE WHITE SALT

Sloane MS (B.M.) 1313 fol. 126v.

To make white salt, take of coarse salt one pint and three pints of water, and put them on the fire until the salt is melted; then strain through a cloth, towel, or sieve. Place on the fire again and make it boil hard and skim it. When it has boiled almost dry, so that the little bubbles which the water throws up are all dry, then take the salt out of the pail and spread it out on a cloth in the sun to dry.

TO MAKE A WATER FOR WASHING THE HANDS AT TABLE

Sloane MS (B.M.) 1313 fol. 126v.

Boil some sage, and pour off the water, and let it cool until it is little more than warm. Add to it camomile or marjoram or rosemary, and boil it with orange peel. Laurel leaves are also good.

TO MAKE WHITE WINE INTO RED AT THE TABLE

Sloane MS (B.M.) 1313 fol. 126v.

Take in spring the flowers that grow in wheat, which are called darnel
or passerose, and dry them until they can be powdered. Put some of
this, without being observed, into the wine glass, and the wine will turn
red.

THE FAMILY'S FOOD

1. Selling Bread and Ale

FARTHING ALE AND FARTHING LOAVES FOR THE LONDON POOR, 1381/82

London, Corporation, *Calendar of Letter-Books*, H, p. 183.

Ordinance by the mayor and aldermen that in order to assist the poor,
bakers shall make bread at a farthing the piece and brewers shall sell
ale by a farthing measure (the mayor and aldermen deeming it equally
necessary to the poor as bread). For this purpose they have caused a
number of such measures to be made and sealed [stamped] with the
letter *F* as a sign of their being farthing measures. And further, in order
that brewers should have no excuse, the said mayor and aldermen have
caused a number of farthings to be made at the Tower to the value of
£80 sterling for distribution among them at the mayor's discretion. A
day appointed for the brewers to come to the Guildhall to fetch away
the measures and the farthings, under penalty. No brewer to refuse
thenceforth to sell on demand that amount of best ale or fail to give
change for a halfpenny.

SHORT-WEIGHT BREAD AT GREENWICH, 1327

Court Roll (P.R.O.) Gen. Ser. 181/14 m. 1 d.

Court of the manor of Greenwich; Assize of Bread taken Saturday before
St. Alphege,[53] 1 Edw. III.

[Presentments by the jurors of bread underweight, including]:
One halfpenny "Cocket" of Alice Makejoye.
One farthing "Wastell" of Alice Makejoye.
One farthing "Wastell" of Alice atte Schoppe.
One farthing "Wastell" of Walkelin le Bakere.
One farthing rye-loaf of the same Walkelin.

[53] The Feast of St. Alphege is April 18.

One halfpenny loaf of the same Walkelin.
One farthing "Cocket" loaf of John Wynter.
One farthing wholemeal[?] loaf (*pan' integ'*) of Alice Simekyns.
One halfpenny wholemeal [?] loaf of Agnes le Pilcheres.
One halfpenny wholemeal [?] loaf of Christine de Hoo.

2. A Well-Stocked Larder

FOOD CONSUMED IN A COUNTRY HOUSEHOLD, MONTH BY MONTH,
1412–1413

The quantity and character of the food eaten varied considerably with the time of year. The following extracts illustrate the monthly fare in a normal month (November), a Lenten month (April), and a harvest month (August) in a country home of considerable size:

Bryene, *Household Book of Dame Alice de Bryene*, pp. 19, 59, 94.

Victuals expended throughout the said month [*November, 1412*]. Wheat baked 5 quarters; wine [blank]; barley and drage malt [54] brewed 10 quarters, whereof 5 quarters drage malt; beef, 1 carcass; 1 pig; 1 young pig; 1 swan; 6 geese; mutton, 11 joints; 3 lambs; 4 capons; 4 chickens; 4 partridges; 147 pigeons; 13 conies; 7 salt fish; 8 stockfish.

Victuals expended throughout the said month [*April, 1413, of which the 1st to the 22d fell in Lent*]. Wheat baked, 6 quarters; wine [blank]; barley and drage malt brewed, 10 quarters, whereof 5 quarters drage malt; beef, 1 carcass; pork, 1 pig and 2 quarters; 3 capons; 6 chickens; 100 pigeons; 8 hundred [*i.e.*, the long hundred of 120] and 90 red herrings; 9 hundred and 100 white herrings; 12¼ salt fish; 24 stockfish.

Victuals expended throughout the month [*August, 1413*]. Wheat baked, 8 quarters 4 bushels; wine [blank]; barley and drage malt brewed, 18 quarters, whereof 9 quarters drage malt; beef, 2 carcasses, 3 quarters; pork, 5 pigs and 1 quarter; 1 young pig; 22 carcasses of mutton; 2 lambs; 1 capon; 336 pigeons; 1 heron; 4 hundred and 60 white herrings; 18½ salt fish; 6 stockfish.

[54] Drage, or dredge, referred to a mixture of various kinds of grain, especially oats and barley, sown together. In the fourteenth century it was called "medylde corne." (*O.E.D.*)

FOOD CONSUMED DAILY IN THE SAME HOUSEHOLD, 1413

In this home fast days were strictly observed, and Saturday was kept as a fish day, in addition to Wednesday and Friday. The following are typical days in the month of May, 1413. The figures denote the number of meals served.

Bryene, *Household Book of Dame Alice de Bryene*, pp. 63–65.

Sunday, May 14: Breakfast 6, dinner 26, supper 20. Sum, 52. The lady [Alice de Bryene] took her meals there [*i.e.*, at Acton in Suffolk] with her household. In addition [guests]: the wife of Ralph Chamberleyn with [a maidservant and four of her household], Richard Scrivener, Richard Hawkyn, the whole day, Margaret Sampson, with two of her household, Grenefeld, Margaret Archeton, 1 repast. Pantry: 66 white, and 8 black, loaves; wine from supply; ale from stock. Kitchen: 1 quarter of beef, 1 quarter of bacon, 1 capon, 20 pigeons. Purchases: beef and pork 4s. 8d., 1 calf, 22d. Provender: hay from stock for 15 horses; fodder for the same, 2 bushels of oats.

Tuesday, May 16: Breakfast 8, dinner 18, supper 18. Sum, 44. [Guests]: John Goldyngham, with one of his household, John Frend, 1 repast, John Blake, the whole day. Pantry: 46 white, and 6 black, loaves; wine from supply; ale from stock. Kitchen: 1 quarter of beef, 1 quarter of bacon, 2 chickens, 16 pigeons. Purchases: 1 calf, 22d. Provender: hay from stock for 9 horses; fodder for the same, 1 bushel, 1 pk. of oats.

Friday, May 19: Breakfast 3, dinner 18, supper 6. Sum, 27. [Guests]: John Blake [with] one of his household, Thomas Barbour, the whole day. Pantry: 36 white, and 5 black, loaves; wine from supply; ale from stock. Kitchen: 20 red herrings, 30 white herrings, half a saltfish, 1 stockfish. Purchases: *nil*. Provender: hay from stock for 6 horses; fodder for the same, 3 pk. of oats.

Saturday, May 20: Breakfast 8, dinner 22, supper 18. Sum, 48. [Guests]: Sir Andrew Boteler with two of his household, 2 friars of Hereford with a clerk, William Waldegrave with one of his household, Robert Mose, 2 laborers, Sir Richard Mauncell with one of his household, 1 repast, John Blake, Thomas Geffrey, the whole day. Pantry: 56 white, and 6 black, loaves; wine from supply; ale from stock. Kitchen: 50 red herrings, 30 white herrings, half a salt fish, 2 stockfish. Purchases: 6 crabs and 2 "Creuys" [cray-fish] 8d.; bread for [the] merchant's horse, ½d. Provender: hay from stock for 11 horses; fodder for the same, 2 bushels of oats.

BREWING AND BAKING IN A COUNTRY HOUSEHOLD DURING A FORT-
NIGHT IN OCTOBER, 1412

Bryene, *Household Book of Dame Alice de Bryene*, pp. 2–6 and 87.

Sun., Oct. 2. The baking: 1 quarter of wheat, whence came 236 white loaves and 36 black loaves.

Mon., Oct. 3. The brewing: 2 quarters of malt, whereof 1 quarter drage, whence came 112 gallons of ale.

Fri., Oct. 7. The baking: 1 quarter of wheat, whence came 236 white loaves and 36 black loaves.

Sat. Oct. 8. The brewing: 2 quarters of malt, whereof 1 quarter drage, whence came 112 gallons of ale.

Wed., Oct. 12. The baking: 1 quarter of wheat, whence came 234 white loaves and 36 black loaves.

Fri., Oct. 14. The brewing: 2 quarters malt, whereof 1 quarter drage, whence came 112 gallons of ale.

> Special provision was made for the harvesters, tenants doing their boon work in the harvest field and receiving meantime certain food, the kind and amount being strictly fixed by custom. Here is an account of a baking and brewing day in August, 1413. The loaves were probably larger than those for household use.

Tues., Aug. 8. The baking: 1 quarter of wheat for the boon workers, whence came 124 loaves. The brewing: 2 quarters of malt, whereof 1 quarter of drage, whence came 112 gallons of ale.

Meals: Breakfast 30, dinner 44, supper 44. Sum, 118. [Guests]: the bailiff of the manor, with the harvest reeve and 14 of the household of the manor, John Scoyl, with 33 boon workers, Saltwell, with his wife, the whole day. Pantry: 50 white, and 6 black loaves, and 26 loaves for the boon workers, newly baked; wine from supply; ale from stock. Kitchen: 1 quarter of beef, 1½ quarters of bacon, 2 carcasses [of mutton], 20 pigeons. Purchases: milk, 2*d*. Provender: hay from stock for 5 horses; fodder for the same, 3 pk. of oats.

3. *The Medieval Love of Spices* .

A GROCER'S BILL, 1380

Common Pleas, Plea Roll 487 m. 438 d.

Robert Passelewe, knight, was summoned to answer Edmund Fraunceys, citizen and grocer of London, in a plea that he pay £6 . . . whereof Edmund says that, whereas Robert, between the Feast of Pentecost, 2

Richard II, and the Feast of Easter following,[55] in the parish of St. Stephen in the ward of Walbrook at divers times purchased of Edmund pepper, saffron, ginger, cloves, dates, almonds, rice, saunders,[56] powder of ginger, powder called "pouderlumbard," powder of cinnamon, figs, raisins, myrrh, and canvas for the said £6, payable on the Feast of the Ascension [May 3] next following the said Easter, though often required, Robert has not paid, and has hitherto refused to pay.

[Robert says he is not bound to pay as above. He wages his law twelve-handed,[57] and goes *sine die*.]

4. *English Recipes*

A MORTREUX OF FLESH, CA. 1450

Austin, ed., *Two Fifteenth-Century Cookery-Books*, pp. 70–71 (from Harl. MS [B.M.] 4016).

Take pork and seethe it enough; and take it up and skin (*bawde*) it, and chop it and grind it and put it in a mortar; and cast thereto grated bread, and then draw the same broth through a strainer. And temper it with ale, and put all in a pot, and let it boil, and allay it with yolks of eggs. And then let it boil no more. And cast thereto powder of ginger and salt, and put it in dishes, in manner of mortars (*mortrewes*) and cast thereto powder of ginger, and serve it forth.

BRUET OF ALMAYNE, CA. 1430–1440

Austin, ed., *Two Fifteenth-Century Cookery-Books*, p. 19 (from Harl. MS [B.M.] 279).

Take almonds and draw a good milk thereof with water. Take capons, coneys, or partridges; cut up the capon, or kid, or chickens, or coneys; the partridge shall be whole. Then blanch the flesh and cast on the milk; take lard (bacon fat) and mince it and cast thereto; take and mince onions and cast thereto enough; put cloves and small raisins thereto; cast whole saffron thereto; then put it to the fire and stir it well. When the flesh is [done] enough, set it off the fire, and put thereto sugar enough. Take powdered ginger, galingale, cinnamon (*canel*) and temper it with vinegar and cast thereto. Season it with salt and serve forth.

[55] That is, between May 29, 1379, and March 25, 1380.
[56] Alexanders, also called horse parsley, formerly cultivated and eaten like celery. (*O.E.D.*)
[57] That is, he and eleven witnesses, or compurgators, swore to his non-indebtedness. (*O.E.D.*)

WAFERS, OR BISCUIT OF PIKE, CA. 1430–1440

Austin, ed., *Two Fifteenth-Century Cookery-Books*, p. 39 (from Harl. MS [B.M.] 279).

Take the belly of a full-grown pike (luce) and seethe it well, and put it on a mortar, and put cheese thereto; grind them together; then take flour and white of eggs and beat together; then take sugar and powder of ginger, and put all together, and look that thine eggs be hot, and lay thereon of thine paste, and then make thin wafers and serve in.

HOW TO COOK CABBAGE, CA. 1430–1440

Austin, ed., *Two Fifteenth-Century Cookery-Books*, p. 6 (Harl. MS [B.M.] 279).

Take fair cabbages, and cut them, and pick them clean, and clean wash them, and parboil them in fair water, and then press them on a fair board; and then chop them, and cast them in a fair pot with good fresh broth, and with marrowbones, and let it boil; then take fair grated bread, and cast thereto saffron and salt; or else take good gruel made of fresh flesh, draw through a strainer, and cast thereto. And when thou servest it in, knock out the marrow of the bones, and lay the marrow two pieces or three in a dish, as seemeth best, and serve forth.[58]

LARDED MILK,[59] CA. 1450

Austin, ed., *Two Fifteenth-Century Cookery-Books*, p. 92 (Harl. MS 4016).

Take milk scalding hot and take eggs, the yolks and the white, and draw them through a strainer and cast to the milk. And then draw the juice of herbs, whichever thou wilt, so that they be good, and draw them through a strainer. And when the milk beginneth to curdle, cast the juice thereto if thou wilt have it green. And if thou wilt have it red, take saunders[60] and cast to the milk when it curdleth, and leave the herbs. And if thou wilt have it yellow, take saffron and cast to the milk when it curdleth, and leave the saunders. And if thou wilt have it of all these colors, take a pot with milk and juice of herbs, and another pot

[58] In view of the prevalence of gardens both in France and in England, it is interesting to know that, contrary to the general idea, a great many vegetables and fruits were eaten. They were, however, always cooked; a specific warning in *The Babees Book* against the use of salad and raw fruit seems to imply that they were not considered wholesome. (*The Babees Book*, ed. by Furnivall, pp. 266–267.)
[59] *Letlardes* in the original.
[60] See p. 88n.

with milk and saffron, and another pot with milk and saunders, and put them all in a linen cloth and press them all together. And if thou wilt have it of one color, take but one cloth and strain it in a cloth in the same manner, and beat on the cloth with a ladle or a skimmer to make it solid and flat. And slice it fair with a knife, and fry the slices in a pan with a little fresh grease, and take a little and put it in a dish and serve it forth.

5. Menus

A FEAST FOR A FRANKLIN, SHORTLY BEFORE 1447

Russell, "The Boke of Nurture," *The Babees Book*, ed. by Furnivall, pp. 170–171.

A franklin may make a feast improberabille: [61]
Brawn with mustard is concordable,
   Bacon served with peas;
Beef or mutton stewed serviceable;
Boiled chicken or capon agreeable,
   Convenient for the season;
Roasted goose and pig full profitable;
Capon bakemeat or custad [62] costable,[63]
   When eggs and cream be plentiful.
Therefore stuff of household is behoveable;
Mortrewes or Jussel [64] are delectable
   For the second course by reason.
Then veal, lamb, kid, or coney,
Chicken or pigeon roasted tenderly,
   Bakemeat or "doucettes" (sweet tarts) with all.
Then following fritters and a leche [65] lovely,
Such service in season is full seemly
   To serve with both chamber and hall.
Then apples and pears with spices delicately,
After the term of the year full daintily,
   With bread and cheer to all.
Spiced cakes and wafers worthily,

[61] Very proper. [Furnivall's note.]   [62] Custard. (*O.E.D.*)
[63] Costly, expensive. (*O.E.D.*)
[64] Iussell. Recipe brede gratyd, and eggs; and mix them together, and add thereto sage, and saffron, and salt; then take good broth, and add it thereto, and boil it. (*The Babees Book*, ed. by Furnivall, p. 53.)
[65] Leach: a dish consisting of sliced meat, eggs, fruits, and spices in jelly or some other coagulating material. (*O.E.D.*)

A WEDDING; *ca.* 1430
New York, Morgan Library, MS 394, fol. 9v

A GENTLEMAN DRESSES IN COMFORT BY THE FIRE
London, Brit. Mus., MS Royal 2 B.VII, fol. 72v

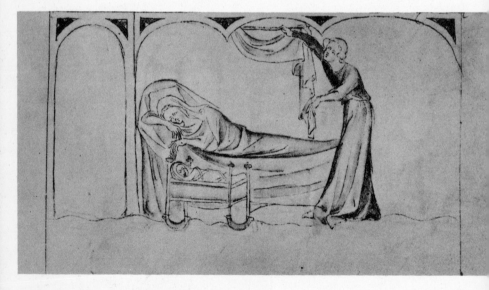

MOTHER, BABE IN CRADLE, AND SERVANT
London, Brit. Mus., Royal 2 B.VII, fol. 290

DOMESTIC SCENES; *ca.* 1320

INFANT BAPTISM
Late fourteenth century
London, Brit. Mus.
MS Add. 29704, fragment 61

INSTRUCTIONS FOR
BRINGING UP CHILDREN
Early fourteenth century
Baltimore, Walters Gallery,
MS W. 144, fol. 41v

THE WORRIES OF
HIGHER EDUCATION
Early fourteenth century
London, Brit. Mus.
MS Burney 275, fol. 143

SCHOOL DAYS

A FATHER ARRANGES FOR
THE EDUCATION OF HIS
SON BY MONKS
Baltimore, Walters Gallery
MS W. 133, fol. 87

With bragget and mead,
Thus men may merrily
Please well both great and small.[66]

A FISH DINNER WITH SUBTLETIES,[67] SHORTLY BEFORE 1447

Russell, "The Boke of Nurture," *The Babees Book*, ed. by Furnivall, pp. 166–168.

The First Course

Musclade of minnows [68] with the salmon bellies, eels, lampern in fere,[69]
Peas with the porpoise are good potage, as I suppose as falleth for time of
    the year;
Baked herring, sugar thereon strewing, fresh millwell [70] dainty and
    not dear;
Pike, lamprey or soles, porpoise roasted on coals, gurnard, lamperns
    baked, a leche,[71] and a fritter;
A seemly subtlety following even there:
            A gallant young man, a wanton wight,
            Piping and singing, loving and light,
            Standing on a cloud, Sanguineus he hight,
            The beginning of the season that cleped is ver.[72]

The Second Course

Dates in comfit, jelly red and white—this is good service;
Conger, salmon, dory, in syrup if they lay with other dishes in serving;
Brett, turbot or halibut, carp, bass, mullet or trout, chevins, bream re-
    newing;

[66] This menu is interesting in the light of Chaucer's franklin's reputation for lavish hospitality. Note that it consists largely of country cooking and that two dishes, mortrewes
and spiced cakes, which might mean gingerbread, are found here and not among the
menus in *Le Ménagier de Paris*. [R.]
[67] " 'Subtleties' . . . [were] trophies or ornaments carried in at the end of a course
or placed as decorations on the table, and were sometimes called 'warners,' as giving warning of the entry of a new course. Though they were often made in sugar, paste, or jelly,
they were not, apparently, allowed to be eaten. . . . 'A Sotelte. Saint Andrew sitting on
an hie Suter of a-state, with beames of golde; afore him knelyng ye Bisshoppe in pontifi-
calibus: his croser kneeling behinde him coped.' " (*The Times*, London, Fri., Jan 7, 1916,
p. 11, col. 3.) Description of subtlety brought in at close of fish course at feast of in-
stallation of John Stafford Abp. of Canter[bury] in 1443.
[68] A mixture of mussels and minnows. [R.]
[69] Together. [R.]   [70] A kind of cod. [R.]
[71] See above, p. 90*n*.   [72] Spring. [R.]

Eels, lamperns roast, a leche, a fritter.
I make now boast the second subtlety serving:

> A man of war seeming he was,
> A rough, a red, angry sire;
> An hasty man standing in fire,
> As hot as summer by his attire,
> His name was thereon, and called Estas.[73]

The Third Course

Cream of almond milk and mawmeny [74] good and fine;
Potage for the third service;
Fresh sturgeon, bream of the sea (*de mer*), perch in jelly, shining and
    clear, whelks, minnows, thus we devise;
Shrimps, fresh herring boiled,[75] "pety perueis" [76] may not be exiled,
leche fritter, a tansey gyse.[77]
The subtlety: a man with sickle in his hand

> In a river of water stand,
> Wrapped in weeds [78] in a wearisome wise,
> Having no desire to dance;
> The third age of man by likeness,
> Harvest we call him, full of weariness;
> Yet there followeth more that we must dress,
> Regards [79] rich that are full of pleasantness.

The Fourth Course of Fruit

Hot apples and pears with sugar candy,
With ginger columbine, minced mannerly,
Wafers with hippocras,
Now this feast is finished for to make glad cheer;
And though so be that the use and manner
Not afore time has been said,

---

[73] Summer. [Furnivall's note.]   [74] Spiced minced chicken. [R.]
[75] The extent to which people of means provided themselves with fish for their tables is
illustrated by the following entry in the Common Plea Rolls: "Richard atte More, sued
by the Abbot of Bylegh for fishing in the Abbot's private (*several*) fishery at Goldhangre,
taking salmones, cunger, merlyng, whityng, codlyng, crabbes, creues, smeltes, shrympes
and other sea fish." (Common Pleas, Plea Roll 490 m. 223.)
[76] Kind of paste puffs. [R.]
[77] A dish of tansey of some kind. [Furnivall's glossary.]
[78] Clothes. [R.]   [79] Things to look at. [Furnivall's note.]

Nevertheless after my simple manner (affection) [80]
I must conclude with the fourth complexion: [81]

> "Yemps," the cold term of the year,
> Winter with his locks gray, feeble, and old,
> Sitting upon the stone both hard and cold,
> Niggard in heart and heavy of cheer.[82]

6. Serving the Meal

EXTRACTS FROM "A GENERAL RULE . . . TO SERVE A LORD OR MASTER," 15TH CENTURY

Chambers, ed., *A Fifteenth-Century Courtesy Book*, pp. 11–15 (from Additional MS [B.M.] 37, 969).

The marshal in the morning ought to come into the hall and see that it be clean . . . the stools, trestles, or else forms . . . set in their own places at meals at the boards, and before and after meals, in corners . . . and all the hangings and costers dressed in their proper places and shaken or beaten with rods. . . . And to perform these things, he shall charge the usher and groom of the hall therewith. . . . The said groom shall also be continually in the hall at the first meat or supper, to bear away dishes, and keep out dogs, and fetch sauces. . . .

Half an hour before the lord goes to meat or supper, the marshal shall take a rod in his hand and command the panterer and ewer to cover . . . and as soon as it is made ready . . . the sewer shall go to the ewery and take a towel upon his shoulder, and the marshal and he go together and show before the lord. . . . And when it pleaseth the lord to ask water, then shall the esquires and the marshal and the sewer go by and by next the lord's basin . . . the marshal shall uncover the basin . . . and hold it in his hands also until the lord have washed, and then make a salutation and take it to the squire that brought it . . . and anon command water for all them that shall sit at the lord's board. . . . And when the lord is set, and the other boards in his presence, the marshal shall fetch in his courses with the sewer. . . . And when all the lord's mess is served, then shall another esquire next the hand serve the other messes at the board or in his presence. And anon . . . the almoner shall bring in the alms dish with a loaf therein and set it beneath the lord's salt, or else upon the cupboard . . . and a little before the second course,

---

[80] Disposition. [Furnivall's note.]   [81] Device. [Furnivall's note.]
[82] Latin inscriptions accompanied each subtlety to explain its character and significance. The subtleties may have been made of sugar or of wax. [R.]

the almoner shall take of every . . . great meat that comes before the lord . . . and put it in the alms dish and send the void dishes to the kitchen. . . .

And when the marshal saith time, that is to say, within three quarters of an hour that the last mess be set in the hall, the marshal shall command to take up, and all the broken meat and broken bread to be cast into the alms vessel. . . .

Note: . . . that all esquires waiters, or yeoman if esquires be lacking, be attendant at meal times upon the commandments of the marshal in all things of the carver, in fetching void dishes or wine. . . . Also, that the marshal, sewer, or esquires waiters at meal times make honest cheer with soft speech to strangers sitting at the lord's board or in his presence, if they may goodly come to them, and as they see time. Also, that in the lord's presence such silence be kept that there be no loud speech save only of the lord and such as he speaketh to. And in the hall such low communication be had that the head officer's voice be heard unto all other officers.

BRINGING UP THE CHILDREN

1. Birth and Baptism

PREPARATIONS FOR THE UPRISING OF QUEEN PHILIPPA AFTER THE BIRTH OF HER ELDEST SON, 1330

Exchequer of Receipt. Warrants for Issues, 2/10.

Edward, by the Grace of God King of England . . . to the treasurer and chamberlains of our Exchequer, greeting. We are sending you enclosed herein a schedule containing many things which will be needed for the uprising of Philippa, Queen of England, our beloved consort, from childbirth. So we command and charge you that you cause payment to be made without delay from our treasure for the provision and purchase of all these things, to our beloved clerk, Master William la Zouche, clerk of Our Great Wardrobe, of all such moneys as shall be needed. And for our honor and that of our said Consort, you should take order as soon as you can, without any excuse, for payment to be made, lest through your fault the things be not ready on the said day of uprising.

Given under our seal at Woodstock, the nineteenth of June in the fourth year of our reign.[83]

[83] Edward the Black Prince was born at Woodstock, Friday, June 15, four days before the date of this warrant.

The schedule. One robe of red velvet of three garments, to wit coat, sur-coat, and mantle, with facings of pure miniver, 6 pieces.

For the churching of my Lady, a coat and hood (*chape*) of cloth of gold, with facings of miniver, 5 pieces.

For the great banquet, a robe embroidered with gold, of five gar-ments, with facings of pure miniver—*the facings are lacking.*[84]

For the evening, a robe of silken cloth worked with fine gold, of 3 garments, coat, surcoat, and mantle, with pure fur, 6 pieces.

A coverlet of scarlet cloth with facing of miniver, for the great cradle for the infant, and a kerchief—*lacking, namely, half a cloth.*

Item, a cloth (*clotet*) for the Queen's Chapel of crimson sendal of Tripoli, 6 pieces.

Item, a coverlet of scarlet for the said Queen, with the facing of pure miniver, and a kerchief for my Lady—*Provided.*

Item, a coverlet of fine cloth of gold with facings for the bed of my said Lady and a kerchief—*not known hitherto.*

Item, bear in mind the cloths of gold for hanging the great chamber; and fueling for the said chamber.

Item, fur of miniver for one robe of the best, of five garments, made for my Lady's person.

Item, for dames and demoiselles of the chamber, 7½ furs of "popr'," 10 furs of "grow," one fur and a half of miniver.

Item, for the dames and demoiselles of the chamber, eight hoods (*chaperons*) of miniver and one hood of miniver of 40 skins.

Item, two coffers for the infant's chamber.

2. *Children at Home and at Play*

OF A GOOD NURSE, 1397 [85]

Bartholomaeus Anglicus, *Mediaeval Lore*, p. 46.

A nurse hath that name of nourishing, for she is ordained to nourish and to feed the child, and therefore like as the mother, the nurse is glad if the child be glad, and heavy if the child be sorry, and taketh the child up if it fall, and giveth it suck; if it weep she kisseth and lulleth it still, and gathereth the limbs, and bindeth them together, and doth cleanse and wash it when it is defiled. And for it cannot speak, the nurse lispeth

---

[84] The comments in italics were added in Latin to the French schedule.
[85] In 1397 John of Trevisa made for Sir Thomas, lord of Berkeley, an English translation of Bartholomaeus Anglicus' *De proprietatibus rerum.* The Latin original was written in the middle of the thirteenth century.

and soundeth the same words to teach more easily the child. . . . And she cheweth meat in her mouth, and maketh it ready to the toothless child . . . and so she feedeth the child when it is an hungered, and pleaseth the child with whispering and songs when it shall sleep, and swatheth it in sweet clothes, and righteth and stretcheth out its limbs, and bindeth them together with cradlebands, to keep and save the child that it have no miscrooked limbs. She batheth and anointeth it with good anointments.

THE CARE-FREE CHILD, 1397

Bartholomaeus Anglicus, *Mediaeval Lore*, pp. 44–45.

Small children be soft of flesh, lithe and pliant of body, quick and light to move, and witty to learn. And they lead their lives without thought or care. They set their hearts only on fun, and are afraid of nothing but being beaten with a rod; and they love an apple better than gold. Whether they be praised, or shamed, or blamed, they care little. . . . They are soon angered, and soon pleased, and easily forgive. . . . Since all children be spotted with bad manners and think only of the present and not of the future, they love plays, games, and vanity and care nothing for profit. . . . They want things that are bad for them, and care more about a doll than a person, and they weep more for the loss of an apple than for the loss of their heritage. . . . They want everything they see, and beg for it with voice and hand. . . . When they be washed they are soon dirty again. When their mother washes and combs them, they kick and sprawl, and put out their feet and hands, and resist with all their might. They are always wanting a drink; they are no sooner out of bed, before they are crying for something to eat.

FROISSART'S BOYHOOD,[86] CA. 1363

Froissart, "L'Espinette amourouse," *Œuvres de Froissart: poésies*, ed. by Scheler, I, 88–95.

In my boyhood I was one who liked too well to have a good time; and I still do. . . . When I was only twelve years old I was very eager for dances and carols, to hear minstrels and lively talk. And I always liked those who loved dogs and birds. And when they sent me to school . . .

[86] Manly says, "That [Chaucer] knew Froissart . . . is practically certain, for Froissart was a member of Queen Philippa's household from 1361 to 1366 . . . and Chaucer was also at this time probably attached to some member of the royal family." (Chaucer, *Canterbury Tales*, ed. by Manly, p. 43.)

there were little girls there of my own age, and I, innocent as I was, gave them pins or an apple or a pear or a little glass ring, and it seemed to me wonderful when they were pleased. (ll. 23–46)

I was never tired of playing the games children play when they are under twelve. For one thing, in a brook I made a little dam with a tile. And I took a small saucer and made it float down. And in a hollow by a brook . . . I often built a mill out of two tiles. Then we played with bits of paper [?] and got our coats and hats and shirts wet in the brook. Sometimes we made a feather fly down the wind, and I have often sifted earth with a shell onto my coat, and I was a clever fellow at making mud balls. Many a time I amused myself making a pipe of straw, and I was very good at chasing butterflies. When I caught them, I tied threads to them; then when I let them go, I could make them fly as I pleased. Dice, chess, tables, and other grown-up games I did not care about, but I liked to make mud pies, round loaves, cakes, and tartlets, and I had an oven of four tiles where I put this stuff. . . .

And when Lent came I had under a stool a great storehouse of shells for which I would not have accepted any money. And then of an afternoon, with the shell which had holes in it, I played with the children of our street; and when we threw it into the air, I would say to them, "Toss it high. . . ." And when the moon was bright, we played at "Pinch Me," and in the spring I was very cross when they interfered with my playing. We played games called "Follow the Leader," and "Trot-trot Merlot," and pebbles [marbles?], and Hockey[?], and "Heads or Tails," I seem to remember; and when we were together, we all ran . . . and played "Robber Enguerrand" and "Brimbetelle" [swinging?] and "Deux Bastons qu'on Restelle" [stilts?]. And I have often made of a stick a horse called Grisel. We used to make helmets of our hats; and often, before the girls, we beat one another with our caps. Sometimes we played at "The King Who Doesn't Lie," [87] at bars [prisoners' base], at "Little Lamb," at "Take (ostés moi) Me Away from Colinet," and at "I Tell on Who Strikes Me." [88] And we played "L'Esbahi" [surprise?], and also at charades (or riddles), at "Avainne" [oats?], at Hide-and-Seek, at "Erbelette" [Little Grass?], "Aux risées," at "Strike the Ball," at "Reculées" [retreat?], at Mule, at "Who Can Jump Highest?" at

[87] Cf. Ernest Langlois, "Mélanges Chabaneau," Rom. Forsch., XXIII (1907), 163–173, for description of this game, which is related to Truth and Consequences.

[88] Cf. a game, Qui féry, found in Le Ménagier de Paris, I, 72, and translated as "hot cockles." (Le Ménagier de Paris [The Goodman of Paris]; tr. by Eileen Power, p. 102.)

"The Cart of Michaut," then at "La Coulee belee" [Run, Sheep, Run], which one makes a gay dance of, at "Hare and Hounds," at "Cluignette" [winking?],[89] at the "Sotte buirette" [silly face?], at "Cow's Horn in the Salt" [*A la corne de buef au sel*], and throwing leaden pennies or pebbles against a fence. And then we rolled nuts; the boy who missed lost his temper. I amused myself night and morning with a spinning top [*Tourpie aux amantins*]; and I've often made soap bubbles in a little pipe, two or three or four or five. I loved to watch them. With such games—there were still others—I have often tired myself out.

When I was a little wiser, I had to control myself, for they made me learn Latin; and if I made mistakes in saying my lessons, I was beaten; and when I was beaten or afraid of being beaten, I did better. Nevertheless, away from my master I could never rest till I fought with the other boys; I was beaten and I beat, and I was so knocked about that often my clothes were torn. I went home and there I was scolded and beaten again, but to be sure one gets used to all that, for I never had the less fun for it. But when I saw my companions passing before me down the street, I dropped everything and ran after them to play. [ll. 148–271]

A NAUGHTY BOY: LYDGATE'S DESCRIPTION OF HIMSELF, CA. 1450

Lydgate, "The Testament," in *Minor Poems*, pp. 352–353 (from Harl. MS [B.M.] 218).

> I had in custom to come to school late
>   Not for to learn but for appearance sake,
> With my fellows ready to debate,
>   To quarrel or joke was set all my pleasure;
>   Whereof rebuked, this was my device [*chevesaunce*].
> To forge a lie, and thereupon to muse,
> When I did wrong, myself to excuse.
>
> To my betters did no reverence,
>   Paid no attention to those over me,
> Became obstinate by disobedience,
>   Ran into gardens, apples there I stole;
>   To gather fruits, spared neither hedge nor wall,
> To pick grapes on other people's vines
> Was more ready than for to say matins.

[89] In *Gargantua*, XXII, Rabelais mentions a game called *clinemuzette*, which Abel Lefranc explains as being "hide and seek."

My pleasure was all to scorn folk and joke,
    Shrewd tricks ever among [them] to use,
To scoff and make faces like a wanton ape,
    When I did wrong, others I could accuse.
    My wits five in waste I did all use,
Rather cherry-stones for to tell [telle] [90]
Than go to church, or hear the holy bell.

Loath to rise, loather to bed at eve,
    With unwashed hands ready to dinner,
    My pater noster, my creed, or my belief
    Cast at the cock, lo, this was my manner!
    Waved with each wind, as doth a reed,
Chidden by my friends who would such faults amend,
Made deaf ear, would not to them attend.

MISHAPS IN CHILDHOOD

London, Coroner, *Calendar of the Coroners Rolls*, pp. 191, 63–64, 30–31, 25, 83.

A lost ball, 1337. On Tuesday in Pentecost week John, son of William atte Noke, chandler, got out of a window in the rent of John de Wynton', plumber, to recover a ball lost in a gutter at play. He slipped and fell, and so injured himself that he died on the Saturday following, of the fall.

Playing on the timber pile, 1322. On the Sunday before the Feast of St. Dunstan,[91] Robert, son of John de St. Botulph, a boy seven years old, Richard, son of John de Chesthunt, and two other boys whose names are unknown were playing on certain pieces of timber in the lane called "Kyrounelane" [where Richard Chaucer [92] had a tavern] in the ward of Vintry, and one piece fell on Robert and broke his right leg. In course of time Johanna his mother arrived and rolled the timber off him and carried him to the shop, where he lingered until the Friday before the Feast of St. Margaret,[93] when he died at the hour of prime, of the broken leg and of no other felony; nor do the jurors suspect anyone of the death, but only the accident and the fracture.

[90] That is, play. Evidently refers to some game played with cherry stones.
[91] The Feast of St. Dunstan is May 19.
[92] The third husband of Chaucer's grandmother; her second husband, Robert le Chaucer, was the poet's grandfather. (Chaucer, *Canterbury Tales*, ed. by Manly, p. 4.)
[93] The Feast of St. Margaret is July 20.

Playing in the street, 1301. On Tuesday the Feast of Sts. Philip and James [May 4] a certain Hugh Picard was riding a white horse after the hour of vespers, when Petronilla, daughter of William de Wyntonia, aged three years, was playing in the street; and the horse, being strong, quickly carried Hugh against his will over Petronilla so that it struck her on her right side with its right forefoot. Petronilla lingered until the next day, when she died, at the hour of vespers, from the blow. Being asked who were present, the jurors know only of those mentioned. The corpse viewed, the right side of which appeared blue and badly bruised, and no other hurt. The horse valued at a mark, for which Richard de Caumpes, the sheriff, will answer. Hugh fled and has no chattels; he afterwards surrendered to John de Boreford (or Burford), sheriff.

A game on the way to school, 1301. On Tuesday [July 19], Richard, son of John le Mazon, who was eight years old, was walking immediately after dinner across London Bridge to school. For fun, he tried to hang by his hands from a beam on the side of the bridge, but his hands giving way, he fell into the water and was drowned. Being asked who were present, the jurors say a great multitude of passers-by, whose names they know not, but they suspect no one of the death except mischance.

A boy thief, 1324. On Monday [in April, 1324] at the hour of vespers John, son of William de Burgh, a boy five years old, was in the house of Richard le Latthere and had taken a parcel of wool and placed it in his cap. Emma, the wife of Richard, chastising him, struck him with her right hand under his left ear so that he cried. On hearing this, Isabella, his mother, raised the hue and carried him thence. He lingered until the hour of curfew of the same day, when he died of the blow and not of any felony. Emma forthwith fled, but where she went or who received her the jurors knew not. Afterwards she surrendered herself to the prison of Newgate.

3. Training and Education

PRECEPTS ON CONDUCT

1. Good Manners for Those That Bide Not Long at School, ca. 1475

The Babees' Book, ed. by Rickert, pp. 21–25.

Whoso will thrive must be courteous, and learn the virtues in his youth, or in his age he is outcast among men. Clerks who know the Seven Sciences say that Courtesy came from heaven when Gabriel greeted our Lady and Elizabeth met with her; and in it are included all virtues, as all vices in rudeness.

Arise betimes from your bed, cross your breast and your forehead, wash your hands and face, comb your hair, and ask the grace of God to speed you in all your works; then go to mass and ask mercy for all your trespasses. Say "Good morning" courteously to whomsoever you meet by the way.

When ye have done, break your fast with good meat and drink, but before eating, cross your mouth; your diet will be the better for it. Then say your grace—it occupies but little time—and thank the Lord Jesus for your food and drink. Say also a *Pater Noster* and an *Ave Maria* for the souls that lie in pain, and then go labor as you are bound to do. Be not idle, for Holy Scripture says to you of Christian faith that if you work, you must eat what you get with your hands. A man's arms are for working, as a bird's wings for flying.

Look you be true in word and deed, the better shall you prosper; for truth never works a man shame, but rather keeps him out of sin. . . .

Make no promise save it be good, and then keep it with all your might, for every promise is a debt that must not be remitted through falsehood. . . .

When your better shows his will, be silent; and in speaking to any man keep your hands and feet quiet, and look up into his face, and be always courteous.

Point not with your finger at anything, nor be ready to tell tidings. If any man speak well of you or of your friends, he must be thanked. Have few words and wisely placed, for so may you win a good name.

Use no swearing or falsehood in buying or selling, else shall you be shamed at the last. Get your money honestly, and keep out of debt and sin. Be eager to please, and so live in peace and quiet. . . .

Hold you pleased with the meat and drink set before you, nor ask for better. . . . Praise your fare, wheresoever you be, for whether it be good or bad it must be taken in good part.

Whether you spit near or far, hold your hand before your mouth to hide it.

Keep your knife clean and sharp, and cleanse it on some cut bread, not on the cloth, I bid you; a courteous man is careful of the cloth. Do not put your spoon in the dish or on the edge of it, as the untaught do, or make a noise when you sup, as do boys. Do not put the meat off your trencher into the dish, but get a voider and empty it into that.

When your better hands you a cup, take it with both hands, lest it fall, and drink yourself and set it by; and if he speaks to you, doff your cap and bow your knee.

Do not scratch yourself at the table so that men call you a jackdaw, or wipe your nose or nostrils, else men will say you are come of churls. Make neither the cat nor the dog your fellow at the table. And do not play with the spoon, or the trencher, or your knife; but lead your life in cleanliness and honest manners.

This book is made for young children that bide not long at the school.[1] It may soon be conned and learned, and will make them good if they be bad. God give them grace to be virtuous, for so may they thrive.

Amen! quoth Kate.[2]

2. *How the Good Wife Taught Her Daughter, ca. 1475*

The Babees' Book, ed. by Rickert, pp. 32–41.

When thou sittest in the church, o'er thy beads bend;
Make thou no jangling with gossip or with friend.
Laugh thou to scorn neither old body nor young,
But be of fair bearing and of good tongue.
    Through thy fair bearing
    Thy worship hath increasing,
      My lief child.

. . .

[1] The inference seems to be that they would learn manners there. [R.]
[2] This name is probably a corruption of *Cato*, unless we have here one of the rare instances of a woman copyist. [R.]

And when thou goest on thy way, go thou not too fast,
Brandish not with thy head, nor with thy shoulders cast,[3]
Have not too many words, from swearing keep aloof,
For all such manners come to an evil proof.
> For he that catcheth to him an evil name,
> It is to him a foul fame,
> My lief child.

Go thou not into the town, as it were agaze,
From one house to another, for to seek the maze;[4]
Nor to sell thy russet,[5] to market shalt thou go,
And then to the tavern to bring thy credit low.
> For they that taverns haunt
> From thrift soon come to want,
> My lief child.

And if thou be in any place where good ale is aloft,[6]
Whether that thou serve thereof or that thou sit soft,
Measurably thou take thereof, that thou fall in no blame,
For if thou be often drunk, it falleth to thy shame.
> For those that be often drunk—
> Thrift is from them sunk
> My lief child.

Go not to the wrestling or shooting at the cock,[7]
As it were a strumpet or a gigggelot;[8]
Dwell at home, daughter, and love thy work much,
And so thou shalt, my lief child, wax the sooner rich.
> A merry thing 'tis evermore,
> A man to be served of his own store,
> My lief child.

And if thy children be rebel and will not bow them low,
If any of them misdo, neither curse them nor blow;[9]

---

[8] Shake or shrug. [R.]

[4] The context seems to demand "maze," connected with "amaze," rather than "maze" meaning labyrinth. [R.]

[5] Coarse brown stuff, homespun, frieze. [R.]   [6] A-going. [R.]

[7] The popular old English pastime of throwing missiles to bring down a cock tied by the leg. [R.]

[8] A giggling girl, expressively spelled. [R.]   [9] Scold. [R.]

But take a smart rod and beat them in a row,
Till they cry mercy and their guilt well know.
　　Dear child, by this lore
　　They will love thee ever more,
　　　My lief child.

And look to thy daughters that none of them be lorn;
From the very time that they are of thee born,
Busy thyself and gather fast for their marriage,
And give them to spousing, as soon as they be of age.
　　Maidens be fair and amiable
　　But in their love full unstable,
　　　My lief child.

3. *How Young People Should Behave in the Household of a Lord or the King, ca. 1475*

The Babees' Book, ed. by Rickert, pp. 2–8.

And first of all, I think to show how you babies who dwell in households should behave yourselves when ye be set at meat, and how when men bid you be merry you should be ready with lovely, sweet, and benign words. . . .

When you enter your lord's place, say "God speed," and with humble cheer greet all who are there present. Do not rush in rudely, but enter with head up and at an easy pace, and kneel on one knee only to your lord or sovereign, whichever he be.

If any speak to you at your coming, look straight at them with a steady eye, and give good ear to their words while they be speaking; and see to it with all your might that ye jangle [10] not, nor let your eyes wander about the house, but pay heed to what is said, with blithe visage and diligent spirit. When ye answer, ye shall be ready with what ye shall say, and speak useful things and give your reasons smoothly, in words that are gentle, but brief and to the point. . . . Take no seat, but be ready to stand until you are bidden to sit down. Keep your hands and feet at rest; do not claw your flesh or lean against a post in the presence of your lord, or handle anything belonging to the house.

Make obeisance to your lord always when you answer; otherwise, stand as still as a stone, unless he speak.

Look with one accord that if ye see any person better than yourself

[10] Chatter. [R.]

come in, ye go backwards anon and give him place, and in nowise turn your face from him, as far forth as you may.

If you see your lord drinking, keep silence, without loud laughter, chattering, whispering, joking, or other insolence.

If he command you to sit in his presence, fulfill his wish at once, and strive not with another about your seat.

When you are set down, tell no dishonest tale; eschew, also, with all your might, to be scornful; and let your cheer be humble, blithe, and merry, not chiding as if ye were ready for a fight.

If you perceive that your better is pleased to commend you, rise up anon and thank him heartily.

If you see your lord and lady speaking of household matters, leave them alone, for that is courtesy, and interfere not with their doing; but be ready, without feigning, to do your lord service, and so shall you get a good name.

Also, to fetch him drink, to hold the light when it is time, and to do whatsoever ought to be done, look ye be ready; for so shall ye full soon get a gentle name in nurture. And if you should ask a boon of God, you can desire no better thing than to be well-mannered.

If your lord is pleased to offer you his own cup to drink, rise when you take it and receive it goodly with both your hands, and when you have done, proffer it to no man else, but render it again to him that brought it, for in nowise should it be used commonly—so wise men teach us.

Now must I tell you shortly what you shall do at noon when your lord goes to his meat. Be ready to fetch him clear water, and some of you hold the towel for him until he has done, and leave not until he be set down and ye have heard grace said. Stand before him until he bids you sit, and be always ready to serve him with clean hands.

When ye be set, keep your own knife clean and sharp, that so ye may carve honestly [11] your own meat.

Let courtesy and silence dwell with you, and tell no foul tales to another.

Cut your bread with your knife and break it not. Lay a clean trencher [12] before you, and when your pottage is brought, take your spoon and eat quietly; and do not leave your spoon in the dish, I pray you.

[11] Decorously. [R.]
[12] Originally a slice of wholemeal bread, four days old, upon which food was served. Later, it was made of wood. [R.]

Look ye be not caught leaning on the table, and keep clear of soiling the cloth.

Do not hang your head over your dish or in any wise drink with full mouth.

Keep from picking your nose, your teeth, your nails at mealtime—so we are taught.

Advise you against taking so much meat into your mouth but that ye may right well answer when men speak to you.

When ye shall drink, wipe your mouth clean with a cloth, and your hands also, so that you shall not in any way soil the cup, for then shall none of your companions be loath to drink with you.

Likewise, do not touch the salt in the salt-cellar with any meat; but lay salt honestly on your trencher, for that is courtesy.

Do not carry your knife to your mouth with food or hold the meat with your hands in any wise; and also if divers good meats are brought to you, look that with all courtesy ye assay of each; and if your dish be taken away with its meat and another brought, courtesy demands that ye shall let it go and not ask for it back again.

And if strangers be set at table with you, and savory meat be brought or sent to you, make them good cheer with part of it, for certainly it is not polite, when others be present at meat with you, to keep all that is brought you and like churls vouchsafe nothing to others.

Do not cut your meat like field men who have such an appetite that they reck not in what wise, where or when or how ungoodly they hack at their meat; but, sweet children, have always your delight in courtesy and in gentleness, and eschew boisterousness with all your might.

When cheese is brought, have a clean trencher, on which with a clean knife ye may cut it; and in your feeding look ye appear goodly and keep your tongue from jangling, for so, indeed, shall ye deserve a name for gentleness and good governance, and always advance yourself in virtue.

When the end of the meal is come, clean your knives, and look you put them up where they ought to be, and keep your seat until you have washed, for so wills honesty.[13]

When ye have done, look, then, that ye rise up without laughter or joking or boisterous word, and go to your lord's table, and there stand, and pass not from him until grace be said and brought to an end.

[13] Propriety. [R.]

Then some of you should go for water, some hold the cloth, some pour upon his hands.

APPRENTICESHIP

1. A Schoolboy to Become an Apprentice

Prerogative Court of Canterbury, 17 Marche.

John Wodecoke, citizen and mercer of London: To my cousin (*cognato*) William Steynford, whom I am exhibiting [14] at the schools (*ad scolas*), to put and make him apprentice, at my executors' discretion, 100*s*.

2. A Curse on Any Who Hinders a Lad's Apprenticeship, 1407

Prerogative Court of Canterbury, 22 Marche.

Will of Thomas de Tyldeslegh of Eccles, Lancaster, and of St. Giles without Cripplegate, London: I bequeath to John Boys, otherwise called by me "Jakke of Tyldeslegh tho [*sic*] yonge," one hundred shillings silver to make him apprentice in some good and honest trade (*arte*), and in no evil one. If anyone hinder this, may God's curse be upon him.

3. Taking a Country Boy to London to Be Apprenticed, 1388

Common Pleas, Plea Roll 510 m. 232 d.

London. John Annotson of Wycliff, junior, was attached to answer both the King and Robert de Wycliff, clerk, for leaving his father's service as a groom before the year was up. John claimed that his father had asked Robert de Wycliff to take him to London and there apprentice him as a tailor, and this he had promised to do.

He put himself on the country, etc.

4. Abuse of Apprentices, 1371

London, Corporation, *Calendar of Plea and Memoranda Rolls, A.D. 1364–1381*, pp. 128–129 (from Plea and Mem. R. A 16. m. 5).

Thomas and William Sewale, sons of Thomas Sewale of Canterbury, who had been apprenticed by their father to John Sharpe, came into court and complained that their master had been for a long time in Newgate and was unable to instruct them, and that his wife Margery had fed them insufficiently, had beaten them maliciously, and had struck William on the left eye so violently that he lost the sight of that eye, wherefore they

[14] Maintaining.

prayed the court to be discharged from their apprenticeship. Evidence having been given that the master was in prison and that neither he nor his wife could support the boys, and as it appeared from a corporal examination that they had been cruelly beaten, the court exonerated them altogether from their apprenticeship.

5. *A Girl Apprentice Beaten and Ill Treated, 1369*

London, Corporation, *Calendar of Plea and Memoranda Rolls, A.D. 1364–1381*, p. 107 (from Plea and Mem. R. A 14, m. 5 b).

John Catour of Reading brought a bill of complaint against Elis Mympe, "broudurer" (embroiderer), of London, to whom his daughter Alice had been apprenticed for five years, for beating and ill treating the girl, and failing to provide for her.

The parties were summoned to appear on March 3, when they announced that they had come to an agreement on terms that the defendant should pay the complainant 13s. 4d. and release the girl from her apprenticeship. Thereupon he released her.

The defendant was then asked why he took the girl for less than seven years, and had not enrolled the indentures, according to the custom of the city and his oath. He put himself on the mercy of the mayor and the aldermen, who gave judgment exonerating the said Alice from her apprenticeship. By order of the court the indentures were surrendered for cancellation.

6. *A Thoughtful Master Provides for His Apprentices, 1383*

Prerogative Court of Canterbury, 1 Rous.

Will of John Vyne, citizen and draper of London: Item, I bequeath to William Cole, my apprentice, £5 6s. 8d.; item, to George, my second apprentice, £5; item, I bequeath to William Chitecroft, my third apprentice, £5; item, I bequeath to William, my fourth apprentice, 10s.

MAKING PROVISION FOR EDUCATION

1. *Bequests for Schooling, 1406–1426*

Prerogative Court of Canterbury, 18 Marche.

Sir Robert Mounteney, Knight, of Inge, Mounteney, Essex, 1406: Item, to Margaret May living in Lime Street, London, £20. Item, to John, the son of the said Margaret, yearly 40s. until he be fifteen to keep him at school if he live, and after the said fifteen years I will that he have 100 marks to keep and prosper him at my executors' discretion.

Prerogative Court of Canterbury, 17 Marche.

John Wykyng, buried in the Chantry chapel of St. Mary of Meere, 1408: I bequeath to the Prior of Staverdale £10 to find [15] John Robyns, son of Robert formerly my groom (*garconis*), at the grammar schools and other schools until the said sum be expended.

Prerogative Court of Canterbury, 8 Marche.

Codicil to Will of John Oteleye, citizen and mercer of London, 1404: I bequeath by these presents to Thomas Wyham, William Lynsy, and Thomas Lynsy, whom I exhibit [16] at the schools out of charity, £15, namely, to each of them 100s. for their exhibition at the schools, their maintenance and their disposal.

Prerogative Court of Canterbury, 35 Marche.

John Brokeman, Esq., of North Mimms, 1416: I bequeath to John, my son, ten pounds of silver for his maintenance and teaching in going to the schools of the University of Oxford or Cambridge . . . and all my books.

Prerogative Court of Canterbury, 7 Luffenam.

John Taillour of Ayssh in Bokelond, 1426: [I bequeath] to poor priests who wish to go to the schools (*scolatizere*) at Oxford, £50.

2. *Prayers in Exchange for Education, 1397–1400*

Prerogative Court of Canterbury, 1 Marche.

Will of Richard Micheldever, 1397: To William, the son of my brother [John Micheldever], to find [17] him at school 100 sheep and 100s., for the love of God, and to pray for my soul, if he be alive.

Drapers' Company Deeds A VIII 336 (2).

Will of Robert Turk, Knight, 1400: To be buried in Holy Trinity Crichurche in the chapel of St. Nicholas next my wife, Alice. To the master and scholars of St. Michael in Cambridge, the tenement which Robert de la Mare held in the parish of St. Lawrence Old Jewry and 6s. 8d. quit-rent from John Trygge the fishmonger's corner house by St. Mary Somerset, for two poor scholars to be called "Turkes-children,"

[15] Support.   [16] Maintain.   [17] Support.

to pray for the souls of the said Robert and Alice and of his father and mother and Beatrice his wife, etc., and the house called Clarehall.

3. *Royal Payments for Scholars, 1343*

Exchequer, King's Remembrancer, Memoranda Roll 119. Precepta. Mich. 17 Edw. III.

The Sheriff of Cambridgeshire and Huntingdonshire craves allowance, and it is permitted to him at the view [of his account as follows]:

£93 15*s.* 2*d.*, which he says he paid to Master Thomas Powys, Warden of the Hall of King's Scholars at Cambridge, namely, £54 5*s.* 10*d.* in part satisfaction of the wages of the same Master Thomas and 34 scholars in the said Hall . . . 53*s.* 4*d.* for the wages of Alan le Mareschal, scholar there, from December 10, 15 Edward III until November 1 following; 21*s.* 8*d.* for the wages of John de Romeseye, scholar there, from July 24, 16 Edward III until November 1 following; each of the said scholars taking 2*d.* a day and 13 marks for 3 robes of the same warden, namely, two with fur (*pellura*) and one with lining (*linura*) for the said 16th year and the first for this 17th year by 5 writs of the King. . . . And £193 7*s.* which he saith he paid to the same Master Thomas, warden of the scholars aforesaid, namely, £9 7*s.* 6*d.* for the wages of the same warden from October 16, 12 Edward III until May 1, 14 [Edward III] for 563 days, the warden taking by the day 4*d.* And £154 16*s.* 6*d.* for the wages of 33 scholars aforesaid for the same time, each taking by the day 2*d.* and [wages of other scholars named for specific times], and £14 for 5 robes of the same warden, namely, 3 with fur (*pellura*) and 2 with lining (*linura*) for the 13th and 14th years and another for the 15th year, and 66*s.* 8*d.* for the rental (*pensione*) of the inn in which the said warden and scholars reside, and 5 marks of the King's gift in aid of the repairs of the said inn.

4. *A Mother Who Had Sacrificed Her Jewels to Make Her Son a Clerk; before 1393*

Prerogative Court of Canterbury, 9 Rous.

Will of Robert de Brauncepeth, clerk of William Rikyll: [18] To be buried in the Cathedral Church of Rochester in the chapel of the Blessed Mary. . . .

---

[18] The judge with whom Chaucer was associated on the Commission of the Peace for Kent, May 27, 1393.

To the shrine of St. Edward the King at Westminster, a necklace (*monile*) of gold with three names (*newynys*) set thereupon and with three shields thereon, two of which are of like arms and the third is azure with three mullets gold, and they were formerly my ancestors'.

To the image of St. Mary the Virgin in the chapel of Rouncesvalles by Charing Cross, a silver brooch with a Saracen's head made therein.

To St. Erkenwald in the Cathedral Church of St. Paul, one other necklace of gold with three names set thereon and also with three red stones, whereof one is broken.

To St. Thomas of Canterbury, one silver seal made after the fashion of a squirrel.

To the Cross of Boxley, a silver seal made after the fashion of a chestnut (*chatene*) for a man's use.

To the image of the Blessed Mary opposite the said Cross in the same church of Boxley, a great purse (*bourse*) of cloth of gold.

To the image of the Blessed Mary in the Cathedral Church of Rochester, one pair of silver beads [a rosary] with a crystal tied thereto.

. . .

And lest anyone should think ill of how the jewels and money in this will bequeathed have come to me, I hereby declare in truth that the said jewels and also a great part of the money were given over to me by the hands of my most beloved mother and of other friends of mine when I went far away from the people loyally dear to me to be schooled; and also another part of the said sum I have by God's grace got together well and faithfully, in good conscience, through my own hard labor.

5. *A Wealthy Citizen Arranges for One of His Sons to Become a Lawyer, and the Other a Merchant, 1389*

Prerogative Court of Canterbury, 2 Rous.

Will of William de Tonge, citizen of London: One hundred marks each to my two sons. And I will that my said two sons shall live upon the profits of the money bequeathed to them above until [they reach] the age of twenty years. And if my said two sons be well learned in grammar and adorned with good manners, which shall be known at the end of twenty years, and the elder son shall wish to practice common law, and if it is known that he would spend his time well in that faculty, I will that over and above the profit of the said one hundred marks he shall have yearly from my rents for the term of seven years five marks. And if he should waste his time aforesaid, or if he should marry foolishly and unsuitably, I will that he receive nothing more of the said five marks.

And if [my] younger son wishes to attend the University of Oxford or to establish himself well in the mystery of a merchant after the age of twenty years, and [if] there be [certain] knowledge of his praiseworthy progress in his faculty or his carefulness (*solercia*) in trading . . . I will that he shall receive five marks yearly in the manner described above for his maintenance, over and above the profit of the said one hundred marks to him bequeathed, for the space of seven years; and if he behave himself otherwise, I will that thereupon (*amodo*) he be excluded from the said five marks. And in case the said bequest of 200 marks to him and his brother shall be annulled so that he shall have nothing therefrom . . . then the said 200 marks shall be spent upon all the yearly chaplains who can be had to celebrate divine service in the church of All Hallows [Barking by the Tower] for my soul [and other souls].

6. *Bills for Two Young Boys Sent to School to the Vicar of Croydon,* *1394–1395*

Schooling provided by Gilbert Maghfeld, a London merchant and moneylender of considerable prominence in the latter years of the fourteenth century, from whom Chaucer himself secured a loan. The items printed below are taken from his account book for the years 1390 to 1395. Although sufficiently wealthy to be one of the rich men who, in 1374, contributed five marks to the King and, in December, 1394, to advance fifty pounds towards the King's expedition to Ireland, by 1398 he had died a bankrupt, and his property had been confiscated by the King.

Professor Rickert, who made an extensive study of Maghfeld's account book, points out that "Like Chaucer's Merchant, Maghfeld engaged extensively in both 'bargaynes' and 'chevisaunce.' " In 1383 he and another man, with two "mariners," undertook to keep the sea between Berwick-on-Tweed and Winchelsea, *i.e.*, to protect English shipping between these limits from pirates and freebooters. Since London was probably in this district, Chaucer, as controller of the customs on which Maghfeld and his partner were entitled to collect a percentage, doubtless knew him at this time. Also like Chaucer's Merchant, he seems to have been "estatly" of his "governaunce," for he had six servants, including a butler, a man cook, two women servants, and two valets. From these and other bits of evidence, including a loan to Chaucer of 26s. 8d., Professor Rickert surmised that Maghfeld might be the original of the Merchant of the *Canterbury Tales* and that this identification "supplies a better motive than any yet given for Chaucer's refusal to tell the Merchant's name: he might have need of another 'chevisaunce.' " [19]

Rickert, "Documents and Records: Extracts from a Fourteenth-Century Account Book," *Modern Philology*, XXIV (1926–1927), 251–252 (from Exchequer, King's Remembrancer, Accounts, 509/19).

[19] Rickert, "Documents and Records: Extracts from a Fourteenth-Century Account Book," *Modern Philology*, XXIV (1926–1927), 111–119 and 249–256 *passim*.

In the seventeenth year [of the reign of Richard II], the month of May, John Frogenhale [20] and William Maghfeld were sent to Croydon to school on the Eve of St. Dunstan [21] [1394], paying by the week, 2s.

Item paid on the Eve of St. Michael [22] in the 18th year, [1394] for 19 weeks	38s.
Item given to their master for their schooling . . .	3s. 4d.
Item paid to him the same day for hose (*chauxsure*) . .	2s.
Item paid upon the Eve of Christmas for 12 weeks . .	24s.
Item for 4 pair of shoes	16d.
Item for 2 pair of hose	16d.
Item delivered at Christmas a book called "Este" which cost	7s.
Item given to the Master for their schooling	3s. 4d.
Item paid for two pair of hose, the two	16d.
Item given to the Vicar of Croydon, February 8, [1395], a cade of herrings, price 6s., and a small basket of figs	16d.

. . .

Item paid for 14 weeks, to wit from Epiphany to Easter [1395]	28s.
Item for 4 pair of shoes	16d.
Item given to the servants in the Vicar's household . .	20d.
Item in expenses of myself and my horses to Croydon	15d.
Item paid to the Schoolmaster for his salary	40d.
Item for 1 pair of hose	12d.

---

[20] "Like Chaucer, Maghfeld had at least one profitable wardship. In 1379 he obtained the wardship and marriage of John, son and heir of John de Frogenhale, whose property included Boclond, Tenham, Lyndestede, Tonge, Ludyngham, Herteye, Osprenge, Davyngton, and Stone by Osprenge, in Kent. This wardship Maghfeld had, without paying anything for it, from one John Kent, a 'yeoman of the buttery' to the King, who had himself received it November 27, 1376. That this John Kent was known to Chaucer seems certain from the positions of the two at court; and some of the lands were within a few miles of the Staplegate property, of which Chaucer was in charge until 1377."

As "the original ward came of age in 1393" and "the school expenses end in 1395, when he was twenty-three years old, it seems probable that the John de Frogenhale who was one of the 'enfantz' [the two children for whom the schooling was provided] was not the original ward, but his young son, Maghfeld having brought about a marriage some time before his ward came of age." (Rickert, "Documents and Records: Extracts from a Fourteenth-Century Account Book," *Modern Philology*, XXIV (1926–1927), 250–251.)

[21] That is, May 18.   [22] That is, September 28.

Item given to the Master for 1 pair of hose .   .   .   .   20*d*.

Item the morrow of St. John the Baptist [23]

paid to the Schoolmaster .   .   .   . 3*s*.   4*d*.

Item the same time to the two children .   .   .   .   8*d*.

Item paid for their commons for 11 weeks, to

wit until July 8, [1395] .   .   .   . 22*s*.

Item for their shoes .   .   .   .   16*d*.

Item for the washerwoman for washing their clothes .   .   16*d*.

Item expended by Frogenhalle on two occasions .   .   .   15*d*.

.   .   .

Item paid for 12 weeks from the day of St. Thomas

Martyr [July 7] until St. Michael [September 29] . 24*s*.

Item to the Master for his salary .   .   .   .   .   .   40*d*.

Item to him for one pair of hose .   .   .   .   .   20*d*.

Item for the children, 4 pair of shoes .   .   .   .   .   16*d*.

Item 4 pair of hose .   .   .   . 2*s*.   3*d*.

Item for the washerwoman .   .   .   .   6*d*.

Item given to the Master one coat of my livery,

furred, against Christmas [1395], price .   .   .   . 11*s*.   8*d*.[24]

THE BOY AT SCHOOL

Of English schools and education in Chaucer's time so little is known that even the unrelated matters grouped below are enlightening.

From Trevisa's account of the coming into use of the English language [25] we see that Chaucer as a boy, a generation earlier, almost certainly construed his Latin into French. Incidentally, it should be observed that Trevisa's phrase "in all the grammar schools of England" implies a large number of such foundations. This is interesting in view of the fact that many of the famous grammar schools of

---

[23] That is, June 25, 1395.

[24] "Apparently the boys were very young. This is shown by the difference in cost between the schoolmaster's hose (20*d*.) and those for the boys (8*d*.), and the low price of their shoes (4*d*. each) and the large number they wore out (sixteen pairs in fifteen months); also, by the low rate of their 'commons' (a shilling a week apiece), the small sum given them, apparently for pocket-money, the low salary paid the master, and the use of the word 'enfantz.'

"The school seems to have been in the house of the Vicar of Croydon. Maghfeld gave the Vicar a cade of herring and a small basket of figs, and he also tipped the servants in the Vicar's house; but the small salary of the schoolmaster (1 mark a year, equivalent to about $100), and the frequent gifts of hose, besides the coat of Maghfeld's livery at Christmas, suggest that he was some poor clerk hired by the Vicar. The board for the boys was probably paid to the Vicar." (Rickert, "Documents and Records: Extracts from a Fourteenth-Century Account Book," *Modern Philology*, XXIV (1926–1927), 251.)

[25] See below, p. 119.

today are believed to have been established in the following century. Perhaps there were more in the fourteenth century than we have been supposing.

The letter from Brother Edmund is illuminating in several ways: (1) it shows that there were boarding schools in England as early as *ca.* 1380 and that one of these was at Oxford; (2) that the child's parents sometimes sent a responsible person (in this case, perhaps a chaplain) to look into the boy's welfare; (3) that the schoolmaster had a wife who at least helped to look after the boys' clothes, and in this case both had an ideal of wholesome simplicity and economy; (4) that the boy was studying Latin grammar in *Donatus;* (5) that the textbook which he needed was a composite volume (that is, contained selections from various authors), which Brother Edmund thought was well worth the twelve shillings asked for it.

But the most vivid picture is given by the rules for the behavior of the boys in Westminster School. Except for the continual reference to the rod, most of them might be in use today. The points which it was thought necessary to mention show that the boys were not so oppressed as we are sometimes given to imagine medieval children to have been. The injunctions show that on the way to church there were unseemly scuffles with—shall we say—passing butcher boys, and surreptitious handling of stray dogs and cats; that in the choir itself there were grinning and chattering and shoving of one another; and that, once in the dormitory, there were certainly such tricks as pulling to pieces the other fellow's bed, to say nothing of pillow fights.

At least one of the three schools mentioned, St. Paul's, had a library, and it is very probable that it was the very collection which is listed here to which Chaucer had access. It is to be hoped, however, that he differed from his fellow students, whose misuse of books is the subject of the famous account by Richard de Bury in 1345.

Last of all, the account of the music student's troubles, while not directly concerned with Chaucer's probable education, is so vivid and amusing as to seem worth including here. [R.]

1. A Chaplain's Report upon His Visit to a Boy at Boarding School, ca. *1380*

The Stonor Letters and Papers, 1290–1483, ed. by Kingsford, I, 21 (from Anct. Correspondence (P.R.O.) xlvi, 18).

Sir and God's servant: Know, if you please, that I have seen your son Edmund and have observed his condition these two nights and a day. His sickness grows less from day to day, and he is no longer in bed. But when the fever returns, he is still a little out of sorts for two hours or so; after which he rises and, according to the demands of the time, goes to school and eats and walks about, well and jolly, so that there seems to be nothing serious in his condition. Of his own accord he himself sent his duty to you and to his lady,[26] and greetings to all the others.

He is beginning to learn *Donatus* [27] slowly, as is right enough so far. He has that copy of *Donatus* which I was afraid was lost.

[26] Mother.   [27] Grammar.

Indeed, I have never seen a boy get such care as he has had during his illness. The master and his wife prefer that some of his clothes should be left at home, because he has far too many, and fewer would be enough; and his clothes, through no fault of theirs, might easily be torn and spoiled.

I enclose descriptive titles of the books in a volume which the owner will not sell for less than twelve shillings. In my opinion and that of others it is worth that; and if he sells it to us, he asks to be paid promptly.

And so, if you please, send me by your boy an answer of your wishes in these matters that I have mentioned.

Farewell, in the power of Christ and in the merits of the Virgin and Mother, Mary,

From your devoted,

Brother Edmund

To the Honorable Sir Edmund de Stonor.

2. *Rules for Conduct at Westminster School, 13th century*

Westminster Abbey, Library, *The Manuscripts of Westminster Abbey*, pp. 67–68.

In the morning let the boys upon rising sign themselves with the holy cross, and let each one say the creed, namely, I believe in God, etc., and the Lord's prayer three times, and the salutation to the Blessed Virgin five times, without shouting and confusion; and if anyone neglects these good things, let him be punished.

Then, after they have made up the beds properly, let them leave their room together quietly, without clattering, and approach the church modestly and with washed hands, not running, or skipping, or even chattering, or having a row with any person or animal; not carrying bow or staff, or stone in the hand, or touching anything with which another could be harmed; but marching along simply and honestly and with ordered step.

Then, as they enter the church, let them sign themselves with the cross, and after they have said the Lord's prayer and the salutation to the Blessed Virgin, with a genuflexion before the crucifix, let them rise and enter the choir two by two, humbly and devoutly; and in the middle of the choir, bowing modestly toward the altar, let each one go to his stall or his seat; and he who makes light of this shall not escape severe punishment.

Whether they are standing or sitting in the choir, let them not have their eyes turned aside to the people, but rather toward the altar; not grinning, or chattering, or laughing aloud; not making fun of another if he does not read or sing psalms well; not hitting one another secretly or openly, or answering rudely if they happen to be asked a question by their elders. Those who break these rules will feel the rod without delay.

. . .

As they go out let them take pains to keep the same manner and bearing as upon entering; and let them conduct themselves upon returning home from church or school in the same way as has been said before. Those who break this rule shall be punished in the same way as for the other transgressions.

Likewise, if anyone who knows Latin dares to speak English or French with his companion, or with any clerk, for every word he shall have a blow with the rod.

Likewise, for rudeness in word or deed anywhere and for any kind of oath let not the rod be spared; but let them use these words as their oath: "Surely," "Of a truth," "Indeed," "I assure you," "No doubt," "God knows." For any kind of falsehood anyone will be disciplined.

Likewise, whoever on festival days has run about the village or into the homes of the farmers or is found outside the court without a definite good reason and without the permission of the elders or in a certain place given to the boys for playing as much as they ought to, will be punished, the day after.

In the same way shall be punished he who on such days goes out of the hall before the long grace to the Lord after dinner has been finished.

At the boys' table, indeed, if one presides for a week, turn about, in the usual way, let him say the blessing over the food set before them and about to be brought, and after the meal is finished, let him give to God the devout thanks due for all his benefits and pray for their benefactors, both the living and the dead.

Again, whoever at bedtime has torn to pieces the bed of his companions, or hidden the bed clothes, or thrown shoes or pillows from corner to corner, or roused anger, or thrown the school into disorder, shall be severely punished in the morning.

In going to bed let them conduct themselves as upon rising, signing themselves and their beds with the sign of the cross.

3. *A Schoolboy's Whipping, 1390*

Common Pleas, Plea Roll 517 m. 340.

Kent. Robert Dryg was attached to answer Robert, son of Thomas Eliot, for assault and wounding, etc., at Harnhill. Robert, son of Thomas, by his guardian, Thomas Dunynton, complained that on Monday before All Saints Day,[28] 10 Richard II [1386], Dryg had assaulted him, etc., and claimed damages of £20. Dryg had also beaten him. Dryg denied everything except the beating and put himself on the country. As to the beating, he said that he was the master of Robert, son of Thomas, to teach him to sing and to read, and he had struck him with a rod (*virga*) for purposes of correction (*causa castigationis et erudicionis*) as he thought good, and therefore no action was taken against him on this account.

4. *A Schoolboy Tricked, 1392*

London, Corporation, *Calendar of Select Pleas and Memoranda*, A.D. *1381–1412*, ed. by Thomas, p. 182 (Plea and Mem. R. A 31, m. 1, July 6, 1392).

Whereas John Harmesthorpe, Master of St. Katherine by the Tower,[29] placed a certain William Gynne, a boy of about ten years of age who was in his wardship, to school with Richard Exton, near the Friars of the Holy Cross,[30] certain friars came to the boy and told him to translate into Latin the words "Y oblisshe me to be a frere of the croys," and when the boy had done so, one of the friars kissed him and said that all the bishops in England could not absolve him from becoming a friar of their order; and so they took the boy away on July 4, 1392 and dressed him in the habit of their order and withdrew him from the custody of the said Richard Exton. And when the latter complained to Edward Dalyngregge, warden of the city, praying for a just remedy, the warden on July 5 ordered the friars to send the boy to him, and next day, on the ground that the boy was of tender age and not of marriageable years and was a servant of the Master of St. Katherine, without whose consent he could not legally bind himself, and further because the friars had gained possession of the boy by deception, the warden sent him back to the Master of St. Katherine.

[28] All Saints Day is November 1.
[29] The Hospital of St. Katherine by the Tower. [Thomas' note].
[30] The house of the crouched or crossed Friars in Hart Street in Aldgate Ward, now called "Crutched" friars. [Thomas' note.]

5. *Ill Effects of Construing Latin into English instead of French,* ca. *1342*

Higden, *Polychronicon*, II, pp. 159, 161.

Children in school, against the usage and manner of all other nations, are compelled to leave their own language and to construe their lessons and their things in French, and so they have done since the Normans came first into England. Also gentlemen's children are taught to speak French from the time that they are rocked in their cradles, and can speak and play with a child's brooch. And uplandish men will liken themselves to gentlemen and with much effort try to speak French, in order to be told of.

Trevisa's note on the changes in construing, 1385. This manner was much used before the first death [31] and is since somewhat changed . . . so that now, the year of our Lord a thousand three hundred and four score and five . . . in all the grammar schools of England children leave the French and construe and learn in English. And they have thereby an advantage on one side and a disadvantage on the other side; their advantage is that they learn their grammar in less time than children were accustomed to do; the disadvantage is that now the children of grammar schools know no more French than their left heel, and that is bad for them if they pass the sea and travel in strange lands and in many other places. Also, gentlemen have now much left off teaching their children French.

6. *On the Care of Books, 1345*

Aungerville,[32] *The Philobiblon of Richard de Bury*, ed. by A. F. West, I, 113–116.

In the first place, there should be a natural decorum in the opening and closing of books, so that they are not unclasped in too great a hurry, or, after they have been looked at, put away not properly clasped. For we ought to take much better care of a book than of a shoe. But scholars as a class are commonly not well brought up, and unless they are held in check by the rules of their elders, are puffed up with all sorts of nonsense. They act on impulse, swell with impudence, and lay down the law on one point after another, when, as a matter of fact, they are inexperienced in everything.

[31] The murrain, or Black Death, of 1349.
[32] Richard Aungerville was known as Richard de Bury.

You may see, perhaps, a headstrong youth sitting lazily over his studies. Because it is winter, and he is chilly, his nose runs, and he does not even bother to wipe it with his kerchief until it has soiled his book. Such a fellow should have, instead of a book, a shoemaker's apron.

He has long fingernails, black as jet, with which he marks passages that he likes. He puts innumerable straws in various parts of the book, so that their stems may help him to find again what his memory cannot retain. These straws, which are never removed, the book cannot digest, and so becomes distended until it bursts its clasps; and there the straws remain, carelessly forgotten until they rot.

Such a fellow does not hesitate to eat fruit or cheese over his open book, or negligently to set his cup here and there on it; and having no alms bag at hand, he leaves the scraps and crumbs in the book. He never stops barking at his fellows with endless chatter, and while he produces an infinitude of reasons void of all sense, he also sprinkles the open book in his lap with sputtering saliva.

What is worse still, he lies on his book with folded arms, supplementing his brief study with a long nap; and by way of smoothing out the wrinkles, he doubles up the pages of the book, to its no small detriment.

When the rain is past and gone and flowers appear on the earth, this so-called scholar will stuff his book with violets, primroses, roses, and even four-leaved clover. Sometimes he paws it over with wet or sweaty hands; or, again, he handles the white parchment with dusty gloves and hunts for his page, line by line, with a forefinger covered with an old piece of skin. And at the prick of a biting flea, he throws aside his precious volume so that it may not be closed again for a month; and by that time it will be so full of dust that it cannot be clasped at all.

It is especially important to keep from contact with our books those impudent boys who, as soon as they have learned to form the letters of the alphabet, immediately become incongruous annotators of the fairest volumes that come their way, and either ornament with a hideous alphabet every wider margin that they find to the text or make free to write with ungoverned pen whatever nonsense comes into their heads. In one place a Latinist, in another a philosopher, or, perhaps, some ignorant scribe tries out his pen—a trick which we have very often seen damage the fairest books in both their utility and their value.

There are also thieves who mutilate books shamefully, cutting off the side margins even into the very letters of the text, to get materials for their own correspondence, or for various uses and abuses steal the fly-leaves which are put there to protect the book.

Again, it is only decent that we scholars, when we return to study after meals, should wash our hands before we begin to read; no greasy finger should turn the leaves or even touch the clasp. No crying child should be allowed to admire the illuminated capitals, lest he defile the parchment with his wet hands, for a child touches whatever he looks at.

Furthermore, the illiterate, who view a book with the same interest whether it is upside down or rightside up, are not at all suitable persons to meddle with books. And let the clerk see to it that no sooty scullion reeking from his unwashed pots touch the leaves of books; but let him who has the care of the precious volumes be always spotlessly clean. . . .

7. *The Books at St. Paul's School, London, 14th century*

Rickert, "Chaucer at School," *Modern Philology*, XXIX (1931–1932), 258–270. In 1328 William de Tolleshunt, almoner and schoolmaster of the Almonry School at St. Paul's Cathedral in London, which Chaucer may have attended,[33] left to the school the following books, mainly works of grammar, logic, natural history, medicine, and law.

1. The better Hugutio; [34]
2. Priscian "Major" and "Minor" bound in one volume; [35]
3. Isidore's Etymologies; [36]
4. All my grammar books except those which Ralph, my clerk, has;
5. All books (*quaterni*) of sermons for the Feast of the Holy Innocents, which the boy bishops were accustomed to recite in my time, to remain forever in the aforesaid almonry for the use of the boys who are there, so that they will in no wise be lent out or sold;
6. Books of the dialectic art . . . the old logic and the new; [37] together with

[33] "It is generally agreed that of the three known London schools of Chaucer's time St. Paul's is the one he is most likely to have attended. It was the cathedral school; it was near his father's house in Thames Street; it was obviously more important than the other two schools, of which little is recorded." (Rickert, "Chaucer at School," *Modern Philology*, XXIX [1931–1932], 258.) See also above, p. 4.

[34] Probably the *Liber derivationum* of Hugutio, or Hugo of Pisa, who was bishop of Ferrara in 1210. According to Abelson, *The Seven Liberal Arts*, pp. 49–50, this work, which was very popular in its time, was so named because the author tried to arrange words according to their derivation. The form of the entry "Hugocionem meliorem" shows that Tolleshunt evidently owned two copies, but left the better one to the school.

[35] Grammars that were standard throughout the Middle Ages.

[36] One of the standard encyclopedias of the Middle Ages, devoted largely to natural science.

[37] The "old logic" (*vetus logica*) consisted of the works studied up to the end of the

7. Books on natural philosophy and other little books of the same art;
8. Several physical books which I have on medicine; and also
9. Books of civil law, *viz.*, the *Instituta*, the *Codex*, the *Digestum vetus*, the *Autentica*,[38] and other legal writings I bequeath for the use of the boys, in the mode and form above mentioned.

> In 1358 William Ravenstone, a later almoner and master at St. Paul's school, left the following books. The emphasis on the classics suggests that Chaucer may have acquired his knowledge of classical authors more directly than has been supposed, not only because the list of works corresponds fairly well with those which Chaucer's writings make it appear he had read, or at least knew from some source, but also because the library regulations seem to have permitted the students to keep the books in their rooms and to borrow them from the school after they had left.[39]

I. 1. A book of natural philosophy which begins thus: "Quoniam autem intelligere"; [40]

II. 2. Two books of logic, both the old and the new [Aristotle, with medieval commentaries]; [41]

III. 3. A book of the new logic, which begins thus: "De sophisticis *autem* elenchis"; [42]

IV. 4. Hugutio, alone; [43]

V. 5. *Magnum doctrinale* [by Alexander de Villa Dei],[44]

6. *Unus omnium* [attributed to John de Garland],[45]

---

twelfth century: Capella's section on logic in his Encyclopedia, Augustine's *Prinicipia dialectica*, the pseudo-Augustinian *Categoriae decem ex Aristotile decerptae* (Ten Classes of Predicables from Aristotle), Cassiodorus's *De Dialectica*, numerous works by Boethius, and Isidore of Seville's section, "De Arte Dialectica" from his *Etymologiae*. The "new logic" (*nova logica*) comprised several works by Aristotle: the *Prior and Posterior Analytics*, the *Topics*, and the *Sophistical Refutations*.

[38] These works, the *Institutes*, the *Code*, the *Old Digest* (or *Pandects*), and the *Authentic or New Constitutions*, were all by Justinian.

[39] Professor Rickert's discussion of these two lists has been much condensed, and her conjectures as to conditions at St. Paul's school have been omitted.

[40] The *incipit* occurs in MS Digby 55: 'Anon. in Aristotle de physico auditu'; also in Gonville and Caius 448.7, Walter Burley's 'Super VIII libros phisicorum.' [R.]

[41] All attributions after titles are Professor Rickert's. This is the same as No. 6 in the list of books left by Tolleshunt.

[42] The *incipit* occurs repeatedly in medieval commentaries on Aristotle: *e.g.*, by William Briton, John Baconthorpe, etc. [R.]

[43] The same as the first item in the list of books left by Tolleshunt.

[44] A grammar in verse, composed in 1199.

[45] According to Hauréau, "Notice sur les œuvres authentiques ou supposées de Jean de Garlande," in L'Institut National de France, *Notices et extraits des manuscrits de la Bibliothèque Nationale et Autres Bibliothèques*, Paris, 1879. XXVII, 64, who gave it the title "Unum omnium," with the *incipit* "Commoda neglectis dum quaerunt," it is very rare.

7. Boethius, *De disciplina scolarium* [46] [pseudo-Boethius; an unknown medieval writer],

8. *Veterem poetriam*,[47]

9. A book of Persius, with six others in one volume;

VI. 10. A glossed Donatus [Ars minor? or Ars gramatica?],[48]

    11. *Magnum doctrinale* [cf. No. 5],

    12. *Grecismus* [by Everard of Béthune],[49] in one volume;

VII. 13. A book of Cato [*Distichs*],

    14. A book of Theodulus [*Eclogues*],

    15. A book of Avianus [*Fables*],

    16. A book of Maximianus [*Elegies*],

    17. A book of Statius [Achilleid],

    18. A book of Claudianus [*De raptu Proserpinae*],

    19. *Parvum doctrinale*,[50] in one volume; [51]

VIII. 20. A book of algorism [by John Holywood (de Sacro Bosco)? or by Alexander de Villa Dei?],[52]

    21. *Magnum doctrinale* [cf. No. 5],

    22. *Grecismus* [cf. No. 12],

    23. Alexander Neckham, with a gloss,[53]

    24. *Phale tholum*,[54]

    25. A book of prayers,[55] together with

There were two copies in the old library of Dover Priory (cf. James, *Ancient Libraries of Canterbury and Dover*, p. 486). [R.]

[46] *On the Training of Scholars.*

[47] The *Ars poetica* of Horace. [R.]

[48] Probably either the *Ars grammatica minor* or the *Ars grammatica major* by Aelius Donatus. Both were very famous texts on grammar in use throughout the middle ages.

[49] A metrical explanation in Latin of Greek terms used in grammar and sophistry.

[50] See p. 125*n.*, below.

[51] The standard "school reader" of the time. Numbers 13–18 were the authors commonly bound together in such a volume during the thirteenth and fourteenth centuries. [R.]

[52] Algorism was a type of mathematics that combined what we understand as arithmetic and algebra.

[53] *De utensilibus?* or *De naturis rerum?* [R.] The *De utensilibus*, or *De nominibus utensilium*, illustrated by means of descriptive passages the meanings of many words used in connection with the household. The *De naturis rerum* described various aspects of the universe.

[54] Described in M. R. James, *A Descriptive Catalogue of the Manuscripts in the Library of Gonville and Caius College;* Cambridge, University Press, 1907–1908, I, 147, as: "Letters of Master Adam Smallbridge to Anselm, Archbishop of Canterbury, de utensilibus cum elucidacione mag. Neckham." Elsewhere, however, it is described differently. [Summarized from Professor Rickert's note.]   [55] *Liber salutum.*

26. A hymnal, and

27. *Accentarius* [by John de Garland],[56] in one volume;

IX. 28. Ovid's *Metamorphoses*, alone,

X. 29. A grammar by Bede, which begins thus: "Litera est minima," [57] alone,

XI. 30. Petrus Helias, *In absoluta*,[58] together with

31. *Antiqua sophismata*,[59] in one volume;

XII. 32. *Compendium artis gramatice* [by John de Garland],[60]

33. *Sermones oracij* [*Satires*],

34. Virgil, *Georgics*, together with

35. A hymnal;

XIII. 36. A book containing both parts of Priscian, alone; [61]

XIV. 37. Priscian, *Construcciones*, alone; [62]

XV. 38. Accentarius [cf. No. 27], together with

39. A large book of Equivocations,[63] in one volume (*quaternus*);

XVI. 40. A little book on grammatical problems, alone; [64]

XVII. 41. Ten books of Lucan, alone in one volume;

XVIII. 42. *Alexander Magnus*, alone; [65]

XIX. 43. Twelve books of Statius, alone [*i.e.*, of the *Thebaid*];

XX. 44. Priscian Minor [cf. Nos. 36, 37], together with

45. A certain compendium which begins thus: "*Gramatica cum algorismo*," [66] and

[56] A poem of 1426 hexameter lines on accent in poetry. Hauréau, "Notice sur les œuvres authentiques ou supposées de Jean de Garlande," in L'Institut National de France, *Notices et extraits des manuscrits de la Bibliothèque Nationale et Autres Bibliothèques*, Paris, 1879, XXVII, 53–54.

[57] Not by Bede. The *incipit* is of Gregory of Huntingdon's *Regulae versificandi*. [R.]

[58] Presumably the commentary *Super Priscianum de constructionibus*. [R.]

[59] Aristotle? [R.]   [60] A summary of grammar in hexameter verse.

[61] *Priscianus major*, Books i–xvi (accidence), and *Priscianus minor*, Books xvii–xviii (syntax). [R.]

[62] Perhaps *Priscianus minor* by itself, or, perhaps, with a commentary such as that of Kilwardby. [R.]

[63] Treatises called *Aequivoca* were written by John de Garland, Matthew de Vendôme, and Geoffrey de Vinsauf. [R.] These works discussed homonyms.

[64] *Unum parvum librum cum dubiis gramaticalibus per se.* "I have not found the exact title. Hugutio wrote *De dubio accentu*; a ninth-century treatise, *De dubiis nominibus*, is mentioned by Keil (*Grammatici Latini*, V, 571 ff.); and there must have been many similar treatises of the sort on difficult points of grammar." [R.]

[65] The *Alphabetum maius* of Alexander de Villa Dei? or the *Alexandreis* or *Gesta Alexandri* of Walter de Castellione (de Insulis?)? [R.]

[66] This *incipit* I have not found. But mathematical and grammatical treatises were often bound in the same volume. [R.]

46. Another compendium beginning thus: "Cum ad cuius-libet sciencie," [67] together with
47. *Distigium* [by John de Garland?]; [68]
48. *Unus omnium* [cf. No. 6], in one volume;

XXI. 49. Juvenal alone;
XXII. 50. Another Juvenal, alone;
XXIII. 51. A *Doctrinale magnum,* alone [cf. No. 5];
XXIV. 52. Another *Doctrinale magnum,* alone;
XXV. 53. A book of Equivocations [cf. No. 39];
54. *Dixionarium* [by John de Garland?]; [69]
55. Alexander Neckham [cf. No. 23], in one volume;
XXVI. 56. A book of Cato, with twelve others besides; [70]
XXVII. 57. A lapidary; [71]
58. *Mysteria* [by John de Garland]; [72]
59. *Accentarius* [cf. No. 38], together with
60. A book of Persius, in one volume;
XXVIII. 61. *Magnum doctrinale* [cf. No. 5], with
62. *Book of Synonyms,*[73] in one volume;
XXIX. 63. *Liber accentus,* alone in one volume (*quaternus*); [74]
XXX. 64. A book on "cantus organicus"; [75]
XXXI. 65. Another book of plain song, *viz.,* a gradual;
XXXII. 66. A book (*quaternus*) on the rules of the art of music;
XXXIII. 67. A pair of concordances to the Bible, arranged by subjects;

[67] The *incipit* in Worcester Cathedral Q.50.II.2 of a work called *Expositio Donati.* The MS is a collection of grammatical treatises. [R.]
[68] But cf. Paul Lehmann, in *Mittelalterliche Bibliothekskataloge Deutschlands und der Schweiz,* II [1928], 14, where this title is given as an alternative for the *Parvum doctrinale* or *Proverbia of Alain de l'Isle.* Cf. No. 19. [R.]
[69] Or Alexander de Hales? [R.]
[70] As the Cato suggests that the volume was another reading book of the type of VII, it is at least possible that besides the usual six authors it contained also works by Ovid and by Virgil. [R.]
[71] Probably in Latin. [R.]
[72] The full title is *Mysteriorum ecclesiae, libri duo* [Two Books of the Mysteries of the Church], or *Carmen de mysteriis* [Song of Mysteries], or *Summa mysteriorum* [Sum of Mysteries.] [R.] It is a mystical explanation in 659 hexameter lines of the rites and vestments of the church. (*DNB,* XX, 437.)
[73] Formerly attributed to John de Garland, but more probably by Matthew de Vendôme or Geoffrey de Vinsauf. [R.] It is a work on synonyms, in verse designed to aid the memory. (Hauréau, *Notices et extraits,* XXVII, Part II, 55–58.)
[74] Priscian, *De accentibus?* [R.]
[75] Part songs, as opposed to plain song? There were many such books at St. Paul's in 1445 (cf. *Archaeologia,* L, 458, 523). [R.]

XXXIV. 68. A little book (*libellum*), with *Merar' equiuoco* and others; [76]

XXXV. 69. A Hymnal,

70. Some glossed sequences;

XXXVI. 71. A little book (*libellum*), *Cum epistola prosaica*,

72. with a *Neutrali*, and

73. with a *Deponentali*, and

74. Merar',

75. *Primis decronis* [for *de dicronis*] *et mediis*; (On Initial and Medial Doubtful Quantities); [77]

XXXVII. 76. A little book (*libellum*) containing the *Exotecon*, which begins thus: "Chere Theoren" [attributed to Alexander de Hales],

77. A gloss to the *Major doctrinale* [cf. No. 5],

78. *Regimina*; [78]

XXXVIII. 79. ⎫
XXXIX. 80. ⎬ Two old psalters;

XL. 81. A nominal and verbal for the reading and use of the boys, that from them they may gain further knowledge;

XLI. 82. Prophecy of the Sybille; [79]

XLII. 83. A little book (*libellum*) of rules and customs of the Church of St. Paul [possibly Ralph de Baldock's, still at St. Paul's];

XLIII. 84. A little book (*libellum*) of allegories and tropologies of certain stories of the Bible;

A chest in the boys' room for keeping their books.

8. *The Music Student, ca. 1325*

Wright, *Reliquiae antiquae*, I, 291–292 (from Arundel MS (B.M.) 292 fol. 71 v).

Uncomely in cloister I cringe full of care,
I look like a lout and listen to my lore,

[76] From the form, which seems to represent "cum Merario equiuoco," as well as from the absence of a comma between *Merar'* and *equiuoco*, I take No. 68 to be a different work from No. 74, though of the same general character. The scribe usually is very careful to separate his titles by commas (though he fails to do so after No. 71). [R.] Professor Beeson suggests that this is probably a book on equivocations by Merarius.

[77] The most puzzling item in the list, though the volume is obviously a collection of grammatical treatises, certainly five, perhaps more (the commas are in the document). [R.]

[78] I have found several treatises with this title. Cf. Corpus Christi (Camb.), 223.4; Add. 37075, fol. 85; and Gonville and Caius 417.3. The rules are grammatical. [R.]

[79] A treatise on a vision of the Judgement Day. [R.]

The notes of the treble make me sigh sore
And sit stuttering over a song a month and more.
I go roaring about just like a gawk,
Many is the sorrowful song I sing upon my book;
I am held so hard that I scarcely dare look;
All the mirth of this world for God I forsook.
I grumble at my *Gradual* and roar like a rook;
Little knew I of it when I thereto took.
Some notes are short, and some a long crook;
Some curl away like a fleshhook.
When I know my lesson [to] my master will I be gone;
Who hears me then say it; he thinks I have well done.
"What hast thou done, Dan Walter, since Saturday at noon?
Thou holdest not a note, by God! in its right tone.
Woe's me, dear Walter, thou shouldest have shame;
Thou stumblest and stickest fast as though thou wert lame;
Thou tonest never a note, whatever its name;
Thou bitest off *B* natural for *B* flat, I thee blame.
Woe's thee, dear Walter, thy work is a wonder;
Like an old bubbling cauldron away thou dost blunder!
Thou dost not sing the notes; thou bitest them asunder;
Hold them up, for shame; thou lettest them all under!"
Then is Walter so woe that well nigh will he bleed,
And goes back to William and hopes he may well speed.
"God it wot!" says William. "Thereof had I need.
Now wot I how *judicare* was set in the Creed."
"I am sad as the bee that bells out his gong;
I ding upon David till dumb is my tongue;
I've not had my lesson since the day men bear palms.
Is there as much sorrow in song as in psalms?"
"Yea, by God! You've said it! That is worse—just try 'em;
I *solfa* and after sing and come never nigh 'em.
I hurl at the notes and off the hinge heave 'em;
Everyone who hears me thinks I should leave 'em.
Of *B* flat and *B* natural—of these knew I naught
When I forsook the world and tried to be taught.
Of *F* and of *E* heard I never before;
I fail fast with the *fa*; it troubles me sore—
Yet there be other notes—*sol*, *ut*, and *la*,

But that rascally wretch that men call *fa*
Oft does torment me and work me full woe;
I never can hit him—too high or too low.
Yet there's a double note; two long tails has he:
For his sake our master makes a ninepin of me.
Full little thou kens what sorrow I feel;
It is but child's play with David to deal
When each note leaps to other and comes to accord,
That we call a measure in *gesolreut3 en haut*.[80]
You'll be sorry you're born if you make a poor show
When our master says, "You good for nothing fellow!"

UNIVERSITY LIFE

1. Student Regulations, Early 15th Century

The life of a university man in Chaucer's time differed from the life of a student at Oxford or Cambridge today chiefly in the studies followed. He was required to attend lectures (three a day the maximum), to read certain books, and after a certain time went through a procedure akin to matriculation. After four years of study in a hall or college, he came up for the examination by which he received the degree of B.A. This examination was entirely oral and consisted of standing in the schools four days, arguing three questions of logic and philosophy against all comers. After receiving this degree, the student who continued at college was expected to teach as well as study; and at the end of three years more, went through various forms and was made M.A. In this capacity he presided over one of the schools for a year, and then might specialize if he pleased. To complete the course in theology, he had to work ten years more; in canon or civil law, eight; in medicine, five, plus two years' practice. Thus, a boy who went to a university at the age of thirteen could not emerge a doctor of theology under thirty, a doctor of laws under twenty-eight, or a doctor of medicine under twenty-seven. The great majority, however, after spending some time in residence, left the university without degrees of any sort.

The regulations for King's College, Cambridge, which were based upon those of New College, Oxford, give a vivid picture of university life at the end of the fourteenth century. The rules here quoted are only a portion of the total number.

Cambridge University, King's College, *The Ancient Laws of the Fifteenth Century, for King's College, Cambridge, and . . . Eton College*, pp. 21, 67–68, 71, 73, 80, 83–84, 118–119, 131, 133–134.

---

[80] Professor Otto Kinkeldey explains that "Gsolreut is a common term in the solmization terminology of Guido of Arezzo and all who followed him. When the parallel and interlocking hexachords were set up in vertical columns to cover the whole scale from Gamma to ee, it became possible to read across the columns and thus to a certain extent locate the particular hexachord (or octave) in which a given note lay. *Gsolreut* occurs in two places. The student singer uses a more specific designation, *Gsolreut en haut*, for the higher position."

1. Each and every student selected for our Royal College at Cambridge must be a poor and indigent clerk who has received the first tonsure, who habitually shows his rank by his good manners, who has an adequate knowledge of grammar, leads a virtuous life, is fitted to be a scholar and desires to advance in his studies, and who has not received a degree in any field of knowledge.

2. In plentiful years, when there is abundance of food . . . each scholar of King's College . . . is to receive sixteen pence for his commons weekly at the hands of the bursar . . . from the common goods of the College. . . . But in times of high prices and lack of food, he shall receive as much as seventeen or eighteen pence, according to the variation in prices.

3. All the scholars, chaplains, and clerks of King's College, sitting at table in the hall daily, shall have the Bible read to them publicly or some of the writings of the holy fathers or doctors. They shall all listen carefully while eating in silence; and no one shall hinder the reading by talking, telling stories, making a noise, laughing, murmuring, or creating any kind of disturbance.

When they speak with each other, whether in the hall, at table, in their rooms, in the church, or anywhere in the precincts or garden of the College, let it be quietly, as becomes clerks. And they shall speak in Latin unless some stranger or layman is present, or for some other good reason. And none of them shall, in any way, hinder anyone in the College from studying, or from sleeping at bed-time, by games, disturbance, or noise of any sort.

4. After meals, without loss of time, when the drink has been passed to those who wish it . . . let the older students of all ranks go to their studies. Nor are the younger students permitted to linger, except at the principal festival days and on solemn double festival days, or the deliberations of the College, or disputations, or other important business concerning King's College, [when] they may be allowed to remain in the hall, or when, out of reverence to God, or his Mother, or any other saint, in winter a fire is provided for the fellows. Then, after dinner or supper, the scholars and fellows are allowed to enjoy themselves in the hall with songs and other honorable pastimes, and to make serious use of poetry, chronicles of nations, the wonders of the world, and anything else which is appropriate for clerks.

5. All fellows and scholars are forbidden to wear red or green shoes secular or curved, or fancy (*modulatis*) hoods inside or outside the uni-

versity, or to carry openly or secretly swords or long knives or arms for assault or defense, or belts or girdles decorated with gold or silver, by order of King's College, either outside or inside the university and the city above-mentioned [Cambridge] . . . except when approved by the president or vice-president, the deans and bursars, in cases of necessity.

All the scholars and fellows aforesaid, moreover, are forbidden to let their hair or beard grow, and all must wear the crown and tonsure belonging to their order, rank, and station, honestly and appropriately, as they should.

6. Because it is not proper for the poor, and especially for those living on alms, to give the bread of children to be eaten by dogs . . . none of the scholars, fellows, chaplains, clerks, or servants of King's College shall have dogs, or nets for hunting or fishing, or ferrets, falcons, or hawks, nor shall practice hunting or fishing, nor among themselves . . . shall they possess in any way an ape, bear, fox, stag, hind, doe, badger, or any other wild animals or strange birds, whether they are useful or harmful.

Moreover, all harmful, disorderly, unlawful and dishonest games of dice, chance, or ball, and especially all games which may cause loss of money, property, possessions, or goods of any servant anywhere within the College or University aforesaid are expressly prohibited. The fellows or scholars aforesaid are expressly forbidden . . . to throw stones, balls, pieces of wood or dirt, spears, or anything else, or play any games or do anything which is not permitted within the college aforesaid, its gates, enclosures, or gardens, or outside, whereby any church, hall, houses, or other buildings of the said college may be broken or suffer damage in its glass windows, walls, roofs, coverings, or anywhere else within or without.

7. Fellows and scholars shall go to chapel quietly, nor shall they murmur, chatter, ridicule, laugh, converse, or make any kind of noise, or through disorderly commotion or the confused sound of voices hinder the devotions or exercises of those who are singing in the choir.

8. Because the deplorable vexation of distracting poverty frequently turns away able scholars from laboring in the field of the Lord and makes them leave their studies . . . £200 are set aside as a fund from which the provost, fellows, and scholars can make loans as follows: the provost, 100s.; the first thirty-five fellows or scholars who apply, 40s.; and the remaining fellows and scholars, 33s. 4d.

9. All chambers and studies in them at King's College . . . shall be ranked and assigned by the president and the vice-president. There shall be at least two fellows in each upper room, as far as the number of fellows in the College extends. In the lower rooms, which have three studies, there shall always be three scholars or fellows, each of whom shall have a separate bed. In each lower room, one fellow, chosen for his maturity, discretion, and greater knowledge, shall superintend the other students and report to the president, vice-president, and deans from time to time, as may be necessary, on their conduct and progress in their studies, in order that they may receive adequate reproof, correction, and punishment.

It is strictly and expressly forbidden that anyone in the upper rooms . . . in washing his head, hands, feet, or anything else, should pour out water, wine, beer, or other liquid so as to disturb either the fellows or the scholars in the lower rooms, in their persons, goods, or property, or trouble them in any way.

2. *Strife among the Students at Oxford, 1388–1389*

Adam of Usk, *Chronicon*, pp. 147–148.

In these days there happened at Oxford a grave misfortune. For, during two whole years there was great strife between the men of the south and the men of Wales on the one side and the northerners on the other, whence arose broils, quarrels, and ofttimes loss of life. In the first year the northerners were driven clean away from the university. And they laid their expulsion chiefly to my charge.[81] But in the second year, in an evil hour, coming back to Oxford, they gathered by night, and denying us passage from our quarters by force of arms, for two days they strove sorely against us, breaking and plundering some of the halls of our side and slaying certain of our men. Howbeit, on the third day our party, bravely strengthened by the help of Merton Hall, forced our adversaries shamefully to fly from the public streets, which for the two days they had held as a camp, and to take refuge in their own quarters. In short, we could not be quieted before many of our number had been indicted for felonious riot; and amongst them I, who am now writing, was indicted, as the chief leader and abettor of the Welsh, and perhaps not unrighteously. And so indicted we were hardly acquitted, being tried by jury

[81] We know little of Adam of Usk's life after 1381. In 1387 he was living at Oxford, probably lecturing on canon law. He seems to have taught there for several years after receiving his doctor's degree. (Adam of Usk, *Chronicon*, p. xii.)

before the King's judge. From that day forth I feared the King, hitherto unknown to me in his power, and his laws, and I put hooks into my jaws.[82]

3. Law Students in a Fray, 1325

London, Coroner, *Calendar of the Coroners Rolls*, pp. 134–135.

On a certain Sunday in November, John de Glemham, apprentice of the Bench,[83] lay dead in a house in the parish of St. Bride of Fleet Street. It was learned that on St. Martin's Eve [84] John de Oxford, clerk, at the request of William de Cornwelle, went to the tavern of Edmund Cosyn in the parish of St. Bride, where he assaulted John Wolfel, Edmund's taverner, on the ground of an old quarrel. John de Wolfel made an outcry, whereupon came John de Glemham and a number of apprentices of the Bench whose names were unknown. [In the fray] a certain William le Taverner struck John de Glemham with his sword, on the fore part of the head, inflicting a wound four inches long and two and a half inches deep. Thus wounded, he returned to his chamber, where he had his ecclesiastical rights, and after lingering until the following Saturday, died.[85]

Many apprentices of the court were present at the inquest.

[82] Knighton, in his *Chronicon*, gives several details of the same event that are omitted by Adam of Usk. The final outbreak occurred during Lent and was settled by the intervention of the Duke of Gloucester. As a result, many of the Welsh were banished from Oxford. On leaving the city, they were obliged to pass through a group of northerners assembled at the gate, to whom they were compelled to offer kisses as they went out. (Knighton, *Chronicon*, II, 309.)

The King's part in quelling this disturbance is further illustrated by the following grant to one of his officials:

To John Elyngeham, the King's sergeant-at-arms, sent in great haste to the town of Oxford with letters under the King's privy seal directed to the Chancellor and Proctors of the University of Oxford for the pacification of certain disputes and dissensions among the scholars there, for his wages and expenses and the hire of horses, by reason of haste, 26s. 8d. (Issue R. 521 m. 23.)

[83] Law student. Although the students involved in this affair were not attending Oxford or Cambridge, they may be regarded as essentially university students, for the Inns of Court "were not merely law schools but rather universities where gentlemen's sons were trained for public careers. Music, dancing, history, and divinity were studied, as well as the law." (Rickert, "Was Chaucer a Student at the Inner Temple?" in *The Manly Anniversary Studies in Language and Literature*, p. 29.)   [84] That is, on November 10.

[85] Part of the interest of this item lies in Speght's statement that Master Buckley said he had seen an entry among the records of the Inner Temple that Chaucer was fined two shillings for beating a Franciscan friar in Fleet Street, and that investigation seems to show that Chaucer was a student at the Inner Temple." (Rickert, "Was Chaucer a Student at the Inner Temple? in *The Manly Anniversary Studies in Language and Literature*, pp. 20–31.)

4. Ordinance on College Gowns, 1358

Anstey, ed., *Munimenta academica*, I, 212–213.

On Sunday, the vigil of the invention of St. Frideswyde,[86] in the year of our Lord 1358, Master John Reygham, chancellor, and Masters Richard Sutton and Walter Wandefforde, proctors at the same time, in a congregation of the regents, all present, it was ordained unanimously by each and all the then regents that any tailor who cut or made a gown to be used in the University should make or cut it properly so that the masters and beadles should have gowns not narrow or short, but wide and reaching to the ankles, as they have been accustomed to wear in times past. For it is decent and consonant with reason that those to whom God had granted the privilege of mental adornment beyond the laity should also be outwardly different in dress from the laity.

If, then, any tailor contravenes this ordinance, he shall be punished with imprisonment and shall not go out of prison until he has made good any part which he cut off and thereby made a gown skimpily and against the dignity of the university.

5. Requirements for the Bachelor's Degree, 1340

Anstey, ed., *Munimenta academica*, I, 142–143.

Item, it was ordained that no one after this year should be licensed to take a degree in arts. . . . unless he first swears that he has read cursorily two books of logic at least, one of the old logic, and the other of the new,[87] or both of the new; and one of the books of physics: namely, the four books "Coeli et mundi" (Of Heaven and Earth), or three books "De anima" (On the Soul), or the four books "Meteororum" (Of Meteors), or the two books "De generatione et corruptione" (Of Birth and Decay), or the books "De sensu et sensatio" (Of Feeling and What Is Felt), with the books "De memoria et reminiscentia" (Of Memory and Recollection), and "De somno et vigilia" (Of Sleep and Waking), or the book "De motu animalium" (Of the Movement of Animals), with two books "De minutis naturalibus" (Of Minor Points in Natural History), and this correctly and rightly according to the form prescribed above.

[86] That is, on October 18.   [87] See above, p. 121*n.*

6. Blacklisted Books [88]

Anstey, ed., *Munimenta academica*, II, 441.

Moroever, the Lord Chancellor, desiring . . . that each and all the scholars of the university and their servants (*subditos*) should be adorned with morals . . . has decreed and ordained as a custom that every master regent in grammar and every other public teacher of grammar shall read his scholars only the book or books dealing principally with grammatical rules and physics, or otherwise dealing with ethics, or metaphors, or decent poetry. To these masters and other teachers the same Lord Chancellor forbids the reading and interpretation of the book of Ovid "De arte amandi" (On the Art of Love), and "Pamphilius," and of any other book which might lure or provoke his scholars to what is forbidden.

7. "Wax Doctors," 1358

Anstey, ed., *Munimenta academica*, I, 207-208.

The words "wax doctors" are of the time of Master Richard Toulworth and Robert Derby, proctors of the University of Oxford. They are called such doctors who try to get degrees from the university by means of letters of great men sealed with wax or in some other way, because just as wax melts in the face of fire, so they run away from the severity of study and work.

But it should be known that such wax doctors in Oxford are always of the orders of the mendicants, of which we have found the reason. For the apples and drink, as people say, they entice and urge into religion little boys whom they do not instruct as professed, as their age demands, but let them get into the way of running about begging and permit them to spend the time when they might be learning in currying favors among friends, ladies, and lords, to the offense of the parents, the danger of the boys, and the detriment of the order. So it is not strange that it happens that those who as children were not compelled to learn against their wills, when they are older presume to teach, wholly unfit and ignorant as they are; and a minor sin in the beginning becomes very great in the end, for thus there grows up among the divine flock a multitude of laymen . . . who undertake the office of preaching the more wickedly in that they do not know what they are talking about . . . who, also, working with a certain confidence and ambition for place, at an early

[88] Anstey includes this in a group of regulations most of which are dated between 1335 and 1344.

age attain to the master's cap and, all unfit, are in many cases made professors of the faculty of divinity, an honor which they reach, not at all step by step in proportion to their ability, but, getting degrees from the university through the letters of great men, climb by leaps and bounds like goats, and when they have scarcely tasted of the great stream, pretend that they have drunk it all from the bottom, although their jaws are scarcely wet.

8. An Apology to Students in the Arts Course [89]

Anstey, ed., *Munimenta academica*, I, 211–212.

When on another occasion in this place I [90] was preaching, in my sermon I distinguished between four kinds of wisdom, as follows: "Some wish to be wise that they may seem so; others, in order that they may know; others, that they may be called so; others, that they may follow the truth." On the first point of this outline I said: "Those studying wisdom that they may appear wise cannot attain to the state of true wisdom. I do not say they are the sophists. . . ."

In my words I foolishly and incautiously and ignorantly gave to understand that these were the sophists who study the arts course, which I ought not to have done, because among all the arts and sciences this is particularly to be commended as the door and entry to all other sciences, as plainly appears from the works and labors, not only of the wise philosophers but also of the holy fathers and doctors, in whose presences I should not be worthy to open my mouth. This I say and affirm as regards that art. As for those who study it, I say that they are studying a course which it is necessary, very useful, and honorable to study, not only for the students themselves but also for all their parents and friends. And may it never happen that on account of any word of mine, which is not the word of virtue or authority, or that of any other, anyone should be led away from his love of that art.

9. On the Pay of Teachers, 1333

Anstey, ed., *Munimenta academica*, I, 128–129.

Granted that no one is supposed to object to proper pay, and that but little corporeal harvest is reaped by those who sow spiritual seeds, and

[89] Anstey includes this between selections dated 1358 and 1360.
[90] A certain preaching friar having attacked the "sophists" in his sermon, a great quarrel ensued between them, and he was obliged to make a retractation in another sermon, as follows. [Anstey's note.]

that still masters of the liberal arts willingly undergo and take upon themselves varied and heavy labors in reading and disputation for the profit and use of their scholars, and on account of the stinginess which in modern times has to an unusual degree become habitual they are not by them paid liberally for work of this kind, as would be fitting and as used to be done in former times,

It is decreed that every scholar of the faculty of arts who lives in a hall on weekly commons shall be bound to pay for the old logic or the new [91] at least twelve pence a year, dividing the sum proportionately among the terms, and for physics eighteen pence at least a year to the masters from whom they regularly hear the said books. . . .

It is decreed that every master of arts, of whatsoever state or condition he may be, except sons of kings, earls, or barons, shall be bound every year by the authority of the statute to collect [his pay]. For otherwise this absurdity will follow, that masters who are poor and of little consequence among the faculties and who need to collect [their pay] will be deprived of their due audiences which they should have by rich masters who do not collect [their pay] because they do not need it.

[91] See above, p. 121n.

4. Careers

SERVICE IN ROYAL AND NOBLE HOUSEHOLDS

1. Richard's Household at Westminster, Late 14th Century

John Hardyng's *Chronicle* was written in the fifteenth century, some time prior to 1465.

In 1394 Richard II began to enlarge and repair Westminster Hall; it was finished in 1398, and a huge feast was held there at Christmas. The extent of the hall and its appurtenances may be inferred from this selection. [R.]

Hardyng, *Chronicle*, pp. 346–347.

> Truly I heard Robert Ireliffe say,
> Clerk of the green cloth,[1] that to the household
> Came every day, for most part alway
> Ten thousand folk by his messes [2] told
> That followed the house, aye, as they would;
> And in the kitchen three hundred servitors
> And in each office many occupiers.
> And ladies fair with their gentlewomen
> Chamberers also and lavenders [3]
> Three hundred of them were occupied then;
> There was great pride among the officers
> And of all men for passing their compeers
> Of rich array and much more costious [4]
> Than was before or since and more precious.

2. Oath of a Herald, 15th century

Dillon, "On a MS Collection of Ordinances of Chivalry of the Fifteenth Century, Belonging to Lord Hastings," *Archaeologia*, LVII (1900), 70.

First ye shall swear that ye shall be true to our high and excellent prince, our sovereign lord that here is, and to him that makes you herald.

[1] The Board of the Green Cloth was a department of the Royal Household consisting of the Lord Steward and his subordinates. It controlled various matters of expenditure, and had legal and judicial authority within the sovereign's court-royal, which extended two hundred yards in each direction from the gate of the palace. Cf. *O.E.D.*
[2] Either a portion of food or a group of persons eating together. Originally it meant each of the small groups, normally of four persons (sitting together and helped from the same dishes), into which the company at a banquet was commonly divided. Cf. *O.E.D.* Also cf. below, p. 142.   [3] Launderers.   [4] Costly.

And if ye have any knowledge or hear any imagination or treason, which God defend [5] that ye should, but in case that ye do, ye shall discover it to his high grace or to his noble council; and counsel [6] it in no manner wise, so help you God and the saints.

Also ye shall promise and swear that ye shall be "connsamit"[?] and serviceable to all gentlemen to do their commandments to their worship [7] of knighthood; and to excuse their worship by your good counsel that God sends you, and ever ready to offer your service to them.

Also ye shall promise and swear to be secret and keep the secrets of knights, squires, ladies and gentlewomen; a confessor of arms; and not discover them in any wise except treason abovesaid.

Also ye shall promise and swear if any fortune befall you in divers lands and countries where ye go or ride, if ye find any gentleman of name and of arms that hath lost his goods in worship of knighthood or in service of his lord and hath fallen into poverty, and if he ask of your goods for his sustenance, ye shall give him of your goods to your power and as ye may bear.

Also ye shall promise and swear if ye be in any place where ye hear language between party and party that is not profitable nor virtuous, that ye keep your mouth close and report it not forth but to their worship and the best.

Also ye shall promise and swear if so be that ye be in any place where ye hear debate or peril between gentleman and gentleman which ye be privy to, if so be that ye be required by prince, judge, or any other to bear witness, ye shall not without license of both parties, and when ye have leave, ye shall [not] for any lust or any good favor or awe, but say the sooth to your knowledge.

Also ye shall promise and swear to be true and secret to gentlewomen, widows, and maidens. And in case that any man would do them wrong, or force them, or disinherit them of their livelihood, and they have no good [friends] to sue for their rights to the princes or judges, if they require of you your support, ye shall support them with your good counsel to princes and judges abovesaid.

Also ye shall promise and swear that ye shall forsake all places of dishonesty and hazard and dishonestly going to common taverns and places of debates and all manner of vices, and take to virtues as much as you

[5] Forbid.
[6] *Counsel* may here mean "hide," by confusion with "conceal."
[7] Respect or honor shown to a person or thing. (*O.E.D.*)

A ROYAL DINNER; late fourteenth century
London, Brit. Mus. MS Royal 1 E. IX, fol. 132v

THE KING AND HIS HERALD
New York, Morgan Library, MS 536, fol. 4

IN THE SERVICE OF THE KING

Late fourteenth century

A MESSENGER TO THE KING
London, Brit. Mus., MS Sloane 2433 (I), fol. 63v

are able. This article and all other articles abovesaid ye shall truly keep, so help you God and the saints.

3. A Herald Carries the King's Letters to Calais, 1386

Exchequer Lord Treasurer's Remembrancer, Exannual Roll 1, London and Middlesex. Debts extracted in 14 Ric. II, dorse.

Marche King Herald, 66s. 8d., advanced to him at the Receipt of the Exchequer on the ninth of June, 9 [Richard II], in moneys delivered to him by his own hand upon his wages [when] sent to Calais with letters of the King directed to the Captain of Calais for certain private (secretis) business of the King there.

4. A Squire's Indentures of Service with John of Gaunt, 1374

John of Gaunt's Register, II, 2–3.

Bordeaux, February 15. This indenture, made between our lord King John [of Castile, etc.] of the one part and Symkyn Molyneux, esquire, of the other part, witnesses that the said Symkyn is retained and will remain with our said lord for peace and for war for the term of his life, as follows: that is to say, the said Symkyn shall be bound to serve our said lord as well in time of peace as of war in whatsoever parts it shall please our said lord, well and fitly arrayed. And he shall be boarded as well in time of peace as of war. And he shall take for his fees by the year, as well in time of peace as of war, ten marks sterling from the issues of the Duchy of Lancaster by the hands of the receiver there who now is or shall be in time to come, at the terms of Easter and Michaelmas by even portions yearly for the whole of his life. And, moreover, our lord has granted to him by the year in time of war five marks sterling by the hands of the treasurer of war for the time being. And his year of war shall begin the day when he shall move from his inn [8] towards our said lord by letters which shall be sent to him thereof, and thenceforward he shall take wages coming and returning by reasonable daily [payments]; and he shall have fitting freightage for him, his men, horses, and other harness within reason, and in respect of his war horses taken and lost in the service of our said lord, and also in respect to prisoners and other profits of war taken or gained by him or any of his men, the said our lord will do to him as to other squires of his rank.

In witness whereof, etc.

Given at Bordeaux, February 15, [1374].

[8] See above, p. 59n.

5. *A Young Squire Who Could Stand Reproof, 1371*

La Tour-Landry, *The Book of the Knight of La Tour-Landry*, pp. 158–159.

There were once two knights . . . brothers . . . of such great renown and worship . . . that they had their say and were listened to in all places where they came. . . . Wherefore, when they saw any young man of their own lineage do anything that was not commendable, they would blame him and correct him before all people. Because of this, the young men feared these knights wherever they went.

One day . . . one of the brothers was at a feast where there was a great number of lords, ladies, knights, squires, and gentlewomen; and there came in a young squire before them that were set at dinner and saluted the company. He was clothed in a coat-hardy [9] after the mode of Germany, and clothed in this wise he came before the lords and ladies and did them goodly reverence. And so this knight called to the young squire . . . before all the estates, and asked him where was his fiddle or his rebec (*ribible*), or such an instrument as belongeth unto a minstrel.

"Sir," said the squire, "I know nothing of such things; it is not my craft or science."

"Sir," said the knight, "I cannot believe what ye say; for ye be counterfeit in your array, and like unto a minstrel. I have known heretofore all your ancestors and the knights and squires of your kin which were all worthy men, but I never saw any of them that were counterfeit or that clothed themselves in such array."

And then the young squire answered the knight and said, "Sir, by as much as it displeaseth you, it shall be amended," and called a follower and gave him the coat-hardy. And he dressed himself in another gown and came again into the hall. Then said the old knight openly, "This young squire shall have honor, for he hath believed and done according to the counsel of his elders, without any contrariness."

6. *A Squire's Letter to His Mother-in-Law, ca. 1396*

Rickert, "Documents and Records: A Leaf from a Fourteenth-Century Letter Book," *Modern Philology*, XXV (1927–1928), 249, 253–254.

As most of the surviving letters of the fourteenth century are of a business character, a special interest attaches to . . . [a] group of eight, which are of an unusually personal tone. They are written on a single leaf of a letter book,[10] badly faded and torn, which seems to have belonged to a lady at the court of Richard II . . . The owner of the book, from internal evidence, was Lady Alice de Bryene,[11] wife of

[9] See above, p. 51*n*.   [10] Now A.C. 51/24, in the Public Record Office, London.
[11] Professor Rickert conjectured that she was "almost certainly known to Chaucer."

Sir Guy the younger and daughter-in-law of Sir Guy the elder—both famous knights of the time. How her letter book came into the hands of the government is at present unknown; but there is also in the Public Record Office a long fragment of a household book of hers, dated some twenty years later.[12] . . .

Perhaps the special interest of the letters lies in the evidence they give that French was still the familiar language of English society at the very end of the fourteenth century. They illustrate also the exaggerated courtesy with which relatives addressed one another; they are indeed more mannered than the contemporary treatises on letter-writing suggest to have been the general practice. . . .

Number 7 was written by Robert Lovell, who had married Lady Alice's daughter Elizabeth. . . . [He] was a wealthy young Essex landowner and a squire at the court of Richard II. He went to Ireland in the King's service, June 30, 1395, with Alexander, Bishop of Meath, Chancellor of Ireland; and again, May 16, 1396, with the same; and May 23, 1397, the last time, with Roger Mortimer, Earl of March, lord lieutenant of Ireland.[13] His letter was almost certainly written soon after he reached Ireland the second time; [14] and it was written at Trim, Mortimer's castle in Meath. Young Lovell was then in the household of the man to whom, directly or indirectly, Chaucer owed his reappointment, that very year, as subforester of Petherton.[15] His letter is particularly charming in its strong expressions of gratitude and love, and of the writer's evident concern about his mother-in-law and his eagerness to hear of her welfare.

My lady and mother, most honored and with all my heart most dearly well-beloved, I commend myself to you as utterly as I know how and best can, desiring earnestly to hear and truly know good and joyous news of you and of your honorable estate, entreating God, the heavenly king, most high and all-powerful, that he may grant me always to hear and know such [things] as you can indeed think and wish for and as my heart most earnestly desires, for certainly my joy is renewed when I have good news of you. Therefore I entreat you that, for the sincere joy and pleasure of my heart, it may please you to inform me of them very often by messengers. And, most-honored lady and mother, because I am quite certain that it would please you much to hear of me and of my health, may it please you to know that at the time of sending this [letter] I am hale and hearty, thank God, and [that I] thank you again and again as much as I can for the very great affection and kindliness that you have had and still have for me, and for the countless other favors which it has pleased you in your very noble kindliness to do and to show me, without my deserving any at all. I entreat you for your good and gracious encouragement to me forever. And if there be anything that I can do for

[12] Cf. pp. 78–79, 85–87. [13] Cf. below, pp. 317–318.
[14] The date—June 3—is too early for his first trip, and it stands in the letter book between two letters of the year 1396. [R.]
[15] That is, North Petherton, Somerset.

your honor or pleasure, may it please you to communicate your gracious wishes and desires, which I am and always will be ready to obey and fulfill to the limit of my small ability, as I am assuredly held and obliged [to do]. My lady and mother, most honored and with all my heart most entirely well-beloved, may the Blessed Trinity have you in its most holy keeping and grant you a good and very long life and the good fulfillment of all your noble desires. Written at Trim in Ireland, the third day of June.

Your humble son—so please you,

Robert Lovell.

7. *Squires of the King's Household, 15th century* [16]

Life-Records of Chaucer, II, 67–70 (from Harl. MS 642, fol. 55).

There are forty squires of the household, or there may be more if it please the king, by the advice of his high council. These men are chosen according to their possessions, social positions, and wisdom. They are also to be of sundry shires in order that the disposition of the counties may be known. Of these squires twenty are to be continually in this court as attendants on the king's person, in riding and going at all times. . . . They are also to help serve his table from the serving board, and from such other places as the man who has general charge of the tables will assign. By common consent, also, they will make assignments among themselves as to which shall serve the king's chamber for any one day, week, or period of time. At another time others will be assigned to serve the hall, of every mess that comes from the dressing board to their hands for such service. There must be nothing withdrawn by these squires, upon pain of demerits that will be awarded by the steward, controller, or other judges at the serving board.

The king may take into his household forty squires in all, and yet, among them all, not twenty are paid full wages for the year. Therefore, the number of persons may be received and suffered the better in the payroll, for a worship, and the king's profit saved.

They eat in the hall, sitting together at one meal as they serve—some at the first meat, some at the latter, by arrangement. This has always been the manner among them, for honor and profit to the king and ease to themselves. Each of them takes for his livery at night half a gallon

[16] Edward IV's Household and Wardrobe Ordinances, the source of this account, were based on those of Edward II, which go back to 1323.

of ale. For the winter season [each] takes two Paris candles and one faggot or else half of talwood.

When any of them is present in court, he is allowed for daily wages in the payroll seven pence halfpenny and his clothing winter and summer, or else forty shillings. The squires in this court have always been especially directed to wear the king's livery, both for personal glory and for the proper worship of this honorable household. Each of them is to be allowed one honest servant in this court and sufficient livery, in the towns or country, for his horses and other servants, by the purveyor. Two gentlemen are to be lodged together as bedfellows by the gentlemen ushers. If any of them be let blood, or be ill, in court or nigh thereto, he takes livery, two loaves, two messes of the principal meat, and one gallon of ale for each of the meat days. They are also to have all the year straw for their beds in court from the sergeant usher of the hall. If any of these squires be sent out of the court by steward, controller, or other of the countinghouse, on matters that concern the household, he has allowed him daily by petition twelve pence. The steward pays also for the squires' carriage of harness in court.

They take no part in the general gifts, neither in chamber nor in hall, unless the giver expressly names them. No squire shall depart from court except by license of steward, treasurer, or sovereign of the countinghouse that know how the king should be attended. They must settle the day when they shall return, upon pain of loss of wages. No sergeant of office, nor squire, nor yeoman, nor groom, except as he be allowed in this book, shall dine or sup out of hall or the king's chamber. Nor are they to withdraw any service or otherwise to hurt or belittle the alms of hall or chamber, upon such pain as the sovereigns of the household will award by the statutes of noble [King] Edward the Third. . . .

The countinghouse in former times made certain commands for festival days. After the king and the queen and their chambers, and the stewards of the household in the hall be served, then some honest yeomen of the household are called or assigned to serve the others from the dresser to the hall. Especially those who are on the payroll are to be called, so that if they neglect any service, they may be corrected for it. These squires of the household of old are accustomed, winter and summer, afternoons and evenings, to gather in the lord's chamber within court. There they keep honest company according to their skill, in talking of chronicles of kings, and other policies, or in piping, or harping, singing, or other martial acts, to help to occupy the court, and accompany strangers, till the time require of departing.

8. *Squires for the King's Chamber, 1323*

Life-Records of Chaucer, II, 18 (from MS Ashmole 1147, fol. 15).

The King shall have twelve squires, besides the youths who serve him as his wards, and the three squires who serve him at the table. Of these twelve squires, one shall be warden in the chamber. Each of them shall have seven pence half-penny wages every day, and two robes in cloth, or forty shillings yearly in money. Each of them, be he well or ill, shall take for allowance one dole of bread, one gallon of beer, one generous meal from the kitchen, and one mess of roast.

9. *Valets of the King's Chamber, 1323*

Life-Records of Chaucer, II, 19 (from MS Ashmole 1147, fol. 16).

There shall be eight valets of the chamber, that is, footmen, who shall make beds, hold and carry torches, and various other things which he and the chamberlain shall command them. These valets shall eat in the chamber before the king. Each of them, be he well or ill, shall have for his allowance one dole of bread, one gallon of beer, an ample meal from the kitchen, and yearly a robe in cloth or a mark in money; and for shoes, each shall have four shillings eight pence at two seasons in the year. If any of them be sent out of the court on the king's business, by his commandment, he shall have four pence a day for his expenses.

10. *A Special Grant to One of Richard II's Valets Transferred to a Squire, 1391*

Chancery Warrants (Privy Seal Writs) 520/6709.

Richard, by the grace of God, King of England and of France and Lord of Ireland. To the Honorable Father in God, the Bishop of Winchester, our Chancellor, greeting. As we formerly, by our especial favor and with the consent of our Council, had granted by our letters patent under our great seal to our beloved servant Henry Chaundeler, one of the valets of our chamber, for his good service ten marks to be taken each year from the income and profits of the fairs and markets of our city of Okeham at certain terms by equal portions for the whole life of the said Henry; and since, on the fourth day of May in the eleventh year of our reign, with the consent of our Council, at the request of the said

Henry and inasmuch as he had returned our said letters patent to be canceled in our Chancellery, we have granted to John de Overton, Esquire, the said ten marks to be taken each year from the income and profits of the fairs and markets aforesaid, at the terms of St. Michael and of Easter by equal portions for the entire life of the said John, as is stated more fully in our aforesaid letters. And by our abundant favor and with the consent of our Council, we have granted to the said John all the income and profits accruing from the fairs and markets aforesaid, to have and to hold all his life, which income and profits have been increased to twenty pounds a year, to which we have agreed. And we now, by our most abundant favor and with the consent of our Council, and since the aforesaid John has offered to return our said letters patent to our Chancellery, we have granted to the same John twenty pounds to be taken each year during his entire life from the income of the County of York,[17] at the hands of our viscount there who now is and for the time will be, at the terms of Easter and of St. Michael, by equal portions. We command that, having received before you our said letters patent made out to the said John as above and likewise our letters with their enrollment canceled in our Chancellery, you cause to be made for the said John, under this our former grant, other similar letters patent of ours under our great seal in due form. Given under our privy seal at Westminster, the eighth day of November, in the fourteenth year of our reign.

11. Wages of One of the King's Sergeants-at-Arms, 1392

Great Britain, Public Record Office, *Calendar of the Patent Rolls*, 1391–1396, p. 65.

May 19, Stamford. Grant for life upon good testimony concerning him, to Thomas Wodyfeld that he be one of the thirty sergeants-at-arms the King lately ordained at the Parliament at Westminster, receiving wages of 12*d.* a day at the Exchequer with a robe yearly at Christmas at the suit of esquires of the household, at the Great Wardrobe.

By p[rivy] s[eal].

12. Will of a Sergeant-at-Arms of the King, 1391

Exchequer King's Remembrancer, Memoranda Roll 169. Hil. Communia, 16 Ric. II.

Enrollment of the will of Thomas atte Melle, the King's Sergeant-at-Arms, dated November 8, 1391.

. . . I bequeath . . . my body to be buried in the chancel of the

[17] Contee deuerwyk.

church of All Hallows of Barking Church, London, next the door which goes towards the chapel of St. Nicholas in the said church. . . . To Sir Nicholas, vicar of the same church, to have my burial there, and so that he take the burden of the execution of my will, 20s. and my girdle barred with silver (*stipatam argenti*) which I was wont to use with a purse (bourse) barred with silver, and also the said purse hanging from the said girdle.

[Pious bequests]. I bequeath to the parishioners there one gilt cup of Paris work, whereof I have three others of the same suit, and 20s. to make a chalice to serve there perpetually to the honor of God and to have my soul for ever in memory. . . . For the maintenance of a lamp before the high cross in the body of the said church, 40d. To the light of the Blessed Mary in the chapel of the Blessed Mary in the churchyard there, 6s. 8d.

To the Abbot and Convent of Bygam my gown of red camlet, lined with red "atteby," to make a vestment and another silver-gilt cup of the said suit for a chalice to have my soul in memory. . . . [Pious bequests.]

I bequeath to Gilbert Maghfeld [18] my sword from Ireland, with a girdle barred with silver, with the letters of my name, and with a knife in "le Stauberk" to take upon him the administration of my will. . . . To Sir John atte Mille my best horse with the saddle and bridle, a habergeon, and a poleaxe. . . . To Tybote, my servant, 13s. 4d. . . . To Isabel, my servant, 40d. . . . To John, my clerk, a furred gown of the livery of the Earl of Salisbury, and my slop bicolored (*bipartitam*) with the scarlet, and 6s. 8d. . . . To John Yonge, my servant, a gown bicolored with white and green, with a hood, and 6s. 8d. To Humbelton, dwelling with the bishop of Salisbury, my two-handed sword. . . . To William Wykes, clerk with the bishop of Durham, my trenchant Bordeaux sword with a buckler. . . . To Hatton, the butler, with the bishop of Salisbury, a gown bicolored with blood and worstederay,[19] furred with foines, with a hood of the same suit. . . . To Thomas Fyshebourne, dwelling with the bishop of Durham, my best slop of silk and one "palet" [20] (head-piece) in a cap (*capicio*) of scarlet. . . . To John Orwell my lance, with a Bordeaux head, and a poleaxe with a case for the head thereof. . . . To Robert Bykerton my "launcegay." [21] Item, I bequeath

---

[18] See above, p. 112.   [19] That is, worsted ray, a striped woollen cloth.

[20] Probably "a piece of armor for the head . . . usually of leather." (*O.E.D.*)

[21] A light, slender lance—apparently of Arabian or Moorish origin. (Chaucer, *Canterbury Tales*, ed. by Manly, p. 631.)

to the shrine of St. Thomas of Canterbury my little silver mace. . . . To Thomas atte Mille, of Cokkyngescrouch, a gown with a hood of the livery of the lord bishop of Durham. . . . To Robert Kyngewode a gown with a hood of the last livery of the lord bishop of St. David. . . . To Robert Kyngewode a gown with a hood of the old livery of the same bishop. . . . To Walter Pette, chaplain of the Order of St. Lazar, 20s. and a habergeon and a poleaxe and "palet" to pray for my soul. . . .

[Residue is bequeathed to Agnes, his wife.]

[The will was proved before the official of the Archdeacon of London. 13 Kal. Jan. 16 Ric. II (1393).]

KNIGHTLY ADVENTURE

1. The Exploits of the Scrope Family, 1386

THE SCROPE-GROSVENOR CASE

The famous suit between Sir Richard le Scrope and Sir Robert Grosvenor concerning the right to use a certain coat-of-arms was an affair that involved hundreds of the most distinguished men of Chaucer's time and the poet himself. As it turned, not upon a question of right, but a point of honor, the hearings were held, not in a court of law, but in a court peculiarly medieval—the Court of Chivalry. Before this body, on October 15, 1386, in the refectory of Westminster Abbey, Chaucer testified what he knew, and in so doing gave us the clue to the date of his birth. In view of the fact that many of the other deponents were his associates and some of them his friends, it is interesting to read what they had to say. Their depositions, moreover, give glimpses of the customs and points of view of the knights of the time. Particularly to be noted are their allusions to fighting in Egypt, the Near-East, and Prussia, with mention of some of the very places named by Chaucer in connection with his Knight, such as Alexandria, Layas (Lyeys), Satalia (Satalye), Prussia (Pruce).

Of the deponents, Clifford, Clanvowe, Neville, and, perhaps, Bukton were well known to Chaucer, probably his friends. Waldegrave was the ancestor of a family one of whose members, in the sixteenth century, wrote his name in the Ellesmere MS of the Canterbury Tales. Among the others, Sabraham is interesting because he had been in so many of the campaigns touched upon by Chaucer, even beyond the "Grete See"; Rither, because he describes how he himself had put a stained glass window in the cathedral of Königsberg, to commemorate the Scrope buried there; and Aton, because he shows how coats-of-arms were used by gentlemen in their homes.

Other depositions, published by Sir Harris Nicolas in both the original French and in translation, are worth reading for their pictures of the times. [R.]

Scrope, De controversia . . . . inter Ricardum Le Scrope et Robertum Grosvenor, II, 377, 323-324, 353-354, 349-350.

(a) Sir Richard Waldegrave, aged forty-eight, armed twenty-five years, deposed that the arms Azure, a bend Or, belonged to the Scropes, who were reputed to be of ancient lineage, as he had heard, in the lifetime of the earl of Northampton. He saw Sir Richard so armed in the expedition of the late King before Paris, and at the same time Sir Henry Scrope with his banner, on which were the said arms with a white label. And also beyond the great sea he saw Sir William Scrope so armed, with a label, in the company of the Earl of Hereford at Satalia in Turkey, at a treaty which was concluded between the King of Cyprus and "le Takka," Lord of Satalia, when the King of Cyprus became Lord of Satalia. At Balyngham Hill the banner of Sir Henry was displayed; and in the expedition into Caux, when the Lord of Lancaster was commander-in-chief. Sir William Scrope, son of the said Sir Richard, was so armed, with a label. The deponent could not say which of the ancestors of Sir Richard first bore the arms, but since this dispute he had heard that his ancestors came direct from the Conquest; and, before this challenge, he had been informed that they were of ancient lineage; but he certainly never heard of any challenge or interruption offered by Sir Robert Grosvenor, or his ancestors, to the bearing of the arms in question.

(*b*) Nicholas Sabraham, Esquire, aged sixty and upwards, armed thirty-nine years, said that the arms Azure, a bend Or, were the arms of Sir Richard Scrope, for he had seen the arms of Scrope on banner and coat-armor in the expedition of Sir Edward Balliol in Scotland, also on a banner in the company of the Earl of Northampton, when he "chevachied" (rode) by torchlight out of Lochmaben as far as Peebles, and had in his company Sir Henry Scrope with his banner. The deponent also said that in the assemblage from all Christian countries at the instance of the King of Cyprus, when he meditated his expedition to Alexandria in ships and galleys, one Sir Stephen Scrope was present, armed in the arms of Scrope, Azure, a bend Or, with a label Argent for difference, and immediately on landing, received in those arms the order of knighthood from the King of Cyprus. He further said that he was armed in Prussia, in Hungary, at Constantinople, "a la bras" of Saint George,[22] and at Messembre, at which latter place there is a church, and therein lies one of the Scropes buried, and beneath him there are depicted on the wall the arms of Scrope, Azure, a bend Or, with a label, and on the three "bezants Gules": he knew them to be the arms of Scrope and to have borne that name, because the wardens of the said church told him so. The deponent saw Sir Henry Scrope armed in France with a banner

[22] Dardanelles.

in the company of the Earl of Northampton, and Sir William Scrope, elder brother of the said Sir Richard, in the same company, armed in the entire arms, or with differences, at the battle of Crécy, at the siege of Calais, in Normandy, in Brittany, in Gascony, and in Spain, and beyond the Great Sea [23] in many places and at many chivalrous exploits: in those places he never heard speak of Sir Robert Grosvenor or of any of his ancestors. He had often heard his ancestors say that the said Sir Richard and his ancestors had a right to the said arms, they having used them from beyond the time of memory, as he learnt from old men, lords, knights, and squires in his country, now no more. He never heard of Sir Robert Grosvenor or of his ancestors, and the only challenge he ever heard of as to the right to the said arms was the challenge of one Carminow, made to the said Sir Richard Scrope before Paris, when the arms were allowed by the King and the late Duke of Lancaster, and both were permitted to bear the arms entire.

(c) John de Rither . . . [deposed concerning] expeditions of the King. . . . Afterwards the noble King made his expedition before Paris: Sir Henry [Scrope] was there with his banner, and the present Sir Richard Scrope was there also, armed in the entire arms, in the company of the Earl of Richmond; Sir Geoffrey Scrope, being then armed in the same with a difference, in company of the late Lord of Lancaster. After that expedition peace was made, when Sir Geoffrey Scrope went, with other knights, into Prussia, and there, in an affair at the siege of Wellon in Lithuania, he died in these arms, and was buried in the Cathedral of Königsberg, where the said arms are painted in a glass window, which the deponent himself caused to be set up, taking the blazon from the arms which the deceased had upon him. Afterwards, when the Prince fought the battle of Najara,[24] in Spain, Sir Richard was so armed in that battle. And in the expedition of the Lord of Lancaster through France into Gascony, the said Sir Richard was so armed during the whole expedition, in company of the Lord of Lancaster, and previously at Balyngham Hill, and at the chevachie in Caux in Normandy. Rither added that he never heard that Sir Robert Grosvenor or any of his ancestors had challenged the arms; nor had he ever heard of Sir Robert Grosvenor or of any of his ancestors; but the only challenge he ever heard of was by one Carminow of Cornwall, who challenged the said Sir Richard when before Paris; and the late King and the Lord of Lancaster agreed that the said

---

[23] Mediterranean Sea.　　　　　　　　[24] Cf. below, pp. 325–329.

Sir Richard should bear the arms entire and that the said Carminow should bear them also; of no other challenge had he ever heard.

(*d*) Sir William Aton, aged eighty-seven, armed sixty-six years, deposed that in his time Sir Henry Scrope, father to the present Sir Richard Scrope, descended of noble and gentle ancestry, was, by consent of his parents, put to the law, and became the King's Justice; but, nevertheless, used in his halls, on his beds, in windows, and on plate, the arms Azure, a bend Or; that the said Sir Henry used these arms as his own, as his father had borne them before him, in tournaments and in other places, as the fashion then was; for he, the deponent, had heard his father and his uncles and ancestors say that the father of Sir Henry Scrope, the Justice, and of Sir Geoffrey Scrope, brother of the said Sir Henry Scrope, and also the King's Justice, was named Sir William Scrope, and that he was in his time the ablest tourneyer of all their country, and always tourneyed in the arms Azure, a bend Or, and had been a good squire and a good servant in arms while a squire, and a good jouster. And, moreover, that he had seen the said Sir Geoffrey Scrope, the brother, who was knighted at the tournament of Northampton in the time of King Edward the Second; which Geoffrey was, in his day, a noble knight and tourneyed at that tournament in the same arms with a white label, performing right nobly, and with his banner, and under his banner other knights, whose names the deponent did not recollect, tourneyed also. And after that reign the late King Edward the Third commenced his wars in Scotland; and there the said Sir Geoffrey was armed with his banner: after which began the wars in France, when the said Sir Geoffrey was in the expedition of the King to Burenfos, and from Burenfos the King went to the siege of Tournay, and there Sir Geoffrey was armed in the retinue of the King, in the said arms with a white label. Sir William Aton added that wherever he had been armed, he always saw one or two of the Scropes bearing the arms in question; that since he had ceased to bear arms, he had always heard that they continued to enjoy them peaceably and with great honor; and that he had heard from his ancestors that the Scropes and their arms came over with Robert de Gant at the Conquest.[25]

[25] See also below, pp. 369–370.

2. *Trial by Combat*

THOMAS, DUKE OF GLOUCESTER, CONSTABLE UNDER RICHARD II, CONCERNING THE MANNER OF CONDUCTING JUDICIAL DUELS, TIME OF RICHARD II

Dillon, "On a MS Collection of Ordinances of Chivalry of the Fifteenth Century, Belonging to Lord Hastings," *Archaeologia*, LVII (1900), 62–66.

In the first place, the quarrels and the bills of the appellant and of the defendant shall be posted in the court before the constable and the marshal. And when they may not prove their cause by witnesses or by any other manner, but must determine their quarrel by strength, the one to prove his intent upon the other and the other in the same manner to defend himself, the constable has power to join the battle as vicar general under God and the king. The battle conjoined by the constable, he shall assign them a day and place, so that the day be not within forty days after the said battle so conjoined, unless it be by the consenting of the said appellant and defendant. Then he shall award them points of arms otherwise called weapons. Either of them shall have, that is to say, long sword, short sword, and dagger. The appellant and the defendant must find sufficient surety and pledges that each of them shall come at his said day. And that this may be done, there shall be given unto the appellant hour, term and so on, to make his prove and dare,[26] and for him to be the first within the lists to quit his pledges.[27] And of the same wise, the defendant. . . .

The king shall find the field to fight in. And the lists shall be made and devised by the constable. It is to be considered that the lists shall be forty paces of length and forty paces of breadth in good manner, and that the earth be firm, stable, and hard, and evenly made without great stones, and that it be flat. And that the lists be strongly barred round about and a gate in the east and another in the west with good and strong barriers of seven foot of height or more. . . .

The day of the battle the king shall be in a raised chair or scaffold and a place shall be made for the constable and marshal at the stair foot of the scaffold. Then shall be asked the pledges of the appellant and defendant to come as prisoners into the lists before the king and those present in the court until the appellant and the defendant have come

[26] That is, to prove his innocence by making good his challenge.
[27] To fulfill his promises.

in the lists and have made their oaths. The appellant shall come to the east gate of the lists in such manner as he will fight, with his arms and weapons assigned to him by the court, and there he shall abide till he be led in by the constable and the marshal. And the constable shall ask him what man he is which is come armed to the gate of the lists and what name he has and for what cause he is come. The appellant shall answer: "I am such a man—A. de K.—the appellant, which is come to this tourney, etc, to do, etc." And then the constable shall open the visor of his basinet so that he may plainly see his visage and if it be the same man that is the appellant. Then shall he open the gates of the lists and make him enter with his said arms, points,[28] victuals, and lawful necessaries upon him and also his council with him; he shall lead him before the king and then to his tent, where he shall abide till the defendant be come.

In the same manner shall be done for the defendant, but that he shall enter in at the west gate of the lists. The constable's clerk shall write and set in the register all these things. . . . Also the constable shall take heed that no other before or behind the appellant or the defendant bring more weapons or victuals than were assigned by the court.

And if it be that the defendant come not on time to his tourney and at the hour and term limited by the court, the constable shall command the marshal to have him called at the four corners of the lists, which shall be done in manner as follows: "Oyez, Oyez, Oyez. C. de B., defendant, come to your tourney which ye have undertaken at this day to acquit [29] your pledges before the king, the constable and marshal in your defense against A. de K., appellant, of that that he has put upon you." And if he come not betimes, he shall be called the second time in the same manner, and at the end he shall say: "Come, the day passes fast"; and if he come not at that time, he shall be called the third time, unless this be between high tierce and noon. . . . But although the constable hath given hour and term unto the defendant to come to his tourney, nevertheless, if that he tarry unto the hour of noon, the judgment should not by right go against him whether it be in case of treason or not. But so is it not of the appellant, for he must hold the hour and term limited by the court without any evasions (*prolonginge*) or excuses whatsoever if it be in case of treason.

The appellant and the defendant being entered into the lists . . . they shall be searched by the constable and marshal of their points of

---

[28] See below, pp. 153 and 154.   [29] That is, to fulfill.

arms that they be genuine (*vowable*) without any manner of deceit on them, and if they be other than reason asks, they shall be taken away, because reason, good faith, and law of arms will suffer neither guile nor deceit in so great a deed. And it is, to wit, that the appellant and the defendant may be armed as much upon their bodies as they will. Then the constable shall send first after the marshal and then for the appellant with his council to make his oath. The constable shall ask him if he will any more protest and that he put forth all his protestations by writing, for from that time forth he shall make none. The constable shall have his clerk ready in his presence that shall lay forth a mass book, open. And the constable shall make his said clerk read out the bill of the appellant. Then the constable shall say to the appellant: "A. de K., thou knowest well this bill and this warrant and pledge that thou gavest in our court. Thou shalt lay thy right hand here upon these saints and shalt swear in manner as follows. Thou, A. de K., this thy bill, is sooth in all points and articles from the beginning continuing therein to the end and that is thine intent to prove this day on the aforesaid C. de B., so God thee help, and these saints." This oath made, he shall be led again to his place. The constable shall make the marshal call the defendant and so shall be done to him in the same manner as to the appellant.

Then the constable shall have the appellant called again and shall make him lay his hand as he did before upon the mass book and shall say: "A. de K., thou swearest that thou neither hast nor shalt have more points or any points on thee or on thy body within these lists, but they that be assigned by the court; that is to say, a long sword, short sword, and dagger, nor any other knife little or big, nor any other instrument or engine of point or otherwise, nor stone of virtue, nor herb of virtue, nor charm, nor experiment,[30] 'nor caract,'[31] nor any other enchantment by thee or for thee by which thou trustest the better to overcome C. de B., thine adversary. . . . Nor that thou trustest in any other thing, but only in God and thy body and on thy rightful quarrel, help thee God and these saints." The oath made, he shall be led again to his place. In the same wise shall be done to the defendant.

These oaths made and their chamberlains and servants put away, the constable shall have called by the marshal the appellant and the defendant also, who shall be led and kept by the men of the constable and the marshal before them. And the constable shall say to both the parties: "Thou, A. de K., appellor, shall take C. de B., defender, by the right

[30] Cf. below, p. 161.   [31] A magical character or symbol; a charm. (Cf. *O.E.D.*)

hand, and he thee. And we forbid you and each of you in the king's name and upon the peril that belongeth thereto and upon the peril of losing your quarrel, whichever one is found in default, that neither of you be so hardy as to do to the other, ill or grievance, thrusting or other harm by the hand, upon the peril aforesaid." This charge given, the constable shall make them place their right hands together and their left hands upon the missal, saying to the appellor: "A. de K., appellor, thou swearest by the faith that thou givest in the hand of thine adversary, C. de B., defender, and by all the saints that thou touchest with thy left hand, that thou this day shall do all thy true power and intent by all the ways that thou best mayst or canst to prove thine intent on C. de B., thine adversary and defender, to make him yield himself up to thine hand vanquished, to cry, or speak, or else to make him die by thine hand before thou wend out of these lists by the time and the sun that thee is assigned by this court, by thy faith, and so help thee God and these saints. C. de B., defender, thou swearest by thy faith that thou givest in the hand of thine adversary, A. de K., appellor, and by all the saints that thou touchest with thy left hand, that today thou shalt do all thy true power and intent by all the ways that thou best mayst or canst to defend thine intent of all that that is put on thee by A. de K., thine adversary, by thy faith, and so help thee God and all these saints."

And then the constable shall command the marshal to cry at the four corners of the lists in manner as follows: "Oyez, Oyez, Oyez. We charge and command by the king's constable and marshal that none of great value and of little estate, of what condition or nation that he be, be so hardy henceforward to come nigh the lists by four feet or to speak or to cry or to make countenance or token or semblance or noise whereby either of these two parties, A. de K., appellor, and C. de B., defender, may take advantage the one upon the other, upon peril of losing life and limb and their goods at the king's will."

And afterward the constable and the marshal shall turn all manner of people out of the lists except their lieutenants and two knights for the constable and marshal which shall be armed upon their bodies, but they shall have neither knife nor sword upon them nor any other weapons whereby the appellant or the defendant may have advantage because of negligence in keeping them. But the two lieutenants shall have in their hands each a spear without iron to separate them if the king will make them leave off in their fighting, whether it be to rest them or other thing whatsoever pleases him. And it is to be known that if any administration should be made to the appellant or to the defendant, of meat or of drink or any other necessary lawful thing after the counsel of friends and servants have been dismissed, the said administration appertains to the heralds and also to all the cries made in the said court; which king's heralds and followers shall have a place for them assigned by the constable and marshal as nigh the lists as may be, so that they may see all the deed and be ready if they be called for, to do anything. The appellant in his place [is] kept by some men assigned by the constable or the marshal, and the defendant in his place, in the same wise, both made ready and arrayed and with fellowship by their keepers abovesaid, the marshal with the one party, and the lieutenant of the constable with the other.

The constable sitting in his place before the king as his vicar general, and the parties made ready to fight as is said by the commandment of the king, the constable shall say with loud voice as follows: "Lessiez les aler"; that is to say, "Let them go and rest a while"; "Lessiez les aler, and rest another while; Lessiez les aler et fair leur devoir de par dieu"; that is to say, "Let them go and do their duty in God's name." And this said, each man shall depart from both parties, so that they may encounter and do that which seems best to them.

Neither the appellant nor the defendant may eat or drink from that time forth without leave and license of the king, for anything that might befall, unless they will do it by consenting between them. From this time forth it is to be considered diligently by the constable whether the king will make the parties fighting depart, rest, or abide, for any cause whatsoever; that he take good care how they are separated, so that they be in the same estate and degree in all things; if the king will sure [32] or make them go together again, and also that he have good harkening and sight unto them if either speak to other, be it of yielding or otherwise; for unto him belongs the witness and the record of the words from that time forth, and to no other.

And if the said battle [be] of treason, he that is convicted and discomfited shall be disarmed in the lists by the commandment of the constable, and a corner of the lists be broken for the reprove of him, by which he shall be drawn out with horses from the same place where he is so disarmed, through the lists unto the place of justice, where he shall be beheaded or hanged after the usage of the country. Which thing appertains to the marshal and to oversee and to perform his said office and

---

[32] To give assurance or promise to [a person]. (*O.E.D.*)

to put him in execution and to go or ride and to be always with him till it be done and all performed and as well of the appellant as of the defendant; for the good faith and right and law of arms will that the appellant suffer the same penalty that the defendant should if he were convicted and discomfited. And if it happen that the king would take the quarrel in his hands and make them agree without more fighting, then the constable, taking the one party, and the marshal, the other, shall lead them before the king, and he showing them his will, the constable and marshal shall lead them to the one side of the lists with all their weapons and armor as they are found and have on when the king took the quarrel in his hands. And so they shall be led out of the gate of the lists equally, so that the one go not before the other in any way nor in any thing; for since the [king] has taken the quarrel in his hands, it should be dishonest that either of the parties should have more dishonor than the other. . . . The fee of the heralds is all the weapons and armor broken, those that have been forfeited or left behind in the lists, as well of the appellant as of the defendant, and all the weapons and armor of him that is discomfited, be it the appellant or the defendant. The fee of the marshal is the lists, the barriers, and the posts of them.

TO ARM A MAN, 15TH CENTURY

Dillon, "On a MS Collection of Ordinances of Chivalry of the Fifteenth Century, Belonging to Lord Hastings," *Archaeologia*, LVII (1900), 43–44.

First ye must set on sabbatons and tie them upon the shoes with small laces so that they will bend; and then greaves; and then cuisses; and then the breech of mail; and then the tonlets; [33] then the breastplate; then the vambraces; then the rerebraces; then the gloves. Then hang his dagger upon his side; then his short sword on the left side in a round ring, all naked to pull it out lightly. Then put his coat upon his back, and then his basinet pinned upon two great staples before the breastplate, with a double buckle behind upon the back, in order to make the helmet sit correctly; and then his long sword in his hand; then his pennant in his hand, painted with Saint George or with Our Lady, to bless him as he goes towards the field and in the field.

[33] Strips of metal to protect the lumbar regions. [Viscount Dillon's note.]

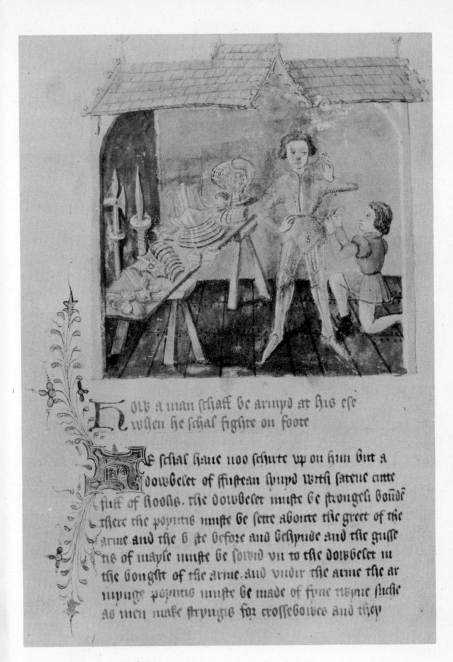

A KNIGHT BEING ARMED FOR COMBAT ON FOOT
Second half of the fifteenth century
New York, Morgan Library, MS 775, fol. 122v

A HERALD; late fourteenth century
Brussels, Bibl. Roy., MS 15652, fol. 122

Dillon, "On a MS Collection of Ordinances of Chivalry of the Fifteenth Century,
Belonging to Lord Hastings," *Archaeologia*, LVII (1900), 43.

He shall have no shirt upon him, but a doublet of fustian lined with
satin, cut full of holes. The doublet must be strongly laced where the
points are set about the great (*greet*) [34] of the arm, and the best (*b ste*)
before and behind, and the gussets of mail must be sewed to the doublet at
the bend of the arm and under the arm. The arming points must be made
of fine twine such as men use to make strings for crossbows, and they must
be tied small and pointed as points. They must be waxed with shoe-
maker's wax, and then they will neither stretch nor break. He shall have
a pair of hose of worsted cloth,[35] and a pair of short pads of thin blanket
to put about his knees to prevent chafing of his leg harness; also a pair of
shoes of thick leather, and they must be fastened with small whipcord,
three knots upon a cord, and three cords must be fast sewed to the [heel]
of the shoe, and fine cords in the middle of the sole of the same shoe,
and there must be between the cords of the heel and those of the middle
of the shoe the space of three fingers.

THE DAY THAT THE APPELLANT AND THE DEFENDANT SHALL FIGHT,
WHAT THEY SHALL HAVE WITH THEM INTO THE FIELD, 15TH CEN-
TURY

Dillon, "On a MS Collection of Ordinances of Chivalry of the Fifteenth Century,
Belonging to Lord Hastings," *Archaeologia*, LVII (1900), 44.

A tent must be pitched in the field,
Also a chair,
Also a basin,
Also six loaves of bread,
Also two gallons of wine,
Also a mess of meat flesh or fish,
Also a board and a pair of trestles on which to set his meat and his drink,
Also a board cloth,
Also a knife to cut his meat,
Also a cup from which to drink,
Also a glass with a drink made,

[34] The chief part. [*O.E.D.*]
[35] "Stamyn sengill," a type of worsted cloth made in Norfolk. [Viscount Dillon's note.]

Also a dozen clasps of arming points,
Also a hammer, pincers, and a bycorne,[36]
Also a dozen small nails,
Also a long sword, and a short, and a dagger,
Also a kerchief to cover the visor of his helmet,
Also a pennant of his cognizance to bear in his hand.

THROWING DOWN THE GAUNTLET, 1388

Sir Nicholas Brembre was a merchant prince, a member of the Grocers' Company of London, and several times lord mayor. As one of the collectors of the wool customs in the port of London, he was closely associated with Chaucer for ten years while the latter was controller of the customs on wool and hides at the same port. He was one of the five councillors who were charged with treason by the lords appellant on November 14, 1387, and were impeached on February 3, 1388. A special charge was brought against Brembre, that he had taken twenty-two prisoners from Newgate and beheaded them without a trial. His claim to the right of trial by battle on the ground that he was a knight was refused, and he was hanged.

Favent, *Historia . . . . mirabilis parliamenti*, p. 16.

And when . . . the said Nicholas Brembre appeared, certain articles having been read before him, he asked to have a copy and counsel and a day, so that he might the better deliberate how to answer, and . . . he was strictly enjoined to answer the charges. For he chose to answer: "Here present do I bear witness that I will do battle within the lists, [that] whatsoever has been charged against me, those things are false."

And this Brembre said, fearing to be executed after the manner of traitors, and he preferred thus to be slain fighting, rather than ignominiously by judgment of Parliament.

Immediately the appellants, with puffed-up countenance, said: "And we offer ourselves and bear witness that we will do battle with thee within the lists to prove that the same things are true," throwing their gloves at the King's feet; but at the same moment there showered down everywhere like snow the gloves of other lords, knights, esquires, and commoners, crying out: "And we take in hand the duel for proving on thy head that what has been said is true."

[36] An anvil with two projecting taper ends. (*O.E.D.*) The various items enumerated were to be used in repairing the armor.

LAW AND GOVERNMENT

1. The Legal Profession

HOW TO BE A SUCCESSFUL LAWYER, CA. 1376–1379

Gower, "Mirour de l'omme," ll. 24,349–24,396.

It is the custom at Westminster
That whoso would learn the trade
Of the law, for this purpose needs
Some money, in order to mount up high.
It is a situation to prize:
According to this practice
On money he will grow wise;
If he makes a start with money,
Later on he will know how to use it
To his own advantage and the harm of others:
By means of money his heart
Is turned to the love of money.
The apprentices in their degree
Taste blood from the beginning,
In pleading at the assizes;
Like dogs they seize as their prey
The silver that is given them,
So that always for the penny
They can run well without check;
I do not say without fault,
For wrong that gives a rich fee
Takes from them the scent of the straight course,
So that they often lose track
And run far from charity.
And then after the apprentice
A certain time has fulfilled
What is sufficient for pleading,
He wishes to have the coif placed
Upon his head, and to his own honor
Wishes to bear the name of sergeant.
But if before this time
In one thing he was greedy,
Now is he a thousand times inflamed;

For he becomes so ravenous
That part is not enough for him:
He must devour the whole country.
But they have also a custom
That the apprentice who is so advanced
To the estate of sergeanty
Must make a donation
Of gold, which is not without meaning;
For the gold that he gives means
That all the rest of his life after
He must be getting it back.
But this will be a great return,
That for giving a single time,
He takes all the bread, by no means holding
The scales in equal balance.

THE MAKING OF A SERGEANT-OF-LAW, 1521

As customs in the inns of court have changed very slowly, it is probable that the
making of a sergeant-of-law in Chaucer's time differed very little from the ceremonies described in the following account from the Inner Temple Records for the
year 1521. [R.]

Inner Temple, London, *A Calendar of the Inner Temple Records*, I, 62–63.

Whereas the King lately directed four writs to four members of the
society, namely, William Rudhale, John Poorte, Baldwin Malett, and
William Shelley, that they in the octaves of St. John should receive the
estate and rank of sergeants-at-law, which same William Rudhale, John
Poorte, and William Shelley, on Friday the 28th June, after vespers,
bade farewell to the society in the manner following. First, all of the
society who were in the city being warned and being assembled in the
hall, the seniors in the upper part and the juniors in the lower, two elder
barristers were sent for the eldest sergeant, to show him that the members would expect his coming and to accompany him into the hall; and
so another two for another sergeant; and so for each of them. Which
being done, and they being come and standing in the chief place of the
society, almost in the middle of the hall on one side, according to their
seniority, the sergeant, being the eldest member, began to deliver to
the society a goodly exhortation, to observe the ordinances and rules
there before used, as well concerning study as other things, admonishing
the younger members to obey their superiors, showing that by so doing
he had come to the rank of a sergeant, declaring to the society his good

will and offering them his service as well with his heart and his mouth, and by his deeds. And having said these words, the second sergeant began his exhortation, and so the third. Which being said, the member who was first in seniority and dignity returned thanks to them in the name of the whole society for their good exhortations and for their teachings now past, beseeching them that although they might be absent in body, nevertheless, they would not be so in spirit and will, and assuring them with humility of the services of the society. Which being said, those three sergeants proceeded to the door of the buttery, where the treasurer delivered to them in the name of the society ten pounds in three pairs of gloves provided for the purpose, namely, to each of them five marks. And if there had been four, they would not have had more, and if only two they would not have had less.[37] And Baldwin Malett, after the delivery of the writ, by the special endeavors of his friends, was discharged, before the rest were sworn, to wit, in Hilary term last.[38]

Then those three sergeants proceeded to the house of the bishop of Ely in Holborn, the society following, from the seniors to the juniors to the number of almost a hundred and sixty, and so they came to a certain parlor on the north side of the hall, where the rest of the sergeants of the other inns had assembled [seven more]. And after all the sergeants had come into the hall there, and sat at the chief table, and the elders of the Inns with them, they had spices and many comfits with wine of every sort. And on Saturday they remained there, and on Sunday the chief justice gave them a goodly exhortation in the great chamber at the end of the hall, and he told them their suits [39] before delivered by the chief prothonotaries.

A CHIEF JUSTICE WHO WORE CHARMS, 1388

Sir Robert Tresilian, the chief justice, was in hiding because he had been convicted of treason. He seems to have returned to London in order to follow the trial of Nicholas Brembre, also accused of treason.[40]

Favent, *Historia . . . . mirabilis parliamenti*, pp. 17–18.

The wretched Tresilian was discovered above the gutter of a certain house next the palace wall [at Westminster] lurking among the tiles to watch the people coming and going to Parliament. And when certain esquires entered the house and, looking about, found no one, one esquire, ad-

---

[37] Because the collection was made by fixed assessment upon each member of the inn.

[38] Just how he got off does not appear, but other records show that he continued to live at the Inn for many years and was one of the governors from 1524 to 1532.

[39] Assigned them their first cases.   [40] See above, p. 158, and below, p. 260.

vancing threateningly upon the master of the house, throttled him by
the hood, with dagger drawn, and said: "Show us where Tresilian is
hid, or your days are short." At once, the trembling man said, "Lo, this
is the place where he always is." And, strange to say, the unhappy
Tresilian was revealed under a round table which for his sake was covered
at that time with cloths. His tunic (*collobium*) of old russet reached to
mid-shin, like an old man's; he had a thick, stiff beard; and was clad in
red hose with Joseph's shoes, so that he resembled rather a pilgrim or
beggar than the King's chief justice. Straightway this came to the hearing
of the lords, and as soon as they heard it, the five appellants hurried from
Parliament without saying why they withdrew. All their adherents in
Parliament were amazed, and many followed them in alarm; and when
they had arrested Tresilian at the gate of the Palace, bringing him to
Parliament, they cried out loud, "We have him! We have him!" . . .

At length Tresilian was bound hand and foot to a hurdle (*cratem*) and,
with an innumerable crowd of lords and commoners, as well on horseback as on foot, was drawn behind horses through the city, resting at
times throughout the length of the journey, out of charity, in case he
should repent. But, alas, he made no public confession; yet what he said
to his friar confessor is unknown, nor is it for us to inquire. . . . And
when he came to the gallows to be executed, he would not climb the ladder; but he was encouraged to climb by blows from fists and whips, and
he said: "So long as I wear certain things about me, I cannot die." Immediately they stripped him and found certain charms (*experimenta*) [41]
and certain signs painted upon them, after the fashion of signs of the
Zodiac, and one demon's head painted, and many names of demons were
written. These were taken away, and he was hanged naked, and to be
more sure of his death, they cut his throat. And night fell, and he hung
until the morrow; and, leave having been begged and obtained by his
wife from the King, he was carried to the Friars Minor and there buried.

A COURT-CRIER SEIZED BY OFFICERS OF A STAPLE, 1395

Coram Rege Roll 538, m. 35 d.

Edmund Hikelyng, "criour," sues William Baddele and wife Maud,
John Olney, and William Knyghtbrugge for assault and imprisonment
at Westminster, attacking him with a stick and imprisoning him for
one hour on Wednesday before St. Martin,[42] 19 Richard II.

Baddele says Mark Faire of Winchester was prosecuting a bill of debt

[41] Cf. above, p. 153.   [42] The Feast of St. Martin is November 11.

for 18s. against Edmund and John More before William Brampton, mayor of the staple of Westminster, and Thomas Alby and William Askham, constables of the said staple, and on that day the Mayor and the constables issued a writ of *capias* against Edmund and John to answer Mark and be before the Mayor and the constables at the next court. This writ was delivered to Baddele as sergeant of the staple, and by virtue of it he took and imprisoned Edmund in the staple. Maud and the others say they aided Baddele by virtue of the said writ.

Edmund does not acknowledge Baddele to be sergeant of the staple or Mark a merchant of the staple or that he was taken in the staple. He is minister of the King's Court of his Bench and is crier (*proclamator*) under Thomas Thorne, the chief crier, his master. Every servant of the court is under special protection while doing his duty or on his way to do it. On the day in question, he was at Westminster carrying his master's staff of office before Hugh Huls, one of the King's justices, and William took him in the presence of the said justice and imprisoned him.

The case is adjourned for consideration from Hilary to Easter.

2. *Attending Parliament*

THE GOOD PARLIAMENT, 1376

The following account of the famous Parliament of 1376, in which the Commons accused members of the King's immediate circle of graft and misgovernment, is taken from the *Anonimalle Chronicle*, written at St. Mary's Abbey, York; it is clearly the work either of an eyewitness of the proceedings or of one who got his information at first-hand. It is interesting not merely for its detailed narrative of what happened but also for its picture of parliamentary procedure, the earliest description known. [R.]

The *Anonimalle Chronicle, 1333–1381*, ed. by Galbraith, pp. 79–90.

In the year 1376 King Edward III held his Parliament in London, which was the longest Parliament ever held; for it began Monday [of] the third week after Easter [43] and lasted until the Translation of St. Benedict [July 11], that is, for ten whole weeks. In this Parliament were assembled the King of England; the Prince of Wales; Sir John of Gaunt, Duke of Lancaster; Sir Edmund de Langley, Earl of Cambridge; Sir Thomas of Woodstock, Earl of Buckingham [the King's four sons]; two archbishops; fourteen bishops; many abbots and priors; the earls of March, Arundel, Salisbury, Warwick, Suffolk, and Stafford; all the barons and bannerets of importance in the land; two hundred and eighty knights and

[43] On April 28, 1376.

squires; and citizens and burgesses of the commonalty in divers cities, boroughs, and counties.

On the aforesaid Monday at the beginning of the Parliament, in the presence of our lord the King and the Lords and Commons, were pronounced the points and articles usual in Parliament by Sir John Knyvet, Chancellor of England, among which, how the realm of England was in danger and on the point of being destroyed by its enemies in France, Spain, Gascony, Flanders, Scotland, and other nations, by land and by sea. Wherefore Sir John asked on the King's behalf aid and succor against his enemies, and that they would kindly grant a tenth from the clergy and a fifteenth from the laity, and the custom from wool and other merchandise for a year or two, to maintain the war.

And on this the Lords and Commons deliberated concerning their response, as the law requires. And at the same time at the end of his speech, Sir John Knyvet, the Chancellor, commanded, on the King's behalf, the knights and burgesses and commons of the shires, on their allegiance and under pain of forfeiture, that if there was anything to redress or amend within the realm or if the realm was badly ruled and governed or treacherously counseled, by their good advice they would find remedy, in so far as they could, how the realm might be more profitably governed to the honor of the King and its own profit. And so ended the first day. And the King went to his chamber, and the other Lords and the Commons to their homes.

And the second day after, the archbishops and bishops and earls and barons assembled and took their places to treat and deliberate in the White Chamber within the King's palace. And to the knights and Commons was assigned the chapter house of Westminster Abbey, where they could deliberate secretly without being disturbed or bothered by other people. And on this second day all the knights and Commons assembled in the chapter house and took their seats in a circle, each beside another; and they began to talk of the business of the points raised in Parliament and said it was well to be sworn, one to another, to keep secret that which was discussed and agreed among them and to treat and ordain loyally for the profit of the realm, without concealment. To do these things they agreed unanimously, and they took oath to be loyal to one another. Then one of them said, "If any of us has anything to say for the advantage of the King or country, it would be well for him to tell what he knows among us, and after each in turn to show what is on his mind."

Then a south country knight rose and went to the lectern in the middle of the chapter house, so that all could hear, and leaning on the lectern, he began to speak as follows:

"*Jube domine benedicere, et cet.* [Lord, bid thy blessing, etc.] Gentlemen, you have heard the points raised in Parliament, how disturbing they are, how our lord the King has asked of the clergy and the Commons a tenth and a fifteenth and the custom on wool and other merchandise for a year or two; and it seems to me that this is a lot to grant, for the Commons are so weakened and impoverished by various tallages and taxes paid heretofore that they cannot bear such a charge at this time, and on the other hand all that we have granted for war we have for a long time lost because it has been wasted by mismanagement and spent dishonestly. Therefore it might be well to consider how our lord King could live and govern his kingdom and maintain the war with his own proper demesnes and without demanding money from his loyal countrymen. As I have heard, there are people who have the wealth and treasure of the King amounting to a great sum of gold and silver, in their hands, without his knowledge and have dishonestly concealed this money and have wickedly and extortionately acquired it to the great injury of the King and country. For the present I shall say no more. *Tu autem domine miserere nostris* [May the Lord have mercy on us!]"—and so went back to his seat among his companions.

Immediately another knight rose and went to the lectern and said: "Gentlemen, our companion has spoken profitably, and I shall tell you another thing for the advantage of the country, so God help me! You have heard how it was decreed by common assent in Parliament that the staple for wool and other merchandise should be only at Calais, to the great advantage of our lord King; for this town has been governed and ruled by English merchants, and they take no recompense for soldiers to continue the war or for the government of the town. Afterward, the staple was suddenly removed to divers cities and towns in England, and the merchants, with their wives and families, were ousted from Calais, without the knowledge or assent of Parliament, for the special profit, contrary to law and statute, made of this, so the Lord Latimer and Richard Lyons of London and others might have their advantages and might raise large sums of evil tax (*male tolle*) by concealing what the King has the right to; for the King spends every year in safeguarding this town as much as eight thousand pounds of gold and silver without any return, where before this time there was no need to spend anything. Wherefore it would be a good idea to find a means by which the staple can be restored to Calais." Without saying more, he went back to his place.

A third rose and went to the lectern and said: "Gentlemen, our companions have spoken well and profitably, and it seems to me that we should not undertake to treat of such great problems and of matters so important for the welfare of the realm without the counsel and aid of the greatest and the wisest; nor would it be advantageous or honorable for us to begin such a process without the assent of the Lords; wherefore it would be well to begin by asking our lord King and his wise council in Parliament to allow and assign to us certain bishops and certain earls and barons and bannerets such as we shall name, to aid and counsel us and to hear and witness what we say."

To this all agreed; and in the same manner two or three others arose in turn and spoke on various motions and points, as will be plain from what follows. And when the speeches were ended and they were seated among their companions, they deliberated how to proceed most successfully in the matter.

Thereupon a knight of the Welsh border, the seneschal of the Earl of March, named Sir Peter de la Mare, began to speak where the others had spoken, and said: "Gentlemen, you have heard the speeches and opinions of our companions and what they think it best to do, and it seems to me they have spoken loyally and wisely." Then he repeated, word for word, all the points they had made, correctly and in good form. Further, he advised them on divers points and articles as will appear more fully in the issue; and so ended the second day.

> Then follows a summary of proceedings in which De la Mare spoke so well and showed himself so much better informed than the others that they asked him to take charge and to express their will in the "great Parliament" before the Lords.[44]

On Friday [May 9], when they were all assembled, the King sent a messenger, Sir Raynalde Bukkeshill, praying them on the King's behalf that they consider his estate; for he was impatient for them to grant the petition and request that he had made the first day of the Parliament so that Parliament might adjourn [45] as soon as possible, for he himself wished to be taking his pleasure elsewhere.

Then it was arranged among them that they should go together in a

[44] This is the first allusion to a speaker of the Commons; in the Parliament the term *vaunt parlour*, i.e., forespeaker, is used for the first time. Cf. the *Parlement of Foules*, ll. 519–525. [R.]

[45] Literally, "be delivered"; cf. the *Parlement of Foules*, ll. 491–495. [R.]

body before the Lords, and what Sir Peter should say, with their assent; this they would all agree to and would support his words. And on that same Friday the Commons tried to enter Parliament and came to the Parliament room. Part of them got in, but the others were pushed back and shut out and went where they would. When Sir Peter and some of his companions had entered and saw that their fellows could not get in, they marvelled greatly at this affair.

Then the Duke of Lancaster, at that time lieutenant of the King and holding Parliament in his absence, and lieutenant of the Prince [of Wales, who was mortally ill], very ill at ease, began to say: "Which of you is the spokesman for that which has been agreed upon among you?"

Sir Peter answered that by common assent he had the right to speak on that day, and the Duke added, "Say what you will."

"Sir," said he, "gladly. Gentlemen, you know and understand that all the Commons who are here have come by the writ of our lord King and by the appointment of the sheriffs of the various counties, and that what one of us says, all say and agree to. Wherefore, first of all, I demand the reason why some are kept outside; and for certain, I shall move no matter until they are all present."

Then the Duke of Lancaster said, "Sir Peter, there is no need of so many of the Commons coming in to give a reply, but two or three at a time are enough, as has been the custom heretofore."

But Sir Peter answered briefly that he would not speak a word until they were all assembled.

So at last the Duke gave orders to go and find out what had become of them; and they were sought in various places for fully two hours before they could all be found and had entered among their companions. And when they were all there, Sir Peter began to say what had been talked of and agreed among them, as follows: "Gentlemen, if you please, you have heard the charge which we have from our lord the King, on our allegiance to treat and ordain concerning his estate and that of the realm, and to redress and amend the defects in so far as in us lies. We have found many defects and grievous matters which it would be to the advantage of King and country to have amended, and we are so simple of wit and of wealth that we cannot redress such great matters without the advice of wise folk. Wherefore we ask you, for the welfare of the realm, that you will grant and associate with us four bishops, four earls, four barons and bannerets, to hear and witness that which we say."

After discussing this, the lords agreed that it was reasonable and advantageous. So the Duke asked Sir Peter, "Whom do you ask for?"

"Sir," he replied, "the bishops of London and Norwich, of Carlisle and Bath; the Earls of March, Warwick, Suffolk, and Stafford; of barons and bannerets, Lord Percy, Sir Roger Beauchamp, Sir Guy de Brian, and Sir Richard de Stafford. And when they have heard and understood our plan, we shall show you our purpose and decision, and this day we shall say no more."

So they took leave of the Lords, commending them to God

> At a meeting with the representatives of the Lords, the Commons explained their course of action, which was approved. They then returned to Parliament.

And when they were all settled and there was no noise, the Duke of Lancaster asked, "Who is to speak?"

And Sir Peter answered [that he was the speaker and summarized the situation, concluding], ". . . we say that if he [the King] had been well governed by his ministers and had spent his money wisely and without waste, there would be no need of such a levy; but he has with him certain counselors and servants who are not loyal or useful to him or the realm, and they have taken advantage by their cleverness in deceiving our lord the King."

At this the Duke of Lancaster wondered and said, "How is this, and who are those who have taken advantage?"

> Sir Peter repeated what was said before about the staple at Calais, concluding that Lord Latimer and Richard Lyons had so many patents granted on the customs, with the King's knowledge, that they could not be counted, and insisting that the staple be restored to Calais.

When Lord Latimer heard these words, he said, "When the staple was removed from Calais, it was by the King and his council."

Sir Peter answered that it was contrary to the law of England and contrary to the statute made about it in Parliament—what was done in Parliament by statute could not be undone without Parliament—and that he would show them the statute. He had a book of the statutes ready with him, and he opened the book and read the statute before all the Lords and Commons so that he could not be contradicted.

There was a great deal of disputing among them, and Sir Peter said: "Sir, we shall tell you more than this pretty soon. Gentlemen, the second point that we wish to make is that Lord Latimer, who is present, and Richard Lyons made a loan to their own great profit and the great damage and loss of the King, when there was no need of a loan; and this loan amounted to twenty thousand marks [equal to something like $2,000,000 today], for which the King had to pay twenty thousand pounds [about $3,000,000], so that those who made the loan gained about ten thousand marks [$1,000,000]." [46]

Then the Duke of Lancaster said that such a case and such a need might arise that the King would be glad to pay ten thousand marks for a loan of twenty thousand.

To this Sir Peter replied that there was no need of a loan at all, for he had heard that there were two London citizens, Adam Franceys and William Walworth, who offered to Sir Richard Lescrope, then treasurer of England, to put into the King's hands fifteen thousand marks, without damage or loss to the King, and to be repaid out of the wool customs at Calais from year to year until the whole sum was paid.

> To prove this, De la Mare asked that the two successive treasurers be questioned on the point. Sir Richard Lescrope (the bishop of Exeter being, perhaps, not present) said that although he was sworn to secrecy by his office, if the King would release him, nothing should prevent him from telling all he knew. It was arranged that the King should be asked to do this, and De la Mare continued.

"The third point is that when our lord the King had borrowed large sums of gold and silver from archbishops, bishops, abbots, priors, citizens, burgesses, and merchants, Lord Latimer and Richard Lyons bargained with some of them to get their tallies and paid them much smaller sums or nothing at all. Cleverly, for their own gain, they got by bargaining the tallies of various people, paying to some £500 for tallies worth £1000, to others £200 for tallies worth £400, and to still others £100 for tallies worth £200. In this way they made enormous sums of money without the knowledge of the King, who should have had these advantages."

"Still another point is that there is a lady or damsel, Dame Alice Perers by name, who has every year from the income of our lord the King two or three thousand pounds [$300,000 or $450,000] of gold and silver from his coffers, without any notable return and to his great injury. It would be a good thing for the country to remove the said lady from the King's company, on grounds of conscience and because of our ill success in war, so that this money could be turned to his advantage. . . ."

> And so presently Parliament adjourned, and when the King had agreed that the treasurers should tell all they knew, the Commons made their plans and returned to

[46] The word used for loan is *chevauns*; cf. *chevisaunce*, practiced by Chaucer's Merchant, *Canterbury Tales*, Prologue, l. 282. [R.]

When they had finished speaking, they rose in a body and went from the chapter house to Parliament and came before the Lords and greeted them and asked for a reply to the petition made to our lord the King.

Then the Duke of Lancaster said, "Have you still some other articles to present?"

Sir Peter replied briefly that they would say nothing more until the truth was made known on the aforesaid points and redress had been given by those who had been guilty of such graft and had kept the King's money, cheating him and the realm. . . .

Then Sir Richard Lescrope was called and confirmed the charge, concluding his speech as follows:

"Gentlemen, you know very well that I was treasurer and in the King's council, and the loan was made, as I suppose, by Lord Latimer, who is present, and Richard Lyons, without my knowledge, when there was no need of a loan, for two London citizens, Adam Franceys and William de Walworth, which William is here present, offered to lend me for the use of our lord the King in his need fifteen thousand marks to be repaid out of the wool customs at Calais, on easy terms, without damage or loss to another; and it would have been a strange thing if all the ministers and counselors of our lord the King could not have advanced the other five, without letting him pay another ten thousand for it."

At this the Duke asked, "Who made the loan?"

The Commons answered: "As we suppose, Lord Latimer and Richard Lyons, as Sir Richard Lescrope has said, and to prove it, William de Walworth knows the truth."

Then the Duke had him called and examined on his allegiance. And the said William declared that he had nothing to do with it but had heard that Richard Lyons and John Pyel made the loan.

"Where is John Pyel?" asked the Duke.

"Sir," they said, "he is at hand."

"Call him to us," said the Duke.

And when he had come before them, the Duke bade him lay his hand on the Book and he did so, and was charged to tell the truth fully how the loan had been made and whether it had been made from his own money or not.

ARPENTERS AND A STONE MASON
:w York, Morgan Library, MS 394, fol. 200v

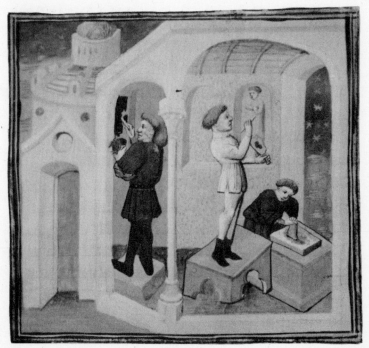

SCO PAINTERS
Morgan Library
MS 394, fol. 145

MEDICAL CARE

A CONSULTATION; late fourteenth century
London, Brit. Mus., MS Royal 20 C.VII, fol. 78v

DRESSING WOUNDS; early fourteenth century
Oxford, Bodl., MS 264. fol. 152v

And he answered, "No, it was not made from my money."

"And how was it made, then, and by whom?" asked the Duke.

"Sir," said he, "by the oath I have taken, as I suppose, it was made out of the King's own money or the money of Lord Latimer, by the assent of Lord Latimer and Richard Lyons."

Then all the Commons cried with one voice: "Monsieur le Duke, now you can clearly see and hear how Lord Latimer and Richard Lyons have played false to their own advantage; wherefore we pray for remedy and redress and that the said Richard may be arrested and put under guard until our lord the King and the council of Parliament have said their will about him."

Lord Latimer said in the hearing of all that this should not be done, for he could find sufficient pledges to answer for him in the future.

At this, Sir Peter de la Mare said that all the goods he had, movables and nonmovables, could not make up the amount he had extorted from our lord the King, "as we shall be ready to prove, and to say more than we have said; and gentlemen, we shall say no more on this day."

So they adjourned until another day, and Lord Latimer was very angry and much disturbed by their speech.

So the Parliament went on until the Commons obtained what they demanded, only to have all they had gained lost the following year in a Parliament judiciously packed with adherents of John of Gaunt.

AN INEFFICIENT PARLIAMENT, 1366

John of Reading, *Chronica*, p. 170.

John of Reading was a chronicler of the Westminster school. In 1265 the chronicle *Flores historiarum* (Flowers of Histories) was brought from St. Albans to Westminster, and was there continued by several writers to 1367, just over a century. Of these writers John of Reading was the last. He says of himself: "The following, indeed, for future [generations] to learn and remember, a certain brother, John de R [Reading, as appears from the Westminster records], monk of Westminster rather in name than in perfected character, deficient in letters as in talent, depending more upon common talk than upon his own study or the letters of great men, never citing ancient writings because of the great mass of things going on now, has woven together with heavy toil and a rude style."

This modest disclaimer notwithstanding, Brother John distinctly fancied his style—perhaps more than we do today; but in spite of his style, his work is valuable, partly because it is the only firsthand chronicle between 1346 and 1367 for many of the events it contains. His reports were undoubtedly often obtained from those who knew, or made from his own observation, as in the case of weather and events in his neighborhood. He seems to have died in 1368/69. Aside from the value of his material, he is worth reading for the glimpses he gives of himself as an honest, narrow-minded, prejudiced, superstitious, irascible, unconsciously amusing individual. [R.]

At this Parliament little else was done except that the brothers of the order of Saint Rouncivalle, upon showing their charters, obtained with all incumbents their possessions with the ancient liberties of the realm of England. Soon after at Westminster, in their property by Charing, they rebuilt their little house, to the scandal of the hospital. For a forged bull of excessive indulgences found in their possession brought infamy upon them (*statum illorum et enfamiam denigravit*) and reduced their oblations and alms.

EXPENSES INCURRED BY THE REPRESENTATIVES OF THE CITY OF LONDON IN ATTENDING PARLIAMENT, 1389

Riley, *Memorials of London*, II, 511–512 (from London Letter-Book H, fol. ccxlv).

Expenses incurred in attending the Parliament at Cambridge by Adam Bamme, Henry Vanner, William Tonge, and John Clenhond:

In the first place—for timber and carpentry, tilers, and daubers,[47] in preparing the house for their lodging, as well the chambers as the hall, buttery, kitchen, and stables for the horses; and for making stools and forms [48] throughout, and for carting out the rubbish, such house being quite ruinous; as also for payment made to the good man of the house, for the said lodging . . . . £6 9s.

Also—for cloth bought for napery, for canvas, dosser, and costers [49] for the hall, of striped worsted; and for all the other utensils, many in number, that pertain to the hall, kitchen, pantry, and buttery; save and except vessels of pewter only, which were bought by the Chamberlain of the Guildhall . . . . £6 16s. 8d.

Also—for firewood, charcoal, turf, and sedge [50] . . . £5 13s.

Also—for the hire of horses, and for hay and oats, and for straw for the beds, as well as for litter for the horses, and for horseshoeing . . . . £12 15s. 7d.

Also—for expenses incurred by the aforesaid Bamme, Vanner, etc., and their servants, in riding on horseback to Cambridge, and back; and for carriage of their wine and all their harness,[51] thither and back . . . . £7 16s. 8d.

---

[47] Layers on, to a framework, of a mixture of straw and mud; like the Devonshire "cob" of the present day. [Riley's note.]   [48] A long seat without a back, a bench. (*O.E.D.*)
[49] A piece of tapestry for the side of a bed or table; or for the side walls of a hall. [Riley's note.]
[50] Turf, and sedge: the latter is still in use at Cambridge for the same purpose. [Riley's note.]
[51] The baggage or portable equipment of an army, a party of travelers, etc. (*O.E.D.*)

Also—for two pipes of red wine taken thither from London and for other wine, bought at Cambridge . . . . £9 2s.

Also—for vesture for them and their servants, arrayed in like suit . . . . £22 15s.

Also—expended at Cambridge throughout the time of the Parliament, on bread, ale, flesh-meat, fish, candles, sauce, the laundryman, and in gifts to the minstrels of the King, and of other lords; together with divers other outlays made . . . . £23 5s. 9d.

Also—for payments made to their officials, such as the steward, butler, cook, and others; and to serving men helping in the kitchen, and elsewhere . . . . £7 13s. 4d.

Sum total . . . . £112 7s.

THE ART OF HEALING

1. Master Surgeons of the City Admitted and Sworn, 1369

Riley, *Memorials of London*, II, 337 (from London Letter-Book G, fol. ccxix).

On Monday next after the Feast of the Purification of the Blessed Virgin Mary,[52] in the forty-third year, etc., Master John Dunheved, Master John Hyndstoke, and Nicholas Kyldesby, surgeons, were admitted in full husting, before Simon de Mordone [mayor], and the aldermen, and sworn, as master surgeons of the city of London, that they would well and faithfully serve the people, in undertaking their cures, would take reasonably from them, etc.,[53] would faithfully follow their calling, and would present to the said mayor and aldermen the defaults of others undertaking cures, so often as should be necessary; and that they would be ready, at all times when they should be warned, to attend the maimed or wounded, and other persons, etc.; and would give truthful information to the officers of the city aforesaid as to such maimed, wounded, and others, whether they be in peril of death or not, etc. And also, faithfully to do all other things touching their calling.

2. A Fourteenth Century Doctor

The famous surgeon and physician, John Arderne, many of whose writings exist today, although only one, *Treatises of Fistula in Ano*, has been published, was almost certainly known to Chaucer. Born in 1307, he seems to have made his reputation as an army doctor in the train of Duke Henry of Lancaster, father of Chaucer's

[52] The Feast of the Purification (of the Virgin Mary) is February 2.
[53] So abbreviated in the original. [Riley's note.] This applies to each use of "etc." in this document.

Duchess. He himself tells how he had cured a knight at Algeciras in 1341/42.[54] After practicing in the town of Newark in Nottinghamshire, he went to London in 1370, and about 1376 wrote his famous treatise, from which the following extracts have been taken.

It is interesting to note that he quotes or refers to twelve of the fifteen famous doctors listed by Chaucer, omitting the mythical Aesculapius, the little-known Rufus, and—oddly enough—his own contemporary, John Gaddesden,[55] who was court physician to Edward II and who lived until 1361.

Although Arderne shared the astrological views of Chaucer's doctor, he had also a large amount of practical common sense, which doubtless contributed to his success. Like Chaucer's doctor, again, he had an eye always to the fee.[56] [R.]

A DOCTOR'S CODE OF PROFESSIONAL ETHICS, CA. 1376

Arderne, *Treatises of Fistula in Ano*, ed. by Power, pp. 4–9.

In the first place, a doctor who wishes to succeed in his profession should always remember God in all his works and should always meekly pray with heart and mouth for his help; and he should from time to time give of his earnings to the poor that they by their prayers may get him grace of the Holy Ghost.

He must not be rash or boastful in speech or in deed. He had better not talk much, especially among great men. And he should answer cannily to all questions so that he may not be tripped up by his own words. If his results do not carry out his words and his promises, he will be looked down upon, and his reputation will suffer. . . .

A doctor should also be careful not to laugh and joke too much; and, as far as he can, he should avoid the company of knaves and dishonest persons.

Let him keep always busy with matters that belong to his profession— reading or writing or studying or praying. The use of books is creditable to a doctor because they both keep him occupied and teach him something. Above all, it is important that he be found always sober; for drunkenness spoils every good thing. . . .

If anyone talks to him about another doctor, he should neither make light of him nor praise or commend him too much, but he may say with all courtesy, "I have no real knowledge of him, but I have heard nothing about him but what is good and to his credit." . . .

A doctor should not look too boldly at the lady of the house or her daughters or other fair women in great men's houses, or offer to kiss

[54] Cf. Prologue of *Canterbury Tales*, ll. 56–57.
[55] *Ibid.*, ll. 429–434.　　　　　　　　[56] *Ibid.*, ll. 442–444.

them, or touch them with his hands, lest he move to indignation the lord or some one of his household.

So far as he can, he should avoid giving offence to servants, but should try to get their love and good will.

Let him refrain from vice, as well in word as in deed, for if he be given to secret vice, some time he will be found out and dishonored for his evil practices. . . .

When sick men or their friends come to consult him, let him be neither too haughty nor too familiar, but adapt his manner to the status of the persons: to some respectful, to others friendly. For wise men say that familiarity breeds contempt.

It is a good thing for him to make up excuses that he cannot do anything for them safely or without causing the indignation of some great person, or because he is too busy. Or he might pretend to be hurt or ill if he wants to get out of undertaking a case. And if he does take up a case, let him make terms for his work and take the money in advance.

He should be careful not to pronounce upon a case until he has seen it and observed what it is. When he has made an examination, even though he may think that the patient can be cured, in his prognosis he should warn him of the danger of deferring treatment. And if he sees that the patient is eager for the cure, let him boldly adjust his fee to the man's position in life. But let him never ask too little; for this is bad for both the market and the patient. For a case of fistula, when it is curable, he may safely ask of an important man a hundred marks or forty pounds with robes and fees amounting to a hundred shillings a year for his life. Of less important men, he might ask forty pounds, or forty marks without fees. But let him never take less than a hundred shillings.[57] For never in my life have I taken less than that sum for the cure of this disease. But every man should, of course, do as he thinks best and most expedient.

If the patients or their friends or servants ask how soon a cure may be expected, the doctor should always say twice as long as he really thinks. . . . For it is better to indicate too long a time than to have the cure drag on. This discourages the patient at a time when faith in the doctor is one of the greatest aids to recovery. If the patient later asks why

[57] Translated into modern terms this means that his fee for great men was approximately $10,000–$7,500, besides a life annuity, in money or in cloth for winter and summer robes, such as were given out in great households, amounting to about $750 more; for lesser men, from about $6,000–$4,000, but without the annuity charge for life. The minimum fee was $750.

the doctor was able to cure him in half the time he mentioned, he may answer that it was because the patient was strong and bore well the severe treatment, and that he was of good complexion,[58] and that his flesh healed quickly, and other things that would please the patient. For patients are, with this kind of talk, made proud and glad.

Furthermore, a doctor should always be well dressed and neat in appearance, not gay like a minstrel but sober like a clerk, because any discreet man dressed like a clerk may sit at a gentleman's table. A doctor should also have clean hands and well-shaped nails, thoroughly cleaned. He should always be courteous at lords' tables and not displease the other guests, either by his words or his manner. He should listen well but say little. . . . And when he does speak, his words should be brief, agreeable, full of sense, and free of oaths. And he should never lie; for if he be found truthful in his speech, few or none will lack confidence in what he does.

A young doctor should also learn good proverbs suited to his profession to comfort his patients. . . . Moreover, he should comfort his patient by admonishing him to be of strong heart. For greatness of heart makes men strong and hardy to suffer sharp and grievous pain. . . .

It is also useful for a doctor to have a stock of good and amusing stories to make the patient laugh, both from the Bible and from other tragedies, and any others that are not objectionable which may make the patient more cheerful.

A doctor should be careful never to betray the secrets of his patients, either men or women, or belittle some to others . . . for if a man knows that other men's secrets are well kept, he will be the readier to trust you with his own.

HINTS TO A PRACTITIONER, CA. 1376

Arderne, *Treatises of Fistula in Ano*, ed. by Power, pp. 15–16.

When, after the preliminary talk, the doctor finds that the patient really wishes to undergo the operation, he should ask leave to make an examination. At this point he should be careful not to show any instruments that might frighten the patient or might be seen by another doctor whom the patient may have brought to spy, as I have often seen to be the case. If the doctor sees that the fistula is curable, he should nonetheless pretend the danger and difficulty of attempting a cure, and give a prognosis

---

[58] That is, characterized by such a combination of the humors, blood, phlegm, choler (yellow bile), and melancholy (black bile), as would produce a quick recovery.

of slow recovery, in case perhaps the patient should not be able to retain medicines, or because he may not be strong enough or may not follow the prescribed rules or diet. The doctor should make up out of his own head such other objections as he thinks necessary. But if the patient persist in wishing to be cured, then the doctor should say, "I doubt not, with the aid of our Lord, if you will be patient and follow directions exactly in doing and leaving undone the things I tell you, that I shall be able to bring this cure to a satisfactory conclusion."

Then let them come to terms about the fee; and of this fee—all excuses put aside—let him take the half in advance. And then he may appoint a day on which he will begin.

In the meantime, he should make ready his medicines and his instruments. He will need two or three sponges at the least, and a razor or very sharp lancet, and the other instruments named before [*i.e.*, in the book],[59] and silk threads and linen cloths and bandages and various other things which will be specified later. He must also have ready a styptic lotion and warm or lukewarm water and other indispensable things. . . . But most important of all is that he do not operate in any time when operation is forbidden by the astronomers.

EXPERIENCE IS BETTER THAN BOOKS, CA. 1376

Arderne, *Treatises of Fistula in Ano*, ed. by Power, p. 23.

The doctor should understand that in operations of this kind he may do more things than he finds written in the books. For not everything that can be done can be put into words; so a skillful doctor uses his own ingenuity, and in addition to what he reads, makes use of his own common sense. For, as Boethius says in his *De disciplina scholarium*, "He has but a poor head who goes on using things that others have found out and never finds out anything for himself."

A GOOD OINTMENT, CA. 1376

Arderne, *Treatises of Fistula in Ano*, ed. by Power, p. 28.

You may use the common white ointment made by apothecaries; but it is well to add powder of bole armenic [60] and *sanguis dragonis* (dragon's

---

[59] Arderne has already listed the following instruments for use in an operation for fistula: the *sequere me*, or flexible probe; the *acus rostrata*, or grooved director, along which the scalpel was passed; the *tendiculum*, or dilator; and the *siringa*, which was probably a clyster-pipe. Power remarks that "Arderne purposely gives fancy names to the instruments he uses as part of a fixed design to keep his methods secret." (Arderne, *Treatises of Fistula in Ano*, ed. by Power, pp. 8–9 and 112.)

[60] Armenian bole. Cf. *Canterbury Tales*, group G, l. 790.

blood), if you have it; also oil of roses and rosewater in which gum arabic has been dissolved, all thoroughly mixed.

COMMON SENSE IN DRESSING A WOUND, CA. 1376

Arderne, *Treatises of Fistula in Ano*, ed. by Power, p. 100.

This ointment [for which the prescription had just been given] I liked especially. With it I cured at London a fisherman the muscle of whose arm had been pierced by a sharp iron on the double doors of the Carmelite Friars. He was almost dead from the aching, swelling, and burning, and because of the unskillful treatment of a barber who had put into the wound a coarse dressing of linen cloth and diachylon. After removing this, about evensong time I applied the above-mentioned ointment and anointed the wound with oil of roses. Before cockcrow the patient was free from aching, and the swelling had begun to go down; and in the morning he was sleeping well and his arm was purged of the foul matter in the wound. But know that I used no dressing in the wound—only the oil of roses and the ointment on it.

A LOCAL ANAESTHETIC, CA. 1376

Arderne, *Treatises of Fistula in Ano*, ed. by Power, pp. 101–102.

A sleeping ointment, with which if any man be anointed, he shall be able to bear cutting in any part of the body without sensation or pain. Take juice of henbane, mandragora, water hemlock, lettuce, poppy, both white and black, and the seeds of all the aforesaid herbs if they can be had, in equal parts; Thebian opium and meconium,[61] one or two drams each; fresh swine's grease as needed. Crush all these well and strongly together in a mortar, and afterward boil them hard and then cool them. And if it be not thick enough, put in a little bee-bread, that is, white wax; and keep it for thy use.

And when thou wilt use thereof, anoint his pulses, his temples, his armpits, and the palms of his hands and the soles of his feet, and very soon he shall sleep so that he shall feel no cutting.

This is also useful if a man cannot sleep for some other cause, as in fevers or something of the sort, for this ointment either shall give him remedy or the patient shall die. Also one grain of Thebian opium to the

[61] "*Opium* is a tear which flows from the wounded heads or leaves of the black poppy, being ripe . . . *Meconium* [is] the gross expressed juice of the whole plant. . . . Opium is the finer gum and the stronger. Meconium is the coarser and weaker, yet the more malign." Thebian, or white, opium was the best grade. [Power's note.]

quantity of half a dram, mixed with a pint of wine or more according to the strength of him that shall drink it, shall make a person sleep. Also the seed of white henbane alone given in wine makes the drinker sleep very soon, so that he shall not feel whatsoever is done to him. And this I myself proved for certain.

And know that it helps to draw him that sleeps by the nose and by the cheeks and by the beard that the spirits be quickened so that he sleep not overrestfully. Also the doctor should beware of giving opium without crocus to drink, for crocus and cassia lignea are the bridles of opium.

To wake a man that sleeps thus, put to his nose gray bread toasted and wet in strong vinegar; or put vinegar and mustard in his nose; or wash his head in strong vinegar; or anoint his temples with the juice of rhubarb. And give him some other things to make him sneeze, and soon he shall wake. And know that it is good to give him afterward castoreum, for it is the cure of henbane and opium and other such things, whether it is given in the mouth, or in drink, or is put in the nose. For castoreum heats and comforts most effectively the sinews that are chilled and loosens the rigidity. And also give him what comforts the brain, for example, castoreum, nutmeg, roses, water-lily, myrtle, and sumac.

3. A Special Surgeon from London, 1373

John of Gaunt's Register, II, 155.

John by the grace of God [king of Castile] to our dear clerks . . . auditors of the accounts of our ministers and officers, greeting! We will and command you . . . to allow to . . . our receiver general five shillings which he paid for two horses for Alfons Surgeon going from London to Hertford by our command to heal Nicholas de la Chambre at the time when he was wounded by Raulyn Grender, which sum the said [receiver general] has paid at our express command.

Dated at the Savoy, April 24, 1373.

4. Suit Concerning an Agreement for Healing an Arm, 1381

Common Pleas, Plea Roll 482 m. 122.

Thomas Wombe of London, taverner, in his own person offered himself against Thomas Leche of London in a plea why, whereas the same Thomas undertook at London well and sufficiently to heal the left arm of the same Thomas Wombe of a certain infirmity whereof it was held, the aforesaid Thomas Leche so negligently and unduly cared for the healing of the arm aforesaid that the arm aforesaid, through the default of the same Thomas Leche, is incurable, so that the same Thomas Wombe cannot in any way work or make his due profit with his arm aforesaid, and [why Thomas Leche] committed other enormities against the said Thomas to his damage in forty pounds.[62]

[Thomas Leche is to be attached to be at the Court of Common Pleas on the Octave of Trinity.]

5. A Woman Doctor at Westminster, late 14th century

During the latter part of the fourteenth century there was at Westminster a woman doctor, Joan de Sutton. She was frequently a party to pleas in the Common Bench, but these did not relate to her profession.

Common Pleas, Plea Roll 509 m. 435 d.

Easter, 1387. Middlesex. Joan de Sutton of Westminster, leech, sues Peter Carpenter of Fleet Street for the return of goods and chattels, to wit belts, silver cups and spoons, and jewelry.

Common Pleas, Plea Roll 524 m. 295.

Hilary, 1392; Middlesex. Thomas de Lincoln sues Joan [altered from *John*] Sutton of Westminster, leech, for forty-two shillings which she [altered from *he*] owes and detains.

Common Pleas, Plea Roll 531 m. 28.

Michaelmas, 1393; Middlesex. Joan de Sutton, leech, sues Alice Coradyn for withdrawing from her service in the town of Westminster without leave within the time agreed for her service.

Common Pleas, Plea Roll 531 m. 467.

Michaelmas, 1393; Middlesex. Joan Sutton, leech, sues Alice Coradyn for breaking the close and houses of the said Joan at Westminster and taking goods worth forty pounds.

[62] Actions of this kind are very common in the Court of Common Pleas at this period. For example, Thomas Butolf, "leech," was sued in 1388 for failure to cure Robert de Sleyme of a megrim for 26s. 8d. (Com. Pleas, Plea R. 509 m. 230), and John Spicer of Canterbury in 1389 for not carrying out his undertaking to cure Isabella wife of John Stryngere within a fixed time for £20 (Com. Pleas, Plea R. 515 m. 462). At times the negligent doctor had been paid in advance, as in the case of Philip Leche of Westminster, who was sued by William Baker of London for £20, because, although William had paid Philip a certain sum to cure him, Philip had not set himself diligently to do so (Com. Pleas, Plea R. 523 m. 278). Such conditions plainly account for the extreme caution advised by John Arderne.

6. A Careless Dentist,[63] 1398

Coram Rege Roll 548 m. 7.

London. A judicial investigation between Isabel Cummay of London, plaintiff, and John atte Hethe of London, barber, to make recognisance whether the said John on Sunday next after the three weeks of St. Michael in the nineteenth year of the now King undertook at London in the parish of St. Nicholas of Acon in the ward of Lombard Street well and sufficiently to extract a certain tooth of the said Isabel, and the said John so negligently and carelessly performed the same that the jaw of the said Isabel through the default of the said John was broken and the life of the said Isabel was despaired of. [He failed to appear, and the case was adjourned.]

7. Veterinary Doctors, 1388 and 1389

Common Pleas, Plea Roll 511 m. 106 d.

London. Robert atte Hay, smith, was summoned because he had not cured a horse of a wound in its left leg, as he had undertaken, in the parish of St. Dunstan's Fleet Street, but neglected it so that it died. The damage claimed was ten pounds.

Common Pleas, Plea Roll 515 m. 45 d.

Somerset. Thomas Crabbe of North Petherton, by his attorney, sued Robert Wycher because he had not cured his horse, valued at one hundred shillings, which was ill at North Petherton, as he had undertaken, but owing to Robert's negligence, the horse had died.

COMMERCE AND BANKING

1. Merchants Who Live beyond Their Means, ca. 1376–1379

Gower, "Mirour de l'omme," ll. 25,813–25,824.

> Formerly when merchants talked
> Of twenty and hundred, they had enough
> Of wealth and of comfort;
> Then they lived on their own goods,
> And in honesty conducted themselves,
> Without cheating anyone:

[63] The regular term for a dentist in the fourteenth century was "toothdrawer." For example: "William Pyry, 'tothedrawer,' charged with robbery," Michaelmas 22 Ric. II [1398] (K.B. Controlment R. 43, m. 7). Formerly the barber was also a regular practitioner in surgery and dentistry, and was sometimes called a barber-surgeon. O.E.D.

But now they're always talking
Of many a thousand; and without doubt,
Of such there are some who, if they paid
Their debts and did no borrowing,
Would have of their own goods not the amount
Of a florin with which to pay them.

2. A Merchant Pays Dear for the Keeping of the Seas, 1383

Ancient Petition 5066, from Record Commission Transcript 111/84.

To our most renowned and powerful lord the King and his lords in
Parliament petitions John Cavendish of London, merchant, that, whereas
Gilbert Maufeld and Robert Parys, merchants, and John Haukyn and
Thomas Horsman, mariners,[64] for a great sum of money [65] paid to them,
and for taking 6d in the pound and 2s from each tun of wine, had
undertaken to keep the sea against the enemies of our said Lord, except
royal power, from the port of Winchelsea as far as the town of Berwick
upon Tweed, as more plainly appears in certain indentures between
our said lord the King and the said wardens—the said wardens and
their deputies, under color of certain commissions from the said King,
without warrant, at Kirkeleyrode, Lowestoft, and Lodynglond in the
County of Suffolk and elsewhere in divers parts of the County of Suffolk
took 3d. in the pound and from each vessel of "tountyl" 3d., from each
man going overseas as a pilgrim 12d., from each chalder [66] of coals 3d.,
and from each thousand of laths(?) [67] 2d., and from every kind of victuals
coming into the said county according to its freight(?) [68] and from every
fishing vessel coasting there as much as each man therein took for a
share, to the great extortion and oppression of the lord King's lieges.
And they were so much occupied with such extortions and oppressions
there for their own profit that through their default and the default of

[64] The men were appointed on May 6, 1383, to protect English shipping for one and a
half years. (See Gt. Brit. P.R.O., *Cal. of the Patent Rolls*, 1381–1385, p. 278.) England's lack of a navy made such an arrangement necessary.

[65] Twenty-five hundred marks (*ibid.*). In terms of modern purchasing power, this is
equivalent to about $25,000. For a concise discussion of fourteenth-century money values
and their modern equivalents see Chaucer, *Canterbury Tales*, ed. by Manly, pp. 63–67.

[66] Chaldron. When used in England for coal and lime, varied in quantity from 32 to 40
bushels, according as the measure was stroked or heaped. Apparently a northern word,
introduced into the London market with coal. (*O.E.D.*) Cf. below, p. 184n.

[67] *Astell's*. Cf. "astelle" in F. E. Godefroy, *Dictionnaire de l'ancienne langue française*,
10 vols., Paris, 1881–1902. All further references to this dictionary are indicated only by
the author's name.   [68] *Lafferant*.

their guard a ship with certain merchandise of the said John Cavendish and diverse merchandise of other persons was taken upon the sea by the enemies of our said lord the King.

Wherefore the said John Cavendish and the rest complaining sued by bill to our lord the King and his lords in the last Parliament held at Westminster against the said wardens to have justice. [The cause was referred to Chancery and the defendants have complained [69] in Parliament to be discharged, against which complaint Cavendish now petitions.]

3. A Fishmonger Exporting Herrings and Importing Wine, ca. 1387

Ancient Petition 4706; queried in Record Commission Transcript 110/3 as 11 Ric. II.

To our most renowned lord the King and to his very noble Council complains your poor servant John Blakeneye, citizen and fishmonger of London, of Sir William de Wyndesore, knight—that, whereas on the 20th of November last past in Southwark, in the church of Our Lady Overee, the said John chartered a ship which belongs to the said Sir William called St. Mary Cog of London from the said Sir William; which ship could then reasonably carry a cargo of 160 tuns of wine, to take her cargo of herrings from Yarmouth to Bordeaux, and from Bordeaux (after unlading the same merchandise) to return to London laden with the wines of the said John; for which freight the said John was to have paid the said Sir William 200 marks, of which the said John paid down £40, as appears by the indentures made between Robert de Sure and Robert de Ouston on behalf of the said Sir William and in his name, and the name of the said John Blakeneye. And then the said John caused the ship to be laden with 65 lasts of herring to the value of 700 marks at Yarmouth. And the ship sailed for Bordeaux, and as she came off Sandwich at Christmas last, the said ship for her unseaworthiness (*foiblesse*) could go no farther; neither would the said Sir William repair her, although he was often requested to do so; but unladed the ship of the said merchandise of the said John and would not carry them farther;

Whereby the said John lost the great part of his said merchandise and the carriage of the said wines which he had at Bordeaux, to his damage in £1,000. . . .

Please your most powerful lordship to cause the said William to come before you and to give the said John recompense. . . .

[69] To make a formal statement of a grievance to or before a competent authority. (*O.E.D.*)

[Endorsed] : The parties present in Parliament were cross-examined [?] (*en furent à travers*) thereupon and were ordered to come to an agreement.

4. *Delivering a Shipload of Coal at the Port of London, 1394*

Rickert, "Documents and Records: Extracts from a Fourteenth-Century Account Book," *Modern Philology*, XXIV (1926–1927), 254–255 (from Excheq. K. R. Accts. 509/19).

This indenture witnesses that Roger de Drayton, burgess and merchant of Great Yarmouth, has purchased, on the day when this was issued at the said Yarmouth, of Tydeman Hare, master of a ship called the *Marieknyth* of Denmark, all the coal in the said ship in the roadstead of Kyrkele to unload and deliver to the said Roger or his attorney at the expense and risk of the said Tydeman in the Pool [70] at the port of London, each chaldron by the measure of London [71] for 6s. 6d. And when the said ship has come into the Pool in the aforesaid port, it will be unloaded, and the master of the ship will be paid 6s. 6d. for each chaldron by the said Roger or his attorney within fourteen work days next following after the arrival of the said ship in the Pool of the aforesaid port. But the master of the ship aforesaid has granted to the said Roger that if he needs four or five days more than the aforesaid fourteen, the said Roger may have them willingly. In witness of which things, the parties aforesaid have both placed their seals on this indenture. Issued at Yarmouth, the third day of February, in the seventeenth year of the reign of our lord King Richard II.[72]

5. *The Oath of the Controller of the Petty Customs at the Port of London, ca. 1376*

Manly and Rickert, "Documents and Records: Recently Discovered Chaucer Documents," *Modern Philology*, XXV (1926–1927), 123 (from Excheq. K.R. Bille in the bundle for 1376).

You swear that you will reside constantly, in your own person or by a sufficient deputy for whom you will be responsible, in the port of Lon-

---

[70] The Thames east of London Bridge; still so called. [R.]

[71] According to the *Oxford English Dictionary*, a "chaldron" was a dry measure of four quarters, *i.e.*, 32 bushels; but as a measure for coal, it was 36 bushels in 1615. As the "measure of London" is specified, evidently the amount varied. [R.]

[72] On the same page as the indenture given above are statements that Tydeman Hare arrived at London with his shipload of coal on March 12 and that on April 10 the coal was sold for 4s. 6d. a chaldron. Professor Rickert comments that "Even so (according to *Calendar of Letter Books, Letter-Book H*, p. 289) it was dear. About 1386 the price of coal was regulated not to exceed 9d. a quarter, *i.e.*, about 3s. a 'chaldron.' "

don, and will supervise (*suruerrez*) the charges on the goods which pay
the petty custom, and as long as you do so (*en qanqe en vous est*), you
will not permit our lord the King to have damage or loss there, and
that you will render a correct account, and will make a correct return of
the issues of the said customs without deceit or fraud in any point, so
help you God and his saints.[73]

6. *The Merchant as Banker or Money Lender, 1390–1395*

Rickert, "Documents and Records: Extracts from a Fourteenth-Century Account
Book," *Modern Philology*, XXIV (1926–1927), 111–119, 256 (from Excheq.
K.R. Accts. 509/19).

The document designated as E 101 509/19 in the Public Record Office of London
seems to be the only one of its kind thus far discovered in that vast collection of
incompletely calendared records. It is a book containing in its present form forty-
seven folios in which a merchant kept account of his financial affairs between 1390
and 1395. Most of these are given under a heading for the year and month,[74] but
at the beginning there is a long list of debts carried over from 46 Edward III (1372)
preceded by a memorandum which explains that they have been transcribed from
another book. . . . There follows a list of about eighty debtors with the sums they
owed, many of the entries being canceled. The name at the head of the list—Sir
Robert Crull—is that of the newly appointed treasurer of Ireland to whom on
May 9, 1386, Chaucer assigned almost two-thirds (£4 out of £6 13s. 6d.) of the
money paid on his annuity. . . .

Concerning the owner of the book . . . Gilbert Maghfeld[75] . . . there is
enough information in the various types of public records to write a short biography.
. . . The first notice of him found thus far[76] shows him as agent in Dantzic for a
London merchant in 1367. . . . His career is perhaps comparable to those of the
better-known Walworth, Philpot, and Brembre, with each of whom he was, in
widely different ways, associated. He was a neighbor of the Walworths in Billingsgate; like Philpot in 1377, in 1383 he and his partner, Robert Parys, with two
"mariners," undertook the keeping of the sea;[77] and when Brembre's enemies in
1388 succeeded in bringing him to the scaffold,[78] Maghfeld obtained some of his
forfeited estates. . . . As controller of the customs . . . Chaucer certainly came
into contact with Maghfeld at this time. . . .

Maghfeld was several times elected alderman, and in 1392 served as sheriff. . . .
As early as 1377 he was one of many rich men who contributed five marks to the
King; [and] in December, 1394, as his account book shows, he advanced fifty pounds

---

[73] Professor Manly points out that "This form is shorter and simpler than the corresponding oath in English, dating from Elizabethan times, published by the Chaucer Society,
and it gives us the very words heard by Chaucer when he took office." (Manly and Rickert,
"Documents and Records: Recently Discovered Chaucer Documents," *Modern Philology*,
XXV (1926–1927), 123 [from Excheq. K.R. Bille in the bundle for 1376]).

[74] In a few cases the date of the loan does not agree with that of the heading under which
it is entered.

[75] The name appears in the account book as Gybon Maghfeld or Maufeld.

[76] That is, in 1926, when Professor Rickert first published this material.

[77] See above, pp. 182–183.   [78] See above, p. 158.

toward the King's expedition to Ireland. Moreover, he and Hugh Sprot (together with John Helmeshale, clerk of the navy, and John Michel, sergeant-of-arms) were appointed, June 16, 1394, to array for the King's use in going to Ireland three ships. . . . These ships were to be fitted out as an armada with artillery and so on. . . . Within three years Maghfeld had died a bankrupt, and his goods and chattels in Billingsgate had been seized into the King's hands—undoubtedly including his account books, of which this one has been preserved ever since among government documents.

Like Chaucer's Merchant, Maghfeld engaged extensively in both "bargaynes" and "chevisaunce." Of the numerous kinds of things in which he dealt, the following list may give some idea: iron, copper, gravel, lead, stones, millstones, wainscot from Prussia, boards, wood, coal, quicklime, rock alum, grain, ginger, saffron, licorice, silk, wool, skins, furs, linen, hats, wines, stockfish, herring, sturgeon, salmon, pearls. . . .

But equally important was his "chevisaunce." Apparently he was a professional money-lender. To what extent he practised the usury complained of in the London Letter-Books cannot be told from his book, as he gives no indication of rate of interest but merely records the sum to be repaid in even pounds, marks, nobles, half-nobles, or shillings. It may safely be assumed that the borrower got less than he had to repay.

It would seem that the merchant's risks must have been considerable. The loan was commonly "par oblig" (*i.e.* obligation); rarely, "par plegg" (bondsman); still more rarely, by sealed indenture. Now and then articles were accepted as security for small loans, as: a "nouche" of silver, a silver girdle, a covered beaker of silver, silver plate, a vestment and chalice, a baselard, a mazer. Once a book was pledged, its title *Tresor de Philosophie.*

The following example of a loan of this type is interesting also because it refers apparently to another set of accounts:

Friar Waulter Somerton borrowed on the Eve of All Saints on [the security of] two little tables of gold, to be repaid on the Purification of Our Lady. . . . xls.[79]

Maghfeld's clients and customers include scores of merchants of London and other English towns, representing more than thirty gilds,[80] besides merchants of Prussia (Hamburg and Königsberg), of La Rochelle, of Bayonne and Bordeaux, of Italy and Spain. In the book are also entries concerning a score or so of knights and squires in royal households, sergeants-of-arms, clerks in the Exchequer and Chancery, several controllers in the Custom House (Chaucer's successors), two "men of law," many chaplains and parsons, including nearly a dozen great ecclesiastics: the warden

[79] The debt ran from October 31, 1394, to February 2, 1395. In the margin to the left is added: "vacat quia in parvo paper" (*i.e.*, void because in the little paper). Here as elsewhere the cancelation of the debt is shown by an irregular line scrawled over the item. Occasionally "sol" (for *solutum* [canceled]) is added in the margin. [R.]

[80] Most of the Londoners appear in the Letter Books, and not a few of them are aldermen and mayors. Of other towns Boston and Dartmouth are perhaps mentioned most frequently. Among the crafts and trades represented may be listed: coppersmith, founder, ironmonger, smith; goldsmith; mason, carpenter, timberman, joiner; millmaker; saddler; bowyer; chandler, waxchandler; dyer, hatter, mercer, draper, linendraper, skinner; shearman; spurrier; shipman, boatman, mariner; glover; limner, scrivener; fishmonger, stockfishmonger, grocer, baker, brewer, vintner, taverner. The names without indication of business undoubtedly cover other occupations not yet worked out. [R.]

and treasurer of Canterbury cathedral; the abbots of Waltham and St. Mary Grace by the Tower; the bishops of Dublin, Ely, Exeter, St. David's, Durham,[81] and Winchester.[82] To the Mayor, the Chamberlain, and the Corporation of London as a body, Maghfeld made loans; and if we may judge from certain entries quoted below (and others like them) he dealt also with the Earl of Derby, the Duke of York, the Duke of Gloucester, and, possibly once, even the King himself.

The following extracts illustrate a few of the many transactions:

Monsieur Thomas Percy owes for a subsidy of 3s. a tun in the ship of Johan Mayhew the fourteenth day of November in the fifteenth year [81] [1391] for 7 tuns of wine . . . . 21s.[84]

Adam Bam, mayor of London, owes on the Monday of Pentecost for one chaplet [85] of silk of Tripoli [86] . . . . . . 13s. 4d.[87]

Johan Hauley of Dartmouth owes on the fifteenth day of November, to be repaid one month later . . . . £40 [88]

On the security of 20,000 of long iron (ferrelonge).

Margerete Spenser, silkwoman, of Soperslane, London, owes by obligation on the sixth day of March in the fifteenth year [1392] for 87¾ lbs. of raw silk, which makes by mercer's weight 65¾ lbs. at 8s. 6d. a pound. Total . . . . £27 18s. to pay at the next Feast of the Nativity of St. John the Baptist,

[81] Walter Skirlawe, with whom Chaucer was associated on an embassy to France in 1377 (*Life Records*, IV, 203f.). The bishop of St. David's here named was successor to the one sent on the same embassy. [R.]

[82] William of Wykeham, the chancellor. [R.]

[83] All regnal years in this series of extracts are of Richard II.

[84] Under the heading November, 1393. Percy was steward of the King's household. In 1377 Chaucer was sent with him to Flanders on a mission (*Life Records*, IV, 201). [R.]

[85] J. B. Ste. Palaye (*Dictionnaire historique de l'ancien langage françois* . . . , Paris, 1875–1882) defines "chapelet" as a type of hat or covering for the head; Godefroy (*Dictionnaire de l'ancienne langue française*), as a small hat.

[86] A city on the seacoast of Palestine. Cf. pp. 286 and 328 and the map of the first crusade of St. Louis, in Jean de Joinville, *Histoire de Saint Louis, suivie du Credo et de la lettre à Louis X*, Paris, 1868.

[87] May, 1391. Canceled. Was the goldsmith who made cups for John of Gaunt to give Philippa Chaucer a dandy? [R.] In 1380, 1381, and 1382, John of Gaunt gave to Chaucer's wife "three silver-gilt cups with covers, each of greater value than the preceding." (Chaucer, *Canterbury Tales*, ed. by Manly, p. 22.)

[88] November, 1391. Canceled, with "alibi" in the left margin. Hauley was the piratical shipowner who may have owned the "Maudelayne" of Dartmouth, of which Chaucer's equally piratical Shipman was captain (see Manly, *Some New Light on Chaucer*). Between August 14 and December 12, 1391, he ceased to be escheator for Devonshire (Gt. Brit., P.R.O. *Cal. of the Close Rolls*, 1389–1392, pp. 386, 420). Does the large loan mean that he expected to need money in settling his accounts? It should not be overlooked that Maghfeld required a pledge to the full value of the loan (one "mille" of "ferre" is listed at 40s.). [R.]

[June 24], £9, 6s. And at the Feast of Michael [September 29] thereafter, £9, 6s. And at the next Feast of the Nativity of Our Lord [December 25] thereafter, £9, 6s. &c. Item, of which received in goods . . . . 22s.[89]

The bishop of Winchester owes for three millstones at £3 a stone, total £9. Of which one stone to Eyscher,[90] one to Farnham, and one remaining at the wharf of G. Maghfeld

Of which received from Lavynton Clerk £3

The fifteenth day of July in the seventeenth year [1393] at the hands of Johan Brymmestone £6

Et Eque [91]

John Clerc of Botelston [92] owes what he received from the Count of Derby which was loaned to him in Prussia with other people of London, Lynne, and Botelston each 10 marks sterling, £6 13s. 4d. just as the said Johan owes what he had received for me

R. de Blomvill . . . . £6 12s. 6d.[93]

Sir Thomas Worston, chancellor of my Lord of York,[94] owes as a loan by obligation the twentieth day of November, to be paid during the fortnight after the following Easter . . . . . . £10 [95]

which belonged to Richard Honyman, as appears hereafter.

Robert Corke, Esquire with the Duke of Gloucester, owes on the

---

[89] February, 1392. Not canceled. In 1370 the silkwoman was living in Soperslane in a tenement belonging to Thomas de Grantham and evidently near the Chaucer property there. Richard Chaucer was one of the executors of the will of John de Grantham, father of Thomas, and Nicholas Chaucer witnessed the discharge of the surviving executor in 1355 (cf. *Life Records*, IV, 148, and London, Corporation, *Calendar of the Letter-Books*, G, pp. 37, 264). [R.]

[90] Esher, in Surrey. The bishop of Winchester purchased the manor of Esher in 1238. It was held by the bishops of Winchester until 1538. Cf. Gover, Mawer, and Stenton in collaboration with Arthur Bonner, *The Place Names of Surrey*, Cambridge, The University Press, 1934, English Place-Name Society, XI, 92–93; P. H. Ditchfield, *The Counties of England*, London, George Allen and Co., 1912, II, 179; and *Victoria County History of Surrey*, III, 448. The manor of Farnham, also in Surrey, was held by the bishops of Winchester as early as the Domesday Book. Cf. *ibid.*, II, 590, and *The Place-Names of Surrey*, p. 169.

[91] Under the heading January, 1391. Canceled. [R.] *O.E.D.* defines "eque" as "A balanced account; an acquittance, receipt. 'So called from the phrase, *et sic aeque*, which was written at the foot of an account when it was closed or settled.' (Jam. *Suppl.*)"

[92] Probably Boston, derived from "St. Botolph's town." Cf. James B. Johnston, *The Place-Names of England and Wales*, London, John Murray, 1915, p. 161.

[93] August, 1391. Canceled. Obscure as this transaction is, it shows Maghfeld repaying an advance made by Henry, Earl of Derby, while in Prussia. [R.]

[94] *Monsieur Deuerwyke*. Probably either the duke or the archbishop of York.

[95] November, 1394. [R.]

twenty-third day of March for freight [96] and *aueryez* [97] of a pipe
of wine which was in the ship of Johan Senches of Spain .   . 12*s*. 4*d*.[98]
Memorandum that I have loaned to the Guildhall, on the twenty-
second day of December in the sixteenth year [1392], which was
paid through the hands of Henry Vanner. . . . 20 marks. 20 marks
Item, loaned to William Staundon, mayor, for the Count of Huntington. . . . 10 marks . . . . 10 marks
Item, loaned for the mumming to the King at Eltham, at the feast
of Christmas . . . . 40*s*.[99]

> This entry is full of interest. Money is lent to the Guildhall as a corporation, pass-
> ing through the hands of Henry Vanner, whom Chaucer knew in 1390,[100] and
> more money is given to the mayor to be paid to the King's half-brother, the Earl
> of Huntington, who had a grant out of the customs. Money is advanced "for the
> mumming to the King at Eltham at the feast of Christmas." [101] This mumming
> it is highly probable Chaucer saw, for on January 9, during the Christmas revels,
> the King gave him ten pounds as a reward for his "good service" during the "present
> year." [102]
> Passing over many other items of interest, we come to two which can hardly
> be omitted. In the first we see Maghfeld acting as a sort of contractor.

Item, by G. Maghfeld for Saint Anton for three quarters of wain-
scot . . . . : . 15*s*.
[Irrelevant item concerning Thomas Blosse]
Item of Gybon Maghfeld, one half hundredweight of wainscot . . 10*s*.
Item, delivered to Macclesfeld for Saint Anton, 20 wainscot .   . . .
    void because paid to R. Honyman
Item, delivered for the paving of Saint Anton, 4,000 paving tile.
Item, paid by J. Schirbrok to two pavers and their servant, and for
wages and lunches (nonsenches) [103] for two days .   .   . 2*s*. 9*d*.[104]

> Maghfeld, then, provided materials for the repair of St. Anthonin, a church in
> the neighborhood of the Chaucers and also for the laying of a pavement in or near
> it, the workmen being given their lunches.

[96] *Frett.* The cost of transporting goods by water. See first definition of "freight" in *O.E.D.*
[97] Any charge or expense over and above the freight incurred in the shipment of goods,
and payable by their owner. (*O.E.D.*)
[98] March, 1394. Unless the squire was speculating in wine, he was probably buying for
the Duke. [R.]
[99] December, 1392. Nothing canceled. [R.]
[100] *Life Records*, IV, 284. [R.]
[101] Translated literally, but the meaning may be that the money was advanced to some
person unnamed for the mumming to be given in the King's presence at Eltham. [R.]
[102] *Life Records*, IV, 315. [R.]
[103] Nonsenche, a variant of "nuncheon"; a slight refreshment of liquor, etc., originally
taken in the afternoon; a light refreshment taken between meals; a lunch. (*O.E.D.*)
[104] 1390–91. Canceled. The line under "vacat," etc., is stricken through. [R.]

The second entry reads:

Memorandum that Gybon Maghfeld has paid at Christmas to porters for the stone for the grave of the Bishop of Exeter, and for one bell and one chest, a total of . . . . 28*d*.

Item, paid to Long Johan [105] for the carriage of the said stone to the ship . . . . 16*d*.

Item, paid for 4 lbs., 6 oz. of green ginger at 26*d*. per pound by his purchaser . . . . 9*s*. 7*d*.

Item, for a messenger for the stone and all . . . . . . 2*s*.

Sir Thomas More, clerk, owes for gold rings . . . . . £4 [106]

The bishop was Thomas Brantingham, bishop of Exeter from 1370 to 1394. In 1369, he was controller of the King's household when Chaucer was a yeoman there, and in 1378 he was the treasurer who disbursed Chaucer's expenses to Italy.[107]

But the entry remains puzzling. Apparently the bishop ordered his gravestone some four years before his death. Perhaps, like Richard II and other notables, he wished to make sure of one to his liking. And the combination with bell and chest and green ginger is strange. The gold rings may have been a different purchase, as the cancellation suggests.

In the book altogether there are thirty to forty names of persons who either appear in the *Life Records* or are in some other way unmistakably associated with Chaucer. Of such items four at least must be given here:

Henri Scoggan owes for a loan on the second day of September, by obligation, to be repaid at the Feast of St. Michael [September 29] next following . . . . 26*s*. 8*d*.[108]

Three entries concern Henry Yevele, chief mason in charge of the works and on Chaucer's payroll when the latter was clerk:[109]

[105] Long John, elsewhere in the book called a "lyghterman," got into the Patent Rolls through an accident. While he was conveying wines and other goods in his barge, a man fell overboard and was drowned. The boat, worth twenty marks, was confiscated; but later, in view of the lighterman's great age and weakness, was restored to him (Gt. Brit., P.R.O., *Cal. of the Patent Rolls*, 1388–1392, p. 508, and *ibid.*, 1391–1396, p. 36). [R.]

[106] December, 1390. Only the last item is canceled. [R.]

[107] *Life Records*, IV, 163, 171, 173, 217.

[108] September 2, 1390. Not canceled. Scogan and three other men—one Roger Elinham or Elmham, Chaucer's successor as clerk of the works in 1391—were bound as mainpernors for a detinue of 106*s*. 8*d*., on September 7, 1390 (Gt. Brit., P.R.O., *Cal. of the Close Rolls*, 1389–92, p. 286). Had this anything to do with Scogan's need of ready money? [R.]

[109] By an appointment dating from July 12, 1389, Chaucer had charge of the Tower, Westminster Palace, and eight other royal residences, besides St. George's Chapel, Windsor —for special repairs in which he was given another commission exactly a year later— five hunting lodges, and the mews for falcons at Charing Cross, as well as of all gardens, ponds, mills, and fences belonging to any of these. He had power to impress workmen, to bring back runaway workmen, to arrest and imprison those who resisted him, to purvey all materials needed for his work, and to make inquisition where such materials could

Master Yevele owes for millstones . . . . £6 [110]

Item, an obligation made by Henri Yevele the eighteenth day of
March in the eighteenth year [1395] to pay on the fifteenth day
of December following for the bishop of Ely . . . . . £130 [111]

Master Henri Yevele owes for a loan for 6 hundredweight, 3 quarters,
and 14 lbs. of lead at 10 marks a fodder [112] . . . . 42s. 3d. [113]

> Was Yevele, then, the master mason in the repair of Westminster Hall, engaged in
> building operations which seem to have been going on at Ely at the end of the four-
> teenth century? In Maghfeld's book, just above the second item about Yevele, we
> find the bishop himself with two parsons giving a recognizance for £119 15s., [114] and
> entries in the Close Rolls show him borrowing elsewhere at this time. [115]
>
> To a "John Gower Esquire" the allusions are as follows:

Memorandum that Gybon Maufeld has paid for Johan Gower,
Esquire, to a shipman for freight [116] of a brass pot brought by
letter (*par lettre*) from Lynne to London . . . . . . 16d.

Item, he has paid previously for carriage of a chest to water [117] (*Ewe*)
to send it to the said Johan at Hull . . . . 4d. [118]

John Gower, Esquire, owes for a loan by obligation on the eve of St.
John the Baptist [i.e., on June 23] to be repaid within the three
weeks following . . . . £3 6s. 8d. [119]

> That this man was the poet it is perhaps impossible to prove; but the "esquire" shows
> that he was not the parson of that name; and the nature of the entries and the amount
> borrowed suggest a person of the poet's rank and means. Perhaps at present no
> more can be said.
>
> The last entry to be quoted concerns Chaucer himself:

---

be procured. He had four or more deputy purveyors and a controller—to check his rolls
as he had checked the rolls of the collectors of the customs—he had a small army of men
in his pay as workmen; and he was paymaster to at least one man of high reputation as an
architect—Henry Yevele, who, before Chaucer's death, restored Westminster Hall and
left it essentially as it [was until World War II], and who also erected the beautiful tombs
of King Richard and Queen Anne still in Westminster Abbey. (Chaucer, *Canterbury Tales*,
ed. by Manly, p. 29.)

[110] September, 1390. Canceled. [R.]

[111] Under the heading August, 1394. Canceled. [R.]

[112] Fodour. Joseph Wright, *The English Dialect Dictionary*, defines "fodder" as "A
weight of lead of varying quantity."

[113] November, 1394. Canceled. [R.]   [114] August, 1394. Canceled. [R.]

[115] Gt. Brit., P.R.O., *Cal. of the Close Rolls*, 1392–1396, pp. 228, 500. [R.]

[116] "Frett." Cf. above, p. 189n.

[117] Evidently the chest was carried from some place inland to water, whence it could be
shipped to Hull.

[118] October, 1392. Canceled. [R.]

[119] Undated; last item, last page. The second item above is dated June 15, 18th year
[1395]. Canceled. [R.]

Geffray Chauxcer [120] owes for a loan on the twenty-eighth day of
July, to be repaid on the following Saturday . . . . 26s. 8d.[121]

As no evidence has been produced to show that there were two Geoffrey Chaucers,
perhaps we may assume that the entry refers to the poet. If so, the curious thing is
that he should have been borrowing this comparatively small sum only fifteen days
after he had received at the Exchequer the large sum of £13 6s. 8d. Perhaps this is
not more odd, however, than that the Exchequer should have left unpaid the small
sum of 12s. 4d. still due on his account as clerk of the works. But as to the sudden
need for money which sent him to a moneylender for an advance of six days we can
only speculate. . . .

Believing, as some of us now do,[122] that Chaucer had the habit of drawing his
figures from the life, we are faced with the question whether Gilbert Maghfeld was
the original of the Merchant. Coincidences must not be pressed, but they may at
least be stated. It can hardly be denied that Maghfeld was a merchant of the type
described by Chaucer. Both were "estatly" of "governaunce" with their "bargaynes"
and their "chevisaunce" (of which Chaucer and many of his associates at court and in
the city took advantage); and if Maghfeld, unlike the Merchant, did not succeed
in concealing the fact that he was in debt until he died a bankrupt, at least there
is no hint of unsound financial status in the printed records. His many dealings with
foreigners . . . would have certainly warranted the line: "Wel coude he in es-
chaunge sheeldes selle." His "Flaundrish bever hat" at once suggests the "bever hat"
worn by Sheriff Newenton (and undoubtedly by Maghfeld) when the two rode
formally to the Tower, September 30, 1392; but we cannot assume that sheriffs
wore the only beaver hats. Still, the "mottelee" and "hye on hors" must be in-
vestigated. Is it possible that to Chaucer's contemporaries they suggested a state
"riding" of city officials? [123] As to the "keeping of the sea," it is usually interpreted
to mean the Merchant's concern for the safety of his wool between Middelburg and
Orwell; but there is no hint in the text (as Mr. Manly shows) that he was a wool
stapler (nor was Maghfeld); and the line may not impossibly be a sly hit at the fact
that several years before, Maghfeld had been one of the four "keepers of the narrow
sea," [124] and since they were ousted within six months, the comment would not
have been without malice.

All in all, while it must be admitted that many another merchant might have
fulfilled the conditions of the picture in the "Prologue," this fragmentary account
book [125] shows that Maghfeld was a familiar figure at court and in the city, hence

[120] This spelling of the name agrees with that of the root word—*chaux*—also used in
the book. [R.] This name is derived from a trade, the making of *chausses*, or hose, but
we have no record that any of the poet's kinsmen actually followed this trade. (Chaucer,
Canterbury Tales, ed. by Manly, p. 3.)

[121] July, 1392. Canceled. [R.]

[122] See Manly, *Some New Light on Chaucer*. [R.]

[123] In at least one other case Chaucer describes a Pilgrim, not as he rode to Canterbury,
but as he looked in his uniform at home: the Yeoman is ready for woodcraft in the forest,
not for a pilgrimage. [R.]

[124] So called in the Rolls; cf. Gt. Brit., P.R.O., *Cal. of the Patent Rolls*, 1396–1399,
p. 207. [R.]

[125] As it was confiscated and preserved among the public records, it may be that the remainder of it and perhaps other account books are among the mass of documents still
uncalendared. [R.]

a likely subject for satire, and it also supplies a better motive than any yet given for Chaucer's refusal to tell the Merchant's name: he might have need of another "chevisaunce"!

CRAFTSMANSHIP

1. *Oath of the Wardens of Crafts, 1376*

Herbert, *The History of the Twelve Great Livery Companies of London*, I, 35 (from City Records, lib. lx, fol. 46).

You shall swear that you shall well and truly oversee the craft of —— [name of craft] whereof you are chosen wardens for the year. And all the good rules and ordinances of the same craft that have been approved here by the court, and no others, you shall keep and have kept. And all the wrongs that you find done in the same craft, you shall well and truly present to the chamberlain of the city for the time being, sparing no man for favor nor harming any person for hate. You shall not do extortion or wrong under color of your office; neither shall you consent to anything that shall be against the state, peace, and profit of our sovereign lord the King or of the city. But for the time that you shall be in office, in all things that shall pertain to the same craft according the laws and franchises of the said city you shall conduct yourself well and lawfully. So help you God and all saints, etc.

2. *Articles of the Cordwainers, or Tawyers, 1375*

Riley, *Memorials of London*, II, 391–392 (from London Letter-Book H, fol. xxvi).

On Monday next after the Feast of St. Andrew the Apostle,[126] came the reputable men of the trade of cordwainers, and presented to John Warde, the mayor, and the aldermen, a certain petition, in these words:

"To the mayor and aldermen of the city of London pray the good folks of the trade of cordwainers of the same city, that it may please you to grant unto them the articles that follow, for the profit of the common people; that so, what is good and right may be done unto all manner of folks, for saving the honor of the city and lawfully governing the said trade.

"In the first place—that if any one of the trade shall sell to any person shoes of bazen [127] as being cordwain, or of calf-leather for ox-leather, in deceit of the common people, and to the scandal of the trade, he shall

[126] The Feast of St. Andrew the Apostle is November 30.
[127] Sheep-skin tanned in oak- or larch-bark; distinguished from roan, which is tanned in sumach. (*O.E.D.*)

pay to the Chamber of the Guildhall, the first time that he shall be convicted thereof, forty pence; the second time, half a mark; and the third time the same, and further, at the discretion of the mayor and aldermen.

"Also—that no one of the trade shall keep house within the franchise [128] if he be not free [129] of the city and one knowing his trade, and that no one shall be admitted to the freedom without the presence of the wardens of the trade bearing witness to his standing, on the pain aforesaid.

"Also—if any one of the trade shall be found offending touching the trade, or rebellious against the wardens thereof, such person shall not make complaint to any one of another trade, by reason of the discord or dissension that may have arisen between them; but he shall be ruled by the good folks of his own trade. And if he shall differ from them as acting against right, then let the offense be adjudged upon before the mayor and aldermen; and if he be found rebellious against the ordinance, let him pay to the Chamber the sum above mentioned.

"Also—that no one of the trade shall entice or purloin the servant of another from the service of his master by paying him more than is ordained by the trade, on the pain aforesaid.

"Also—that no one shall carry out of his house any wares connected with his trade for sale in market or elsewhere except only at a certain place situated between Sopereslane [130] and the Conduit; [131] and that at a certain time of the day, that is to say, between prime [132] and noon. And that no shoes shall exceed the measure of seven inches,[133] so that the wares may be surveyed by the good folks of the trade, because of the

---

[128] The district over which the privilege of a corporation or an individual extends. (*O.E.D.*)

[129] Invested with the rights or immunities *of*, admitted to the privileges *of* (a chartered company, corporation, city, or the like). (*O.E.D.*)

[130] On the site of the present Queen Street, Cheapside. It took the name from the Sopers, or makers of "sope" (soap). [Riley's note, p. 33.]

[131] The Great Conduit at the junction of Cheapside and the Poultry, was the chief source of London's water supply. Water was piped underground from Tyburn to a lead tank in the Conduit, and was delivered to the public by means of pipes and brass taps in the stone framework. [Cf. Charles Pendrill, *London Life in the 14th Century*, New York, Adelphi Co., n.d., p. 37.]

[132] The first hour of the day, beginning either at six o'clock throughout the year, or at the varying time of sunrise; also sometimes used for the period between the first hour and tierce, the end of which period (about nine o'clock) is believed to have been *high prime*, or *prime large*. [*O.E.D.*]

[133] Possibly there may be something omitted here; as the measure of 7 inches (which cannot have been the length) bears no reference to what follows. [Riley's note.]

deceit upon the common people that might ensue and the scandal of the trade, on the pain aforesaid.

"Also—that no one shall expose his wares openly for sale in market on Sundays at any place, but only within his own dwelling to serve the common people, on the pain aforesaid.

"Also—that if any one sells old shoes, he shall not mix new shoes among the old in deceit of the common people and to the scandal of the trade, on the pain aforesaid.

3. *Journeymen Cordwainers Charged with Making an Illegal Fraternity, 1387*

Riley, Memorials of London, II, 495–496 (from London Letter-Book H, fol. ccxix).

John Clerk, Henry Duntone, and John Hychene were attached on the seventeenth day of August, in the eleventh year [of Richard II], etc., at the suit of Robert de York, Thomas Bryel, Thomas Gloucestre, and William Midenhale, overseers of the trade of cordwainers, and other reputable men of the same trade, appearing before Nicholas Extone, mayor, and the aldermen in the Chamber of the Guildhall of London; and were charged by the said prosecutors for that, whereas it was enacted and proclaimed in the said city, on behalf of our lord the King, that no person should make congregations, alliances, or covins of the people privily or openly; and that those belonging to the trades, more than other men, should not, without leave of the mayor, make alliances, confederacies, or conspiracies; the aforesaid John Clerk, Henry Duntone, and John Hychene, serving men of the said trade of cordwainers, together with others, their accomplices, on the Feast of the Assumption of the Blessed Virgin [August 15] last past, at the Friars Preachers [134] in the said city brought together a great congregation of men like unto themselves and there did conspire and confederate to hold together, to the damage of the commonalty and the prejudice of the trade before mentioned and in rebellion against the overseers aforesaid; and there, because Richard Bonet, of the trade aforesaid, would not agree with them, made assault upon him so that he hardly escaped with his life, to the great disturbance of the peace of our lord the King and to the alarm of the neighbors there and against the oath by which they had before been bound, not to make such congregations, or unions, or sects, for avoiding the dangers resulting therefrom.

[134] The House of Black Friars. [Riley's note.]

And the said persons, being examined and interrogated thereon, could not deny the same; but they further confessed that a certain Friar Preacher, "Brother William Bartone" by name, had made an agreement with their companions and had given security to them that he would make suit in the Court of Rome for confirmation of that fraternity by the Pope; so that, on pain of excommunication and of still more grievous sentence afterwards to be fulminated, no man should dare to interfere with the well-being of the fraternity. For doing which he had received a certain sum of money which had been collected among their said companions, a deed which notoriously redounds to the weakening of the liberties of the said city, and of the power of the officers of the same. Wherefore, by award of the said mayor and aldermen, it was determined that the said John Clerk, Henry Duntone, and John Hychene should be confined in the Prison of Newgate until they should have been better advised what further ought to be done with them.

4. Regulations for Bakers, 1378

London, Corporation, *Calendar of Letter-Books, Letter Book H*, ed. by Sharpe, pp. 106–107.

Articles given in charge to bakers of white bread and of brown bread,[135] which they are bound on oath to keep, *viz.*:

First that every baker swear to charge his servants to bolt their meal twice, that is to say with a large bolter and a smaller one, and that he will use his diligence to make his servants work well in kneading, as well as to keep the proper time for so doing.

Also that if anyone be found to be ignorant or unwilling to make bread in the manner aforesaid, let him be put out of the mystery.[136]

Also that they make four loaves for a penny of the flour that is bolted with the smaller bolter.

Also that they bake not with water from the fountains,[137] under the penalty ordained.

Also that they buy not bad meal to mix with good, under the penalty ordained.

[135] "Tourte," a coarse brown bread made of unbolted meal, and very different from the modern "tourte" or tart. [Sharpe's note.]
[136] That is, out of the gild of the bakers.
[137] It has been suggested that spring water was too hard for the proper kneading of bread. [Sharpe's note.]

Also that no baker sell to hucksters more than thirteen loaves for twelve without gift or other "courtesy." [138]

Also that no brown-bread baker handle a bolter or make white bread.

Also that bread of the poorer leaven be made bolted.

Also that no horse bread be made except of pure beans and peas without mixture of other grain or other bran, under heavy penalty.

5. *Ordinance of the Writers of Text-Letter, Limners, and Others Who Bind and Sell Books, 1403*

Riley, *Memorials of London*, II, 557–558 (from London Letter-Book I, fol. xxv).

Be it remembered that on the twelfth day of July, in the fourth year [of Henry IV], etc., the reputable men of the craft of writers of text-letter, those commonly called "limners," and other good folks, citizens of London, who were wont to bind and to sell books, presented here unto John Walcote, mayor, and the aldermen of London a certain petition in these words:

"Unto the honorable lords, and wise, the mayor and aldermen of the city of London, pray very humbly all the good folks, freemen of the said city, of the trades of writers of text-letter, limners, and other folks of London who are wont to bind and to sell books, that it may please your great sagenesses [139] to grant unto them that they may elect yearly two reputable men, the one a limner, the other a text-writer, to be wardens of the said trades, and that the names of the wardens so elected may be presented each year before the mayor for the time being, and they be there sworn well and diligently to oversee that good rule and governance is had and exercised by all folks of the same trades in all works unto the said trades pertaining, to the praise and good fame of the loyal good men of the said trades and to the shame and blame of the bad and disloyal men of the same. And that the same wardens may call together all the men of the said trades honorably and peaceably when need shall be, as well for the good rule and governance of the said city as of the trades aforesaid. And that the same wardens, in performing their due office, may present from time to time all the defaults of the said bad and dis-

---

[138] It appears to have been the custom at one time for bakers to give to each huckster who dealt with them six-pence each Monday morning by way of *estrene* or present, and three-pence on Fridays as "curtesye" money; but this practice had been forbidden early in the fourteenth century, and the more ancient usage of giving "a baker's dozen" reverted to. [Sharpe's note.]

[139] *Tressagesses.* [Riley's note.]

loyal men to the chamberlain at the Guildhall for the time being, to the
end that the same may there, according to the wise and prudent discretion of the governors of the said city, be corrected, punished, and duly
redressed. And that all who are rebellious against the said wardens as
to the survey and good rule of the same trades may be punished according to the general ordinance made as to rebellious persons in trades of
the said city, as set forth in Book G, fol. cxxxv.[140] And that it may please
you to command that this petition, by your sagenesses granted, may be
entered of record for time to come, for the love of God and as a work of
charity."

Which petition having been read before the said mayor and aldermen, and fully understood, for the reason especially that it concerned
the common weal and profit, that transgressors of the ordinance aforesaid should be severely punished, as before stated; it was unanimously
granted by them that the ordinance should thereafter be faithfully observed and that transgressors should be punished in manner as above
stated.

6. Skilled Labor for the King's Works, 1350

Rymer, *Foedera*, 2d ed., V, 670.

The King to all and singular, the sheriffs, mayors, bailiffs, and his other
lieges, as well within the liberties [141] as without, to whom greeting. Know
ye that we have appointed our beloved Hugh de St. Albans, master of
the painters assigned for the works to be executed in our chapel at our
palace at Westminster, to take and choose as many painters and other
workmen as may be required for performing those works in any places
where it may be expedient, either within the liberties or without, in the
counties of Kent, Middlesex, Essex, Surrey, and Sussex, and to cause
those workmen to come to our palace aforesaid, there to remain in our
service at our wages as long as may be necessary. And therefore we command you to be counseling and assisting this Hugh in doing and completing what has been stated, as often and in such manner as the said
Hugh may require.

[140] Also it is ordained that all the mysteries of the City be lawfully ruled and governed,
each in its kind, so that no deceit or false work be found therein by good men elected and
sworn from each mystery. And if any be rebellious against them, let him be fined and imprisoned in manner prescribed. (London, Corporation, *Calendar of Letter-Books, Letter-
Book G*, p. 174.)
[141] In England before 1850, a district within the limits of a county, but exempt from
the jurisdiction of the sheriff, and having a separate commission of the peace. (*O.E.D.*)

AGRICULTURE

1. Goods and Stock of a Well-to-Do Yeoman Farmer, 1381

Powell, *The Rising in East Anglia in 1381*, pp. 143–145 (from Excheq. K.R. Escheators' Inq. Series I. File 1167).

Inquisition taken at Ipswich, August 8, 5 Richard II . . . by the oath of jurors, who say upon their oath that Thomas Sampson,[142] who for certain treasons and felonies by him committed against his allegiance [143] was condemned to death, had . . . goods and chattels in the county of Suffolk, namely:

At Kersey in the said county, 6 stots, 30s.; 4 oxen, 40s.; 5 bullocks, 15s.; 3 foals, 10s.; 8 pigs, 8s.; 20 geese, 3s. 4d.; 2 quarters of wheat (*frumenti*) in the granary, 10s.; 2 quarters of malt, 8s.; 16 acres of [growing] wheat, 40s.; 8 acres of dredge,[144] 11s. 8d.; 24 acres of peas and oats, 32s.; 2 cart loads of hay, 4s.; 1 tumbrel with a *cartebonke*,[145] 2s.; old timber, 2s.

. . . At Harkstead . . . [where he evidently lived], in his chamber, 3 beds with sheets (*linthiaminibus*) and other necessaries, 53s. 4d.; 2 basins with a ewer(?) (*peluvia cum lavatore*); 3 copper pots and other copper vessels, 30s.; 1 silver dish with 6 silver spoons, 12s.; 2 table-napkins with 2 towels, 3s. 4d.; 2 dozen pewter vessels, 6s. 8d.; 2 pewter pots and 2 pewter saltcellars (*selers*) 16d.; 2 leaden [vessels], 10s.; wooden vessels, 6s. 8d.; 6 oxen, 60s.; 8 stots, 40s.; 8 cows, 40s.; 2 bulls, 6s. 8d.; 2 bullocks, 6s.; 6 calves, 6s.; 300 ewes (*multones oves matrices*) and lambs, £15; 6 pigs, 6s.; 6 geese, 12d.; 10 capons, 20d.; 18 acres of wheat, 45s.; 17 acres of rye,[146] 34s.; 23 acres of barley, 57s. 6d.; 26 acres of peas and oats, 33s. 8d.; 8 cart-loads of hay, 16s.; 2 carts, whereof 1 is iron-[tired],[147] 13s. 4d.; 2 tumbrels, 3s. 4d.; 2 plows with all the equipment, 2s.

[142] This man was a leader of the rebels at Ipswich and East Suffolk, where Chaucer's cousins must have been in danger of losing their property through his followers.
[143] *Ligeanciam.* A feudal term denoting the oath of fidelity by which a vassal was bound to his lord. See C. D. DuCange, *Glossarium mediae et infimae Latinitatis*, 10 vols., Niort, 1883–1887. All further references to this dictionary are indicated by the author's name only.
[144] See above, p. 85n.
[145] Probably a *char-à-banc*, "a kind of long and light vehicle with transverse seats looking forward." (*O.E.D.*)
[146] *Siliginis.* Although in classical Latin *siligo* meant winter wheat, in Baxter and Johnson, *Medieval Latin Word List* it is glossed as "rye."
[147] "Unde j ferri."

. . . At Freston . . . [where he had a third farm], 4 stots, 20*s.*; 2 oxen, 20*s.*; 15 cows with 1 bull, £4; 100 hoggasters, 75*s.*; 2 acres of wheat, 5*s.*; 5 acres of rye, 10*s.*; 22 acres of peas and oats, 29*s.* 4*d.*; 2 cartloads of hay, 4*s.*; 1 cart, broken (*debilem*), 2*s.* 6*d.*; 1 plow with equipment, 12*d.*

Item, they say that the said Thomas had . . . one-eighth of a certain ship called "Waynpayn" of Harwich, 53*s.* 4*d.*

• • •

Sum of the particulars of Kersey	£10 16*s.*
Sum of the particulars of Harkstead	£39 16*s.* 6*d.*
Sum of the particulars of Freston	£15 0*s.* 2*d.*[148]
The ship	53*s.*
[Total	£65 13*s.*]

CROOKS WHO LIVE BY THEIR WITS

1. Proclamation against Vagrants, 1359

Riley, *Memorials of London*, I, 304–305 (from London Letter-Book G, fol. lxxviii).

Forasmuch as many men and women, and others, of divers counties, who might work, to the help of the common people, have betaken themselves from out of their own country to the city of London and do go about begging there so as to have their own ease and repose, not wishing to labor or work for their sustenance, to the great damage of the common people; and also do waste divers alms which would otherwise be given to many poor folks, such as lepers, blind, halt, and persons oppressed with old age and divers other maladies, to the destruction of the support of the same—we do command on behalf of our lord the King, whom may God preserve and bless, that all those who go about begging in the said city and who are able to labor and work for the profit of the common people shall quit the said city between now and Monday next ensuing. And if any such shall be found begging after the day aforesaid, the same shall be taken and put in the stocks on Cornhill for half a day the first time, and the second time he shall remain in the stocks one whole day, and the third time he shall be taken and shall remain in prison for forty days and shall then forswear the said city forever. And every constable and the beadle of every ward of the said city shall be em-

[148] This includes the value of Sampson's share of the "Waynpayn." The property at Freston was worth £12 6*s.* 10*d.*

powered to arrest such manner of folks and to put them in the stocks in manner aforesaid.

2. Dumb Impostors, 1380

Riley, *Memorials of London*, II, 445–446 (from London Letter-Book H, fol. cxxv).

On October 24, John Warde, of the County of York, and Richard Lynham, of Somerset County, two impostors, were brought to the hall of the Guildhall before the mayor, aldermen, and sheriffs and questioned why, although they were stout enough to work for their food and raiment and had their tongues to talk with, they pretended that they were mutes and had been deprived of their tongues, and went about in divers places of the city carrying in their hands two ell measures, an iron hook and pincers, and a piece of leather shaped like part of a tongue, edged with silver and with writing around it to this effect: "This is the tongue of John Warde." With which instruments and by means of divers signs they gave many persons to understand that they were traders, in token whereof they carried the ell measure, that they had been plundered by robbers of their goods, and that their tongues had been drawn out with the said hook and then cut off with the pincers, they making a horrible noise like unto a roaring, and opening their mouths, so that it seemed to all who examined the same that their tongues had been cut off, to the defrauding of other poor and infirm persons and in manifest deceit of the whole of the people.

Wherefore they were asked how they would acquit themselves thereof; upon which they acknowledged that they had done all the things above imputed to them. And it was awarded that they should be put upon the pillory on three different days, each time for one hour in the day, the said instruments being hung about their necks each day.

3. Games of Chance, 1376

Riley, *Memorials of London*, II, 395–396 (from London Letter-Book H, fol. xxxii).

Many times between Christmas and the first Sunday in Lent, Nicholas Prestone, tailor, and John Outlawe went to John atte Hille and his brother William and asked them if they would like to make some money at tables or checkers, commonly called "quek."

Upon their saying "Yes," John Outlawe told them to follow him and he would show them a place and a man from whom they could easily win; and he offered to be their partner, to win or to lose.

They followed him to the house of Nicholas Prestone in Friday Street, and there they found Nicholas with a pair of tables on the outside of which was painted a checker board called a "quek." Nicholas asked them if they would play at tables [149] for money. They agreed and played with John Outlawe and lost a sum of money, because the dice were loaded.

John then left them to play alone, and they continued to lose. The tables were then turned, and they played "quek" with Nicholas until they had lost at both games 39s. 2d. Then, wondering at their continued losing, they examined the board and found that in three quarters of it all the black squares were lower than the whites, and in the fourth part, the reverse. They found also that the dice were loaded (false and deceptive). And because they would play no longer, Nicholas and John Outlawe stripped John atte Hille of a cloak valued at 16s. . . .

The checker board was shown in court, and Nicholas was asked if it was his. He said that it was not; that it had been given him as a pledge for 5s., by a man of the town of——, together with two spoons and a mazer; that he had never played with it and did not know it was false.

The men were found guilty, had to return the 39s. 2d., and restore the cloak or pay for it, and had also to stand in the pillory while the checker board was burnt beneath them and then to remain in prison until the mayor and aldermen should order their release.

4. Magic and False Accusation, 1382

Riley, *Memorials of London*, II, 472–473 (from London Letter-Book H, fol. clv).

On October 4, . . . Robert Berewold was attached to make answer, as well to the mayor and commonwealth of the city of London as to Johanna Wolsy, in a plea of deceit and falsehood, etc. Who made plaint that a certain mazer having been stolen from the house of Matilda de Eye in the parish of St. Mildred Poultry in London, at the request of one Alan, a water-bearer, the said Robert asserted and promised that he would let the same Alan know who had stolen the same.

And thereupon he took a loaf and fixed in the top of it a round peg

---

[149] The game at the "tables," played with dice upon the inside of the board, probably resembled our backgammon; that on the outer side, or the "checkers," was probably played with rounded pebbles rolled upon the squares, the one party staking on the white squares, the other on the black; perhaps similar to the game called "checkstone" at a later date. In the present instance, the odds in favor of the black squares would be three to one, supposing that the object was to hit the squares. [Riley's note.]

of wood and four knives at the four sides of the same in form like a cross, and then did soothsaying and the art magic over them. Which done, he alleged that the said Johanna had stolen the cup, falsely and maliciously lying therein and unjustly defaming her, to Johanna's scandal and manifest disgrace and grievance.

And the said Robert, being questioned as to the matters aforesaid, how he would acquit himself thereof, said that he could not deny the same. . . . And because by such soothsaying, magic arts, and falsities good and lawful men and women might easily and without deserving it incur injury in their name and good repute, and seeing that such sorcery is manifestly opposed to the doctrine of Holy Writ, and in order that others might beware of doing the like, it was adjudged that the said Robert should be put upon the pillory the same day, there to remain for one hour of the day, the said loaf, with the peg and knives stuck in it, being hung from his neck. . . .

And further, because the said Alan, from the faith he put in the words of the same Robert, had oftentimes defamed the said Johanna in the same parish, calling her a thief, it was adjudged that on the Sunday next ensuing he should go to the said church and at the hour of mass, in the presence of the parishioners and other neighbors, say and confess that he had falsely defamed the said Johanna.[150]

5. A Sleeping Powder Used by Rogues, ca. 1376

Arderne, *Treatises of Fistula in Ano*, ed. by Power, pp. 100–101.

A powder to make a man sleep against his will, used by rogues and vagabonds who fall into company along the road with pilgrims so that they may rob them of silver when they are asleep: Take equal quantities of seed of henbane, darnel, black poppy, and dried briony root; pound it together in a brass mortar very fine. Put some in his soup, or in a piece of bread, or in his drink, and he shall sleep at once, whether he wishes to

---

[150] A similar case is recorded earlier in the same year, in which Henry Pot was attached to answer to the same accusation as that confronting Robert Berewold, "that whereas one Simon Gardiner had lately lost a mazer cup, the said Henry came to him and promised that he would let him know who had stolen the cup, and so cause him to regain it. And hereupon, the same Henry made thirty-two balls of white clay, and over them did sorcery, or his magic art; which done, he said that the same Cristina [who, with her husband, Nicholas Fremen, brought the accusation against him] had stolen the cup, falsely and maliciously lying therein." Henry acknowledged his guilt and was sentenced to the pillory "for one hour of the day. And the sheriffs were ordered to have proclamation made as to the reason for the same." (Riley, *Memorials of London*, II, 462–463 [from London Letter-Book H, fol. cxliii].)

or not, all day or longer, according to the amount that has been given to him.[151]

6. A Canon's Downfall, 1395

King's Bench, Controlment Roll 42, m. 11 d.

Proceedings before the justices of the peace against Thomas Honlot of Forncett, clerk, formerly servant of John de Toyngton, a monk of Bingham priory, for giving his said master a drink mixed with poison, whereof he died at once; and as a canon of Walsingham, breaking into a small room at Walsingham Parva in the priory of Walsingham and stealing divers goods of the cellarer there, and at Walsingham Parva breaking into a box (*pixidem*) of the sacristan at the altar of St. Katherine and taking ten shillings in silver, and for other thefts and a rape.

7. A Smooth-Tongued Villain, 1387

Riley, *Memorials of London*, II, 496–498 (from Letter-Book H, fol. ccxix).

On Tuesday, September 17 . . . before Nicholas Extone, mayor, and the aldermen, in the Chamber of the Guildhall of London, . . . William Frenkysshe, of the County of Stafford, was attached to make answer, as well to our lord the King and his people as to John Tylneye, of the County of Norfolk, in a plea of deceit and falsehood, etc.; and as to which the same John made plaint that the said William came to him at Tylneye and said that he was the son of the Earl of Ormond, and because our lord the King wished to have him married to one of the Queen's damsels against his will, he had fled from the court and was now concealing himself in those parts; as, contrary to the King's will, it was his own wish to marry elsewhere as he might feel disposed; and he asked the same John if he would find him lodging and decent clothes, such as suited his rank, until such time as he should be able otherwise to make provision, from the profits of his castles and houses, for the same; and then, he said, he would take to wife Katherine, the daughter of the said John, a child then seven years of age, and make her a countess; and he would have her taken care of in one of the nunneries founded by his ancestors until she should arrive at full age for him to marry her, etc. Wherefore John Tylneye, giving full credence to his words, sold divers lands, tenements, and other goods and chattels of his, to support and find the said William in food and clothing.

[151] The ribald's potion would not have done much harm even in considerable doses. [Power's note.]

After this, the same William said that John and his daughter must go with him to the neighborhood of Cambridge, where he had two castles, and there they would stay until he should have made other arrangements as to his estate and future management. John Tylneye, in like manner giving credence to these words of his, together with his daughter and the said William, went to Cambridge; and then, with other false and deceiving words, the same William told him that they must go to London, to the King's Council there, on various business of his, and for prosecuting his suits there. Accordingly they came to London, to a hostelry there in Eastcheap called the Bell on the Hoop, where this same William requested John to let him have a handsome chamber and one befitting his rank; which John Tylneye accordingly did, and called for bread, wine, ale, and other victuals at the command of the said William; and paid for the same, as well as all their other expenses, both there and everywhere else; and in the same chamber he made the said Katherine lie with him in his bed for one night. And so, continuing such malevolence and falsehood, this William maliciously and falsely continued and persevered in the same, etc., in contempt of our lord the King, and in manifest deceit of his people, and to the no small damage and grievance of the same John, and the impoverishment of his estate.

The said William, questioned thereupon . . . acknowledged that he was in every way guilty of all the falsehood and deceit aforesaid save and except the words imputed to him as having been spoken about our lord the King; and he put himself upon the favor of the Court as to the same. For his falsehood and deceit aforesaid, so committed, and in London especially, and in order that others might beware of doing the like . . . it was adjudged that the said William should be put upon the pillory the same day, there to remain for three hours, a whetstone, in token of his being a liar, being hung from his neck. And precept was given to the sheriffs to have the reason for the said punishment publicly proclaimed. After that, they were to take him back to the prison of Newgate, where he was to remain until he should have satisfied the said John Tylneye as to the damages awarded to him in the sheriffs' court . . . and also until the mayor should have been more fully advised as to his release.

8. A Thief and Murderer Who Abjured the Realm, 1347

Chancery Miscellanea, Writs and Returns, 104/4.

Memorandum that on July 6, [21 Edward III], Henry de Roseye abjured the realm of England before John Bernard, the King's coroner, at the church of Tendele in the County of Kent [where he had taken sanctuary] [152] in form following:

Hear this, O lord the coroner, that I, Henry de Roseye, have stolen an ox and a cow of the widow of John Welsshe of Retherfeld; and I have stolen eighteen beasts from divers men in the said county. And I acknowledge that I have feloniously killed Roger le Swan in the town of Strete in the hundred [153] of Strete in the rape [154] of Lewes and that I am a felon of the lord King of England. And because I have committed many ill deeds and thefts in his land, I abjure the land of the Lord Edward King of England, and [I acknowledge] that I ought to hasten to the port of Hastings, which thou hast given me, and that I ought not to depart from the way, and if I do so I am willing to be taken as a thief and felon of the lord King, and that at Hastings I will diligently seek passage, and that I will not wait there save for the flood and one ebb if I can have passage; and if I cannot have passage within that period, I will go up to the knees into the sea every day, endeavoring to cross; and unless I can do so within forty days, I will return at once to the church, as a thief and a felon of the lord King, so help me God.[155]

[152] A church or other sacred place in which, by the law of the medieval church, a fugitive from justice, or a debtor, was entitled to immunity from arrest. . . . By English law, a fugitive charged with any offence but sacrilege and treason might escape punishment by taking refuge in a sanctuary, and within forty days confessing his crime and taking an oath which subjected him to perpetual banishment. (O.E.D.)
[153] In England . . . a subdivision of a county or shire having its own court. (O.E.D.)
[154] One of the six administrative districts into which Sussex is divided, each comprising several hundreds. (O.E.D.)   [155] Cf. below, pp. 284–285.

5. Entertainment

Judging from the records and considering the cramped quarters in which the majority of the people lived in the fourteenth century, their recreation must have taken place largely outside the home. The nobles and the rich merchants, of course, with their huge halls, could and did entertain lavishly at feasts, where some form of entertainment, such as that provided by dancers or minstrels, accompanied the incredibly elaborate dinner. At many such feasts Chaucer must certainly have been present, but as far as we know he was never in a position to give them, though his father may have done so.

The social life of the poorer middle and lower classes centered in the market place and tavern, while for entertainment they thronged to watch those colorful and varied public ridings and processions which marked the many religious and secular holidays, the tournaments and jousts when held in public places, such as Cheapside, the wrestling matches, horse races, and various other public sports. When some more active form of amusement was wanted, it was always easy to pick a quarrel or reopen an old feud; and then, as the coroner's reports show, excitement enough immediately followed. [R.]

TOURNAMENTS AND FEATS OF ARMS

1. A Knight's Equipment for a Friendly Joust, 15th Century

Dillon, "On a MS Collection of Ordinances of Chivalry of the Fifteenth Century, Belonging to Lord Hastings," *Archaeologia,* LVII (1900), pp. 40–41.

First a helmet well padded and adorned with his crest.
A pair of plates, and thirty guiders.[1]
A "hanscement for the body with sleeves." [2]
A button to attach the front of the helmet to the breastplate, with a fastening for it.[3]
A shield covered with his device.

[1] The pair of plates are the breast and back to which the helmet was fastened, and the thirty guiders were either attachments such as hooks and eyes for closing the front to the back, in fact girders, or they may have been, as some have suggested, pieces of chain mail to cover the parts left exposed by the plate protection. [Viscount Dillon's note.]
[2] A close-fitting garment worn immediately beneath the armor to protect the body from the hard metal. It was probably of thin leather or some stout woollen material. [Viscount Dillon's note.]
[3] Probably the arrangement of a cord and button by which the front of the helmet was fastened to the breastplate as in military effigies (for example, the Warwick one) a buckle and strap were used. For the stout blows of a joust a cord would probably be stronger than a leather strap. [Viscount Dillon's note.]

A rerebrace with a roll of leather well stuffed.[4]

A large bridle gauntlet with a ring.[5]

A rerebrace for the right arm, with a movable shield to protect the armpit.[6]

A vambrace, a small gauntlet, two brickettes,[7] two dozen tresses,[8] six vamplates, twelve grapers,[9] twelve coronels,[10] and forty spears.

An armorer, with a hammer, pincers, nails, and a bickern.[11]

A good rough-shod courser with a soft bit and a great halter for the rein of the bridle.

A saddle well stuffed.[12]

A pair of "jambus." [13]

Three double girths with double buckles, and a double surcingle with double buckles, and a rein of Hungarian leather tied from the horse's head to the girths between his legs, to keep the saddle from slipping backward.

[4] Probably a padded protection for the left upper arm against which the [shield] would rest. [Viscount Dillon's note.]

[5] The *main-de-fer* or large bridle gauntlet, which in sixteenth-century examples has a fixed buckle at the top. This serves as would the ring for suspension of the *main-de-fer* from the arm, its large size making its retention in place more difficult. The gauntlet underneath it would be holding the reins, and the suspension of the *main-de-fer* would relieve the left hand of some of its work. [Viscount Dillon's note.]

[6] This shield "would cover the right armpit when it might, from the handling of the lance, become exposed." [Viscount Dillon's note.]

[7] Taces or brickettes were part of the body armor, what in some inventories is called a petticoat of mail. (Samuel R. Meyrick, "Remarks on the Ancient Mode of Putting on Armour," *Archaeologia*, XX (1824), 500 and Plate XX. The *O.E.D.* defines "tasse," of which "tace" is an obsolete variant, as follows: "A series of articulated splints or plates depending from the corslet, placed so that each slightly overlapped the one below it, forming a sort of kilt of armor to protect the thighs and the lower part of the trunk."

[8] Arming points for attaching various parts of the armor. [Viscount Dillon's note.]

[9] Viscount Dillon defines them as "metal rings with points to stick into the wooden blocks in the lance rests," and explains that "the object of these spikes was to keep the lance steady in the rest, the lance being held so that these spikes pressed into a wooden block in the lance rest. The shock of the blow was thus distributed over the whole body of the rider instead of depending only on the strength of the wrist of the jouster." [Pp. 42 and 35.]

[10] Lance-heads consisting of a socket and three or more diamond-shaped points, which without penetrating the opponent's armor would bite the surface and be less liable to glance off than would the single point. [Viscount Dillon's note.]

[11] An anvil with two projecting taper ends. (*O.E.D.*)

[12] One of those in which the jouster almost stood upright. [Viscount Dillon's note.]

[13] No doubt . . . . the long saddle steels . . . . sufficient to protect the rider's unarmed legs, for . . . . no armor is mentioned for the lower limbs. [Viscount Dillon's note.] The *O.E.D.* defines "jambeau" as a piece of armor for the leg.

A "rennyng for paytrell." [14]
A crupper of Hungarian leather.
A trapper for the courser. [15]
Two servants on horseback, well equipped.
Six servants on foot, all in the same livery.

2. *To Proclaim a Friendly Joust, 15th Century*

Dillon, "On a MS Collection of Ordinances of Chivalry of the Fifteenth Century, Belonging to Lord Hastings," *Archaeologia*, LVII (1900), 39.

We heralds of arms, bearing coats of arms, here proclaim to all gentlemen of family and of arms that there are six gentlemen of family and of arms who because of their great desire and honor have agreed to appear on the third day of next May before the high, mighty, and worshipful ladies and gentlewomen of this high and most honorable court, and to joust against all comers from nine of the bell before noon until six of the bell in the afternoon.

Then a diamond worth forty pounds is to be given to the stranger knight who in the opinion of the said ladies and gentlewomen is the best jouster, and to the next best a ruby worth twenty pounds, and to the third best jouster a sapphire worth ten pounds.

And on that day there shall be officers of arms to take the measure of their spears as they are fitted out, that is, with coronal, vamplate, and grapers [16] all of the size that they shall joust with. The said comers may take the length of the said spears in consultation with the said officers of arms, who shall be impartial toward all parties on the said day.

3. *Coming into the Field, 15th Century*

Dillon, "On a MS Collection of Ordinances of Chivalry of the Fifteenth Century, Belonging to Lord Hastings," *Archaeologia*, LVII (1900), 39.

The six gentlemen must come into the field unhelmed, with their helms carried before them. Their servants shall be on horseback, each of them carrying a spear ready to use (garniste), [17] and the said six servants shall

[14] Viscount Dillon describes this merely as part of the harness [p. 43]. *O.E.D.* gives "paytrell" as a variant of "peitrel," which it defines as "a piece of armor to protect the breast of a horse (often richly ornamented, and retained for ornament after its defensive use had passed away).

[15] A covering put over a horse or other beast of burden, made of metal or leather for purpose of defense, or of cloth for shelter and adornment. (*O.E.D.*)

[16] See above, p. 208*n*.

[17] That is, provided with coronal, vamplate, and grapers. See above, p. 208*n*.

ride before them into the field. As the six gentlemen shall come before the ladies and gentlewomen, a herald of arms shall be sent to the ladies and gentlewomen, and shall say, "High and mighty, honorable and right worshipful ladies and gentlewomen, these six gentlemen have come into your presence commending themselves as humbly as they can to your grace, beseeching you to give a diamond, a ruby, and a sapphire to the three best jousters from without, those that you think best deserve them."

When this message is finished, the six gentlemen shall go into the tilt-house [18] and put on their helms. And when the heralds cry, "To your quarters! to your quarters," then shall all the six gentlemen in the lists take off their helms, go home to their lodgings, and change [their clothing].

4. Bestowing the Prize, 15th Century

Dillon, "On a MS Collection of Ordinances of Chivalry of the Fifteenth Century, Belonging to Lord Hastings," *Archaeologia*, LVII (1900), 40.

Then, with the advice of all the ladies and gentlewomen, a lady comes forth and gives the diamond to the best of the jousters from without, saying: "Sir, these ladies and gentlewomen thank you for the pleasure you have given them and for your great labor this day in their presence. These ladies and gentlewomen say that you have jousted best this day; therefore they give you this diamond and wish you much honor and joy with your lady." The gift of the ruby and of the sapphire shall be made to the next two jousters in the same way.

Then shall the herald of arms stand up on high and say in a loud voice: "John has jousted well, Richard has jousted better, and Thomas has jousted best of all."

Then shall he to whom the diamond was given take a lady by the hand and begin the dance. And when the ladies have danced as long as they please, then spices and wine and drink [shall be served], and [the company] shall depart.

[18] "Tellws." "Probably a kind of shed or stall, for the convenience of the combatants. . . . It may have been so called from its having consisted chiefly of a sloping roof, in old French, *teil*, or *taulisse*, the sides being closed by curtains or blinds." (Albert Way, "Illustrations of Medieval Manners," *Archaeological Journal*, IV [1847], 232.)

5. The Jousting at Smithfield, 1390

Froissart, *The Chronicle of Froissart*, tr. by Berners, ed. by Ker, V, 419–424.

King Richard of England and his three uncles . . . arranged a great feast to be held at the city of London, where there should be jousts [19] and sixty knights to await all comers, and with them sixty ladies freshly appareled, to keep them company. These knights should joust two days besides Sunday, and the challenge should begin the next Sunday after the Feast of Saint Michael,[20] in the year of our Lord God 1390, on which Sunday the said sixty knights and sixty ladies at two o'clock in the afternoon should issue out of the Tower of London, and come along the city through Cheapside, and so to Smithfield; and that day twelve knights should be there ready to await all stranger knights who would joust.

This Sunday was called the Sunday of the Feast of Challenge. On the Monday next after, the said sixty knights should be in the same place ready to joust and await all comers courteously to encounter them with blunt-headed lances (rokettes).[21] To the best jouster from the outside should be given for a prize a rich crown of gold; and the best jouster of the inside, in the opinion of the ladies of the Queen's chamber, should have for a prize a rich girdle of gold.

On the Tuesday following, the knights should be again in the same place, to meet all manner of stranger squires and others who would joust with blunt-headed lances; and the best jouster on the outside should have for his prize a courser saddled; and the chief jouster of the inside should have a falcon.

The manner of this feast was thus arranged and devised,[22] and heralds were charged to cry and publish this feast in England, in Scot-

---

[19] As clerk of the King's works, Chaucer had charge of erecting the scaffolds or seats for this tournament.

[20] The Feast of St. Michael is September 29, which fell on a Thursday in 1390. The jousts therefore began on October 2.

[21] Cf. *O.E.D.* under "ratchet."

[22] On September 23, 1390, the following order was sent to each of the London aldermen: For the safe-keeping and maintenance of the peace of our lord the King, and for saving the honor of this city, we do command and charge you, strictly enjoining that you shall order in your ward that sufficient watch be made by persons able for defense, well arrayed, every night during the time that the revels and jousts now approaching shall be continued; and this in such manner that by your default no danger or disgrace shall befall the city aforesaid. (Riley, *Memorials of London*, II, 521–522 [from London Letter-Book H, fol. cclii].)

land, in Germany, in Flanders, in Brabant, in Hainaut, and in France. The heralds departed, some in one direction, and some in another. These tidings spread abroad into divers countries as the heralds had day and time sufficient. Knights and squires in various lands prepared themselves to be at this feast, some to see what England was like, and some to joust. . . .

> Among them was William of Hainaut,[23] the young earl of Ostervant, cousin of King Richard.

Then the Earl of Ostervant passed over [the Channel] on a Thursday and so came to Canterbury. On Friday he visited St. Thomas's shrine and offered there in the morning, and remained [in Canterbury] all that day. The next day he rode to Rochester; and because he had so large a company and so many carriages, he made the journey in easy stages to save his horses. On Sunday he rode to Dartford for dinner, and after dinner to London to be at the feast, which began the same day.

On the Sunday next after the Feast of St. Michael this feast and triumph were to begin, and that day were to take place in Smithfield the jousts called the Challenge. So the same Sunday, about three o'clock in the afternoon, there issued out of the Tower of London first threescore coursers ready for the jousts, and on every one a squire of honor, riding an easy pace. Then issued out threescore ladies of honor, mounted on fair palfreys, riding on the one side, richly appareled for the jousts; and every lady led a knight with a chain of silver, which knights were appareled to joust.

Thus they came riding along the streets of London with a great many trumpeters and other minstrels, and so came to Smithfield, where the Queen of England and other ladies and damsels were ready in chambers richly adorned to see the jousts, and the King was with the Queen. When the ladies that led the knights were come to the place, they were taken down from their palfreys, and they mounted up into chambers ready prepared for them.

Then the squires of honor alighted from the coursers, and the knights in good order mounted on them. Their helms were set on and made ready at all points.

Thither came the Earl of Saint Pol, nobly accompanied by knights and squires, all armed, for the jousts to begin the feast, which immediately commenced; and there jousted all the stranger knights (knyghtes

[23] Also known as William of Bavaria.

straungers) who wished to do so and had time before the night came on. Thus these jousts of challenge began and continued till it was dark. Then knights and ladies withdrew, and the Queen was lodged beside [St.] Paul's in the bishop's Palace, and there the supper was prepared. The same evening the Count of Ostervant came and was nobly received.

Now for these jousts on Sunday: for the answerer without, the Earl Walleran of St. Pol had the prize; and of the challengers, the Earl of Huntingdon [King Richard's half-brother]. There was goodly dancing in the Queen's lodging in the presence of the King and his uncles and other barons of England and ladies and damsels, continuing till it was day. . . .

On the next day, which was Monday, you might have seen in many places of the city of London, squires and varlets [24] going about with harness and doing other business of their masters. After noon King Richard came to the place all armed, richly appareled, accompanied with dukes, earls, lords, and knights; he was one of the inner party. The Queen, well attended with ladies and damsels, came to the place where the jousts were to be, and mounted into chambers and scaffolds prepared for them. Then the Earl of Ostervant, well attended by knights of his country, came into the field, and all were ready to joust. . . .

Then the jousts began. Every man strove to obtain honor. Some were struck down from their horses. These jousts continued till it was nearly night. Then all the people withdrew to their lodgings, knights and ladies, and at the hour of supper every man went to the court. There was a goodly supper, well prepared. For that day the prize was given to the Earl of Ostervant as the best jouster of the outer party, and well he deserved it. The prize was given him by the ladies, lords, and heralds who were appointed to be judges. Of the inner party, a knight of England called Sir Hugh Spenser had the prize.

The next day, Tuesday, there were jousts again in the same place, by all manner of squires, which lasted till it was night, in the presence of the King, the Queen, lords, and ladies. Then all the men withdrew to their lodgings as they had done the days before; and at supper they returned to the bishop's Palace, where the King, the Queen, and the ladies were. There was a goodly and costly supper, and afterward great dancing, continuing all night.

On Wednesday, after dinner, they jousted in the same place, all manner of knights and squires who would joust. That was a sore and a

[24] An attendant on a knight or other person of military importance. (*O.E.D.*)

rude joust, lasting till night. Then they withdrew, and at the hour of supper went where they had supped before. On Thursday the King gave a supper to all knights and gentlemen strangers, and the Queen to all ladies and damsels. Then on Friday the Duke of Lancaster gave a dinner for all stranger knights and squires, which was a goodly dinner.

On Saturday the King and all the lords departed from London for Windsor. The Earl of Ostervant and the Count of St. Pol, with all other stranger knights and squires, were requested to accompany the King to Windsor. Every man rode as it was convenient to the castle of Windsor. Then there began again great feasts, with dinners and suppers given by the King; and especially, the King did great honor to the Earl of Ostervant, his cousin, who was requested by the King and his uncles to take on him the Order of the Garter . . .

[He was accordingly made Knight of the Garter.]

6. *A Goodly Feat of Arms, 1381*

Froissart, *The Chronicle of Froissart*, tr. by Berners, ed. by Ker, III, 182–183.

Then came forth Edward Beauchamp and Clarence . . . of Savoy, who was a squire very hardy and strong and bigger in all his members than the Englishman was; so they came against each other and met fiercely and struck each other on the breast in such a way that Edward Beauchamp was overthrown backward, whereat the Englishmen were sorely displeased. And when he was up again, he took his spear and came again against Clarence, and so [they] met again, and there Edward Beauchamp was again overthrown to the earth, wherewith the Englishmen were more sorely displeased and said that Edward was too weak to contend with the French squire; the devil was on him to joust against him. So then they were parted, and told that they should do no more.

And when Clarence saw this, desiring to do deeds of arms, he said, "Lords, you do me wrong; and since you will that Edward shall do no more, then set some other against me in his place, that I may perform my enterprise." The Earl of Buckingham asked what he said, and it was told him; then he said the Frenchman spoke valiantly.

Then stepped forth an English squire . . . and came before the earl and kneeled down and desired that he might perform the battle; and the earl agreed thereto. Then this [squire] came forth and armed himself completely and took his spear, and Clarence his, and so they came against each and foined and thrust so sorely at each other that the spears flew all to pieces over their heads. And at the second encounter they did likewise, and at the third also, so that their spears were broken; and all the lords on both sides thought this deed a goodly feat of arms. Then they took their swords, which were very big, and in six strokes they broke four swords. And then they would have fought with axes, but the earl would not let them and said he would not see them fight to the finish, saying they had done enough. Then they drew back and others came forth.

7. A Foul Stroke, 1381

Froissart, *The Chronicle of Froissart*, tr. by Berners, ed. by Ker, III, 183–184.

Then came forth one Jenkin Clinton, an Englishman, a squire of honor with the Earl of Buckingham and very near to him, to joust with Johan de Castell Morant, a Frenchman. But the earl did not wish that his squire, who was small and slender of body, should have to contend in arms with so big a man as Johan de Castell Morant was; nevertheless, they were put together to make trial of each other, and so they came right fiercely together. The Englishman could not hold out against the Frenchman, but with their foining the Englishman was overthrown to the earth. Then the Earl of Buckingham said they were not at all evenly matched, and commanded his squire to go and rest; and so they parted.

Johan de Castell Morant, seeing this, said, "Sirs, if you think that your squire is too little to deal with me, send another to me at your pleasure, in order that I may perform my enterprise, or else it should be to my disgrace; and also I should have wrong if I should depart without doing any deeds of arms."

Then the constable and the marshal of the host said to all the knights thereabout, "Sirs, is there any of you that will satisfy this knight?"

To which answered Sir William of Faringdon, "Tell the knight that he shall not depart hence without doing deeds of arms; if it please him to rest a little, he shall soon be satisfied, for I shall arm myself against him." This answer pleased Johan de Castell Morant much, and so he went and sat down to rest. Soon the English knight was ready and came into the place.

So the two knights came afoot against each other fiercely, with their spears low couched,[25] to strike each other within the four quarters.[26]

[25] To couch was to lower (a spear, a lance, etc.) to the position of attack, grasping it in the right hand with the point directed forwards. (*O.E.D.*)
[26] The French original is "entre les IIII membres," literally, within the four limbs, *i.e.*, in the trunk of the body.

Johan de Castell Morant struck the English knight on the breast so that he stumbled and bowed, for his foot failed him a little; he held his spear low with both his hands and could not avoid striking Sir Johan in the thigh, so that the spear went clean through and the head was seen a hand's breadth on the other side. And with the stroke Sir Johan reeled, but did not fall. Then the English knights and squires were very sorely displeased and said it was a foul stroke. But the English knight excused himself and said that he was sorry for what had happened and that if he had known it would be so, he would never have begun it, saying that he could not avoid it because of the slipping of his foot, on account of the great stroke that Sir Johan had given. So the Frenchmen departed and took leave of the earl and of the other lords and took with them in a litter Sir Johan de Castell Morant.

8. *A Fatal Passage at Arms, 1389*

Continuation of Higden, *Polychronicon*, IX, 219–220.

The King kept Christmas at Woodstock. There, on the last day of December, the Earl of Pembroke, a young man not quite seventeen years old, insisted upon trying out his horse with another knight, Sir John Saint John, in preparation for the next tournament. When the two met, the knight, at the earl's bidding, flung his lance from one side. The part which he gripped hit the ground and stuck, while the other end flew up in the air. At this the earl's horse took fright and flung him with great force, so that the spear entered his body near the groin and inflicted a mortal wound. His helmet being knocked off at the same time, he was knocked senseless and died about noon.

Thereupon laughter was turned into tears, and there was universal mourning. The King was overcome with grief, and the Queen and her women shut themselves in her chamber and gave themselves up to their sorrow. The earl's servants could not think what would become of them and wondered whether life was better than death. The funeral was held at Hereford with great ceremony, and the earl was buried by the side of his father. The knight who had wounded him took to flight; if he had remained, he would undoubtedly have lost his own life.

9. *A Knight Injured in a Tournament, 1380*

Common Pleas, Plea Roll 480 m. 15 d.

Middlesex. Michaelmas,[27] 4 Richard II. Robert Lucas, citizen and gold-smith of London, brings a plea of debt (of £40) against John de Agnes-ford, knight. The plea is adjourned to February 3, 5 Richard II [1382], when he finds mainpernors, who later come and testify that the said John de Agnesford at the tournament on the Feast of St. George [April 23] last past at Windsor, in the King's presence, was so seriously broken and crushed in the legs and thighs that by reason thereof he can neither be carried nor can appear in court. . . .

10. *The Women Ape the Men, 1348*

Knighton, *Chronicon*, II, 57–58.

In these days a rumor and a great complaint arose among the people that when tournaments were held, in every place a company of ladies appeared, somewhat like performers during the time between combats (*quasi comes interludii*), in the diverse and marvelous dress of a man, to the number sometimes of about forty, sometimes fifty, ladies from the more handsome and the more beautiful, but not the better ones, of the entire kingdom; in divided tunics, that is, one part of one kind and the other of another kind, with small hoods and liripipes flying about the head in the manner of cords, and well encircled with silver or gold, even having across their stomachs, below the middle, knives which they vulgarly called daggers placed in pouches from above. Thus they came, on excellent chargers or other horses splendidly adorned, to the place of the tournament. And in such manner they spent and wasted their riches and injured their bodies with abuses and ludicrous wantonness that the common voice of the people exclaimed. Thus, they neither re-spected God nor blushed on account of the modest outcries of the people, having freed themselves from the restraint of matrimonial chastity. . . . But God against these as against all others appeared with a marvelous remedy, putting their frivolity to rout, for at the places and times designed for this vanity, he defeated them with heavy rainstorms, thunder, and the flash of lightning, and with the fury (*ventilatione*) of diverse extraor-dinary tempests.

[27] One of the four terms during which the superior courts of England were open. The Michaelmas term ran from November 2 to 25.

SPORTS

1. Hunting

The Master of Game was written between 1406 and 1413 by Edward, the second Duke of York, first cousin of two kings, Richard II and Henry IV. In Shakespeare's *Richard II* he is the treacherous Duke of Aumerle, and he worked at his book while in prison because of a plot to assassinate Henry IV. It is, therefore, the more interesting to observe that he dedicated his book to the son of this king, Shakespeare's Prince Hal. The duke was later released and died in the vanguard of the English army at Agincourt, one of the very few Englishmen slain there (cf. Shakespeare, *Henry V*, Act IV, scene vi).

The greatest part of his book is a translation from the French of the famous hunter and nobleman, Gaston, count de Foix, of whose court Froissart has left so vivid a picture. The Duke of York was, however, expert on the subject of hunting, and his three added chapters at the end, on hunting the hare and the hart, show this and show also how these sports were conducted in England.

Original, too, are the prologue and the epilogue, which are to be found in only one manuscript. Most interesting of all is the allusion to Chaucer and the quotation from memory of two lines from the *Legend of Good Women*. [R.]

THE MASTER OF GAME, 1406–1413

Edward, second duke of York, *The Master of Game*, ed. by Baillie-Grohman, pp. 1–3, 8–11.

To the honor and reverence of you, my right worshipful and dread lord, Henry, by the grace of God, son and heir unto the high excellent and Christian Prince, Henry IV, by the aforesaid grace, King of England and of France, Prince of Wales, Duke of Guienne, of Lancaster, and of Cornwall, and earl of Chester.

I, your own in all humility, have ventured to make this little simple book, which I recommend and submit to your noble and wise correction, which book, if it pleases your Lordship, shall be called *Master of Game*. And for this cause: that this book treats of what in every season of the year is most lasting, and to my thinking to every gentle heart most enjoyable of all games, that is to say, hunting. For though hawking with gentle hounds and hawks for the heron and the river [28] be noble and commendable, it seldom lasts at most more than half a year. For though men find from May to Lammas (August 1) game enough to hawk at, no one will find hawks to hawk with.[29] But as to hunting, there is no

[28] Water birds. "Not 'river' but the French *rivière*. *Rivière* originally meant 'the bank of a stream' . . . then 'hawking for waterfowl.' . . . By a further development the word came to mean 'waterfowl hunted with hawks.' " (Chaucer, *Canterbury Tales*, ed. by Manly, pp. 630–631.)

[29] "As the hawks would be mewing and unfit to fly." [Baillie-Grohman's note.]

JOUSTING; early fourteenth century
Baltimore, Walters Gallery (fragment of an ivory casket)

CHESS
Oxford, Bodl., MS 264, fol. 112

HUNTING THE HARE
Baltimore, Walters Gallery
MS W. 88, fol. 157v

BOY SHOOTING AT BIRD
Baltimore, Walters Gallery
MS W. 88, fol. 98

THE KING HUNTING THE HART
London, Brit. Mus., MS Royal 10 E. IV, fol. 253v

INDOOR AND OUTDOOR AMUSEMENTS
Early fourteenth century

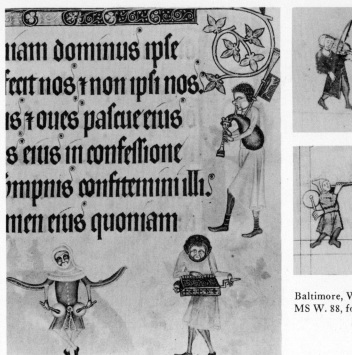

Baltimore, Walters Gallery
MS W. 88, fols. 60 and 156v

London, Brit. Mus., MS Add. 42130, fol. 176

E nsi ua qui amours demaine a son commant

Oxford, Bodl., MS 264, fol. 181v

MINSTRELS AND MUMMERS

Early fourteenth century

CORPUS CHRISTI PROCESSION; *ca.* 1400
London, Brit. Mus., MS Harl. 7026, fol. 13

season of all the year in which game may not be found in every good country, also hounds ready to chase it. And since this book shall deal entirely with hunting, which is so noble a game, and lasts through all the year, of various animals that grow according to the season for the gladdening of man, I think I may well call it *Master of Game*.

And though it be true, my dear lord, that many could better and more ably have treated this matter than I, yet there are two things that have principally emboldened and caused me to undertake this work. The first is trust of your noble correction, to which, as I said before, I submit this little and simple book. The second is that, though I be unworthy, I am master of this game with that noble prince your father, our all dear sovereign and liege lord aforesaid. And as I would not that his hunters nor yours that now are or that should come hereafter did not know the perfection of this art, I shall leave for these this simple memorial, for, as Chaucer says in his prologue of "The 25 Good Women," [30] "By writing have men mind of things passed, for writing is the key of all good remembrance." [31]

.   .   .

Now I shall prove how hunters live in this world more joyfully than any other men. For when the hunter rises in the morning, and sees a sweet and fair morn and clear, bright weather, and hears the song of the small birds, which sing so sweetly with great melody and full of love, each in its own language in the best way that it can; and when the sun is up and he sees fresh dew upon the small twigs and grasses, and the sun by his power makes them shine—that is great joy and pleasure to the hunter's heart.

And when he shall go to his quest or searching, he shall see or soon meet with the hart without great seeking and shall harbor [32] him well and readily within a little compass. It is great joy and pleasure to the hunter.

And afterward, when he shall come to the assembly or gathering and shall report before the lord and his company what he has seen . . . every man shall say, "Lo, here is a great hart and a deer of high feeding or

[30] *The Legend of Good Women*, which is referred to in the Retraction to the *Canterbury Tales* as "the book of the 25 Ladies."
[31] This is a paraphrase of ll. 25–26 of the Prologue to *The Legend of Good Women*, which are as follows:

> And if that olde bokes were a-weye,
> Y-loren were of remembraunce the keye.

[32] Trace the deer to its lair. [Baillie-Grohman's note.]

pasturing; let us go and move him." These things I shall describe later; then can one say that the hunter has great joy.

When he begins to hunt, and has hunted only a little, and shall hear or see the hart start before him, and shall know well that it is the right one, and his hounds that shall this day be finders shall come to the lair (bed), or to the fues (track), and shall there be uncoupled, and shall all run well and hunt, then has the hunter great joy and great pleasure. Afterwards he leaps on horseback, if he be of appropriate rank, otherwise on foot, with great haste to follow his hounds.

And in case by accident the hounds shall have gone far from where he uncoupled, he seeks some opportunity to get in front of them. And then he shall see the hart pass before him, and shall holloa and shout mightily, and shall see which hounds come in the van-chase,[33] and in the middle, and which are *parfitours*,[34] according to the order in which they shall come.

When all the hounds have passed before him, then he shall ride after them and shout and blow as loudly as he can, with great joy and great pleasure, and I assure you he thinks of no sin or other evil thing.

When the hart is overcome and at bay, he shall be glad. And later, when the hart is spayed [35] and dead, he cuts him up, makes his curée,[36] and rewards his hounds, and so he shall have great pleasure; and when he comes home, he comes joyfully, for his lord has given him some of his good wine to drink at the curée.

And when he has come home he shall doff his clothes and his shoes and his hose, and shall wash his thighs and legs, and perhaps all his body. In the meanwhile he shall order his supper, of vegetables and the neck of the hart and other good meats and good wine or ale. And when he has eaten and drunk, he shall be glad and well and at his ease. Then he shall take the air in the evening, because of the great heat he has endured. And then he shall go and drink and lie in his bed in fresh clothes, and shall sleep well and soundly all night, without any evil thoughts of sin. Therefore I say that hunters go into Paradise when they die, and live in this world more joyfully than any other men.

[33] The first in the chase. [Baillie-Grohman's glossary.]
[34] The last relay of hounds uncoupled during the chase of the stag. [Baillie-Grohman's appendix.]
[35] Despatched with a sword or knife. [Baillie-Grohman's note.]
[36] The portions of an animal slain in the chase that were given to the hounds; the cutting up and disemboweling of the game. (*O.E.D.*)

HUNTING THE HARE, 1406–1413

Edward, second duke of York, *The Master of Game*, ed. by Baillie-Grohman, pp. 181–186.

Now to speak of the hare, how he shall be sought and found and chased with hounds. . . .

When the door of the kennel is opened, the hunter shall say loudly, "Ho, ho, arere [Back there!]" so that his hounds will not come out too quickly.

When he uncouples his hounds, he shall say to them when he comes into the field, "Sto, mon amy, sto atrete [Hark, my friend, hark]." But when he has come out into the field, he shall blow three motes [37] and uncouple the hounds; then he shall speak twice to his hounds in this manner, "Hors de couple, avaunt cy, avaunt [Out of couples, forward there, forward]"; and then he shall say thrice, "So how"—and no more.

Afterward he shall say loudly, "Sa say cy avaunt [Forward, sir, forward]," and then, "Sa cy avaunt, sa cy avaunt so how"; and if he see the hounds draw rapidly from him and wish to run, he shall say to them, "How, amy—how, amy, [Ho, friend—ho, friend]," and then he shall say, "Swef, mon amy, swef [Softly, my friend, softly]" to make them go quietly, and between always blow three motes.

If any of his hounds find the scent where the hare has been, he shall say to them, "Oyez a Beaumont, le vaillant! [Listen to Beaumont, the brave]," or whatever the hound is called.

And if he sees that the hare has been feeding in green corn, or in any other place, and his hounds find [the scent] of her and fall well in the enquest [hunt] and chase it well, then he shall say, "La Douce, la il a este [Softly, he has been there]," and also, "So how!" with a high voice; and if his hounds do not chase as he wants them to, and if they hunt where the hare has not fed, then the hunter shall say "Illeoqs, illeoqs [Here, Here]" in the same place while they seek her.

. . .

And then the horsemen should keep well to one side and somewhat to the front, with long rods in their hands, to meet with the hare, and so blow a mote and rechase,[38] and holloa and set the hounds in the right if

[37] A mote was "a single note, which might be sounded long or short." [Baillie-Grohman's Appendix.]

[38] "A four-syllabled sound succeeded by an interval, blown three times." It was used to call back the hounds or put them on the right scent. [Baillie-Grohman's Appendix and Glossary.]

they see her, and also to prevent any hound following sheep or other animals, and if they do, to scold them severely and dismount and take them up and lash them well, saying loudly, "Ware, ware, ha ha ware," and lash them back to their fellows.

.   .   .

And whenever any hound catches (the scent), the hunter should shout to him by his name, and direct him to his fellows, as before is said, but not rechase till the hare is found, or someone meets her and blows the rights [39] and holloas, or else until he finds her pointing or pricking.[40] And if he finds that, he can well blow the rights and holloa and call three or four times and cry loud "Le voy, le voy!" [See her, see her!], till the hounds come thither and have well caught it. And (when) she is retrieved, blow and holloa and shout to the hounds, as it is said you should do at the finding, and let everyone follow after as fast as he can.

And if it happen when men hunt her and hounds chase her that she squat anywhere before the hounds, and that any hunter find her squatting, if the hounds are near, he should blow a mote and rechase and start her, and then holloa and shout to them, as is said above.

And if he find her squat, and the hounds are far from him, then he should blow as I last said before, and afterward, two motes for the hounds; and the berners [41] that hear him should answer him thus, "Trut, trut, trut!" [42] and draw all towards him with the hounds as fast as they can, saying to their hounds, "So-howe, mon amy, so-howe!" And when they are there and the hounds have all come up, they should check them with one of their rods; and when the hare is started, they should blow, holloa, and shout to the dogs as before is said. . . .

When she has been well chased and well retrieved, notwithstanding her rusing [43] and squatting and reseating, so that by strength at last she is bitten by the hounds,[44] whoever is nearest should start to take her whole from them, and hold her in one hand high over his head, and blow the death so that men may gather thither; and when they have come,

[39] The scent, the track. (*O.E.D.*)

[40] Track. [Baillie-Grohman's Vocabulary.]

[41] A man who has the charge of hounds, a huntsman, or, perhaps, would be more accurately described as a kennelman. [Baillie-Grohman's Appendix.]

[42] That is, with three motes.

[43] Making a detour or other movement in order to escape from the dogs. (*O.E.D.*)

[44] Hunting by strength of hounds meant hunting with dogs following a scent, as illustrated by this selection. Cf. Patrick Chalmers, *The History of Hunting*, London, n.d., p. 201.

then she should be stripped [of her skin], all save the head and the gall and the paunch cast away, and the remnant laid on a great staff or on a board, if somebody has one, or on the earth, and then it should be chopped as fine as it can be, so that it hang together. And when this has been done, then one of the berners should take it up with the head and hold it as high as he is able in his hands, and then whoever is most master should blow the death,[45] and as soon as he begins, every man should help and holloa.

And when the hounds have bayed as long as the master wishes, the berner should pull as high as he can every piece from the other and cast to every hound his reward. Then the master should blow a mote and stroke [46] if he thinks that the hounds have done enough; and also if the hounds are hot, he should rest until they are cooled, and then lead them to the water to lap. . . .

HOW THE KING SHALL HUNT THE HART, 1406–1413

Edward, second duke of York, *The Master of Game*, ed. by Baillie-Grohman, pp. 188–195.

The master of the game shall arrange with the master forester or parker where the king is to hunt on such a day, and if the tract be wide, the forester or parker must warn the sheriff of the shire where the hunting is to be, to order stations [47] enough, and also carts to bring the slain deer to the place where the curées at hunts have usually been held. Then he should tell the hunters and fewterers [48] where they are to come, and the forester should have men ready there to meet them, so that they would go no farther nor straggle about, for fear of frightening the game before the king comes. If the hunting is to be in a park, all the men should remain at the park gate except [those at] the stations, who should be placed by the foresters or parkers before the king arrives.

Early in the morning the master of game should be at the wood to see that everything is ready, and he or his lieutenant or such hunters as he assigns should choose the greyhounds, and those that are to be teasers [49] to the king or queen, or their attendants. . . .

[45] We have no description of the notes. [Baillie-Grohman's Appendix.]

[46] The stroke must have been [a] grouping of short and long notes, but of this we have no record. [Baillie-Grohman's Appendix.]

[47] Men and hounds stationed at different places, usually on the boundaries of the district in which the game was to be roused and hunted, or at convenient passes from whence the hounds could be slipped at the game. [Baillie-Grohman's note.]

[48] The men who let loose the greyhounds. [Baillie-Grohman's note.]

[49] Small hounds to tease forth or put up the game. [Baillie-Grohman's note.]

The master forester or parker ought to show him the king's standing if the king wishes to stand with his bow, and where all the other bows are to stand. The yeoman for the king's bows ought to be there . . . and the grooms that keep the king's dogs. . . .

When all this is done, the master of the game should take horse and meet the king, bring him to his standing, and tell him what game is within the set [50] . . . how the greyhounds are placed, the stations, and where it is best for him to stand with his bow or his greyhounds. . . . The two fewterers ought to make fair lodges of green boughs at the tryst [51] to keep the king and queen and ladies and gentlewomen and also the greyhounds from the sun or bad weather.

When the king is at his standing or at his tryst . . . and the master of game or his lieutenant has set the bows and assigned who shall lead the queen to her tryst, then he should blow the three long motes for the uncoupling. . . .

Then the harrier [52] should uncouple his hounds and blow three motes and seek forth, saying loud and long: "Hoo, sto ho, sto, mon amy! Ho, sto!"

. . . As often as he passes within the set from one quarter to another, he should blow drawing,[53] and when he has passed the boundary of the quarter and entered a new quarter, he should blow three motes and seek forth; but if his hounds pursue anything as he wishes, and if any hound happen to find the scent of the king's [game], he should shout to him by his name and say loudly: "Oyez a Bemond [or whatever the hound is named], oyez-oyez! Assemble! assemble!" and holloa and rally.

If it be a hart and any of the hart hounds meet with it, they should blow a mote and rechase and relay, and go forth therewith, all rechasing at the same time. And if it come to the bows or the greyhounds and be dead, he should blow the death when he is come thither, and reward his hounds a little, and couple them up and go again to his place. And if the hart has escaped, he should no longer rechase, but blow drawing and draw in again, and in the best way that he can, take up his hounds and get in front of them. . . . Then the sergeant and the berners of the

[50] That quarter of the forest or park around which are set or stationed the men and hounds. [Baillie-Grohman's note.]
[51] The place or stand where the hunter took up his position to await the game he wished to shoot. [Baillie-Grohman's Appendix.]
[52] It was the harrier's business to drive away from the trysts any animals that should not be hunted. Cf. Patrick Chalmers, The History of Hunting, p. 209.
[53] Drawing was the hound's tracking of the game by the scent. (O.E.D.)

hart hounds should blow three motes, one after the other, uncouple where they suppose the best lair is for a hart, and seek as before is said.

.   .   .

[When] they find the great old wily deer that will not lightly go away, they hunt him well and lustily and make him run before bows and greyhounds, so that they fully do their duty. And all the while that the hunting lasts, the carts should go about from place to place to bring the deer to the curée. There the server of the hall should be to arrange the curées and to lay the game in a row, all the heads one way—and every deer's feet to the other's back. . . .

Then the master of the game should lead the king to the curée and show it him, and no man . . . should come within until the king has told the master of the game which deer he will give away and to whom. If the king wishes to stay on, he may; nevertheless, he usually goes home when he has done this.

2. *Outdoor Sports and Entertainments in London*

Although it is not certain that Chaucer was born in London, a sufficient number of the recorded facts of his life are associated with the city and its suburbs to show that by far the greater part of his fifty-odd years was spent there.

Of the London of his time there is extant neither a detailed contemporary description nor a map, so that the only picture we can get of it is a patchwork of bits taken from different sources and periods. It is interesting to observe in such a composite description how little the main outlines change during the four centuries between 1200 and 1600.

The earliest and also the most picturesque account of London life, from which the two following passages and that on horse-racing (p. 228) are taken, was written by William Fitzstephen, learned scholar and himself a citizen of London, as a preface to his history of Thomas à Becket, in whose household he lived as clerk and trusted friend. Although he wrote before 1200, the London he described is probably very largely as Chaucer knew it one hundred and fifty years later. [R.]

PLAYS, 12TH CENTURY

Stow, *A Survey of London*, I, 92–93.

"London, in place of the ancient theatrical shows and scenic entertainments, has devout plays, representations of the miracles which the holy fathers have wrought, or of the passions by which the martyrs revealed their constancy. . . ." [54] These or the like exercises have been continued

[54] Stow quotes this statement from Fitzstephen. His assertion that the plays were still given in Chaucer's time receives additional support in the proclamation made on August 12, 1385, by the mayor and aldermen, "forbidding any wrestling matches within seven miles of the city, either privily or openly, and also the performance of the play that customarily

till our time, namely in stage plays, whereof you may read in the year 1391 a play by the parish clerks of London at the Skinners' Well beside Smithfield, which continued for three days together, the King, Queen, and nobles of the realm being present.

YOUNG PEOPLE'S GAMES, 12TH CENTURY

Stow, *A Survey of London*, II, 226–228.

After dinner, all the youth of the city go to the fields for a popular game of ball. Pupils in different classes play with their own balls . . . various city officials with theirs. The aldermen, fathers, and the city magnates come on their horses to watch the sports of the young ones, and in their own way grow young with them; a natural heat seems to be stirred in them by watching so much movement and by sharing the pleasures of freer youth.

On certain Sundays in Lent after dinner "a fresh crowd of young men" go out into the fields on horses of first rank in war, of which each is "a steed fitted and trained to run the course." Sons of citizens who are laymen pour out of the gates in crowds, equipped with lances and war shields. The younger boys with split spear shafts from which the iron has been removed "stir up a pretence of war," play at battles in the field, and practice the methods of war. There come also many members of the [royal] household, if the king happens to be in the neighborhood, and of the retinues of bishops and [other] officials, and the attendants of barons, not yet girded for knighthood—all for love of fighting. The hope of victory excites them; the wild horses whinny, their limbs tremble, they champ their bits; impatient of delay, they cannot be made to stand still. When at last the hoofs of the horses beat the earth, the young riders, in divided troops, all try to overtake those in front and not to be left behind; they catch up with their fellows, unhorse them, and fly past.

During the Easter holidays they play at a kind of naval battle. A shield is fixed firmly into the middle of a tree, and a small boat, moved swiftly by hard rowing and the current of the river, has on its high stern a boy [ready] to pierce it with his lance. If he strikes his lance

took place at Skinners' Well, or any other such play, until further news arrived of the King's exploit. . . ." (London, Corporation, *Cal. of Letter-Books*, Letter-Book H, p. 272.) "The King's exploit" referred to is Richard II's expedition to Scotland. Stow says that the Skinners' Well was so named because the London skinners gave Scripture plays there each year. (Stow, *A Survey of London*, I, 16.)

against the shield, breaks it, and keeps his footing, he is successful; but if he strikes [too] hard and his lance is unbroken, he is thrown into the flowing river, and the boat by its motion carries him past the mark. Behind the shield, however, there are two boats at anchor, and in them many boys to seize the player as he goes under water, as soon as he comes up, or blows bubbles on the crest of a wave. On the bridge and in the solars [55] above the river there are onlookers ready to laugh heartily.

On holidays all the summer the boys play at archery practice, running, jumping, wrestling, putting the stone, sending missiles attached with thongs [slingshots?] beyond a mark, and duelling with bucklers. The girls Cytherea leads in dancing until moonrise, and the earth is beaten with the lively foot.

In winter on almost all holidays before dinner, foaming boars and pigs armed with gleaming teeth are made to fight for their heads so that they may be added to the flitches of bacon, or fat hooved bulls or huge bears are made to fight with dogs set upon them.

When the great swamp that borders the northern wall of the city is frozen over, crowds of boys go out for fun on the ice. Some take long runs and slide far across toward the other side. Others make themselves seats out of lumps of ice like great stones; and many running ahead, hand in hand, draw the one who is seated thus. With such a slippery speed of movement, sometimes they all lose their balance and fall head-long. Some know how to have [still] better sport on the ice: they fit to their feet and bind about their ankles bones, such as the thigh bones of animals, and take in their hands stakes tipped with iron; when they strike these on the ice, they are carried on with the speed of a flying bird or of a dart from a sling. Sometimes from a great distance, by agreement, two advance [in this way] from opposite sides; they come together, they lift their sticks, they strike at one another; one falls or both, not without bodily hurt; for after the fall even, by the very force of the motion they are carried far, and where they strike the ice they are skinned and bruised. Often the one who falls breaks an arm or a leg by falling on it; but youth is eager for glory, youth is greedy for victory, and in order to be the braver in real battles, they practise these mock battles.

[55] An upper room or apartment in a house or other dwelling. (*O.E.D.*)

A FATAL GAME, 1337

London, Coroner, *Calendar of the Coroners Rolls*, p. 196.

One Sunday in August, Walter de Mordone and his whole household were playing in the fields after dinner, except William Russel and John Paul, who were left behind to guard the house. As these two were having a friendly game, William Russel fell over John Paul; and as he fell, the point of John's knife, which had come through its sheath, pierced William's body and made a wound an inch deep and half an inch broad. William and John continued to live together in the same house for three weeks, having no idea that William would not recover; but when John saw that William was succumbing to the wound, he ran away, no one knew where. And William died of the wound about sunset on Wednesday after the Feast of the Nativity of the Blessed Mary.[56]

HORSE-RACING AT SMITHFIELD, 12TH CENTURY

Robertson, ed., *Materials for the History of Thomas Becket*, III, 6–7.

Just outside one of the city gates there is a field which is as smooth in fact as in name [Smithfield]. Here every Friday unless it is a major festival, there is a wonderful show of fine horses for sale. All the earls, barons, and knights who happen to be in the city and many of the citizens come either to look on or to buy. It is a pleasing sight to behold the ambling nags, so smoothly moving by raising and putting down alternately the two side feet together. The great coursers for armed men move more roughly but yet quickly, lifting up and putting down the two opposite fore and hind feet together. Splendid young colts, not accustomed to the bridle, proudly prancing kick about with their legs. Here are packhorses with strong, stout legs. There are the shapely, valuable steeds, beautiful in build and noble of stature, with ears and necks erect and plump haunches. In the movements of these, what the buyers chiefly watch is, first, an easy, pleasant walk, and then the gallop, when the two fore feet are raised and put down together and the hind feet in like manner alternately.

When a race is to be run by these horses and by such of the draft horses as are also good runners, the common beasts are led away with a great shouting and hullabaloo. The riders are boys, sometimes three, sometimes sets of two according to arrangement, all trained in managing horses. They have special bits for the unbroken animals; the great point

[56] This feast was celebrated September 8.

is not to let a competitor get in their way. The horses too are so eager for the race that their limbs tremble and they chafe at the delay; they cannot stand still. At the signal they leap forward and continue at a steady speed. The riders, urged on by love of praise and hope of victory, use spur and whip, and shout at their beasts. You would think that, as Heraclitus says, the whole world was moving, and that Zeno was altogether wrong in saying there is no such thing as motion and therefore it is impossible to reach the goal.

FOOTBALL AND COCKFIGHTING, 1409

London, Corporation, *Calendar of Select Pleas and Memoranda*, 1381–1412, pp. 291–292 (from Plea and Mem. R., A 40, m. 2 b).

Six men, citizens and tapisers, and two others, citizens and parishioners of St. Denis Bakchirche, were forced to give a bond of twenty pounds to the city chamberlain for their good behavior towards "the kind and good men of the mystery of Cordwainers" and that they would not collect money for a football (*pro pila pedali*) nor money called "cocksilver" for cocks, hens, capons, or other birds, or thrash any cock,[57] etc., in the streets or lanes of the city. March 4, 1409.

GAMES OF SKILL AND CHANCE

1. A Game of Chess, 1341

Froissart, *The Chronicle of Froissart*, tr. by Berners, ed. by Ker, I, lxxiii–lxxv.

So he called for chess, and the lady [58] had it brought in. Then the King asked the lady to play with him, and she consented gladly, for she wished to entertain him as well as she might. And that was her duty, for the King had done her good service in raising the siege of the Scots before the castle, and he was her right and natural lord in fealty and homage.

At the beginning of the game of chess, the King, who wished that the lady might win something of his, laughingly challenged her and said, "Madam, what will your stake be at the game?"

And she answered, "And yours, sir?"

Then the King set down on the board a beautiful ring with a large ruby that he wore.

Then said the Countess, "Sir, sir, I have no ring so rich as yours is."

[57] Whipping or thrashing the cock, a sport practised at wakes and fairs . . . in which carters, armed with their whips, were blindfolded, and set round a cock, to whip at random. (*O.E.D.*)

[58] The Countess of Salisbury. The king is Edward III.

"Madam," said the King, "set down what you have, and do not be so concerned over its value."

Then the Countess, to please the King, drew from her finger a light ring of gold of no great value. And they played chess together, the lady with all the wit and skill she could, that the King might not think her too simple and ignorant. The King, however, deliberately played poorly, and would not play as well as he knew how. There was hardly a pause between the moves, but the King looked so hard at the lady that she was very much embarrassed, and made mistakes in her play. When the King saw that she had lost a rook or a knight or some other piece, he would lose also, to restore the lady's game.

They played on till at last the King lost, and was checkmate with a bishop. Then the lady rose and called for the wine and comfits, for the King seemed about to leave. She took her ring and put it on her finger, and wanted the King to take his back also. She gave it to him, saying, "Sir, it is not appropriate that in my house I should take anything of yours, but instead, you should take something of mine."

"No, madam," said the King, "but the game has made it so. You may be sure that if I had won, I should have carried away something of yours."

The Countess would not urge the King further, but going to one of her damsels, gave her the ring and said, "When you see that the King has gone out and has taken leave of me, and is about to mount his horse, go up to him and courteously give him his ring again, and say that I will certainly not keep it, for it is not mine." And the damsel answered that she would do so.

At this, the wine and comfits were brought in. The King would not take of them before the lady, nor the lady before him, and there was a great debate all in mirth between them. Finally it was agreed, to make it short, that they should partake together, one as soon as the other. After this, and when the King's knights had all drunk, the King took leave of the lady and said to her aloud, so that no one should comment upon it, "Madam, you remain in your house, and I will go to follow my enemies." [59] At these words the lady courtesied low before the King, and the King freely took her by the hand and pressed it a little, for his pleasure, in sign of love. And he watched until the knights and damsels were busy taking leave of one another. Then he came forward again to

[59] The Scots.

say two words alone: "My dear lady, to God I commend you till I return again . . . and I hope you will feel otherwise than you have said to me."

"My dear lord," answered the lady, "God the Father glorious be your guide, and put you out of all base and dishonorable thoughts, for I am and ever shall be ready to serve you to your honor and mine."

Then the King went out of the room, and the Countess also, and she conducted him to the hall where his palfrey was. Then the King said that he would not mount while the lady was there; so, to make it short, the Countess took her full and final leave of the King and his knights, and returned to her bower with her maidens.

When the King was about to mount, the damsel whom the Countess had instructed came to the King and knelt; and when the King saw her, he raised her up quickly, and thought she would have spoken of another matter than she did. Then she said, "My lord, here is the ring which my lady returns to you, and prays you not to consider it as discourtesy, for she does not wish to have it remaining with her. You have done so much for her in other ways that she is bound, she says, to be your servant always."

When the King heard the damsel and saw that she had his ring, and was told of the wish and the excuse of the Countess, he was amazed. Nevertheless, he made up his mind quickly; and in order that the ring might remain in that house as he had intended, he answered briefly . . . "Mistress, since your lady does not like the little gain that she won from me, let it remain in your possession."

Then he mounted quickly and rode out of the castle to the lawn where his knights were. . . . Then they all set out together. . . . And the damsel returned and told the King's answer, and gave back the ring that the King had lost at chess. But the Countess would not have it, and claimed no right to it. The King had given it to the damsel; let her take it and welcome. So the King's ring was left with the damsel.[60]

2. *Money for Dicing, 1375*

John of Gaunt's Register, II, 315.

John [king of Castile] to our dear and well beloved. . . . clerk of our Great Wardrobe. We will and command you to pay and deliver . . .

---

[60] The passage above is an episode that "did not find its way into the vulgate text of Froissart, and so did not reach Lord Berners." [Ker's note.]

to ourselves and into our own hands £45 10s. 8d. to play at dice and for our other privy expenses and necessary occasions.

Given at the Savoy, September 20, 49 [Edward III].

MINSTRELSY

1. Traveling Minstrels and Bears, 1372

John of Gaunt's Register, II, 98.

John by the grace of God [king of Castile] to our beloved . . . steward of our town of Newcastle-under-Lyme . . . . Whereas it was found by inquisition before you . . . that William de Brompton, our burgess of the said town, and Margery his wife and all the ancestors of the said Margery have been wont and ought to have from time immemorial from every minstrel coming to the said town at the Feast of St. Giles [September 1] to make his minstrelsy, four and a half pence, and from every bear coming to the same town to be baited (chace) one course, we . . . command you . . . to cause the perquisites and privileges (choses et liberties) aforesaid to be delivered to them. . . .

Given at the Savoy, November 26, 46 Edward III.

2. Minstrels from Brabant Return Home, 1368

Chancery, Warrants (Privy Seal Bills) 918/2.

On the King's behalf let writs be made in due form under our Great Seal for Myttok, king of the minstrels of Brabant, Guynaud the Blind, Swankyn, and Rolether, minstrels, to pass in the port of Dover towards Calais with 6 horses, the same which they brought over with them, and no others, one horse price under 6 marks, one hackney price under 40s., their grooms (garceons) Clynkes and Wauter, 40 marks by exchange, and each of the said minstrels with 20 shillings (soldz) for expenses.

Given under our Privy Seal at Westminster, July 8, 42 Edward III.

3. A Raise in Salary for the Minstrels of John of Gaunt, 1374[61]

John of Gaunt's Register, II, 219.

John [king of Castile] to our receiver of Leicester . . . greeting. Whereas we have given to Hans Gough, piper, Henry Hultescrane, piper, Smeltes, piper, and James Sanche [or Sauthe], clarioner, our minstrels, to each of them 100s. by the year to be taken from the honor of Leicester by the hands of the receiver there . . . at the terms of St.

[61] This item is undated, but it occurs among several entries for 1374.

Michael and Easter by equal portions . . . we will and command you to pay and deliver 200s. each by the year for their lives to each of the said Hans, Henry, Smeltes, and James, taking acquittance from them for what you shall pay them. . . .

Given at the Savoy, the [blank] day of June.

4. A Christmas Mumming, 1377

Harleian MS (B.M.) 247 fol. 172v.

At the same time the commons of London made great sport and solemnity to the Prince.[62] For upon the Monday next before the Purification of Our Lady,[63] at night, and in the night, one hundred and thirty men were disguised and well mounted on horseback to go mumming to the said Prince, riding from Newgate through Cheapside, where many people could see them, with great noise of minstrelsy, trumpets, cornets,[64] and shawms, and a great many wax torches lighted. The first forty-eight rode like esquires, two and two together, in coats and cloaks of red say or sendal, and had their faces covered with vizards, well and handsomely made. After these esquires came forty-eight like knights, well arrayed in the same manner. After the knights came one excellently arrayed and well mounted, as though he were an emperor; after him some one hundred paces came one nobly arrayed as a pope; after him came twenty-four arrayed like cardinals; and after the cardinals came eight or ten arrayed and with black masks like devils not at all amiable, seeming like legates. All these rode through London and over London bridge to Kennington, where the young Prince lived with his mother. The Duke of Lancaster, the earls of Cambridge, Hertford, Warwick, and Suffolk, and many other lords were there with him to behold the solemnity.

When they reached the manor, they alighted and entered the hall. Soon afterward, the Prince with his mother and the other lords came out of the chambers into the hall, and the said mummers saluted them, showing a pair of dice upon a table to play with the Prince. These dice

[62] Richard, who became king later that year.

[63] The Feast of the Purification was celebrated on February 2. It was not uncommon for the festivities of the Christmas season to be extended to this date. Cf. John Brand, *Observations on the Popular Antiquities of Great Britain*, London, George Bell and Sons, Vol. I; Stow, *Survey of London*, I, 96–97.

[64] The medieval cornet was an entirely different instrument from that which today bears the name, for it was short and either straight or slightly curved, and had several holes bored in one side to make possible the sounding of more tones than the simple tube could produce.

were subtly made so that when the Prince threw he would win. And the said players and mummers set before the Prince three jewels in succession: first a ball of gold, then a cup of gold, then a gold ring. The Prince won these at three casts, as had been previously arranged. Then they set before the Prince's mother, the Duke of Lancaster, and the other earls, a gold ring apiece, and the mother and the lords won them. After this the Prince had wine brought, and they drank with great joy, commanding the minstrels to play. The trumpets began to sound and other instruments to pipe, etc., and the Prince and the lords danced on the one side and the mummers on the other a long time. Then they drank and took their leave, and so departed toward London.

PROCESSIONS AND FEASTS

1. The Whitmonday Procession to St. Paul's, before 1419

London, Corporation, *Munimenta Gildhallae Londoniensis; Liber albus*, I, 29.

When Monday in the Feast of Pentecost had at length arrived, before dinner and between nine and ten by the clock it was the custom for the mayor, aldermen, and sheriffs, arrayed in their suits, to meet in the church of St. Peter upon Cornhill, as also all those of the livery of the sheriffs as well as of the mayor. From which place the rectors of London heading the procession, those who were of the sheriffs' livery followed, and next to them, preceding the mayor, those who were of his livery, after whom came the mayor with the recorder and the aldermen in order of precedence. The procession passed through Cheapside to the churchyard of St. Paul's. Entering this on the north side, they were met in procession by the officials of the church; and then passing out by the south side of the churchyard and through the close of Watling Street, they entered the church by the great door on the west side; which done, they came to a stand in the nave while the hymn *Veni Creator* was chanted by the vicars to the music of the organ in alternate verses, an angel censing from above.[65] This ended, the mayor and aldermen, ascending to the altar, made their offerings, after which they returned each to his home. And observe that the archdeacon of London used to give to the sergeants-at-mace with the mayor and the sheriffs, as also to those of the Chamber, two nobles equally to be divided among them, for preserving the procession of the rectors from the pressure of the throng.

[65] That is, an acolyte dressed as an angel.

2. *Livery Worn in Processions, 1357*

London, Corporation, *Munimenta Gildhallae Londoniensis; Liber albus*, I, 35.

The mayor, sheriffs, and aldermen were all accustomed to array themselves in a like suit on two occasions in the year: first, when the mayor
rode, that is to say, to have the oath administered at Westminster on
the morrow of the apostles Simon and Jude; [66] such vestments being
trimmed with proper furs. Again it was the usage to be arrayed in a like
suit for the Feast of Pentecost,[67] the linings being then of silk. Hence . . .
an ordinance was made in [1357] by the mayor and aldermen that whenever . . . [they] should be arrayed in such a suit, no one of them should
give or part with his robe within that year on pain of forfeiting one hundred shillings to the use of the community without any remission thereof.

3. *Gild Processions*

TO HONOR THE FINDING OF THE CROSS, 1378

Chancery, Miscellanea, Gild Certificate 446.[68]

The Gild of St. Helen and St. Mary, Beverley, have yearly on St. Helen's
day [September 3] a procession headed by one old man with a cross and
another with a spade and then a youth dressed as Queen Helen—all in
token of the finding of the cross. The gild brethren and sisters follow to
the church, where a solemn mass is sung, and each offers one penny.

A CORPUS CHRISTI PROCESSION, CA. 1339

Chancery, Miscellanea, Gild Certificate 109.

The Gild of Corpus Christi, at Grantham, was begun in honor of Corpus
Christi out of devotion of the townspeople. Before the time of procession
on Corpus Christi Day they assemble at the church; the two priests in
the sacred vestments carry the Body of the Lord attended by two boys in
albs carrying the gild candles, followed by the brethren and sisters with
candles. At the mass each offers as he pleases. After the mass the two
candles are carried to the high altar by the boys and remain there. Of
the other candles, two burn daily at the high altar and one at the Corpus

[66] The day of the apostles Simon and Jude is October 28.
[67] The seventh Sunday after Easter.
[68] Unless otherwise indicated, for all references to Gild Certificates cf. Westlake, *Parish Gilds of Mediaeval England*, pp. 138–238. The Gild Certificates were returns made to the articles of inquiry under the Statute of 1389. The date of the foundation of the gild has been used in all cases where it is known. Where such a date is not available, "*ca.* 1389" has been used, to indicate that the situation described existed about that time.

Christi altar during mass. After the (Corpus Christi) mass they eat together, and each couple—*i.e.*, husband and wife, gives food to a poor man. To the Friars Minor who go in front of the procession they give fourteen loaves, a sheep, half a calf, etc.

4. *Activities of a Woman's Gild, ca. 1366*

Chancery, Miscellanea, Gild Certificate 76.

The gild of St. John the Baptist at Baston, in the county of Lincoln, was founded about 1366 in honor of Jesus Christ, the Blessed Virgin Mary, St. John the Baptist, and All Saints, for the increase of divine worship and the devotion of man. They find [69] twenty-six candles yearly before the altar of St. John the Baptist. When their goods suffice, they will have a chaplain. All attend the funerals of every member of the gild and pay one half penny in soul alms.

All the sisters come together on St. John the Baptist's Day [June 24] to dance with each other, on pain of a fine. The sisters attend vespers and matins of the Vigil of St. John the Baptist and carry lights, as they do also when they dance. They may be excused on the ground of old age or sickness.

5. *Some Gild Feasts*

The following items concerning some gild feasts are summarized from Gild Certificates.

HOLY TRINITY GILD, GRIMSBY, 1341

Chancery, Miscellanea, Gild Certificate 116.

A loving cup at the feast. The alderman has 2 gallons of ale, the farthingman [70] and dean 1 gallon each. Ordinances as to . . . keeping place, speaking reasonably, and bringing guests.

HOLY CROSS, HULTOFT, LINCOLNSHIRE, 1350

Chancery, Miscellanea, Gild Certificate 129.

The gild feast consists of bread, cheese, and 30 gallons of ale. The residue goes to the poor.

GILD OF THE BLESSED VIRGIN MARY, HULTOFT, 1356

Chancery, Miscellanea, Gild Certificate 131.

The brethren pay for the gild feast in turn.

[69] Provide.   [70] The man who convened the gild members. Cf. *O.E.D.*

GILD OF ST. LAWRENCE, LINCOLN, CA. 1389

Chancery, Miscellanea, Gild Certificate 142.

At the first feast there are to be as many poor as brethren, to eat and drink good bread and ale and a dish of meat or fish.

GILD OF CORPUS CHRISTI, MULTON, NORFOLK, 1368

Chancery, Miscellanea, Gild Certificate 288.

Each brother and sister pays 6d. and a capon to the general feast.

GILD OF THE ASCENSION, GREAT YARMOUTH, 1356

Chancery, Miscellanea, Gild Certificate 368.

At the gild feast 13 poor men receive 1d. each. The sick members have their portions sent to them, and are to pray if they can. Absentees send a deputy.

ST. BOTOLPH, BURY ST. EDMUND'S, CA. 1389

Chancery, Miscellanea, Gild Certificate 404.

The brothers and sisters meet yearly to eat bread and cheese and to drink ale together on the eve and Feast of St. Botolph.[71]

CONVIVIAL LIFE

1. The Tavern, ca. 1393

Le Ménagier de Paris, ed. by Pichon, I, 48.

The tavern is the church (*moustier*) of the Devil, where his disciples go to serve him and where he works his miracles. For when people go there, they walk straight and talk well and wisely, with moderation and discretion, and when they come home, they cannot stand up or talk; they are either silly or crazy (*enragiés*) and come back swearing and beating and abusing one another.

2. Fixed Prices and Hours, 1376

London, Corporation, *Calendar of the Letter-Books, Letter-Book H,* ed. by Sharpe, p. 27 (from London Letter-Book H, fol. xxxv).

Monday the Feast of St. Dunstan [May 19] proclamation was made to the effect that no taverner or other person should sell a gallon of wine of Gascony or "Ryve" [72] for more than 10d.; or a gallon of wine of "la

---

[71] The Feast of St. Botolph is June 17.

[72] Probably the same as "Ryvere," *i.e.,* Rhenish wine. [Sharpe's note.]

Rochele" or of France for more than 8*d*.; and further that no taverner should keep his hostel open after the tenth hour [73] has been sounded by the bell called "la clocke," [74] under penalty.

3. *Tavern Fixtures, 1374*

London, Corporation, *Calendar of Plea and Memoranda Rolls*, A.D. 1364–1381, p. 172 (Plea and Mem. R., A 19, mem. 5b.).

John Parker, butcher, was summoned to answer Clement Spray in a plea of trespass, wherein the latter complained that the said John, who had hired a tavern at the corner of St. Martin-le-Grand from him for fifteen months, had committed waste and damage therein, although by the custom of the city no tenant for a term of years was entitled to destroy any portion of the buildings or fixtures let to him.

He alleged that the defendant had taken down the doorpost of the tavern and also of the shop, the boarded door of a partition of the tavern, a seat in the tavern, a plastered partition wall, the stone flooring in the chamber, the hearth of the kitchen, and the mantelpiece above it, a partition in the kitchen, two doors and other partitions, of a total value of £4 1*s*. 8*d*., and to his damage, £20.

The defendant denied the trespass and put himself on the country. Afterwards a jury . . . found the defendant guilty of the aforesaid trespass to the plaintiff's damage, 40*d*. Judgment was given for that amount and a fine of 1*s*. to the King, which the defendant paid immediately in court.

4. *The Stock in Two Taverns Belonging to Richard Lyons, 1376*

Exchequer King's Remembrancer, Sheriffs' Accounts 25/70.

THE TAVERN CALLED "LA GALEYE OF LOMBARD STREET":

The quantity of 2 tuns of red Gascon wine in 4 tuns, price	8 marks	
Item, 1 butt full of Rhenish wine, and 3 residues of vernage, romney, and malmsey which amounted to another butt, estimated	20*s*.	
Item, 2 residues of Rhone wine and 1 residue of wine, all price	6*s*.	8*d*.

---

[73] Approximately 10 P.M. The length of an hour varied, being one-twelfth of the time from sunrise to sunset. Cf. *O.E.D.*

[74] This hung in the tower of the church of St. Pancras, in Soper Lane. (Cf. Charles Pendrill, *London Life in the 14th Century*, p. 40.)

Item, 6 tuns, 1 pipe of *vordor* . . . . 3*s.*

Item, a leaden laver, price . . . . 6*s.* 8*d.*

Item, 7 tables with the seats, price . . . . . . 5*s.*

Item, 1 table, 2 trestles, 1 long bench, price . . . 16*d.*

Item, 6 quart pots, 4 pottle pots, and 1 pint, of
  pewter, price . . . . 4*s.*

Item, 1 stool, price . . . . 6*d.*

Item, 7 canvases for the seats, price . . . . . 21*d.*

[Total . . . £7 15*s.* 7*d.*]

THE TAVERN CALLED "CHICHESTRE SELER":

Item, ½ butt of vernage, price . . . . 40*s.*

Item, 1 tun of red wine less 12 *pouz*   and

Item, ½ tun of red wine, price . . . . 40*s.*

Item, ½ tun of Oseye wine, price . . . . . . 6*s.* 8*d.*

Item, ½ butt of romney, price . . . . 46*s.* 8*d.*

Item, ¾ butt of malmsey wine, price . . . . . 5*s.*

Item, ½ butt of vernage, price . . . . 40*s.*[75]

Item, 1 residue of Rhenish wine . . . . . . 40*d.*

Item, 1 empty pipe, 4 empty roundels, price . . . 4*s.* 2*d.*

Item, 1 large wooden funnel, 1 small pewter funnel,
  1 wicker basket (*potte* [76] *de wikeres*), price . . . 10*d.*

Item, 1 gallon pot, 2 pottle pots, 2 pint pots, price . . 4*s.*

[Total . . . £7 10*s.* 8*d.*]

5. *A Lawyer's Drinking Song, ca. 1371*

The Latin original of these verses was written by Strethay, an attorney chiefly
concerned with Gloucestershire cases in the Court of Common Pleas, at the head of
one of the membranes of Plea Roll No. 480.

Common Pleas, Plea Roll 480 m. 266.

> Twice two full quarts we lawyers need,
>   To fill a legal jug.
> With one, we're gay; with two, we teach;
>   With three, we prophesy.
> And four good quarts it takes to bind
> Legal senses, legal tongues,
>   A lawyer's hands and mind.

[75] Struck out because above.

[76] The *O.E.D.* lists "potte" as a variant of "pot" and gives as one definition, "A wicker
basket used as a trap for fish or crustaceans; a fish-pot, lobster pot, etc."

6. *A Rector's Drinking Cup, 1405*

Prerogative Court of Canterbury, 9 Marche.

Will of John Wytloff, rector of Lodiwell in the diocese of Exeter, 1405.
. . . Item, I bequeath to Robert Vrensche my leathern bottles for
wine, my silver cup with cover to drink wine therefrom, and one hundred shillings to buy himself wine, because I can no longer drink wine
with him, unless God wills.

7. *A Tricky Taverner, ca. 1376–1379*

Gower, "Mirour de l'omme," ll. 26,065–26,112.

When I go to the tavern,
If I call for a taste of wine,
The taverner, in the beginning,
Of his good wine gives me a sample;
But if I fill my bottles,
When of the good wine I am certain,
At once he slips one over on me,
For of quite another quality will be
The bad wine that I carry home.
He who trusts in such a neighbor,
In the end should be well persuaded
That his friendship is not real.
If you wish to know the utmost
Of Fraud, you shall find example
In his piment and in his claret,
And in the fresh hippocras
With which he makes his purse so fat.
When the ladies of the city,
Going to church or market
In the morning, to the tavern
On their way come tripping,
Fraud makes money of them,
For all his wines are sampled
Unless they are pure vinegar.
And Fraud will assure them
That they shall have, if they'll wait a bit,
Vernage, Greek, and malmsey;
To make them spend the more,

Many a wine he names to them;
Candia, ribolla, and rumney,
Provence and Montross has he,
He says, in his tavern,
Rivere and muscatel for sale;
But he hasn't the third part of them;
He says so for the novelty
That may induce them to go on drinking.
From a single tun he draws them
Ten kinds of wine, if so he can keep them
Sitting there in their chairs.
And he says to them, "Oh, my very dear
Mesdames, you are welcome.
Drink now at your pleasure;
To serve you we have leisure."
But then Fraud has his desire
When with such assistants
The dames cheat their husbands;
It's nothing to him, if he can grow rich on it,
That the women's husbands are defrauded.

8. A Tavern Brawl, 1322

London, Coroner, *Calendar of the Coroners Rolls*, pp. 49–50.

Monday after the Feast of St. Mark,[77] 1322, it happened that a certain Luke atte Hetthe, avener, lay dead of a death other than his rightful death near the Leadenhall [78] in the parish of St. Peter of Cornhill in the ward of Lyme Street. On hearing this, the sheriffs and the coroner proceeded thither, and having summoned good men of that ward and of the three nearest wards, *viz.*, Cornhill, Bishopgate, and Aldgate, they diligently enquired how it happened. The jurors say that when, on the preceding Sunday, at the hour of vespers, Luke atte Hetthe and a certain John le Avener, clerk to the Earl of Chester, and William de Wircestre, John's groom, were sitting drinking in a solar of the tavern held by John de Oxenford of William de Wengrave in the parish, a quarrel arose between them, so that John le Avener took in his hand a

---

[77] The Feast of St. Mark is April 25.
[78] A hall near the intersection of Gracechurch Street and Cornhill, used as a market and for various other purposes. It received its name from its roof of lead, which was uncommon at the time.

certain wooden measure called a quart and struck Luke therewith on the top of his head, inflicting a wound that was not mortal, two inches long and reaching to his skull. Thereupon, William de Wircestre feloniously threw Luke on to the stair of the solar so that he mortally injured his neck and shoulders; and Luke, thus injured, was carried thence by his friends to the place where he died and where he had his ecclesiastical rights; he lingered until midprime [79] on Monday, at which hour he died of the injury. Being asked who were present when it happened, they say no one except those three and a certain Roger Ote. Being asked if the said Roger abetted the felony, they say no; nor do they suspect any man or woman of the death of Luke save John and William, who had no chattels so far as they could learn. Being asked what became of John and William, the jurors say that John forthwith fled, but whither he went or who received him they know not; and William was captured and committed to Newgate prison. The corpse was viewed, on which the injuries appeared and no other hurt. The measure was appraised by the said jurors at a half-penny, and the stair at two-pence, for which Richard de Hakeneye would answer. Precept to the sheriffs to attach John le Avener when found in their bailiwick, and also Roger Ote because he was present.

9. *A Wild Night in a London Brewhouse, 1325*

London, Coroner, *Calendar of the Coroners Rolls*, pp. 115–116.

On a Sunday in March, at the hour of compline, Walter de Benygtone, tailor, with seventeen companions whose names were unknown, went to the brewhouse of Gilbert de Mordone, stockfishmonger, in Bridge Ward, with stones in their hoods, and with swords, knives, and other weapons. They sat there and drank four gallons of beer, lying in wait to seize and carry off Emma, daughter of the late Robert Porte, who was then in Gilbert's charge.

Seeing this, Mabel, Gilbert's wife, and Geoffrey, his brewer, begged Walter and his comrades to leave. They answered that they would stay there whether wanted or not, to spend their money, as the house was public.

Mabel, seeing their folly, went back to her chamber, taking Emma with her. Then Walter and his companions became angry and assaulted

[79] Probably about 7:30 A.M., as "prime" denoted the period from 6:00 A.M., or sunrise, to about 9:00 A.M. Cf. *O.E.D.*

Geoffrey and Robert de Mordone [80] and other inmates of the house, and struck Robert on the head with stones, so that he raised the cry and ran out into the High Street. Walter, with a knife in one hand and a dagger in the other, followed him to kill him. When Benedict de Warde and other neighbors came up to pacify them, Walter assaulted Benedict with his weapons and refused to surrender to the King's peace. Then Benedict, seizing a "balstaf" [81] from a stranger, struck Walter on the top of his head so that he fell to the ground at the end of the lane of Gilbert de Mordon.

He was carried thence by Walter de Arderne and Christiana, his wife, to the lane of St. Michael and there laid on the pavement near the fountain. He lay there the whole of the night, and on the morrow was carried to the house of Geoffrey de Warde, where he died.

There were present Geoffrey le Brewere, Robert de Mordone, Walter and Benedict, and a number of others whose names were unknown. Benedict fled and had no chattels.

[80] Nicholas de Copton, first cousin to Chaucer's mother, Agnes, in 1349 bequeathed a rent to his "sister" Mary, daughter of a Robert de Mordon. (Husting R. 77, No. 107.)
[81] See above, p. 16.

6. Travel

ON THE ROAD

1. Keeping up with the Court, 1395

FROISSART'S JOURNEY TO PRESENT TO RICHARD II HIS TRAITÉS
AMOUREUX

Froissart, *The Chronicle of Froissart*, tr. by Berners, ed. by Ker, VI, 129–147.

True it was that I, Sir John Froissart (as at that time treasurer and
canon of Chimay, in the county of Hainault, in the diocese of Liège), had
great affection to go and see the realm of England when I had been in
Abbeville, and saw that truce was taken between the realms of England
and France. . . .

The Lords of Brabant counseled me to take this journey and gave me
letters of recommendation to the King of England and to his uncles. . . .
And I had engrossed in a fair book, well illumined, all the matters of
amours and moralities that in four and twenty years I had made and
compiled. . . . I had great desire to go into England to see the King
and his uncles. Also I had this fair book, well covered with velvet,
garnished with clasps of silver and gilt, thereof to make a present to
the King, at my first coming to his presence. I had such desire to go this
voyage that the pain and travail grieved me nothing. Thus provided of
horses and other necessaries, I passed the sea at Calais and came to Dover
the twelfth day of the month of July. . . . I abode half a day and all
a night at Dover. It was on a Tuesday, and the next day by nine of the
clock I came to Canterbury, to Saint Thomas's shrine, and to the tomb
of the noble Prince of Wales, who is there interred right richly. There
I heard mass and made mine offering to the holy Saint, and then dined
at my lodging.

And there I was informed how King Richard should be there the next
day on pilgrimage, which was after his return out of Ireland. . . . The
King had a devotion to visit Saint Thomas's shrine, and also because the
Prince his father was there buried. Then I thought to abide the King
there, and so I did.

And the next day the King came thither with a noble company of
lords, ladies, and damsels. And when I was among them, they seemed to

TRAVEL

me all new folks; I knew no person. And with the King as then was none of his uncles; the Duke of Lancaster was in Aquitaine, and the dukes of York and Gloucester were in other businesses, so that I was at first all abashed, for if I had seen any ancient knight that had been with King Edward or with the Prince, I had been well comforted and would have gone to him; but I could see none such.

Then I asked for a knight called Sir Richard Stury, whether he were alive or not; and it was showed me yes, but he was at London. Then I thought to go to the Lord Thomas Percy, great seneschal of England, who was there with the King. So I acquainted me with him, and I found him right honorable and gracious. And he offered to present me and my letters to the King, whereof I was right joyful, for it behooved me to have some means to bring me to the presence of such a prince as the King of England. He went to the King's chamber, at which time the King was gone to sleep, and so he showed me, and bade me return to my lodging and come again, and so I did. And when I came to the Bishop's palace, I found the Lord Thomas Percy ready to ride to Ospringe. And he counseled me to make as then no knowledge of my being there but to follow the Court; and said he would cause me ever to be well lodged till the King should be at the fair castle of Leeds in Kent.

I ordered me after his counsel and rode before to Ospringe. And by adventure I was lodged in an house where was lodged a gentle knight of England called Sir William Lisle. He was tarried there behind the King because he had pain in his head all the night before. He was one of the King's privy chamber. And when he saw that I was a stranger, and, as he thought, of the marches of France because of my language, we fell in acquaintance together; for gentlemen of England are courteous, accessible (*treatable*), and glad of acquaintance. Then he demanded what I was and what business I had to do in those parts. I showed him a great part of my coming thither and all that the Lord Thomas Percy had said to me and ordered me to do. He then answered and said how I could not have a better means, and that on the Friday the King should be at the Castle of Leeds. And he showed me that when I came there I should find the Duke of York, the King's uncle, whereof I was right glad because I had letters directed to him, and also that in his youth he had seen me in the court of the noble King Edward, his father, and with the Queen, his mother.

Then on the Friday in the morning Sir William Lisle and I rode together, and on the way I demanded of him if he had been with the King

in the voyage into Ireland. He answered me yes. Then I demanded of
him the manner of the hole that is in Ireland called Saint Patrick's
Purgatory, if it were true what was said of it or not. Then he said that of
a surety such a hole there was, and that he himself and another knight of
England had been there while the King lay at Dublin, and said how
they entered into the hole and were closed in at the sun's going down and
abode there all night, and the next morning issued out again at the sun's
rising.

Then I demanded if he had any such strange sights or visions as
were spoken of. Then he said how that when he and his fellows were
entered and passed the gate that was called the Purgatory of Saint
Patrick, and that they were descended and gone down three or four
paces, descending down as into a cellar, a certain hot vapor rose against
them and struck so into their heads that they were fain to sit down on the
stairs, which are of stone. And after they had sat there a season, they
had great desire to sleep, and so fell asleep and slept there all night.
. . . And in the morning they issued out and within a short season clean
forgot their dreams and visions; wherefore he said he thought all that
matter was but a fantasy. . . . I would fain have known of him what
was done in the voyage in Ireland . . . but then company of other
knights came and fell in communication with him. . . . Thus we rode
to Leeds, and thither came the King and all his company, and there I
found the Lord Edmund, Duke of York. Then I went to him and delivered my letters from the [Count] of Hainaut, his cousin, and from
the [Count] of Ostervant.

The Duke knew me well and made me good cheer, and said: "Sir
John, hold you always near to us, and we shall show you love and
courtesy. We are bound thereto for the love of time past, and for love of
my lady, the old Queen my mother, in whose court ye were. We have
good remembrance thereof." Then I thanked him as reason required.

So I was advanced by reason of him and Sir Thomas Percy and Sir
William Lisle. By their means I was brought into the King's chamber,
and into his presence by means of his uncle, the Duke of York. Then I
delivered my letters to the King, and he took them and read them at good
leisure. Then he said to me that I was welcome, as he that had been and
is of the English court. As on that day I showed not the King the book
that I had brought for him; he was so sore occupied with great affairs
that I had as then no leisure to present my book. . . . To have counsel
of two great matters [the project for his marriage and the answer to a

petition from Aquitaine against the recent gift of that duchy to John of Gaunt], the King had sent for the most part of the prelates and lords of England, to be at the feast of Magdalentide, at a manor of the King's called Eltham. . . . And when they had tarried at Leeds four days, the King returned to Rochester and so to Eltham; and so I rode forth in the King's company. . . .

In riding the way between Leeds and Eltham, I demanded of Sir William Lisle and Sir John of Grailly, captain of Bouteville, the cause . . . why that great council should assemble at Eltham. . . . And all the way between Leeds and Eltham I rode most part in [the] company of Sir John of Grailly and with Sir William Lisle. Thus the King came to Eltham on a Tuesday, and on the Wednesday the lords of all sides began to assemble. . . . On the Thursday . . . after dinner I fell in acquaintance with an ancient knight whom I knew in King Edward's days, and he was then of King Richard's Privy Council; he was called Sir Richard Stury. He knew me anon and yet in twenty-four years he had not seen me before, which was at Codenberg and at Brussels in the house of Duke Wencelas of Brabant and of the Duchess Jeanne of Brabant. This knight, Sir Richard Stury, made me a good cheer and inquired of me many things; and I answered him as I knew. And as I walked up and down with him in a gallery before the King's chamber, I questioned him of that Council. . . .

As soon as [the King] had said his sentence [in Council] and that he saw some murmured in the King's chamber and that the prelates and lords talked together two and two, he issued out of the chamber and the Earl of Derby with him, and came into the hall at Eltham and made a cloth to be laid on a table and so sat down to dinner and left all others still talking together. . . . And so it was that on the Sunday following all such as had been there were departed and all their counselors, except the Duke of York, who abode still about the King. And the Lord Thomas Percy and Sir Richard Stury showed my business to the King.

Then the King desired to see my book that I had brought for him. So he saw it in his chamber, for I had laid it there ready on his bed. When the King opened it, it pleased him well, for it was fair illumined and written, and covered with crimson velvet, with ten buttons of silver and gilt, and roses of gold in the midst, with two great clasps gilt, richly wrought.

Then the King demanded me whereof it treated, and I showed him how it treated of matters of love. Whereof the King was glad and looked in it and read it in many places, for he could speak and read French very well. And he took it to a knight of his chamber named Sir Richard Creadon, to bear it into his secret chamber.

And the same Sunday I fell in acquaintance with a squire of England called Henry Castyde, an honest man and a wise, who could well speak French. He companied with me because he saw the King and other lords made me good cheer, and also he had seen the book that I gave to the King; also, Sir Richard Stury had showed him how I was a maker of histories.

2. *Moving a Nobleman's Household, 1409*

AN ACCOUNT FOR MOVING THE HOUSEHOLD OF EDWARD, DUKE OF YORK, FROM THE CASTLE OF CARDIFF TO HANDLEY CASTLE IN WORCESTERSHIRE

Household Account of Edward, duke of York, 1409 (fols. 4–7).[1]

Wed. Oct. 16 [*1409*]. In carting 14 cartloads of fuel from [Cardiff] Castle to the Friars and two cartloads of the lord's harness, 14*d*.

In carting 10 cartloads of the lord's harness from the water at Cardiff to the Friars and thence to the water, when the lord went for London, and 46 cartloads of victuals and fuel from the castle to the Friars, 4*s*. 8*d*.

In carting 14 cartloads of victuals and fuel from the Castle to the Friars, 14*d*.

In carting 2 cartloads of household utensils to the ship, 2*d*.

In hiring the same [man] to make hoops from the lord's wood together with the hire of packing pipes, hogsheads, and barrels with the victuals and utensils from Cardiff to Handley for 18 days, 6*s*.

In carting 4 wagon loads of the lord's harness in the removal of the household from the Friars to the water at Cardiff, 16*d*.

In carting 6 cartloads of the lord's harness from the Friars to the water, 4*d*.

In carting 2 wagon loads of harness and victuals from the inn to the water, 8*d*.

In carting 14 wagon loads of utensils and victuals of the household from the Friars to the water at Cardiff, 4*s*. 8*d*.

In carting 3 cartloads of utensils from the inn to the water, 3*d*. . . .

[1] Published by the kind permission of the Right Honorable the earl of Westmorland.

[*Fri. Oct. 25.*] *Newport for supper and the whole night.* In bread bought, 5*d.*; wine bought, 14½*d.*; 2 lbs. candles bought, 4*d.*; milk bought, 1*d.*; 1 quart of metheglin bought, 1½*d.*

In hay bought for 6 horses of the lord and the [chariot] horses and 24 hackneys, 23*d.*; 7 bbl. of oats bought, 2*s.* 4*d.*

In the wages of 5 scullery men there, 17*d.*

In one guide hired throughout the way, 6*d.*

In beds hired, 8*d.*; fuel bought, 3*d.*; fish bought for the washer-woman, 3*d.*

In horsebread [2] bought from the governor of the chariot horses, 3*d.*

In one horse hired to carry the pannier (*sporta*) with the fish from Cardiff to Newport for use on the Saturday, 6*d.*

Sat. Oct. 26. At Monmouth for dinner and the whole night. [Expenses as at Newport with additional payments for fish, eggs, butter, and pears for dinner.]

Sun. Oct. 27. At Ross for dinner. [Payments for bread, ale, beef, mutton, geese, chicken, fuel, fodder, milk] and:

In one "gyde" hired from Monmouth to Ross, 4*d.*

In the ferrying of the chariot and all the horses at Wye, 20*d.*

At Ledbury, the same day at supper and for the whole night. [Pay-ments for bread, ale, 2½ pounds of Paris candles, beef, veal and pork, chicken, fuel, fodder and litter, wages of seven scullery-men, beds hired, milk, shoeing horses] and:

In one "gyde" hired for "le chariot" from Ross to Ledbury, 4*d.*

[*Mon. Oct. 28 at Handley.*] *Foreign expenses.* In the wages of David Kymro, John Boys, one page of the kitchen, one page of the brewhouse, and one page of the bakehouse traveling from Cardiff to Handley to make arrangements for their offices towards the coming of the household for 9 days, 8*s.* 2*d.*

In John ap Hoell and his fellows hired to drive and lead 10 beeves and 25 bullocks of the household, 5 heifers and cows received from the receiver of Newport, and 18 bullocks bought of Spernore from Cardiff to Handley, in gross 14*s.* 2*d.*

[2] Bread made of beans, bran, etc. for the food of horses. (*O.E.D.*)

In the wages of Martyn the Chaplain and John Chesterfelle traveling from Cardiff to Handley by water with the harness for 5 days, 3s. 4d.

In wages of Henry Shawe and the washerwoman's husband by water for the same time, 2s. 6d.

In wages of John Bysschop by water the same time, 15d.

In wages of the poultry pages for the same time, 10d.

In 15 men hired for the lord's household service, traveling from Cardiff to Handley for 5 days, whereof two for 7 days each, 26s. 4d.

In 6 men hired to travel with the household from Cardiff to Handley to guard the said household by the way at the lord's pay, and from Handley to Cardiff on [the] return journey for 2 days, 7s.

In expenses of 12 of the said men from Handley to Cardiff for 2 days with 5d. for ferrying at the Wye, 6s. 5d.

In a reward to Edward Stone traveling by water with the harness and victuals of the household from Cardiff to Bristol and thence to Handley, 3s. 4d.

In the freight of parcel of the harness and victuals from Cardiff to Bristol, [25s.]

In the freight of the said harness and victuals from Bristol to Handley, 22s. 6d.

Item, in a gift to two charioteers of the lord from Coytyf driving the Lord Henry from Cardiff to Handley, with 5s. 3d. for the expenses of themselves and 5 horses from Handley to Coytyf on [their] return journey for 3 days and 3 nights and 3d. for the ferry, 25s.

In the expenses of Henry Shawe, traveling from Cardiff to Newport to arrange for hackneys there for the household servants, 4d.

In the expenses of Stephen Peynton [and 4 others named] traveling from Cardiff to Handley on foot, 11s. 1d.

. . .

In the wages of the same [comptroller of the household] traveling from Cardiff to Handley to take order for divers necessaries there towards the coming of the household for 21 days with a horse and 5 days without a horse before the household came to Handley, 11s. 9d.

In the wages of the same traveling from Cardiff to Handley with the great wardrobe of the lord for 3 days with a horse and being at Handley for 10 days without a horse before the coming of the household, 4s.

. . .

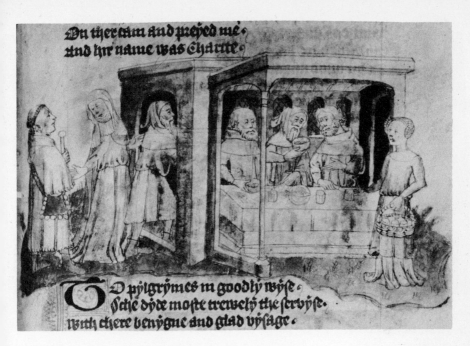

HOSPITALITY TO WAYFARERS; early fifteenth century
London, Brit. Mus., MS Cott. Tib. A.VII, fol. 93

A PILGRIM WELCÓMED AT A ROADSIDE TAVERN
Early fourteenth century
London, Brit. Mus., MS Royal 10 E.IV, fol. 114v

LODGING AND REFRESHMENT

TWO-WHEELED MILITARY CART; *ca.* 1300
New York, Morgan Library, MS 806, fol. 170

Et iusticia illius in filios filiorū:
hiis qui seruant testamentum eius.
Et memores sunt mandatorum
ipsius: ipsius: ad faciendum ea.

TRAVELING COACH AND FIVE; *ca.* 1340
London, Brit. Mus., MS Add. 42130, fol. 181v-182

SHIPS; *ca.* 1415
Baltimore, Walters Gallery
MS W. 219, fol. 245

A HORSE LITTER; *ca.* 1400
London, Brit. Mus., MS Sloane 2433 (111), fol. 122

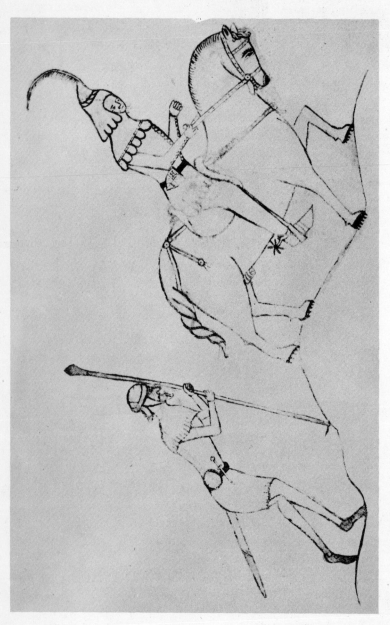

THE KING'S MESSENGER AND HIS RUNNER; sketched in an expense account of *ca.* 1360
London, Public Record Office, E 101/309/11 (34 E III)

In carting 33 wagon loads of victuals, utensils, and harness of the household from "le bakes" [3] at Handley to the inn (*hospicium*) there, 5s. 6d.

In carting 2 wagon loads from "le bakes" at Handley to the inn there, 4d.

. . .

In wages of John Baker traveling from Cardiff to Handley to take order for the bakery and brewery and other offices there, and for vessels, towards the coming of the household, for 26 days, 13s. 4d.

3. *A Traveler, His Horse, and His Dog, 1361–1366*

ARGUMENT BETWEEN FROISSART'S HORSE AND HIS HOUND, ON THE WAY
FROM SCOTLAND

Froissart, "Le Débat dou cheval et dou lévrier," *Œuvres de Froissart, Poésies,* ed. by Scheler, II, 216–219.

> Froissart from Scotland was on his way,
> Riding upon a horse that was gray.
> A white hound on a leash he led;
> "Oh, but I'm tired," the little dog said.
> "Grisel, when shall we rest our feet?
> It is our usual time to eat."
> "Tired, you say," the horse replied;
> "If you'd carried a man and his trunk beside,
> Over the hills and dales all day,
> Then you might have some cause to say
> You 'wish you'd never been born, you do.' "
> The little dog said, "That's very true,
> But big and heavy and strong are you.
> Your four feet are shod with iron, too,
> And I must trot along footbare;
> That's why I have so much more care
> Than you, who are so stout and tall,
> While I have only a body small;
> For haven't they named me 'lévrier'? [4]
> My business in life with folks to play;
> And you are built quite strong enough

[3] The landing place at Handley.
[4] Greyhound, harrier.

To carry a man and all his stuff.
When you our master have safely brought
To the inn, without any other thought
He brings your oats—a good full measure,
And if he thinks you've earned your leisure
Over your back he will throw his cloak,
And then your sides he will idly stroke.
And all I can do is to sit on my haunches;
It's no fun for fellows with empty paunches."
"I can well believe it," Grisel replied,
"But you count only the things on my side;
On your side I could name some, too.
Would God I were a dog like you,
Exactly as nature made you," he said;
"Then I should have both butter and bread
A-mornings, and soup of good fat meat.
For supper I know what he'll give you to eat:
If he has no more than one good bite,
You'll get your muzzle in it all right!
And if you like to go gadding about,
There's no one to spur you or give you a clout;
But unless I go at a jolly good clip,
Never a word have I from his lip;
But with feet like claws he deeply pricks,
And into my side his spur he sticks;
It's sometimes enough to make me neigh;
If you had to suffer in such a way
As I do, by St. Honestas,
You'd be ready to say, 'I'm tired. Alas!' "
Said the dog: "You've naught to complain about;
As quick as a man puts a candle out
They begin to rub you and curry and scratch
And cover you lest some disease you catch;
And then they take to cleaning your feet,
And if they see it will be a treat
They stroke you on your back [and chest]
And say to you, 'Now take your rest,
Grisel, for you have earned this day

The oats that you are munching away.'
And then your bed for you they make
Of clean white straw or [fragrant] brake,
And then you go to sleep no doubt.
But I've other things to think about;
For behind the door they make me stay,
And often before a passageway:
'Now watch the house,' they say to me.
And if anything happens it's sure to be
I that am given many a slap;
For if bread and meat in a cloth they wrap—
Butter and cheese or milk when they can—
Both the maid and the serving man,
Although they eat it, as sure as can be,
All the blame they will put on me,
And 'Who's been here?' is the song they sing;
'That dog!' And I haven't touched a thing.
So it happens to me—it's always the same—
That I am beaten, though not to blame.
But all that they ever ask of you
Is well to put your journey through.
By the way, you'd better get on, I say;
For directly in front of us, in the way,
Is a town with a high church tower. Get up!
Our master there will want to sup,
And oats enough shall you have there,
And I also my simple fare;
So I pray you and so I beg
You'll show how you can shake a leg."
Grisel replied, "And so I will,
For sure I want to eat my fill."
So came Froissart to the town,
And all their talking died adown.

4. *Riding a Horse to Death, 1387*

Common Pleas, Plea Roll 505 m. 124 d.

William Spicer of Hungerford sued Peter "that was William's servant Pedewell" for damages, because, when he had delivered a certain horse to Peter to ride from London to Hungerford and back, Peter had ridden the horse so fast and excessively that the horse was killed, etc., to the said William's great damage.

5. *Heavy Traffic in the Town Streets, 1352*

CUSTOMS, TO BE LEVIED TOWARDS THE ENCLOSING OF THE TOWN OF IPSWICH, UPON GOODS COMING THITHER FOR SALE

Chancery Files, Drafts and Surrenders of Patents, 15/72.

From every packload of corn coming for sale, ¼*d.*; every cartload of corn, ½*d.*; every horse, mare, ox, and cow, ¼*d.*; every hide of horse, mare, ox, and cow, fresh, salt, or tanned, ¼*d.*; every cart carrying meat, salt or fresh, ½*d.*; five bacons, ½*d.*; 3 salmon, fresh or salt, ¼*d.*; 10 sheep, goats, or pigs, ½*d.*; every sack of wool, ½*d.*; 10 fleeces, ¼*d.*; every hundred sheepfells [and other] skins, ½*d.*; every hundred skins of lambs, kids, hares, rabbits, foxes, cats, and squirrels, ¼*d.*; every packload of cloths, ½*d.*; every whole cloth, ¼*d.*; every hundred of linen cloth, canvas, Irish "Galeweth," and worsted cloths, ½*d.*; every tun of wine, 1*d.*; every cartload of honey, ½*d.*; every bundle of cloths brought by cart, 2*d.*; every cartload of iron, ½*d.*; every packload of iron, ½*d.*; every cartload of lead, 1*d.*; goods by the pound, [*i.e.*, groceries], 1*d.* the hundred [pounds]; every wey of tallow and fat, ¼*d.*; every quarter of woad, ½*d.*; every hundred of alum, [etc.], ¼*d.*; every two thousand of rushes, ¼*d.*; and ten sheaves of garlic, ¼*d.*; every thousand herrings, ¼*d.*; every cartload of sea fish, ½*d.*; every packload of sea fish, ¼*d.*; every hundred of boards, ½*d.*; every grindstone, ¼*d.*; every thousand of faggots, ½*d.*; every quarter of salt, ¼*d.*; every wey of cheese or butter, ¼*d.*; every cartload of brushwood and [char]coal, ½*d.* per week; every thousand of cartnails, ½*d.*; every hundred of horseshoes and cartclouts, ¼*d.*; every quarter of tan, ¼*d.*; every bundle of wares of what sort soever coming to the said town for sale, over the total of 5*s.*, ¼*d.*; every hundred of tin, brass, and copper, ½*d.*; every hundred gads of steel, ¼*d.*; everything else for sale, of the value of five shillings, not expressed above, coming to the said town, ¼*d.*

6. *Wanderings of a Conspirator, 1402*

A TREASONABLE LETTER AND GOSSIP WITH A BARBER, FOR WHICH
NICHOLAS LOUTHE, A CHAPLAIN, WAS HANGED AT TYBURN

Coram Rege Roll, Trinity, 3 Henry IV, Rex, m. 4 d.

Nicholas Louthe, chaplain, acknowledged [before the King's coroner, the King himself, and his Council] that he came to Walkerne in the county of Hertford on Tuesday after the Feast of the Ascension last past [5] to the house of a "barbour," to him unknown, and there the said "barbour" asked him: "What news?" And he told him that Richard who was of late King of England was alive and that he was of late at St. James's by Westminster and there was seen and recognized by women by a "werte" on his face and that he had a white livery-cloth upon that "werte."

And, moreover, he said that the Duke of Lancaster, who calls himself King of England, was no more than a collector and bailiff to the said King Richard and in a short time would render account to him for his kingdom.

And that the said late King had forty harts ready prepared and that they were grazing happily and amicably at Wodesore.

And, moreover, he acknowledged that he wrote a letter to Sir Walter Baldok, prior of Laund [in Leicestershire], which letter follows:

"Greeting to my dear friend, Sir Walter, that I have had much trouble in this country because I have inquired after you and that I would fain know of your welfare, because it was told me that I should find you here in this town or else here I should know where you were. Wherefore I have gone [through] many countries, both in Kent and in Sussex and in Surrey and all Norfolk and Suffolk and all Essex and all Middlesex, and now I am gone to London to inquire and to know the end of the counsel, and then I shall go from thence northward. But now at this time I might not speak with you, but by the grace of God I shall speak with you at a nigh time not far distant (longe to). And the most [*sic*] friend that we loved and we shall come so strong that the Earl of Derby that now is the king shall not know where he shall hold him or abide, and therefore I pray you that you pray for your liege lord, King Richard, and for all his men. And therefore I have no more to speak to you at this time but that you shall keep well your tongue and be still, but

[5] That is, on May 9, 1402.

God keep you and save you. Another day I shall tell you my name [and] wherefore I was afraid (for wy was dredand) to tell you what I was."

7. *Wayfarers Robbed on the King's Highway, 1388/89*

CONFESSIONS OF THOMAS MORYS, AN IRISHMAN, AND RICHARD BRE-
TOUN, WHO TURNED INFORMERS

Chancery Miscellanea, Transcripts of Records, 88/3 No. 59.

On Saturday after the feast of the Conversion of St. Paul,[6] 12 Richard II [1388/89], Thomas Morys of Ireland [a prisoner in Newgate] came before the sheriffs and the coroner of London at Milk Street and acknowledged that he was a thief and a felon of the lord King, because he, together with John Burton, "travelyngman," and David Esmound, on Tuesday in Passion Week,[7] 11 Richard II . . . in a certain valley between Dartford and Swanscombe, after the ninth hour, feloniously robbed a certain man of Canterbury, whose name he knoweth not, of twenty shillings in gold and silver money and of a certain black horse, together with a saddle and bridle, price 20s. Whereof the said Thomas Morys had for his share 15s., and the said John Burton and David Esmond had all the rest. And thus the said Thomas Morys became approver of the lord King and appealed the said John Burton and David concerning the said felony.

[He informed similarly of the following robberies in the highway by himself and divers others]:

An unknown man from Coventry, this side Barnet, Middlesex, about the third hour of the day, of a bay horse with saddle and bridle, a leather bag (*mantuca*) and money.

A dyer of Stepney, of two basins and two ewers and of cloaks of divers colors, at Stepney by night.

At a wood by the highway two leagues this side of Stony Stratford, Bucks, a chapman of Gloucestershire, of a pack of linen cloth and 10 marks in money.

Two leagues this side of Merton in Surrey, at sundown, a fisherman of the prior of Merton, of a baselard harnessed with silver and 3s.

A stranger by Lewes in Sussex, of two bay horses.

Between Towcester and Daventry, Northants, an unknown chapman of a pack of shoes (*caligularum*) and woolen cloths of divers colors, a gold seal called "Synet," [8] and 4 marks.

[6] The Feast of the Conversion of St. Paul is January 25.
[7] That is, on March 24, 1387/88.   [8] Signet.

About sundown an unknown man at Shetkonde by Oxford, of two horses, a sword, a bow and a sheaf of arrows.

.   .   .

On Thursday February 11, 12 Richard II, Richard Bretoun, informer, similarly appealed divers persons of highway robberies, as follows:

Between Newmarket and St. Edmondsbury, Suffolk, after the ninth hour, a chaplain, of a dun-colored horse with a black streak and with saddle and bridle, a book called "portehors" (breviary), price 13s. 4d., and 40s. in silver.

Between Northburgh and Leicester, a chapman from Beverley, of 22 yards of linen cloth of "Weskernecloth," price £10.

Between Oxford and Bicester, a servant of the prior of Bicester, of two horses, a "portehors," price 24s., and 3s. 4d.

At Royston, by night, from a Cambridge chapman, 400 stockfish and 2 cades of red herring.

Between Melton Mowbray and Dalby on the Wolds, county Leicester, a monk and his yeoman, of 13s. 4d. in money.

Between Grantham and Stamford, about the ninth hour, an esquire of Richard Scrope, canon of Lincoln, of £5 in gold and silver money.

> The dangers of highway travel are further illustrated in this King's Bench case, summarized from Coram Rege Roll 552, Rex, m. 1 d.

Middlesex.—Jurors in Hilary term, 22 Richard II [1398/99], Coram Rege, Westminster, presented that at Feast of SS. Fabian and Sebastian [January 20], 21 Richard II [1397/98], John Suoring, alias John Gelle of Walsingham, at night killed Geoffrey Blogate of Norfolk and took goods and chattels to the value of £10 from his purse and is a common thief; and that Thomas Walsham, alias Coke, late canon of Walsingham, on same date raped against her will Emma, wife of William Bole of Walsingham, coming on pilgrimage to Canterbury, and took goods and chattels from her purse to the value of £20, and is a common thief.

Suoring and Walsham secured mainpernors; they were finally acquitted.

LODGINGS BY THE WAY

1. Putting up at a Southwark Inn, 1381

PROCEEDINGS RELATING TO THE ROBBERY OF THE SHERIFF OF SOMER-
SET AND DORSET AT AN INN IN SOUTHWARK

Common Pleas, Plea Roll 483 m. 590.

John Trentedeus of Southwark was summoned to answer William
Latymer touching a plea why, whereas according to the law and custom
of the realm of England, innkeepers who keep a common inn are bound
to keep safely by day and by night without reduction or loss men
who are passing through the parts where such inns are and lodging
their goods within those inns, so that, by default of the innkeepers
or their servants, no damage should in any way happen to such their
guests. . . .

On Monday after the Feast of the Purification of the Virgin Mary [9]
in the fourth year of the now King [1380/81] by default of the said
John, certain malefactors took and carried away two small portable chests
with 40 marks and also with charters and writings, to wit two writings
obligatory, in the one of which is contained that a certain Robert Bour
is bound to the said William in £100 and in the other that a certain John
Pusele is bound to the same William in £40 . . . and with other muniments of the same William, to wit his return of all the writs of the lord
King for the counties of Somerset and Dorset, whereof the same William
was then sheriff, for the morrow of the Purification of the Blessed Mary
the Virgin in the year aforesaid, as well before the same lord the King
in his Chancery and in his Bench as before the justices of the King's
Common Bench and his barons of his Exchequer, returnable at Westminster on the said morrow, and likewise the rolls of the court of Crane-
stock for all the courts held there from the first year of the reign of the
said lord the King until the said Monday, contained in the same chests
being lodged within the inn of the same John at Southwark. . . .

And the said John . . . says that on the said Monday about the
second hour after noon the said William entered his inn to be lodged
there, and at once when he entered, the same John assigned to the said
William a certain chamber being in that inn, fitting for his rank, with a
door and a lock affixed to the same door with sufficient nails, so that he
should lie there and put and keep his things there, and delivered to the

[9] The Feast of the Purification (of the Virgin Mary) is February 2.

said William the key to the door of the said chamber, which chamber the said William accepted. . . .

William says that . . . when the said John had delivered to him the said chamber and key as above, the same William, being occupied about divers businesses to be done in the city of London, went out from the said inn into the city to expedite the said businesses and handed over the key of the door to a certain servant of the said William to take care of it meantime, ordering the servant to remain in the inn meanwhile and to take care of his horses there; and afterwards, when night was falling, the same William being in the city and the key still in the keeping of the said servant, the wife of the said John called unto her into her hall the said servant who had the key, giving him food and drink with a merry countenance and asking him divers questions and occupying him thus for a long time, until the staple of the lock of the door aforesaid was thrust on one side out of its right place and the door of the chamber was thereby opened and his goods, being in the inn of the said John, were taken and carried off by the said malefactors. . . . The said John says . . . [that his wife did not call the servant into the hall, but that] when the said servant came into the said hall and asked his wife for bread and ale and other necessaries to be brought to the said chamber of his master, his wife immediately and without any delay delivered to the same servant the things for which he asked . . . protesting that no goods of the same William in the said inn were carried away by the said John his servants or any strange malefactors other than the persons of the household of the said William.

GOING ON PILGRIMAGE

1. Royal Pilgrimages

EDWARD III'S ALMS AND GIFTS AT CANTERBURY, MAY, 1369

Exchequer, King's Remembrancer Accounts, 396/11. fols. 13v, 19r (Controlment Roll of John de Ipre, Controller of the King's Household, 13 Feb. to 27 June, 43 Edw. III).

Alms: In oblations of the lord King made at the Requiem Mass celebrated in his presence in the chapel [of St. George, Windsor] on the morrow of St. George,[10] 6s. 8d. In oblations of the lord King made at the Shrine of St. Thomas the Martyr in Christchurch, Canterbury, May 14, the price of three gold nobles, 20s. In like oblations of the lord King made at the

[10] That is, on April 24.

head of St. Thomas there, the same day, the price of one gold noble, 6s. 8d. In oblations of the lord King made at the image of the Blessed Mary Undercroft in the same church, the same day, the price of three gold nobles, 20s. In like oblations of the lord King made at the old tomb of St. Thomas the Martyr there, the same day, the price of one gold noble, 6s. 8d. In like oblations of the lord King made at the Point of the Sword in the same church the same day, the price of one gold noble, 6s. 8d. In like oblations of the lord King made at the shrine of St. Augustine in the church of St. Augustine of Canterbury, the same day, the price of three gold nobles, 20s. In like oblations of the lord King made at the shrine of St. Mildred the Virgin there, the same day, the price of one gold noble, 6s. 8d. In like oblations of the lord King made at the head of St. Augustine there the same day, 6s. 8d. In oblations of the Lord King made at the shrine of St. Adrian there, the same day, 6s. 8d. In oblations at the High Mass celebrated in the King's presence in the chapel within his castle of Windsor on the day of Pentecost [May 20], 10d.

Gifts: To Hanekyn Fytheler, making his minstrelsy before the image of the Blessed Mary Undercroft in Christchurch, Canterbury, at the time when the King was offering there, of the King's gift, the fourteenth day of May, 6s. 8d. To John Harpour, harping in the church of St. Augustine, Canterbury, at the time when the King was offering there, of the gift of the lord King, the same day, 3s. 4d.

RICHARD II AND HIS FRIENDS ON PILGRIMAGE TO ST. EDWARD'S SHRINE AT WESTMINSTER, NOVEMBER 10, 1387

Continuation of Higden, *Polychronicon,* IX, 104.

The King, delighted with such an answer [from the mayor and citizens, that they would stand by him], entered the city of London on the tenth day of November; and the mayor and the rest of the citizens of the said city, clad all of one suit of white and red, went forth to meet him with ceremony and rode in procession before him through the midst of the city as far as the Mews at Charing Cross.

There the King loosed his shoes and the bishop of York, Robert de Vere, Duke of Ireland, and Michael de la Pole, Earl of Suffolk [with Robert Tresilian, the chief justice, and Sir Nicholas Brembre, the five councilors appealed of treason three days later] [11] went in procession

[11] Cf. Favent, *Historia . . . mirabilis parliamenti,* pp. 9–10. See also above, pp. 161–162 and 158.

with him, barefoot likewise, to the church of St. Peter, Westminster. The abbot and convent of the said monastery also came to meet him in solemn manner in their copes, as far as the King's Gate, and brought him upon carpets laid before him from that place to the church. And when he had made devotions in the customary fashion, he withdrew to his palace.

2. *The Pilgrims at Canterbury*,[12] *early 15th Century*

Prologue to *The Tale of Beryn*, ed. by Furnivall, pp. 1–14.

They took their inn and lodged them at midmorn, I trow,
At the Checker-on-the-Hoop, which many a man doth know.
Their host of Southwark went with them, as ye have heard before,
Who was ruler of them all, were they less or were they more;
He ordered their dinner wisely before to church they went,
Such victuals as he found in town and for no others sent.

The Pardoner saw the waiters busy the great folk to obey,
Who quietly ignored him and looked another way.
The Innkeeper was shouted at, in one place and another.

(ll. 13–21)

. . .

When the pilgrims were all lodged as right would and reason,
Each according to his degree, to church then was the season
To turn their way and wend, and to make their offering,
Devoutly as each would of silver brooch and ring.
But at the church door courtesy bade them stay
Till the knight, who, of his gentry, knew full well the way,
Pushed forward the prelates two, the Parson and his peer,
The Monk, who took the sprinkler with a manly cheer,
And did as the manner is, moistened all their pates,
Each one after other, according to their estates.
The Friar pretended cunningly to pick the sprinkler up
To use upon the others. He would not for his cope
Have missed that occupation in that holy place;

[12] From the Prologue to *The Tale of Beryn*. Both the Prologue and the story were evidently designed as a continuation of Chaucer's incomplete *Canterbury Tales*. They are found only in Northumberland manuscript 55. The rhythm is as bad in the original as in the modernization. The story abounds in vivid description, lively incident, and real, though primitive, humor. [R.]

So longed his holy conscience to see the Nun's face.
The Knight went with his compeers towards the holy shrine
To do what they were come for and after for to dine.
The Pardoner and the Miller and the other stupid sots
Went wandering about the church just like silly goats,
Peered fast and pored, on the glass above them high,
Counterfeiting gentlemen, blazoning heraldry,
Pointing out the painter and the story with as deep
Understanding of the matter as old hornéd sheep.
"He bears a quarter-staff," said one, "or else the end of a rake."
"Now where's your mind?" said the Miller. "That's a big mistake.
It's a spear, if you use your eyes, with a spur tied on before,
To push adown the enemy and through his shoulder bore."
"Peace!" said the Host of Southwark. "Let be these windows glazed;
Go up and make your offerings. Ye seem like folk amazed.
Since ye be in company of honest men and good,
Imitate their manners, as rules of breeding would.
Enough for this time now! I hold it for the best,
For he who does as others do may keep his mind at rest."

Then on they went boisterously, goggling here and there,
Kneeled adown before the shrine, said heartily their prayer;
They prayed to Saint Thomas in such wise as they knew,
And then the holy relics, each man kissed them, too,
As from the goodly monk the name of each they learned;
And then to other places of holiness they turned,
And were at their devotions till the service was sung through.
And then as it was near noon, to dinner-ward they drew.
But first, as manner and custom is, pilgrims' signs they bought;
For men from home should know the saint whose shrine they have sought.
Each man laid out his silver in the things that he liked best.
                                        (ll. 131–173)

                        .   .   .

They set their tokens on their heads, some on their caps did pin,
And then to the dinner-ward went back to their inn.
                                        (ll. 191–192)

                        .   .   .

At dinner the friar reminds the host that he has invited the whole company to
supper that same evening. The host repeats his invitation and the party breaks up for
the afternoon, each to amuse himself in his own way.

The Knight arose therewith, cast on a fresher gown,
And his son, another, to walk about the town;
And so did all the others who were of that array
Who had their changes with them; they made them fresh and gay,
Went off in groups together, as their pleasures lay,
As they were wont to do in traveling by the way.

The Knight with his companions went to see the wall
And defences of the town, as do these knights all;
Observing attentively the strong points thereabout,
And all the weak places to his son pointing out,
For shot of arbalest and bow and shot of gun,
In the defences of the town and how it might be won,
And how defended there, he worked out in his head
And declared compendiously. . . .

(ll. 231–244)

. . .

The Wife of Bath was so weary, to walk she had no mind;
She took the Prioress' hand: "Madam, are ye inclined
To stroll a bit in the garden to see the flowers grow,
And afterwards to rest in our hostess' parlor go?
I will treat you to wine and ye shall treat me, too,
For till we go to supper, we have nothing else to do."

The Prioress, as gentlewoman born and bred, could say
No nay to that proposal, and forth they went their way,
Passing out softly where many an herb there grew
In the herb-garden, for surgery and for stew;
And all the garden paths adorned and railed full fair,
The sage and the hyssop staked and protected there,
And other flower-beds about them freshly dight,
For visitors at the inn a very pretty sight.

(ll. 281–294)

. . .

The supper at an end,
The people who were sober and sensible did wend
Without more ado to take their rest soon.
But the Miller and the Cook sat drinking by the moon;

They drank twice to each other in the silence there;
And when the Pardoner spied them, he began to hum an air;
"Double me this burden," chuckling in his throat,
Hoping that Tapster would hear his merry note.
He called to him the Summoner, his own disciple true,
The Yeoman and the Reeve, and the Manciple, too;
And there they stood a-bellowing; for nothing would they leave,
Until an hour when it was well within the eve.

(ll. 407–418)

3. *Lollard Scorn for Pilgrimages, 1407*

EXAMINATION OF WILLIAM THORPE BEFORE ARCHBISHOP ARUNDEL
AT SALTWOOD CASTLE ON SUNDAY, AUGUST 7, 1407

Foxe, *Acts and Monuments*, III, 267–268.[18]

[Archbishop]. What sayest thou to the third point that is certified against thee, preaching openly in Shrewsbury that "pilgrimage is not lawful?" And, over this, thou saidest that "Those men and women that go on pilgrimages to Canterbury, to Beverley, to Carlington, to Walsingham, and to other such places are accursed and made foolish spending their goods in waste.

> William, distinguishing between the virtuous pilgrim, who, approaching heaven step by step, delights to hear of the good examples of the saints, and the majority of pilgrims, who cannot say their Pater Noster, Ave Maria, nor Creed in any manner of language, and go on pilgrimage more for the health of their bodies than their souls, continues:

Also, sir, I know well that when divers men and women will go thus after their own wills, finding out one pilgrimage, they will ordain with them before to have with them both men and women that can well sing wanton songs; and some other pilgrims will have with them bagpipes; so that every town that they come through, what with the noise of their singing and with the sound of their piping and with the jangling of their Canterbury bells and with the barking out of dogs after them, they make more noise than if the King came there away with all his clarions and many other minstrels. And if these men and women be a month out on their pilgrimage, many of them shall be, a half year after, great janglers, tale-tellers, and liars.

[Archbishop]. Lewd losel! thou seest not far enough in this matter!

[18] The whole examination is printed in A. W. Pollard, ed., *An English Garner, Fifteenth Century Prose and Verse*, New York, 1903, pp. 97–174.

For thou considerest not the great travail of pilgrims; therefore thou blamest that thing that is praiseworthy. I say to thee that it is right well done that pilgrims have with them both singers and also pipers; that when one of them that goeth barefoot striketh his toe against a stone and hurteth him sore and maketh him to bleed, it is well done that he or his fellow begin then a song, or else take out of his bosom a bagpipe for to drive away with such mirth the hurt of his fellow; for with such solace the travail and weariness of pilgrims is lightly and merrily borne out.

4. *Pilgrims on Shipboard* (*a Pilgrimage to the Shrine of St. James de Compostela*), *time of Henry VI*

Wright, *Reliquiae antiquae*, I, 2–3 (from Trinity College, Cambridge, MS R. 3. 19).

> Men may leave off all games,
> Who sail to Saint James;
> For many their trouble tames
>   When they begin to sail.
>
> For when they have taken the sea,
> At Sandwich or at Winchelsea,
> At Bristol or wheresoe'er it be,
>   Their hearts begin to fail.
>
> Anon the master commandeth fast
> To his shipmen in all haste,
> To line up soon about the mast,
>   Their tackling to get out.
>
> With "Ho! Hoist now!" then they cry.
> "What ho, mate! thou stand'st too nigh;
> Thy fellow may not haul thee by":
>   Thus they begin to shout.
>
> A boy or two anon climb nigh
> And overthwart the sailyard lie.
> "Yo ho! Tally there!" the others cry,
>   And pull with all their might.
>
> "Come, stow the boat, boatswain, anon,
> That our pilgrims may play thereon;
> For some are like to cough and groan,
>   Ere it be full midnight."

"Haul the bowline! Now veer the sheet!
Cook, make ready anon our meat.
Our pilgrims have no wish to eat;
    I pray God give them rest."

"Go to the helm! What ho! [Come] not near?
Steward, fellow! a pot of beer!"
"Ye shall have, sir, with good cheer,
    Anon all of the best."

"Yo ho! Furl 'em! Haul in the brails!
Thou haulest not; by God, thou fails't!
Oh, see how well our good ship sails!"
    And thus they say among.

"Haul in the wartake!" [14] "It shall be done."
"Steward! Cover the board anon,
And set bread and salt thereon,
    And tarry not too long."

Comes one and says, "Be merry all;
You're going to have a storm or squall."
"Hold your tongue and cease to bawl;
    Thou meddlest wonder sore."

In the meanwhile the pilgrims lie,
And have their basins near them by,
And after hot malmsey they cry,
    "Help us to restore."

And some would have a salted toast,
For they could eat neither boiled nor roast;
A man could soon pay what they cost
    For the first day or two.

One laid his book upon his knee,
And read till he could no more see.
"Alas! my head will split in three!"
    Says another, and it's true.

Then comes our master like a lord,
And speaketh many a royal word,

[14] Some particular kind of tack or rope. (*O.E.D.*)

And sits him down at the high board
    To see all things be well.

Anon he calls a carpenter
And bids him bring along his gear,
To make the cabins here and there
    With many a fragile cell.

A sack of straw was there right good,
For some must lie with but a hood;
I had as lief be in the wood
    With neither meat nor drink.

For when that we shall go to bed,
The pump is nigh to our bed's head;
A man might just as well be dead
    As smell thereof the stink.

5. *Pilgrimage by Proxy, 1388–1417*

It was a common custom to send someone else to fulfill a vow of pilgrimage, or to go on pilgrimage to pray for the soul of a dead person. Here are some excerpts from wills and testaments containing bequests for these purposes:

Prerogative Court of Canterbury, 2 Rous.

May 2, 1388. John de Multon, knight.— My body to be buried in the Monastery of the Blessed Mary of Lincoln. . . . Item, I bequeath to one man going for my soul as far as Jerusalem, 5 marks.

Prerogative Court of Canterbury, 3 Rous.

February 10, 1394. John Blakeney, citizen and fishmonger of London, buried at Charterhouse.— I bequeath 20 marks to hire one chaplain to go on pilgrimage to Rome and there to remain throughout one year, to celebrate and pray for my soul and the souls for whom I am bound [to pray], and £10 to hire two men to go on pilgrimage for my soul to St. James in Galicia,[15] to fulfill my vow.

Prerogative Court of Canterbury, 3 Rous.

August 2, 1394. Sir Richard atte Leese, knight, buried in the chapel of St. Mary in Sheldewych church.— Item, [I bequeath] to find [16] one pilgrim to St. James, 100*s.* Item, to find one pilgrim to Walsingham, 13*s.* 4*d.*

[15] The Shrine of St. James de Compostela. See above, p. 265.
[16] To provide for.

Commissary of London, 456 Courtenay.

1400. Alice, widow of Thomas Hose, taverner.— [I bequeath] to my son Thomas 10s. to perform my pilgrimage to Walsingham.

Commissary of London, 459 Courtenay.

1400. Margaret Deloe, widow.— [I bequeath] two nobles for two pilgrimages to Walsingham.

Prerogative Court of Canterbury, 45 Marche.

1417. Sir Richard Arundel, knight, buried in St. Mary's Abbey, Rochester. — My executors to find a man after my death to go for the good of my soul to the Court of Rome, the Holy Land and the Sepulchre of Our Lord, and to the Holy Blood in Germany.[17]

6. Gild Provisions for Pilgrims and Other Travelers

MASS BEFORE STARTING, 1350

Chancery Miscellanea, Gild Certificate 391.[18]

Certain men and women founded a fraternity of St. Thomas the Martyr in the Church of St. Mary, Oxford, to the end that scholars of the university and visitors coming there to sleep could hear a mass between five and six in the morning.[19]

MASS FOR TRAVELERS, 1260

Chancery Miscellanea, Gild Certificate 87.

The Gild of the Blessed Virgin Mary [Boston, Lincs.] provided that, since it was impossible to attain the Gate of Salvation without the aid of the "Star of the Sea" . . . , one priest should say mass at dawn and another at nine o'clock, in order that those leaving the town or returning late to it might not be prevented from hearing mass by reason of the lack of celebration.

[17] Cf. Provision made in will of John de Holegh, hosier, 1351/52.—To be buried in the church of St. Mary-le-Bow. . . . To anyone going on a pilgrimage to the Holy Sepulchre in Jerusalem and to the tomb of St. Katherine on Mt. Sinai [I bequeath] £20, and to anyone making a pilgrimage to St. James in Galicia, £7; and if my executors be unable to find anyone to undertake such pilgrimages, then one half of the legacies to be distributed among the poor, the other to be devoted to the repair of roads within twenty miles of London. (London, Court of Hustings, Calendar of Wills, I, 656–658.)

[18] For all references to Gild Certificates cf. Westlake, The Parish Gilds of Mediaeval England, pp. 138–238.

[19] Cf. Gild of St. Peter, Southgate Chapel, Grantham, which provided mass for travelers passing through the town. Chancery Miscellanea, Gild Certificate 115.

A PILGRIM'S SEND-OFF AND WELCOME HOME, 1350

Chancery Miscellanea, Gild Certificate 135.

The Corpus Christi Gild of St. Michael on the Hill, Lincoln, founded in 1350, ordained (*inter alia*) that if a member went on pilgrimage to Jerusalem, each brother should give him 1*d*. If he went to St. James or to St. Peter and St. Paul, all the brethren should lead him to the Cross before the Hospital of the Holy Innocents without Lincoln, and when he returned should meet him there and bring him to the Mother Church [*i.e.*, cathedral] of Lincoln.

LODGINGS FOR POOR PILGRIMS, 1340

Chancery Miscellanea, Gild Certificate 439.

The Gild Merchant of Coventry provided a hostel with thirteen beds for poor men passing on pilgrimage. A governor presided over it, and there was a woman to keep it clean. The upkeep was £10 a year.

PERILS OF THE JOURNEY, CA. 1365

Chancery Miscellanea, Gild Certificate 91.

Five men [of the borough of St. James, Lincs.] had vowed a pilgrimage to the land of St. James, and while returning after its completion were in great danger from a storm at sea. They vowed that, if by the intercession of St. James they were preserved . . . they would build in his honor an altar in the church of St. Peter. When they had made their vow, the storm ceased, and by the Saint's intercession they came to the desired haven. Upon coming to their homes and being asked by their neighbors how they had fared, they told of the tempest and of their vow. All combined to help build the altar.

CANTERBURY PILGRIMS FOUND A GILD [20]

Chancery Miscellanea, Gild Certificate 272.

The Gild of St. Thomas the Martyr, Lynn, Norfolk, was founded by six of the town who made pilgrimage to Canterbury. They were accustomed to find a candle in honor of St. Thomas and to attend the funeral services of a deceased brother, offering ½*d*. and providing thirteen masses for his soul.

[20] In the returns of 1389 this gild is described as having been founded "lately." Cf. Westlake, *Parish Gilds*, p. 198.

JOURNEYS ON THE KING'S BUSINESS

1. A Yeoman of the Chamber Acting as Confidential Messenger between Richard II and the Archbishop of Canterbury, 1382

Archbishops' Registers (Lambeth), Courtenay, fol. 328.

THE KING'S LETTER, SENT BY THOMAS HATEFELD, A YEOMAN OF THE CHAMBER

Very Reverend Father in God and our dear Cousin: Be pleased to know that our messengers whom we sent recently to Flanders have returned and have set before us three articles, which Philip Artevelde has sent to us in the name of the Commonalty of Flanders.

> The articles follow, desiring that an alliance be made between England and Flanders, and that the wool staple be fixed at Bruges until the haven of Ghent be completed.

Thus, we beg, very Reverend Father, for your love towards us, that you would send us your good and wise counsel upon the whole of this matter, by your [letters] and by the bearer of these, as soon as you conveniently can. For you are well aware that this matter is very great and onerous and that it is fitting that order should be taken therein speedily. . . . God have you in his safe keeping. Given under our signet at our manor of Henle[y] upon le Hethe, July 20 [1382].

THE ARCHBISHOP'S REPLY

My very excellent and redoubtable Sire: I commend myself to your most high Majesty, to the height of my power. And my most redoubtable Sire, may it please your very gracious Lordship to know that I received your most honorable letters addressed to me, your humble chaplain and orator, on the twenty-second of July by the hands of Thomas Hatefeld, yeoman of your chamber; whereby I have quite understood everything therein contained. . . .

> He comments upon the three articles in detail and advises the King to take counsel with those who have most knowledge of the Staple, as to what would best profit the kingdom.

Written at my Manor of Otford, July 23.

2. The Steward of the Royal Household Traveling to Borrow Money, 1377–1378

Exchequer of Receipt, Issue Roll 471 m. 7.

Thursday, November 11 [1378]. [Paid] to Hugh Segrave, knight [steward of the household], late sent by ordinance of the Council upon divers occasions to certain parts upon the King's business; namely, sent upon one occasion to the towns of Glastonbury, Bristol, and divers other places in the counties of Somerset, Dorset, Wiltshire, Gloucestershire, Oxfordshire, and Berkshire, to borrow moneys for the use of the King for the making of the voyage to sea [undertaken] by the Earl of Buckingham as captain, in the winter last past.

And upon two other occasions sent to Sandwich to John, Duke of Lancaster, the Duke of Brittany, and other magnates of his company, at Sandwich . . . to expedite their passage.

For his wages for 33 days, namely, for every day upon which he was occupied in the said businesses, 10s.

3. A Bishop Going Abroad with His Train, 1365

Exchequer, King's Remembrancer, Accounts Various, 315/2.

The account of Simon, bishop of London, going from London towards the parts of Flanders in the company of Bartholomew de Burghersh to treat of the King's business with the Council of Flanders, from Friday, February 21, 39 Edward III [1365], until Wednesday, March 26 in the year aforesaid:

In wages of the said Simon the bishop from February 21, when he left London, until March 25, both days included, for 34 days, receiving by the day 66s. 8d.

Sum, £113 6s. 8d.

In one ship hired for the bishop and his household servants from Dover to Calais, £3 13s. 4d. Item, in one ship hired for the horses of the lord and of his household and their stuff, from Dover to Calais, £3 13s. 4d.

Sum, £7 6s. 8d.

In the pontage of 32 horses at Dover, 2s. 8d. In portage, carriage, and boat-hire of the said Simon the bishop, his household and stuff from his inn to the ship at Dover, 2s. 6d. In [the like] to his inn at Calais, 8s. 6d. In pontage of 32 horses landing there, for every horse, 2d.— 5s. 4d.

Sum, 19s.

In one ship hired for the lord, his household, and their stuff, returning from Calais to Dover, £3 13s. 4d. In one ship hired for the horses, 31s. 6d.

Sum, 104s. 10d.

In the pontage of 28 horses at Calais on the return, for every horse, 2*d.*—4*s.* 8*d.* In pontage, carriage, and boat-hire at Calais, returning from the inn to the ship, 5*s.* 6*d.* In pontage of 28 horses landing at Dover, 2*s.* 4*d.* In portage, carriage, and boat hire of the said Simon, his household, and their stuff there, 8*s.* 7*d.*

Sum, 21*s.* 1*d.*

In carriage of the stuff of the said Simon and his household from Bruges to Sluys and from Sluys to London by water, 23*s.* 10½*d.*[21]

Sum of all the expenses . . . . £127 18*s.* 3*d.*

4. *A Journey to Pavia with Horses, 1368*

Exchequer, King's Remembrancer, Accounts Various, 105/38.

Particulars of the Account of Edmund Rose [one of Chaucer's fellow esquires of the Household], of his expenses in taking seventeen horses and eighteen men and seven hounds from Calais to Milan, by command of the lord King, from January 27 [1368] to March 20 following:
He accounts for:

Payment for the pontage from the ship . . . . 40*s.*
Carriage of saddles and other harness from the ship . . . . 6*d.*

Upon Thursday, January 27, at Calais in expenses of 13 palfreys, one sumpter-horse, and 14 men for leading them, and also one man as sergeant of the hounds, and for the keep of 7 hounds, each of the 14 men and horses taking 18*d.* the day, the sergeant of hounds 8*d.* the day, and each hound 2*d.* the day . . . . 22*s.* 10*d.*

Item, in white wine for physic for the said horses, for 3 gallons, 2*s.*, and for a tip to the man who brought the said physic . . . . . 8*d.*

Item [expenses at 22*s.* 10*d.* a day, as follows]:

Friday at Calais, Saturday at Calais; Sunday at Boulogne; Monday at Menteneye; Tuesday at Flixecourt; Wednesday at Amyas; Thursday at Seintynte; Friday to Saturday at Menyanbry, and for white wine bought for the horses' physic there, 8*d.*; and for honey, linseed, and cumin bought for the horses' physic, 2*s.* Sunday at Creil; Monday to Wednesday at Paris (with physic for the horses there); Thursday at Fontenay en Brie; Friday at Petitparis; Saturday at Provins en Brie (with physic for the horses); Sunday at Villenece Legraunt; Monday at Amery; Tuesday to Wednesday at Troyes (with physic); Thursday at Bas-sur-Sone; Friday at Agenay; Saturday to Tuesday at Degeon (with physic);

[21] This item disallowed at the audit.

Wednesday at St. Jean de Losne, and for the ferrying of men, horses, and hounds there, 40s.

Paid wages of a man-at-arms of France for the safe conduct of the said palfreys from Paris to St. Jean de Losne, for 13 days in the company of the said Edmund, taking by the day for himself and two horses, 6s. 8d. . . . . £4 6s. 8d.

Thursday at Chalyn; Friday to Saturday at Bogaille (with physic); Sunday at Jonii; Monday to Tuesday at Lausanne; Wednesday at S. Mons (with physic); Thursday at Martyn; Friday at Sote, and for toll there, 10s.; Saturday to Sunday at Mountbrigge and for toll there, 6s. 8d.; Monday at Seintpyoun; Tuesday to Wednesday at Dome (with physic); Thursday at Parraunce and for the ferry there, 20s.; Friday to Saturday at Caresk (with physic); Sunday at Some; Monday to Tuesday at Viadegrace (with physic); Wednesday at Casille; Thursday to Friday at Venaske [22] (with physic); Saturday at Pavia; paid a man as guide from St. Jean de Losne to Pavia, 40s., and for his expenses at 8d. a day, 16s.; for shoeing the horses at ¼d. the day, 18s. 5d.

His own wages and those of 2 men and 3 horses of his from London to the Lord of Milan residing in Pavia, from January 23 to March 20 . . . . £18 13s. 4d.

In wages of Hans Henxstman [the henchman], sent from Pavia to the lord King of England, from March 23, when he left Pavia, until May 7, for himself and his horse at 14d. by the day . . . . 52s. 6d.

And in one ship hired for the passage from Calais to Dover for the same time, 20s.

5. A Knight's Visit to the Pope at Avignon, 1366

Exchequer, King's Remembrancer, Accounts Various, 315/16.

Particulars of the account of Bartholomew de Burghersh, knight, going on the King's business to Avignon, staying there and returning to England, from May 19, 40 Edw. III [1366], to September 26 following, for 131 days, taking £4 by the day £524

For allowance of one ship for the horses of the said B. from Dover to Calais . . . . £4 10s. 4d.

For allowance of one barge for the said B. and his household from Dover to Calais . . . . 46s. 8d.

In carriage, portage, and boat-hire of the said B., his men and their stuff from Dover to the ship . . . . 7s.

22 Probably modern Binasco.

[The like] from the ship to Calais . . . . 10s. 7d.

Paid for wages to Massy, servant of the King of France, going with the said B., Richard Stafford, knight, Master Thomas de Bokton, and Master John de Carleton, to guide them from Paris to Avignon, and returning to Poitiers from June 1 until September 1 . . . . by the day, 6s. 8d. . . . . £30 13s. 4d.* [23]

Paid to the said Massy for his reward . . . . £6 13s. 4d.*

In divers boat hirings for the said B., his men, their stuff, and their horses from the said town of Calais to the said town of Avignon, and thence to St. Malo in Brittany . . . . 13s. 4d.*

To divers men guiding the said B. and his men upon occasion . 12s.*

Paid to Massyot, sergeant-at-arms of the lord Pope, for his service and toil in going with the said B., Richard, Thomas, and John, throughout the time when they remained in Avignon . . . . . £4 10s.*

To divers officers and ushers of the lord Pope . £16 13s. 4d.*

To a certain usher of the Chamber of the lord Pope, bringing the news that the bishop of Ely was chosen by the lord Pope to be Archbishop . . . . £16 13s. 4d.*

Paid to John Pheffane, a merchant of the Company of Lucca, for divers letters sent upon divers occasions to England . . . £4 16s. 8d.*

To Master Thomas de Bokton, remaining behind at Avignon upon the King's business . . . . £10 *

Paid to Master Nicholas de Chaddesdon, going with the said embassy . . . . £6 13s. 4d.*

For allowance of a certain ship taking the said B., his men, horses, and their stuff from St. Malo in Brittany to [Sout]hampton . £26 13s. 4d.

In divers expenses for the repair of the said ship for the horses of the said B. . . . . 71s.

In carriage, portage, and boat-hire of the said B., his men, and their stuff from St. Malo to the ship . . . . 9s.

In boat-hire of the said B., his men, and their stuff from the ship to the town of [Sout]hampton and boat-hire for the horses of the said B. . . . . 8s. 4d.

[The last four] items are admitted . . . by command of the King's Council, because . . . the said B. had with him many men and horses for the said business . . . and because he landed [at Southampton] on account of the danger from French enemies.

[23] Items followed by an asterisk were disallowed because paid without warrant.

6. *Journeys of One of the King's Esquires, 1370–1375*

Exchequer, King's Remembrancer, Accounts Various, 316/12.

Particulars of the account of Geoffrey Styvecle, the King's esquire, of all his journeys in the King's service, going as the King's messenger as well to parts beyond the seas as to divers places within the realm of England, for which journeys the same Geoffrey hath not hitherto accounted. He accounts for:

His wages at 3*s.* 4*d.* by the day from December 8, 44 Edward III [1370], on which day he left Westminster for the parts of Gascony to the lord Prince, whom he met at sea off Plymouth, until April 8 following, when he returned to the King at Sheen,[24] deducting 6 days on which he returned to the King upon six occasions within the same time; and thus for 116 days (including the first and last) . . £19 6*s.* 8*d.*

His wages at 3*s.* 4*d.* by the day from March 24, 48 Edward III [1374], on which day he left London for Plymouth and Dartmouth to oversee the muster and array of men-at-arms and archers of the retinue of Philip de Courtenay, admiral of the Western Fleet . . . until May 4 following.

His wages at 13*s.* 4*d.* by the day from March 10, 49 Edward III [1375], when he left London for Bruges in Flanders to report to the King's Council concerning the progress of the treaty of peace between the ambassadors of the lord King and the ambassadors of his adversary of France, until April 13 following, when he returned there.

His wages at 13*s.* 4*d.* by the day from April 18, 49 Edward III, when he set out from London to the said town of Bruges for secret business of the lord King concerning the said treaty, namely, on his second journey towards those parts, until May 8 following, when he returned there.

His wages at 13*s.* 4*d.* by the day from May 23, 49 Edward III, when he left London for the said parts of Flanders for the secret business of the King, on his third journey, until June 4 following, when he returned to the King at Sheen.

His wages at 13*s.* 4*d.* by the day from June 5, 49 Edward III, when he left London for the said parts of Flanders for the secret business of the King, until June 18 following, when he returned there.

His wages at 13*s.* 4*d.* by the day from July 2, 49 Edward III, when he left London for the said parts of Flanders for the said business, on his fifth journey to the said parts, until the 18th day of the said month, when he returned there. . . .

[24] Now Richmond.

[In each case, except for the first two items, he has also allowances for passage and repassage of the sea.]

7. *A Herald Sent to Procure Safe-Conducts for the King's Envoys and to Deliver Them from Captivity, 1379–1385*

Exchequer, King's Remembrancer, Accounts Various, 318/11.

Particulars of the account of Richard Hereford, Herald of Arms . . . for divers voyages by him made going in the service of King Richard II as envoy of the said lord King to parts beyond the seas, namely, from the time of the coronation of the same King until January 19, [1386]:

He accounts for his wages at 10s. by the day going as the King's envoy to the parts of Flanders with certain letters directed to the Count of Flanders for certain business of the lord King touching the wars, and also to obtain letters of safe conduct for William de Gunthorp, Edward de Berkele, and Richard de Wodhale, deputed by the King to [negotiate] reparations for attacks between the King and the Count, viz., from January 27, 2 Richard II [1379], when he left the city of London for Flanders, until March 16, when he returned there .   .   .   .   £24 10s.

In the expenses of the said Richard in his passage of the sea between Dover and Calais with his two men and three horses within the same time, viz., for each man with a horse, 5s. .   .   .   .   15s.

And in like expenses in his repassage and also for his men and horses between Calais and Dover within the said time .   .   .   .   .   .   15s.

And in like wages of the same Richard going a second time as a like envoy of the same King to the parts of Flanders with letters directed to the Count of Flanders to procure letters of safe conduct from the same count for Michael de la Pole [and others], envoys of the same lord King to the Court of Rome, viz., from March 28, 2 Richard II [1379], when he left London . . . until April 28 following, when he returned £16

[Expenses with two men and horses as above, 30s.]

And in like wages of the same Richard going as the King's envoy to the parts of Germany for the deliverance of the said Michael de la Pole and John de Burley, knights, late sent as the King's envoys to the Court of Rome and taken and imprisoned upon their return in the said parts, viz., from December 14, 3 Richard II [1379], when he left London, until February 23 following [1380], when he returned £36

[Expenses with two men and three horses from Dover to Calais and back, 30s.]

[Three similar journeys to obtain letters of safe conduct from the Count of Flanders]:

And in like wages of the same Richard going as the King's envoy to the parts of Paris for certain secret business of the lord King, namely, from the second of March, 8 Richard II [1385], when he left London, until April 30 following, when he returned there. £30

[Expenses of the passage and repassage of two men and three horses between Dover and Calais and back, 30s.]

8. *The King's Henchman Gets His Outfit to Go to Sea, 1387*

Exchequer, King's Remembrancer, Accounts Various, 401/16.

Delivered to [John Wyse, henchman of the lord King], upon his apparel against his [going upon a] voyage made by sea by the lord Earl of Arundel and others of his company, in the month of March in the tenth year of Richard II [1387]; namely, for the making of a jacket of Camacca lined with blue silk, padded with flock and cotton wool; and upon the padding, lining and stretching; together with linen of Brabant . . . and for one basinet of the . . . gift of the King . . .

2¾   ells—blue Camacca
4¾   ells—blue silk
3¾   ells—Brabant linen
4   lbs.—flock
3   lbs.—cotton wool
1   basinet with aventail

PRIVATE TRAVEL BEYOND THE SEAS

1. Travel the Essence of Good Breeding in the World of Chivalry, 1389–1399

Christine de Pisan, "Ballade," *Archaeologia*, XX (1824), 165–166 (French original from MS Harl. 4431, fol. 47a and 47b).

O man of gentle birth! Thou who wouldst prowess share,
Hark, whilst I tell to thee, how thou shouldst have a care
In many a land to be, where thou canst warfare dare,
Yet toward thine adversary, ever good faith to bear,
Never the fight to shun, nor cunning flight prepare.

.   .   .

By frequent journeyings, thine shall be joys most rare.
Far through strange realms and courts thus shalt thou fare.
All kingly policies shalt thou learn there.

2. A Medieval Itinerary, London to Rome, 1401/2

Adam of Usk, *Chronicon*, pp. 242–243.

On the nineteenth day of February in the year of our Lord 1401/2, I, the writer of this history, as by the will of God I determined, took ship at Billingsgate in London and with a favoring wind crossed the sea, and, within the space of a day landing at Bergen-op-Zoom in Brabant, the country which I sought, I set my face towards Rome. Thence passing through Diest, Maastricht, Aachen, Cologne, Bonn, Coblentz, Worms, Speyer, Strassburg, Breisach, Basel, Bern, Lucerne, and its wonderful lake, Mont St. Gotthard, and the hermitage on its summit, where I was drawn in an ox-wagon half dead with cold and with mine eyes blind-folded lest I should see the dangers of the pass, on the eve of Palm Sunday,[25] I arrived at Bellinzona in Lombardy. Thence through Como, Milan, Piacenza, Borgo-San-Donnino, Pontremoli, Carrara, Pietrasanta, Pisa, Siena, and Viterbo, turning aside from Bologna, Florence, and Perugia on account of the raging wars and sieges of the duke of Milan —of whom hereafter and the perils thereof—and halting for two days at every best inn for refreshment of myself and men and still more of my horses, on the fifth day of April by the favor of God and the fear of our archer-guards I came safely through all to Rome.

3. A Conversational Manual for Travelers in France, ca. 1400

Stengel, "Die ältesten Anleitungsschriften zur Erlernung der französischen Sprache," *Zeitschrift für neufranzösische Sprache und Literatur*, I (1879), 11–13.

To ask the right road:

"Sir, God give you good day," or, "God give you good health and good luck," or, "Madam, God give you good evening," or, "God commend you and guard you from evil, my friend."

"Sir, you be welcome."

"What hour of the day is it, prime or tierce, noon or nones?—What time is it?"

"Between six and seven."

"How far is it from here to Paris?"

"Twelve leagues and far enough."

"Is the road good?"

"Yes, so God help me."

[25] That is, on March 9.

"Of these two, is this the right road?"

"God help me, sweet sir, no."

"Is this the wrong road? And tell me how many leagues it is from here there."

"I told you twelve or around that."

"Is the road safe from robbers?"

"So God help me, sir, not at all. Some people have been robbed recently."

"In truth?"

"Indeed, sir, truly."

"Tell me the name of that town. Who is the lord of it? Say, where do he and his lady live? Say, is their daughter married? Tell me, have we enough of day to arrive there?"

"Sir, you must ride hard."

"Is the road safe?"

"Indeed, sir, you can pass well enough."

"Is there no danger at all of robbers?"

"Certes, sir, we do not hear of many."

"And in which direction should I go?"

"Take the right-hand road and then the left-hand, then keep always to the right."

"Sir, God keep you in his care."

"Sir, may you have good luck."

"Let us go buy our dinner."

"It will be prepared now."

"What is the right way to Canterbers [*sic*]? And say, is there any danger of robbers, or can I pass safely?"

"Sir, it is safe enough by day, but at night it is dangerous. For that reason, wait till tomorrow. And then we shall have breakfast together. When you have done everything, then you will depart. God give you a good journey and increase you in wealth."

To make enquiry concerning lodgings:

DIALOGUE I

"Say, porter, where is the lady of the house?"

"Sir, in her room or in her chamber."

"Go, take my message to her."

"Sir, what shall I say to her?"

"Tell her I am here."

"Madam, a man wants to talk with you."

"Do you know who he is?"

"Yes, you know him well."

"Tell him I will come at once."

"Madam, God give you good day."

"Sir, good day to you."

"Madam, have you lodging for us three fellows?"

"Sir, how long would you stay?"

"Madam, we don't know."

"Then what would you pay for your board (*table*) by the day?"

"Madam, what would you take for each of us?"

"Sir, not less than six pence (*deniers*) a day."

"Madam, we are willing to pay that."

"Sir, by God, you are welcome."

"Then, madam, we will send our things here. . . . Will you have them put upstairs?"

"Sir, they shall be kept safe."

"Then, madam, we shall go about our business."

"Sir, will you drink before you go?"

"Madam, for God's sake, have something brought to us."

"Sir, take the hanap; you drink first."

"Madam, I will not before you."

"Indeed, sir, you shall."

"Marry, this is good drink."

"Well, sir, may it do you much good."

"Madam, to God I commend you."

"Sir, may God be with you."

DIALOGUE 2

"God save this fair company! Tell me where there's a good inn."

"Sir, ahead of you, at the sign of the Swan (*sine*)."

"God be with you —Sir, or madam, lodging for charity and for the Holy Cross."

"Sir, come in, in God's name."

"Madam, have you good wine?"

"Indeed, sir, much."

"What kind?"

"Both white and red."

"At what price?"

"At sixteen, twelve, ten, eight, six, four, two."

"And hay and oats and other things we need?"

"Yes, sir, plenty."

"Madam, how do you sell beer?"

"At three 'mailles' (penny and a half) a gallon."

"Madam, have some beer brought. Fill the hanap, and bring us glasses and goblets for the wine. Get us some supper, madam. Let us have some food."

"Now, my gentlemen, good appetite (*Faitez bonne chere*)!"

"Madam, let us have some cheese.— Take away the tablecloth. Let us settle up. How much does it come to? Does that include everything? — Madam, are our beds made? Then let us go to sleep. . . . Show us our room."

"Boy, go with them."

"Well, how do you like it, sirs?"

"Madam, we are well pleased."

"Well, you shall not lack anything."

"Madam, call your clerk."

"Here I am, sir."

"Are you the clerk of this place, my friend?"

"Yes, sir, if you please."

"How much does our bill come to?"

"Sir, there's 'en meilleur,' four pence, and for wine, eight, which makes twelve; and in the kitchen, sixteen pence, which makes two shillings (*souls*) four pence; and for fruit, four pence, which makes two shillings eight pence; and for cheese, two pence, and for 'belle chere,' four pence, which makes three shillings two pence."

"And how much for hay and oats, and what do you get for beds and for litter [for six horses]?"

"Nothing for the beds, sir, but four pence for litter, which makes three shillings six pence."

"Well, is that all now?"

"Yes, sir, I think so."

"Madam, are our beds ready?"

"Yes, sir, upstairs."

"Well, see to it that we have good sheets and enough covers, and that our horses are well looked after.—Clerk, give us a drink and then we shall go to bed."

"Sir, God give you good night," etc.

4. The Suite of an Attendant of the Duke of Clarence Setting Out from Dover for Lombardy, 1368

Chancery, Warrants (Privy Seal Bills), 915/22.

Let a writ be made under our Great Seal in due form for our beloved and faithful William Bourcher to pass with one esquire, eight yeomen, and nine horses, their armor and other stuff, six bows and twelve sheaves of shafts, and twenty shillings for their expenses to our most beloved son, the Duke of Clarence, to go in his company to the parts of Lombardy, from Dover, with £100 in exchange.

5. The Duke's Baggage Is Sent from London via Sluys, 1368

Chancery, Warrants (Privy Seal Bills), 915/22.

Let a writ be made under our Great Seal in due form for John Gryme, Robert Chelsham, Walter of the Buttery, William Baker, and William Wyleys, yeoman, Maurice Laweles, and Hugyn Richokson, grooms, and two pages of our son, the Duke of Clarence, to pass from the port of London to Sluys in Flanders with two sets of hangings for halls, four great beds with all the appurtenances, the Great Wardrobe of robes and other necessaries, five suits of vestments for the chapel, with all the ornaments, to wit, a square of silver for an alms dish, two silver-gilt images, four silver basins, four silver phials, books, crosses, relics, jewels and other like necessaries, armor, to wit, four suits of plate [armor], three habergeons, eight basinets with aventails, three helms with crests, four kettlehats [26] . . . a trapping of mail for a warhorse . . . thirty banners, a dozen pennons, a dozen swords, a dozen lances, with three shields, a jousting saddle, with thirty other saddles, six pairs of trussing coffers, with divers stuff therein, six whole cloths of scarlet, four whole cloths of black, and one cloth of white, four other whole cloths of divers colors of our said son, together with £10 of gold and silver for their expenses.

[26] A kind of helmet used in the fourteenth and fifteenth centuries. (O.E.D.)

6. A Chaplain Goes to the Roman Court, 1367

Great Britain, Public Record Office, *Calendar of the Patent Rolls*, 1367–1370, p. 52.

License for Thomas West, chaplain, to cross from the ports of London, Sandwich, or Dover to the Roman Court with a hackney under the price of 40s., a letter of credit for 25 marks by John de Wilteshire, "spicer," a denizen, and 14s. 3d. for expenses. . . .
Westminster, October 15, 1367

7. An Esquire Goes to Lombardy, 1368

Great Britain, Public Record Office, *Calendar of the Patent Rolls*, 1367–1370, p. 130.

License for John de Wilton, esquire, to cross from the port of Dover to the ports of Lombardy with four yeomen [*sic*] each under the price of 40s., a letter of exchange of Silvester Nicholas of Lombardy for £20, and 20s. for expenses.
Westminster, February 21, 1368.

8. Going to Paris in the Service of a Prince, 1368

Great Britain, Public Record Office, *Calendar of the Patent Rolls*, 1367–1370, p. 129.

Philip de Popham, "chivaler," from the port of Dover to Paris and Lombardy in the service of Lionel, Duke of Clarence, the King's son, with nine persons, ten horses, a letter of exchange for £20 payable at Calais and 20s. for expenses.
Westminster, February 15, 1368.

9. A Letter of Protection, 1368

Chancery, Warrants (Privy Seal) No. 15.

William de Hornby granted letter of protection for pilgrimage to St. James' shrine [Galicia]; 20s. for expenses.—July 17, 1368.

10. Traveling to See the World, 1390

Great Britain, Public Record Office, *Calendar of the Patent Rolls*, 1388–1392, p. 188.

License, at the request of the King's uncle, the Duke of Gloucester, for William Arundell, knight, Simon Felbrigg, knight, and Robert Teye, who propose to visit and see the world in divers places, to pass beyond the sea from London, Dover, Sandwich or elsewhere with their men and twelve horses and to change £300 of money for expenses.
Westminster, February 3, 1390.[27]

[27] Numerous other items concerning foreign travel are found in the Patent Rolls, the Chancery Warrants, etc.

11. *Pipers and a Drummer Going Overseas to Train, 1377*

Exchequer, King's Remembrancer, Accounts Various, 398/8 (Account of John de Fordham, Chamberlain to Richard II, before his accession).

To Henry and Petirkyn, pipers (*fistulatoribus*), and to Master John, nakerer, going with the leave of the lord [28] to parts beyond the seas, to the schools, at the time of Lent, as a gift made to them for this purpose. . . . February 18, 1377—60s.

12. *An Exile's Journey from Waltham Holy Cross to Dover, 1391*

King's Bench, Controlment Roll 38, m. 13 d.

Walter atte Gore, on Friday next after the Feast of the Translation of St. Thomas the Martyr,[29] 15 Richard II, was found a fugitive in the parish church of Waltham Holy Cross, and there on that same day Edmund atte Chambre, the Coroner of the Liberty . . . of the half hundred of Waltham, approached. And the said Walter was examined by the said Edmund the Coroner why and for what cause he kept himself in the said church, and if he would be willing to surrender to the King's peace or not. And he said not, and utterly refused to surrender to the said peace. And before the said coroner, four men, the reeves of the four neighboring towns, and other faithful subjects of the King there present, he acknowledged that he was a thief and felon of the lord King, in that he, on the Feast of the Purification (of the Virgin Mary) [February 2], in the said fifteenth year,[30] broke the house of John Motte at Nettleswell in the county of Essex and there feloniously took and carried away a coverlet, price 2s., a blanket, price 8d., 3 sheets, price 18d., 3 silver rings, price 3d., one silver spoon, price 8d.

And thereupon the said Walter, touching the Holy Gospels, abjured the realm of England, and port was assigned to him at Dover, to be there upon Friday [31] next following and to make his way on that same Friday [July 14] to the town of Hackney, and on the Saturday to the town of Dartford, and on the Sunday to the town of Rochester, and on the Monday to the town of Ospringe, and on the Tuesday to the town of Canterbury, and on the Wednesday to the port aforesaid, there to take

---

[28] Richard, Prince of Wales. [29] Friday next after this feast was, in 1391, July 14.
[30] Evidently 1390/91 is meant; February 2 of 15 Richard II came in 1391/92.
[31] *Sic;* presumably this included three days' grace at Dover: Wednesday, Thursday, and Friday.

ship and never to return to England without special licence of the lord King.[32]

[The rest indicates that he had previously broken gaol.]

13. The Search at Dover, 1378–1379

A PILGRIM CAUGHT SMUGGLING MONEY OUT OF THE COUNTRY

Exchequer, King's Remembrancer, Customs Accounts, 181/10.

Particulars of the account of John Seford and others, searchers in all towns and ports in Kent . . . touching their search for gold and silver in coin or in bullion and for jewels and letters of exchange taken out of England to the parts overseas contrary to the proclamation of the King thereof made; and also touching the goods and chattels of men of the Court of Rome or other parts beyond the seas, coming to this kingdom of England or traveling from this kingdom and carrying letters patent and bulls with processes or other matters prejudicial to the King or to his said kingdom or to his subjects, contrary to the form of the late statute; and by the said searchers to be stayed at the King's command, namely, from October 18, 2 Richard II [1378], to the feast of St. Michael [September 29] following.

The same [searchers] account for ten shillings of gold and silver in coin, by them found during the said time of this account, sewn into the cloak of a certain pilgrim in the port of Dover who was about to set out for parts beyond the seas, contrary to the said proclamation.

[32] Cf. above, pp. 205–206.

7. War

MAKING PREPARATION

1. A Burgess's Armor, 1393

Prerogative Court of Canterbury, 3 Rous.

An extract from the will of John Polymond, burgess of Southampton, dated the Saturday after St. Martin,[1] 1393:

Item, I bequeath to Thomas Skore . . . 1 silver girdle, 1 basinet, 1 hauberk (*loricam*), 1 breastplate, 1 pair of leg armor, vambrace (*vaunbras*) and rerebrace (*cerebras* [sic]), and one pair of plate gauntlets (*cerotecarx de plate*), which were for my body.[2] Item, I bequeath to Gilbert Moyne . . . one suit of armor sufficient for his body. . . . Item, I bequeath . . . to Alexander Deye a suit of armor sufficient for his body. Item, I bequeath to William Colet . . . a suit of armor sufficient for his body.[3]

2. Collecting Archers from the Forest, 1373

John of Gaunt's Register, II, 148–149.

John by the grace of God [King of Castile] to our beloved Simon de Shirford, our forester within our frith of Leicester, greeting. We will and command that you cause to be delivered to our beloved Walter de Legh [and four others, named], to each of them two oaks within your bailiwick if they will come with us in this next expedition; [4] but if any of them comes not with us in this same expedition, we command that no oak be delivered to him. And, moreover, we command you to warn the said archers to be with us at Plymouth on the tenth of May, quite ready and appareled to pass with us on the same expedition without delay. . . .

Given at our Castle of Hertford, May 19, 47 [Edward III].

[1] St. Martin's day is November 11.

[2] With this may be compared the following, which comprised an esquire's livery: 1 habergeon, 1 basinet with aventail, 1 pair of plate gauntlets, 1 jack, 1 doublet, and 1 pair of knee armor. (Excheq. K. R. Accts. 396/15.)

[3] Cf. above, p. 44.

[4] An invasion of France, the immediate purpose of which was to recoup English military fortunes there, but the ultimate object, at least in the mind of John of Gaunt, was to win for himself the throne of Castile. Neither end was achieved. This same expedition is referred to on p. 288, below.

3. *Taking Service with a Knight, 1380*

Common Pleas, Plea Roll 488 m. 118.

Part of a plea between Henry Ferrers, knight, and John Botesham, citizen and gold-smith of London, who stood surety that the two squires would fulfil their agreement.

[John Botesham says that] it was witnessed by indenture dated at London June 14, 3 Richard II, that Henry Van the Ryve and Walter Grete of Gelderlond, esquires, were retained with the said Henry de Ferrers as men sufficiently arrayed for war as pertains to their degree to serve Henry de Ferrers in war towards the parts of Brittany and France or elsewhere where Henry de Ferrers should be appointed, for one whole year from the time of the making of the said indenture; and that Henry Van [the Ryve] and Walter came before Henry de Ferrers on the Monday after the making of the said indenture at London in the parish of St. Vedast in the Ward of Cheap and declared to Henry de Ferrers how their armor and their other harness were at Calais, seeking leave from him to go to Calais before the said Henry and await his coming there; and Henry willingly gave them leave to do this, whereupon they, on the Friday next following at London, namely, at Billingsgate in the parish of St. Mary at Hill in Billingsgate Ward, took passage in a certain ship towards Calais and crossed over to that town; and immediately afterwards Henry de Ferrers came to Calais in the company of Thomas, Earl of Buckingham, assigned by the lord King to lead an army into France in the name of the lord King and there to wage war in his name, whereupon the said Henry and Walter met Henry de Ferrers, sufficiently arrayed, and went with the said Henry and served him there in the said war in accordance with the form of the indenture.

[Henry de Ferrers denies that they left Billingsgate and served as above.]

[Adjourned to Easter.]

4. *Edward III's Military Band, ca. 1344*

Stowe MS (B.M.) 570 fol. 229.

The expeditionary force of Edward III in France included the following musicians, ranked among the archers of the royal household:

5 trumpeters, 1 citoler,[5] 5 pipers, 1 taborer, 2 clarioners, 1 nakerer, 1 fiddler, 3 waits.[6]

[5] The citole was a plucked string instrument with three or four wire strings, which were vibrated by a plectrum. It had a pear-shaped body with a flat back.
[6] These men played the shawm, a wind instrument with a double reed and a conical tube which flared out into a wide bell.

5. *Repairs by the King's Clerk of Array, 1379*

Exchequer, King's Remembrancer, Memoranda Roll 160, Brevia, m. 1.

To account faithfully with the King's clerk, John de Haytfeld, formerly Clerk of Array of the barges of Edward III, until he was appointed Keeper of the Privy Wardrobe of Richard II in the Tower, and pay him his expenses for the repair of habergeons, kettle hats, plates, basinets, jacks, doublets, worsted stuffs, targets, lances, arras, seats, streamers, standards, banners, chests, and other expenses as Clerk of Array.

6. *Preparing Engines of War, 1373*

John of Gaunt's Register, II, 157–158.

John by the grace of God [King of Castile] to our beloved . . . receiver of Tutbury, greeting. Whereas we have great need in this next expedition . . . beyond the seas of certain craftsmen, we pray you in particular, charging you to . . . send four carpenters, two masons, and two iron-workers to make and work engines and trebuchets (*trepgeutes*) and other such things wanted for the same expedition, and so far as you can, see that they are good archers and suitable, and that they are with us at the sea on the twelfth of May at the latest with such tools of their crafts as they can easily carry, knowing that we shall do by them so that they will reasonably be satisfied, and at their coming to the sea they shall be paid their wages at once. And we will that these men be sent to us over and above the number of archers for whom we have already sent to your parts. Moreover, we will and command that you pay from the issues of your receipt to each of the said carpenters, masons, and ironworkers forty pence by way of imprest.

Given at our manor of the Savoy, April 24, 47 [Edward III].

7. *Buying Horses for the Baggage Train, 1373*

John of Gaunt's Register, II, 150.

John by the grace of God [king of Castile] to our beloved clerk, Sir Adam Pope, our avener, greeting. We will and command you to buy for our use two hundred horses for our carriage and baggage. And more-over we command you to pay for the charges and expenses of the keepers of the said horses, and for all manner of charges for the same horses until they are brought to us.

Given at the Savoy, March 1, 47 [Edward III].

8. Providing Carts for Victuals and Armor, 1384

Common Pleas, Plea Roll 493, m. 258 d.

William Wyndesore, knight,[7] [sues] John Norman, whelere,[8] in a plea why, whereas the same John undertook at Southwark to make three wagons (*curros*) for carting the victuals and harness of the same William to parts overseas, for a certain sum of money whereof he received part in advance, and within a certain time agreed between them, the same John did not see to it that he made the wagons within the said time, whereby the said William entirely lost divers victuals to the value of one hundred marks, which for default of the said wagons could not be carted in the said wagons, to his great damage.

9. Arresting a Spy, 1388

Chancery, Miscellanea, Writs and Returns, 111/18.

Answer of sheriffs of London to writ of February 18, 11 Richard II— Clement Clayssm of Frankeburgh [9] was taken and imprisoned in the King's prison of Newgate because he was brought to the counter of one of [his] high sheriffs by Roger Carneford, constable of Dowgate Ward, upon the information of Henry Bailly of Ducheland for suspicion of being a spy.[10]

MAINTAINING GARRISONS

1. At Ghent, 1385

Exchequer of Receipt, Issue Roll 508, mm. 18–20, 22.

PAYMENTS FROM THE EXCHEQUER OF RECEIPT:

Saturday, July 15: [11]

To John, Lord de Boursser, by the hands of John Pecbrigg, knight, and Thomas Hattfeld for wages of war and reward of 100 men at arms and 300 bowmen with him in the King's service at the town of Ghent, by privy seal . . . . £2,792 14s.

To the said John, 40s. a day, ordered to be paid by the King and

[7] He was captain of the town and castle of Cherbourg. (Com. Pleas, Plea Roll 494, m. 258.)
[8] Wheeler, a wheelwright or wheel-maker. Cf. *O.E.D.*
[9] There were several cities named Frankenberg in what is now Germany.
[10] A number of such returns denotes an outbreak of "spy-mania" early in this reign. [R.]
[11] The previous entry is July 14.

Council so long as he remained in the King's service in the said
town £200

To him for lances, bows and arrows, etc., for munitioning the said
town and for buying chests, barrels, etc., for the carriage of the same
artillery from the city of London to Ghent .   .   .   .   . £53 18s. 4d.

[Payments for the week ending] July 24:

To Ralph Steynour of Westminster, sent to Scotland with letters of
the captain of Calais and of the good men of the town of Ghent directed
to the King and other lords in his company concerning the ordinance of
the King of the French against the men of Ghent and concerning the
town of Damme, for his wages .   .   .   . 26s. 8d.

[Between July 15 and 24]:

Paid by John Hereford, the King's sergeant at arms, by order of the
King's Council for a boat hired in the port of London for the carriage of
artillery from London to the port of Orwell, there to be delivered to
John Pecbrigg, knight, and Thomas Hattfeld, attorneys of John, lord
de Boursser, waiting in the said port with certain men at arms and bowmen for their passage to Ghent, by writ of Privy Seal .   .   . 26s. 8d.

[Between July 24 and 29]:

To Lawrence Chesse and William Wodeward, seamen of Greenwich,
by agreement with them made by certain lords of the King's Council for
their wages and expenses and for those of 60 men at arms and 40 bowmen to go with them in the King's service in a barge [12] and a balinger
to Flanders for the safe conduct of 100 men at arms and 200 bowmen
from the port of Orwell to the town of Ghent, there to remain in the
King's service at war in the company of John, lord de Boursser, for
the strengthening (*fortificacione*) of the said town, by writ .   .   . £50.

[Between July 29 and August 17]:

To John Orewell, the King's sergeant at arms, sent to the town of
Ghent by order of the King and his Council with letters of credence of
the King to the good men of the said town, for his wages and expenses,
and for hire of men and boats for his safe conduct, for fear of the King's
enemies in Flanders .   .   .   . £17 10s.

[Between August 17 and September 18]:

To Simon Berry, master of a ship called "La Mighell" of Dartmouth,
and to Richard Malangre, master of "La Julian" of the same, by advice

[12] A small sea-going vessel with sails: used specifically for one next in size above the
balinger. (*O.E.D.*)

of the King's Council, in subsidy, customs, and expense of themselves, and their associates, 32 seamen, waiting under arrest by Sir Robert Knoll, Nicholas Brembre, Mayor of London, and William Walworth, knight, in the port of London because of a certain voyage ordered at the time when the King with his army was in Scotland, both for keeping the sea and coasts and for strengthening (*fortificacione*) the towns of Ghent and Damme . . . . £4.

2. At Calais Castle, 1386–1389

Exchequer, King's Remembrancer, Accounts Various, 181/12.

Account of Edmund Pole, controller of Roger Walden, treasurer of Calais, 10–11 Richard II [1386–1388]: Oureus Sukoryn, crossbowman of Genoa, for his wages and those of 39 of his fellow crossbowmen in the garrison of Calais, in the time of Simon de Burgh, former treasurer.[13]

Exchequer, King's Remembrancer, Accounts Various, 183/9.

October 19, 13 Richard II [1389]

The King to Roger de Walden, treasurer of Calais: Whereas our dear and faithful Philip la Vache, knight,[14] was retained in our service on April 7, 11 Richard II [1388] as warden of Calais Castle for three years beginning on the day he had livery [15] of the said castle; and he was to have for its safekeeping 10 horsemen at arms, of whom he himself was knight, 20 footmen at arms, 10 archers mounted and 10 on foot; he should take for each of the said other 9 horsemen at arms 12*d.* a day, for each of the footmen at arms and each mounted archer 8*d.*, for each archer on foot 6*d.*, for the 9 horsemen at arms the accustomed reward and half [as much again], and for himself as a special reward 10 marks the quarter. (Conditions are set out in case of peace or a long truce.)

(Walden is to make the payments accordingly.)

[13] Amount of payment not indicated.
[14] The man to whom Chaucer addressed his poem "Truth: Balade de Bon Conseyl." A soldier and a country gentleman, he "prospered and grew steadily in honor and in wealth," except for a short period, from 1387 to 1390, when he was abroad, perhaps "because Gloucester was, for a time, in control of the government." It was during this period that he was captain of the Castle of Calais. "Association with Chaucer is suggested . . . by the fact that he married Elizabeth, the daughter of Chaucer's friend, Sir Lewis Clifford."

Professor Rickert once suggested that Philip la Vache may have furnished some of the details for Chaucer's picture of the Franklin, especially his lavish hospitality, the public offices he held, and his feudal rank of vavasor. (Rickert, "Thou Vache," *Modern Philology*, XI (1913–1914), 209–225.)
[15] The action of handing over or conveying into a person's hands. (*O.E.D.*)

Exchequer, King's Remembrancer, Accounts Various, 183/9.

October 23, 13 Richard II [1389]

Richard II to the treasurer of Calais: Whereas we have ordained that our beloved and faithful Philip la Vache, captain of our Castle of Calais, should have with him for the safekeeping of the said castle during the present truce 6 extra footmen at arms, you are to pay the same Philip for them the same wages as for his other footmen at arms.

BATTLES AND MILITARY EXPEDITIONS

1. England Invades France

TRIALS OF A FRENCH PRIOR, 1358

Quicherat, ed., "Récit des tribulations d'un religieux de diocèse de Sens pendant l'invasion Anglaise de 1358," *Bibliothèque de l'École des Chartes*, III, ser. 4 (1857), 359–360.

In the year of our Lord 1358 came the English to Chantecocq, and on the eve of All Saints [16] they captured the castle and that same night set fire to almost all the countryside; afterward they brought the whole country under their rule, ordering all the owners of both great and small estates to pay ransom for themselves, that is to say, for their lives, their goods, and their chattels, or their houses would be burned—and this they did in many places. Roused and terrified by this, very many people came to the English and agreed to buy themselves back, promising to give florins and flour and oats and many other necessaries for food if they would cease for a little while their persecutions, because they were killing many men in divers places; some they kept in unknown prisons, threatening them every day with death, and some they tortured unceasingly with scourgings and blows, hunger and dire want, beyond the possibility of belief. Others, indeed, having nothing with which to redeem themselves, unwilling to submit to the power [of their foes], and wanting to escape from their hands, made huts in the woods, there eating their bit of bread in fear, sadness, and great grief. But this was found out by the English, and you may be sure many searched the woods till they found these huts, and of the many people hiding there they killed some and took others prisoners, but some got away. Among them I, Hugues de Montgeron, prior of Brailet in the parish of Domats, in the canton of Courtenay, diocese of Sens, had built a hut in the wood of Cauda, above the swamp of the lord of Villabeonis, and there I was staying with many of my

[16] That is, on October 31, 1358.

neighbors, daily seeing and hearing about the base and horrible deeds of our enemies, that is to say, of houses burnt and of the many dead left lying about the villages and hamlets, as is their bestial custom. Seeing and hearing these things, I had made up my mind to go to the city on the Sunday after St. Lucy's day,[17] meaning to stay there. But it happened that on the very same night those cursed English were brought secretly to my hut, our guards being but little on the watch, so that they very nearly took me as I slept; but by the grace of God and the aid of the Blessed Virgin Mary, in the confusion I managed to get away, and naked as I was I escaped, taking nothing with me in my hurry but my tunic and my hood. Crossing through the fen, I stayed there, trembling with fear and shivering with the great cold, long enough to see my hut completely stripped. Afterward, I went to Sens to the home of Johannes Paganus, a clerk, a kinsman of mine, who welcomed me very kindly and gave me so generously of the goods granted to him by God that my tongue could never tell it all. All the while the [English] never ceased going to our house, sending me letters, threatening to bring upon me all sorts of ills and to burn [the priory] unless I went to them by the safe conduct they sent me. And at last I did go to them and obtained the promise of a truce to last from the Feast of the Throne of St. Peter [February 22] to the Feast of St. John the Baptist [June 24], but little did it profit me, for the captain who was then there was captured by the French, and so my trouble was all for nothing.

And so in such tribulation have I lived from the said Feast of All Saints until the Feast of St. John the Baptist. Once, indeed, they captured me, but recognizing me, they let me go, because they were so few; for which praise be to God! But at that time they spoiled all the furniture of my house, drank four casks of wine, carried off a peck of oats, by Courtenay measure, took all my clothes, and stole the horses; on two different occasions they stole my money, and they killed my pigeons at Easter and on the Sunday after the Feast of Sts. Peter and Paul.[18] And so, by the grace of God, I escaped from their hands, in the name of the Lord, until then; but unless I am willing to lose thirty acres of the best wheat, I must settle with them yet, or my condition will be worse than it is now.

Written on Thursday, the summer Feast of St. Martin [July 4], in the year 1359, behind my grange, because it is not safe anywhere else.

---

[17] That is, on December 16, 1358.
[18] The Feast of Saints Peter and Paul is June 29.

Did you ever see trouble like mine, you who dwell safe in cities and castles? Adieu.

                                                                    Hugues

A MILITARY EXPEDITION INTO FRANCE (CHAUCER'S CAMPAIGN), 1359–1360

Gray, *Scalacronica*, pp. 145–160.

King Edward led an expedition out of England with all the great men of his realm . . . and arrived at Sandwich on the [Feast of] the Nativity of our Lady [September 8]. He was grievously delayed for want of ships, wherefore he could land [his forces] neither all at once nor at the place he intended. So he divided the crossing, sending the duke of Lancaster with his retinue to Calais. . . .

The King arrived at Calais on Monday next before All Saints,[19] where he remained eight days. He divided his army into three [columns]: one he kept with himself; another column he gave to his eldest son, the Prince of Wales; [20] the third column he intended for the Duke of Lancaster. He marched from Calais on the Monday before Martinmas,[21] when the said Duke of Lancaster met him on the Sunday, having spent five weeks afield in much want of bread and wine.

The three columns marched by different routes. The King kept the way by Saint Omer, near Arras . . . through . . . Champagne to Rheims. The Prince . . . held the route by Montreuil . . . through Ponthieu and Picardy, across the river Somme . . . into Vermandois . . . by Saint-Quentin and Retieris,[22] where the enemy himself fired the town to obstruct his crossing. [But] the Prince's people forced a passage at Chateau-Porcien, whence he marched through Champagne to join his father's column before Rheims.

The Duke of Lancaster followed a route between the King and his son [*i.e.*, the Black Prince], and the three columns formed a junction before Rheims, lying all around the city in hamlets for a month at Christmastime. From the column of the said Prince the town of Cormicy was taken by escalade and the castle won, the keep being mined and thrown down by

---

[19] All Saints day is November 1.   [20] That is, Edward, the Black Prince.
[21] Martinmas is November 11.
[22] Réthel or Retters. In a foray on this town Chaucer was taken prisoner. About March 1, 1360, he was ransomed. In the Scrope-Grosvenor trial, in 1386, at which he was a witness, Chaucer testified that he had seen Sir Henry and Sir Richard Scrope at Retters using the coat of arms claimed by the Grosvenors of Cheshire. (Chaucer, *Canterbury Tales*, ed. by Manly, pp. 10 and 26–27.)

the people of the Prince. On the challenge of the French in Rheims, Bartholomew de Burghersh, an officer of the Duke of Lancaster's army, fought there to the death by formal arrangement, where one Frenchman was killed and two others wounded by lance-point.

From the King's column, the Duke of Lancaster and the Earls of Richmond and March captured two fortified market towns, Otrey and Semay, on the river Aisne and the border of Lorraine.

Lords and knights of the King's column made a raid from Rheims nearly to Paris. They ambushed themselves and sent their scouts up to the gates of the city. They made such an uproar in the suburbs that those within the city had not the courage to come forth.

The King of England afterwards broke up from before Rheims and marched towards Chalons. . . . Having caused the bridge over the river Marne to be repaired, and over other very great rivers also, [he] marched to the neighborhood of Troyes. . . . [He] crossed the Seine near Méry-sur-Seine and held his way by Sens and Pontigny into Burgundy. His son the Prince followed him, and the Duke of Lancaster also; but for want of forage for the horses, his son left the route of his father and quartered himself at Ligny-le-Châtel, near Auxerre, where the Prince's army suffered more from the enemy than in any other part of this expedition hitherto. Several of his knights and squires were killed at night in their quarters, and his foraging parties taken in the fields, although the country was more deserted before them than in all the other districts, so that they scarcely saw a soldier outside the fortresses.

Five English esquires belonging to the army of the Prince, without [defensive] armor except their helmets and shields, having only one coat-of-mail and three archers, were in a corn mill near Regentz, a fortress held by the English not far from Auxerre. Fifty men-at-arms, the troop and pennon of the Lord of Hanget, came to attack them; but the five defeated the fifty, taking eleven prisoners; wherefore even the French of the other garrisons called this in mockery the exploit of fifty against five.

The said King remained at Golion near Montreal in Burgundy, to negotiate a treaty with the Duke of Burgundy; and here Roger Mortimer,[23] Earl of March and marshal of the army and most in the confidence of the King, died on the twenty-sixth day of February.

A three years' truce was taken with Burgundy, on payment to the

[23] This was Roger Mortimer V. Cf. below, p. 317.

King of England at three terms of [the sum of] 200,000 florins moutons,[24] the florin at 4*s*. sterling.

. . .

At this time French, Norman, and Picard knights, with others of the commonalty, three thousand fighting men, made an expedition into England . . . with a show of remaining there so as to cause the King of England to withdraw from France in order to relieve his own country. These Frenchmen arrived at Winchelsea on Sunday in mid-Lent of the aforesaid year [1360], remained in the said town a day and a night, set fire to it on leaving, and, in going off in their ships, they lost two ships which had run aground, and about three hundred men [killed] by the commonalty who attacked them. . . .

In Passion Week of the same season, the King of England marched through Beauce, where the monasteries were almost all fortified and stocked with the provender of the country. Some of these were taken by assault, and others surrendered as soon as the siege-engines were in position, whereby the whole army was greatly refreshed with victual. . . .

The King of England took up his quarters before Paris on Wednesday in Easter week . . . 1360, in the villages adjacent to the suburb of Saint-Cloud, across the Seine above Paris. He remained there five days, and in departing displayed himself before the King of France's son, who was regent of the country and was in the city with a strong armed force. The Prince of Wales . . . who commanded the advance guard, and the Duke of Lancaster, with another column, marched close in front of the suburbs from sunrise till midday and set them on fire. The King's other columns kept a little farther off. A [certain] French knight, Pelerin de Vadencourt, was captured at the city barriers, where his horse, being wounded by an arrow, had thrown him. Knights of the Prince's retinue, newly dubbed that day, concealed themselves among the suburbs when the columns marched off, and remained there till some [knights] came out of the city, then spurred forth and charged them. Richard de Baskerville, the younger, an English knight, was thrown to the ground, and springing to his feet, wounded the horses of the Frenchmen with his sword, and defended himself gallantly until

[24] The original florins, coined at Florence in 1252, were imitated in many countries. The florin *mouton* was doubtless the same as the *Florenus de agnello*, or lambkyn, which was valued in England at 4*s*. sterling. (Cf. W. H. Prior, "Notes on the Weights and Measures of Medieval England," *Archivum Latinitatis medii aevi*, I [1924], 162–164.)

he was rescued with his horse by his comrades, who speedily drove back into their fortress the Frenchmen who had come out. . . .

The King marched off, spreading fire everywhere along his route, and took up quarters near Montereau with his army round him. On Sunday, April 13, it became necessary to make a very long march toward Beauce because of lack of fodder for the horses. The weather was desperately bad, with rain, hail, and snow, and so cold that many weakly men and horses perished in the field. They abandoned many vehicles and much baggage on account of the cold, the wind, and the wet, which happened to be worse this season than any old memory could recall. . . .

The King of England remained in Beauce, near Orleans, fifteen days, for a treaty of peace which the Council of France proposed to him . . . The English of the King's army had encounters, some with loss and others with gain. Certain knights in the following of the Duke of Lancaster, disguising themselves as brigands or pillaging soldiers, without lances, rode in pretended disarray in order to give the enemy spirit and courage to tackle them, as several of their foragers had been taken during the preceding days. Some of them, the knights Edmund Pierpont and Baldwyn Malet, overdid the said counterfeit to such an extent in running risks from the French that they came to grief; thus, they were taken and put on parole. . . .

On the seventh day of May [1360], a treaty of peace was made near Chartres and agreed to by the King of England and his Council . . . and by the Regent and Council of France and the commons.

2. *France Threatens to Invade England*

LONDON CALLED TO ARMS, 1385

London, Corporation, *Calendar of Letter-Books*, H, p. 269 (from London Letter-Book H, fol. cxciii b).

A proclamation made to the effect that those able and willing to go to the sea-coast in defence of the realm and the City should come to the Guildhall to the Mayor and Chamberlain and receive their pay, *viz.*, twelve pence a day for men-at-arms properly arrayed and six pence for archers; that no freeman leave the City without special permission, and that those freemen then absent should return within eight days; that no armorer, bowyer, or fletcher enhance the price of his wares in consequence of this proclamation; that those men-at-arms and archers who were able, but not willing, to go should be arrested as traitors to the King and the City;

that no foreigner of any nation whatsoever carry knife, baselard, sword, or any arms; and that no one wander about the City after nine o'clock. Those who were to go on the expedition were to be ready to join Robert Knolles, their leader, by Saturday next for the neighborhood of Sandwich.

Whereas Nicholas Brembre, the Mayor, and the Aldermen had heard from William Beauchamp, Captain of Calais, and others, that a great number of ships of France and Flanders were being prepared for a descent on England, the said Mayor and Aldermen, in the absence of the King on the borders of Scotland, caused good men of each ward to meet in the Council Chamber of the Guildhall on July 18, 9 Richard II [1385], to take steps for safeguarding the realm.[25]

PREPARATIONS IN FRANCE AND ENGLAND, 1386

Froissart, *The Chronicle of Froissart*, tr. by Berners, ed by Ker, IV, 305-362.

The young King, Charles [VI] of France, had great desire to go with an army into the realm of England. All the knights and squires of France were well agreed thereto, and specially his uncle, the Duke of Burgundy, and the Constable of France,—even though he had as his wife the sister of King Richard of England,—and also the Lord of Coucy. These lords and most of the chivalry of France said, "Why should we not at once go into England to see the country and the people there, and teach them in the [same] way as they have done in France?"

And so in the year of Our Lord 1386, partly to break the Duke of Lancaster's voyage [to Spain] and cause him to return out of Castile, and partly to frighten the Englishmen, great preparations for that voyage were made in France, and taxes and tallages were levied in cities and towns, and in the country, so that in a hundred years before there were none such seen, and also great preparations were made by the sea all the summer. Till the month of September they did nothing else on the seacoast but grind corn and bake biscuit, and at Tournai, Lille, Douai, Arras, Amiens, Bethune, Saint Omer, and all the towns about Sluys; for the

---

[25] These steps consisted of electing from two to nine men from each of London's twenty-four wards, who, with the mayor and the aldermen, "agreed that there should be levied with all speed in the city and suburbs a sum amounting to two-fifteenths, the same to be raised by an impost on victuals and merchandise as of old accustomed, an impost of twelve pence in the pound of rent belonging to those who do not share the city's charges and six pence in the pound in the case of freemen. This decision was thereupon announced to all the other good folk who were present, and they signified their assent." (London, Corporation, *Calendar of Letter-Books*, H, pp. 269–271. Cf. above, pp. 43–46.

BATTLE AT GATES OF CITY
Late fourteenth century
London, Brit. Mus., MS Stowe 54, fol. 83

NAVAL BATTLE AT SLUYS; *ca.* 1400
New York, Morgan Library, MS 804, fol. 44v

BATTLE OF POITIERS; *ca.* 1400
New York, Morgan Library, MS 804, fol. 128

WAR AT HOME
AND ABROAD

ATTACKING A CITY WITH ENGINES OF WAR
Late fourteenth century
London, Brit. Mus., MS Sloane 2433 (II), fol. 113

DIGGING THE MOAT TO PROTECT A CITY
Early fifteenth century
New York, Morgan Library, MS 526, fol. 6

TRANSPORTING ARMOR BY HORSE AND BY WAGON; early fourteenth century
Oxford, Bodl., MS 264, fol. 102

LOOTING A HOUSE; late fourteenth century
London, Brit. Mus., Royal 20 C.VII, fol. 41v

French King's intention and plan was to embark at Sluys, and so enter England to destroy the country. To aid this voyage the rich men in the realm of France were taxed to the third and fourth part of their goods; and many paid more than they were worth besides, to pay for the men of war.

From Spain and the port of Seville to Prussia there was no great ship on the sea that the Frenchmen could lay their hands on, nor under their control, that was not retained for the French King and his men. Provisions came from all directions and arrived in Flanders: wine, salt, meat, hay, oats, onions, biscuits, flour, casks of eggs, and all manner of things that one could think of; so that in time to come it could not be believed but by those that saw it.

Lords, knights, squires, and men of war were written to and asked to come and serve the King in his journey, out of Savoy, Germany, and from the sun's going down to the land of the Count of Armagnac. These lords of far countries, like the Count of Savoy, were retained with five hundred spears, also the Count of Armagnac and the Dauphin of Auvergne. And these lords, though they were of far countries and did not know what end this war should come to, made their preparations so lavishly that it was astounding to think of, and it was wonderful to consider from whence all such supplies came, both by land and by sea into Flanders, to Bruges, to Damme, and to Sluys.

And so all manner of ships that could be of any service were sent for into Holland, Zeeland, Middelburg, Ziericksee, Dordrecht, Escounehove, and to all other towns on the seacoast, and to the rivers entering the sea; and all the ships were brought to Sluys. But the Hollanders and Zee-landers said to those who engaged them, "If you will have our service, pay us our wages clearly, or else we will go nowhere." So they were paid, wherein they did wisely. I am sure that since God created the world there were never seen so many great ships together as were that year at Sluys and Blankenberg, for in September of that year there were twelve hundred and eighty-seven ships; their masts looked like a great forest in the sea. . . .

Whoever had been then at Bruges, at Damme, or at Sluys, and had seen the activity there in loading ships with hay, sacking biscuit, and loading in onions, peas, beans, barley, candles, hose, shoes, spurs, knives, daggers, battle axes, axes to hew with, mattocks, nails, beds, couches, horse-shoes, pots, pans, candlesticks, and all kinds of necessaries for kitchen, buttery, and all other offices, and everything that could be thought necessary to serve man and horse—all were put into ships in one thing or other—whoever had seen it, if he had been sick, I think he would clean have forgotten all the pain.[26] The French counted on nothing else, when they talked among themselves, but that the realm of England should be entirely lost and ruined without recovery, all the men slain, and the women and children carried into France and there held in servitude. . . .

Now let us return to the preparations that were made at this time at Damme and at Sluys. Nothing like them has ever been seen or heard of in the memory of man or in writing. Gold and silver were no more spared than though they had rained out of the clouds or scummed out of the sea. The great lords of France sent their servants to Sluys, to prepare their necessaries and ships, and to furnish them with everything needful. The King himself, as young as he was, was more eager for this journey than anyone else, and continued so to the end. Every man helped someone else prepare and furnish his ships and paint them with his arms. Painters had a good season then, for they were paid whatever they asked, and yet enough could not be gotten for money. They made banners, pennons, and standards of silk so excellent that they were marvelous to see. Also the masts of the ships, from one end to the other, glittered with gold and devices and arms. . . . The paintings that were made cost more than two thousand francs. . . . And the poor people of the realm paid for everything, for the tallages to pay for this expedition were so great that those who were richest sorrowed on account of them, and the poor fled because of them.

All that was done in France, Flanders, and other places . . . was well known in England, and it was rumored to be much greater than it was in reality. Because of this, the people in various parts of the realm were aghast, and there were general processions in every town and city by prelates and men of the church three times every week. These were made in great devotion of heart, with holy prayers and orisons to God to deliver them from that peril.

There were in England, however, a hundred thousand people who desired heartily that the Frenchmen might come and arrive in England; and such thoughtless fellows, in reassuring themselves and those that were frightened said, "Let these Frenchmen come. Not one coward of them shall return to France."

Those who were in debt and could not or would not pay were very

---

[26] Froissart, *Œuvres . . . chroniques*, ed. by Lettenhove, XI, 361: "even if he has had a fever or toothache."

happy over the coming of the Frenchmen, and said to their creditors when they demanded payment, "Sirs, be quiet. They are forging new florins in France, with which you shall be paid." Hoping for this, they lived and spent lavishly. And when they were refused credit, they would say, "What would you have of us? It is better for you that we should freely spend than have the Frenchmen take the goods of this realm." And so, in that way, a thousand pounds sterling were spent extravagantly in England. . . .

When the lords of England and the prelates and the people of the towns and cities and the commons of the realm were accurately and reliably informed that the French King was ready to come into England to destroy it, they assembled in council. Then the King's uncles wrote to him that he should come to London, telling him that the commons of his realm were discontented with him and his Council.

The King and his Council dared not refuse to go, but departed from the marches of Wales, where they had been for a long time, and the Queen also, and so came to Windsor and remained several days. Then the King, leaving the Queen at Windsor, went to his palace at Westminster and remained there. And all those who were concerned in the situation came to him, and there they took counsel how they should act, in view of this journey of the French King.

Then the Earl of Salisbury, who was a very valiant and prudent knight, said before the King and his uncles, and before all the prelates and lords of England that were present: "Sir, my sovereign lord, and all ye my lords and others, we should not be surprised if our adversary, the French King, comes and attacks us; for since the death of the last noble and puissant King Edward, of noble memory, this realm has been in great danger of being lost and destroyed by the deeds of wicked men; and also it is well known in France that we are not all agreed; wherefore this trouble appears, which is not little, for he is but a fool who does not fear his enemies. As long as the realm of England was in unity, the King with his people and they with him, we prospered and reigned victoriously, and we saw nor found none that did us any great wrong. Therefore it is now needful—never did greater need appear in England—that we reform ourselves in love and unity if we wish to live in honor. . . . Then every man agreed that this should be done. . . .

They arranged to guard the havens and ports where they supposed that the Frenchmen would arrive. The Earl of Salisbury, because part of his land came near to the Isle of Wight, which is directly across from Nor-

mandy and the country of Caux, was set there with his men and archers
of the country. The Earl of Devonshire [was] to be at Hampton with
200 men of arms and 600 archers to keep the haven; the Earl of
Northumberland at Rye, with 200 men of arms and 600 archers; the
Earl of Cambridge at Dover, with 500 men of arms and 1200 archers;
and his brother, the Earl of Buckingham, at Sandwich, with 600 men of
arms and 1200 archers. The Earl of Stafford and the Earl of Pembroke
were sent to Orwell haven with 500 men of arms and 1200 archers; Sir
Henry Percy and Ralph Percy were at Yarmouth with 300 men of arms
and 600 archers; and Sir Simon Burley was Captain of Dover Castle.

All the havens and ports between the Humber and Cornwall were
strengthened with men of war and archers. On the mountains and hills
adjoining the sea on the coast opposite Flanders and France watchmen and
watchers were placed in various ways. They had empty pipes [wine
tuns] filled with sand, one set on another, and on the top were places
for men to sit. Night and day they kept watch, looking across the sea.
They were charged that if they saw the French navy approach the land,
they should make fires on the hills, to arouse the people of the country to
come to that part of the coast where the fires appeared.

It was arranged that they should allow the French King and all his
men to land peaceably, and to march into the interior for three or four
days. Then they would first go to the sea where he had landed, fight with
the ships and win them if they could, destroy them and take all their
supplies, and then follow the Frenchmen, not to fight with them immediately, but to harry them and keep them waking, prevent them from
foraging, and destroy all of them that were abroad in the country. . . .
Rochester bridge was broken where there is a large river running from
Arundel into the country of Essex. . . . This bridge the Londoners beat
down to be more secure. And whereas taxes and tallages were great in
France on the men of the towns, likewise they were great at that time
in England; so that the realm sorrowed for it a long time afterward,
but they were glad to pay the soldiers in order to be defended. There were
ready in England 100,000 archers and 10,000 men of arms, besides the
great company that the Duke of Lancaster had in Castile. . . .

When the middle of August came and the time for the expedition approached, in order to make those from distant countries hasten, and to
show that the French King was very eager for his venture, the King took
his leave of the Queen, his wife, and of Queen Blanche,[27] and of the

27 The widow of Charles IV, who had been King of France from 1322 to 1328.

Duchess of Orleans, and of the other ladies of France, and heard mass solemnly at Notre Dame in Paris. His intention was never to return to Paris until he had been in England. So the King rode to Senlis. . . .

Then the French King came to Compiègne, and so to Noyon, and from thence Peronne, and to Bapaume, and so to Arras. Daily there came down people from all parts, so many that the country was completely eaten up. Nothing was left abroad in the country but it was taken without payment, so that the poor common people that had gathered their corn had nothing left them but straw; and if they complained of it, they were beaten or slain. Their waters were fished, and their houses beaten down for firewood. If the Englishmen had arrived in the country, they could not nor would not have caused so great destruction or hurt as the Frenchmen themselves did.

And the French said to the poor men, "Sirs, we have now no silver to pay, but when we return we shall have enough, and then you shall surely be paid."

But the poor people, when they saw their goods taken away and durst not protest, cursed between their teeth, saying, "Go into England or to the devil, and never return again."

.   .   .

And always the time passed, and the winter approached, and the lords lay there in great cold and peril. The Flemings gladly would not have had them return again through their country, and they said to each other: "Why the devil does not the French King pass over into England? Why does he delay so long in this country? Are we not in poverty enough, without the Frenchmen making us poorer? We think they will not pass into England this year, for the realm of England is not easily won. Englishmen are not like Frenchmen. What will they do in England? When the English were in France and overran their countries, they hid themselves in their fortresses and fled before them as the lark does before the hawk." . . .

Finally the Duke of Berry came to Sluys to the King, and the King said to him: "Ah, fair uncle, how anxious I have been to see you! Why have you delayed so long? We would have been in England now and have fought with our enemies if you had come sooner."

The Duke began to smile and to excuse himself, and did not show at once what was in his mind. First he thought he would learn what preparations had been made, and see the navy that was said to be so excellent.

So they were there seven days, and every day it was said, "We shall depart tomorrow." . . .

Then the King's Council met to consider how they should carry out their plans. But the Duke of Berry disrupted them, and showed so many good reasons that those who had been most eager to go were greatly discouraged. He said it was a great folly to counsel the French King, who was still only a child, to embark in that season of the year and go to fight with a people whose condition, and the way thither, they did not know.

"And as it is said," [he continued], "it is an evil country to make war in. For though we all landed there, yet they would fight with us only when they wished, and we would not dare to leave our supplies behind us, for if we did, they would be lost. And those who wish to make so long a voyage should begin in the middle of summer, and not in winter. Call all the mariners together, and see if they will not say that my opinion is right. For though we now have 1500 ships, yet before we arrived, we should not have 300. Then see what peril we should put ourselves in. I say this not because I would have the journey abandoned, but by way of counsel. Since the largest part of the realm wishes to undertake this journey, I suggest, fair brother of Burgundy, that you and I go, but I would not advise that the King should go, for if any misfortune should occur, it would be laid to us."

"Well," said the French King, who was present at all these words, "if none will go, I will go!"

Then the lords began to smile, and said, "The King has a courageous heart."

They decided to postpone the voyage until the next April or May; and to keep their provisions, such as biscuit, salt meat, and wine, till then. They also arranged that the lords and their companies should return to that place in March. At once this was known, and so the voyage, which cost the realm of France thirty times one hundred thousand francs,[28] was given up for that time.

THE KING PAYS SOLDIERS GATHERED TO RESIST INVASION IN 1386

Exchequer of Receipt, Issue Roll 541 m. 17.

To Henry, earl of Derby, late coming to the King, at the King's command, at the Feast of St. Michael [September 29], 10 Richard II, with 47 knights, 516 squires, and 1,316 bowmen of his retinue, to resist the

[28] Froissart, Œuvres . . . chroniques, ed. by Lettenhove, XII, 27: "trois fois cent mille frans."

malice of the King's enemies [who had] arranged with a huge army to land at several ports of England in which men did not dwell or inhabit (*moram non traxherunt nec inhabitati fuerunt*) within the limits of 60 miles from the city of London, by the oath of the earl's attorneys, taken before the treasurer and the chamberlain; in money delivered to the earl by the hands of John Leventhorpe, his squire, by assignment made this day for wages of war of the same men at arms and bowmen, *viz.*, in full satisfaction of £1,902 due to the said earl and to be delivered for the King's customary wages of the said men at arms and bowmen, by 30 days, within the space of one month after the said feast, during which 30 days they were coming to London and there lodged (*hospitati*) in the parts adjacent (*in partibus comitivis*), were waiting, and were returning, by the King's command, by Privy Seal among the mandates of the term of St. Michael 10 Richard II. £52 13s. 4d.[29]

3. *The Siege of Calais*

CALAIS CAPITULATES TO THE ENGLISH, 1347 [30]

Baker, *Chronicon Galfridi le Baker de Swynebroke*,[31] ed. by Thompson, p. 267.

In the meantime, those who were besieged made known their situation to the French King [32] by signs and tokens, for when he first came, those within the town set up his ancient on the chief tower of the castle, and also set out banners of the dukes and earls of France. A little after dark they made a great light on the top of one of the highest towers which faced towards the army of the Frenchmen, and in addition made a great shout and noise with trumpets and drums. The second night they did the same, but somewhat less. The third night they made a very small fire, and uttered at the same time a sorrowful cry, indicating thereby that their strength for keeping the town was quite spent and done. And the same night they took in all their flags and ancients except their standard. At the last, the day of battle drew on, in preparation for which there came out of England and Germany (*ligua Teutonica*) to help King Edward [III], seventeen thousand fighting men, whereupon the French King

[29] This was the final balance of the £1,902 due the earl of Derby, and was said to be "in full satisfaction" because the rest of the money had already been paid. Since, however, this money was said to be delivered "by assignment" [*i.e.*, of some of the revenues of the Crown], the earl may not have received the money at this time, the entry being merely for purposes of bookkeeping.

[30] This and the following item deal with the same event, but the first is by an English chronicler, whereas the second is by a Frenchman.

[31] See below, p. 320.   [32] Philip VI, of Valois.

early in the morning of the second day of August, after burning his tents, fled, whose rear the Duke of Lancaster and the Earl of Northampton cutting off, they slew and took many of them.

When the defenders of Calais saw this, they took their standard down, and with great sorrow cast it from the tower into the ditch; and on the Saturday following, John de Vienne, their captain, a man very skillful in warlike affairs, opening the gates of the town, came out to the King of England, sitting on a little nag, because he walked with difficulty on account of lameness, with an halter about his neck, and the other burgesses and soldiers following on foot, bareheaded and barefooted, having halters about their necks. The captain, coming thus before the King, offered him a warlike sword, as to the chief prince of arms among all Christian kings and as to one who had taken that town from the mightiest Christian king by noble chivalry. Then he delivered to him the keys of the town. Thirdly, requesting of him pity, he asked pardon and delivered him the sword of peace, wherewith he should give right judgment, treat the humble and lowly with forbearance, and chasten the proud-hearted. The King, receiving that which was offered him, sent the captain, with fifteen knights and as many burgesses, into England, enriching them with large gifts. The common sort of people and such as he found in the town, after they had been somewhat refreshed with the King's alms, he commanded to be conducted safely to the castle of Guines.

QUEEN PHILIPPA PLEADS FOR THE BURGESSES OF CALAIS, 1347

Froissart, *Œuvres . . . chroniques*, ed. by Lettenhove, V, 215–216.

Then the noble Queen of England, who was far gone with child, humbled herself and wept so bitterly that they could not support her. She flung herself on her knees before her lord the King [33] and said, "Ha, dear sir, since I have crossed the sea hither in great peril, as you know, I have not made one request nor asked one gift of you. Now I beg you humbly and ask of you the gift that for the sake of the Son and Blessed Mary and for love of me, you will have on these six men mercy."

The King hesitated and looked at the good lady his wife, on her knees before him and in tears. His heart softened, for he would rather not have been angry where she was, and when he spoke he said: "Ha, madame, I wish you were somewhere else. You pray so earnestly that I dare not refuse the gift you ask; and no matter how unwilling I may be, I grant it you, and do with it as you please."

[33] Edward III.

The brave lady answered: "Monseigneur, very great thanks!"

Then she rose and had the six burgesses set on their feet and took away the ropes from their necks and led them with her to her hostel and had them clothed and set at dinner and made comfortable that day. And in the morning, she gave each six nobles and had them led out of the army by Monsieur Sanse d'Aubrecicourt and Monsieur Paon de Roet,[34] as far as they could and until it seemed to the two knights that they would be out of danger; and at parting the knights commended them to God and returned to the army, and the burgesses went to St. Omer.

4. The Capture of Guines, 1352

Baker, *Chronicon Galfridi le Baker de Swynebroke,* ed. by Thompson, pp. 284–286.

About the beginning of January, the Frenchmen being occupied in repairing the walls of Guines town, which had been destroyed by the Englishmen, some men of arms of Calais, understanding what they were doing, planned how they might overthrow the work in this way. There was an archer named John Dancaster in prison in the castle of Guines, who, not having money to pay his ransom, was freed on condition that he should work there among the Frenchmen. This fellow chanced to lie with a laundress, a strumpet, and learned from her where, beyond the principal ditch, from the bottom of the ditch there was a wall two feet broad stretching from the ramparts across to the edge of the ditch so that, being covered with water, it could not be seen, yet not so submerged but that a man walking along the top of it would not be wet past the knees. It was made for the use of fishers, and therefore in the middle there was a two-foot gap. The archer (his harlot shewing it to him) measured the height of the wall with a thread.

After he had learned these things, one day, slipping down from the wall, he crossed the ditch by that hidden wall, and, lying hid in the marsh till evening, came in the night near to Calais, where, waiting for daylight, he went into the town. . . . Here he told those who were greedy for prey and were eager to scale the castle, how they could enter it. They had ladders made to the length which the archer told them. Thirty men, plotting together, clothed themselves in black armor without any brightness, went to the castle by the guiding of the said John de Dancaster, and, climbing the wall with their ladders, they slew the watch-

[34] Probably Chaucer's father-in-law.

men and threw them down headlong beside the wall. After this, in the hall, they slew many whom they found unarmed, playing chess and hazard. They then broke into the chambers and turrets upon the ladies and knights that lay there asleep, and so became masters of all that was within. Shutting all the prisoners into a strong chamber and taking away all their armor, they released the Englishmen that had been taken the year before and kept there in prison, and, after they had relieved them well with meat and drink, they made them guardians over those who had had them in custody; and so they won all the fortresses of the castle. . . .

The Earl of Guines came to the castle and demanded of those within, as at other times, in whose name they kept it. As they constantly affirmed that they kept it in the name of John Dancaster, he asked whether the same John were the King of England's liegeman or would obey him, and when the said John answered that he did not know what messengers had been in England, the earl offered for the castle, besides all the treasure found in it, many thousands of crowns, or possessions for exchange, and a perpetual peace with the King of France. To this the defenders replied that, before taking that castle, they had been Englishmen by nation, but by their demerits banished for the peace of the King of England; wherefore the place which they thus held they would willingly sell or exchange, but to none sooner than to their natural King of England, to whom they said they would sell their castle to obtain their peace; but if he would not buy it, then they would sell it to the King of France or to whosoever would give most for it. The earl being thus shifted off, the King of England bought it, indeed, and so had that place which he greatly desired.

5. Sea Fights

SLUYS, 1340

Baker, *Chronicon Galfridi le Baker de Swynebroke*, ed. by Thompson, pp. 242–243.

King Edward [III] kept his Whitsuntide at Ipswich, because he intended from thence to make his passage into Flanders; but, being informed that the French King had sent a great navy of Spanish ships and also the whole fleet of France to stop his passage, he caused his ships of the Cinque Ports and others to be assembled, so that he had in his fleet, great and small, 260 ships.

Wherefore, on the Thursday before the Nativity of Saint John the

Baptist,[35] having a favorable wind, he began to sail; and the next day, in the even of the said feast, they descried the French fleet lying in Swine haven. Wherefore the King caused all his fleet to come to anchor.

The next day, being the Feast of Saint John the Baptist, early in the morning the French fleet divided themselves into three parts, withdrew about a mile, and then approached the King's fleet. When the King saw this, about nine o'clock, having the wind and sun on his back, [he] set forward and met his enemies as he would have wished; at which the whole fleet gave a terrible shout, and a shower of arrows out of long wooden bows so poured down on the Frenchmen that thousands were slain in that meeting. At length they closed and came to hand blows with pikes, poleaxes, and swords, and some threw stones from the tops of ships, wherewith many were brained. The size and height of the Spanish ships caused many Englishmen to strike many a blow in vain. But, to be short, the first part of the French ships being overcome and all the men spent, the Englishmen entered and took them. The French ships were chained together in such a way that they could not be separated from each other, so that a few Englishmen kept that part of the fleet. They then set upon the second part and with great difficulty made the attack; but when this had been done, the second part was sooner overcome than the first, because many of the Frenchmen abandoned their ships and leaped overboard. The Englishmen, having thus overcome the first and second parts of the fleet, and now finding night drawing on, partly for want of light and partly because they were weary, determined to take some rest till the next morning. On this account, during the night thirty ships of the third part fled away, but a large ship called the "James" of Dieppe, thinking to have carried away a certain ship of Sandwich belonging to the prior of Canterbury, was stopped, for the sailors so stoutly defended themselves by the help of the Earl of Huntingdon that they saved themselves and their ship from the Frenchmen.

The fight continued all night, and in the morning, the Normans being overcome and taken, there were found in the ship 400 men slain. Moreover, the King, understanding that the ships were fled, sent forty well-equipped ships to follow them. . . . In the first group of ships that were taken they found these conquered ships: the "Denis," the "George," the "Christopher," and the "Blacke Cocke," all of which had been captured by Frenchmen at Sluys and carried into Normandy. The number

[35] The nativity of St. John the Baptist is June 24.

of ships of war that were taken was about 230 barges; the number of enemies that were slain and drowned was about 25,000, and of English-men about 4,000, among whom were four knights: Sir Thomas Mor-timer, the King's cousin; Sir Thomas Latimer, his son; Sir William But-ler of Seortkorne; and Sir Thomas Poynings.

ESPAGNOLS-SUR-MER, 1350

Baker, *Chronicon Galfridi le Baker de Swynebroke*, ed. by Thompson, p. 280.

In the summer following, variance rising between the fleets of England and Spain, the Spaniards beset the English Channel with forty-four great ships of war, with which they sank ten English ships coming from Gascony towards England, after they had taken and plundered them; and thus, their former injuries [36] being revenged, they entered Sluys in Flanders. King Edward, hearing of this, furnished his navy with fifty ships and pinnaces, planning to meet the Spaniards on their return. He had in his company the Prince of Wales, the Earls of Lancaster, North-ampton, Warwick, Salisbury, Arundale, Huntington, and Gloucester,[37] and other barons and knights with their servants and archers.

Upon the Feast of the Decollation of St. John [August 29], about evensong time, the navies met at Winchelsea, where the great Spanish vessels, as much larger than our ships and foists as castles are larger than cottages, sharply assailed our men. The stones and quarrels flying from the top sorely and cruelly wounded our men, who, no less busy to fight aloof with lance and sword and with the foreguard, manfully defended themselves; at length our archers pierced their arbalesters with a further reach than they could strike again, and thereby compelled them to for-sake their place, and caused others, fighting from the hatches, to protect themselves with planks of the ships, and compelled those who threw stones from the tops so to hide themselves that they durst not show their heads, but let their stones fall on their comrades. Then our men, enter-ing the Spanish vessels with swords and halberds, killed those they met, in a little while emptying the vessels and filling them with Englishmen, until, being overtaken by nightfall, they could not see the twenty-seven ships yet remaining untaken. Our men cast anchor, thinking of the hoped-for battle, supposing nothing finished while anything remained undone,

[36] Probably those sustained in the Battle of Sluys, at which Spanish ships fought with the French against the English. Cf. above, p. 308.

[37] Baker is wrong in including the Earl of Gloucester among those present. The title had become extinct . . . in 1347. [Thompson's note.]

tending the wounded, throwing the miserable Spaniards into the sea, refreshing themselves with food and sleep, and setting an armed band to keep vigilant watch. The night having passed, the Englishmen prepared—but in vain—for a new battle; for when the sun began to appear, they, viewing the seas, could perceive no sign of resistance; for twenty-seven ships flying away by night left seventeen plundered in the evening to the King's pleasure, but against their will.

6. Personal Adventures in Warfare

THE BISHOP OF DURHAM AS MILITARY COMMANDER, 1388

Froissart, *The Chronicle of Froissart*, tr. by Berners, ed. by Ker, V, 225-231.

The same evening that the Percys departed from Newcastle, . . . the Bishop of Durham, with the rearband, came to Newcastle and supped. And as he sat at the table, he felt that it was not to his credit to be within the town while the Englishmen were in the field. At once he caused the table to be taken away, and commanded that his horses should be saddled, the trumpets sounded, and men in the town called up to arm themselves and mount their horses, and foot soldiers to prepare themselves to depart. Thus all the men left the town, to the number of seven thousand, two thousand on horseback and five thousand afoot.

They took their way toward Otterburn, where the battle had been. By the time they had gone two miles from Newcastle, tidings came to them that their men were fighting with the Scotch. Because of this, the Bishop rested there, and at once more men came fleeing so fast that they were out of breath. When they were asked how the battle went, they answered, "Very badly. We are all put to flight. Here come the Scotch chasing us."

These tidings troubled the Englishmen, and [they] began to doubt. Again a third time men came fleeing as fast as they could. When the men of the bishopric of Durham heard these evil tidings, they were so frightened that they broke their array, and the bishop could not hold five hundred of them together. It was thought that, since it was night and the Englishmen were so frightened, if the Scotch had followed them in any number in entering the town, the Scotch would have won it.

The bishop of Durham, being in the field, would have helped the Englishmen and encouraged his men as much as he could, but he saw his own men flee as well as others. Then he asked Sir William Lucy and Sir Thomas Clifford and other knights what would be best to do. These knights for their honor would give him no advice; for they thought that to go back without doing anything would sound little to their credit, and to go ahead might be to their great harm; so they stood still and would give no answer. And the longer they stood, the fewer they were; for some kept stealing away.

Then the bishop said, "Sirs, all things considered, it is no honor to put all in peril, nor to make one evil into two. We hear that our company is put to flight, and we cannot remedy it. For if we go to help them, we do not know with whom nor with what number we shall meet. Let us return safely for this night to Newcastle, and tomorrow we will draw together and go look for our enemies."

Every man answered, "As God will, so be it."

Therewith they returned to Newcastle.

Thus a man may consider the great fault that is in men who are frightened and confused. For if they had kept together and had caused those who fled to turn again, they would have defeated the Scotch: this was the opinion of several. And because they did not do this, the Scotch had the victory. . . .

When the bishop of Durham had come again to Newcastle and was in his lodging, he was very sad and did not know what to say or do, for he heard a report that his cousins the Percys were slain or taken and all the knights that were with them.

Then he sent for all the knights and squires that were in the town; and when they had come, he demanded of them whether they should leave the matter as it stood, and said, "Sirs, we shall be severely blamed if we thus return without looking on our enemies."

Then they decided that by sunrise every man should be armed, and on horseback or afoot should leave the town and go to Otterburn to fight with the Scotch.

This was announced through the town by a trumpet, and all the men armed themselves and assembled before the bridge. By sunrise they departed by the gate towards Berwick and took the way towards Otterburn, to the number of ten thousand, some afoot and some on horseback. . . .

When the knights of Scotland were told that the bishop of Durham was coming against them with ten thousand men, they formed a council to see what was best for them to do, whether to depart or to await the encounter. All things considered, they decided to wait, for they said they could not be in a better nor a stronger place than they were in already. They had many prisoners, and could not carry them away if they departed; and also many of their men were hurt, and some of their prisoners, whom they did not wish to leave behind them.

They drew together and arranged their field so that there was only one entry; and they put all their prisoners together and made them to promise that, rescue or no rescue, they would be their prisoners. After that, they had all their minstrels play at once and make the greatest revel in the world. It is an established custom of the Scotch that when they are thus assembled together in arms, the foot soldiers carry horns around their necks as though they were hunters, some great, some small, and of all sorts, so that when they all blow at once, they make such a noise that it may be heard nearly four miles away. This they do to frighten their enemies and to cheer themselves.

When the bishop of Durham with his banner and ten thousand men had come within a league, the Scotch blew their horns in such a way that it seemed as though all the devils in hell were among them, so that those who heard them and did not know of their custom were very badly frightened. This blowing and noise lasted a long time and then ceased.

By that time the Englishmen were within less than a mile. Then the Scotch began to blow again and made a great noise, which lasted as long as it did before.

The bishop approached with his soldiers well ranged in good order, and came within sight of the Scotch, to within two bowshot or less. Then the Scotch again blew their horns for a long time.

The bishop stood still to see what the Scotch would do. He looked at them carefully and saw that they were in a strong position, greatly to their advantage. Then the bishop took counsel what it would be best for him to do. After all things had been considered, they decided not to attack the Scotch, but to return without doing anything, for they saw they might lose rather than win. When the Scotch saw the Englishmen retreat and that they should have no battle, they went to their lodgings and made merry, and then prepared to depart.

A CAPTOR CAPTURED, 1388

Froissart, *The Chronicle of Froissart*, tr. by Berners, ed. by Ker, V, 226–229.

I shall tell you of Sir Matthew Redman [Captain of Berwick], who was on horseback to save himself, for he alone could not remedy the matter.[38] At his departing, Sir James Lindsay [cousin of Douglas] was near him

[38] The English defeat by the Scotch at the battle of Otterburn.

and saw how he left. And this Sir James, to win honor, pursued Sir Matthew Redman and came so near him that he might have struck him with his spear if he had wished. Then he said, "Ah, sir knight, turn; it is a shame thus to fly. I am James of Lindsay. If you will not turn, I shall strike you on the back with my spear."

Sir Matthew said nothing, but struck his horse with the spurs harder than he did before.

In this manner the chase lasted more than three miles, and at last Sir Matthew Redman's horse foundered and fell under him. Then he sprang to his feet, drew out his sword, and took courage to defend himself. The Scot intended to strike him on the breast, but Sir Matthew Redman dodged the stroke, and the spear point entered the earth. Then Sir Matthew cut the spear in two with his sword.

When Sir James Lindsay saw that he had lost his spear, he threw away the shaft, lighted afoot, took a little battle axe that he carried at his back, and handled it with one hand very skilfully, in which feat the Scotch are very expert. Then he set upon Sir Matthew, who defended himself with great bravery. Thus they tourneyed together, one with an axe and the other with a sword, a long time, and no one stopped them.

Finally Sir James Lindsay gave the knight such strokes and pressed him so hard that he was put out of breath and yielded himself, saying, "Sir James Lindsay, I yield myself to you."

"Well," said he, "I receive you, rescue or no rescue."

"I am content," said Redman, "if you treat me like a good companion."

"I shall not fail in that," said Lindsay, and so put up his sword.

"Well, sir," said Redman, "what do you wish me to do now? I am your prisoner. You have conquered me. I would like to return to Newcastle, and within fifteen days I shall come to you in Scotland wherever you designate."

"I am content," said Lindsay. "You shall promise by your faith to present yourself within the next three weeks at Edinburgh, and wherever you go, to acknowledge yourself my prisoner."

All this Sir Matthew swore and promised to fulfill. Then each took his horse, and took leave of the other. Sir James returned, intending to go to his own company the same way that he came, and Sir Matthew Redman to Newcastle.

Sir James [Lindsay] could not keep the same way as he came. It was dark and misty, and he had not ridden half a mile when he met face to face the bishop of Durham and more than five hundred Englishmen with him. He might well have escaped if he would, but he supposed it was his own company that had pursued the Englishmen. When he was among them, someone asked him who he was.

"I am Sir James Lindsay," he said.

The bishop heard those words and stepped up to him and said, "Lindsay, you are taken. Yield yourself to me."

"Who are you?" asked Lindsay.

"I am the bishop of Durham," he replied.

"And from whence come you, sir?" asked Lindsay.

"I come from the battle," said the bishop, "but I struck never a stroke there. I am going back to Newcastle for this night, and you shall go with me."

"I may not choose," said Lindsay, "since you will have it so. I have taken, and I am taken: such are the adventures of arms."

"Whom have you taken?" asked the bishop.

"Sir," said he, "I took Sir Matthew Redman in the chase."

"And where is he?" asked the bishop.

"By my faith, sir, he has returned to Newcastle. He asked me to trust him on his faith for three weeks, and I have done so."

"Well," said the bishop, "let us go to Newcastle, and there you shall speak with him."

Thus they rode to Newcastle together, and Sir James Lindsay was prisoner to the bishop of Durham. . . .

After Sir Matthew Redman had returned to Newcastle and had told several people how he had been taken prisoner by Sir James Lindsay, he was told that the bishop of Durham had taken Sir James Lindsay, and that he was there in the town as his prisoner.

As soon as the bishop had departed,[39] Sir Matthew Redman went to the bishop's lodging to see his master. He found him in a study, lying in a window, and said, "What, Sir James Lindsay? What are you doing here?"

Then Sir James came out of the study to him and greeted him and said: "By my faith, Sir Matthew, fortune has brought me here. For as soon as I had left you, I met by chance the bishop of Durham, to whom I am prisoner, as you are to me. I believe you will not need to come to Edinburgh to me to pay your ransom. I think that instead we shall make an exchange, one for the other, if the bishop is willing."

"Well, sir," said Redman, "we shall agree very well together. You

[39] For Otterburn. Cf. above, p. 311.

shall dine today with me. The bishop and our men have gone out to fight with your men. I cannot tell what will happen. We shall know when they return."

"I am content to dine with you," said Lindsay.

Thus these two knights dined together in Newcastle.

SIR WILLIAM DE BEAUCHAUMPE SELLS A PRISONER, 1376

Riley, *Memorials of London*, I, 392–393 (from London Letter-Book H, fol. xxviii).

To all persons who these letters shall see or hear, William de Beauchaumpe, greeting. Whereas Messire Thomas de Feltone is bound unto me, and obligated, in four thousand marks, by Statute Staple made, and the Staple of Westminster, the same to pay at a certain term, as by the said Statute more clearly appears, by reason of the purchase of Messire Berard de la Bret, my prisoner. And, nevertheless, by a certain indenture made between the said Messire Thomas and myself, I have granted that if he shall pay, or cause to be paid, himself or by persons by him deputed, unto me, my heirs, or my executors, or to my attorneys ready to deliver sufficient acquittance for the same, in the Guildhall of London, in presence of the mayor for the time being, two thousand marks, that is to say, at the Feast of Our Lord's Circumcision [January 1] in the forty-eighth year of the reign of King Edward [1375] etc., six hundred marks; at the Feast of Easter then next ensuing, four hundred marks; at the Feast of St. Michael [September 29], then next ensuing, five hundred marks; and on the Day of Our Lord's Circumcision then following, five hundred marks, then the said Statute Staple shall lose its force, as by the said indenture more fully appears: I, the aforesaid William, do hereby make known unto all people that I have received, on the last Day of Our Lord's Circumcision comprised in the said indenture, in presence of the mayor and the recorder, five hundred marks of Sir John Smel, chaplain, and Thomas Wailand, citizen and draper of London, in the name of the said Thomas de Feltone, as the last instalment of payment of all the sum of two thousand marks aforesaid. And of the said sum of five hundred marks, and of all other sums comprised in the said indenture, I do will and grant that the said Messire Thomas, his heirs, and his executors shall be acquitted and discharged by these present letters; and that I myself, my heirs, and my executors be ousted forever hereby from all manner of action by reason of the said Statute, or by reason of the purchase of the said Messire Berard, my prisoner. In witness whereof, to these letters I have set my seal with my arms. Given in the Guildhall of London, the eighth day of January, in the forty-ninth year [1376] of the reign of King Edward, after the Conquest the Third.

DEATH OF ROGER MORTIMER, EARL OF MARCH, 1398

As a boy, Chaucer served as page in the household of the Countess of Ulster, wife of Prince Lionel, second son of Edward III. Their daughter Philippa was married in 1368 to Edmund Mortimer, Earl of March, and their grandson Roger [40] is the subject of this description. Especially to be noted is the fact that the office of keeper of the forest of North Petherton in Somerset was hereditary in the Mortimer family and that in 1391 Chaucer was appointed deputy forester in that place. Whether Adam of Usk was right in regard to the enmity of the King and his riotous associates toward Mortimer it is, of course, impossible to say. [R.] [41]

Adam of Usk, *Chronicon*, ed. by Thompson, pp. 164–165.

To this parliament [42] was summoned and came that noble knight, the Earl of March, lieutenant of Ireland, a youth of exceeding uprightness, who had no part or share in such designs and wanton deeds of the King.[43] The people received him with joy and delight, going forth to meet him to the number of twenty thousand, clad in hoods of his colors, red and white, and hoping through him for deliverance from the grievous evil of such a king. But he bore himself wisely and with prudence; for the King and others who were only half-friends, envying his virtue, laid snares for him, seeking occasions of complaint against him. But he, as though he cared not for the turmoil among the people, feigned in the King's presence, pretending that his deeds [the King's] were pleasing to him, although in very truth they displeased him much. Yet the King mistrusted, and being ever evil-minded against him, because others dared not do so, plotted to slay him with his own hands. And, with others thereto sworn, the King constantly sought occasion to destroy him, excusing his evil purpose on the grounds that the earl had received in Ireland, some time after his banishment, Sir Thomas Mortimer, a bold knight, his uncle, who had been banished by them and whom they greatly

[40] He was Roger Mortimer VI, the grandson of Roger Mortimer V, who died February 26, 1360. Cf. above, p. 295n.

[41] Roger Mortimer VI was, because of Richard II's childlessness, next in succession to the throne. That may explain Richard's alleged designs upon him.

[42] The parliament of 1397–1398, in which many persons of high rank, including Thomas, the Archbishop of Canterbury; Richard, earl of Arundel; Sir Thomas Mortimer; Thomas de Beauchamp, earl of Warwick; and John de Cobham, as one of the twelve commissioners of the kingdom, were condemned or banished as traitors.

[43] Richard II had levied extremely heavy taxes for the duration of his life: a tenth and a half from the clergy, a fifteenth and a half from the people, 5s. on every tun of wine, and 5 marks on every sack of wool.

feared, and had also, before his departure, furnished him with money. And so in secret among themselves they doomed the earl, striving to find a time to destroy him, and boasting that they would share his lands among themselves. To that end they sent into Ireland, as their lieutenant, to take him, my lord of Surrey before mentioned, his wife's brother, who hated him bitterly.[44] But alas! on Saint Margaret's day [July 20], near Kells in Ireland, while, too bold in his warlike valor, he had rashly outstripped his own troops, he fell by the accident of war into the hands of his enemies and was slain, to the great sorrow of the realm of England, and to the no small joy and delight of his rivals and adversaries.

THE EARL OF FLANDERS HIDES HIMSELF, 1382

Froissart, *The Chronicle of Froissart*, tr. by Berners, ed. by Ker, III, 319–321.

Then several of the Earl's men said, "Sir, go no farther, for the Gauntoise [45] are in control of the marketplace and of the town [of Bruges]. If you enter the marketplace you are in danger of being killed or taken. Many of the Gauntoise are going from street to street, looking for their enemies. They have some of the townspeople with them, to guide them from house to house where their enemies might be. And sir, you cannot leave by any of the gates, for the Gauntoise are holding them, nor can you return to your own lodging, for many Gauntoise are going there."

When the earl heard this news he was greatly frightened, and realized what danger he was in. He believed what he was told and would go no farther, but decided to save himself if he could, and so made his own plan. He ordered that all the lights which they carried should be put out, and said to those who were with him, "I see clearly that there is no alternative. Let every man depart and save himself if he can." And what he ordered was done. . . .

The earl then went into a back lane, made a servant of his unarm him, threw away his armor, put on an old cloak of his servant's, and then said to him, "Go and save yourself if you can. Be careful of what you say if you fall into the hands of your enemies. If they ask you about me, do not tell them that I am in the town."

He answered, "Sir, if I were to die for it, I would say nothing about you."

Thus, the Earl of Flanders waited all alone. He might then, indeed,

[44] Roger Mortimer, Earl of March, married Eleanor, sister of Thomas Holland, Duke of Surrey. [Thompson's note.]
[45] The men of Ghent.

say that he was in great danger and peril, for if he had then fallen into the hands of his enemies, he would have been in danger of death. For the Gauntoise went from house to house searching for the earl's friends; and whenever they found any, they brought them into the marketplace, and there without alternative . . . they were put to death.

About midnight the earl went from street to street and by back lanes until at last he was forced to enter a house, or else he would have been found by the Gauntoise. As he went about the town, he entered a poor woman's house which was not appropriate for such a lord. There was neither hall, palace, nor chamber; it was only a poor smoky house; there was nothing but a poor hall, black with smoke, and above, a small loft and a ladder of seven steps to climb up; and in the loft there was a poor couch, where the poor woman's children slept.[46]

Then the earl, exceedingly frightened and trembling as he entered, said, "O, good woman, save me. I am your lord, the Earl of Flanders, but now I must hide, for my enemies are pursuing me. If you help me now, I shall reward you hereafter for it."

The poor woman knew him well, for she had often been at his gate for alms and had often seen him as he went in and out hunting. And so she answered at once, for if she had hesitated at all he would have been captured talking with her by the fire. "Sir, climb this ladder and lie under the bed that you will find there, where my children sleep." And then the woman sat down by the fire with another child that she had in her arms.

The earl climbed the ladder as quickly as he could, crept in between the couch and the straw, and lay as flat as possible. Even while he was doing this some of the men of Ghent entered the house, for some of them said that they had seen a man go in before them. But all they found was the woman sitting by the fire with her child. Then they said, "Good woman, where is the man that we saw enter this house before us, and shut the door after him?"

"Sirs," she said, "I saw no man enter this house tonight. I went out just now and threw out a little water, and closed my door again. If any one were here, I would not know where to hide him. You see all the room that I have in this house. Here is my bed, and above in this loft my poor children are sleeping."

Then one of them took a candle, climbed up the ladder, put up his

---

[46] Professor Manly points out the similarity of this cottage to the one which Chaucer describes in the "Nun's Priest's Tale." (Chaucer, *Canterbury Tales*, ed. by Manly, p. 637.)

head into the loft, and saw there nothing but the poor couch, where her children were sleeping. He looked all about and then said to his company, "We might as well go; we are losing the more for the less. The poor woman is telling the truth: there is nobody here but her and her children." Then they left the house.

After that no one entered to do any harm. The earl heard plainly all that was said where he lay under the poor couch. You may be sure that he was in great fear of his life.

7. *Battles*

POITIERS, 1356

Baker, *Chronicon Galfridi le Baker de Swynebroke*, ed. by Thompson, pp. 305–306.

Of Geoffrey le Baker we know from a colophon at the end of one of his works this: "Memorandum that on Friday, the Feast of St. Margaret [July 20], at Osney [now a part of Oxford], A.D. 1347, and the twenty-first year of the reign of King Edward the third since the Conquest, Geoffrey le Baker of Swynebroke [Swinbrook, now a village not far from Oxford], clerk, at the request of Sir Thomas de la More, knight, wrote this little chronicle."

Baker's patron was repeatedly a member of Parliament for Oxfordshire and was connected with the court in such a way that he was able to give the chronicler interesting information. In fact, Baker refers to him as his authority for the account of the deposition of King Edward II, which de la More evidently witnessed.

The "little chronicle" is a mere summary, a pendant to Baker's larger work, which is good authority for the period between 1320 and 1347. Especially interesting are his accounts of the great battles of that time, which he seems to have obtained from eyewitnesses. His description of the Battle of Poitiers (1356) is regarded as the best authority for that great victory in which the King of France and many other French princes and lords were taken prisoner by the Black Prince.

Among the heroes of the day were the Earl of Salisbury and one of the French prisoners, Sir Guichard d'Angle, who later went over to the English and became military tutor to Prince Richard. With these two, Chaucer was sent on an embassy in 1377. [R.]

The Prince [47] therefore committed the vanguard of the army to the earls of Warwick and Oxford, the middle section he kept under his own command, and the rearguard was led by the earls of Salisbury and Suffolk. In the Prince's entire army there were not more than four thousand men of arms, one thousand armed soldiers, and two thousand archers. . . .

The armies being prepared on both sides to fight early on Sunday morning, which was extremely fair, the Cardinal of Perigord came and urged the Prince, in the name of God who was crucified, that he should defer the war for a time, both for ecclesiastical peace and also for the

[47] Edward, the Black Prince.

sparing of Christian blood, and to the end that there might be a treaty of peace, which he promised should be made with great honor on both sides. The Prince neither feared nor refused peace, but modestly agreed to the request of this father.

All this day, which was now set aside for arranging of peace, the army of the Frenchmen increased by a thousand men of arms and also a great many others. The next day the Cardinal came again from the French King, in his behalf to request a truce which should last for one year. This the Prince refused, yet, at the urgent request of that cardinal, he granted a truce to last until the next Christmas. Therefore the Cardinal, returning to the French King, asked him to agree to such a truce; but Marshal Dawdenam, Geoffrey de Charney, and Douglas the Scot persuaded him that common sense showed that the Englishmen could not win then, especially because they were only a few, were in a strange country, were wearied out miserably with their toil in travel, and therefore unable to withstand so large a number of the Frenchmen, who were defending their own land. . . .

The Prince of Wales,[48] being assured that the captain of the French would accept no kind of peace but such as he could get by force of arms, called his men together and made a speech to them, first to the army as a whole and then to his archers. . . .

Having spoken these words, he saw that there was a hill nearby, at one side, quite encompassed by hedges and ditches on the outside; within, however, it was divided up; that is, there was a pasture on one side, thick with brambles, on the other side was a vineyard, and the rest was arable land. On the top of this hill he supposed the army of the French lay. Between our men and the hill there were large and low valleys and a piece of marshy ground. One company of the Prince, discovering a narrow passage, entered the valley and took the hill, where they hid themselves among the bushes, taking advantage of the place. The field wherein our men lay, that is, the vanguard and middle guard, was divided from the plain where the French army lay by a long hedge and ditch, one end of which extended down to the marsh aforesaid. The Earl of Warwick, captain of the vanguard, kept the side of the hill next the marsh. In the upper part of the hedge, toward the top of the hill, there was a great gap, a stone's throw from which stood our rearguard. Over this the Earl of Salisbury was captain.

Our enemies, seeing that our Prince's standard was displayed and

[48] That is, Edward, the Black Prince.

frequently moved from place to place and because the hill was sometimes entirely out of sight, supposed that the Prince fled; yet Douglas the Scot and Marshal de Clarimount said that it was not so, but Marshal Dawdenam, who was mistaken, thought otherwise, urging still to follow and chase the Prince now fleeing, and with him also Douglas, who wished to get preferment and a worthy name by his military service. But Clarimount, to counteract men's suspicions concerning his fidelity, urged them forward all the more vehemently, for they had been put in charge of the vanguard. . . .

Those who were in charge of our rearguard, making haste to take the gap and keep the enemy from passing that way, bore the first brunt of the battle. Then began a terrible encounter between the armed men, who laid on hard with swords and spears. Neither did the archers neglect their duty, but, standing safely behind a rampart, across the ditch and beyond the hedge they forced their arrows to prevail against the military arms, and also quarrels from their crossbows repeatedly and in great numbers. Thus, our rearguard, slaying the enemies who came straggling to the gap, and the vanguard, which lay on the slope of the hill toward the marsh, commanded by the Earl of Warwick, were always ready and met with the Frenchmen, beating them down.

The archers of the vanguard were placed in the marsh out of danger from the horsemen, yet for all that they were somewhat successful, even though the horsemen had been charged solely with the duty of trampling down the archers. The Earl of Oxford, considering the harm that might come of this, left the Prince's guard, and, leading with him the archers, placed them on one side of the Frenchmen, commanding them to shoot at the hindquarters of the horses, so that the horses, being galled and wounded, started to fall with those that sat on their backs, or else turned back and ran upon those who followed them, causing great slaughter among their own masters. The horsemen being thus beaten back, the archers retired towards the place from which they came, shooting and galling the sides of the Frenchmen who fought opposite them. . . .

After a time a new army of the Frenchmen marched out, led by the eldest son of the French King, the Dauphin of Vienne. The order and array of this army was more terrible and fierce than the appearance of that which had previously been driven back, yet for all that it could not make our men afraid, as they were very desirous of honor and also of revenge, both for themselves and their fellows who shortly before had been slain and wounded. Therefore they went to it boldly on both sides, shouting and crying out, "Saint George be our aid," and "Saint Denis for us." Soon they were fighting man to man, and, every man ready to die, [they] fought now to save their lives. The breeding lion does not scatter the wolves more fiercely, nor is the tiger more terrible than our lusty gentlemen were to their enemies. And though this battalion withstood our men longer than the first, yet, after they had lost a large number of their men, they saved many by a piece of strategy, not by running away, but by a pretended retreat, which the Frenchmen are accustomed to use. But our men, believing that victory was doubtful as long as the French King might be nearby with his army, which lay half hid in a valley close at hand, would not, therefore, when they chased any who fled, go out of the field. . . .

In the meantime some of our men laid their wounded under bushes and hedges out of the way; others, having worn out their weapons, took the spears and swords from those whom they had overcome; and the archers, lacking arrows, made haste to draw them from poor wretches that were but half dead. There was not one of them all who was neither wounded nor thoroughly wearied with great labor, except four hundred men who, keeping the chief standard, had been held in reserve to meet the French King.

The Dauphin being thus put to flight, an onlooker came to the French King and said, "My lord King, the field has fallen to the Englishmen, and your eldest son has retreated"; to whom the French King answered with an oath that he would not that day forsake the field unless he were taken or slain, and so by that means carried away by force. On this account the standard-bearers were commanded to march forward into a wide field, followed by two great companies of armed men, who showed themselves to our men and struck such great terror into their hearts that they lost all hope of victory. A man of great worth, standing by the Prince, cried out in a tone of lamentation, "Alas, we poor wretches are overcome." But the Prince, having great trust and faith in Christ, checked him, saying, "You lie, you dastardly fellow, for you cannot say that we can be overcome as long as I live." . . .

Then the Prince commanded his standard-bearer, Sir Walter Woodland, to advance toward his enemies, and with a few fresh men he joined battle with the great army of the French King. Instantly they sounded their trumpets, one answering another. They made such a noise that the walls of Poitiers echoed with the sound like a wood, so that a man would have thought that the hills had bellowed out to the valleys, that from the clouds had come most terrible thunder and cruel lightning, while the air shone on the bright armor and spears dashing against shining harness. Then came on the cruel company of crossbowmen, making a darkness in the skies with the multitude of quarrels which they shot; and against them came a worthy company of English bowmen. Out flew also darts of ash which struck the enemy at a distance, but the French army, being composed of closely-packed troops defending their breasts with their shields, proceeded forward against their enemies. Therefore our archers, having emptied their quivers in vain and being armed only with swords and light shields, were forced to encounter heavily armed soldiers. Then the worthy Prince of Wales bestirred himself, cutting and hewing the Frenchmen with a sharp sword. . . .

The Prince with great courage charged the French army again, wishing to break their ranks before [Captain de la Buche] should make a flank attack. The Prince, lustily encountering his enemies, penetrated to the middle of the throng, and where he saw most adversaries, there he laid about him on every side. . . .

This was the courage of the Prince, who at length penetrated the throngs of those who guarded the French King. . . . Then the standards began to reel, the bearers of them to fall down. . . . The blood of slaves and princes ran mingled together into the waters which were near. Thus raged the Boar of Cornwall, who would have no other way to the French King's standard than by blood. When they came there, however, they found a company of stout men to oppose them. The Englishmen fought, and the Frenchmen fought back, but at length, Fortune making haste to turn her wheel, the Prince pressed forward on his enemies, and, like a fierce lion beating down the proud, he forced the French King to surrender.

The Frenchmen being scattered abroad in the fields of Poitiers, seeing that the standard with the fleur-de-lis was beaten down, fled with all speed towards the town, which was not far off. The English, seeing they were in flight, though they themselves were either badly wounded or much fatigued, pursued them to the very gates of Poitiers, where in a great and very dangerous skirmish they slew a large number of Frenchmen.

At last, our men being called back with the sound of trumpets, and assembling together, pavilions and tents were set up in the fields, and the whole company eagerly turned to providing for the wounded, for the quiet rest of those that were wearied, for guarding the prisoners, and for the refreshing of those who were almost famished, until they discovered who and how many were missing.

NÁJERA, 1367

Chandos Herald, *Life of the Black Prince*, ed. by Pope and Lodge, pp. 161–165.

The English victory at Nájera, April 3, 1367, entirely overshadowed today by the great battles of Sluys, Crécy, and Poitiers, was of great personal interest to Chaucer. The English army, headed by the Black Prince and accompanied by John of Gaunt, left Bordeaux immediately after the birth of Richard (later the king) and, after enduring many hardships in the long, hard climb over the Pyrenees in winter, met and conquered a Spanish army not far from the city of Burgos.

The invasion grew out of a desire to restore to the throne of Castile, King Pedro the Cruel, who, after reigning since 1362, had been driven off his throne by a party headed by his bastard brother, Henry of Trastamare. He had fled to Bordeaux with such treasure as he could save, and his family, including his daughters Constance and Isabel, who in 1371 married John of Gaunt and his brother Edmund of Langley (Earl of Cambridge, later Duke of York).

But Don Pedro, who (according to Chandos Herald) was "of so proud a disposition that he had fear of no man, but weened well that none could do him any hurt, howsoever great his power might be," continued on his throne only two years and was then defeated by his brother and murdered (cf. *Canterbury Tales*, B ^{2} 3565–3580).

In November, 1371, John of Gaunt landed at Plymouth with his Spanish bride, the "Queen of Castile"; and by August 30, 1372, he had appointed Philippa Chaucer one of her ladies in waiting. It is not improbable that Chaucer's "Man of Law's Tale," which relates the sufferings of an exiled princess named Constance and is full of religious allusions, was written for the Spanish Princess, whose chief attribute seems to have been her piety (cf. *Canterbury Tales*, B 134 ff., especially, ll. 652–658).

In addition to these sources of interest, Chaucer had many personal friends and acquaintances in the battle. Among them were Sir Guichard d'Angle, Sir Thomas Percy, and Sir John Devereux, whom he later accompanied at different times on foreign embassies and must have known well as his superiors in the royal household; Sir William Beauchamp, with whom he was certainly on intimate terms, and Beauchamp's brothers-in-law, Sir Matthew Gournay, one of the famous knights of the time, and Ralph, Earl of Stafford.

In this battle the English were aided by the King of Navarre; and the Spanish Bastard, by a French force under the great leader Bertrand du Guesclin, whose capture by Sir John Chandos was the crowning point of the campaign.

The account of the battle was written about 1386 by an eyewitness, the herald (whose name is unknown) who accompanied the greatest of the English heroes, Sir John Chandos. There can be little doubt that Chaucer read, if he did not hear, the narrative as we have it today. [R.]

Now the matter was settled, and all their host marshaled, and the Prince [49] without delay came down from the mountain. When one army saw the other, each knew well that nothing remained but to fight; of this they were certain. No one would wait for the next day. Sir John

[49] Edward, the Black Prince.

Chandos came at once to the Prince and brought him his banner, which was of silk, rich and brave.[50] Very courteously he spoke to him thus: "Sire," said he, "mercy for God, I have served you in the past, and every-thing that God has given me comes from you. You know well that I am wholly yours and will be always. If it seems to you the time and place for me to raise my banner, I have enough means of my own, that God has given me to hold, with which to maintain it. Now do your pleasure in the matter. Behold it; I present it to you."

Then at once the Prince, the King Don Pedro, and the Duke of Lancaster also unfurled his banner, handed it to him by the shaft, and said to him forthwith: "God grant that you gain honor thereby." Chandos took his banner, set it among his companions, and said to them with great joy, "Fair sirs, behold my banner. Guard it well as your own, for indeed it is yours as much as ours." . . .

The English dismounted, aflame with desire to win and achieve honor, and the Prince said to them that day: "Sirs, there is no other end. You know well that we are nearly overtaken by famine, for lack of food, and you see there our enemies who have plenty of provisions, bread and wine, salt and fresh fish, both from fresh water and the sea, but we must con-quer them with blow of lance and sword. Now let us so act this day that we may depart in honor."

Then the valiant Prince clasped his hands to heaven and said: "True, sovereign Father, who hast made and created us, as truly as Thou dost know that I have come here only for the maintenance of right, and for prowess and nobility which urge and incite me to gain a life of honor, I beseech Thee that Thou wilt this day guard me and my men." And when the Prince, fair to look upon, had made his prayer to God, he said, "Forward banner! God help us to our right!"

And then the Prince took the King Don Pedro by the hand and said to him: "Sire King, today you shall know whether you shall ever have Castile again. Have firm faith in God." Thus spake the valiant-hearted Prince.

In the vanguard went forward the noble and brave Duke of Lancaster.

[50] Chandos had been made a banneret in 1360, when he received the estate of Saint-Sauveur-le-Viconte, but was now displaying his banner for the first time in battle. That this was no new honor conferred upon him is borne out by the fact that he is said to have brought his banner to the Prince, who merely unfurled it; not, as a later historian [Barnes] has said, cut off its tail, which would have signified the conversion of a pennon into a banner. Chandos could not have brought his banner to the Prince if he were still only a simple knight. [Pope and Lodge's note.]

The good knight Chandos knighted there without delay Curson, Prior, Eliton, William de Ferinton, Aimery de Rochechouart, Gaillard de la Motte, and Messire Robert Briquet. Many a knight was made who was full of valor and came of noble and puissant lineage.

On the field the Duke of Lancaster said to William Beauchamp, "See, there are our enemies. But so help me Jesus Christ, today you shall see me a good knight if death does not hinder me." Then he said, "Forward, forward banner! Let us take the Lord God for our Protector, and let each one acquit himself honorably." The noble and valiant duke placed himself before his men; more than a hundred he made bolder-hearted than they were before. In that hour the Duke knighted Jean d'Ypres of the proud heart.

Now began fierce battle, and the dust commenced to rise. Archers shot swiftly, thicker than rain falls. Like a valiant man the Duke of Lancaster led the way. After him went Thomas d'Ufford and the stalwart Hugh de Hastings, each one with his banner unfurled, each one holding his lance couched. On the right hand were Chandos, who won great renown that day, Stephen Cosinton, and John Devereux, a noble knight; and there was the good Guichard d'Angle, who was always in the forefront. With him he had his two sons and other knights of renown, who did their duty stoutly; and there was the right noble lord of Rays.

There might one see the companions coming, all close together, banners and pennons. Each one held lance in hand, and they made fierce onslaught to attack their enemies. The archers kept on shooting, and the crossbow-men on the other side, who were with the Bastard; [51] but all advanced so far on foot that they met together with Bertrand [Du Guesclin's] division, which caused them much harm. There might you see thrust of lance as they came together; each one strove to acquit himself well. Then, surely, was no heart in the world so bold as not to be amazed at the mighty blows they dealt with the great axes they bore, and the swords and daggers. It was no mere pastime, for you might see many a good knight fall to the ground.

Great were the din and reek. There was neither banner nor pennon that was not cast down. At one time that day Chandos was thrown to the ground; and upon him fell a Castilian, a large man named Martin Fernandez, who strove desperately to slay him, and wounded him through the vizor. Chandos boldly took a dagger from his side and thrust

[51] Henry of Trastamare, an illegitimate son of Alfonso XI. [Pope and Lodge's note.] See above, p. 325.

the sharp blade into the Castilian's body. The Castilian stretched himself
out dead, and Chandos leapt to his feet. He grasped his sword with both
hands and plunged into the fray, which was fierce and terrible and marvelous to behold. He who was struck by him might be certain of death.

Elsewhere the noble Duke of Lancaster, filled with valor, fought so
nobly that every one marveled, seeing his great prowess, how he put
himself in jeopardy by his noble valor; for I think that no man, rich or
poor, pressed so far forward as he did. Neither did the Prince falter, but
hastened to the battle. . . .

Fiercer waxed the battle, which began on all sides. The Spaniards
hurled with might archegays,[52] lances, and darts. Each one strove to
acquit himself well, for archers shot thicker than rain falls in winter time.
They wounded their horses and men, and the Spaniards saw clearly
that they could no longer endure; they began to turn their horses and
took to flight. When the Bastard Henry saw them, he was filled with
wrath. Three times he made them rally, saying, "Sirs, help me, for God's
sake, for you have made me king and have also sworn to help me loyally."
But his speech was of no avail, for the attack continually grew fiercer.

What would you have me tell you? There was not in the Prince's following any man, however small, who was not as bold and as fierce as a
lion; one cannot make comparison with Oliver and Roland. The Spaniards turned in flight; each one loosened his rein. When the Bastard saw
them, he was much grieved and very angry, but they had to flee or they
would all have been taken and slain. Then the terrible onslaught began,
and then might you see the foot soldiers slain with point and blade. The
Bastard fled down a valley. The French, Bretons, and Normans still
stood their ground, but their pride lasted only a short while, for they
were speedily routed. The cry, "Guyenne! St. George," was raised loudly
in many places.

Messire Bertrand [du Guesclin] was taken and the noble Marshal
d'Audrehem of such great valor, and a count of great renown, the Count
of Denia by name. Count Sancho, doubt not, was taken there, who was a
leader, together with Le Begue de Villaines, Messire Jean de Neufville,
and more than two thousand others; and, to make true report, Le Begue
de Villiers was slain, and several others whose names I cannot mention;
but according to the report five hundred [French] men-at-arms or more
died on the strip of land where the battle was hand to hand. Also on the
side of the English died a perfect knight, the Lord of Ferrers. The glori-

[52] An iron-pointed wooden dart. (*O.E.D.*)

ous God and St. Peter receive the souls of the dead. Sirs, for God, now listen.

The battlefield was on a fair and beautiful plain, whereon was neither bush nor tree for a full league round, along a fine river, very rapid and fierce, which caused the Castilians much damage that day, for the pursuit lasted up to the river. More than two thousand were drowned there. In front of Nájera, on the bridge, I assure you that the pursuit was very terrible and fierce. There you might see knights leap into the water for fear, and die one on the other; and it was said that the river was red with the blood that flowed from the bodies of dead men and horses. So great was the defeat that methinks never could any creature have seen the like, so God help me. So great was the mortality that the number was reported as about seven thousand and seven hundred, and moreover I assure you that the Prince's followers entered the town. More than a thousand were slain; and there the Grand Master of Calatrava was taken in a cellar; and the Prior of St. John, who caused them much mischief, and the master of St. Jacques also. These two had retreated without delay beside a high wall; there they were not safe, for men-at-arms climbed up to attack them, but they yielded humbly, for they dared not await them. Thus were they slain and taken prisoner, whereat the noble and valiant Prince rejoiced greatly. He remained in the open and raised his banner, round which his men gathered.

My lords, the time I am telling you of was on a Saturday, the third day of April, when sweet and gentle birds begin to renew their songs in meadows, woods, and fields. It was at that time that the great battle before Nájera occurred, just as you have heard.

That night the Prince occupied the very lodging in which King Henry himself had been the night before. There they held high revel and thanked God the Father, the Son, and his blessed Mother for the grace he had done them, for you must know that they found there at once wine and bread—all the camp was well furnished therewith—coffers, vessels, gold and silver, whereat many people were much pleased.

WAR'S AFTERMATH

1. Bringing Back the Dead, ca. 1435

Prerogative Court of Canterbury, 2 Stokton.

From the will of Sir Forthe Elton (?): Executors to arrange with my lord of Arundel as to 1,000 marks and 4d.[?], owed for bringing back

the bones of Lord John, Arundel's brother,[53] and their deliverance out
of the Frenchmen's hands. When paid, the bones to be buried at Arundel.

2. *Prayers for the Slain, 1426*

Prerogative Court of Canterbury, 5, 6 Luffenam.

Will of Henry Lounde, Esquire, of Yorkshire, May 1, 1426: 100s. left
for masses to be celebrated in the Church of Cave, in the Isle of Cave,
Yorkshire, for a year after my death, for my soul and the souls of John
Myndrom and John Jalby and the souls of all my servants who were
killed in the King's wars beyond the seas.

3. *Provision for Ransom, 1455*

Prerogative Court of Canterbury, 3 Stokton.

Will of Eleanor, countess of Arundel, lady of Mautravers and Hungerford [widow of John, earl of Arundel]: Left to Sir Robert Hungerford,
knight, Lord de Moleyns, a prisoner in France, wool at the manor of
Hastesbury to the value of 100 marks towards his ransom, on certain
conditions.

[53] After distinguished participation in the French wars, he died in Beauvais on June 12,
1435, and was buried in the Grey Friars there.

8. The Rich and the Poor

THE RICH

1. Houses and Households

A NOBLEMAN'S COUNTRY MANOR, 1397

Chancery, Miscellaneous Inquisition 265, 21 Richard II, 5, m. 6.

Extent of the manor of Keevil in the county of Wiltshire, which was of the Earl of Arundel: Within that manor are a certain hall, a chief chamber, and a little chamber next thereunto with a certain latrine at the back of the same hall, roofed with tiles. Item, a certain chamber below the said great chamber with a certain other chamber and latrine next thereunto. Item, a certain chapel and a cellar below the chapel. Item, a certain chamber called "le warderobe" likewise at the end of the hall, and the entrance thereof is a certain great chamber with a latrine, and below that chamber is a certain pantry and buttery. Item, there is there a great kitchen newly repaired. Item, a certain long house called "kyghtenchambre." Item, a certain house for the office of bakery and two chambers for grooms (*valettis*). Item, a certain chamber beyond the gate (*portam*) with a latrine, entirely roofed with tiles. Item, there is there a certain long stable and a certain little stable and a certain barn partly roofed anew with straw, which is of no value by the year, but is in great need of repair. Item, there is there a certain dovecote and two gardens. . . .

RANKS OF EVERY ESTATE AT TABLE, CA. 1447

Russell, "Book of Nurture," *The Babees Book*, ed. by Furnivall, pp. 188–192 (from Harl. MS [B.M.] 4011, fol. 171).

The pope, an emperor, king, cardinal, prince with a golden royal rod, archbishop in his pall,—all these for their dignity ought not to dine in the hall.

A bishop, viscount, marquis, goodly earl may sit at two messes [*sic*] if they be agreeable thereunto.

The mayor of London, a baron, a mitred abbot, the three chief justices, the speaker of Parliament,—all these estates are great and honorable, and they may sit together in chamber or hall, two or three at a mess, if it so please them.

The other estates, three or four to a mess equal to a knight's are: un-mitred abbot or prior, dean, archdeacon, master of the Rolls, all the under judges and barons of the king's Exchequer, a provincial, a doctor of divinity or of both laws, a prothonotary, or the pope's collector, if he be there, and the mayor of the Staple.

Other ranks may be set four to a mess, of persons equal to a squire in dignity, sergeants-at-law, and ex-mayors of London, the masters of Chancery, all preachers, residencers, and parsons, apprentices of the law, merchants and franklins,—these may sit properly at a squire's table.

Each estate shall sit at meat by itself, not seeing the others, at mealtime or in the field or in the town; and each must sit alone in the chamber or in the pavilion.

* * *

A marshal is often puzzled how to rank lords of royal blood who are poor, and others not of royal blood who are rich, also ladies of royal blood wedded to knights, and poor ladies marrying those of royal blood. The lady of royal blood shall keep her rank, the lady of low blood and degree shall take her husband's rank. The substance of property is not so worthy of reverence as royal blood, wherefore this prevails in chamber and hall, for some day blood royal might attain to the kingship.

* * *

A marshal must honor foreign visitors and strangers to this land, even when they are resident here.

If the king send any messenger to any lord, if he be a knight, squire, yeoman of the crown, groom, page, or child, he must be received honor-ably as a baron, knight, squire, yeoman, or groom, and so forth, from highest degree to the lowest, for a king's groom may dine with a knight or a marshal.

* * *

The estate of a knight of blood and wealth is not the same as that of a simple and poor knight.

2. *Fashions for Men*

STYLES FROM FLANDERS, CA. 1345

Continuation of *The Brut*, ed. by Brie, II, 296–297 (from Corpus Christi Coll. Cambridge, MS 174).[1]

In this time Englishmen so much haunted and cleaved to the madness and folly of the foreigners that, from the time of the coming of the Hainaut people eighteen years past, they ordained and changed them every year divers shapes of disguisings of clothing, of long, large, and wide clothes, destitute and desert from old honest and good usage; and another time short clothes and strait-waisted, dagged and cut, and on every side desslattered [2] and boned, with sleeves and tapets [3] of surcoats and hoods over long and large and overmuch hanging, that if I sooth shall say, they were more like to devils and tormenters in their clothing and shoeing and other array than to men. And the women were arrayed more curiously than the men, for their clothes were so narrow that they let hang fox tails sewed beneath within to hide their arse, which disguisings and pride peradventure afterward brought forth and caused many mishaps and mischiefs in the realm of England.

EXTREMES OF FASHION, 1365

John of Reading, *Chronica*, ed. by Tait, p. 167.

And in these times the Devil appeared in the shape of a monster. No wonder; for the frivolity of the English, always taking up the folly of foreigners in the variety of their clothes and not foreseeing future evils

---

[1] The English *Brut* was one of the most popular chronicles of the Middle Ages. Not less than 167 manuscripts have been found, and this large number is in itself an indication that there were many more. First printed in 1480, it went into ten editions in the next fifty years. It related English history only, unlike many other chronicles of the time which attempted to cover the history of the world.

The first source of the *Brut* was an Anglo-Norman chronicle of the same title which was compiled from two Anglo-Norman writers, Wace and Geoffrey Gaimar, and which ended with 1066. In 1333 it was continued in French to the battle of Halidon Hill. Not until 1307, when it began to draw its information from contemporary accounts of the events described, is it of any historical value; but after 1307 it introduced much valuable information which would otherwise have been lost. Between 1346 and 1361 the main source of the work is the chronicle of John of Reading (see above, p. 171); after 1361, other sources were used. Between 1350 and 1380, or thereabouts, the chronicle was translated into English. Of the translator and of the compiler nothing is known. It is safe to believe that both were ecclesiastics. [R.]

[2] *Slatter*, to slash or slit (clothes). (*O.E.D.*)   [3] Perhaps *tippet* is meant here.

coming through this, they began to wear hoods so small that they barely covered the shoulder [much less the head], laced and buttoned close to the chin, with tippets like cords, over paltocks, some very short and of woolen cloth, others of thin [silk] stuffed and sewed all over . . . hose even longer than their thighs fastened to the short jackets with points which they called harlots, gadlings, and lorels,[4] shoes pointed sideways (*lateraliter*),[5] and long knives hanging between their thighs, and cloth hats turned back and fitted like hose or gloves. The monstrosity and tightness of these garments did not permit them to kneel to God or the saints or to do reverence to their lords or to help themselves without great discomfort; how many indeed put them to the test in hostile combat?

APING THE FASHIONS OF THE RICH, 1411–1412

Hoccleve, *The Regement of Princes*, pp. 16 20.

But this me thinketh an abusion,
To see one walk in gowns of scarlet,
Twelve yards wide, with pendant sleeves down
On the ground, and the rich fur therein set
Amounting to twenty pound or bet;
And if he for it have paid, he no good
Hath left him wherewith for to buy a hood.

For though he strut forth among the press,
And look down on every poor wight,
His coffer and his purse are penniless;
He hath no more than he walks in right.
For land, rent, or cattle he may go light;
The bulk of them not so much weighs
As doth his gown: is such array to praise?

Nay soothly, son, it is all amiss, me thinketh,
So poor a wight his lord to imitate

---

[4] The short jacket (paltock), which did not reach the loins, was attached to the hose by latchets or points, "which in derision of the character of the wearers were popularly called harlots, gadlings, or lorels (losels), all of which were current words for a worthless, idle fellow." [Tait's note.]

[5] Probably the peaked shoes called "crakowes." "If the word 'crakowes' is correctly derived from the Polish town of Cracow it seems probable that the fashion, like that of the *coat-hardie*, was brought to England from Germany, either directly or through France." [Tait's note.] Cf. above, p. 51*n.* and 140.

In his array; for to my mind it stinketh.
> Surely blameworthy are the nobles great,
> If I dare say, who their retainers let
> > Usurp such a lordly apparel;
> > It is not right, my child, without fail.

. . .

> Also there is another style set,
> A foul waste of cloth and an excessive;
There goeth no less into a man's tippet
> > Than a full yard of broadcloth, as I live.
> > Me thinketh this a very incentive
> > > To theft: let them beware of Hempen Lane,
> > > For theft is paid for by strangling bane.

. . .

> What would a lord without attendants be?
> Supposing that his foemen him assail
Suddenly in a street,—what help will he
> > Whose sleeves so wide and cumbrous trail
> > Give to his lord? He is of no avail.
> > > He helpeth no more than a woman can;
> > > He can not stand to aid him like a man.

> His two good arms have right enough to do,
> And somewhat more, his sleeves to uphold.
The tailors, trow I, must hereafter too
> > Work in the field; they shall not spread and fold
> > Out on their board, when they have all unrolled,
> > > The cloth that shall into a gown be wrought;
> > > Take an whole cloth is best, for less is naught.

. . .

> He who can bear most on his back at once
> Of cloth and rich fur hath a fresh renown;
He is called "a lusty fellow" for the nonce;
> > But drapers, yes, and skinners of the town
> > Have for such folk a special prayer all their own,
> > > Which sprinkled is with curses here and there,
> > > And will be, till they get pay for their ware.

. . .

Now have these lords but little need of brooms
To sweep away the filth out of the street,
Since the long sleeves of impecunious grooms
Will lick it up, whether it be dry or wet.
O England, stand upright and firmly set !
Such waste among such simple folk prevent,
Or sorely thou shalt in due time repent.

"LIONS IN THE HALL AND HARES IN THE FIELD," 1362

Eulogium historiarum . . . a monacho quodam Malmesburiensi, III, 230–231.

In this year and last year Englishmen have gone stark mad over fashions
in dress. First came wide surcoats that reached no farther than the hips;
then others that came clear down to the heels, not open in front as becomes a man but spread out at the sides to arm's length, so that when
their backs are turned you think they are women rather than men. This
garment is called "goun" in the mother tongue and rightly so . . . for
the name is applied in open derision. They wear also small hoods fastened
right up under the chin in womanish fashion. Besides, they are embroidered all about with gold, silver, and precious stones. Their liripipes,
dagged in the manner of fools, reach to their ankles.

They have another garment of silk, commonly called a paltock,
so handsomely adorned as to be suitable rather for ecclesiastics than
for laymen. It is said in the Book of Kings that Solomon in all his life
was never arrayed in such a manner (*talibus non est usus*).

They wear also tight two-piece hose,[6] which they fasten with latchets
to their paltocks; [7] these are called "harlots," [8] and so one harlot serves
another. . . . They wear costly gold and silver girdles . . . though
they have not so much as twenty pence saved up.

Their shoes, which they call "crakows," have curved peaks more than
a finger in length,[9] resembling the claws of demons rather than ornaments for human beings. Wearers of such attire ought to be considered
players and worthless fellows rather than barons, actors rather than
knights, buffoons rather than squires. They are lions in the hall and hares
in the field.[10]

[6] Cf. William Camden, *Remaines, concerning Britaine*, London, 1614, pp. 232–233. Camden translates this passage as follows: "hose of two colors, or pied with more."

[7] Camden adds, "without any breeches."   [8] See above, p. 334*n*.

[9] Camden inserts, "fastened to the knees with chains of gold and silver."

[10] Camden adds: "The Book of Worcester reporteth that in the year of our Lord 1369
they began to use caps of divers colors, especially red with costly linings; and in 1372

A SQUIRE'S ARRAY

Exchequer, King's Remembrancer, Accounts Various, 402/17.

Outfit for the King's Esquire, Otho de Granson,[11] *1394*

For 19 pairs of shoes	9s.	6d.
For 2 reins, 2 poitrels, 2 pairs of stirrups, 1 panel, 3 cingles,		
and for the repair of the same	8s.	
For a red and black chaplet	2s.	
To his groom who looked after his horses—		
for various services	8s.	6d.
For 2 dozen points		6d.
For 4 pairs of soles[?] (*souz*)		6d.
For 3 pairs of hose	5s.	
To the maker of a hart (*le fesur dun cerf*) [12]		16d.
For a hand towel		12d.
To the laundress for various services		16d.
To the barber for various services		10d.
For 1 pair of spurs		10d.
For 1 pair of pencels[?] (*enceines*)		6d.
For a sword	2s.	6d.
Total	42s.	6d.

A SQUIRE'S TAILOR'S BILL, 1397

Common Pleas, Plea Roll 547 m. 546.

Henry Hervyle, Esquire, summoned to answer the executors of the will of John Dymmok, late citizen and tailor of London, concerning a debt of £7 0s. 14d. for the following goods, which they say he bought from John Dymmok in the parish of St. Swithin, Walbrook, April 12, 9 Richard II [1386]:

1½ yards 1 nail of red cloth for	9s.	4d.
1½ yards 1 nail of black cloth for	7s.	10d.

---

they first began to wanton it in a new round curtal (short) weed which they called a 'cloak,' and in Latin *armilausa*, as only covering the shoulders. Here you may see when gowns, cloaks, and caps first came into use, though doubtless they had some such like attire in different names."

[11] "Chaucer . . . mentions with praise, in a way that suggests personal acquaintance, Otho de Granson, a knight of Savoy who fought on the side of the English as early as 1372 and in 1393 was pensioned by Richard. Three of his poems Chaucer translated and combined into the *Compleynt of Venus.*" (Chaucer, *Canterbury Tales*, ed. by Manly, p. 43.)

[12] Possibly a heraldic device.

2 yards of rayed cloth, blue ground (*le champ blew*) for .   4s.   8d.

1¼ yards of red cloth for . . . . 3s.   9d.

3 yards of rayed cloth for . . . .   5s.   11d.

1 pair of chausses (*caligularum*) of russet cloth for . .   20d.

1 pair of chausses of black cloth for . . . . . .   2s.   2d.

For the making of a long cloak of black cloth and a cloak

    of black fustian, the same day and place . . .   9s.   8d.

3 yards of red cloth and 1 pair of sleeves (*manicarum*)

    of fustian for . . . .   14s.   2d.

For the making of 1 cloak with a hood of red cloth, with

    a robe of say, 1 cloak of russet furred with calaber

    (*calabre*), 1 hood of scarlet, 1 doublet of worsted

    and 1 pair of chausses of scarlet, 1 cloak of russet

    furred with marten (*foynes*), 1 green cloak, 1 pair

    of points[?] (*poynettus*) of blood and white

    baudekin for . . . . £4   0s.   18d.

The esquire's attorney denies the debt and is commanded to have his master here in person to wage his law.[13]

A SQUIRE'S CLOTHES SEIZED FOR DEBT, 1398

City of London, Mayor's Court, Original Bills, bdle. 2, No. 177.

Articles attached upon Nicholas Colfox, Squier, at suit of Roger Colney, draper, in a plea of debt, October 31, 22 Richard II [1398]:

1 hat of straw with a dagged chaplet . . . . . price   6d.

1 pair of sleeves of fustian . . . .   6d.

2 pairs of old points and 1 pair of

    sleeves of baudekin . . . .   2d.

1 pair of points of baudekin . . . .   12d.

2 pairs of spurs . . . .   8d.

2 pencels (*stremers*) . . . .   4d.

1 pair of socks . . . .   1d.

2 recorders . . . .   8d.

1 gown of gold . . . .   22s.   8d.

1 gown of green damask . . . .   6s.   8d.

1 belt of baudekin . . . .   12s.   8d.

1 quire of paper . . . .   1d.

[13] See above, p. 88*n*.

EXTREMES IN THE MONASTERIES, CA. 1363

Benedictines in England, *Documents Illustrating the Activities* .... *of the English Black Monks, 1215–1540,* II, 67–68.

Moreover, in the color of hoods and frocks we decree and order conformity henceforward in every monastery and church and in the wearing by every monk of our order; so that red, brown (*burnetum*), purple (*bluetum*), and every such color be absolutely relinquished, and everyone be clad simply in hoods and frocks of unrelieved black. We shall not be called red, or brown, or purple, but black monks, thus keeping our true name. . . . Also, we absolutely forbid, both for the monks and for prelates of this province, boots which are pointed (*rostratas*) or too narrow, together with silk girdles, or girdles of any such material, or with silver adornments, and hoods ornamented with silk or sendal of green or blue or any other color but plain black; nor do we allow any monk, whether inferior or superior, to ride forth with a cloak or bell-shaped cape (*rotundello*) or any such dishonest apparel, or in hood or other outer garment alone; but we command that whenever monks are to ride forth they shall be clad outwardly according to the ancient custom of our cloister in honest capes having their hoods sewn on.

3. *Fashions for Women*

KEEPING UP WITH THE FASHIONS, 1371

La Tour-Landry, *The Book of the Knight of La Tour-Landry,* pp. 29–31.

Fair daughters, I pray you that you be not the first to take new fashions and guises of array of women of strange countries, as I will tell you. There was a debate between a baroness that dwelt in Guienne and a lord that was a wise and a malicious knight. For the baroness said to him, "Cousin, I come out of Brittany, and there I have seen my cousin your wife, but she is not arrayed as ladies of this country of Guienne are, nor of divers other places hereabout, for her hoods, tails, and sleeves are not furred enough after the present fashion."

And the knight answered: "Since she is not arrayed in your guise and because you think her array and her fur too little and you blame me for it, indeed you shall have no more cause to blame me. For I will array her as nobly as any of you and as finely; for you have only half your hoods and coats furred with ermine or minever, and I will do better by her, for I will fur her gown, collars, sleeves, and coats, the hair outward;

thus she shall be better purfled and furred than other ladies and gentle-women. And be sure that I will see her arrayed after the state of the good and honorable women of France, not of them of this country that have taken the state of the unthrifty, evil women . . . for they were the first that brought in this fashion that you use, of great purfles and slit coats. . . . And I consider a person poorly advised who first takes up the fashion introduced by such women. And as to my wife, she shall not; but the princesses and ladies of England have taken up the said state and guise, and they may well hold it if they like." . . . And therefore, daughters . . . it is good to hold the intermediate estate of the good women and the common estate of the realm, that is to say, the state that most good women use. . . .

And know that whoever first takes up a new fashion is much spoken of, but nowadays if a woman hears of a new fashion, she will never be in peace till she has the same. And the wives say to their husbands every day, "Sir, such and such a wife has certain fashionable clothes that become her well, and I pray you I may have the same." And if her husband says, "Wife, even if such and such a one has such clothes, some that are wiser than they have them not," she will say, "Good reason why, for they cannot wear them." . . . And thus with her words her husband must needs give her what she desires; otherwise he will never have peace with her, for she will find so many reasons why she will not be refused. But such women are not wisest nor know best their good, but they have more thought for pleasing the world than for their husband's welfare.

And there is a fashion which is common now among serving women of low estate: for they fur their collars that hang down into the middle of the back, and they fur their heels, which are daubed with dirt, and [their clothing] is single about their breast. This fashion I praise not in winter nor summer, for it would be better for them to take the fur that hangs about their heels in the winter and set it about their stomachs, for the latter have more need of heat than their heels; and in summer it were better away, for flies hide in it.

HOW TO WEAR YOUR CLOTHES, CA. 1393

Le Ménagier de Paris, ed. by Pichon, I, 13–15.

Know, dear sister, that if you wish to follow my advice you will have great care and regard for what you and I can afford to do, according to our estate. Have a care that you be well dressed, without new fal-lals and without too much or too little frippery. And before you leave your chamber or house, take care first that the collars of your shift and of your *blanchet* [14] [and of your] gown and cloak do not hang out one over the other, as happens with certain drunken, foolish, or ignorant women who have no care for their honor or for the honesty of their estate or that of their husbands, and who walk with wandering eyes and head horribly reared up like a lion's, their hair straggling out from their wimples, and the collars of their shifts and gowns crumpled the one upon the other, and who walk mannishly and bear themselves uncouthly before folk without shame. And if one speaks to them about it, they excuse themselves on the ground of their industry and humility, saying that they are so busy, hardworking, and humble that they take no care for themselves. But they lie; they care so much for themselves that if they were in an honorable company, never would they be willing that men should pay less attention to them than to the wiser ladies of like rank with themselves, or that they should have fewer greetings, bows, courtesies, and conversations than the rest, but rather they desire more. And they are unworthy of it, for they know not how to maintain their own honorable fame, nay, or the fame of their husbands and of their lineage, which they dishonor. Therefore, fair sister, have a care that your hair, wimple, kerchief and hood, and all the rest of your attire be well arranged and simply ordered, that none who see you can laugh or mock at you, but that all the others may find in you an example of fair array and simplicity and honesty in all other matters.

PUNISHMENT FOR PAINTING THE FACE, 1371

La Tour-Landry, *The Book of the Knight of La Tour-Landry*, ed. by Wright, pp. 69–70.

I will tell you a tale that was told me of a lady that I knew, who, folk said, painted herself. . . . And for a long time she was a lady of great authority, honored and made much of. And she had formerly more than eighty gowns, but at the end of her life she had fewer, for her lord died and she had not wherewith to sustain her estate and array, and she died in poverty. And when she was dead I have heard say that her visage became so hideous and foul that no man might know she ever had a visage and no one knew what her features were like, for nobody might endure to look thereon for horribleness. And I suppose, and so did others,

[14] *Blanchet*, a short garment, a kind of camisole . . . worn over the chemise. [Translated from Pichon's note.]

that God gave through her that example and punishment because she painted her face and plucked her forehead ("popped, painted, plucked, and farded her head").

Wherefore, fair daughters, take warning and hold it in your heart that you use nothing to paint or color your visages, which are made after God's image, otherwise than your creator and nature have ordained; and that you pluck not your brows nor temples nor forehead; and also that you wash not the hair of your head in any other thing but lye and water. For you shall find of miracles that have been done in the church of Our Lady of Rochmadame,[15] divers tresses of ladies and gentlewomen that had been washed in wine and other things to make the hair a different color than God made it; for the ladies that owned the tresses were coming thither on pilgrimage, but they might never have power to come within the church door until they had cut off the tresses of their hair, which are hung there before the image of Our Lady.

A MEDIEVAL POWDER BOX, 1413

Archdeaconry of London, Register I, fol. 313.

Will of Agnes, widow of Geoffrey Creke, formerly citizen and physician of London:—

I bequeath to Joan my daughter a graven standing cup with cover, silver-gilt, two salts of silver, one cup called "note," [16] with a cover, silver-gilt, one "pouderboxe" inscribed with these words in English: "Strawe on pouder enough." [17]

A GIRDLE WITH BELLS, 1407

Prerogative Court of Canterbury, 17 Marche.

Will of Alice, late wife of John Barbour, brazier [buried in the church of St. Edmund, Salisbury]:

I bequeath to John my son . . . my fifth ring of gold and a green girdle appareled with bells.

[15] In the original it is *Nostre Dame de Rochemadour*. This was a well-known place of pilgrimage near Cahors famous in the middle ages for the miracles performed there. [Wright's note.]

[16] *Nut*, a cup formed from the shell of a cocoanut mounted in metal; also one made of other materials to resemble this. (*O.E.D.*)

[17] Cf. will of John Baret of Bury, 1463 (prob. May 2, 1467): Item, [I bequeath] to Don John Wulfpet my best powder box of silver and a farthing of gold (Tymms, ed. *Wills and Inventories from the Registers of the Commissary of Bury St. Edmunds and the Archdeacon of Sudbury*, p. 15).—"Probably for perfumed powder, which was much used for clothes; or, a caster, like a modern pepper-box, for powdering, or seasoning meat." [Tymms' note.]

JEWELS

Common Pleas, Plea Roll 579 m. 380.

A debt for jewels, 1390. London. Matilda de Veer, Countess of Oxford, summoned to answer John Leysetre, citizen and merchant of London, who claims £66 14s. from the countess for jewelry bought on the nineteenth of December, 12 Richard II [1388], in the parish of St. Nicholas Acon, ward of Langborne: gold necklaces (*monilia*) with precious stones, *viz.*, margarites and "popyngeayes," fixed on them, purses (*bursas*) called "pauteners," [18] and silver rings.

Countess denies the debt. (To Easter term.)

Archdeaconry of London, Register I, fol. 186 d.

A unicorn's horn in a ring, 1407. Will of Isabella Nichel, widow of Henry Nichel, September 2, 1407. I bequeath to the wife of William Venour a gold ring "cum ossa unicorn," weighing one noble.

Prerogative Court of Canterbury, 52 Marche.

Beads gauded with gold, 1421. Will of Joan Elveden, widow [buried in the church of the Friars Minor, Newgate]: I bequeath to the Duchess of Clarence one pair of coral beads gauded with gold; to her daughter my lady Joan, a diamond; to her daughter my lady Margaret, one pair of beads of jet containing 180 jet stones gauded with gold.

4. *Shopping in London*

BILL FOR CLOTH, CA. 1380

The Stonor Letters and Papers, 1290–1483, ed. by Kingsford, I, 28 (from Chan. Misc. 37/1 [26]).

Account between Edmund de Stonor and Raulyn de Swanton [bill for cloth bought] . . . the 14th day of November, delivered to Thomas, his valet.

First, for 2¼ yards of sanguine m [19] . . . ,
price per yard, 4s. 8d. . . . . 10s. 6d.
Item, for 2½ yards of . . . tawny medley,
price per yard, 4s. 8d. . . . . 11s. 6d.
Item, for 3½ yards of ray, brown ground,
price per yard, 2s. 6d. . . . . 8s. 9d.
Item, for 3 yards of tawny parted with ray,
price per yard, 3s. 4d. . . . . 10s.

[18] Pautener, a small bag, wallet, scrip, or purse. (*O.E.D.*)
[19] Manuscript "somewhat damaged." [Kingsford's note.]

Item, for 1½ yards of ray for a groom,
    price per yard, 22*d.* . . . . 2*s.* 9*d.*
Item, for 1 yard of tawny parted with ray. . . . . . 2*s.* 2*d.*
    Total . . . . 45*s.* 8*d.*
Item, for one pair of hose of scarlet for
    Christmas[?] (skarlet a countre Nowel). . . . [6?]*s.* 8*d.*

PURCHASES FROM A MERCER, 1382

Common Pleas, Plea Roll 486 m. 503.

Thomas Tryvet, knight, was summoned to answer Richard Northebury, citizen and mercer of London, in a plea that he pay £16 0*s.* 7*d.* which he owes. Richard says that whereas the said Thomas purchased from him in the ward of Eastcheap [the following articles]:

Oct. 10, 1378, a piece of baudekin, 2 ells of red worsted;

Dec 13, 1378, 5 ells of westfall,[20] 2½ ells of linen cloth, 1 yard of bokeram (buckram), ½ yard of velvet;

Dec. 24, 1378, 10 ells of linen cloth, 1 ell of westfall, 1 piece of green carda (*carde veridi*); [21]

Jan. 1, 1378/9, 6 ells of linen cloth, 16 ells of westfall, 2 "quyltes" of the greater assize, 4 "yperlynges," 1 bed, 12 ells of westfall, 6½ yards of ribbon of gold, 3 ells of canvas, 2 pieces of fustian, 1 piece of baudekyn and 1 mattress,

for £16 0*s.* 7*d.* payable to the said Richard on the Feast of Pentecost [22] then following, he has not paid, although often asked to do so.

[Judgment for the mercer with damages, 100*s.*, of which he remits 33*s.* 4*d.* as an act of grace.]

COMMISSIONS FOR A LADY

Rickert, "Some English Personal Letters of 1402," *Review of English Studies*, VIII (1932), 260–262 (Excheq. K. R. Accts. 512/10).
Letters of Lady Elizabeth Zouche [23] from Eaton Bray in Bedfordshire to her friend John Bore in London.

A gift of cheap damask, March 18, 1402: Right well beloved friend, I greet you. . . . Also I pray you that you will go and buy a cloth of

---

[20] A variety of cloth of Westphalian origin. (*O.E.D.*)
[21] A kind of muslin. (*O.E.D.*)
[22] Seventh Sunday after Easter; in 1379 Pentecost fell on May 29.
[23] Elizabeth, Lady Zouche, was the widow of Sir John Arundel (died 1391) and of William, Lord Zouche (died 1396); she died in 1408, and if her will was carried out, is buried in Tewkesbury Abbey. . . . Through both her husbands she must have been

damask (or two if necessary) of green or red or pale [color], of the
lowest price, and bear it to the good lord and pray him that he will make
the reels for Chicheley and Skot, as he promised me now[?] at Eaton.
I pray you, as I trust you, that you fail me not of this cloth, for truly I
would not fail Mr.[?] [B?]rook at this time for ten times more than it
is worth. . . .

Elizabeth Lady Zouche.

[*Endorsed in French*]:

By order of this letter John Bore hath bought one cloth of blue
damask which cost 51s. 8d., and it hath been delivered to William, lord
Zouche,[24] by the said John Bore, and for this the said John hath a release general of debt covenant and trespass for him and his heirs for ever.
And also two deeds of gift of the body of Thomas Scot, prisoner, to the
said lord made to the said lady [his stepmother], which two deeds the
said John Bore delivered to the said lady in the embattled chamber at
Eaton, Saturday before Philip and James,[25] 3 Henry [IV], [1402].

A corse of silk for a horn, May 29, 1402: And also I pray you that you
will send me nineteen arrays of this same ray that the bearer of this letter
shall take you, and as much cloth of color thereto according, and that you
send it hither by the bearer of this letter and the price therewith, and [by]
the next man [that] goeth between I shall pay you, by my troth. And also
I pray you for my love that you will send me two yards of the breadth
that is marked here [   ] for a corse of silk for a horn. . . .

Elizabeth Lady Zouche.

More as to the same, July 7, 1402: And as touching Bampton the taylor,
whatever agreement that you make with him in any degree I assent fully
thereto. And as touching all other matters, I pray you that you will do
what you think is good; and concerning the clothing and the horn which

---

of the Court circle; and she was related by marriage to Sir William Beauchamp, whose
friendship with Chaucer seems now an assured fact. . . .

Her "right well beloved friend," John Bore, whom she finds so useful in executing
small commissions, is not certainly identified. A man of that name appears frequently in
the Patent Rolls and Close Rolls as King's clerk and dean of the chapel of the royal
household. . . . But as this man died in April, 1402, between the writing of the first
and second letters, the Bore of the letters may have been a younger kinsman of the King's
Chaplain. (From Professor Rickert's introduction to "Some English Personal Letters of
1402," *Review of English Studies*, VIII [1932], 257–258).

[24] Stepson of Lady Zouche.
[25] The feast of Philip is celebrated on May 1, together with that of James the Younger.

I sent to you before, I pray you that you will do your business that I might have it. . . .

E. la Zouche.

[*Endorsed in French*]:

A corse of silk such as within was sent to my lady by Thomas [blank], groom to the said lady the bearer of this letter, which cost 3s. 8d.

A paternoster of gold at any price, St. Giles Eve,[26] *1402:* Right well beloved friend, I greet you well, and gladly would I hear of your welfare, and I pray you that you will take a leisure that Frome[27] and you might come hither together and set, I pray, this house in better governance, for I think[28] to God it is ever longer the worse; and that you would do it in haste, for I would prepare me to ride to my lady my mother. And also I would pray you that you would have ordered for me a pair of beads of gold for my lady my mother with the quaintest paternoster that you can find, whatsoever they cost; and also I pray you that you will order me a pipe of white wine as I spoke to you of; also I pray you that you will send me word what the price [is] of a whole cloth of black velvet and as my trust is in you, fail me not, especially of my beads. . . .

E. la Zouche.

[*Endorsed in French*]:

There was delivered by the said John Bore to Thomas, Chicheley's man, bearer of this letter, the fifth of September in the third year [of Henry IV] one pipe of white wine, which cost 35s. 8d.[29]

And for barreling[?] the same, 7d. And for drawing out of the cellar, 12d. And for carriage of the same between the cellar and Smithfield, 12d. And delivered to the said Thomas for his charges, 8d.

Item, sent to my Lady la Zouche by the said bearer one pair of gold beads weighing one ounce and half an ounce save forty [*sic*] pennyweight, which cost in all 38s.

5. *Fat Pets and Famished People, 1371*

La Tour-Landry, *Book of the Knight of La Tour-Landry,* pp. 28–29.

There was a lady that had two little dogs, and she loved them so that she took great pleasure in the sight and feeding of them. And every day she made for them dishes with sops of milk, and afterward gave them flesh.

[26] That is, August 31.
[27] One of her first husband's executors.
[28] *panke* in original; error for *penke?*
[29] The eight pence stroked through. As appears below, it was the tip to Thomas.

THE RICH AND THE POOR, a medieval interpretation
of the parable of Dives and Lazarus; *ca.* 1425
Baltimore, Walters Gallery, MS W. 174, fol. 125

KNIGHT AND LADY
IN GARDEN
London, Brit. Mus.,
MS Harl. 4431, fol. 376

FASHIONABLE DRESS

Early fifteenth century

CHAUCER'S SQUIRE
San Mareno, Huntington Library.
MS 26. c. 9 (The Ellesmere
Chaucer), fol. 121v

CRIPPLE BEGGING
Baltimore, Walters Gallery, **MS W.** 88, fol. 97v

THE POOR; early fourteenth century

ALMONER GIVING ALMS
New York, Morgan Library, MS 456, fol. 93

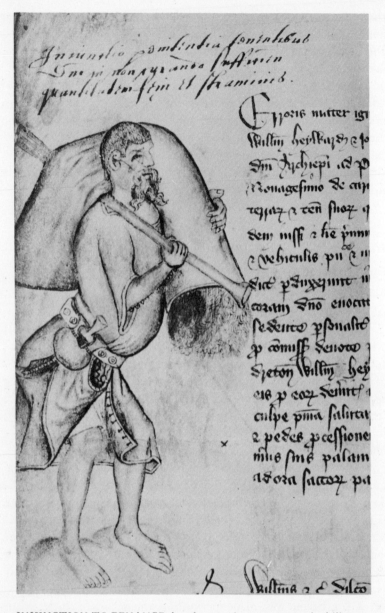

INJUNCTION TO PENANCE, late fourteenth century; marginal illustration accompanying the text quoted from Courtenay's Register on page 392. The superscription in the original handwriting reads: "Injunctio poenitentiae tenentibus domini nostri non curando sufficientem quantitatem foeni et straminis." Reproduced from the original MS in Lambeth Library, London, by the kind permission of His Grace the Archbishop of Canterbury.

But there was once a friar that said to her that it was not well done that the dogs were fed and made so fat, and the poor people so lean and famished for hunger. And so the lady for his saying was wroth with him, but she would not amend it.

And afterward it happened that she died, and there fell a wonderful marvelous sight, for there were seen ever on her bed two little black dogs, and in her dying they were about her mouth and licked it, and when she was dead, where the dogs had licked it was all black as coal. . . . Therefore here is a good example that neither ladies nor gentlewomen should have their pleasure in such beasts, nor give them that which poor people might be sustained with who die of hunger.

THE POOR

1. Hard Times

FAMINE IN THE LAND, 1390

Knighton, *Chronicon*, II, 314–315.

In that year there was great want in all parts of England, and that want, or scarcity of grain, began under the Sickle and lasted until the Feast of St. Peter ad Vincula [August 1], that is, until the new harvest. Want fell upon many people, chiefly the commons and paupers; for you would see infants and children in highways and houses, wailing and clamoring on account of hunger, begging for bread, nor was the mother able to help them. . . . The cause of that want was believed to be the great scarcity of money among the majority, for money was lacking in those days mainly because the wool of the kingdom remained without a buyer, some of it for two years, some for three. A statute had been enacted in a certain parliament that the English merchants should not go from the kingdom with wool and other goods, but that they should take those things to twelve places alloted for this business within the kingdom, so that the foreign merchants, flocking together with their goods at the designated places, would through soliciting exchange their goods for ours. On account of this statute the English merchants refused to buy wool and other merchandise, until at last in the second parliament following, a concession was made permitting them to sell their goods wherever they chose.

In those days wool sold cheap; one stone[30] of wool sold for three shillings, and at the gate of Leicester sometimes for two shillings or

[30] Usually 14 lbs.; of wool, 24 lbs. (*O.E.D.*)

twenty pence. The pinch of hunger was felt most sharply in the county of Leicester and in the central parts of the kingdom. Even if the scarcity was great, the price of grain was not very high. The top price for a quarter of grain in Leicester was sixteen shillings eight pence at one exchange; generally the price was one mark or fourteen shillings. In London, indeed, and in many other parts of the kingdom a quarter of grain was sold for ten shillings or thereabout. Eleven ships loaded with an abundance of provisions were sent out to different parts of the country for the relief of the people. The citizens of London contributed two thousand marks to purchase provisions for a common box for orphans. And the twenty-four aldermen added twenty pounds for similar purchases on account of the fear of famine about to come to the city, and they located at different places suitable conveniences for the people, so that the needy could come and buy at a fixed price what would suffice for maintaining themselves and their families. Those who did not at the time have any money would make payment in the following year, and thus they were relieved so that no one because of the famine perished.

NEEDY NEIGHBORS, LATE 14TH CENTURY

Piers the Plowman, ed. by Skeat, III, 161–163 (C-text, Passus X, ll. 71–97); done into modern English by L. F. Salzman, *English Life in the Middle Ages*, p. 28.

The neediest are our neighbors if we give heed to them,
Prisoners in the dungeon, the poor in the cottage,
Charged with a crew of children and with a landlord's rent.
What they win by their spinning to make their porridge with,
Milk and meal, to satisfy the babes,
The babes that continually cry for food—
This they must spend on the rent of their houses;
Aye, and themselves suffer with hunger,
With woe in winter, rising a-nights
In the narrow room to rock the cradle.
Pitiful it is to read the cottage women's woe,
Aye and many another that puts a good face on it,
Ashamed to beg, ashamed to let neighbors know
All that they need, noontide and evening.
Many the children, and nought but a man's hands
To clothe and feed them; and few pennies come in,
And many mouths to eat the pennies up.

Bread and thin ale are for them a banquet,
Cold flesh and cold fish are like roast venison;
A farthing's worth of mussels, a farthing's worth of cockles,
Were a feast for them on Friday or fast-days;
It were charity to help these that be at heavy charges,
To comfort the cottager, the crooked and the blind.

2. Care of the Poor and the Sick

A CHEST FOR THE POOR, 1349

White, "Ancient Records and Antiquities of the Parishes of St. Swithin, London Stone, and St. Mary Bothaw," *Transactions of the London and Middlesex Archaeological Society*, I (1905), 209.

John, son of Adam de Salisbury, pepperer, to be buried in the Church of St. Mary Bothaw. . . . An ironbound chest is to be deposited in the aforesaid church, and in it are to be placed forty pounds sterling, to be lent to poor parishioners of the same upon certain securities to be repaid at a fixed time so that no loan exceed sixty shillings, and the security must be greater than the loan. Three parishioners to have each a key to the said chest, so that it might be opened and closed, with the consent of all three, and one of the executors to have one of the keys in his custody, so long as he shall reside in the parish.

A CRUSH AT THE DISTRIBUTION OF ALMS, 1315

City of London, Guildhall Library MS 126, fol. 78, from London Coroner's R. Mich. 9 Edw. II.

The coroner was informed that a certain Alice de Lincoln [with three other women and five men, including Henry le Dumbe], poor persons and beggars, lay dead of other than their right deaths in the entrance of the rent of John Paulin in the parish of St. Andrew in the ward of Castle Baynard. Having heard this, the coroner and sheriffs proceeded thither, when they called together the good men of the same ward and of neighboring wards diligently to inquire how this happened. The jurors said that, whereas on the preceding Tuesday Sir Walter de Frhysney (Frysney?) and Sir Robert de Waleby, chaplains, executors of the will of Robert de Retford deceased, and a certain Thomas de Marnham caused a distribution of money to be made for the soul of the testator, according to custom, in the said rent, there assembled a great multitude of poor beggars and, for greed of receiving the money, they entered running swiftly into the said entry, among whom were the deceased; and because they were weaker than the others, they fell and were immediately trampled under the feet of the said poor people and crushed to death.

A SIMILAR INCIDENT, 1322

London, Coroner, *Calendar of the Coroners Rolls*, 1300–1378, ed. by Sharpe, p. 61.

When at daybreak of the Feast of the Translation of St. Thomas [July 3] a great multitude of poor people were assembled at the gate of the Friars Preachers seeking alms, Robert Fynel, Simon, Robert, and William his sons, and twenty-two other male persons, names unknown, Matilda, daughter of Robert le Carpenter, Beatrix Cole, Johanna "le Peyntures" [woman painter], Alice la Norice, and twenty-two other women, names unknown, whilst entering the gate were crushed to death in the crowd, and immediately died thereof and of no other felony. The jurors suspect no one of their death except the misadventure and crushing. As regards who were present or who first saw the corpses, they are unable to say, owing to the crowd and its being nighttime. The corpses so crushed were viewed, on which no other hurt, wound, or bruise appeared.[31]

A POOR PENSIONER, 1437

Prerogative Court of Canterbury, 22 Luffenam.

Will of Elizabeth, widow of Robert Lovell, Esquire, of Devonshire: . . . [I bequeath] to William Juddes 6*d.* a week for his life.

A BEQUEST TO POOR HUSBANDMEN, 1419

Prerogative Court of Canterbury, 47 Marche.

Will of Edmund Holes: . . . I will that 20[?] marks shall be distributed among poor men and to *pauperes agricultores* in Cheshire and 5 marks to sundry poor men in Hertfordshire.

NO BEGGARS AT THE DOOR, 1447

Prerogative Court of Canterbury, 35 Luffenam.

Will of Roger Leveden, merchant of Bristol: . . . And of the remnant of my goods I bequeath for my soul and for all Christian souls £10 to be divided among poor men that goeth not from door to door, but to poor householders and to bedridden men and to blind men and to lame men.

---

[31] The occasion of this disaster, which caused the death of fifty-five men and children, was the distribution of alms for the soul of Henry Fingrie, late fishmonger and sheriff (A.D. 1299–1300), by his executor.—"Annales Paulini" (Rolls Series, No. 76), I, 304. [Sharpe's note.]

GILD BENEFITS FOR THE POOR, THE SICK, AND THE AGED, 1340–
CA. 1389

The following items concerning the care of the poor and the sick are summarized
from Gild Certificates.[32]

Chancery Miscellanea, Gild Certificate 439.

The Gild Merchant of Coventry, [1340], buries its members at the Gild
expense in need. In unmerited poverty it helps members get started in
trade and gives assistance in sickness. It maintains thirty-one brothers
and sisters who cannot work, at a yearly cost of £35 3s.

Chancery Miscellanea, Gild Certificate 369.

The Gild of St. George the Martyr, in the Charnel House next St.
Nicholas church, Great Yarmouth, [ca. 1389], finds for its members in
poverty 7½d. per week, a tunic with a hood and other clothing, and also
burial at the Gild's expense in need.

Chancery Miscellanea, Gild Certificate 308.

The Tailors' Gild of the Ascension, Norwich, [1350], gives 7d. a week
to the poor, blind, etc. so long as they are not proved thieves.

Chancery Miscellanea, Gild Certificate 296.

The Gild of St. George in the Cathedral Church of Norwich, [1385],
pays 8d. a week to members in poverty, toward which each member of
the gild subscribes ¼d. a week. The balance goes toward the making of
an image of St. George.

Chancery Miscellanea, Gild Certificate 321.

The Gild of St. James, Sall, Norfolk, [1358], provides for every poor
person coming to the gild-feast a meal and ¼d.

Chancery Miscellanea, Gild Certificate 59.

The Corpus Christi Gild of Walden, Essex, [1377/78], pays 8d. a week
to its members in accidental poverty, sickness, or other mishap. Poor
strangers are buried at the Gild's expense. Poor women with child coming
into the town have a chrism and a penny to offer at their purification.

Chancery Miscellanea, Gild Certificate 96.

All Saints Gild, Crowland, [ca. 1389], provides its members who are sick
or in need with 40d. a year and with a tunic and hood of russet.

Chancery Miscellanea, Gild Certificate 189.

Gild of the Conception B.V.M., church of the Carmelites, London,

[32] See above, p. 235n.

[1365], keeps a common box into which each brother and sister pays 3*d.* quarterly. In infirmity or detention in prison or other adversity members receive 7*d.* a week from the box.

Chancery Miscellanea, Gild Certificate 190.

Gild of the Holy Cross in St. Lawrence Jewry, London, [1370], pays to members in infirmity by reason of mutilation of limbs or because of old age 14*d.* a week; but the brothers so helped must have paid their quarterage (4*d.* a quarter) for 7 years.

Chancery Miscellanea, Gild Certificate 242.

Gild of the Holy Cross at Lynn, [*ca.* 1389], sends a gallon of ale to a brother who is sick, or who is going on pilgrimage.

Chancery Miscellanea, Gild Certificate 325.

Gild of All Saints, Stoke Ferry, Norfolk, [1359], finds a halfpenny and a loaf for each member who is in sickness at the time of the gild-feast.

Chancery Miscellanea, Gild Certificate 342.

Gild of St. John Evangelist, Upwell, Norfolk, [1382/83], collects ¼*d.* a week from each brother to provide for members suffering poverty, blindness, paralysis, etc.

HOSPITALS

Common Pleas, Plea Roll 526 m. 158.

Mortuary in a hospital, 13—. John Mildenhale, prior of the Hospital of the Blessed Mary without Bishopsgate, summoned to answer Robert Hodel, clerk, touching a breviary worth £10, which belonged to William Morwyn, late parson of St. Michael Queenhithe, who died in the Hospital. The prior says that it is the custom for the Hospital to take as mortuary the best thing of anyone who dies there. Robert Hodel says the book was given to him by Morwyn before he died. Judgment for Hodel.

Prerogative Court of Canterbury, 1 Marche.

Hospital beds, 1401. Will of Richard Baret, burgess of Gloucester: . . . Item, I bequeath for constructing beds (*pro lect' faciend'*) in the Hospital of St. Bartholomew, Gloucester, especially for the poor, sick, and feeble, 100*s.*

LONDON LEPERS, 1403

Prerogative Court of Canterbury, 4 Marche.

Will of John Bygonet of Holborn: . . . Item, I bequeath to the house of lepers by Saint George in Southwark, called "Loke," one "masseboke" for celebrating divine service. Item, to John Fythelar, a leper dwelling there, a bed of the best with a coverlet and a tester and two blankets, two sheets, and a mattress. Item, I bequeath to his five brethren lepers, 10s. . . . Item, I bequeath to the lepers of St. Giles without Holborn, 20s.

A DRAPER'S BEQUEST TO LONDON HOSPITALS, 1411.

Prerogative Court of Canterbury, 23 Marche.

Will of Peter Briklesworth, citizen and draper of London, who dwelt within the close of the Hospital of St. Thomas the Martyr, Southwark: Item, I bequeath to be divided among the lepers and the poor bedridden, as my executors shall ordain, 100s. Item, to every sister of the Hospital of the Blessed Mary without Bishopsgate, 3s. 4d. Item, to the Master of the Hospital of St. Thomas the Martyr of Southwark, for my tithes and oblations and all things else by me of right to him belonging, 10s. Item, to every brother there, 20d., and to every chaplain celebrating divine service in the said Hospital of St. Thomas the Martyr to pray for my soul, 12d. . . . [Testator's executors include John Weryng, who dwelt within the close of the same Hospital.]

LEPERS IN "LES MESELCOTES," 1401

Prerogative Court of Canterbury, 3 Marche.

Will of Bartholomew Neve, citizen and clothier of London: Item, I bequeath to each leper living in "les Meselcotes" [33] in Kent Street of Southwark a tunic of russet and 20d. . . . To each leper living in "les Meselcotes" of Holborn, one pair of shoes, two water-buckets (j par sitularum), and 12d. . . .

3. Troubles of the Workingman

LABORERS IMPRISONED FOR ACCEPTING ILLEGALLY HIGH WAGES, 1349

Knighton, *Chronicon*, II, 63–64.

Meanwhile the King sent word among the separate companies of the kingdom that reapers and other workers should not take more than they

[33] *Mesel-cote*, leper-house. (*O.E.D.*)

were accustomed to receive under penalty of the fixed statute, and in conformity with this he renewed the statute. The artisans, however, so puffed up and contrary, would not heed the mandate of the King, but if anyone wished to have them it was necessary to pay them according to their wish and either to lose his produce and his crops or satisfy the proud and greedy desire of the workers. Wherefore, when it was known to the King that employers would not obey his mandate and that they granted greater payments to the laborers, he imposed heavy fines upon the abbots and the priors, and upon the greater and lesser knights, and upon others, the more as well as the less important of the kingdom; from some [he exacted] one hundred shillings, from some forty shillings, from some twenty shillings, from each and every person what he could give. . . . Then the King set about to arrest many of the laborers and send them to prison; many such withdrew and hid in the forests and woods for the time, and those who were captured were heavily fined. The greater part of them were bound under oath that they would not take daily payments beyond the old custom, and thus they were freed from prison. In a similar way it happened to the other artisans in the towns and villages.

THE BLACK DEATH OF 1348–1349

The Black Death, which took a heavy toll from all classes of society but probably the heaviest from the working classes, was the cause of the labor problems which Knighton describes. (For attempted governmental regulation, see below, pp. 357–358.) Three contemporary descriptions of this most terrible of plagues follow.

Baker, *Galfridi Le Baker de Swinbroke, Chronicon Angliae,* ed. by Giles, p. 189.

There began amongst the East Indians and Tartarians a certain pestilence, which at length waxed so general, infecting the middle region of the air so greatly, that it destroyed the Saracens, Turks, Syrians, Palestinians, and the Grecians with a wonderful or rather incredible death, insomuch that those peoples, being exceedingly dismayed with the terror thereof, consulted amongst themselves and thought it good to receive the Christian faith and sacraments, for they had intelligence that the Christians which dwelt on this side of the Greekish sea were not so greatly (more than common custom was) troubled with sickness and mortality. At length this terrible slaughter passed over into those countries which are on this side of the Alps, and from thence to the parts of France which are called Hesperia, and so by order along into Germany and Dutchland. And the seventh year after it began, it came into England and first began in the towns and ports joining on the seacoasts, in Dorsetshire, where, ever as in other countries, it made the country quite void of inhabitants, so that there were almost none left alive. From thence it passed into Devonshire and Somersetshire, even unto Bristol, and raged in such sort that the Gloucestershire men would not suffer the Bristol men to have any access unto them or into their country by any means. But at length it came to Gloucester, yea even to Oxford and London, and finally it spread over all England and so wasted and spoiled the people that scarce the tenth person of all sorts was left alive.

Continuation of Higden, *Polychronicon*, VIII, 345, 347.

This year fell great rain from the Feast of the Nativity of St. John [June 24] and lasted till midwinter next thereafter, so that hardly any day passed but it rained by day or by night. That time fell great death of men in all the world wide and began in the southeast part of the country so that hardly half the people were left alive. And in a certain house of religion out of twenty but two were left. . . . Also that year began great dearth of things that should be sold, so that the sale of things was for double the customary price. Also the sea and the land began to wax more barren than they had been before.

Knighton, *Chronicon*, II, 58–59, 61–63.

In this year [1348 and the year following] there was a general mortality among men throughout the world. It began first in India, and then appeared in Tharsis, then among the Saracens, and at last among the Christians and Jews, so that in the space of one year, namely, from Easter to Easter, eight thousand legions of men, according to widely prevalent rumors in the Court of Rome, died in those remote regions, besides Christians. The King of Tharsis, seeing such a sudden and unheard of mortality among his people, set out with a great multitude of nobles, intending to seek out the Pope at Avignon and have himself baptised as a Christian, believing the vengeance of God to have overtaken his people because of their sinful disbelief. But when he had traveled twenty days he heard along the road that the plague had invaded the ranks of the Christians as well as other nations, and therefore he turned about to go back to his own country. But the Christians, following the Tharsians, attacked them from the rear and slew two thousand of them. . . .

The dreadful pestilence penetrated the seacoast by Southampton and came to Bristol, and there almost the whole population of the town perished, as if it had been seized by sudden death; for few kept their beds more than two or three days, or even half a day. Then this cruel death spread everywhere around, following the course of the sun. And there died at Leicester in the small parish of St. Leonard more than three hundred and eighty persons, in the parish of Holy Cross, four hundred, in the parish of St. Margaret's, Leicester, seven hundred; and so in every parish, a great multitude. Then the bishop of London sent word throughout his whole diocese giving general power to each and every priest, regular as well as secular, to hear confessions and to give absolution to all persons with full episcopal authority, except only in case of debt. In this case, the debtor was to pay the debt, if he was able, while he lived, or others were to fulfill his obligations from his property after his death. Likewise the Pope granted full remission of all sins to anyone receiving absolution when in danger of death, and granted that this power should last until Easter next following, and that every one might choose whatever confessor he pleased.

In the same year there was a great murrain of sheep everywhere in the kingdom, so that in one place in a single pasture more than five thousand sheep died; and they putrefied so that neither bird nor beast would touch them. Everything was low in price because of the fear of death, for very few people took any care of riches or property of any kind. A man could have a horse that had been worth 40s. for half a mark [6s. 8d.], a fat ox for 4s., a cow for 12d., a heifer for 6d., a fat wether for 4d., a sheep for 3d., a lamb for 2d., a large pig for 5d.; a stone of wool [24 lbs.] was worth 9d. Sheep and cattle ran at large through the fields and among the crops, and there was none to drive them off or herd them; for lack of care they perished in ditches and hedges in incalculable numbers throughout all districts, and none knew what to do. For there was no memory of death so stern and cruel since the time of Vortigern, king of the Britons, in whose day, as Bede testifies, the living did not suffice to bury the dead.

In the following autumn a reaper was not to be had for a lower wage than 8d., with his meals; a mower for not less than 10d., with meals. Wherefore many crops wasted in the fields for lack of harvesters. But in the year of the pestilence, as has been said above, there was so great an abundance of every kind of grain that almost no one cared for it.

The Scots, hearing of the dreadful plague among the English, suspected that it had come about through the vengeance of God, and, according to the common report, they were accustomed to swear "be the foul deth of Engelond." Believing that the wrath of God had befallen the English, they assembled in Selkirk forest with the intention of invading the kingdom, when the fierce mortality overtook them, and in a short time about five thousand perished. As the rest, the strong and the feeble, were preparing to return to their own country, they were followed and attacked by the English, who slew countless numbers of them.

INFRINGEMENT OF THE STATUTE OF LABORERS BY TWO PLOWMEN, 1352–1353

Latin original printed in Putnam, *The Enforcement of the Statutes of Labourers, 1349–1359*, p. 196 * (from Assize R. 524 m. 2).

The scarcity of labor as a result of the Black Death resulted in exorbitant wages and the consequent inability of landowners to till their lands. Parliament being unable to meet on account of the pestilence, the responsibility of dealing with the emergency fell upon the King's Council; the result was the issue on June 18, 1349, of the famous ordinance of laborers, which attempted to regulate both wages and prices. The main object of the Statute was to secure an adequate supply of laborers at the rate of wages prevailing before the catastrophe.[34]

Lincolnshire. Item, they [the jurors] present that a certain John Skit was in the service of Sir John Dargentene as plowman last summer, and a certain Roger Swynflete, warden of the manor of the Abbot of Seleby at Stallingborough, hired the said John Skit out of his [Dargentene's] service in this winter for six shillings and for the sake of unmixed wheat and as much land as he could sow with two bushels, London measure, of wheat for one crop and also one acre of peas sown for one crop, and for the sake of so great a gain he withdrew from the service of the said Sir John until the Feast of St. Martin last past. And afterwards the said John Skit suspected that he would be indicted before the justices; so he dared not remain, but withdrew to other parts, and thus the said Sir John lost the service of the said servant by the fault and malice of the said Roger and against the Statute of the lord King.

Item, they present that William de Caburn of Lymburgh, plowman, will not take service except by the day and with board (*ad mensam*), and will not eat salt meat but fresh, and for the sake of this he has withdrawn from the town because no one dared hire him after this manner and against the Statute of the lord King.

DEMANDS FOR HIGHER WAGES—REFUSALS TO WORK, 1357

Latin original printed in Putnam, *The Enforcement of the Statutes of Labourers, 1349–1359*, pp. 224*–225* (from Assize R. 971 m. 1 d).

It was against such offenses as the following that the Statute of Laborers was enforced. "The endeavor to check the mobility even of the free laborer seems at first sight an extension of the whole theory of villeinage; but it is to be emphasized that

[34] Putnam, *The Enforcement of the Statutes of Labourers, 1349–1359*, pp. 2–3, 219, 8*–12*.

this provision was merely aimed at preventing a given laborer from refusing the legal wages offered in his own district and going to a place where he could obtain higher wages." [35]

Warwickshire. Divers constables [of Coventry] present . . . that Agnes who has been servant of William Bray will not serve by the year for less than 30s. . . .

The constable of Wyleby presents that William le Cok [and five others] hold only a quarter of land and will not take service. . . .

[The constables] of [Kirkeby] present that . . . Cristiana, wife of Roger Ferst, went away to another town in autumn after she had been required to reap in that town where she dwelt, and took 12d. in excess.

Roger de Barton [of Bulkington] took in excess in autumn 2s. and is unoccupied and will not work or serve. . . .

William Martyn has long been out of work (vacuus) and could work, but he refuses absolutely to do so.

A PREFERENCE FOR BOND SERVICE, 1350

Latin original printed in Putnam, *The Enforcement of the Statutes of Labourers, 1349–1359*, pp. 249*–250* (from Chan. County Placita, Surrey, No. 8 <Wokyngg>, 24 Edward III).

Surrey. William atte Merre of Merrow was attached to answer Peter Semere of a plea why [he refused to serve]—whereas it is ordained that any man and woman of the lord King's realm of England, being able of body and below the age of sixty years, not living by trade or practicing any specific mystery or having his own land about the tilling of which he can occupy himself, not being a servant to another, if he should be required to serve in a service considered fitting to his estate, shall be bound to serve him who so requests and shall take only the wages, liveries, rewards, or salaries which were in force, in the place where he should serve, in the twentieth year of the lord King [36] or the average in the five or six preceding years. The same Peter says that he, on Monday after the Purification of the Blessed Mary [37] in the 24th year aforesaid [1350], at Merrow in the presence of John atte Dene and William Hereward, offered the said William fitting service to serve the said Peter in the town of Merrow, William to receive from the said Peter as is declared in the statute aforesaid, and the said William refused absolutely to serve the said Peter in form aforesaid, and still refuses, in contempt

[35] Putnam, *The Enforcement of the Statutes of Labourers, 1349–1359*, p. 222.
[36] That is, in 1346, well before the Black Death.
[37] The Feast of the Purification (of the Virgin Mary) is February 2.

of the lord King and against the ordinance of the said statute and to the damage of the said Peter in 100s. . . .

And the said William . . . says that he cannot serve the said Peter, because, he says, he is a villein (*nativus*) of the prior and convent of the Blessed Mary of Boxgrave, of their manor of Merrow, and that the prior of the church aforesaid who now is was seised of him as of his villein and of his services as villein in right of his church . . . and that the said prior and all his predecessors from time immemorial have been seised of him and of all his ancestors as of their villein, to tallage them high and low, and to take from them redemptions for the marriage of their daughters as in right of their said church; and he says that the prior and convent let the said manor with the appurtenances to John Chene . . . for his life, and that the said John Chene has the said William in his necessary service in the said manor. . . .

And because the judges had their suspicions as to the admissions of the said William, they offered him a book to swear that he was speaking truth concerning the above matters; and he took his oath as above. Wherefore it was adjudged that the said Peter should take nothing by his complaint, and that the said William should serve the said John Chene as his lord. Thereupon he is delivered to Walter de Wernham, the bailiff of the said John Chene, to serve him according to statute and the custom of the said manor.

RECOVERING A VILLEIN, 1381

Common Pleas, Plea Roll 482 m. 198.

London. John Lovell, knight, was attached to answer Walter Ethulf in a plea why he assaulted the said Walter at London by force and arms and beat, wounded, and imprisoned him, ill-treated him, and committed other enormities against him to the grave damage of the said Walter and against the King's peace. And whereof Walter complains in person that the said John on the first day of April in the fourth year of the now King [1381] by force and arms, to wit, with swords and bows and arrows, assaulted the said Walter at London in the parish of St. Bride in the ward of Farringdon Without, and beat, wounded, and imprisoned him, namely, from the said first day of April and for the two days following . . . whereof he has damages of £10. . . .

And the said John in his own person comes and says that the said Walter ought not to be answered to his said writ because he says that the same Walter is his villein as of his manor of Southmere in the county of

Norfolk and that he and his ancestors, lords of the manor aforesaid, have been seised of the said Walter and his ancestors as of their villeins belonging to the manor aforesaid from time without mind. And this he is ready to prove; whereof he seeks judgment whether the same Walter ought to be answered to the writ aforesaid.

And the said Walter says that he cannot deny that he is villein of the aforenamed John Lovell belonging to his manor aforesaid, as the same John in his pleading above has alleged. Therefore it is adjudged that the said John go *sine die* and the said Walter take nothing by his writ, but let him be in mercy.

4. *The Rising of the Peasants* [38]

JOHN BALL AND HIS PREACHING, 1381

Walsingham, *Historia Anglicana*, II, 32-34.

In this time John Ball, priest, who had been taken by men of Coventry and brought to St. Alban's and into the presence of his majesty the King, and who had confessed to the most shameful of evil deeds, was convicted . . . and sentenced by [the judge], Sir Robert Tresilian, to be drawn, hanged, beheaded, disemboweled, and quartered. His death was delayed through the intervention of Sir William, bishop of London, who, being solicitous concerning the salvation of his soul, secured for him time for repentance. For twenty years and more this man had been all the time preaching in various places things which he knew were pleasing to the common people, speaking evil of both ecclesiastics and secular lords, and had won the benevolence of the common people rather than merit in the sight of God. For he taught the people that tithes ought not to be paid unless he who should give them was richer than the vicar or rector who received them; and that tithes and oblations ought to be withheld if the parishioner was known to be a better man than his curate; and also that none are fit for the Kingdom of God who are not born in matrimony. He taught, moreover, the perverse doctrines of the perfidious John Wycliffe, his opinions and his follies, with many other things that it would be tedious to recite. Wherefore, being prohibited by the bishops from preaching in churches, he began speaking in

[38] "That Chaucer was in London during the Peasants' Revolt of 1381 is indicated by the fact that during this very time he quit-claimed his father's house in Thames Street to Henry Herbury (one of the collectors of the poll tax that had brought about the revolt); but that he was involved in it is unknown." (Chaucer, *Canterbury Tales*, ed. by Manly, p. 21; cf. *Life-Records of Chaucer*, IV, 232.)

streets and villages and in the open fields. Nor did he lack hearers among the common people, whom he always strove to entice to his sermons by slander of the prelates and by pleasing words. At last, having been excommunicated because he would not desist, he was imprisoned, whereupon he predicted that he would be liberated by twenty thousand of his friends —which afterwards happened in the great disturbances, when the commons broke open all the prisons and set the prisoners free.

And when he had thus been set free, he followed them, instigating them to perpetrate greater evils and saying that such things must surely be done. And, to corrupt the more with his doctrine, at Blackheath, where twenty thousand of the commons were gathered together, he began a discourse in this fashion:

"When Adam delved and Eve span,
    Who was then a gentleman?"

And continuing the sermon he strove to prove, by the words of the proverb that he had taken for his theme, that from the beginning all men were created equal by nature and that servitude had been introduced by the unjust oppressions of evil men, against the will of God, who, if it had pleased him to create serfs, surely in the beginning of the world would have determined who should be a serf and who a lord. Let them consider, therefore, that a time was now given them by God, a time in which they might lay aside the yoke of long servitude and, if they wished, enjoy their liberty. Wherefore they should be prudent men, and, with a love of a good husbandman tilling his field and uprooting the tares that are wont to destroy the grain, they should first kill the great lords of the kingdom, then slay the lawyers, justices, and jurors, and finally root out everyone who they knew would be harmful to the community in the future. Thus they would obtain peace and security in the future, if, when the great ones had been removed, there were among them equal liberty and nobility, and like dignity and power.

And when he had preached this and much other nonsense, the common people held him in such high favor that they acclaimed him the future archbishop and chancellor of the realm, for, they said, he alone was worthy of the office, the present archbishop being a traitor to the realm and the commons, who should be beheaded wherever in England he could be seized.

Moreover, he sent a letter to the commons in Essex, full of enigmatic statements, urging them to finish what they had begun; this was afterwards found upon a man who was to be hanged for taking part in the disturbance, and ran as follows: "John Schep, sometime priest of St. Mary's, York, and now of Colchester, greeteth well John Nameless and John the Miller and John Carter, and biddeth them that they beware of guile in the town and stand together in God's name; and biddeth Piers Plowman go to his work and chastise well Hob the Robber, and take with you John Trueman and all his fellows and no more, and look sharp to your own head, and no more.

> "John the Miller hath ground small, small, small:
> The King's Son of heaven shall pay for all;
> Beware, or ye will be in woe,
> Knoweth your friend from your foe;
> Haveth enough and sayeth 'Ho.'
> And do well and better and fleeth sin
> And seeketh peace, and hold therein,
> And so biddeth John Trueman and all his fellows."

The said John Ball confessed that he had written this letter and sent it to the commons and owned that he had written many more. Wherefore he was drawn, hanged, and beheaded at St. Albans on the 15th of July, in the King's presence; and his corpse was quartered and sent into four parts of the kingdom.

WAT TYLER'S INSURRECTION, 1381

The Anonimalle Chronicle, 1333–1381, ed. by Galbraith, pp. 141–143.

The following account of the Peasants' Revolt is commonly agreed to be the best. It was interpolated in the *Anonimalle Chronicle* of St. Mary's, York, but is believed to be based on a London account which was in part that of an eyewitness. As the narrative is far too long to be quoted in full, the most interesting parts which concern London itself have been chosen. [R.]

At the same time the commons took their way to London and did no harm or damage until they came to Fleet Street. There, it was said, the commons of London had set fire to and burned the fair manor of Savoy before the arrival of the mob from the country.

In Fleet Street the commons from Kent broke open Fleet Prison and took out all the prisoners and let them go where they would. Then they stopped and pulled down to earth and set fire to a chandler's shop and a blacksmith's shop in the middle of the street, where, it was supposed, there would never be a shop because of spoiling the beauty of the street.

Afterwards they went to the Temple to destroy the tenants of the

Temple; and they pulled down the houses to earth and tore off all the tiles so that they were unroofed and in bad condition. Then they went to the church and took all the books and rolls and records which were in their chests within the Temple of the apprentices of the law and carried them to the great chimney and there burned them.

And in going towards the Savoy they destroyed all the houses which belonged to the Master of the Hospital of St. John. Then they went to the palace of the bishop of Chester, near the church of St. Mary-of-the-Strand, where was living Sir John Fordham, bishop-elect of Durham and clerk of the privy seal; and they rolled tuns of wine out of his cellar and drank their fill and so departed without doing more harm.

Then they went to the Savoy and set fire to divers houses of various people . . . on the west. At last they came to the Savoy itself and broke open the gates and entered the place [court?] and came to the wardrobe and took all the torches they could find and put them in the fire; [39] and all the cloths and coverlets and beds and hangings of great value, whereof one with *escutes* [40] was said to be worth a thousand marks, and all the napery and other goods which they could find they carried into the hall and set fire to them with the torches, and they burned the hall and chambers and all the rooms within the gates belonging to the place or manor, which the London mob had left without guard. And it was said that they found three barrels of gunpowder, and, thinking it was gold or silver, they threw it into the fire, and it exploded and set the hall on fire and in flame more quickly than the other did, to the great discomfort and damage of the Duke of Lancaster.

The commons of Kent were blamed for the fire, but some said that the London people did it from hatred of the duke.

Then a party of them went to Westminster and set afire a place belonging to John de Butterwyk, sub-sheriff of Middlesex, and houses of various other people and took away all prisoners condemned by the law and returned to London by way of Holborn. Before the church of St. Sepulchre they set afire the houses of Symond Hosteler and several other houses, and they broke into Newgate and took out all the prisoners, regardless of the cause for which they had been imprisoned.

That same Thursday the mob went to St. Martin's-le-Grand and took out of the church, from the high altar, one Roger Legett, chief tailor, and led him to Cheapside and there beheaded him. That same day eighteen persons were beheaded in different parts of the town.

[39] That is, to light them. [40] Scutes,—heraldic shields, escutcheons. (Godefroy; *O.E.D.*)

At that time a large part of the mob went to the Tower of London to speak with the King, and, as they could not get a hearing, they set siege to the Tower from the side of St. Katherine's on the south. Another part of them who were in the city went to the Hospital of St. John of Clerkenwell, and . . . burned the place and the houses of Roger Legett, questmonger, who had been beheaded in Cheapside. . . . Afterwards they went to the fair priory of the Hospital and set it afire and burned also several fair and pleasant rooms in the priory itself, with great and horrible damage for all time to come. Afterwards they returned to London, to rest or to get into mischief.

During this time the King, being in a turret of the great Tower of London, saw the manor of the Savoy and Clerkenwell and the houses of Symond Hosteler by Newgate and the place of John de Butterwyk in flames, and he called all the lords about him into a room and asked their advice as to what should be done in such a crisis. None of them could or would suggest anything; whereupon the young King said he would order the Mayor of the City to command the sheriffs and aldermen to have cried in their wards that everyone between the ages of fifteen and sixty, on pain of life and limb, should be on the morrow at Mile End and meet him there at seven of the bell.

ANOTHER ACCOUNT OF THE SAME, 1381

Riley, *Memorials of London*, II, 449–451 (from London Letter-Book H, fol. cxxxiii).

Among the most wondrous and hitherto unheard-of prodigies that have ever happened in the city of London, that which took place there on the Feast of Corpus Christi,[41] the thirteenth day of June in the fourth year of the reign of King Richard the Second [1381], seems deserving to be committed to writing that it may be not unknown to those to come.

For on that day, while the King was holding his council in the Tower of London, countless companies of the commoners and persons of the lowest grade from Kent and Essex suddenly approached the said city, the one body coming to the town of Southwark and the other to the place called Mile End, without Aldgate. By the aid within the city of perfidious commoners of their own conditions, who rose in countless numbers there, they suddenly entered the city together, and, passing straight through it, went to the Duke of Lancaster's mansion, called the Savoy,

[41] The feast of Corpus Christi is observed on the Thursday after Trinity Sunday.

and completely leveled the same with the ground and burned it. From thence they turned to the church of the Hospital of St. John of Jerusalem, without Smithfield, and burnt and leveled nearly all the houses there, the church excepted.

On the next morning all the men from Kent and Essex met at the said place called Mile End, together with some of the perfidious persons of the city aforesaid, whose numbers in all were past reckoning. And there the King came to them from the Tower, accompanied by many knights and esquires and citizens on horseback, the lady his mother [42] also following him in a chariot.[43] There at the prayer of the infuriated rout our lord the King granted that they might take those who were traitors against him and slay them, wheresoever they might be found. And from thence the King rode to his wardrobe,[44] which is situate near to Castle Baynard, while the whole of the infuriated rout took its way towards the Tower of London. Entering it by force, they dragged forth Sir Simon, archbishop of Canterbury, chancellor of our lord the King, and Brother Robert Hales, prior of the said Hospital of St. John of Jerusalem, the King's treasurer; and, together with them, Brother William Appeltone of the Order of Friars Minor, and John Leg, sergeant-at-arms to the King, and also one Richard Somenour of the parish of Stebenhithe. All of these they beheaded in the place called Tower Hill without the said Tower, and then carrying their heads through the city upon lances, they set them up on London Bridge, fixing them there on stakes.

Upon the same day there was also no little slaughter within the city, as well of natives as of aliens. Richard Lions, citizen and vintner of the said city, and many others were beheaded in Cheapside. In the Vintry also there was a very great massacre of Flemings, and in one heap there were lying about forty headless bodies of persons who had been dragged forth from the churches and from their houses; and hardly was there a street in the city in which there were not bodies lying of those who had been slain. Some of the houses also in the said city were pulled down, others in the suburbs destroyed, and others burnt.

[42] Joan, countess of Kent, known as "the fair maid of Kent." She was married to Edward, "the Black Prince," in 1361.
[43] Or *whirlicote*, as the ladies' chariots were called in those days. [Riley's note.]
[44] The building in which the officers of the wardrobe department of a royal or noble household conduct their business. (*O.E.D.*)

Such tribulation as this, greater and more horrible than could be believed by those who had not seen it, lasted down to the hour of vespers on the following day, which was Saturday the fifteenth of June. On this day God sent remedy for the same and His own gracious aid, by the hand of the most renowned man Sir William Walworth,[45] the then mayor, who in Smithfield in the presence of our lord the King and those standing by him, lords, knights, esquires, and citizens on horseback, on the one side, and the whole of this infuriated rout on the other, most manfully by himself rushed upon the captain of the said multitude, Walter Tyler by name, and, as he was altercating with the King and the nobles, first wounded him in the neck with his sword and then hurled him from his horse, mortally pierced in the breast. And further, by favor of divine grace, he so defended himself from those who had come with him, both on foot and on horseback, that he departed from thence unhurt and rode on with our lord the King and his people towards a field near to the spring that is called Whittewellebeche; in which place, while the whole of the infuriated multitude in warlike manner was making ready against our lord the King and his people, refusing to treat of peace except on condition that they should first have the head of the said mayor, the mayor himself, who had gone into the city at the instance of our lord the King, in the space of half an hour sent and led forth therefrom so great a force of citizen warriors in aid of his lord the King that the whole multitude of madmen was surrounded and hemmed in; and not one of them would have escaped, if our lord the King had not given orders to allow them to depart.

Therefore our lord the king returned into the city of London with the greatest of glory and honor, and the whole of this profane multitude in confusion fled forthwith for concealment in their affright.

For this same deed our lord the King, beneath his standard in the said field, with his own hands decorated with the order of knighthood the said mayor and Sir Nicholas Brembre [46] and Sir John Philipot, who had already been mayors of the said city, as also Sir Robert Laund.

[45] Sir William Walworth, Sir Nicholas Brembre, and Sir John Philipot were all collectors of the customs while Chaucer was controller—the two latter for many years. Walworth, with Brembre and Philipot, was knighted for his gallant conduct during the Wat Tyler rebellion. (Chaucer, *Canterbury Tales*, ed. by Manly, p. 42.)

[46] See above, p. 158.

ANOTHER ACCOUNT OF THE SAME (WRITTEN BY THE ALMONER
OF BURY ABBEY), 1381

Powell, *The Rising in East Anglia in 1381*, p. 139 (from Cott. Claud. A xii [B.M.]
fol. 131 b).

In that year . . . . well ten days before the Feast of St. John the
Baptist [47] because of the burdensome tax on the Kingdom, namely, 12*d*.
per head from the fifteenth year upwards, the accursed company of
country villeins and of the rustics in the Eastern coast that is Kent,
Essex, Suffolk, Norfolk, and from the counties of Cambridgeshire and
Hertfordshire, rose and thought to extinguish the King's council, the
lawyers, gentlemen, and the powerful throughout the kingdom. From
the Tower of London, where the King was present, they dragged the
archbishop of Canterbury, then chancellor of England, and the master
of the Hospital of St. John, a knight, treasurer of England, and beheaded
them upon the Hill near the Tower. They put to death cruelly many
others, especially those from Flanders; they burned to the ground the
stately mansion called the Savoy, which belonged to the Duke of Lancaster, and the Hospital of St. John; and as these did in London who
were mostly from Kent, so others at the same time rose in the said counties
and performed like evil deeds.

[The rest concerns attacks on the Monks of St. Edmund.]

A STREET SCENE IN THE RISING, 1381

Common Pleas, Plea Roll 480 m. 252 d.

In Michaelmas term, 4 Richard II [1381], John de Salesbury, gold-
smith, sued William de Denton, chaplain, as to three messuages in
Southwark. The case was adjourned until [eventually] in Michaelmas
term, 5 Richard II [1382], William answered that the writ ought to
be quashed because, pending the action, John had entered the premises.
John replied: In the detestable tumult, which recently arose, many malefactors, overthrowers of society, pulled down and destroyed a messuage
next to the said tenements, whereupon the said John, fearing that the
malefactors would pull down and destroy the said tenements, went on
his knees before them in the street, telling them that the said tenements
had been at one time his ancestors' and that he had a certain writ pending
concerning these tenements in the King's Court against the said William,

---

[47] The Feast of St. John the Baptist is June 24.

begging and praying them especially for the love of God not to do any damage to the said tenements, and he did not enter the tenements.

[Judgment for John.]

AN ECHO OF THE PEASANTS' RISING, 1382

Common Pleas, Plea Roll 486 m. 349.

Kent. Geoffrey Cartere of Sittingbourne was attached to answer Simon Hey in a plea why he, together with William Coupere of Kekkyngbourne, John Flecchere of Ospringe, William Coupere that was Jak servant Strowe,[48] and John Date Soutere, by force and arms broke the close and houses of Simon at Ospringe and burned the timber from the said houses to the value of £10 and took away his goods and chattels to the value of £20 and £32 in money there, and consumed two tuns of wine of the same Simon to the value of £10, which they found there. . . .

Whereof he complained that the said Geoffrey together with [the rest] on the morrow of Trinity [49] in the fourth year of the now King [1381] by force and arms, to wit with swords and bows and arrows, broke the close of the said Simon at Ospringe and burned the timber from the said houses, namely, posts, beams, ties, rafters, doors, and windows to the value of [£10] and took his linen and woollen cloths, brass and copper vessels, gold and silver rings [50] to the value of [£20] and £32 of money and consumed two tuns of red wine of the said Simon.

[He pleaded not guilty; the case was adjourned.]

[48] Jack Straw's servant (?).
[49] That is, June 9.   [50] These are formal descriptions of goods stolen.

9. Religion

CHURCH AND CHURCHMEN

1. A Parson's Reminiscences of His Old Church, 1386

Scrope, De controversia . . . inter Ricardum Le Scrope et Robertum Grosvenor, I, 129–130.

Sir Simon, parson of the church of Winslow, of the age of sixty and upwards, said that certainly the arms azure, a bend or, appertained to Sir Richard Scrope, for they were in his church of Winslow in certain glass windows of that church, of which Sir Richard was patron; and on the west gable window of the said church were the entire arms of Sir Richard Scrope in a glass window, the setting up of which arms was beyond the memory of man. The said arms were also in divers other parts of the said church, and in his chancel in a glass window, and in the east gable also were the said arms placed amongst the arms of great lords, such as the King, the Earl of Northumberland, the Lord of Neville, the Earl of Warren. He said also that there was a tomb in the cemetery of Simon Scrope, as might be seen by the inscription on the tomb, who was buried in the ancient fashion in a stone chest, with the inscription "Cy gist [1] Simond le Scrope," without date. And after Simon Scrope lieth one Henry Scrope, son of the said Simon, in the same manner as his father, next the side of his father, in the same cemetery. And after him lieth William, son of the said Henry Scrope, who lieth in the manner aforesaid beneath the stone, and there is graven thereon "Ycy gist William le Scrope," without date, for the bad weather, wind, snow, and rain had so defaced it that no man could make out the remainder of the writing, so old and defaced was it. Several others of his lineage and name were buried there, one after the other, under large square stones, which being so massive were sunk into the earth, so that no more of the stone than the summit of it could be seen; and many more of their sons and daughters were buried under great stones. From William came Henry Scrope, knight, who lieth in the abbey of St. Agatha, armed in the arms azure, a bend or, which Sir Henry was founder of the said abbey; and Sir William Scrope, elder brother of Sir Richard that now is, lieth in the

[1] *Ci gît,* here lies.

same abbey in the same arms depicted, but not painted. The said Sir Simon placed before the commissioners an alb with flaps (*aube ove pairuers*), upon which were embroidered the arms of the Scropes entire, the making of which arms and the name of the donor were beyond the memory of man. He added that the patronage of his church of Winslow had always been vested in Sir Richard Scrope, beyond the memory of man; and that the arms azure, a bend or, had always been reputed to belong to him and his ancestors, and he never heard to the contrary; he had never heard that the arms had been challenged, or of Sir Richard Grosvenor or any of his ancestors.

2. A Church Shrine: a Tourist's Description of the Tomb of Thomas à Becket, time of Henry VII

A Relation . . . of the Island of England, tr. by Sneyd, pp. 30–31.

But the magnificence of the tomb of St. Thomas the Martyr, archbishop of Canterbury, is that which surpasses all belief. This, notwithstanding its great size, is entirely covered over with plates of pure gold; but the gold is scarcely visible from the variety of precious stones with which it is studded, such as sapphires, diamonds, rubies, balasrubies, and emeralds; and on every side that the eye turns something more beautiful than the other appears. And these beauties of nature are enhanced by human skill, for the gold is carved and engraved in beautiful designs, both large and small, and agates, jaspers, and carnelians set in relievo, some of the cameos being of such a size that I do not dare to mention it; but everything is left far behind by a ruby, not larger than a man's thumbnail, which is set to the right of the altar. The church is rather dark, and particularly so where the shrine is placed, and when we went to see it the sun was nearly gone down, and the weather was cloudy; yet I saw that ruby as well as if I had it in my hand; they say that it was the gift of a king of France.

3. Church Relics: Recovery of the Head of St. Hugh of Lincoln, 1364

Knighton, *Chronicon*, II, 120.

At the same time thieves and robbers increased in the kingdom and plundered churches, biers of the saints, and carried off the relics, namely, from the abbacy of Thornton, the image of the Lord at Merivale and the image of the Lord at Monkskirby and at many other places. Many of them were taken captive and hanged. Likewise the head of St. Hugh of Lincoln [2] was stolen, and, after taking the silver and gold and precious stones, they threw the head in a certain field. And as is wonderful to relate, a certain raven, as the story went, guarded this until it was known through these same robbers and carried to Lincoln.

4. Sermons

PREACHING AT PAUL'S CROSS, 1398

Stow, *A Survey of London*, I, 167–168.

And here is to be noted that time out of mind it hath been a laudable custom that on Good Friday in the afternoon some especial learned man, by appointment of the prelates, hath preached a sermon at Paul's Cross, treating of Christ's passion; and upon the three next Easter holy days, Monday, Tuesday, and Wednesday, the like learned men, by the like appointment have used to preach on the forenoons at the said Spittle [3] to persuade the Article of Christ's resurrection; and then on Low Sunday one other learned man at Paul's Cross, to make rehearsal of those four sermons, either commending or reproving them, as to him by judgment of the learned divines was thought convenient. And that done, he was to make a sermon of his own study, which in all were five sermons in one. At these sermons so severally preached, the mayor and his brethren the aldermen were accustomed to be present in their violets at Paul's on Good Friday, and in their scarlets at the Spittle in the Holy days, except Wednesday in violet, and the mayor with his brethren on Low Sunday in scarlet, at Paul's Cross. . . .

Touching the antiquity of this custom, I find that in the year 1398 King Richard, having procured from Rome confirmation of such statutes and ordinances as were made in the Parliament begun at Westminster and ended at Shrewsbury, caused the same confirmation to be read and pronounced at Paul's Cross and at St. Mary Spittle in the sermons before all the people.

[2] Two saints were known as St. Hugh of Lincoln. The first, known also as Hugh of Avalon (1140?–1200), a member of the Carthusian Order, rebuilt Lincoln cathedral after the earthquake of 1185. His shrine was located in the south transept. The second St. Hugh is the English boy saint asserted to have been slain by Jews of Lincoln in 1255. His remains were credited with miracles, and his shrine was erected in the south choir aisle of the minster. Chaucer tells the story of his death in the "Prioress's Tale." To which St. Hugh Knighton refers in the above passage it is impossible to say.

[3] Saint Mary Spittle, founded 1197 (*spittle, spital*, a hospital).

AN EXEMPLUM FROM A MEDIEVAL SERMON, EARLY 13TH CENTURY

Jacobus de Vitriaco, *The Exempla*, pp. 22, 157 (from "Exempla ex sermonibus vulgaribus Jacobi Vitriacensis," Bib. Nat. MS Lat. 17509, fol. 50).

There was once a priest who thought he sang well, although he had a horrible voice like an ass's. On a certain day a woman who heard him sing began to weep. The priest, thinking his sweet voice incited her to tears and devotion, sang the louder. The woman wept the more. Then he asked her why she wept, and she said: "Sir, I am that wretched woman whose ass the wolf devoured the other day, and when I hear you singing, I remember that my ass was wont to sing so." The priest, having heard this, reddened; from whence he thought to receive praise he received shamefacedness instead.

5. *Some Medieval Churchmen*

BISHOP

John of Reading, *Chronica*, pp. 177–178.

Although John of Reading's opinion concerning William of Wykeham, bishop of Winchester and chancellor of England, may be narrow-minded or even prejudiced, it represents one side of a considerable controversy between church and state which arose at the time of Wykeham's election to the bishopric in 1366. Wykeham had become a most influential figure at the court of Edward III, and it was at the King's instance that the monks of Winchester chose Wykeham, already rewarded by the King with many rich livings, prebends, and deaneries. The pope (Urban V) delayed investiture of the bishop-elect for some time, possibly because of Wykeham's reputation as a mighty pluralist. The reforming element of the church also opposed him; Wycliffe growled at the preferment of clerks "wise in building castles or worldly doing." Nevertheless, through the insistence of Edward, Wykeham was made bishop.

The duties of his high office he fulfilled honorably. James Tait, editor of John of Reading's *Chronica*, drawing from other contemporary sources than the *Chronica* (*e.g.*, *Chronicon Angliae* and *Historia Anglicana*) in his article on Wykeham in the *Dictionary of National Biography* (LXIII, 225–231), shows the bishop to have been gentle and moderate, generous and kindly to the poor and the old of his see and much interested in education. He is well known as the founder of New College, Oxford (built 1380–1386), and of Winchester College (built 1388–1394). Wykeham had earlier (1356) been clerk of the king's works, a position which Chaucer held from 1389–1391.

Bishops good and bad, 1366. In this year, in the month of October, the see of Winchester was deprived of its good bishop by the death of Sir William de Edington, who before his death distributed alms and gifts most generously. . . . For which see the pope, influenced by golden letters [4] as well as entreaties, provided [by appointing] a certain servant of the lord King, William Wykeham, influenced more by fear than by

[4] Bribes.

love, and setting aside more worthy men who had been chosen before.
Alas! the mammon of iniquity raises the unworthy to be prelates.

MONK

Gower, "Mirour de l'omme," ll. 20,953–20,976.

"A Fish Out of Water," [5] *ca. 1376–1379*

> That monk is not a good cloisterer
> Who is made keeper or seneschal
> Of some office which is outside;
> For he must have horse and saddle
> To run about the lands
> And he spends with generous hand;
> He keeps for himself the best of the grain,
> And like a wretch leaves to the others
> The straw, and so like a lord
> The monk becomes silly and vain.
> With an empty grange and a full stomach
> No account will be kept balanced.
> Of charity that is incomplete,
> "All is ours," says this monk,
> When he is keeper of a manor.
> This is part of the truth but not all;
> For he with his mad appetite
> Would have more than seven others.
> Such a keeper, to speak truth,
> The cloister had better drive out than keep,
> Since he takes from others their profit.
> Saint Bernard it is who tells us
> It is an evil thing to see
> A bailiff in monk's habit.

FRIAR

Gower, "Mirour de l'omme," ll. 21,373–21,384.

A greedy friar, ca. 1376–1379

> Oh, how the friar behaves himself
> When he comes to the house of a poor man!
> Oh, well he knows how to preach!

[5] Cf. Chaucer, *Canterbury Tales*, A, ll. 179–181.

Though the woman has little or nothing,
No less for that does he refrain
From claiming, praying, adjuring;
The halfpenny he takes if there's no penny,
Even the only egg there is for supper—
He has to have something.
"Woe," says God, "upon the vagabond
Who comes thus to visit
The house that a poor woman keeps!"

John of Reading, *Chronica*, p. 119.

An opinion about friars, 1354. In this year, the week before Pentecost, in Avignon, certain Friars Minor were burned to death on account of certain heretical opinions. This horrible punishment ought to be inflicted upon the Order of Mendicants, because in their sermons and disputations they have always maintained heretical and other opinions contrary to holy faith and the church. If they persist in these and other perverse views of this kind, even if they are not burned in material fire, they will undoubtedly, unless they recant, descend into eternal fire.

Song against the friars, ca. 1380

Wright (ed.), *Political Poems and Songs*, I, 263–268 (from Cott. MS Cleop. B. ii [B.M.] fol. 62b).

Priest, nor monk, nor yet canon,
  Nor any man of religion,
  Gives himself so to devotion
    As do these holy friars.
For some give them to chivalry,
  Some to riot and ribaldry;
  But friars give them to great study,
    And to great prayers.
Whoso keeps their rules all,
    Both in word and deed,
I am full certain that he shall
    Have Heaven's bliss for meed.

Men may see by their countenance
That they are men of great penance,
And also that their sustenance
    Simple is and weak.

I have lived now forty years,
And fatter men about the ears
Saw I never than are these friars,
   In countries that they seek.
Meatless so meager are they made,
   And penance so puts them down,
That each one is a full horse-load,
   When he shall truss from town.

Alas! that ever it should be so,
Such clerks as they about should go,
From town to town by two and two,
   To seek their sustenance.
By God that all this world won,
He that that Order first began,
Methinketh certes it was a man
   Of simple ordinance.
For they have nought to live by;
   They wander here and there,
And deal with divers mercery,
   As if they pedlars were.

They deal with purses, pins, and knives,
With girdles, gloves, for maids and wives;
But ever the worse the husband thrives
   As long as they haunt him still.
For when the goodman is from hame,
And the friar comes to our dame,
He spares neither for sin nor shame,
   But that he does his will.
If they no help of housewives had,
   When husbands are not in,
The friars' welfare were full bad,
   For they should brew full thin.

Some friars carry furs about,
For great ladies and maids stout,
To reverse [6] there with their clothes without,—

6 Trim (?).

All after that they are.
For some *vair*, and some *gris*,
For some *budge*, and for some *bis* [7]
And also many a divers spice,
 In bags about they bear.
All that for woman is pleasant
 Full ready certes have they;
But little care they for the husband
 That for all shall pay.

Tricks they ken and many a joke;
For some can with a pound of soap
Get them a kirtle and a cope,
 And somewhat else thereto.
Whereto should I oaths swear?
There is no pedlar that pack can bear,
That half so dear can sell his gear,
 As a friar can do.
For if he give a wife a knife
 That cost but pennies two,
Worth ten knives, so may I thrive,
 He will have ere he go.

Each man that here shall lead his life,
That has a fair daughter or a wife,
Beware that no friar them shrive,
 Neither loud nor still.
Though women seem of heart full stable
With fair behest and with fable
They can make their hearts changeable,
 And their likings fulfill.
Beware aye with the limitour,
 And with his fellow too;
If they have mastery in thy bower,
 It shall thee undo.

They say that they destroy sin,
 And they maintain men most therein;

[7] All of these terms refer to kinds of fur.

For had a man slain all his kin,
　Go shrive him at a friar
And for less than a pair of shoon
He will assoil him clean and soon,
And say the sin that he has done
　His soul shall not injure.
It seems sooth what men say of them
　In many a diverse land,
That that caitif cursed Caim
　First this Order found.

Now see the sooth of what they say:
The Carmelites come of a *k*,
The Austin Friars come of an *a*,
　Friar Jacobins of *i*,
Of *m* come the Friars Minors;
Thus founded Kaim these four Orders,
That fill the world full of errors,
　And of hypocrisy.
All wickedness that men can tell
　Reigns them among;
There shall no soul have room in Hell,
　Of friars there is such throng.

They labor hard and busily
To bring down the clergy;
Speaking thereof ay villainy,
　And thereof they do wrong.
Whoso lives on for many years
Shall see it shall befall with friars
As it did with the Templars
　That dwelled here us among.
For they held no religion,
　But lived after their liking;
They were destroyed and brought adown
　Through ordinance of the king.

These friars do a dreadful thing
That never shall come to good ending:

One friar for eight or nine shall sing,
  For ten or for eleven.
And when his term is fully gone,
Conscience then has he none;
He dares to take from everyone
  Marks full six or seven.
Such revenue has made these friars
  So prosperous and so gay,
That there may no possessioners
  Maintain their array.

Their lot is to live all by purchase,[8]
By alms-getting from place to place,
And for everyone who helped them has,
  Should they pray and sing.
But now so through the land they fare
That scarcely may a priest secular
Get any service because of a friar.
  That is a wonder thing,
This is a quaint custom
  Ordained them among,
That friars shall annual priests become
  And thuswise sell their song.

Full wisely can they preach and say;
But as they preach nothing do they.
I was a friar full many a day,
  Therefore the truth I know.
But when I saw that their living
Accorded not with their preaching,
Off I cast my friar's clothing,
  And quickly away did go.
Other leave took I none,
  From them when I went,
But left them to the devil, each one,
  The prior and the convent.

---

[8] *Purchase* originally meant "property obtained in any way except by inheritance or the mere act of law." The word was often used with a suggestion of fraud. (Chaucer, *Canterbury Tales*, ed. by Manly, p. 513.)

PARDONER.

Catholic Church, Councils, *Sacrorum conciliorum . . . collectio*, Vol. XXVI.

Attempts to restrain the evil practices of pardoners, 1348, 1368, 1374.
Because questors of alms (pardoners) in their preaching advocate many
evil practices by which they often deceive the simple-minded and because
they distort that which is good by their subtle and fraudulent character
and at the same time do much evil through their manifold deceptions,
we have determined and do ordain that no pardoners whatever be permitted without letters of their archbishop or of their bishop; and that
the welfare of souls may the more carefully be provided for, we rule that
the words of this decree be inserted in their letters. . . . Nor by any
other way, except by canonical law, are they to be permitted to operate.
Priests who, by any other than the aforesaid way, voluntarily and knowingly permit pardoners to preach are *ipso facto* prohibited for a year
from celebrating masses; and the pardoners themselves who attempt to
contravene this decree are *ipso facto* excommunicated. If for forty days
they persist in their course, they may, at the command of the bishop, be
seized and imprisoned, until such time as their case may otherwise be
disposed of by the local diocesan. Letters of any kind granted previously
to pardoners are hereby revoked. [Col. 117.]

Concerning questors for churches, hospitals, or bridges we decree by these
presents and through the authority of the Council that without letters
from us or from their bishops none are to be received. Nor are they to
be permitted to preach. . . . And if they should presume to preach,
they may be seized and corrected in such a way that their punishment
will serve as an example to others. [Col. 541.] [9]

Exchequer, King's Remembrancer, Writs, 52. Mich. 45 Edw. III.

A forged bull, 1371. Precept is issued to sheriffs of London and Middlesex to distrain Walter de Serleby and John de Halle to account for
moneys collected from many faithful for the remission of sin by a bull
forged by Ralph Churcheman, proctor of William Warden of the Hospital of St. Mary of Bethlehem without Bishopsgate.

[9] This decree, of 1368, was repeated in 1374 with slight changes in wording.

Common Pleas, Plea Roll 515 m. 568 d.

A thieving pardoner, 1389. Middlesex. John Gibbes of Baldurton, by his attorney, brings suit against Richard Arderne, pardoner, for taking goods and chattels to the value of 40 marks in the parish of St. Sepulchre, outside the Bar of West Smithfield, London, [etc.].

CANON

Chancery Warrants (Privy Seal Writs) 555/10218, 10211.

A pugnacious canon, 1395. Petition of Robert Chircheman, citizen and stockfishmonger of London, that, whereas he went peaceably to Waltham Holy Cross on Saturday Eve of the Assumption of Blessed Virgin Mary,[10] 19 Richard II, with a warranty for security directed to the abbot's bailiff Thomas Chamberleyn, William Double, smith of Waltham, [who had been] procured by Chircheman's enemies, William Harleston, Canon of Waltham, and Peter Clerk, called Hereford, aided and abetted by other servants of the abbot, dressed as women, beat him with sticks and broke two of his ribs and cast him into a ditch, leaving him for dead.

September 11, 19 Richard II. Warrant [Privy Seal] to the King's sergeant-at-arms, John Elingeham, to arrest the canon, the smith, and the rest and to bring them into the King's presence to answer as to certain matters.

Exchequer, King's Remembrancer, Memoranda Roll 164, Recorda, East. 11 Ric. II.

A pilfering canon, 1388. Memorandum that the Treasurer, learning that Brother Geoffrey Stafford, canon of Routon, late farmer of the alien priory of Abberbury, *alias* New Abbey next Abberbury, took from the Abbey, while he was farmer, a chalice and a priest's vestment and put them in pledge at Shrewsbury, committed him to the Fleet,[11] [etc.].

PARSON

Riley, *Memorials of London*, II, 463 (from London Letter-Book H, fol. cxliv).

Greedy parsons, 1382. Forasmuch as farthings [have been refused] heretofore by parsons of churches in the city for the purpose of putting a stop to the currency of such small money and also in order to make people offer more than a farthing, it is ordained by the mayor, the aldermen, and the common council that thenceforth no one shall offer at vigils of the dead or like case more than one farthing a mass, and if he fail to ob-

[10] The Assumption of the Blessed Virgin Mary is celebrated on August 15.
[11] A prison outside the walls of London; it was encircled by a ditch filled from the Fleet River.

tain change for a halfpenny, he shall leave without making any offering.

Common Pleas, Plea Roll 485 m. 111 d.

A hunting parson, 1381. Sir John de Cobham brings a plea against William Symme, clerk, for breaking his free warren at Couling on Monday after St. Leonard, 1 Richard II,[12] and hunting hares, rabbits, pheasants, and partridges continually from that day until the Feast of Holy Trinity [June 9], 4 Richard II [1381].

Common Pleas, Plea Roll 504 m. 52.

A poaching parson, 1387. Herts. Henry Welwyn, clerk, by his attorney, against Simon "the parisshe clerk" of Welwyn: Simon, together with James Boxforde, parson of the church of Welwyn, broke *vi et armis* [13] into close of said Henry at Welwyn and into his several fisheries there, where they fished and took fish to value of 100s.

Common Pleas, Plea Roll 486 m. 199.

A parson sued by his chaplain, 1382. London. Thomas, parson of the church of Aydrop Rothing, was summoned to answer Richard de Coventry, chaplain, in a plea that he pay him £10 which he unjustly detains. And whereof the same Richard . . . says that whereas on the Feast of St. Michael the Archangel [September 29] in the fourth year of the now King [1380], at Aydrop Rothing in Essex, he was retained with the said Thomas to serve him there in the office of parish chaplain from the Feast of St. Michael aforesaid until the same feast next following for one whole year, taking for his salary 10 marks and a robe of the value of 13s. 4d. or 13s. 4d. for the said robe to be paid to him there at the end of the said term. And also the said Thomas at Aydrop Rothing on the said Feast of St. Michael borrowed from the said Richard 4 marks, the residue of the said sum of £10, to be paid on the Feast of St. Martin [November 11] then next to come, and although often requested to pay the said £10, the said Thomas has not yet paid it.

[Thomas denies the debt, and is to wage his law twelve-handed.[14]]

Common Pleas, Plea Roll 485 m. 113 d.

A country parson's home, 1382. William Symme, parson of the church of Couling, county Kent, was summoned to answer Sir John de Cobham, knight, who says that on March 1, 48 Edward III [1374], at Couling he requested the said William to put into repair divers houses in the rectory

[12] That is, on November 9, 1377.   [13] By strength and with arms.
[14] See above, p. 88n.

of the said church, namely, a hall, a chamber, a kitchen, two barns, and a stable which were ruinous; whereupon it was agreed that Sir John should cause the houses to be repaired and that William should pay the charges thereof. William denies that he was bound to pay £40, which John alleges he paid about the repairs.

William is given day in the Octave of Trinity to make his law twelve-handed.[15]

PRIEST

Canterbury, Prerogative Court, *North Country Wills, 1383–1558*, pp. 2–5.

A wealthy priest, 1407/8. January 19, 1407/8. William, son of John de Escrik, ordained priest: I will that my body be buried in Selby church next to the grave of my parents. I bequeath for my mortuary the customary sum. I leave £15 to buy wax, from which are to be made 5 tapers to be burned about my body, according to custom. . . . I leave for distribution to the poor of the town of Selby, the more needy to be chosen according to the discretion of the executors of my will, 100s. I leave to the parochial chaplain of Selby, 20d.; to Lord John de Shirburn, chaplain, 6s. 8d.; to any other chaplain coming to my exequies and praying for my soul, 16d. To David, abbot of Selby, 13s. 4d. and to the lord prior of the same, 6s. 8d. To Dompnus de Cresseby, monk, 56s. 8d.; to any other monk of the Monastery of Selby, 3s. 4d. *Item*, to the said abbot and the assembly of Selby, one covered cup of gilt, ornamented with vine leaves. To the Monastery of Selby, one cap of cloth of gold "de Lukes." To the parochial priest of Selby, 7d. For a pittance to the canons of Drax, 13s. 4d. For a pittance to the monks of Appleton, 13s. 8d. To master Ada of the Order of the Carmelite Friars of York, 13s. 4d. To Brother Richard, associate, 6s. 8d. To the brothers of the said order in York, 20s., and to the brothers of the Order of Preachers, likewise 20s., and to the brothers of the Order of Minors, likewise 20s., and to the brothers of the Order of St. Augustine, likewise 20s. I leave to the fabric of the Cathedral Church of York, 20s. *Item*, to the prior of the Hospital of St. Leonard, York, 13s. 4d.; to the fabric of the smaller church of Selby, 26s. 8d.; to the repair of roads in Selby, 13s. 4d. To Beatrice, my sister, 56s. 8d., 12 ells of new linen cloth, and one gown of scarlet, furred with byse.[16] To Agnes, who was the wife of my father, 40s. and one gown of

---

[15] See above, p. 88*n*.

[16] Some kind of (?brown) fur, much used in the 15th century for trimming gowns, etc. (*O.E.D.*)

"mustre-vilers," [17] furred with byse. To Joanna, my maidservant, 15s. and one plain gown. To Richard, my servant, 56s. 8d. and one gray horse with "cella" [18] and bridle. To Thomas Bryan, those 4m. which Alicia, his mother, owes to me. To William, son of my brother, £10 in good money, to be kept in the custody of Lord John of Burgoyne, chaplain, for ministering to the same William according to need. To John de Brun, 6s. 8d. To my church of St. Felicitas one whole vestment with appurtenances of cloth of gold embroidered with deer and greyhounds, and one cap of blue satin ornamented with X's, and two service books. For distributing to the poor of my parish, 100s. I absolve the prior of St. Nicholas in Exeter of all the debt for which he is bound to me, and I bequeath to that same prior 6s. 8d. To any monk in the aforesaid place, 3s. 4d. I will that my executors cause to be returned to that same prior all his goblets which I have in my custody. To lord Robert Peyntor, chaplain, 40s. and one silver cup with cover, value 20s. To Lord John de Burgoyne, chaplain, 100s. and one silver cup with cover, value 4m. To John Bikbury, 100s. and one silver cup with cover, which is in London. To John Taverner, my junior uncle, 100s. To John Taverner, my senior uncle (great-uncle?), 13s. 4d. To his wife, a gown of scarlet lined with muslin. To Isabel Scut, 3s. 4d. and one double gown. To Lord Reginald, my uncle, 20s. and one gown of worsted. I absolve that same Reginald and Beatrice, my sister, of all the debt for which to me they are bound. To Emma Botiller, 3s. 4d. To Reginald, son of John de Whytmore, 56s. 8d., to be placed in the custody of Lord John de Burgoyne for ministering to this same Reginald. To John de Whytmore, 6s. 8d. To Richard de Roudon and Joan his wife, one silver cup with cover, value 40s. To Alicia, their daughter, one silver cup with cover, value 2m., or 2m. for them and one pair of coral beads with a gold ring appended, or 6s. 8d. for them, according to their wishes. To William de Wessyngton, 6s. 8d. To John de Lathes, 3s. 4d. To John Hasand, 3s. 4d. To Richard de Drax, 10s., and to Margaret his wife, one pair of beads, or 3s. 4d.; and to Isabel, daughter of the same Richard, one head-band with silver ornaments, value 3s. 4d., or that much money. To Lord Luce, my steward, 40s. To master William Tollarn, my chaplain, 20s. To Lord Paul, chaplain, 13s. 4d. To the priest, Lord John of Schyrburn, 6d. To William de Scolowe, 2s. To Elaine, daughter of Isabel Scut, 6s. 8d. To Alicia, daughter of Oliver Burdelen,

[17] Variant of "musterdevillers," a kind of mixed grey woolen cloth, much used in the fourteenth and fifteenth centuries. (O.E.D.)
[18] Lat. sella, seat, saddle.

13*s*. 4*d*. To Matilda Watson, 3*s*. 4*d*. I release Richard Roide of £10 of the £43 13*s*. 4*d*. for which he is bound to me by the Statute of Merchants, on condition that he absolve the aforesaid Lord Robert Peyntor of £20 13*s*. 4*d*., and on certain days agreed upon, £12 13*s*. 4*d*., in order that the aforesaid Robert may be able to make arrangements concerning the aforesaid money [to provide] for my soul. Of the £20 13*s*. 4*d*., for which Thomas de Selby, residing at Calais, is bound to me through an obligatory writing, in the same way in which he has pledged to me for 5*m*. a beaver fur, a sword, and a girdle ornamented with silver—of the above-mentioned sum I absolve this same Thomas of £7 6*s*. 8*d*., on condition that he release to [my] executors £13 6*s*. 8*d*. To Isabel, wife of Thomas Smallwood, my sister, that messuage in Selby, adjacent to the town called Micklegate, in which the said Thomas and Isabel reside, to be held by the said Isabel throughout her whole life; after the death of this same Isabel, the aforesaid messuage shall go to Lord Robert Peyntor above mentioned, to be sold by him at as high a price as possible and the money thence obtained to be converted to pious uses for my soul. To the said Lord Robert, for the repair of buildings on the said messuage, 106*s*. 8*d*. All those tenements in Selby which Christina de Chester holds, and which I hold through the gift of my father, to be sold soon after the death of the said Christina, and the money thence obtained to be used in the celebration of masses. To that same Robert £6 10*s*. 8*d*. which the lord Abbot of Selby [owes] me in payment of 20*m*. for which John de Birne is obligated to me for the abbot, that he [Robert] may provide for my soul. I will that the same Lord Robert by his own authority appoint in my name executors for all my property in the diocese of York, and the said John de Burgoyne and John de Bikbury upon their own authority to appoint executors in the province of Canterbury; but [this arrangement] not to hinder Lord John and John from transmitting to the aforesaid Lord Robert at Selby with all possible speed such a sum of English money as will make it possible that my will be fully executed, and that they cause to be released to the said Robert all charters and documents concerning my tenements within the diocese of York. *Item*, I will that the same Lord John and John buy a marble stone for my tomb, in which shall be graven the image of the Blessed Virgin Mary, seated on a throne, holding the Son in her left arm; at whose feet shall be made an image like to a priest kneeling, holding in his hands a scroll with these words: Jesus, Son of God, have mercy on me. I will that my executors thence make provision for my soul, with the stipulation that two parts of the property at Selby, where my body is to be buried, be converted to pious uses by the aforesaid Lord Robert. My seal I have caused to be affixed in evidence of matters set forth. Witnesses: Richard de Drax, John de Brun, Richard de Upton, John Taverner of Selby, [and] others. Dated at Selby.

Proved March 17, 1407/8.

Wycliffe, *Tractatus de officio pastorali*, pp. 7-13, 19-21, 26, 31-32 (from Vienna MS No. 4302 [DCCCII]).

A good shepherd as seen by Wycliffe, 1367-1378. Every pastor or curate must, before all things else, be instructed in the three divine virtues, which are faith, hope, and charity, and fundamentally the Lord Jesus Christ. For otherwise he would not have the likeness of Christ for laying his soul before his sheep and for teaching them faithfully. . . . Verily, the life of Christ is an example and a mirror to us, which we must imitate as far as lies in our strength. . . . (Cf. Chapter I.) [19]

From that principle of faith, which for a sign may be called *golden* by the faithful, is plainly derived the rule. . . . Everyone ought to follow Christ in his way of life to the utmost of his strength. But every priest, curate, or pastor has the strength thus to follow Christ in his mode of life; therefore he should do so. And this [rule] moved the apostles and other priests of the Lord after them to imitate Christ in that evangelical poverty. For the Apostle [Timothy] understands by "alimenta" food and drink which suffice for nourishment. He does not say luxury or superfluity of nourishment, but he says simply "alimenta," that is, enough to feed the body so that it can serve God as it should. And he means by "tegumenta" clothing for the body as well as suitable homes which shall protect from storms and heat for that faithful service. What more, I ask, would he do for a traveler? And since we have that pilgrimage from the Lord in order to attain blessedness, it follows that everything more than this would be superfluous and sinful. (Chapters III, XVIII.)

From this it is concluded that all curates inducted according to the law of the Lord ought to live entirely on the physical alms of their parishioners. For if they have income or sufficient worldly wealth, they ought to relinquish these for the physical alms of their flock, and lacking support from any other source, they ought to live in the recompense of

[19] The chapter references here are to F. D. Matthew's edition of the English version of the Latin tract from which this selection is translated (Wycliffe, *The English Works of Wyclif*, pp. 405-457). The two tracts are substantially the same; Wycliffe must have published his argument in both Latin and English in order to reach different classes of readers.

charity from alms of their parishioners; so on both sides alms are dispensed, the more worthy because they are spiritual. . . . (Chapter V.)

Whence the conclusion that a curate ought not to extort tithes from his people by excommunication or other censure is clear in this way, that a curate ought not to contend with his charge about such matters.[20] For a sign of which, Christ and his Apostles did not demand tithes, but were content with the food and clothing that were their due. Indeed, in the New Testament we rarely read about tithes. . . . No one should excommunicate his parishioner or persecute him by other forms of censure except in the name of love to destroy medicinally his folly. It is better, according to the teaching of Christ, to forgive parishioners such injury and to live more frugally in office. Accordingly, the priest ought to do this in the likeness of Christ. . . . Nowhere is excommunication or persecution for the sake of tithes enjoined. . . . There is no doubt that according to the rules of the church such extortion does not agree with charity. Therefore, let a priest move his parishioners by patience, humility, and all the works of charity so that they will give him of temporal things what is necessary for the proper support of life. . . . (Chapter VI.)

. . . For Christ ordained that his shepherds should live among their sheep, teaching them the way of the Lord as much by works as by preaching. . . .

Wherefore priests, and especially curates, ought to be poor and weak. They ought to be poor, inasmuch as they are clerics. And although they may happen to have good bodily strength, still they are too weak to carry out their pastoral duty and with this to live in their own persons and those of their fellows by the labor of their hands. . . .

But to this Antichrist replies, finding excuse for sins: It is permitted such a curate not to dwell in his own parish, if he provide a suitable substitute, and to devote himself to prayer and meditation, which is a duty more excellent and useful to the church. . . . But if that curate is zealous for prayer and contemplation, let him give up his office and name; for there is no reason why he should falsely bear the name of priest, except that he may be the spiritual vicar of Antichrist. . . . The care of a parish is enough for the duty of a priest. . . . (Chapter XII.)

And the same judgment holds of curates [namely, that they are ravenous wolves who strangle their sheep, body and soul] who remain in the

[20] Cf. Chaucer, *Canterbury Tales*, A, ll. 486–490.

court of Rome to get other benefices or privileges for taking the alms of their poor parishioners, or who dwell in London or other places of pleasure outside their parishes, at the cost of the same. . . . (Chapter XIX.)

The priest has a triple duty: first, to feed his sheep spiritually with the word of God, so that they may be led through pastures ever green to the blessedness of their Home. The second pastoral duty is prudently to cleanse his sheep from the scab, lest they infect still more themselves and others. And the third is that a pastor should defend his sheep from greedy wolves, those of the flesh as well as those of the spirit. And on every side the principal duty of the pastor seems to be to spread the word of God among his sheep. For a suitable reason God ordains that the teaching of a pastor by his own life should be a more efficacious sermon to his flock, since it would affect them more than bare preaching in a sermon. . . . Therefore, the life of a good pastor is a mirror to be imitated by his sheep. For the best pastor could not fall from rectitude in his work or preaching for the reason that his manner of life is as it were a vital spirit such as is to be observed among Christians here and there and especially among the priests who say that they are the vicars of Christ. And for a sign of this, that life and works are more important than preaching for a pastor, uprightness of life is necessary for every one of those who are to be saved. (Chapter XXI.)

Knighton, *Chronicon*, II, 184–185.

Opposition to Wycliffe and the Lollards, 1382. By the common people the disciples of Wycliffe were called Wycliffians or Lollards. For his sect they gained more and more followers, who were thus vainly deceived. The principal pseudo-Lollards, at the time this abominable sect was introduced, adopted russet attire generally, their outward [appearance] manifesting, as it were, simplicity of heart. They would thus subtly attract the attention of those who beheld them, and they would set about the task of teaching and disseminating their senseless doctrine with more security. Concerning such things, indeed, the Lord said in the gospel, teaching his [people] to guard against these, "Take heed of the false prophets who come among you in sheep's garments; inward, nevertheless, they are ravenous wolves."

PERSONAL RELIGION

1. Church Attendance

A GIFT TO INSURE ATTENDANCE AT CHURCH, 1456

Prerogative Court of Canterbury, 6 Stokton.

Will of Alice Palmer: She forgives William Chester, baker, a debt of £27 13*s*. 4*d*. on condition "that he from hence forward duly and continually keep and come to his parish church and there abide and hear service as other good and faithful men of the same church."

AN AFFRAY ABOUT PEWS

City of London, Mayor's Court, Original Bills, bdle. 1, No. 38.

John Hokle, spicer of London, complains of William Stanes, cutler, that William on Thursday last in the church of St. Uwayn [21] in the city threatened to kill him with a knife, calling him "faux Selter of Talage" before all the parishioners; also, he commanded his wife to sit in the place of the wife of the complainant, John, in the said church, where the complainant's wife had sat for thirteen years past. The said William caused an affray in the church, so that the parson could not proceed with the mass which he was about to celebrate.

2. Tithes: Statute of Archbishop of Canterbury Regarding Tithes, ca. 1305

Ely, Eng. (Archdeaconry). *...us liber archidiaconi Eliensis*, pp. 179–180.

Since, because of diverse customs in asking tithes in different churches, quarrels, contentions, scandals, and hatreds arise between the rectors of the churches and their parishioners, we wish that in all the churches the levying of tithes and of produce for the churches be uniform. Especially we will that a tenth part of the crops, not after the expenses have been deducted, but of the whole amount without any deduction, be counted: both of the fruits of the trees and of seed crops, and of all garden produce unless parishioners make a sufficient recompense therefor. We will also that the hay, wherever it may be, whether in large meadows or small, be delivered and claimed according to the convenience of the church. Of the foods from animals, that is, of lambs, we will that for six lambs and less, six halfpennies be given for a tenth. If there be a seventh lamb and upward, let always be given a tenth. However, the rector of the church

[21] St. Ewin[e], Faringdon Ward Within.

who receives the seventh lamb shall give to the parishioner from whom he receives the seventh lamb three halfpennies in compensation; who receives the eighth shall pay a penny and who receives the ninth shall give a halfpenny or let the rector wait, if he wishes, until another year when he shall be able to receive his full tenth. And because he shall thus wait, let him always demand the second best lamb or at least the third best of the lambs of the second year. . . . And so may it be understood about the tenth of the wool. . . . If the sheep be fattened in one place in summer and in another in winter, then the tenth must be divided. If anyone keeps them in the meantime or sells them and it is certain from what parish those sheep came, the tenth must be divided according as they belong to two places. Of milk we will and decree that a tenth part be rendered while it lasts, both of cheese in its season and of milk in autumn and winter, unless parishioners wish to make sufficient compensation for such tithes and this at the convenience of the church. Of the products of mills, we will that a tenth part be rendered. From artisans, likewise from merchants, of the gain from their business, similarly from carpenters, stone-masons, blacksmiths, weavers, and all other workmen and wage-earners, clearly a tenth part of their wages may be demanded unless the wage-earners wish to give annually a certain sum for the candles in the church or for the work of the church, if it please the rector. From autumn grazing and from pasturage, whether common or not common, we decree that a tenth be faithfully rendered and this according to the number of animals and of days as the church declares, nor may lords and parishioners have just cause of complaint [of this]. Of fall fishing and of the products of bees, as of all other goods duly acquired, accordingly as they are renewed we will and decree that a tenth be rendered. . . .

3. *Relics, Paternosters, Breviaries*

SOME OF THE RELICS OWNED BY EDWARD III, 1332

Additional MS (B.M.) 35181 fol. 8v.

A crystal vessel enclosed after the fashion of the Temple, partly of gold and ornamented with divers gems, in which are relics.

A chest from York in which are four crystal vessels enclosed in silver containing divers relics, namely, in one, [part] of the chasuble and alb of St. Edmund the Confessor, and in another a bone of the arm of St. Amphibalis, in the third [some] of the blood of St. George.

Another chest of wood covered with cloth in which are two crystal vessels enclosed in silver gilt containing the relics of Stephen in the one, and in the other a tooth of St. Adrian, and a cross of silver with part of black wood in the middle. . . .

A "bourse" (purse) containing [part] of the column to which Christ was bound. . . .

A very small "bourse" in which are contained two very small bones. . . .

A great bone of St. Geronimus.

PIECES OF THE HOLY CROSS WILLED TO WIFE AND CHILDREN, 1428

Prerogative Court of Canterbury, 14 Luffenam.

Will of Richard Poynings, knight, eldest son of Robert, Lord de Poynings: My body to be buried in the burial ground of Poynings, before the north door of the church, if my wife pleases, or where else she pleases. . . . I bequeath to my beloved wife, Lady of Arundel and Maltravers, a cross containing a large piece of the Holy Cross. This is now in pledge; when it is recovered, each of my children is to have a piece, with the divine blessing and my blessing "ex toto corde meo," but my wife is to have the larger piece for her life. Afterwards the cross and the larger piece of the Holy Cross to go to the church of Stokecours, forever. . . . And I appoint John Belney and Walter Cury, Esquires, my executors.
[Proved, October 31, 1430.]

PRAYER BEADS OF SILVER, GILT, AND AMBER, 1389

Chancery Enrolments of Extents on Debts, 38/16.

Included among goods of Thomas Cuteler, citizen and grocer of London, extended for debt: one pair of paternosters of silver, price 3s. 4d.; one pair of paternosters of gilt with a crucifix, price 4s.; one pair of paternosters of amber, price 20d.

BREVIARIES BEQUEATHED, 1405

Prerogative Court of Canterbury, 9 Marche.

Will of John Wodewey, clerk: I bequeath to the church of Weston in Lewes my tablet painted with the story of the Day of Judgment, two curtains painted with angels . . . and one book called Legendary. . . . I bequeath to Lacy . . . a new breviary and I will that [another] breviary remain in the custody of my kinsmen. . . . [An ordinal also is mentioned.]

4. Confession

FALSE CONFESSORS, CA. 1383

Wycliffe, *The English Works of Wyclif*, pp. 159–160.

[Evil curates] deceive Christian men in the doing of true penance; for they dare not tell the truth how men must needs forsake all falseness in business, in oaths, and all sin, according to their knowledge and power, and must not for the sake of any earthly good wittingly and willfully work against God's commands, either for gain or on account of fear of death. God will not forgive men their sins because of confessions of mouth, made without true contrition, nor will he forgive them through the assoiling of priests or through bulls of pardon or through letters of fraternity or through the prayers of any creature in earth or in heaven, unless there be true contrition. Curates speak much of tithes and offerings at the confession and little of restitution and the doing of alms to poor men. Rather they speak of the mass pence and of church gains (gayness), and in this way they teach people to trust that their sins are forgiven because of the priest's assoiling, though they do not true penance, as God himself teaches. . . . Although God himself says that in that hour when a sinner has inward sorrow and true contrition for his sins he shall be saved, curates will make this word false, saying that a man shall not be saved be he ever so contrite, unless he has made shrift to one of them. In this case they be the procurators of the fiend, deceiving men through their pride and ignorance and covetousness.

CHOICE OF CONFESSORS, 1366

Great Britain, Public Record Office, *Calendar of Entries in the Papal Registers, 1342–1419*, pp. 521–526.

Numerous instances of petitions for leave to choose confessors may be found in the *Papal Registers*. The following, for the year 1366, are typical:

Joan, Princess of Aquitaine and Wales, petitions the Pope (Urban V) for an indult to choose her confessor. (Granted.)

Ralph Basset, for indult to choose his confessors during life. (Granted for six years.)

John, Baron of Woodhull, for license to choose his confessor during journey to the Holy Sepulchre and to other holy places beyond the seas. (Granted, during his going, returning, and remaining.)

5. *Penance*

PENANCE ENJOINED FOR NOT BRINGING STRAW TO THE ARCHBISHOP'S
HORSE, 1390

Foxe, *Acts and Monuments*, ed. by Pratt, III, 315–316 (from Archbishops' Register [Lambeth], Courtenay).

Ignorance, the mother of error, so much hath blinded and deceived certain persons, to wit, Hugh Pennie, John Forstall, John Boy, John Wanderton, William Hayward, and John White, tenants of the lord of Wingham, that they, against the coming of [William Courtenay], archbishop, to his palace of Canterbury on Palm Sunday eve, the year of our Lord 1390, being warned by the bailiff to convey and carry hay, straw, and other litter to the aforesaid palace, as they were bound by the tenor [22] of their lands which they hold of the see of Canterbury, refused and disdained to do their due service as they were accustomed, and brought their straw and other litter, not in carts and wains openly and sufficiently, but by piecemeal and closely in bags and sacks, in contempt of their lord and derogation of the right and title of the see of Canterbury. Whereupon, they being cited and presented before the archbishop, sitting in judgment at his manor of Saltwood, yielded and submitted themselves to his lordship's pleasure, humbly craving pardon of their trespass. Then the aforesaid archbishop absolved the above named Hugh Pennie, etc., they swearing to obey the laws and ordinances of the Holy Church, and to do the punishment that should be appointed them for their deserts: that is, that on the next Lord's day following, the said penitents, bare of head and foot, should with slow steps go humbly and devoutly before the procession made at the collegiate church of Wingham, each penitent carrying openly on his shoulder his bag stuffed with hay and straw, so that the said hay and straw should appear hanging out, the mouths of the sacks being open.[23]

---

[22] Obs. form of *tenure*. (*O.E.D.*)

[23] Foxe appends the following lines, which must not be understood as forming an extract from the Register, but were probably the production of his pen:

> "This bag full of straw I bear on my back,
> Because my lord's horse his litter did lack;
> If ye be not good to my lord grace's horse,
> Ye are like to go barefoot before the cross."
>   [Pratt's note.]

6. *Excommunication and Compurgation*

EXCOMMUNICATION, LATE 13TH CENTURY

Excommunication might be the lesser (medicinal) or the greater (mortal excommunication or anathema). A church member upon whom had been imposed the sentence of minor excommunication would be excluded from the observance of the sacraments; if under sentence of major excommunication, he would be excluded from all graces and blessings of the church; mass could not be celebrated in his presence, he could not hold a benefice, or receive Christian burial. Intercourse with the faithful was denied except in certain specified cases.[24]

Ely, Eng. (Archdeaconry), *Vetus liber archidiaconi Eliensis*, pp. 27–28.

General and universal sentence of the church [to be read] thrice yearly: By the authority of God the Father and of the Son and of the Holy Spirit and of all the saints of God and of the Holy Church of God, we excommunicate, damn, anathematize, and exclude from the threshold of the Holy Mother Church: those who disturb the peace of the realm; those who flout the laws, liberties, and customs of the church or steal the goods of the church; all those who by force or a show of violence have resisted the rights of the church; all usurers; incendiaries zealous in evil; those who have knowingly and wittingly sworn falsely by those things most sacred; those who commit sacrilege; counterfeiters and clippers of coins; those who have interfered with legacies left by the dead; those who have by treachery brought about the death or disinheritance of their superiors or inferiors; followers after heresy; those who, inspired by some grace, sell such grace; [25] those who knowingly prevent conception or cause abortion, who beget false heirs, that is, heirs conceived in adultery; all those who commit, or in their conscience consent to, theft or pillage, or knowingly and wittingly have profited, or have expected to profit, or are expecting to profit from theft or pillage; moreover, those who through lies spread scandal harmful to the good name of another, from which he suffers everlasting injury, and likewise those who are backbiters, odious to God; those who fraudulently retain the tithes and customary church offerings; and all those who "give aid, counsel, or countenance to these offenders."

May the holy and indivisible Trinity, the one God, curse all these

[24] Cf. F. E. Hyland, *Excommunication: Its Nature, Historical Developments, and Effects* (Washington, 1928), pp. 18–25; E. Friedberg, "Excommunication," *The New Schaff-Herzog Encyclopaedia of Religious Knowledge* (New York, 1909), IV, 236–237.
[25] Reference apparently to false pardoners (quaestors). The Latin is *inspiratos aliqua gratia illam vendentes*.

aforesaid evildoers. May the Holy Mother of God curse them. May Saint Michael, Saint Gabriel, Saint Raphael, and all the holy angels and archangels curse them. Amen. May the patriarchs Abraham, Isaac, and Jacob, and all the rest of the patriarchs curse them. May Saint John the Baptist and all the other prophets curse them. May Saints Peter, Paul, and Andrew, with all the rest of the apostles and evangelists, curse them. May Saint Stephen and all the other martyrs as well as Saint Martin and all the rest of the confessors curse them. May Saint Mary Magadalene, Saint Agnes, with all the virgin saints, curse them. May all the saints curse them.

May they be accursed withindoors and withoutdoors, going in and coming out, eating, drinking, sleeping, waking, standing, sitting, walking, talking. May they remain excommunicated, damned, accursed. As these lamps are extinguished, so may their souls be extinguished in hell with the devil and his angels—unless they repent and come to make worthy penance and restitution. Let it be done. Let it be done. Amen.

COMPURGATION, MIDDLE 14TH CENTURY

Ely, Eng. (Archdeaconry), *Vetus liber archidiaconi Eliensis*, p. 171.

The official of the Lord Archdeacon of Ely to the Dean or Parochial Chaplain of T., greetings: On this day by these presents we commit to you our duty of receiving in the church of T. the canonical and solemn purgation of John of Rich., accused of the crime of adultery or incontinence with Margery, wife of Thomas de Careleton. . . . Dated at Cambridge, etc.[26]

7. *Chantries and Masses for the Soul* [27]

A BENEFACTOR OF ST. MARY-LE-BOW, 1352

London, Court of Hustings, *Calendar of Wills*, I, 656–658.

Will of John de Holegh, hosier: To be buried in the chancel of St. Nicholas the Bishop in the church of St. Mary-le-Bow in the tomb of

---

[26] Adultery was classed as one of the gravest of offenses, for which a severe penalty might be imposed. Crimes less grave than adultery were, according to *Vetus liber archidiaconi Eliensis*, p. 196, fornication, with the special interpretation of intercourse with widows, prostitutes, or concubines; defilement, properly the illicit defloration of virgins; likewise, perjury and injury to faith.

Crimes which were more serious than adultery and for which, according to canonical law, a more severe penalty might be imposed were heresy, simony, idolatry, apostasy, sacrilege, blasphemy of God and of the saints, divination, homicide, incest, and the violation of avowed chastity.   [27] See also below, pp. 419–423.

PRIEST ADMINISTERING THE
SACRAMENT; *ca.* 1425
Baltimore, Walters Gallery, MS W. 174, fol. 124

THREE OF THE SEVEN SACRAMENTS—Confirmation, Confession, Ordination
Early fifteenth century
New York, Morgan Library, MS 359, fols. 112v, 113, 114v

BISHOP TEACHING; late fourteenth century
London, Brit. Mus., MS Add. 29704, fragment 82

MASS FOR THE DEAD; in roundels: EXTREME UNCTION, AND
PREPARATION OF CORPSE FOR BURIAL; early fifteenth century
New York, Morgan Library, MS 359, fol. 119v

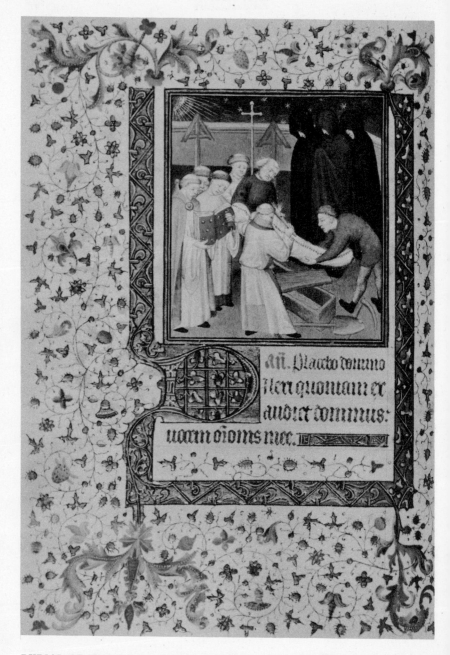

BURIAL OF THE DEAD; early fifteenth century
New York, Morgan Library, MS 455, fol. 121v

Alice, his late wife, over which tomb he wishes a marble stone to be placed with two images of latten having letters written around asking for prayers for the benefit of their souls. Bequests to the new work of the belfry of St. Mary-le-Bow and for the purchase of a bell for the same. A tenement . . . to be devoted to the maintenance of chantries in the same church for the good of his soul and the souls of Alice, his late wife, and others, for the service of which he also leaves money for the purchase of a missal, a silver cup weighing forty shillings to be fashioned into a chalice, and divers sums of money for the purchase of vestments, towels,[28] and other ornaments. . . .

This his testament is to remain in the custody of four honest parishioners of St. Mary-le-Bow, and a copy of it is to be written in a missal which is to be used at the high altar in this church and for the purchase of which he leaves one hundred shillings.

For painting an image of the Blessed Mary in the choir and for the purchase of a crown to be placed on her head he leaves sixty shillings. He wills also that all the articles of his testament affecting the church of St. Mary-le-Bow be written on a sheet of parchment and placed on a tablet fixed at the foot of the image of the Blessed Mary aforesaid in the choir.

A BENEFACTOR OF ST. MARTIN VINTRY, 1350

London, Court of Hustings, *Calendar of Wills*, ed. by Sharpe, I, 643–644.

Will of John de Gisors:[29] To be buried before the rood in the church of St. Martin in the Vintry. . . . Provision was made for a chantry in this church for the souls of the testator, Isabella his wife, John and Margery his father and mother, John his grandfather, and others. The mayor of the city of London for the time being to present[30] to the same, under certain circumstances, and in case there should be no such mayor, the dean and chapter of St. Paul's. The chaplain of the said chantry to have a chamber allotted to him and to be provided with a chalice . . . a missal in two volumes, to wit, a gradual with epistles and communion

[28] Cloths of linen for use at communion, or of silk for use in covering the altar at other times. (*O.E.D.*)
[29] John de Gisors was mayor of London in 1311, 1312, and 1314. In his will, an extract of which appears here, he is described as a vintner, like most of his family, but elsewhere is called a pepperer. As a vintner and resident of the Vintry in London, he was probably well known to the Chaucer family (see above, p. 4). He died in 1351. Henry de Gisors, who may have been related to John de Gisors, succeeded Chaucer as Controller of the Petty Customs in the port of London in 1386. (See *Life-Records of Chaucer*, IV, 268; Stow, *A Survey of London*, II, 354–355.)
[30] To name a suitable cleric for a benefice. (*O.E.D.*)

of the saints with divers special masses, and the other volume containing the gospels appertaining to the said missal; also a portifory with notations of the use of St. Paul's; a psalter with manual combined; a vestment with apparel complete and a cope of fine linen; for the deacon a white amice and stole; and for the sub-deacon a white amice and maniple, a cascorporas,[31] corporas, three towels, and a surplice, two cruets, a pyx, one chaufepoun [32] for winter, a cloth of silk and gold, and a chest for keeping the same.

GREAT TRENTAL OF ST. GREGORY TO BE SUNG, 1428

"Documents Relative to the Families of Bryan, Fitzpain, Ponynges, and Others, the Coheirs of Sir Guy Bryan, K.G.," *Collectanea topographica et genealogica*, III (1836), 260.

Will of Sir Richard Poynings: . . . I will that wherever [my and my wife's] bodies be buried twenty shillings be given to each of the places where our bodies lie for holding of the "mendys" [33] and that a priest be found two years to sing the great trental of St. Gregory for our souls especially and for my lady my mother and for Sir John, Lord of Arundel and of Maltrevers, the husband of my wife that was. And I pray you both, John Bolne and William Russell,[34] that ye do your duty and perform my will, and better if you can, as ye will answer before God.

DEVOTIONAL GILDS

1. *Prayer to Be Said at Every Meeting of the Gild, 1384, Fraternity of St. Christopher, Norwich*

Chancery Miscellanea, Gild Certificate 295 (printed in Smith, *English Gilds*, pp. 22–23).

In the worship of Jesus Christ and of his dear Mother and of St. Christopher the holy martyr and of all holy heaven devoutly we begin this fraternity. . . .

In the beginning we shall pray devoutly for the state of the Holy Church and for the peace of the land; for the pope of Rome and his cardinals; for the patriarch of Jerusalem; for the Holy Land and for the Holy Cross, that God by his might and his mercy bring it out of heathen

[31] A case for sacramental cloths. [Sharpe's note.]
[32] Warming apparatus.
[33] The month's mind, or commemoration service held on the thirtieth day after burial. (*O.E.D.*)
[34] A squire and a clerk who were to be the guardians of Poynings' children and the executors of his will.

power into rule of Holy Church; and for all archbishops and bishops and especially for our bishop of Norwich; and for all parsons and priests, and all orders of Holy Church, that God of his mercy save them and keep them, body and soul, and give them grace here, order to keep and so to rule Holy Church and man's soul that it be to God's worship and to salvation of their souls and of all Christian men; for our lord the King, for our lady the Queen, dukes, earls, barons, and bachelors [35] of the land, that God of his grace save them and keep them from deadly sin and give them grace the realm and Holy Church and their own souls so to rule and keep that it be worship to God and to all Christian men salvation; for all knights, squires, citizens, and burghers, franklins, all true tillers and all men of craft, widows, maidens, wives, and for the commonalty and Christian people that God of his mercy save them and keep them that in this world live with truth, and give them grace so to do that it be worship to God and salvation to their souls; and for all true shipmen and all true pilgrims that God for his grace give them weathering and passage, that they may safely come and go; for the fruit of the land and of the sea; for all the men that be in false belief and would be in good belief, God give them grace to come to their desire; for our fathers' souls and mothers' and brothers' and sisters' souls and for the souls of all the brethren and sisters of the gild, and for all Christian souls. Amen.

And also it is ordained that this bead [36] and prayer shall be rehearsed every time that the alderman and the brethren be together.

2. *A Gild for the Worship of Our Lady, 1384/85, Gild of the Assumption, Wiggenhall, Norfolk*

Chancery Miscellanea, Gild Certificate 356 (printed in Smith, *English Gilds*, pp. 111–112).

In the worship of Jesus Christ and of his dear Mother, Saint Mary, and the holy fellowship of heaven and especially of Our Lady Saint Mary of the Assumption, this fraternity is begun in the town of Wiggenhall for the worship of Our Lady. In the worship of God and of His Mother, in amendment of our lives and salvation of our souls, [this fraternity] says a paternoster and an ave for charity.[37]

[35] Candidates for knighthood.
[36] Supplication, prayer.
[37] The prayer with which this Gild Certificate begins is described by Westlake as "a kind of bidding prayer." (*Parish Gilds*, p. 216.)

Laudemus Deum, etc. Benedicamus pater, etc. Benedictus es, etc. Per signum sancte, etc.

Maria virgo semper letare, que meruisti Christum portare, celi et terre conditorem, quem de utero tuo protulisti, mundi saluatorem. Deo gratias.

Beseech we the mercy of Jesus Christ for the state of the Holy Church and all that thereto belongs. Also, we beseech for our lord, King Richard of England, and for the Queen and for all the baronage and for all that to them belongs the gift of grace to overcome their enemies. Also we beseech for the pope of Rome and for the patriarch of Jerusalem and for all the Holy Church and all that to it belongs. Also we beseech for the Holy Land, that Jesus Christ for his great mercy bring it into Christian power. Also we beseech for the fruit that is in the earth, that God send it such weathering that it may turn to the profit of Christian men. And for shipmen and for all men that travel, by sea and by land. And for all that this fraternity first began and that uphold it. And they to say a paternoster for charity.

Deus miseriatur nostri, etc. Gloria patri, etc. Kyrieleison, etc. Pater noster, etc. Dies fuit, etc. Habundat quemcumque. Deus a quo, etc.

And also beseech we Jesus' mercy for our fathers' souls and for our mothers' souls and for the Christian souls that be in the bitter pain of purgatory and for the souls of all the brothers and sisters that to this fraternity belong and that maintain it for the worship of Our Lady. We say a paternoster, etc. *De profundis, etc. Oremus. Incline Domine ne fidelis, etc. Benedicite dominus, etc. Ille nos benedicat.* May God's help be among us. Amen.

3. *The Paternoster Gild of York, ca. 1389* [38]

Chancery Miscellanea, Gild Certificate 454 (printed in Smith, *English Gilds*, pp. 137–139).

As to the beginning of the said gild, be it known that once on a time a play setting forth the goodness of the Lord's Prayer was played in the city of York, in which play all manner of vices and sins were held up to scorn and the virtues were held up to praise. This play met with such favor that many said: "Would that this play could be kept up in this city, for the health of souls and for the comfort of citizens and neighbors." Hence the keeping up of that play in times to come, for the health and amendment of the souls as well of the upholders as of the hearers (*audientium*)

[38] See above, p. 235n.

of it, became the whole and sole cause of the beginning and fellowship of the brethren of this brotherhood. And so the main charge of the gild is to keep up this play, to the glory of God the maker of the said prayer and for the holding up of sins and vices to scorn. . . .

Also, the brethren are bound to make, and as often as need be to renew, a table showing the whole meaning and use of the Lord's Prayer and to keep this hanging against a pillar in the cathedral church. Also they are bound, as often as the said play of the Lord's Prayer is played in the city of York, to ride with the players thereof through the chief streets of the city of York; and the more becomingly to mark themselves while thus riding, they must all be clad in one suit. And to insure good order during the said play, some of the brethren are bound to ride or to walk with the players until the play is wholly ended. . . .

There do not belong to the gild any rents of land, or any tenements, or any goods, save only the properties needed in the playing of the before-named play; which properties are of little or no worth for any other purpose than the said play. And the gild has one wooden chest, in which the said properties are kept.

4. *The Sick to Join in Gild Prayers, 1356*

Chancery Miscellanea, Gild Certificate 368.

The Gild of the Ascension was founded at Great Yarmouth in honor of God, St. Mary, and Holy Church and for the amendment of the living and the dead furnishes a candle at the first vespers, matins, mass, and second vespers of the Ascension. On the Sunday after Ascension Day [39] the members hear masses and say six paternosters, six aves, and one credo. On the Friday after vespers they come together and say five paternosters and five aves, etc. All attend funeral services and say the psalter of Our Lady, attend the corpse to church, offer $\frac{1}{4}d.$ at mass, and give $\frac{1}{4}d.$ in soul-alms. One dying at sea [40] or away shall have soul-alms and 60 masses.

The sick to have their portions sent from the gild-feast and to pray if they can. Absentees to send a deputy.

[39] Holy Thursday, the fortieth day after Easter.
[40] Then as now Great Yarmouth was the center of the herring fishery.

5. *A Devotional Gild in the Custom House Church, ca. 1389* [41]

Chancery Miscellanea, Gild Certificate 204.

The Gild of Our Lady in the church of St. Dunstan by the Tower exists for devotion to Our Lady and the good of the people. It finds a chaplain to sing mass daily and provides lights and ornaments for the altar of Our Lady.

6. *A Devotional Gild in the Hospital of Roncesvalles, 1385 (?)*

Chancery Miscellanea, Gild Certificate 212.

The Gild of St. Mary Roncesvalles was founded in honor of the Holy Trinity, the glorious Virgin, and All Saints, and was designed chiefly to celebrate the Feast of the Nativity in the chapel of Roncesvalles at Charing Cross. The gild has no assemblies or quarrels,[42] but exists solely for devotion and prayer in honor of God and the Blessed Virgin and for the safety of souls. It offers on the Feast of the Nativity and keeps a light burning at the daily mass.

7. *A Chaplain Provided to Sing in Honor of God, Time of Edward III.*

Chancery Miscellanea, Gild Certificate 63 (i).

The Gild of St. Katherine, Tewkesbury, was founded to provide a chaplain to sing in honor of God, Our Lady, and St. Katherine, for all members of the fraternity, and for all Christians. Other members have since joined in order to share in the prayers of the chaplain.

8. *Visitation of the Sick, ca. 1349*

Chancery Miscellanea, Gild Certificate 279.

In the great pestilence which at Lynn was in 1349, in which the greater part of the people of that town died, three men, [seeing that] the venerated sacrament of the Body of Christ was being carried through the town with only a single candle of poor wax burning in front of it, whereas two torches made of the best wax hardly suffice, thought this so improper that they ordained certain lights for it when carried by night or by day in the visitation of the sick.

[41] Earliest deed of feoffment quoted is dated 2 Richard II [1378–79]. (Westlake, *Parish Gilds*, p. 184.)
[42] Complaints. (*O.E.D.*)

10. Death and Burial

THE BURIAL RITES

1. Funerals of Some of Chaucer's Associates

INSTRUCTIONS FOR THE BURIAL OF ONE OF CHAUCER'S FELLOWS IN
THE HOUSEHOLD OF EDWARD III, 1380

John de Beverley was one of King Edward's favorite squires and must have been
well known to Chaucer. His importance at court is attested by numerous entries in
the Patent Rolls. On October 4, 1368, he was given a grant for life, "for kindly
services long rendered freely by him not without danger to body and expense of
substance," that he and his heirs might hunt hares and all kinds of vermin with
dogs in all the king's forests, chases, parks, and warrens, using a parti-colored horn
of russet and black which the King had given him as a sign of such hunting, to be
returned to the King upon failure of heirs male; if the horn was stolen or lost,
Beverley was still privileged to hunt. He was permitted to take one or two deer,
with or without horn, and not be molested. He was exempt for life, "lest he be
hindered at all from such game," from assizes, juries, inquisitions, recognitions
before stewards of the household, barons of the exchequer, justices and other king's
ministers, from appointment as mayor, sheriff, escheator, coroner, customer, taxer,
collector, receiver of wools, tenths or other subsidies, arrayer, or leader of men-at-
arms, hobblers or archers, or other bailiff, justice, or King's minister, and from being
compelled to knighthood.[1]

Some recorded gifts from the King to Beverley include the following: all the
goods of William, son of Hugh Penne, which were forfeit to the King on account
of a felony for which he had been outlawed (January 1, 1365); two tuns of wine
yearly, one at Christmas and the other at Easter, of the King's right prises [customs
(O.E.D.)] of wine (May 3, 1365); grant for life of the manor of Mendlesdene
(Minsden), county Hertford, which the King had recovered from Edward de Ken-
dale, "chivaler" (July 20, 1365); grant to Beverley and Amice, his wife, and their
heirs, of the reversion of the manor of Bokenhull, Co. Oxford, expectant on the demise of Richard Damory, knight (March 20, 1366); £30 yearly, to replace the
wardship of the manor of Melton, Co. Kent, which the King had by mistake granted
to Beverley, "not recollecting" the letters patent by which he had previously granted
this same manor to Alice, late the wife of John de Staunton (September 16, 1366).[2]
[R].

Archbishops' Registers (Lambeth), Sudbury, fol. 105 b.

In the name of God, Amen. I, John de Beverley, being of good memory,
on the fourth day of May, 1380,[3] do make my will in this manner. *In*

---

[1] Gt. Brit., P.R.O., *Cal. of the Patent Rolls*, 1367–1370, p. 181.
[2] Gt. Brit., P.R.O., *Cal. of the Patent Rolls*, 1364–1367, pp. 56, 104, 158, 162, 196, 225,
324.
[3] Proved, Aug. 11, 1380, Lambeth.

primis, I bequeath my soul to God Almighty and my body to be buried in the Conventual Church of Westminster upon the south side of the tomb of the noble King Edward. *Item,* I bequeath for the burial of my body and [that] of Amice my wife [4] and for the soul of the noble King Edward and for the souls of myself [and] Amice aforesaid and also of our parents (*parentum*) and all the faithful departed, to the said Conventual church 100*s.*; and that upon condition that the monks of Westminster come to fetch [my] body wheresoever in London it may be, in procession, to be buried in the above place and the body of Amice my wife when [her death] shall occur. *Item,* I bequeath £20 for the maintenance of a chaplain to celebrate at the altar of the said King Edward in the Conventual church aforesaid for three years to come from the time of my burial for the soul of the noble King Edward and for the souls [as above] with this special clause saying in the collect of the daily mass "pro anima famuli tui Regis," etc. . . . I will that upon the day of my burial there shall be over my body a black pall with a white cross "ycrucid cum pedibus." I will that my body shall be drawn from my inn by two male asses, if they can be found, otherwise by two horses, to the Conventual church where the body shall be buried, and that no men shall carry my body by the way save two boys in black, barefoot and unshod (*cum pede albo et sine caligis*), of whom the one shall go before the body leading an ass, and the other after, as far as Westminster. *Item,* I will that two poor men shall carry two torches, one on either side of the body, clad in black and barefoot. *Item,* I will that all my yeomen (*valecti*) wearing my livery shall go in the same livery from my inn about my body as far as my place of burial, not carrying nor touching my body. I will that a "bedeman" go from my inn before my body ringing a little bell as far as Westminster, clad in black and barefoot.[5]

SIR LEWIS CLIFFORD'S BURIAL "IN THE FARTHEST CORNER OF THE CHURCHYARD," 1404

With Sir Lewis Clifford, a younger son of the baronial family of that name, a distinguished soldier and a member of the King's council, Chaucer was closely acquainted. Early in 1386 Clifford, upon his return from France, brought to Chaucer a poetical tribute in the form of a ballade addressed to him by Eustache Deschamps. Clifford may have been godfather to Chaucer's son, "litell Lowis," for whom the *Astrolabe* was compiled.[6]

[4] She survived him.
[5] Cf. abstract in *Early Lincoln Wills,* ed. by Alfred Gibbons, p. 34 (Bishop Buckingham's Register, 1363–1398, Lincoln).
[6] Cf. Chaucer, *Canterbury Tales,* ed. by Manly, pp. 22, 36, 40, 41.

Sir Nicholas Harris Nicolas, editor of *De controversia*, from which we have taken Clifford's will, writes the following note: "One of the most memorable events in Sir Lewis Clifford's career is his having become a convert to the doctrines of the Lollards; but towards the close of his existence he recanted his errors and renounced their tenets. His religious opinions, in May 1389, induced him to become a party to the letter which several other eminent individuals addressed to the Pontiff, respecting the excesses of the Court of Rome. . . .

"About 1402 Sir Lewis Clifford withdrew from the Lollards, and it is said that in his confession he disclosed the names of the chief persons of that sect. That this act arose from the desire to atone for his errors rather than from a worse motive may be inferred from his will, an instrument in which men are seldom hypocritical, wherein he evinces the deepest contrition for his apostasy. It was prepared shortly before his decease and betrays the poignant remorse under which he labored in so striking a manner that a copy of it is a necessary illustration of his life." [7]

Scrope, *De controversia . . . inter Ricardum Le Scrope et Robertum Grosvenor*, II, 430–431.

Sir Lewis's will: In nomine Patris et Filii et Spiritus Sancti, Amen. The seventeenth day of September, the year of our Lord Jesus Christ one thousand four hundred and four, I, Lewis Clifford, false and traitor to my Lord God and to all the blessed company of Heaven and unworthy to be called a Christian man, make and ordain my testament and my last will in this manner. At the beginning I, most unworthy and God's traitor, recommend my wretched and sinful soul wholly to the grace and to the mercy of the blessed Trinity, and my wretched carrion to be buried in the farthest corner of the churchyard in which parish my wretched soul departeth from my body, and I pray and charge my survivors (*i.e.*, supervisors) and executors, as they will answer before God, and as my whole trust in this matter is in them, that on my stinking carrion be laid neither cloth of gold nor of silk, but a black cloth; and a taper at my head and another at my feet; nor stone nor other thing whereby any man may know where my stinking carrion lieth. And to that church do mine executors all things which ought duly in such cases to be done, without any more cost, save to poor men. And also I pray my survivors and mine executors that any debt that any man can ask me by true title, that it be paid. And if any man can truly say that I have done him any harm in body or in property that ye pay fully his claim ("make largely his gree") while the goods will stretch. And I will also that none of my executors meddle with or administer anything of my goods without the advice and consent of my survivors, or some of them.

[7] Scrope, *De controversia . . . inter Ricardum Le Scrope et Robertum Grosvenor*, II, 429–430; cf. Chaucer, *Canterbury Tales*, ed. by Manly, p. 657.

The Will of Sir Philip la Vache: [8] In the name of God, Amen. I, Philip la Vache, knight, being of sound mind, on the twenty-fifth day of the month of April in the year of our Lord one thousand four hundred and seven and in the eighth year of the reign of King Henry the fourth after the Conquest, make my testament in the following manner. In the first place, I bequeath my soul to Almighty God and to the blessed Mary his mother and to all the saints, and my body to be buried in the church of St. Giles at Chalfont. And because by a certain form I have arranged for my lands to be sold and the profits from them to be disposed of in certain ways to carry out this my testament, as in a certain indentured document of my declared will is plainly shown, I will that first of all my debts shall be paid, and that to whomsoever I have done any injury, or my father has done any, just and due recompense shall be made, as well of lands and tenements, goods and chattels, as of all other actions whatsoever.

And that a black cloth shall be arrayed to be placed on my body and five wax candles be burned on the day of my decease, in honor of the five wounds of Jesus Christ. *Item,* I will that a thousand poor folk in special need shall have by way of alms, as quickly as can be done justly, four pence, each of them. *Item,* I will that the expenses of my funeral shall be according to the disposition of the supervisors of this my testament and of my executors.

Item, I give and bequeath to the fabric of the church of St. Giles at Chalfont ten marks, and I will that my servants for whom I have made no provision in this my testament shall be rewarded according to the ordinance of my executors and supervisors.

Item, I give and bequeath to Elizabeth my wife thirty-six silver dishes, with twelve silver sauce dishes and six chargers of silver, four silver pots, each of a pottle, and two silver pots, each of a quart. *Item,* I give and bequeath to Elizabeth my wife a small silver pot standing on three lions together with its base. *Item,* twenty-four silver spoons, twelve silver-gilt cups with their covers, and two cups with their covers, one of which, of gold, my said wife had of the gift of Isabella, late queen of England, and the other my said wife had on the day of her marriage of the gift of Lady Joan, late princess of Wales. *Item,* six plain[?] silver cups with their covers. *Item,* I give and bequeath to the said Elizabeth my wife

[8] See above, p. 291*n.*

two silver basins marked in the centre with a cow's foot [for Vache], with their two ewers, and a round silver basin with the ewer belonging to it. *Item*, I give and bequeath to the said Elizabeth my wife two salt cellars of silver and four silver candelabra.

Item, I give and bequeath to the said Elizabeth my wife a new missal, a chalice with a paten of silver, two silver cruets, an osculatory of silver, two sets of vestments, with all the furnishings of the chapel.

Item, I give and bequeath to the said Elizabeth my wife all my several beds, all the sheets, curtains, coverlets, bolsters, embroidered[?] pillows, and all featherbed coverings whatsoever, with all the furnishings belonging to my chamber or chambers, except a bed of silk embroidered with knots.

Item, I give and bequeath to the said Elizabeth my wife all my napery which belongs to the offices of the pantry and buttery, and all other utensils belonging to the said offices. And likewise all my utensils or vessels of lead, pewter, brass, and iron belonging to the offices of the kitchen and the brewhouse.

Item, I give and bequeath to the said Elizabeth my wife all my own gems and jewels, whatsoever belongs to her apparel, now in her possession or mine.

Item, I give and bequeath to the said Elizabeth my wife all my carts with all the horses and their harness. *Item*, I give and bequeath to the said Elizabeth my wife all the crops of my land and the pasturage, fruits now sown and to be sown. *Item*, I give and bequeath to the said Elizabeth my wife all my sheep, as well male as female, with all the lambs, pasturing on the manor La Vache. *Item*, I give and bequeath to the said Elizabeth my wife all the cows and bulls of my dairy. *Item*, I give and bequeath to the said Elizabeth my wife all the hogs, pigs, and sows which are on the said manor La Vache.

Item, I give and bequeath to the said Elizabeth my wife my chariot with the horses, cushions, curtains, and all the equipment belonging to it.

Item, I give and bequeath to the said Elizabeth my wife all the furnishings of my hall, with the curtains, cushions, and all other things of every kind belonging to the hall or halls.

And since Alice Spigurnell has a certain annual pension of four marks and a certain other pension of six marks to be taken from my lands for her whole life, I will that it be in the choice of the said Alice whether after my death she wishes to keep the said pensions or to give them up and release her right to them, that if she releases her said right to them and gives up the said pensions within the first half year after my decease, I will and bequeath forty pounds sterling to be paid and delivered to the said Alice in lieu of the said pensions, so that it be the choice of the said Alice to enjoy the said pensions according to the form of her title or to have the forty pounds in their stead.

And the residue, if there be any residue beyond my aforesaid ordinances, I will that this remain with my executors to be expended for my soul, according to the assent, disposition, and ordinance of my supervisors, and especially of Elizabeth my wife. So, namely, that my several tenants, the more needy, who hold of me on the day of my death, shall have part of this residue as a work of charity.

And if there shall be any further residue, I desire further that with a part of it some memorial be made and established perpetually for the salvation of my soul and for the soul of my wife, and for the souls of my parents, in the said church of St. Giles, at the disposition of my supervisors and executors, by a chaplain or other poor man as to them shall seem most profitable to do.

Item, I desire that Maud, late wife of Henry Kyng, Maud Melward, John Kynge, Dionisia Fuller, John Lincoln and Constance his wife shall have of my charity for the period of their lives food and clothing so that they shall not be in great need, provided they live well and honestly, behave themselves, and conduct themselves to the honor of God, and whatsoever more shall remain of this residue I give and bequeath to the said Elizabeth my wife to be expended and used for my soul as my said wife shall deem most expedient.

I desire further that all charters, fines, and muniments, which are in my hands as in my keeping, which are not my own, immediately after my death shall be delivered to those who have the right to them.

Item, I give and bequeath to a certain tenant of mine called Rydyng forty shillings. *Item*, I bequeath to be distributed for the soul of Sir Guichard d'Angle forty-six shillings and eight pence.

Item, since William Molyns, squire, is bound by a certain deed for the sum of one thousand marks, which deed is in my keeping, I will that the said deed be delivered to this William under the form and condition which follows, namely, that if the said William Molyns shall pardon and hold clear, as regards our most excellent lord the King, Lady Margery de Molyns and others in a certain deed of obligation for the sum of three hundred marks. I desire further that William Alberd shall be given a deed of his now in my custody.

And to fulfill and carry out this my testament I appoint as my executors Master John Medilton, clerk, William Assh, Richard Wyot, Walter Gayton, Thomas Barbow, John Skrevan, John Kynwalmerssh, John Buktofte, and Robert Seman, chaplains. To supervise and accomplish this my aforesaid will and testament, I appoint and ordain and as a work of charity I entreat as my supervisors Elizabeth my wife, Thomas Clanvowe,[9] and Edmund Hamden [for the supervising and carrying out of this my last will and testament] as appears plainly in a certain indenture. And I will that my administrators shall have, each of them, beyond the usual costs, ten marks of silver for his labor in carrying out my aforesaid will and testament. Given on the day and year named above. And I have signed my name with my own hand.

> This will was probated before Master John Perche, commissar, etc., the twenty-second day of the month of June, *anno Domini* one thousand four hundred and eight. And the administration of all the goods of the deceased was given to John Kynwalmerssh and Sir John Buktofte, chaplain, executors named in this will, etc.

2. *The Burial of an Earl and His Son, 1462*

> Society of Antiquaries of London, *A Collection of Ordinances and Regulations for the Government of the Royal Household*, pp. 131–133.

The interment of the Earl of Salisbury at Breshall, in the shire of Buckingham, [was made] the fifteenth day of February in the second year of King Edward the Fourth, and of Sir Thomas his son, in two coffins in one chariot with six horses in trappings, the first in St. George's arms, the other covered in black, a banner of St. George before him, and two behind. First, before the conveying of the body and bones of the said earl and his son, the Earl of Warwick, son and heir of the said earl, rode after the chariot, Lord Montague on the right side afoot, Lord Latimer, his son, on the left hand with many knights and squires afoot on every side to the number of sixteen; the earl's banner and standard came next and immediately after the chariot; and before the Earl of Warwick, meeting with the corpses a mile without the town, came two heralds and two kings of arms, bearing the coats of arms of the said earl at every

---

[9] Sir Thomas Clanvowe was author of *The Cuckoo and the Nightingale*, written in palpable imitation of Chaucer. He was a member of the court circle and a kinsman of Sir John Clanvowe, distinguished soldier and diplomat and friend of Chaucer's. (Chaucer, *Canterbury Tales*, ed. by Manly, p. 41.)

corner of the chariot. . . . At the place [of interment] they received
the bodies and the bones so coffered. The bishop of Exeter, chancellor
of England, the bishop of Salisbury, the bishop of St. Asaph, and two
other abbots mitered, in solemn procession accompanied by the Lord
Hastings, the King's chamberlain, the Lord Fitz-Hugh, and many other
knights and squires in great number, conveyed the corpses, the son before
the father, into the choir, where the hearse [10] of the said earl . . . was
prepared and ordained in solemn and honorable wise, as appertained to
the estate of an earl . . . the pall and parclose being covered with black.
. . . The earls within the parclose and pall covered with black, where
the coffer with the bones of the earl's son, Sir Thomas, was laid under the
coffer of the earl his father, were the lords that followeth: the Duke of
Clarence, the King's brother, the Duke of Suffolk, the Earl of Warwick,
the Earl of Worcester, the Lord Montague, the Lord Hastings, the
Lord Fitz-Hugh, with many other knights and nobles without. At the
corners of the head of the said hearse, on the right side of the banner,
stood Garter king of arms in the coat of the said earl's arms; on the left
side of the standard there stood Clarenceux king of arms; and at the
corners of the feet of the said hearse were two other heralds, Windsor
and Chester, in coats of the said earl's arms, with many other heralds
and pursuivants, during the observance of the dirge till the void was
done.

Also, on the morrow after, the states, princes, lords and ladies came
to the high mass. The said kings of arms and heralds brought out of the
vestry solemnly and honorably every one of [the arms], that is to say,
Garter, the coat of arms, Clarenceux, the shield, Windsor, the sword,
Chester, the helm and timber,[11] and conveyed them to the head of the
said earl's hearse, holding the coat of arms and the sword; on the right
side the shield, on the left side the helm and timber. *Item,* after the
gospel of the mass, the two kings went forth to the west door of the
church, where there was ready a man armed on horseback trapped, with
an axe in his right hand, the point downward; the said herald received
him and conveyed him to the choir door of the church, where he alighted,
holding in his hand the said horse trapped in the arms of the said earl.
Item, at the offering, the Earl of Warwick, conveyed between two noble

[10] Hearse: a framework intended to carry a large number of lighted tapers over the
bier or coffin while placed in the church at funerals. (*O.E.D.*)
[11] The crest of a helmet; hence, the crest or exterior additions placed over the shield in
heraldic arms. (*O.E.D.*)

and worshipful knights, offered the mass-penny and stood apart on the right side of the bishop.

Item, the king of arms, proceeding to the offering with the coat of arms before the Earl of Worcester, delivered the said coat to the earl with due reverence, offering the said coat. Afterwards the said bishop delivered the said coat to the Earl of Warwick as heir, in tokening that the said coat belonged in right to him; after which deliverance, the said Earl of Warwick delivered the said coat to the said king of arms, as it appertaineth to his office to do; the said king of arms standing apart on the right side with the said coat. *Item*, the shield borne by a king of arms before the Lord Montague in reverent wise was delivered, as was said before, to the heir, and redelivered again to the king of arms to do as it appertained, as before was said. *Item*, the sword borne by the herald before the Lord Hastings in like wise was delivered, redelivered, and offered to the said herald, as before was said. *Item*, the timber and helm borne before the Lord Fitz-Hugh by an herald, as before was said, was delivered, offered, and redelivered to the said herald, the king of arms and heralds on the right hand, the other on the left side, to the end of the offering. *Item*, the residue of the heralds and pursuivants came before the man of arms and horse trapped; the said man of arms, conveyed between two barons, was by them presented, and he offered his arms and horse to the church; and afterwards he was conveyed through the church to the vestry, where he was received and unarmed. *Item*, then the Duke of Clarence, conveyed between two barons to the offering, offered a noble. *Item*, the Duchess of Suffolk and the Duke together each offered a skull.[12] *Item*, the Earl of Warwick, coming again, for himself offered twenty pence. *Item*, the residue of ladies and gentlewomen with other knights and esquires and gentlemen offered, the lords and ladies returning into the hearse before said. *Item*, the lords returned into the pall and parclose of the hearse and made their presentation and offering of cloths of gold of baudekin unto the corpses then present; that is to say, one a length (along) the corpses and the other over, like a cross; the youngest baron first, the two barons after, and so the third. Every baron offered one cloth, every earl two, the Duke of Suffolk three, the Duke of Clarence four; the earls after the barons, the dukes after the earls, at every time till they had offered their cloths; the youngest of estate first beginning, the most noble the richest cloths. *Item*, when the offering was done, the said kings of arms and heralds in most humble and

12 Possibly an error for *shull*[*ing*], shilling. Cf. *O.E.D.*

reverent wise bare forth the said coat of arms, shield, sword, and helm and timber, unto the sepulchre where the corpses should be buried, and with due reverence set there on the tomb in the midst the coat of arms, at the head above the helm and timber, the shield underneath the sword hanging by the banner on the right side at the head, the standard at the same side at the foot; and, this observance done, they did off their coats. *Item,* in token that the coat was delivered and redelivered by the heir, the said earl's herald in the said coat revested stood before the hearse in the presence of the said lords during the remnant of the said mass unto the burying of the said corpses.

3. The Wake

NO MASKS AT THE WAKE, 1284 [13]

Chancery Miscellanea, Gild Certificate 392.

Members of the Gild of Palmers of St. Mary, Ludlow, all attend all the burial offices for a dead member and pray devoutly for the soul of the deceased and of all the faithful in Christ. A man, but not a woman, unless of the household of the deceased, may be allowed to keep watch by the dead during the night, but must not presume to don hideous masks, to make mock of the body or of the reputation of the deceased, or to try any other improper games.[14]

VICTUALS AND ALMS AT A FUNERAL, before 1425

The following fragment of an account seems to refer to the funeral of Joan Hampden, daughter of Sir Robert Bealknap, whose second husband, Edmund Hampden, was a neighbor and kinsman by marriage of Thomas Chaucer. The expense account belonged to his step-son, Thomas Stonor, who was a ward of Thomas Chaucer. Chaucer, indeed, paid £200 for the custody of Stonor's lands and the control of his marriage. [R.]

The Stonor Letters and Papers, 1290–1438, ed. by Kingsford, I, 39–40 (from Chancery Miscellanea 37/1 [35]).

Paid to the [black]smith of Rippinghale

Item primis: For two fiches . . .   [sum omitted]

Paid to the smith of Rippinghale for divers things . . .   11*d.*

[13] See above, p. 235*n.*
[14] Original Latin for the last clause: "Dumtamen nec monstra larvarum inducere, nec corporis vel fame sue ludibria, nec ludos alios inhonestos, presumat aliqualiter attemptare." The phrase *monstra larvarum inducere* is translated by Toulmin Smith "to call up ghosts." (Smith, *English Gilds,* pp. 194–195; cf. Westlake, *The Parish Gilds of Mediaeval England,* p. 19.)

Paid to Ralph Fool . . . . 2*d.*

Paid for half a beef . . . . 5*s.* 4*d.*

Paid for bread . . . . 8*s.*

Paid for wax [for candles] at 7*d.* the pound . . . £10 5*s.* 10*d.*

    and the residue of the wax here anon

Paid for 3 torches . . . . 8*s.*

For fish at Bury . . . . 13*d.*

For fish at Stamford . . . . [sum omitted]

For wine . . . . 22*d.*

For claret wine, 2 gallons . . . . 16*d.*

For a veal . . . . 3*s.* 4*d.*

For a brawn . . . . 3*s.* 4*d.*

For 2 geese . . . . 10*d.*

For 3 pigs . . . . 12½*d.* [xij. d. ob.]

For plovers . . . . 7*d.*

For black cotton for the hearse cloth, 7 yards . . . . . 2*s.* 11*d.*

For an ell of linen cloth . . . . 5*d.*

The vii[th] Day

Memorandum delivered to William Wayrd to be dealt in alms for my mother's soul [11 places are named and the total sum is just under a pound. There follows:]

Delivered to the priests of the 7th day . . . . 6*s.* 8*d.*

To clerks and children and poor people, the same day . . . 10*s.*

For nine dozen of bread the burying day . . . . . 9*s.*

For a veal, the 7th day . . . . 2*s.* 8*d.*

For 2 swans, 3 geese, 3 capons, 3 pigs, half a

    hox (ox), and 6 couple of conies . . . . . [sum omitted]

The xxxth Day Dealt in Alms

[The same places are named and the total amount is 22*s.* 8*d.*]

Victuals the Same Day

Half an ox . . . . 4*s.*

Half a pork . . . . 12*d.*

Also crop of beef and the sirloin . . . . 10*d.*

A swan, 4 geese, 2 pigs, 3 capons, 5 couple of

    conies, 16 plovers, a mutton . . . . . . [sum omitted]

The Burying Day

Received of my mother's money in gold and silver this sum following:

In King Harry's pence this sum	30s. 12d.
In gold	£5
In groats and two-penny pieces	13s. 4d.
Sum total	£7 4s. 4d.
Paid to the sheriff's servants for sheriff's tenth	2s. 6d.
Paid for two boxes of conserves, treacle, and sugar candy .	10d.

Delivered for Wages to the Herdsmen and Others

To the cowherd for his quarter wages	20d.
To Richard Clay	7d.
Paid to John Hosbourne [Osbourne] for a quarter wages	[sum omitted]
Paid for coloring (dyeing) of 22 yards of cloth	2s. 10d.
Paid to the cleaner (fuller) for cleaning of the same stuff	[sum omitted]

Endorsements

In groats, 15s. In pence and two-penny pieces . . .	£4 7s. 6d.
Paid of my money this sum following the burying day and the seventh day—summa	£3 14s. 6d.

4. *The Poor at the Burial*

PSALMS AND PRAYERS BY THE POOR, 1392

Prerogative Court of Canterbury, 6 Rous.

Will of John de Donewich, warden of Clare Hall, Cambridge, dated April 6, 1392:— I desire . . . to be buried at the south door of the church of St. John in Melde Street. I will that about my hearse forty poor learned clerks shall sit, saying their psalters, and sixty poor men and women shall sit round saying their psalters of the glorious Virgin Mary, praying for my soul until my body is brought to the tomb, and for the souls of all the faithful departed . . . and my executors shall allow none to be present with them in the church except those who are willing to pray.

A BLACK AND WHITE FUNERAL, 1404

Prerogative Court of Canterbury, 9 Marche.

Will of Matilda, formerly wife of Robert de la Mare, knight:—My body to be buried in the chapel of the Blessed Mary in the church of Steeple

Lavinton. I will that . . . twelve torches and twelve poor persons carrying the said torches and clad in white tunics with black hoods and with new shoes be present at the exequies and masses. . . . I will . . . that the poor be well fed and every beggar coming on the day of my burial shall have a penny for the sake of charity.

SHOES AND RUSSET FOR THE POOR, 1411

Prerogative Court of Canterbury, 23 Marche.

Will of John Rychard, burgess of the town of Bristol:— I bequeath to twenty-four poor persons on the day of my burial twenty-four pairs of shoes. . . . I will that thirteen poor persons be clothed in Welsh russet on that same day.

5. *Poor Men's Funerals*

GILD PROVISIONS, 1306–CA.1389.[15]

Chancery Miscellanea, Gild Certificate 440.

The Gild of Holy Cross, Stratford-on-Avon, [*ca.* 1389], has a candle which burns at mass before the Holy Cross. This candle, with eight smaller ones, is taken to the house of a dead brother and carried back with him to the church, where all members attend the ceremonies and pray for his soul. The gild also supplies a sheet and a carpet for the coffin of any poor man or stranger dying in the town.

Chancery Miscellanea, Gild Certificate 64.

The Gild of St. Mary the Virgin at Barkway in Hertfordshire, [1306], pays ¼d. in soul-alms and 1d. for masses at the burial of members. The burial, if necessary, is at the gild's expense. A dead brother or sister shall be brought home if within ten miles of the town.

Chancery Miscellanea, Gild Certificate 135.

The Gild of Corpus Christi in St. Michael on the Hill, Lincoln, [1350], pays for the burial of a brother, if need be. It provides four soul-candles with others to burn round the hearse. At the funeral mass the "graceman" and warden of the gild offer 1d. each from the gild fund, and each brother offers as he will. The gild banner is taken to the house of a dead brother and there displayed publicly to show that he was a member of the gild. Thence with the great light it precedes the corpse to the church. Mass for living and dead brothers is celebrated on the octave of Corpus Christi, the bell tolling on vigil.

[15] See above, p. 235*n.*

Chancery Miscellanea, Gild Certificate 261.

The Gild of St. Margaret, Lynn, [1354], for a dead brother gives ½d. in offering and 40 masses and all the gild candles. A dead sister has *all* the candles by special grace. The son of a brother has the largest candle only. A brother dying within three miles is brought home at gild's expense, if necessary.

6. *Miscarriage of Plans for a Felon's Burial, 1345*

Chancery Miscellanea, Writs and Returns, 122/6.

Return made by the bailiffs of Norwich to a writ to show the cause of imprisonment of Thomas Davy, clerk.

Thomas Davy, clerk, was taken within the City by the Sheriff of Norfolk, because on Tuesday after Holy Trinity last [1345] he cut down from the gallows Henry, son of John le Saltere, who had been convicted of felony before the justices for the delivery of Norwich Castle and had been hanged; and as clerk and attorney of the Prior of the Hospital of St. John of Jerusalem in England, Thomas Davy took the said man who had been hanged at the place where he was hanged and caused him to be brought by the friends of the hanged man to the church of St. Margaret of Fybridge Gate within the city for burial as if dead, as is the custom; which hanged man within the bounds of the church breathed and recovered. Being given to understand this, and because the sheriff had encroached upon our liberties, we [the bailiffs] took the said Thomas Davy and put him in the King's prison of the said city, and detain him there.

7. *Horse Taken for a Mortuary, 1384*

Common Pleas, Plea Roll 493 m. 418.

Richard Everdon, clerk, attached to answer Robert Echyngham and others concerning a horse worth 60s. which they say he found and took in the parish of St. Bennet in Baynard Castle Ward, London, answers that a certain John Haukherst, clerk, came riding upon the said horse into the parish aforesaid and was there detained by such an infirmity that he died there thereof. And that the horse at the time of his death was his own horse and that he himself [Richard Everdon] is parson of the church aforesaid, and took and led away the same horse as a mortuary, as [he was] parson of the said church and it was the best beast of John Haukherst, as well he might.

THE TOMB

1. Orders for Making the Tomb of the Duchess Blanche,[16] *1374–1375*

John of Gaunt's Register, II, 212–213, 296.

The Savoy, June 18, 1374. John [king of Castile] to our . . . receiver of Tutbury, greeting. We command you that you take order for six wagons loaded for London with alabaster for the new work of the tomb of the Lady Blanche, formerly our consort, upon whom God have mercy, with all the speed you can at our charge, so that they be in London this season. Given at the Savoy, the eighteenth of June, 48 [Edward III]. And we will that the said alabaster shall be such as the bearer of these [letters] will choose, and in case you have no alabaster of the alabaster in our demesne fit for an image, take order for alabaster from some other fit place for the said image, according to what the bearer shall tell you; and for the charges and for the carriage of these letters this shall be your warrant, for we understand that you have no alabaster except for one image, and we desire to have two.

John [king of Castile] to our beloved . . . clerk of our Wardrobe . . . We command you to pay . . . to Henry Yevele,[17] mason, £108 by the year by equal portions at the Feasts of St. Michael [September 29] and Easter, beginning the first payment at the Feast of St. Michael last past, until such time as you have paid in full £486 assigned to him for a tomb to be made in the church of St. Paul of London for our very dear and beloved consort Blanche, on whom God have mercy. . . .

Given at the Savoy, January 26, 49 [Edw. III, 1375].

2. Orders for Making the Tomb of Richard II and Queen Anne, 1395

In 1395 Richard contracted for the construction and ornamentation of a tomb for himself and Queen Anne, who had died the previous year. The following extracts from two indentures for the work are interesting because of their particulars as well as because Henry Yevele, one of the two masons named, was master mason under Chaucer when he was clerk of the King's works, 1389–1391. [R.]

Rymer, *Foedera*, 2d ed., VII, 795–796.

---

[16] Professor Manly conjectured that undoubtedly "both Geoffrey and Philippa Chaucer were among the mourners at the funeral of . . . the Duchess Blanche; and Chaucer's first long original poem must have been written soon after this date." The Duchess died on September 12, 1369. (Chaucer, *Canterbury Tales*, ed. by Manly, p. 14.) See also below, pp. 419–420.

[17] See above, pp. 190–191.

MASONRY

This indenture is made between our lord King Richard on the one part and Henry Yevele and Stephen Lote, citizens and masons of London on the other. Witness that the above-mentioned masons have covenanted and undertaken to make to the honor and profit of our lord the King a tomb of fine marble for our lord the King and the excellent Lady Anne, the late Queen of England.

Which tomb shall be made of fine marble and constructed according to the manner and form of a plan in the hands of the said masons bearing the seal of the treasurer of England.

And the said masons shall make niches for twelve images, namely, six on one side and six on the other side of the said tomb, and the rest of the said tomb shall be made with shields, corresponding to and similar to the said niches, for images to complete the tomb and containing spaces for escutcheons of copper and brass, to be assigned by the advice of the said treasurer.

Which tomb shall be placed in Westminster, containing in length all the space between the pillars where the said Queen is interred, and it shall be duly proportioned to sustain the superincumbent metal work which shall be placed thereon. And the said masons shall make the tomb of the same height off the ground as the tomb of King Edward III.

Which work shall be done and all ready at Westminster, where the Queen lies between the two pillars above mentioned, before the feast of St. Michael the Archangel [September 29] in the year 1397, provided the said masons shall be reasonably paid on the days below specified.

For which tomb made according to agreement in the above form our lord the King wills that the said masons shall be paid two hundred fifty pounds as follows: [Payments in instalments follow]. And besides the said masons shall have a gratuity of twenty pounds over and above this amount if the work is well and faithfully performed in every respect in the manner and form above stated.

IMAGES AND ADORNMENT

This indenture is made between the very excellent and most noble lord King Richard on the one part and Nicholas Broker and Godfrey Prest, citizens and coppersmiths of London, on the other part.

Witness that the above-named have covenanted to make or cause to be made images herein described, namely, two images of copper and brass, gilt, and crowned, close together and with right hands joined and holding sceptres in their left hands, and a ball and a cross between the said images. The one image a likeness of our lord the King, the other, of that excellent and noble lady, Anne. . . .

And a slab of the same metal, gilt, on which the figures shall be placed, the which slab shall be ornamented with a fret of fleur-de-lis, lions, eagles, leopards; and the said slab shall be as long as the space between the two pillars at Westminster where the said queen is interred and wide in due proportion.

And there shall be canopies called hovels or *gabletz* of the same gilt metal at the sides, and double jambs on each side.

And [there shall be] two lions at the feet of the King and an eagle and a leopard at the feet of the Queen, all in gilt metal. And also twelve images, of gilt metal, of such saints as shall be named and chosen by our lord the King or his treasurer, of uniform size on the two sides of the tomb to make it in the form above described, duly proportioned to the whole, and eight angels around the tomb. And also an inscription to be engraved around the tomb such as may be furnished to Nicholas and Godfrey, suitable to that tomb.

And also they shall make such escutcheons well proportioned, of the same gilt metal engraved and enameled with divers arms, uniform around the tomb, as to the said Nicholas and Godfrey shall be assigned by our lord the King or his treasurer.

These aforesaid things shall be made and finished in the above manner according to plans shown to the said Nicholas and Godfrey, which now are in the possession of the treasurer and under the seals of the treasurer and the said Nicholas and Godfrey, before the Feast of St. Michael the Archangel next coming after the date of this, providing the said Nicholas and Godfrey shall be reasonably paid on the days below stated. [They are to receive £400 in instalments.]

Given April 24, 1395.

3. The Tomb of a Wealthy Priest, 1407

Prerogative Court of Canterbury, 16 Marche.

Will of William, son of John de Escrik of Selby, ordained priest, dated January 19, 1407/8; to be buried in Selby church: I will that [my executors] buy a marble stone for my tomb, in which shall be graven the image of the blessed Virgin Mary, seated on a throne, holding the Son in her left arm; at whose feet shall be made an image like to a priest kneeling, holding in his hands a scroll with these words: Jesus, Son of God, have mercy on me.[18]

4. *Copying a Neighbor's Tomb, 1426*

Prerogative Court of Canterbury, 6 Luffenam.

Will of William Hanyngfeld, Esquire, [with English codicil]. . . . I will that I have a tomb like Sir Thomas More's, and thereupon a broad stone with four pillars, and the broad stone graven with "Laton [19] of Cisisly," and [the names of] seven children, that is to say, a son and six daughters, John and two children, Agnes and two children. Cost to be 50 marks.

Proved in 1427.

5. *Burial beneath the Pavement, 1415*

Prerogative Court of Canterbury, 40 Marche.

Will of Thomas Broke of Holdich. . . . I will that I be buried in Thomecombe church key, as men go over into the church at the south entrance, where they may step on me. And a flat stone, plain save my name engraved thereon, that men may the rather have mind on me and pray for me. . . . These two lines I write with mine own hand.

6. *A Likeness of the Deceased to be Placed over the Tomb, 1395*

Bishop of London, Register Braybrook, fol. ccccx.

Will of Thomas Grey, rector of the church of Weathersfield. I will that I be buried before the high altar in the chapel of the Virgin in the church of Holy Trinity, Hadenham. The chapel at my cost to be decorated with painted tiles. I will that a good stone of marble with an image . . . representing a likeness of me be placed above me. In the north of the chapel I will that a new and good window . . . be made as wide and as high as the wall extends, and I will that the story of Jesse be told in glass. And I will that in one [part] be made a likeness of me kneeling upon my armorial shield and holding a roll in my hands.

7. *Draping the Tomb on the Anniversary, 1408*

Prerogative Court of Canterbury, 16 Marche.

Will of Thomas de Molynton, knight and lord of Wem: [I bequeath] to the College [of Crutched Friars, London], one green cloth of gold to

---

[18] For the entire will, see above, pp. 382–385.
[19] Possibly latten, a kind of brasslike alloy, formerly much used for monumental brasses.

use and place every year upon my tomb on the day of my death forever for an ornament.

[He was buried in the chapel of St. Mary there.]

MOURNING

1. Livery for the Funeral, 1403

Prerogative Court of Canterbury, 4 Marche.

Will of William Parker, citizen and mercer of London: I will that twenty-four garments be made of blue cloth lined with blanket,[20] the one half for men and the other half for women, and that they be given to the poorest where need shall be. *Item,* I will that no more livery be made for my burial save only my wife, my children, brethren, the people of my household, and my executors.

2. Mourning for a Priest, 1410

Prerogative Court of Canterbury, 21 Marche.

Will of Robert Rygge, priest [of Exeter]: I will that thirteen poor persons and all the people of my household be clothed; I leave the color to the discretion of my executors. *Item,* I will that my executors who are willing to take upon them the execution of my will be clothed the same day [of my funeral].

3. No Mourning by Request, 1413

Source unknown.

Will of William Marchford, citizen and mercer of London, December 1, 1413: I ordain that none of my executors, apprentices, or any other of my servants or anyone else whatever be clothed or clad in black cloth by reason of me or my funeral rites, except only my wife.

PROVISION FOR THE SOUL

1. Setting up an Altar for the Soul of the Duchess Blanche,[21] 1372

John of Gaunt's Register, II, 23–25.

John [of Gaunt] to our . . . receiver general, greeting. Whereas we have ordained and assigned two chaplains to sing for the soul of Blanche of Lancaster, formerly our consort, on whose soul God have mercy, in the church of St. Paul of London where the body of the said Blanche is buried, we command that from the issues of your receipt you cause to be

[20] A white or undyed woollen stuff used for clothing. (*O.E.D.*)
[21] See above, p. 415n.

paid to the said chaplains for the time being £20 by the year. . . . And moreover pay from the said issues to Master Robert, joiner of London, who has made an altar next the tomb of our said consort in the said church, by advice of our council, where the said chaplains shall say their masses, 100s. 8d., receiving from him the particulars under his seal . . . and pay similarly for a missal which our clerk, Sir John de Yerdebur, clerk of our Wardrobe, has bought to be used at the said altar, £6 16s. 8d.; item, for a chalice bought by him for the same reason, 65s. 8d.; and these our letters shall be your warrant.

Given at the Savoy, the nineteenth day of February of the year [1372].

2. Masses by the Thousand, 1404

Prerogative Court of Canterbury, 5 Marche; codicil, 8 Marche.

Nuncupative will of Thomas Weylond, citizen and draper of London: He bequeathed to a thousand chaplains a thousand groats (grossos) sterling, to each of them one groat (grossum), to celebrate four masses for his soul and the souls of all faithful departed as speedily as they could conveniently be celebrated after his death.

3. Masses for the Souls of Knights of the Garter, 1375

John of Gaunt's Register, II, 312.

John [King of Castile] to our well beloved . . . clerk of our Great Wardrobe: We . . . command you . . . to pay . . . 10 marks for one missal bought for the use of our chapel. And, moreover, to pay to Fr. Walter Disse, our confessor, 2005d. for as many masses which he has had sung for the souls of five of our companions of the Garter who have passed away.

Given at the Savoy, October 12, 49 [Edward III].

4. Works of Charity for the Soul, 1405

Prerogative Court of Canterbury, 13 Marche.

Will of Thomas Wyltord, citizen and fishmonger of London, dated 1405, proved 1407: If my widow marry again, my lands and tenements shall be sold and the money distributed for my soul and the souls of my parents, friends, and benefactors to the poorest people in divers townships of divers counties of England upon "Upland," namely, to plowmen, carters, the infirm, the bedridden, widows, scholars (pupillis), orphan girls for their marriage, and prisoners.

5. *Ditch Cleaning and Prayers for the Soul, 1375*

Riley, *Memorials of London*, II, 384–385 (from London Letter-Book H, fol. xxi).

Be it remembered that on Friday, the last day of August, 49 Edward III . . . the chamberlain of the Guildhall received from . . . the vendors of the tenements which belonged to Thomas Legge [22] and disposers of the moneys arising therefrom, £100 of such moneys; which they . . . granted unto the mayor and commonalty for cleansing the fosses of the city; on condition that the chaplains celebrating in the Chapel of St. Mary at the Guildhall should have the soul of the said Thomas and the souls of Alice, Margery, and Simon Legge in their masses and prayers commended unto God.

6. *Mass for the Peace of the Kingdom, 1390*

Prerogative Court of Canterbury, 9 Rous.

Will of John Ravenser, rector of Algarkirk, diocese of Lincoln, and prebendary of Castre in Lincoln Cathedral, September 2, 14 Richard II: I bequeath 400 marks stirling to be paid to as many chaplains as it may suffice for their stipends to celebrate for the peace and tranquility of the kingdom of England and for the good and healthful estate of the King and Queen and of all princes and nobles of the kingdom aforesaid and of all my kinsmen, parishioners, and benefactors, and also for my soul and the souls of my father John and my mother Sybil and for the souls of King Edward III and Philippa, late Queen of England, of John de Thoresby, late archbishop of York, and of Sir Richard de Ravenser, late archdeacon of Lincoln, my most dear master.

7. *Library Sold to Pay for Prayers, 1402–1403*

Prerogative Court of Canterbury, 4 Marche.

Will of Thomas de Walynton, citizen and clothier of London: To be buried at St. Benet, Paul's Wharf. I will that my library, existing in two volumes, one catholicon,[23] one book called Sydrac [24] . . . be sold and the money given to poor scholars to pray for my soul.

[22] Thomas Legge was twice mayor of the city, and evidently a canny man, who knew how to make his money serve more than one purpose. [R.]

[23] The *O.E.D.* defines "catholicon" as "a comprehensive treatise" and states that the term was "applied by Johannes de Balbis de Janua, as the title of his celebrated Latin Grammar and Dictionary, the Catholicon or Summa, made in 1286; whence in later times [it was] given to various vocabularies of Latin and some vernacular."

[24] Probably the book sometimes called *La Fontaine de toutes sciences*, a catechism of medieval science. Because it tells how Sydrac converted Boctus, king of the Bactrians about 1200 B.C., to the Trinitarian faith, it is also known as *Sydrac and Boctus*. It occurs

8. A Gild of the Resurrection, 1354

Chancery Miscellanea, Gild Certificate 136.

The Gild of the Resurrection, in St. Martin's church, Lincoln, finds yearly 24 square candles and four mortuary candles round the [Easter] Sepulchre, of which four square and four mortuary candles burn from the Burial to the Resurrection, when all are lighted in honor of the Burial and Resurrection and for the safety of the souls of members living and dead. They find also 20 candles with the mortuary candles round the hearse of a dead brother and at the funeral mass, at which the "graceman" and two wardens offer 2d. of the gild fund and each brother 1d., so that there may be as many masses as there are brethren.

9. Chantry Chapels in St. Paul's, 1345

Chantry Chapels, endowed by the rich for the salvation of their souls, added considerably to the magnificence and importance of a church. In St. Paul's, the Mother church of London, the number of these increased so greatly that in the fourteenth century forty-four of them were incorporated because their endowment was inadequate to provide for individual priests.

The following letter from the mayor and aldermen to the dean and chapter of St. Paul's complains as early as 1345 of neglected chantries. [R.]

Riley, *Memorials of London*, I, 224–225 (from London Letter-Book F, fol. ciii).

Whereas it is well known that many men and women of the city have devised in their testaments and given in other ways to the dean and chapter of the same church and to their successors many tenements and rents in the said city for founding and maintaining divers chantries in the same church and for offering up prayers and other devotions perpetually for their souls . . . and whereas we have fully understood and also do see it daily with our own eyes when we pass by your church of St. Paul . . . that there are but few chaplains to sing there in proportion to the chantries which in the said church have been founded, to the great peril of your souls who ought to oversee the said chantries and maintain and support the same: we do pray and request you . . . that you will cause such defaults to be amended and redressed in your time . . . not having regard to the words of any person who shall wish to gainsay the said matter. . . . And to the end that persons may have the greater feelings

in British Museum MS Additional 16,563. An early fourteenth-century copy on vellum is in the Library of Lambeth Palace. See British Museum, *Catalogue of Romances*, ed. by Ward, I, 93, and Lambeth Palace, Library, *A Descriptive Catalogue of the Manuscripts in the Library of Lambeth Palace*, ed. by James and Jenkins, pp. 418–419.

of devotion and may bestow alms, honors, and other bounty upon your church aforesaid, let no person who holds a benefice or chantry elsewhere hold any chantry in the same church, and then only a single chantry, at the which he may be personally in attendance, to do what shall thereunto pertain.

That chaplains sometimes had difficulty in securing pay for their services in behalf of the souls of the deceased, or that they made false claims for such services, is shown by the following Common Pleas cases:

Common Pleas, Plea Roll 505 m. 133 d.

Somerset, 1386. John Spyne summoned to answer Henry Lowes, chaplain, on plea of debt for seven marks. Lowes stated by his attorney that he had been engaged by John to serve in the office of priest to say matins, masses, and vespers in the parish church of South Petherton for the souls of John's father and mother, etc., for a whole year, and had done so faithfully. John denied the arrangement. Both placed themselves on the country.

Common Pleas, Plea Roll 520 m. 142 d.

London, 1390. A London chaplain sued John Curson of Ketellston for 14 marks in payment for celebrating masses for the soul of John Curson, knight [father of the defendant?]. Both parties put themselves on the country. Judgment was brought against the chaplain for making a false claim.

Bibliography

MANUSCRIPT SOURCES

Public Records (at Public Record Office)

CHANCERY

Criminal Inquisitions, 41/9.
Miscellaneous Inquisition 265, 21 Ric. II 5, m. 6.
Enrolments of Extents on Debts, 38/16.
Files, Series H (Drafts and Surrenders of Patents) 15/72.
Miscellanea, Gild Certificates 59, 63(i), 64, 76, 87, 91, 96, 109, 115, 116, 129, 131, 135, 136, 142, 189, 190, 204, 212, 242, 261, 272, 279, 288, 295, 296, 308, 321, 325, 342, 356, 368, 369, 391, 392, 404, 439, 440, 446, 454.
Miscellanea, Transcripts of Records, 88/3, no. 59.
Miscellanea, Writs and Returns, 104/4, 111/18, 122/6.
Warrants (Privy Seal Bills) 915/22, 918/2.
Warrants (Privy Seal Writs) 520/6709, 555/10211, 555/10218.
Warrants (Privy Seal) 15. Reference incomplete.
Warrants (Internal) 1767/31.

EXCHEQUER

King's Remembrancer, Accounts Various, 105/38, 181/12, 183/9, 315/2, 315/16, 316/12, 318/11, 396/11, 396/15, 398/8, 401/16, 402/17, 406/15.
*King's Remembrancer, Memoranda Roll 119. Precepta, Mich. 17 Edw. III.
King's Remembrancer, Memoranda Roll 160. Brevia, Membrane 1.
King's Remembrancer, Memoranda Roll 164. Recorda, Easter 11 Ric. II.
King's Remembrancer, Memoranda Roll 169. Communia, Hil. 16 Ric. II.
King's Remembrancer, Customs Accounts, 181/10.
King's Remembrancer, Sheriffs' Accounts, 25/70.
King's Remembrancer, Writs, bdle. 52, Michaelmas Term, 45 Edw. III.
Lord's Treasurer's Remembrancer, Exannual Roll 1, London and Middlesex. Debts extracted in 14 Ric. II.
Exchequer of Receipt, Issue Rolls 471 m. 7; 508 m. 17–22; 521 m. 23; 541 m. 17.
Exchequer of Receipt, Warrants for Issues 2/10.

COURTS OF LAW

King's Bench, Coram Rege Rolls 538, 548, 552, 553, 565.
King's Bench, Controlment Rolls 38, 42, 43.
Common Pleas, Plea Roll 476, Deeds Enrolled.
Common Pleas, Plea Rolls 480, 482, 483, 485, 486, 487, 488, 490, 493, 494, 502, 504, 505, 509, 510, 511, 515, 516, 517, 519, 520, 523, 524, 526, 530, 531, 547, 548, 551, 561, 579.
Court Roll (P.R.O.) General Series 181/14.

TRANSCRIPTS (MODERN) OF RECORDS

Ancient Petition 4706, from Record Commission Transcript 110/3.
Ancient Petition 5066, from Record Commission Transcript 111/84.

City of London Records (at the Guildhall)

City of London, Guildhall Library MS 126.
City of London, Mayor's Court, Original Bills, bdle. 1, no. 38; bdle. 2, no. 177.
London Letter-Book H.
London Bridge Estate Deeds, G 16, 17.

City Company Records

The Drapers' Company (at Drapers' Hall). Drapers' Company Deeds, A viii 336(2).

Episcopal Records

Archbishop of Canterbury (at Lambeth Palace Library). Archbishops' Registers (Lambeth), Courtenay, Sudbury.
Bishop of London (at St. Paul's). Register Braybrook.

Testamentary Records (Central Probate Registry, Somerset House)

Prerogative Court of Canterbury. Registers of Wills, Luffenam, Marche, Rous, Stokton.
Commissary of London. Register of Wills, Courtenay.
Archdeaconry of London. Register I.

Collections

British Museum, Department of Manuscripts. Sloane MS 1313.
—— Additional MS 35,181.
—— Harleian MS 247.
—— Harleian Charter 55 C 18.
—— Stowe MS 570.
Earl of Westmorland. Household Account of Edward, Duke of York, 1409.

PRINTED SOURCES

Adam of Usk. Chronicon Adae de Usk, A.D. 1377–1421. Ed. by E. M. Thompson. 2d ed. London, 1904.

Anonimalle Chronicle, 1333–1381, The. Ed. by V. H. Galbraith. Manchester, 1927. Publications of the University of Manchester; Historical Ser., XLV.

Anstey, Henry, ed. Munimenta academica. 2 vols. London, 1868. Rerum Britannicarum medii aevi scriptores, L.

Arderne, John. Treatises of Fistula in Ano, Haemorrhoids, and Clysters. Ed. by D'Arcy Power. London, 1910. EETS, Orig. Ser., CXXXIX.

Aungerville, Richard d', known as De Bury. The Philobiblon of Richard de Bury. Ed. by A. F. West. 2 vols. New York, 1889. The Grolier Club.

Austin, Thomas, ed. Two Fifteenth-Century Cookery-Books. London, 1888. EETS, Orig. Ser., XCI.

Babees Book, The. Ed. by F. J. Furnivall. London, 1868. EETS, Orig. Ser., XXXII.

Babees' Book, The. Ed. by Edith Rickert. London, New York, 1908. The New Medieval Library, IV.

Baker, Geoffrey. Chronicon Galfridi le Baker de Swynebroke. Ed. by E. M. Thompson. Oxford, 1889.

—— Galfridi le Baker de Swinbroke, Chronicon Angliae. Ed. by J. A. Giles. London, 1847.

Bartholomaeus Anglicus. Mediaeval Lore. Ed. by Robert Steele. London, 1893.

Benedictines in England. Documents Illustrating the Activities of the General and Provincial Chapters of the English Black Monks, 1215–1540. Ed. by W. A. Pantin. 3 vols. London, 1931–1937. Publications of the Royal Historical Society. Camden Third Ser., XLV, XLVII, LIV.

Brut, The; or, The Chronicles of England. Ed. by F. W. D. Brie. 2 vols. London, 1906–1908. EETS, Orig. Ser., CXXXI, CXXXVI.

Bryene, Dame Alice (de Bures) de. Household Book of Dame Alice de Bryene, of Acton Hall, Suffolk, September 1412–September 1413. Ed. by V. B. Redstone. Ipswich, 1931. Suffolk Institute of Archaeology and Natural History.

Cambridge University, King's College. The Ancient Laws of the Fifteenth Century, for King's College, Cambridge, and for the Public School of Eton College. Ed. by James Heywood and Thomas Wright. London, 1850.

Canterbury, Prerogative Court. North Country Wills, 1383–1558. [Ed. by J. W. Clay.] Durham, 1908. Publications of the Surtees Society, CXVI.

Catholic Church, Councils. Sacrorum conciliorum nova et amplissima collectio. Ed. by Giovanni Mansi. 53 vols. Florence and Venice, 1759–1798, 1901–1927.

Chambers, R. W., ed. A Fifteenth-Century Courtesy Book. London, 1914. EETS, Orig. Ser., CXXXXVIII.

Chandos Herald. Life of the Black Prince. Ed. by M. K. Pope and E. C. Lodge. Oxford, 1910.

Chaucer, Geoffrey. Canterbury Tales. Ed. by J. M. Manly. New York, 1928.

Christine de Pisan. "Ballade" printed in "Translation of a French Metrical History of the Deposition of King Richard the Second," tr. by John Webb, *Archaeologia*, XX (1824), 1–442.

Dillon, Harold Arthur, Viscount. "On a MS Collection of Ordinances of Chivalry of the Fifteenth Century, Belonging to Lord Hastings," *Archaeologia*, LVII, Pt. 1 (1900), 29–70.

"Documents Relative to the Families of Bryan, Fitzpain, Ponynges, and Others, the Coheirs of Sir Guy Bryan, K.G.," *Collectanea topographica et genealogica*, III (1836), 259–260.

"Early Deeds Relating to Shropshire," *Collectanea topographica et genealogica*, V (1838), 180–181.

Edward, Second Duke of York. The Master of Game. Ed. by W. A. Baillie-Grohman and F. Baillie-Grohman. London, 1909.

Ely, Eng. (Archdeaconry). Vetus liber archidiaconi Eliensis. Ed. by C. L. Feltoe and E. H. Minns. Cambridge, 1917. Publications of the Cambridge Antiquarian Society, Octavo Ser., XLVIII.

Eulogium (historiarum sive temporis): chronicon . . . . a monacho quodam Malmesburiensi exaratum. 3 vols. London, 1858–1863. Ed. by F. S. Haydon. Rerum Britannicarum medii aevi scriptores, IX.

Favent, Thomas. Historia . . . . mirabilis parliamenti. Ed. by May McKisack. London, 1926. Publications of the Royal Historical Society. Camden Third Ser., XXXVII.

Foxe, John. Acts and Monuments. Ed. by Josiah Pratt. 3d ed., rev. 8 vols. London, 1870.

Froissart, Jean. The Chronicle of Froissart. Tr. by John Bourchier, Lord Berners; ed. by W. P. Ker. 6 vols. London, 1901–1903.

—— Œuvres de Froissart . . . . chroniques. Ed. by Kervyn de Lettenhove. 25 vols. in 26. Bruxelles, 1867–1877.

—— Œuvres de Froissart: poésies. Ed. by Auguste Scheler. 3 vols. Bruxelles, 1870–1872.

Furnivall, Frederick J., ed. The Fifty Earliest English Wills in the Court of Probate, London. London, 1882. EETS, Orig. Ser., LXXVIII.

Gardener, Ion. "A Fifteenth Century Treatise on Gardening," *Archaeologia*, LIV, Pt. 1 (1894), 157–172.

Gower, John. "Mirour de l'omme," in The Complete Works of John Gower: the French Works, ed. by G. C. Macaulay, Oxford, 1899.

Gray, Sir Thomas. Scalacronica. Tr. by Sir Herbert Maxwell. Glasgow, 1907.

Great Britain, Public Record Office. Calendar of Entries in the Papal Registers Relating to Great Britain and Ireland: Petitions to the Pope. Ed. by W. H. Bliss. Vol. 1, A.D. 1342–1419—. London, 1896—.

—— Calendar of the Fine Rolls. Ed. by H. C. Maxwell Lyte. Vol. 1, A.D. 1272–1307—. London, 1911—.

—— Calendar of the Patent Rolls. Ed. by H. C. Maxwell Lyte. Vol. 1, A.D. 1216–1225—. London, 1901—.

—— Descriptive Catalogue of Ancient Deeds. Ed. by H. C. Maxwell Lyte. 6 vols. London, 1890–1915.

Halliwell-Phillipps, J. O., ed. Early English Miscellanies, in Prose and Verse. London, 1855. Publications of the Warton Club, II.

Hardynge, John. Chronicle. Ed. by Henry Ellis. London, 1812.

Herbert, William. The History of the Twelve Great Livery Companies of London. London, 1837.

Higden, Ranulf. Polychronicon Ranulphi Higden . . . . together with the English Translations of John Trevisa . . . [and with Continuations by Caxton and Johannes Malverne]. Vols. 1–2 ed. by Churchill Babington; Vols. III–IX ed. by J. R. Lumby. 9 vols. London, 1865–1886. Rerum Britannicarum medii aevi scriptores, XLI.

Hoccleve, Thomas. The Regement of Princes. Ed. by F. J. Furnivall. London, 1897. EETS, Extra Ser., LXXII.

Inner Temple, London. A Calendar of the Inner Temple Records. Ed. by F. A. Inderwick. 3 vols. London, 1896–1901.

Jacobus de Vitriaco, Cardinal. The Exempla or Illustrative Stories from the Sermones Vulgares of Jacques de Vitry. Ed. by T. F. Crane. London, 1890. Publications of the Folk-lore Society, XXVI.

John of Gaunt, Duke of Lancaster. John of Gaunt's Register. Ed. by Sidney Armitage-Smith. 2 vols. London, 1911. Publications of the Royal Historical Society. Camden Third Ser., XX–XXI.

John of Reading. Chronica Johannis de Reading . . . 1346–1367. Ed. by James Tait. Manchester, 1914. Publications of the University of Manchester. Historical Ser., XX.

Kingsford, C. L. "A London Merchant's House and Its Owners, 1360–1614," Archaeologia, LXXIV (1923–1924), [137]–158.

Knighton, Henry, Canon of Leicester. Chronicon Henrici Knighton. Ed. by J. R. Lumby. 2 vols. London, 1889–1895. Rerum Britannicarum medii aevi scriptores, XCII.

Laborde, L. E. S. J., Marquis de. Les Ducs de Bourgogne; études sur les lettres, les arts, et l'industrie pendant le XVe siècle. Seconde Partie. 3 tomes. Paris, 1849–1852.

BIBLIOGRAPHY

La Tour-Landry, Geoffrey de. Book of the Knight of La Tour-Landry. Ed. by Thomas Wright. London, 1868. EETS, Orig. Ser., XXXIII.

Life-Records of Chaucer. Parts I and III ed. by W. D. Selby; Part II ed. by F. J. Furnivall; Part IV ed. by R. E. G. Kirk. London, 1900. Chaucer Society. Publications. Second Ser., XII, XIV, XXI, XXXII.

London, Coroner. Calendar of the Coroners Rolls, A.D. 1300–1378. Ed. by R. R. Sharpe. London, 1913.

London, Corporation. Calendar of Letter-Books . . . . Letter-Book A-L. Ed. by R. R. Sharpe. 11 vols. London, 1899–1912.

—— Calendar of Plea and Memoranda Rolls . . . . A.D. 1323–1381. Ed. by A. H. Thomas. 2 vols. Cambridge, 1926–1929.

—— Calendar of Select Pleas and Memoranda, A.D. 1381–1412. Ed. by A. H. Thomas. Cambridge, 1932.

—— Munimenta Gildhallae Londoniensis: Liber albus, Liber custumarum, et Liber horn. Ed. by H. T. Riley. 3 vols. in 4. London, 1859–1862. Rerum Britannicarum medii aevi scriptores, XII.

London, Court of Hustings. Calendar of Wills Proved and Enrolled in the Court of Husting, London, A.D. 1258–A.D. 1688. Ed. by R. R. Sharpe. 2 vols. London, 1889–1890.

London, Lord Mayor's Court. Calendar of Early Mayor's Court Rolls, A.D. 1298–1307. Ed. by A. H. Thomas. Cambridge, 1924.

"London Lickpenny," attributed to John Lydgate. Ed. by N. H. Nicolas in A Chronicle of London. London, 1827.

Lydgate, John. "The Testament," The Minor Poems of John Lydgate. Ed. by H. N. MacCracken. 2 vols. London, 1908–1910. EETS, Orig. Ser., CXCII; Extra Ser., CVII.

Madden, Frederic. "Agreement between the Dean and Chapter of St. Paul's London, and Walter the Orgoner, of Southwark, Relating to a Clock in St. Paul's Church," Archaeological Journal, XII (1855), [173]–177.

Maidstone, Richard de. De concordia inter Ricardum Secundum et civitatem London. Ed. by Thomas Wright in Alliterative Poem on the Deposition of King Richard II, and Maydiston, Ricardi, De concordia . . . London, 1838.

Manly, John M. Some New Light on Chaucer. New York, 1926.

Manly, John M., and Edith Rickert. "Documents and Records: Recently Discovered Chaucer Documents," Modern Philology, XXV (1927–1928), 121–123.

Ménagier de Paris, Le. Ed. by Jérôme Pichon. 2 vols. Paris, 1846.

Piers the Plowman. Ed. by W. W. Skeat. 3 vols. London, 1873. EETS, Orig. Ser., LIIII.

Powell, Edgar. The Rising in East Anglia in 1381. Cambridge, 1896.

Putnam, Bertha H. The Enforcement of the Statutes of Laborers, 1349–59.

New York, 1908. Columbia University Studies in History, Economics and
Public Law, XXXII.

Quicherat, J., ed. "Récit des tribulations d'un religieux de diocèse de Sens
pendant l'invasion Anglaise de 1358," *Bibliothèque de l'École des Chartes*,
III, ser. 4 (1857), 357–360.

Relation, A, or, Rather a True Account, of the Island of England. Trans. by
C. A. Sneyd. London, 1847. Publications of the Camden Society, XXXVII.

Rickert, Edith. "Chaucer at School," *Modern Philology*, XXIX (1931–
1932), 257–274.

—— "Documents and Records: a Leaf from a Fourteenth-Century Letter
Book," *Modern Philology*, XXV (1927–1928), 249–255.

—— "Documents and Records: Extracts from a Fourteenth-Century Account Book," *Modern Philology*, XXIV (1926–1927), 111–119, 249–
256.

—— "Some English Personal Letters of 1402," *Review of English Studies*,
VIII (1932), 257–263.

—— "Thou Vache," *Modern Philology*, XI (1913–1914), 209–225.

—— "Was Chaucer a Student at the Inner Temple?" in The Manly Anniversary Studies in Language and Literature. Chicago, 1923.

Riley, H. T., ed. Chronicles of the Mayors and Sheriffs of London, A.D. 1188
to A.D. 1274 . . . . The French Chronicle of London, A.D. 1259 to
A.D. 1343. London, 1863.

—— Memorials of London and London Life. 2 vols. London, 1868.

Robertson, J. C., ed. Materials for the History of Thomas Becket, Archbishop of Canterbury. 7 vols. London, 1875–1885. Rerum Britannicarum
medii aevi scriptores, LXVII.

Rymer, Thomas. Foedera. 2d ed. 20 vols. London, 1726–1735.

Salzman, L. F. English Life in the Middle Ages. London, 1926.

Scrope, Sir Richard le. De controversia in curia militari inter Ricardum le
Scrope et Robertum Grosvenor milites. Ed. by N. H. Nicolas. 2 vols. London, 1832.

Simpson, W. S. "St. Paul's Cathedral, London," *Transactions of the London
and Middlesex Archaeological Society*, V (1881), 311–326.

Smith, Toulmin, and L. T. Smith, eds. English Gilds. London, 1870. EETS,
Orig. Ser., XL.

Smyth, W. H. "Description of an Astrological Clock Belonging to the Society
of Antiquaries of London," *Archaeologia*, XXXIII (1849), 8–35.

—— "Supplement to the Description of an Astrological Clock Belonging to
the Society of Antiquaries," *Archaeologia*, XXXIV (1852), [1]–20.

Society of Antiquaries of London. A Collection of Ordinances and Regulations
for the Government of the Royal Household. London, 1790.

Stapleton, Thomas. "A Brief Summary of the Wardrobe Accounts of the

Tenth, Eleventh, and Fourteenth Years of King Edward the Second," *Archaeologia*, XXVI (1836), 318–345.

Stengel, E. "Die ältesten Anleitungsschriften zur Erlernung der französischen Sprache," *Zeitschrift für Neufranzösische Sprache und Literatur*, I (1879), 11–13.

Stephens, George. "Extracts in Prose and Verse from an Old English Medical Manuscript, Preserved in the Royal Library at Stockholm," *Archaeologia*, XXX (1844), 349–418.

Stonor Letters and Papers, 1290–1483, The. Ed. by C. L. Kingsford. 2 vols. London, 1919. Publications of the Royal Historical Society. Camden Third Ser., XXIX–XXX.

Stow, John. A Survey of London. Ed. by C. L. Kingsford. 2 vols. Oxford, 1908.

Tale of Beryn, The. Ed. by F. J. Furnivall. London, 1887. Chaucer Society. Publications. Second Ser., XVII, XXIV.

Times, The. London, Fri., Jan. 7, 1916, p. 11, col. 3.

Tymms, Samuel, ed. Wills and Inventories from the Registers of the Commissary of Bury St. Edmunds and the Archdeacon of Sudbury. London, 1850. Publications of the Camden Society, XLIX.

Walsingham, Thomas. Thomae Walsingham, Quondam Monachi S. Albani, Historia Anglicana. Ed. by H. T. Riley. 2 vols. London, 1863–1864. Rerum Britannicarum medii aevi scriptores, XXVIII: Chronica Monasterii St. Albani, Pt. I.

Westlake, H. F. The Parish Gilds of Mediaeval England. London, 1919.

Westminster Abbey, Library. The Manuscripts of Westminster Abbey. Ed. by J. A. Robinson and M. R. James. Cambridge, 1909. Notes and Documents Relating to Westminster Abbey, I.

White, J. G. "Ancient Records and Antiquities of the Parishes of St. Swithin, London Stone, and St. Mary Bothaw," *Transactions of the London and Middlesex Archaeological Society*, I (1905), 183–209.

Wilkins, David. Concilia Magnae Britanniae et Hiberniae. 4 vols. London, 1737.

Wright, Thomas, ed. Political Poems and Songs. 2 vols. London, 1859–1861. Rerum Britannicarum medii aevi scriptores, XIV.

Wright, Thomas, and J. O. Halliwell, eds. Reliquiae antiquae. 2 vols. London, 1841–1843.

Wycliffe, John. The English Works of Wyclif. Ed. by F. D. Matthew. London, 1880. EETS, Orig. Ser., LXXIV.

—— Tractatus de officio pastorali. Ed. by G. V. Lechler. Leipzig, 1863.

Index

Edward, Duke of York (*Cont.*)
 Handley Castle in Worcestershire, 248-51
Eelskins, fight about, 15
Egypt, 147
Eleanor, Countess of Arundel, 330
Elingeham, John, 132*n*, 380
Elinham (or Elmham), Roger, 190*n*
Eliton, knighted, 327
Eltham, great council assembled at, 247
Elton, Sir Forthe, 329
Ely, John Barnet, Bishop of, chosen to be Archbishop, 274
Ely, John Fordham, Bishop of, 191
Ely, building operations, 191
Elyngeham, *see* Elingeham
Engines of war, preparing, 288
England, in danger, 164; invades France, 292-97; truce with Burgundy, 295; treaty with France, 297; France threatens to invade, 297-305; preparations, 298; processions, prayers, and orisons, 300; aided by Germany, 305; victory at Nájera, 325
Entertainment, 207-43; tournaments and feats of arms, 207-17; sports, 218-29; outdoor sports in London, 225; games of skill and chance, 229-32; minstrelsy, 232-34; processions and feasts, 234-37; convivial life, 237-43
"Eque," 188*n*
Escrik, William de, tomb, 417
Espagnols-sur-Mer, 310
Espayne, Domengo de, 5
Esquire, contents of house of, 59; livery, 286*n*
Estate, ranks of every, at table, 331
Esturmy, Sir William, 66
Ethics, doctor's code of professional, 174-76
Ethulf, Walter, 359
Eve-cheapings, 26
Evening markets in streets, 25
Evenynge, Ralph, 12
Eve of St. Dunstan, 113
Excommunication, 48, 393
Exemplum from a medieval sermon, 372
Exeter, George Neville, Bishop of, 408
Exile's journey from Waltham Holy Cross to Dover, 284
Exton, Richard, 118

Extone, Nicholas, 195, 204
Extortion and oppression, 182
Eyscher, manor of, in Surrey, 188

Faire, Mark, 162
Family life, 71-84; husband and wife, 71-75; servant question, 76-78; life by candlelight, 78-80; toilet and home remedies, 80-83; household hints, 83-84; food, 84-94; *see also* Food
Famine, 347
Faringdon, Sir William of, 215
Farmer, goods and stock of a well-to-do yeoman, 199
Farnaham, John, 9
Farnham manor, Surrey, 188
Farringdon, Nicholas de, 43
Farringdon Without, ward, 10
Farthing measures, 84
Fashions, for rich men, 333-39; Englishmen stark mad over, 336; for rich women, 339-43; how to wear clothes, 340
Feast for a franklin, 90
Feasts, 207, 234-37; gild, 236
Feats of arms, 207-17
"Feats of Gardeninge, The," 68*n*
Felbrigg, Simon, 283
Felon's burial, miscarriage of plans for a, 414
Felstede, Richard de, 8
Feltone, Thomas de, 316
Ferinton, William de, knighted, 327
Fernandez, Martin, 327
Fernham, Adam, 25
Ferrers, Lord of, 328
Ferrers, Henry, 287
Ferst, Cristiana, 358
Fifty against five, exploit of, 295
Fire, carrying about the house, 79
Fire regulations, 41
Firewood, buying for resale forbidden, 21
Fish dinner with subtleties, 91
Fishmonger, inventory of household goods, 59; exporting herrings and importing wines, 183
"Fish out of water, A," 373
Fistula, treatise on, 173 ff.; fee for cure of, 175; operation for, 177
Fitz-Hugh, Lord, 408, 409
Fitzstephen, William, 225

M.A., degree of, 128
Macclesfeld, 189
Maghfeld (or Maufeld), Gilbert (or Gybon), 113n, 114n, 146, 182, 188, 189, 190, 191; was he the original of Chaucer's Merchant? 112, 192; career, 185
Maghfeld, William, 113
Magic and false accusation, 202
Makkeney, William, 54
Malangre, Richard, 290
Malet, Baldwyn, 297
Malett, Baldwin, 160, 161
Manly, John M., quoted, 4, 12, 53n, 54n, 55n, 59n, 96n, 99n, 182n, 185n, 191n, 192n, 218n, 294n, 319n, 337n, 360n, 366n, 378n, 403n, 407n, 414n
Manners, good, for those that bide not long at school, 101-2
"Man of Law's Tale" (Chaucer), 325
Marbrer, William le, 7, 8
March, Edmund II de Mortimer, Third Earl of, 163, 168, 317
March, Eleanor Mortimer, Countess of, 318n
March, Roger de Mortimer V, Second Earl of, death, 295
March, Roger de Mortimer VI, Fourth Earl of, 141; death, 317; King's reputed enmity toward, 317n; married Eleanor Holland, 318n
Mare, de la, see De la Mare
Market gardeners, place fixed for, 23
Markets, London, 25
Marnham, Thomas de, 349
Marny, Robert and Alice de, 5
Marriage, 50-56; control through feudal tenure a financial asset, 53; King's ministers hasten to secure, of a wealthy heiress, 54; persons abducted because of marriageable value, 54; a student's, 55; customs, 56; settlement including quarters with bride's father, 57
Marshal, puzzled how to rank estates, 332
Masks not allowed at wake, 410
Mason, specification for vaulted cellars, 7
Masses, for travelers, 268; for the soul, 394-96; bequests for, 420, 421
Master of Game, The (Edward, 2d duke of York), 218-25
Maufeld, Gybon, see Maghfeld, Gilbert
Maukel, Robert, 53

Maukel, Roger, 53
Mayor's show, 39-40
Mazelyner, John le, 4
Meal, serving, 93-94
Meconium, 178n
Medicine, doctor of, see Doctor
Medieval itinerary, London to Rome, 278
Melburne, John, 55
Melburne, William, 55
Melle, Agnes, 147
Melle, Thomas atte, 145, 147
Melton, Robert, 58
Memorials of London . . . (Riley), 20
Men, fashions for, 333-39
Mendicants, Order of, 374
Menus, 90-93
Mercer, purchases from a, 344
Merchants, in cathedral, 48; who live beyond their means, 181; keeping of the seas, 182, 185; as banker or money lender, 185-93; things in which, dealt, 186
Merchant's house next the customs wharf, London, 5-7
Meryet, George, 59
"Meselcotes, Les," lepers in, 353
Messembre, 148
Meters of sea-coal, 20
Michel, John, 186
Micheldever, John, 109
Micheldever, Richard, 109
Micheldever, William, 109
Midenhale, William, 195
Midsummer watch, 40
Mikelfeld, John, 58
Mikelfeld, Margaret, 58
Mikelfeld, Thomas de, 57, 58
Mildenhale, John, 352
Military band, Edward III's, 287
Military expeditions, 292-329
Mille, Sir John atte, 146
Mille, Thomas atte, 147
Minstrels, 17
Minstrelsy, 232-34
Mirour de l'omme (Gower), excerpts, 27, 159, 181, 240, 373
Mocking, Thomas, 59, 62
Molyneux, Symkyn, 139
Molyns, Lady Margery de, 406
Molyns, William, 406